A HISTORY

OF

THE CHURCH KNOWN AS THE

MORAVIAN CHURCH

AMS PRESS

NEW YORK

NICHOLAS LOUIS VON ZINZENDORF.

A HISTORY

OF

THE CHURCH KNOWN AS THE

MORAVIAN CHURCH,

OR

THE UNITAS FRATRUM,

OR

THE UNITY OF THE BRETHREN,

DURING THE EIGHTEENTH AND NINETEENTH
CENTURIES.

BY

J. TAYLOR HAMILTON,

PROFESSOR OF CHURCH HISTORY IN THE MORAVIAN THEOLOGICAL SEMINARY,
BETHLEHEM, PA.

BETHLEHEM, PA.
TIMES PUBLISHING COMPANY, PRINTERS.
1900.

Reprinted from the edition of 1900, Bethlehem, Pa.
First AMS EDITION published 1971
Manufactured in the United States of America

International Standard Book Number: 0-404-08427-3

Library of Congress Catalog Number: 70-134379

AMS PRESS INC.
NEW YORK, N.Y. 10003

PREFACE.

Completed in the year memorable as the bicentenary of the birth of Nicholas Louis Count Zinzendorf, the instrument in God's hand for the resuscitation of the almost extinct evangelical Church of the Bohemian and Moravian Brethren, this attempt to trace the renewal and development of its life and the spread of its missionary undertakings in all parts of the world during the two hundred years that followed, is reverently dedicated to his memory.   It enters upon what is in large part a new field of history; hence its author craves lenient judgment.

Special thanks are due and are herewith cordially tendered to Bishop J. M. Levering, of Bethlehem, Pa., Archivist of the Moravian Church in America (North); to the Rev. Alexander Glitsch, Archivist of the Brethren's Unity, at Herrnhut; to the Rev. Leonard G. Hasse, Director of the Moravian College and Theological Seminary at Fairfield, in England; and to the Rev. Charles J. Klesel, Secretary of Moravian Missions, in London, England.   To their kind assistance much valuable information is to be ascribed.

Bethlehem, Pennsylvania, June 18, 1900.

BIBLIOGRAPHY.

The following are the chief sources for the history of the Moravian Church, during the eighteenth and nineteenth centuries:

MANUSCRIPT SOURCES.

The very extensive archives of the Moravian Church at Bethlehem, Pennsylvania, are exceedingly rich in original documents—autobiographies, biographies, letters, congregation diaries, minutes of various synods, conferences, etc., giving a vast amount of information from the very inception of the work of the Moravian Church in America, together with correspondence, and copies of documents of first importance for the history of the Moravian Church abroad.   The following are of primary importance;

The Diary of the Congregation at Bethlehem, Penna., 1742–1899.

Journals of the "Pennsylvania Synods," 1742–1748.

Diarium der Hütten, 1747–1755.

Jüngerhaus Diarium, 1756–1760.

Gemeinhaus Diarium, 1761–1764.

Gemein Nachrichten, 1765–1818.

Reports of the Proceedings of the General Synods of the Moravian Church, 1746–1836.

Original Minutes and Documents of the Provincial Synods of the American Moravian Church, North, 1748–1898.

Monatliche Nachrichten aus der Unitäts Aeltesten Conferenz, 1764–1858.

Monatliche Nachrichten aus der Provinzial Helfer Conferenz, 1802–1848.

PRINTED SOURCES.

REICHEL, WILLIAM C., Memorials of the Moravian Church.   (Contains documents from 1742 to 1757.)   Philadelphia, J. B. Lippincott and Co., 1870.

SPANGENBERG, AUGUSTUS GOTTLIEB, Darlegung richtiger Antworten, etc., Leipzig and Görlitz, 1751.

ZINZENDORF, NICHOLAS LUDWIG VON, Die Büdingische Sammlung einiger in die Kirchen-Historie einschlagender sonderlich neuerer Schrifften. Three vols., Büdingen, Joh. Chr. Stöhr, 1742–1745.

————, Pennsylvanische Nachrichten von dem Reiche Christi, 1742.

————, Ludwigs von Zinzendorf, ΠΕΡΙ ΕΑΥΤΟΥ. Das ist: Naturelle Reflexiones über allerhand Materien.   1746.

————, Reden, Berlinische, des Ordinarii Fratrum, etc., London and Barby, Second Edition, 1758.   (Translated. Sixteen Discourses on Jesus Christ our Lord, Being an Exposition of the Second Part of the Creed, preached at Berlin by the Right Rev. Lewis, Bishop of the Ancient Brethren's Church.   London, 1755.)

——, Theologische und darin einschlagende Bedenken. Büdingen, Johann Christoph Stöhr, 1742.

——, Acta Fratrum Unitatis in Anglia. London, 1749.

DIARY OF DAVID ZEISBERGER, 1781–1798. Translated by Eugene F. Bliss, and printed by Robert Clarke for the Historical and Philosophical Society of Ohio. Two vols., Cincinnati, 1885.

Periodical Accounts Relating to the Missions Established by the Protestant Church of the Unitas Fratrum. Quarterly, London, 1790-1900.

Verlässe, und Verhandlungen von, und Mitteilungen aus den Allgemeinen Synoden der Brüder-Unität, 1836-1899.

Journals of the Provincial Synods of the American Moravian Church, North, 1847-1898.

Reports of the Society for Propagating the Gospel among the Heathen, 1849-1899.

The United Brethren's Missionary Intelligencer. Quarterly, 1822-1848.

The Moravian Church Miscellany. Monthly, 1850-1855.

Das Brüder Blatt. Monthly, 1854-1861.

The Moravian. Weekly, 1856-1900.

Der Brüder-Botschafter. Weekly, 1866-1900.

Das Missions-Blatt. Monthly, 1837-1900.

Der Brüder-Bote. Monthly, 1862-1898.

Mitteilungen aus der Brüder Gemeine. Monthly, 1895-1900.

HISTORIES AND BIOGRAPHIES.

MANUSCRIPT.

PLITT, JOHANNES, *Denkwürdigkeiten aus der Geschichte der Brüder-Unität*, 1841. (The part relating to the history since 1722 fills three voluminous and closely written quarto vols. A copy is in the Library of the Moravian Theological Seminary, Bethlehem, Pa. Very valuable. As archivist of the Moravian Church at Herrnhut, Professor Plitt draws from and largely quotes original documents.)

SCHWEINITZ, EDMUND DE, S. T. D., Lectures delivered in the Moravian Theological Seminary, 1876-1877.

PRINTED.

BECKER, BERNHARD, D.D., Zinzendorf im Verhältnis zu Philosophie und Kirchentum seiner Zeit. Leipzig, I. C. Hinrichs'sche Buchhandlung, 1886.

BENHAM, DANIEL, Memoirs of James Hutton. London, Hamilton, Adams & Co., 1856.

BOVET, FELIX, Le Comte de Zinzendorf, Deuxiéme édition, revué et augmentée. Paris, 1865. (Translated. The Banished Count. By Rev. John Gill. London, James Nisbet and Co., 1865.)

BUCHNER, C., Acht Monate in Süd Africa. Gütersloh. C. Bertelsmann, 1894.

BURKHARDT, G., Zinzendorf und die Brüdergemeine seiner Zeit. Gotha, Rud. Besser, 1886.

————, Die Brüdergemeine. Erster Teil, Entstehung und geschichtliche Entwickelung der Brüdergemeine. Gnadau, 1893. Zweiter Teil, Die Brüdergemeine in ihrer gegenwärtigen Gestalt. Gnadau, 1897.

————, Die Mission der Brüdergemeine in Missionstunden. Grönland und Alaska, (H. G. Schneider) 1897. Suriname, 1898. Deutsch-Ostafrika, Nyassa-Gebiet, 1898. Leipzig, Friedrich Jansa.

CRANZ, DAVID, Alte und Neue Brüder-Historie. Barby, H. D. Ebers, 1771. (Translated. The Ancient and Modern History of the Brethren. By Benjamin La Trobe. London, W. and A. Strahan.)

CRÖGER, E. W., Geschichte der erneuerten Brüderkirche. Three vols., Gnadau, 1852-1854.

GEDENKTAGE DER ERNEUERTEN BRÜDERKIRCHE. Gnadau, 1821. Translated. The Memorial Days of the Renewed Church of the Unitas Fratrum. Ashton-under-Lyne, 1822.

DEWITZ, A. VON, In Dänisch - Westindien. Herrnhut, zweite Auflage, Schneider, 1882.

————, An der Küste Labradors, zweite Auflage, Herrnhut, 1891.

GLITSCH, ALEXANDER, Geschichte der Brüdergemeine Sarepta im östlichen Russland während ihres hundertjährigen Bestehens. Nisky, L. Glitsch, 1865.

HEGNER, J. K., Fortsetzung von David Cranzens Brüder historie. Drei Abschnitte, 1769-1775, 1775-1782, 1782-1789. Barby, 1791, 1804.

HOLMES, REV. JOHN, History of the Protestant Church of the United Brethren. Two vols. London, 1825, 1830.

————, Historical Sketches of the Missions of the United Brethren for Propagating the Gospel among the Heathen, from their Commencement to the Year 1817. Second edition, London, 1827.

KÖLBING, FRIEDRICH LUDWIG, Nachricht von dem Anfange der bischöflichen Ordination in der erneuerten evangelischen Brüderkirche. Gnadau, C. D. Hans, 1835.

LOCKWOOD, REV. J. P., Memorials of the Life of Peter Böhler, Bishop of the Church of the United Brethren. With an Introduction by the Rev. Thomas Jackson. London, Wesleyan Conference Office, 1868.

LOSKIEL, GEORG HEINRICH, Geschichte der Mission der evangelischen Brüder unter den Indianern in Nord Amerika. Barby, 1789. (Translated. History of the Mission of the United Brethren among the Indians in North America. By George Henry Loskiel. Translated from the German by Christian Ignatius La Trobe. London, 1794.)

OLDENDORP, C. G. A., Geschichte der Mission der Evangelischen Brüder auf den Caraibischen Inseln, S. Thomas, S. Croix, und S. Jan. Barby, Johannes Jacob Bossart, 1777.

PLITT, HERMANN, D.D., Zinzendorf's Theologie. Gotha, F. A. Perthes, 1869, 1871, 1874.

————, Die Gemeine Gottes in ihrem Geist, und ihren Formen mit besonderer Beziehung auf die Brüdergemeine. Gotha, F. A. Perthes, 1859.

————, Die Brüdergemeine und die Lutherische Kirche in Livland. Gotha, F. A. Perthes, 1861.

REICHEL, REV. LEVIN T., The Moravians in North Carolina; An Authentic History. Salem, N. C., O. A. Keehln, 1857.

————, The Early History of the Church of the United Brethren in North America, A.D. 1734–1748. (Vol. 3 of the Transactions of the Moravian Historical Society.) Nazareth, Pa., 1888.

REICHEL, WILLIAM C., Memorial of the Dedication of Monuments erected by the Moravian Historical Society to mark the Sites of Ancient Missionary Stations in New York and Connecticut. Philadelphia, Collins, 1860.

RISLER, JEREMIAS, Leben August Gottlieb Spangenbergs, Bischofs der evangelischen Brüderkirche. Barby, 1794.

RITTER, ABRAHAM, History of the Moravian Church in Philadelphia, from its Foundation in 1742 to the Present Time. Philadelphia, C. Sherman and Son, 1857.

SCHNEIDER, HERMANN, Ein Missionsbild aus dem Westlichen Himalaya. Gnadau, 1880. (Translated. Working and Waiting for Tibet. Arthur Ward. London, Morgan and Scott.)

————, Missionsarbeit der Brüdergemeine in Australien. Gnadau, 1882.

————, Gnadenthal. Stuttgart, Roth, 1892.

————, Die Buschneger Surinams. Herrnhut, 1893.

————, Moskito. Zur Errinnerung an die Feier des fünfzigjährigen Bestehens der Mission der Brüdergemeine in Mittel-Amerika. Herrnhut, 1899.

SCHRAUTENBACH, LUDWIG CARL, FREIHERR VON, Der Graf Zinzendorf und die Brüdergemeine seiner Zeit. Herausgegeben von F. W. Kölbing. Gnadau, H. L. Menz, 1851.

SCHULTZE, A., D.D., Die Missionsfelder der erneuerten Brüderkirche. Bethlehem, Pa., 1890.

SCHWEINITZ, EDMUND DE, S. T. D., The Moravian Manual. Second, enlarged Edition, Bethlehem, Pennsylvania, A. C. and H. T. Clauder, 1869.

————, The Life and Times of David Zeisberger, the Western Pioneer and Apostle of the Indians. Philadelphia, J. B. Lippincott and Co., 1870.

————, The Centennial Anniversary of the Society of the United Brethren for Propagating the Gospel among the Heathen. Bethlehem, 1887.

————, The Financial History of the American Province of the Unitas Fratrum, and of its Sustentation Fund. Bethlehem, 1887.

SPANGENBERG, AUGUSTUS GOTTLIEB, Leben des Herrn Nicolaus Ludwig Grafen und Herrn von Zinzendorf und Pottendorf. Acht Theile in drei Bänden. Barby, 1772-1775. (Translated. The Life of Nicholas Louis, Count Zinzendorf. By Samuel Jackson. With an Introductory Preface by the Rev. P. La Trobe. London, Samuel Holdsworth, 1838.)

THOMPSON, AUGUSTUS, D. D., Moravian Missions. New York, Charles Scribner's Sons, 1882.

TRANSACTIONS OF THE MORAVIAN HISTORICAL SOCIETY. Nazareth, Pa., 1859 to 1900.

VERBEEK, JACOB WILHELM, Des Grafen Nicolaus Ludwig von Zinzendorf Leben und Charakter, in kurzgefasster Darstellung nach A. G. Spangenbergs Biographie desselben und Quellen aus dem Archiv der evangelischen Brüder-Unität. Gnadau, H. L. Menz, 1845.

TABLE OF CONTENTS.

ILLUSTRATIONS.

CHAPTER I.

For the Ancient Unitas Fratrum the outcome of the terrific convulsions of the Thirty Years' War was the practical annihilation of its congregations in the twin lands of its birth, amidst persecutions that disgraced the Christian name, though scattered individuals loyally held to the doctrines and discipline of their fathers in hope against hope. For the rest of the parties to the struggle, the Peace of Westphalia may briefly be described as having put a restraint upon their battlings with the sword by placing the Lutherans and Reformed and Roman Catholics practically on the same footing throughout the various dominions of Germany, so far as concerned the right to worship. In fact efforts were made to bring about a union between the Lutherans and the Roman Catholics and also between the Lutherans and the Reformed. Although such well meant, if unpractical, efforts of Calixtus and others not only failed to achieve this desired result, and instead intensified the extreme aversion with which the adherents of one confession regarded those of another, nevertheless there were men who plainly perceived that Christian ethics had been only too sadly ignored in the battling of theologians and their partisans concerning dogma. Amongst these there now arose a longing for the spread of true godliness rather than for obtaining assent to exact definitions of dogmatic theology. Such prominent personages as Ernst the Pious, Duke of Saxe-Gotha, and Pastor Paul Gerhard, the hymn-writer, strove most earnestly to raise the standard of Christian life. The need of a new reformation came to be recognized, in which prominence should be given to the culture of personal piety. Thus the Protestants of Germany began to approach what had ever been the standpoint of the Brethren's Church.

Schrautenbach gives a graphic picture of the age. "How surprisingly different from our own were those times that have

2

scarcely disappeared. Culture, enlightenment, general intelligence far less than at present. Less intercourse of peoples with
one another, throughout the great world. A veneration of respectable darkness in many things; everything not so mingled,
made common, everything more definite in its bounds and con-
trasts. Everything scientific made less popular; more labor
and toil in every province of life: and hence fixed impressions
and convictions. The manners rough, with ever a step nearer
to nature; and therefore impetuosity, irritability, energy. Many
of the scholars of the Church and the clergy intolerant and
masterful, accustomed to deal arbitrarily and with great power,
being secure in the possession of their livings, and taking positions without being asked by anyone, 'What are you about?'
Those men who sought for an improvement (not the comfortable, fortunate, well-to-do pious, who are made for the world
and the world for them, but the perplexed and earnest seek-
ers), for the most part deeply wounded at the proceedings of
the influential, bearing their griefs within them, mistrustful and
stubborn; yet a general longing amongst these men for union,
though from very indistinct reasons."

The man providentially destined to turn such longings into
a definite channel was Philip Jacob Spener, born January 13,
1635, at Rappoltsweiler near Colmar in Alsace. His religious
life began at thirteen, by the death-bed of his mother. Indebted
for both religious training and intellectual culture to Joachim
Stoll, subsequently his brother-in-law and from 1645 chaplain
to the Counts of Rappolstein, he was educated in the University of Strasburg, and in this city he commenced his ministerial
career. In 1666 he received an appointment as pastor
in Frankfort-on-the-Main. Deeply in earnest and fully convinced that the dogmatic disquisitions and theological polemics
which made up the sermons of the day could be of very little
profit to the people, his great object was to set forth the saving power of the Gospel. In his discourses he therefore
avoided all technical terms, and he also sought to again bring
into repute catechetical instruction, which had been left by most
pastors to the indifference of the parish school-teachers. In
order to exercise a more effectual influence over individual
souls, in 1670 he began to hold private meetings at his own
house. In these informal gatherings he repeated the substance
of the Sunday sermons, explained and expounded passages

from the New Testament, and gave those present an opportunity to ask questions and express their views. In 1675 he published his famous *"Pia Desideria,"* embodying his opinions with regard to the need of a reformation of the public instructions and a resuscitation of personal piety in the Lutheran Church, and the manner in which these ends were to be attained. General attention was attracted to the author of the work. *"Collegia Pietatis,"* as he called his gatherings for the culture of the spiritual life, were introduced in many places.

In 1686 Spener was called to Dresden as chief court chaplain. Here he rendered important services in securing, in particular, the general introduction of catechetical instruction and examinations throughout the Electorate of Saxony. The resumption of exegetical lectures at Leipsic and Wittenberg was also due to his influence.

At the former University three young Masters of Arts, Augustus Herman Francke, John Caspar Schade, and Paul Anton, imbibed his spirit and entered into his plans very cordially. Like him, they began to give lectures on the books of the Bible in the German language, in which they sought not learned exposition, but the awakening of genuine piety. Large numbers of students and citizens came to hear them. The jealous enmity of the pastors was aroused, more especially because these followers of Spener taught that worldly amusements, the dance, the theater, the card-table, fashions, etc., were unlawful for true Christians, whereas the regular pastors countenanced them. The members of the Theological Faculty also took an antagonistic position, notably Benedict Carpzov, who believed he had delivered a sufficient reply to the efforts of these men in his biting epigram, *"satis pii sed satis indocti."*

Stigmatized as "Pietists," the three Masters were driven from Leipsic after a legal investigation in 1691. Spener himself also incurred the displeasure of the Elector of Saxony through the freedom with which he had censured the morals of the court and the drunken sensuality of the ruler. Hence he was glad in the same year to accept a call to Berlin. Here he labored faithfully until his death, February 5, 1705.

"The three fundamental truths underlying his system of doctrine were, Man's total depravity, God's revelation to man, and Man's communion with God. By nature we are estranged from Him. We must be born again. There is a fundamental distinction between the regenerate and the unregenerate state. When men have been born again, holiness must follow as a consequence. This consists neither in the feelings nor in an emotional religion, but living a genuinely devout life. Out of this doctrinal system grew his practical ideas with regard to the spread of true religion. Christianity can be apprehended and communicated only by those who have experienced its power through repentance and faith. Only a regenerate man can be a true theologian, and a real minister. Theological studies must be based on the Bible, and not on Church creeds. Scripture must be explained by Scripture. A separation from the Church is to be carefully avoided; but *ecclesiolae in ecclesia* are to be organized. By this term Spener meant little associations of living members within a regular parish, to act as a leaven among the membership. Awakened and regenerate persons are to institute a special fellowship among themselves, and to uphold certain regular rules in view of personal piety and family religion; but at the same time they are to remain in the full communion of the Church."

Orthodox Lutherans objected to various ideas of the Pietists, particularly to the principle that the theology of the unregenerate is no true theology. They contended, on the other hand, that the unregenerate man could comprehend the truths of vital religion, and could efficiently do the work of the ministry, the former being a phase of philosophy and the latter a profession. They alleged that at bottom the Pietists sought justification by works. Moreover both shortly before and during the Pietistic Controversy, many fanatics made their appearance, some of whom had a certain affinity to the Pietists, which gave the Orthodox an opportunity to place Pietism in the same category with these forms of fanaticism, though these errors were neither a necessary nor a legitimate outcome of Spener's position.

Its more just development is to be seen in the life-work of Augustus Herman Francke. Born March 23, 1663, at Lübeck, he had been educated at Erfurt and at Leipsic, where he had for a time lectured after obtaining his Master's degree. Dismissed for his Pietism, together with his friends, Paul Anton and John Justus Breithaupt, he had been invited to the new University of Halle, in 1692. At first Professor of Oriental languages, he was afterwards the occupant of the chair of Theology, and pastor of Glaucha, a suburb of the city. Here God used him for large service, in connection with the establishment of a charity-school, which he opened first of all in his own house. The number of children admitted rapidly increased from year to year. In 1698 was laid the corner-stone of the first edifice of the vast rows of structures that astonish the visitor to-day. Funds were received in unexpected ways from all quarters, till in time his institutions comprised a College, an Orphan asylum, a Home for poor, a Bible-house, a Seminary for the training of teachers, a Divinity-school, a Foreign missionary Society, a Book-store, a Printing-office, an Apothecary shop, and an Infirmary. Anton and Breithaupt assisted him; Baron Canstein established the Bible-house. Ziegenbalg and Plütshau were the first missionaries sent out by the society in 1706, to Tranquebar.

These institutions of Francke mightily worked for the spread of Pietism. Soon the influence of this system made itself felt not only in the world of dogma but also in the theory of education, and in social life by the organization of *ecclesioloe* throughout various parts of Germany. As regards the system of education, to its praise it sought to combine personal piety with a preparation for highest usefulness, but was one-sided and overloaded with religious exercises. The chief centers of learning which were affected by Pietism were those at Halle, Jena and Tübingen. At Jena, Buddæus began to exert a special influence among the students, encouraging the formation of religious associations amongst them, and used all his influence to revive discipline in the Church and the personal care of souls. Devoting himself especially to researches in Ecclesiastical History, he published, amongst other works, the *Ratio Disciplinae* of Comenius, and recommended the discipline of the Unitas Fratrum to the Church of Germany. From the University of Jena scholarly graduates were destined hereafter to cast in their lot with the loyal adherents of the Church of the Bohemian and Moravian Brethren, and became men prominently identified with the resuscitation of the *Unitas Fratrum*. Tübingen was similarly under the influence of moderate Pietism, promoted by Professor Bengel, Chancellor Pfaff, and others. This University likewise contributed its men to the ministry of the Unity in later decades.

The influence of Pietism on personal religion was very one-sided, the fundamental mistake being that practically one and the same mode of conversion was insisted on in every case. The terms *Durchbruch, Busskampf* and *Rettende Gnade* became its shibboleths. Yet its faults deserve to be forgotten over-against the general good which Pietism accomplished. The *ecclesiolae* in the time of Spener existed especially amongst the better class of noble families, and thus wielded a powerful in-fluence for righteousness. After the death of Spener these *ecclesiolae* continued to spread through the exertions of Francke. This was the case especially in Central Germany, Saxony, Sile-sia, Denmark, Livonia and Switzerland. The ultimate gain for Germany may be estimated from the assertion of Professor Tholuck that never were there so many pious pastors and zealous laymen to be found amongst Protestants of Germany as during the first forty years of the eighteenth century.

Not unnaturally many of the conservatives amongst the clergy bitterly opposed all these new tendencies. A keen feud broke out especially between Halle and Wittenberg. Gradu-ally, however, the differences between the parties became less marked, and some of Spener's principles have won universal sway throughout evangelical Christendom. Long before this an inner decay of the Pietistic system itself began to appear. Zinzendorf said, that if the Pietists had remained united and strong, the Saviour would have had no need of a resuscitation of the Brethren's Church.

To suppress in Bohemia and Moravia all organic ecclesias-tical life other than the Roman Catholic was within the power of the unholy alliance of the House of Austria and the Jesuits; but though the Peace of Westphalia had confirmed them in their rigorously tyrannical religious policy, they could not deprive the evangelicals of the sorrowful right of emigration. Hence a significant body of emigrants is to be noted as proceeding thereafter at intervals from Bohemia to Silesia and Lusatia. In 1650 these exiles were so numerous in Dresden as to re-ceive for their use the Johannis-Kirche. Others settled at Wesgau near Barby. The Bohemian colony at Zittau in-creased in numbers remarkably. A Bohemian congregation was organized at Charselz on the Spree, and another at Gebhards-dorf, near Messersdorf, about the year 1670. Though their ritual was Lutheran, it proves nothing with respect to their antecedents; for what other uses would have then been tolerated in strictly orthodox Saxony? Similarly, too, in the first decades of the eighteenth century several Bohemian families lived at Gerlachsheim, between Görlitz and Messersdorf, whose pastor Augustine Schulze became in 1728; and Bohemians were to be found about the same time at Gross Hennersdorf, to whom such considerable accessions arrived, that when, deprived in 1732 of their homes at this place, they set out for Berlin, their numbers amounted to about five hundred persons.

These facts have no unquestionably direct bearing upon the fortunes of the Unitas Fratrum in the ancient lands. Yet indirectly their significance is considerable, and of a two-fold character. If the adherents of the other confessions managed to so preserve a secret attachment to their traditional faith and usages as to furnish the material for such emigrations after years of seemingly successful suppression, it is to be reasonably supposed in the first place, that the members of the Brethren's Church were not less tenacious of what they prized, and not less adroit in perpetuating the truth in concealment. And in the second place, it is evident that the stream of emigration which later set in from Moravia to Herrnhut was in no wise anomalous or unique. Rather, like the flight of the Huguenots from France, the exodus of the Schwenkfelder from Silesia, and the exile of the Salzburger from their southern home, it was a characteristic feature of the stern necessities of that illiberal age.

Furthermore the history of the archbishopric of Salzburg well illustrates the truth, that rigorous persecution does not necessarily involve the extirpation of an intelligent faith. Though from the outset its rulers stringently and energetically opposed the Reformation, when the edict of Firmian shut up the evangelicals to one of two alternatives, the success of a secret propagation of the faith was demonstrated in that 30,000 industrious and peaceful citizens chose to forsake all things rather than compromise with conscience. If Lollardy, in an age before the printing press multiplied copies of the Scriptures, of the hymnals and of catechisms, had vitality enough in spite of bitter persecutions to survive in Scotland to such an extent that Knox claimed the Lollards of Ayrshire as the forerunners of the Scotch Reformation, it would be setting a poor estimate upon the quality of the stalwart Bohemian Brethren, to believe it possible for them to utterly and altogether vanish within a century after the inception of the Counter-Reformation. In a matter like this, even absence of records can not well be counted an incontrovertible argument for non-existence of facts, from the very nature of the case. For it is one thing for monarchs and cabinets and the hierarchy to crush out organic congregational life, and to suppress a prohibited cultus amongst the nobility, and quite another thing to extinguish the embers of a cherished faith amongst those of humbler walk, if intelligent and possessed of books. Clergy who have propagated, and nobility who have patronized the true doctrine, may be tortured and entombed in perpetual imprisonment or furnished with the fiery chariot of martyrdom; yet the common man will long find means to elude the vigilance of the most cunning inquisitors, by reason of the numbers in which he exists and the countenance and abetment which he may perhaps obtain from friendly neighbors who are not utterly without bowels of mercy, even though perverts to the domineering, persecuting faith.

Hence a student of history readily believes that insight into the not merely exceptional is afforded by the narratives that have come down to posterity through the diligence of a pastor like Augustin Schulze, and of Bohemian refugees like Zacharias and Tobias Hirschel and John Bittman, and of Moravian refugees like David Nitschmann, the Syndic, and Frederick Neisser, and of the restlessly indefatigable itinerant Christian David, and that have been preserved and made known through the providential accident of the connection of these men with the Brethren's congregations at Rixdorf and Herrnhut. It would seem more than probable, and in accord with human nature, that the families and individuals who are mentioned by these as having cherished the doctrines and usages of the Brethren in Bohemia and Moravia rather furnished instances of fidelity that had their counterpart elsewhere, but which has not been chronicled in history from a failure to attain connection later with the Brethren whose emigration to the foot of the Hutberg was destined by God to once more bring into prominence and world-wide usefulness the organization which had been so long and so thoroughly tempered by persecution.

In the month of April, 1756, a so-called "Moravian Synod" was held at Herrnhut, preparatory to a General Synod of the

Church. A committee of nine was by it appointed, to draw up lists of all Brethren and Sisters of Moravian and Bohemian extraction, secure accounts of their experiences when fleeing from their fatherland, and record their labors in behalf of the resuscitated Unity. Thus sources for history were furnished which Kölbing used in writing the *Memorial Days*, and his *Bischöfliche Ordination*, etc. From a passage in the *Jüngerhaus Diarium* of May 1, 1756, in conjunction with a passage in Plitt's manuscript History, and Neisser's manuscript *Fasciculus*, it seems that at this time, viz. in 1756, 1014 members were living who had been born in Moravia or were of Moravian parentage, and 629 members born in Bohemia or of Bohemian parentage—the latter residing chiefly in Berlin and Rixdorf. Zinzendorf himself is here recorded to have declared that up to this time thirty-eight brethren and forty-five sisters of Moravian extraction had departed this life after serving in the ministry at home or in mission fields. Plitt's manuscript and Neisser's Fasciculus indicated that three hundred and thirteen Moravians and Bohemians had already passed away. This would give a total of nearly 2000 members of Bohemian-Moravian birth up to 1756, not reckoning the departed to whom Zinzendorf refers.

It is known that Synods of the Polish branch of the Brethren's Unity as such met statedly at Lissa until 1699; and that in 1710 the Brethren and the Reformed met at Warsaw in a Union Synod, and continued to hold such in future. In the interval, it is known, Bishop Jablonski called frequent Synods to strengthen the things that remained, and that he utilized his position as court preacher in Berlin to aid the Brethren in Poland, Russia, and Hungary in every manner. Doubtless the Polish Synods prior to the beginning of the eighteenth century must have endeavored to keep track of their Brethren who secretly held to the faith in Moravia and Bohemia, and must have endeavored to encourage them. Certain it is that friendly relations were early maintained between the resuscitated Unity and the old Polish congregations of the Brethren.

Unfortunately it is impossible to ascertain with accuracy the complete number of exiled Moravians and Bohemians who entered into connection with Zinzendorf and his co-laborers. It is known that they came from about twenty different places in Bohemia and from about eighteen different towns and villages in Moravia. But the *Fasciculus* of George Neisser, which seems to be just such a list and appended collection of memorabilia as this "Synod" of 1756 called for, is evidently incomplete.

This much can be definitely substantiated. Just as in Poland and Polish Prussia there yet remained at least fifteen parishes in the year 1715, in spite of every catastrophe and the repeated disasters that had befallen Lissa, the central point of their activity; and just as these were an element of sufficient importance in the religious life of those lands to be granted representatives at the Union Synod at Danzig in 1718, and to maintain their episcopate; so, too, up to the same date in Bohemia, around Landskron and Leitomischl, and Hermanitz and Rothwasser, and in Moravia around Zerawic, Fulneck, Zauchtenthal, Kunwalde, and Sehlen, the irrepressible adherents of the Unity of the Brethren dared the stake and the dungeon, that they might serve God according to conscience and after their fathers' mode.

The Diary of the congregation in Berlin and Rixdorf for May, 1754, reads: "On May 18 Brother Hirschel began to draw up an account of our Bohemian Congregation. Several things of importance appear from it.

1. That the most of our members originate from around Leitomischl and Lititz, where were formerly the chief seats of the Bohemian Brethren.

2. That their awakening took place about the year 1720, and was therefore contemporaneous with the awakening in Moravia.

3. That they maintained the knowledge of the Saviour and intelligence concerning the Brethren's Unity throughout the entire seventeenth century by the traditions of their forefathers which they passed on to their descendants.

4. Their first connection with the Moravian Brethren at Herrnhut was through visits of Christian David and Christopher Demuth in 1726 and especially through that of Melchior Nitschmann in 1728."

Jacob and John Pechatschek, father and son, John Schallman, Wenzel Kleych and his extensive colporteur work from 1708 on, are not to be forgotten; nor the thorough revival in the village of Hermanitz and its vicinity from the years 1720-1722, quite independent indeed of the similar revival in the Moravian Kuhländl, and followed by such cruel persecution that after enduring the knout the track of the confessors going homeward from the castle was to be traced by the blood that dripped from them.

Then in Moravia, the Kutschera family of Zerawic; and the Schneiders of Zauchenthal—with their venerable sire, aged Martin, the contemporary of Comenius, who frequently had services, including the Lord's Supper, at his house, when a clergyman came stealthily from the Brethren's parish of Skalic, in Hungary, and his grandson, Samuel Schneider, who often himself preached, and who on his death-bed in 1710, after repulsing his offer of the viaticum respectfully but firmly, with a glorious testimony of assured salvation, won from the Romish priest the confession, "Let my soul strive after a death such as that of this righteous man." And in fellowship with the Schneiders were the Kunz and Beyer and Stach and Zeisberger and Tanneberger families of Zauchtenthal, and the Jaeschke and Neisser families of Sehlen and Seitendorf, and the Grasmann family of Senftleben, and the Nitschmanns of Kunwalde. But there were others in both lands not so well known. For example, the memoir of Thomas Piesch, born at Birlitz in Silesia in 1702, and later active in England, states that his father made it his business to take evangelical books thence into Moravia, and was arrested and persecuted therefor. It also appears from this memoir that he had a connection with the well-known Schneider family. Persecution could not effectually stamp out Bible reading and secret conventicles. Born in 1675, at Schönau in Moravia, from youth up George Haberland was diligent in reading the Scriptures. Rosina Kisselowa, m. n. Hirschel, of Lippstadt in Bohemia, relates that she often heard of the so-called Waldenses (a misnomer often anciently applied to the Bohemian Brethren), who held their services and celebrated the Lord's Supper in the surrounding villages. Paul Wottmar was born in Bohemia on June 28, 1705. His ancestors had uninterruptedly maintained the faith and usages of the Brethren's Unity in secret, and in childhood implanted the truth in him. He died in Berlin in 1755. Tobias Kutschera was born in Moravia in 1671. His parents were both descended from members of the old Unity, his mother being a granddaughter of a presbyter of the Church and his father's father also a minister, being pastor at Zerawic, where the Synod of 1616 assembled. Here, moreover during the days of Tobias

Kutschera himself, a meeting-house of the Brethren still stood. As late as 1680 services of the Brethren were still openly held in this part of Moravia (so says his memoir). In the house of his father the Brethren later had worship three times every Sunday. But the persecution became more severe and public meetings were stopped. The memoir of old father David Nitschmann of Zauchtenthal, the uncle of the Bishop, who was born in 1676, records that his father John held services in his own house every Sunday, when the rooms were all so full that there were not seats for all the people. They sang hymns from the old Brethren's Hymn-book, and read whatever ser· mons they had on hand. When a new priest came, named Schlimman, who dealt with them severely, they still maintained their worship—but with great secrecy. This must have been before 1692, for about that year the old parents died. George Pakota, born at Steinern Sedlitz, near Leitomischl, in 1699, relates that his parents were loyal adherents of the Brethren's Church; that when he was a child his father often told him of the evangelical preachers who were formerly in Bohemia, sighing over the tale of their suppression. Later his father read to him out of the New Testament and out of a book by John Hus, from which he himself derived a permanent blessing.

Why did these at all remain in the lands of narrow bigotry and dreadful oppression? It is recorded that they often contemplated emigration, the more so because their fathers had frequently spoken· of the liberty of conscience and religion to be enjoyed when the Lord should lead them out of their "Babylonian captivity." But the elusive expectation of better times, like a mirage on their horizon, and the dangers attendant upon attempted but detected and arrested flight, and the not unnatural love of the beautiful fatherland, and a shrinking from the surrender of all property and the loss of all certain opportunity to earn a livelihood, involved in the venture, from the sure confiscation of everything which they could not carry with them, served as not inexcusably deterrent arguments. Meantime, however, the reading of the Scriptures and sermons and other evangelical literature, and family worship and the careful training of their children in the traditional way, did not cease. And with it all, dawn was nearer than they dreamed.

God saw fit to search out two extremes of society for the chief agents in the fulfillment of the touching prayer of Comenius, a quondam shepherd and carpenter, and a noble who was even more princely in character than in hereditary rank. It was the former who first came into touch with the remnant of the Brethren, Christian David, born of Roman Catholic parents at Senftleben, between the Carpathians that separate Moravia and Hungary, not far from Neutitschein, and the Kuhländl, memorable as the scene of the first scholastic labors of Comenius. Early showing great zeal for the observances required by the priests, and indefatigable in his adoration of pictures of the Virgin, as he himself expressed it, he was wont to burn with devotion like a stove. The family with which he was apprenticed at Holeschau were in secret evangelical, and taught him to lose his faith in the pictures of the saints and in pilgrimages, and the fidelity of certain Protestants who were thrown into a prison for their faith's sake, also made a great impression on his mind. But he had been completely torn away from his moorings. At length, in 1710, he came into the possession of a Bible, a book about which he had heard, but which he had never yet seen. That he diligently searched it is proved by his subsequent style of speech, and by his handwriting which imitated the printed letters of the German Bible. The result of his searchings determined him to seek fellowship with some evangelical body of believers. Hence he set out on his travels throughout Hungary, Austria, Bohemia, Silesia, Saxony, and Brandenburg. At various places the Lutheran pastors refused his application to be received into their Church, for fear of Catholic persecutors; in others he was himself so shocked at the loose morals of their members that he had no desire for fellowship with them. Fearful distress of mind ensued, in the midst of which he enlisted in the army which Frederick of Brandenburg was collecting for the war against Charles XII of Sweden, thinking that he would have more leisure to serve Christ as a soldier than when working at his trade. Pastor Schmidt, of Berlin, furthermore received him into the Lutheran Church before the army left the city. After having participated in the siege of Stralsund, and its capture on December 12, 1715, he was thankful to obtain his discharge, having been sadly deceived in his expectations about the opportunities of growing in Christian knowledge as a soldier.

Whilst proceeding afterwards to Breslau, he fell seriously ill, but in time managed to reach that city.   Here his illness again came on him, and he was taken to the hospital.   After his recovery he worked at his trade, having however a very uncomfortable time of it, owing to the persecutions of the Jesuits. These varied experiences all proved of educational value.   At Görlitz he next learnt to know Melchior Schaeffer, the pastor of Holy Trinity Church, and his friend John Andrew Rothe, a candidate of theology, as also John Christopher Schwedler, of Nieder-Wiese.   The latter was particularly interested in the lot of those who came to his Church from Roman Catholic sections of country.   This was in the year 1717.   Through his intercourse with these men Christian David at last found the assurance of salvation which he had been so long seeking. And with it he felt an inner call to evangelistic work.   Across the Austrian border there were many of his countrymen, he knew, as little satisfied with the superstitions of Rome as he had himself been.   Was he not under obligation to bring them to a knowledge of that truth which he had himself found so precious ?

Accordingly, in this same year, 1717, he made a first visit to his fatherland.   In the course of his fourth visit, in 1719, he came to Sehlen, near Neutitschein, where he became acquainted with the five brothers Neisser.   Perceiving the fervor and power of this man who was but a layman, they became filled with a longing for a home in a land where there were doubtless many such as he, and where the pastors, it was to be supposed, could clear up all their difficulties and satisfy all the hunger of their souls.   It was a peculiar coincidence that their grandfather, George Jaeschke, whose family had belonged to the Unity since the 15th century, had been a most godly man, a veritable patriarch amongst the remnant of Brethren who cherished the past in secret, and that on his death-bed he had uttered almost prophetic words concerning the restoration of the Brethren's Unity.   The result of this intercourse was that the Neissers began to think seriously of emigrating, and on Christian David's third visit they told him that they were very anxious to find a refuge in a Protestant country. He therefore promised to do what he could, and directed them to pastors Steinmetz, Muthmann and Sassadius, of Teschen. Returning to Görlitz, he made known the wish of the Neissers to Schaeffer and other friends. But time passed before it could be realized. Then came, however, God's time. In the spring of 1722 a young Saxon noble and government official, Count Nicholas Louis von Zinzendorf, in the course of a conversation with Rothe, his future parish minister, heard of Christian David and of his efforts to find an asylum for a few Moravians. The Count became interested, and sent for Christian David, who gave a full account of his visits to Moravia. Zinzendorf promised to find a place for the Neissers, where they could worship God in peace; and till he should succeed in doing this, he offered to receive them on his own estate, without intending to keep them there. He first of all wrote to others, especially to Count Reuss of Kostritz, and when he found no suitable spot, desired to lease a domain near Ebersdorf, and let them settle on that. But God overruled these plans, and caused the few intending refugees to be forever linked to his own career.

Immediately on receiving the Count's promise, Christian David visited Moravia, and arrived at Sehlen on Whit-Monday, May 25, 1722. Augustine and Jacob Neisser at once resolved to emigrate, abandoning home and all worldly goods, but the others preferred to wait until they received news of the successful issue of the undertaking of these pioneers. Their mother had fainted when told what was in contemplation. Nevertheless at 10 oclock, on the next Wednesday night, the two brave brothers, with their wives and children, viz., a son six years old, a daughter three years old and twins of twelve weeks, together with Michael Jaeschke and Martha Neisser, niece of Augustine's wife, ten souls in all, set out from Sehlen secretly, led by Christian David, to seek the God of their fathers in a new land. Traveling all night along byways, they crossed the Silesian frontier, and followed the Oder to Nieder-Wiese, where they were welcomed by pastor Schwedler. Thence they crossed into Saxony. At Leube the Von Schweinitz family hospitably entertained them, and here they met Rothe, their future pastor. At Görlitz the families were left with pastor Schaeffer. Zinzendorf being at Dresden, the two Neissers and Christian David on the 8th of June visited Gross Hennersdorf to interview Lady Gersdorf, Zinzendorf's grandmother. She received them coldly and declined to have anything to do with them; but at the earnest pleas

of the family tutor, Marche, she was however finally induced to
send them to Berthelsdorf and put them under the care of Heitz,
the steward of Zinzendorf's estate. Thus the first representa ·
tives of the Church had reached the ground on which its resusci ·
tation was destined to be effected.

CHAPTER II.

THE ANTECEDENTS AND EARLY LIFE OF COUNT ZINZENDORF.

In the distant century that witnessed the decline of the Hohenstauffen and the rise of the Hapsburger, a grim old castle in Austria cradled the ancestors of the man who should offer succor to refugees from Austrian tyranny and bigotry five hundred years later. The Reformation brought them, like many other families of distinction, into the valley of decision, and during the lifetime of the great Reformer one branch renounced the corruptions and superstitions of Rome. In consequence Count Maximilian Erasmus von Zinzendorf had to leave his ancestral home for the sake of conscience. His place of refuge was Oberberg, near Nuremberg, where he died in 1672. His three daughters formed alliances with the Counts of Orthenburg and Pollheim and Castell, Franconian nobles, whilst his two sons entered the service of the Saxon Elector, the one dying childless in 1718 as a Saxon field-marshall, and the other, the younger, enjoying a brief career as a minister of state under the Electors John George the Fourth and Augustus the Second. This second son, George Louis, won as his second wife Charlotte Justina von Gersdorf, a lady equally distinguished for her noble lineage. Her father, Nicholas von Gersdorf, was Prefect of Upper Lusatia, and an ancestor of the same name had held Bautzen for the Bohemian King at the outbreak of the Thirty Years' War. Well mated in their birth, George Louis von Zinzendorf and Charlotte Justina were kindred in character. Personal friends of Spener, they were in full sympathy with his devout purposes; an *ecclesiola* was established in their home at Dresden, and they selected the father of Pietism as a sponsor for their son, Nicholas Louis, born on May 26, 1700.

From the first peculiar experiences shaped the character and influenced the future of the boy, fashioning him into an instru-

3

ment for extraordinary work. When he was only six weeks old he lost his father by consumption. Next year the young widow returned to the home of her family, the castle of Gross·Hennersdorf, in Upper Lusatia, once a hunting lodge of the Bohemian kings. Here her mother in turn became a widow in August, 1702. Then in 1704 Lady Zinzendorf married again, her second husband being the Prussian Marshall von Nazmer. Thenceforth Berlin became her home, and she saw comparatively little of her son. The boy, on whose head Spener had laid his hands in anticipation setting him apart for the furtherance of Christ's kingdom, became a ward of his grandmother and his aunt Henrietta, now a young woman of twenty.

Lady Henrietta Catharine Gersdorf, the grandmother of Nicholas Louis, was a lady of exceptional parts, and was distinguished for firmness of character. On one occasion when it was necessary for her to undergo the operation of trepanning, rather than cause her husband any anxiety she quietly withdrew from the official life of Dresden to their country home, submitted to the skill of the surgeon, and let him know what had been done only on her recovery. A highly talented and cultured lady, a poetess and proficient in music and painting, she occupied a position of wide influence through her extensive circle of acquaintances and correspondents in all parts of the empire. Personally devout, her doors were thrown open for the meetings of an *ecclesiola*. Spener, Francke, Canstein, and especially Anton were her frequent guests. Yet she did not champion their movement to the exclusion of an appreciation of earnestness and genuine service of Christ amongst the adherents of the school of Wittenberg. Her daughter Henrietta, a lively and sanguine young woman, had inherited many of her characteristics. Naturally, therefore, at an early age they gave careful attention to the religious training of their young charge; and the results of his intimacy with these ladies were very early manifested in the delicacy and tenderness of his nature. Love to Jesus began to show with the first awakening of his self-consciousness, and though when only nine years of age he was precociously tormented with doubts and with a sense of his own depravity, his marvelous apprehension of the love of Jesus proved savingly victorious.

When in the year 1706 the Swedes overwhelmed Saxony, a detachment of their soldiers came to Hennersdorf to demand supplies. Entering into the castle, they pressed into the room where the young Count was engaged in his customary devotions. The sight of this child and the freedom with which he earnestly delivered his exhortations so impressed them, that they almost forgot the purpose of their hostile visit.

Though he inherited from his father a delicate constitution, he had an ardor and a powerful will that rapidly carried him through the tasks set by his tutors—Edeling, Kriebel and Hofmann. If a too vivid imagination and volatility and impatient irrepressibility were likely to affect his scholarship unfavorably, to offset these he possessed wonderful powers of concentration, ready apprehension, a reliable memory, sound judgment, exactness of expression, and a capacity for deep reflection.

His relatives could not help noting his high endowments and destined him for distinguished office in the state. For this purpose his uncle and guardian would have preferred the course of training usual in the case of young noblemen, but yielded to the representations of his mother and grandmother, who desired him to be placed under positively Christian influences in Francke's Paedagogium at Halle. This institution was now at its zenith. Its founder was still at the head, and was assisted by a corps of able and like-minded men.

This school young Zinzendorf accordingly entered at the early age of ten, his well-intentioned grandmother giving him a doubtful recommendation as "a very sharp and intelligent youth who must be held in with a tight rein, for fear of his becoming proud and presuming too much on his abilities." It brought no undue mitigation of the severity which characterized the paedagogics of that age. His tutors, Hofmann and Crisenius, with whom he lived until his fourteenth year, indelibly impressed upon his memory their senseless harshness--to use no stronger term. Moreover, the uncouth horse-play of his comrades caused the first five years of his stay at Halle to be a decidedly unhappy period. Nevertheless he managed to make satisfactory progress in his studies, especially in Latin and French, acquiring sufficient facility in the former to deliver extemporaneous speeches by his sixteenth year. Meantime the unfeigned sincerity of his personal piety showed itself in repeated efforts to prove helpful to his comrades in bringing them to a satisfactory knowledge of Christ. Seven little associations for prayer and edification were formed by him during these school days, some unattended with success but some of permanent significance and all of them manifesting the natural bent of the lad. With four comrades in particular he entered into closer relations—Von Sohlenthal, Wallbaum, Von Tonz and De Watteville—covenanting that they would in after life labor for the conversion of the heathen, and especially in behalf of those for whom no one else cared. Reports from the Malabar mission in 1714 appear to have been influential in connection with this resolution. They did not indeed expect to accomplish this by their own personal efforts, but hoped to play the part of patrons of missions, in imitation of Baron Canstein. Later the idea developed into the conception of a spiritual knighthood, their fraternity being known by turns as "Slaves of Virtue" and "Confessors of Christ" and finally as the "Order of the Grain of Mustard Seed."

But Zinzendorf's guardian, Count Otto Christian, had no notion that the gifted scion of their house should become a mere religious enthusiast. Hence at sixteen he caused him to be transferred to the University of Wittenberg, where Francke's peculiarities were stoutly opposed. Crisenius moreover received most precise instructions respecting the conduct and the studies of his ward. With military precision the hours were mapped out—so many to be devoted to law, to the fencing-hall, the riding-school and the dancing-master. In dutiful obedience Zinzendorf accepted this curriculum, but devoted his free time to the study of theology, philosophy and natural science, though scrupulously refraining from attendance at lectures in the forbidden branches. As at Halle, he stood very much alone. In the course of time his Hallensian prejudices against the divines at Wittenberg wore off, as intimate knowledge disclosed the true worth of these men. Then it was in accordance with his chivalrous spirit and innate syncretism to seek single-handed to heal the breach between Halle and Wittenberg. He wrote letters to Drs. Francke and Lange and Anton with this end in view, and did succeed in bringing about a colloquy at Merseburg between Francke and Superintendent Löscher of Dresden, with no practical result. He himself was to have conducted Dr. Wernsdorf of Wittenberg to Halle in order to introduce him to Francke, when his tutor shabbily spoilt his plan by writing to Madame Nazmer and putting his alleged ambition and presumption in so unfavorable a light as to call forth a positive injunction on her part, a prohibition which a dutiful son was compelled to heed.

In the spring of 1719 it was decided in the family councils that Zinzendorf's legal studies could now be best pursued in the most famous foreign schools, and the finish be given to his education by an extensive foreign tour, as was the mode for young noblemen. Accompanied by his new tutor, Riederer, and for a time also by his elder half-brother, Count Frederick Christian, after visiting his mother and bidding farewell to his grandmother, he proceeded by way of Dresden, Leipsic, Eisenach and Frankfort-on-the-Main to Mayence, Utrecht being his first destination. It was during this tour that the sight of an *Ecce Homo* in the picture gallery at Düsseldorf deepened and developed the determination formed in childhood, to devote his life to the service of Christ. Here and at Amsterdam, where he made the acquaintance of the Prince of Nassau and the Prince of Orange, and formed a life-friendship with Count Henry 24th Reuss, he learnt to appreciate the good in the position of the Reformed Church. The closing days of the year found him in Paris, and the winter was spent amid the courtly scenes of the gay capital. The mother of the Regent, the Duke of Orleans, took a special fancy to him, and he formed the acquaintance of Cardinal Noailles and the appellant bishops. But the temptations of his situation had no allurement; the rather did the hollow unreality of pomp and pleasure disclose itself. Leaving Paris at the end of April, Basel, Zürich and the Black Forest were in turn enjoyed, and his aunts, the Countesses of Pollheim and Castell, visited.

During this visit in Franconia an episode transpired which had an important influence upon his future views of married life.

With the eldest daughter of the Countess of Castell, Theodora, young Zinzendorf fell in love. In January, 1721, he informed her mother of his feelings, and she was entirely satisfied. But his cousin did not really reciprocate his attachment, and only half yielded to the persuasions of her mother in his behalf. He himself, however, did not perceive this, and hastened to Hennersdorf to gain his grandmother's consent to their betrothal. This obtained, he hurried back to Castell. On the way thither his carriage met with an accident at the River Elster. This compelled him to stop at the neighboring estate, which happened to be the home of his friend, Count Reuss. By a strange coincidence the latter had been secretly desirous to marry Theodora Castell, but had refrained from overtures when he heard of Zinzendorf's intentions. In the course of conversation concerning his expected marriage, when the latter discovered the state of his friend's heart, he adopted a sudden and romantic resolution. He declared himself willing to relinquish Theodora to his friend, if it proved a fact that her secret preference was for him. Reuss accepted the magnanimous offer, and the two friends proceeded to Castell. To Zinzendorf's dismay, he then learnt that his cousin had never really loved him. Reuss and Theodora were betrothed on the ninth of March. By this time Zinzendorf had so mastered his feelings as to be at peace, and on this interesting occasion offered a touching prayer in behalf of the betrothed.

Unquestionably this experience helped to develop his character, deepening his self-denial. Moreover by giving a bias to his mind in connection with marriage and the claims of Christ's service in relation to family life, it contributed towards his adoption of those peculiar principles respecting family life in religious communities, which for a long time marked the Brethren's Church.

On his return to Hennersdorf, shortly before he became of age, Zinzendorf found changes in the home of his boyhood. Lady Gersdorf, his grandmother, was now in the seventies, enjoying retirement with her sister, Lady von Mausebach, as her companion. Her daughter Henrietta, still unmarried, administered the estates of Hennersdorf and Berthelsdorf with masculine firmness. Two daughters of privy councillor Gottlob von Gersdorf were also members of the household, and with them their tutor, Christian Gottfried Marche. An orphanage and a home for the poor had been founded at Hennersdorf. An *ecclesiola* was still maintained, but an intimacy had also been established with Pastor John Christian Schwedler of the Silesian frontier parish of Nieder-Wiese, though a Wittenberger, and with Pastor Melchior Schaeffer of the cloister church at Görlitz, and with his friend John Andrew Rothe, a candidate of theology and at present a tutor in the Von Schweinitz family at Leube.

In autumn, in obedience to the wishes of his grandmother, though his own tastes and inclinations were far otherwise,

Zinzendorf at length entered upon the public career which lay open to one of his rank, becoming first of all a councillor and justiciary in the service of the electoral government. As such in Dresden he everywhere maintained the consistently outspoken Christian course which had distinguished him hitherto, in spite of the ridicule it drew down at the irreligious court of Augustus the Strong. But his present ambition was to secure an estate which he might make the center of an influence in Lusatia like that which went forth from Halle, and therefore he purchased Berthelsdorf from his grandmother in April, 1722. This village had existed as a separate parish since the year 1346, when it formed part of the diocese of Löbau. During the negotiation of the sale the pastor, John Horn, died from a stroke, and Zinzendorf secured Rothe in his place, a man whose disposition and talents gave promise of hearty coöperation. Though a number of years had transpired since his leaving the University of Leipsic, conscientious scruples with regard to his own fitness for the pastoral office had hitherto caused him to avoid a call to any parish. For several years he had filled the pulpit of Trinity Church in Görlitz with great acceptance. As manager of his new property Zinzendorf appointed John George Heitz, a Swiss, formerly steward of his aunt the Countess of Pollheim. In his case also the earnest and outspoken character of his religious life was a chief recommendation.

Finally on the 7th of September a most important step was taken by Zinzendorf in connection with his plans, his marriage with Countess Erdmuth Dorothy Reuss, the sister of his friend Count Henry. She was equally devoted with himself to the furtherance of Pietistic institutions, Ebersdorf being in connection with Halle, and was fully in sympathy with his disinterested designs. To her at the time of their marriage he made over his entire possessions in a formal and legal document—purely from a chivalrous spirit of devotion, but as the event proved, providentially. After their tour the young couple made their home in apartments in Dresden, whilst Heitz commenced the erection of a mansion for their permanent residence at Berthelsdorf.

CHAPTER III.

THE FIVE LOYAL SONS OF THE UNITY AND THEIR DREAMS OF
A RESUSCITATION.

At length the new home at Berthelsdorf was habitable, and in it Zinzendorf enjoyed a retreat from the uncongenial life of officialdom. From July to November, 1723, he began to feel at leisure to enter upon the project which had influenced the purchase of his Lusatian estate, the promotion of vital godliness along the lines of activity suggested and developed by the Pietistic movement. Accordingly in August certain members of the *ecclesiola* previously established in his household were banded together into what became known as "The Covenant of the Four Brethren," in effect a renewal of the "Order of the Grain of Mustard Seed," but with definite aims. De Watteville, Rothe, and Schaeffer were his coadjutors. The first, a man of most attractive parts—affable, benevolent, frank, unaffected, cheerful, inviting confidence, energetic—was in the glow of first love for Christ, having reached a wholesome assurance of personal salvation only half a year before. Rothe's fervid piety was kindling a new light among the Lusatian villages, and Schaeffer of Görlitz was manifesting likeness of spirit with them. These men covenanted together to seek the power of the Holy Ghost for their own renewal in holiness and for the exaltation of the actual and practical sway of Christ throughout the land, and purposed to attain their aim by personal correspondence, by securing the allegiance· of pulpits pledged to seek to promote revivals of religion, by the publication of suitable literature, by the reformation of pastoral methods and of the inner life of the churches, by the itinerancy of evangelists, and by the founding and maintenance of a college distinctively religious in its educational methods. Dresden, where Zinzendorf held religious services in his apartments, Görlitz, and especially Berthelsdorf were to be the first centers of this activity.

Before the close of the year a printer at Pirna, Ludwig by name, was found willing to manage the publication house, if proper capital were provided; but a prohibitory decree of the Saxon cabinet in May, 1724, necessitated its establishment outside the country.

The educational enterprise seemed more feasible. In the autumn of 1723 Zinzendorf, De Watteville and Schaeffer had made a tour through Lower Silesia, during which the project had been discussed with friends, and a gratifying measure of approval secured. At Leube Captain von Schweinitz had given great encouragement, and had expressed his willingness to send his two sons as pupils. A prospective principal had been secured, John Christian Gutbier, a physician of Schmiedeberg enjoying an extensive practice. Hence on January 31, 1724, a written agreement was drawn up and signed by the four "brethren" and their wives, to provide the money needed for a commencement. The sum of two hundred thaler was subscribed by each, and in addition Captain von Schweinitz donated one hundred. A further sum of seven hundred was borrowed at six per cent.

When it came to the choice of a site, the village of Berthelsdorf was not itself selected, but a plot of ground not far from the humble homes of the Moravian refugees on the highway from Löbau to Zittau. Yet their coöperation was taken into the calculations in only a secondary way. Nevertheless God meant the plan of the titled owner of the land to fail, and designed the promotion of the interests of the obscure exiles through the attempted founding of this very college.

It was the foresight of an experienced man, blessed by the guidance of God, that had been employed in selecting the site for the new settlement.

When Lady Gersdorf had turned over the first refugees from Moravia to the care of Heitz, it was his first purpose to lodge them on a leasehold farm held by his employer. But whilst the men were absent, having returned to Görlitz to bring their wives and children, he consulted further with the Baroness. They came to an agreement that the newcomers should settle in some spot by themselves, and not in the already existing village. The Baroness proposed a place where there were

good springs, but Heitz preferred a point on the highway
from Löbau to Zittau, as affording better opportunity to live
by their trade. Lady Gersdorf objected that water could not
be found there. But Heitz was confident that God would help
and Marche agreed with him. Next morning at sunrise therefore Heitz went to the Hutberg, a prominent hill of basalt
south-west of Berthelsdorf. From its summit a charming outlook was to be had, the larger part of Upper Lusatia standing
out in all the beauty of alternate hill and valley, field and forest
and village, castle and spire. To the south and south-east rise
the Oderwitz Spitzberg, the Hochwald and the crags and
peaks of Saxon Switzerland, separating Lusatia from Bohemia,
and in the blue distance of the east the Isarkamm and the
Riesengebirge. To the west and north the nearer Kottmar
and Sohlander Rothstein and the distant Konigshain. A
noble panorama of well-tilled valleys and wooded slopes! But
the shrewd man of affairs who has seized on the strategic value
of the southern slopes of the Hutberg, where the highway skirts
its base, as the site of future industries, is less concerned with
the charms of sunrise from this favored spot, and more with
the rising of mists from the lower ground, that he may learn
where water is likely to be found. He accompanies his observations with fervent prayer. Lo! an abundant mist hangs over
a spot not far from the foot of the hill. Gratefully he vows,
"Upon this spot will I in Thy name build them the first house."
True, it is now a wild marshy stretch of unimproved land.
Tangled forest, bushes and briars are on every side. The very
highway is so poor that wagons sometimes sink axle-deep in
mud. But faith and energy will work wonders. Augustine
Neisser's wife will at first exclaim, "Where shall we find bread
in this wilderness?" But Christian David's recitation of the
third verse of the eighty-fourth Psalm, as he plunges his axe
into the first tree to be felled, shall be typical of a spirit that
can make the wilderness blossom as the garden of the Lord.

So in spite of all manner of trying circumstances the first
house has been completed before the young Count has come
to his new mansion, and by this time the Neissers and their
families are not the only expatriated strangers, and the place
has obtained a name. Already in July, 1722, Heitz when writing to the Count had named the spot Herrnhut, expressing
the prayer that at the foot of the Hutberg a city might rise,

CHRISTIAN DAVID.

which should not only be *"Unter des Herrn Hut"* (Under the Lord's watch-care) but also *"Auf des Herrn Hut"* (On the watch for the Lord).

Moreover the news sent home by the first refugees had encouraged their brothers to emigrate and join them. And the characteristic treatment received at the hands of the Austrian authorities had served as an additional stimulus; for in lieu of the fugitives who were beyond reach, they had been imprisoned, and had afterwards received a curt refusal when asking for permission to leave the land unmolested. Hence it was that when Hans Quitt and Frederick Riedel arrived at Herrnhut soon after Easter, 1723, they announced that the remainder of the Neisser family might shortly be expected. And this was only the beginning of emigrations.

In fulfillment of a vow connected with his wife's recovery from serious sickness in December, 1723, Christian David set out for Moravia, bearing a letter to Christian Jaeschke from his relatives at Herrnhut encouraging him to join them. He and his wife and five children arrived next month. Meantime Christian David was busy in Zauchtenthal and Kunwalde. In the former village he was welcomed into the home of David Schneider, whose father and grandfather had faithfully cherished the traditions of the Unitas Fratrum. The time for an appeal for decisions was most propitious. For the past year or two a deep current of spirituality had been making itself felt, and had been promoted by Schneider and David Nitschmann, a wagoner of Kunwalde, and others, who enjoyed the sympathy of Pastor Steinmetz of Teschen, just across the Silesian border. Kunwalde had been fortunate in having for fifteen years a priest who tolerated the conventicles, and his curate had been of like mind. Both these priests had recently died, and their successors were bigoted Papists, whilst a magistrate named Dietrich seconded the severity of the new men in their attempts to suppress private services. The commencement of persecutions and the fervid preaching of Christian David contemporaneous with it caused the smouldering fire of religious revival to burst out into flames. Card-playing, dancing, worldly amusements and the patronage of places of drinking practically ceased. Hundreds gathered openly for evangelical worship. Young men led in impressive prayer-meetings, and undertook house to house visitation to win others for

Christ. The opponents discovered that ridicule was unable to check the movement. Imprisonments began. The ordinary places of confinement proved inadequate to hold the confessors of the faith. All sorts of prisons were contrived—cellars, stables, the upper portions of castle-towers, loathsome holes. Some were compelled to work on the roads with their legs shackled. Others were transported to distant localities, where it was difficult to earn a living. Naturally, equal firmness was not displayed by all; but many proved true in spite of every inducement to recant. Emigration finally became the resource of the most determined, emigration even at the cost of all earthly possessions.

Yet hitherto the question with the refugees had been a question only of personal liberty of conscience. Although all five sons of George Neisser, who had stood beside the death-bed of father Jaeschke, and to whom he had foretold the renewal of the church of their forefathers, were now at the place where the resuscitation was to take place, not even do they appear to have contemplated anything more than the securing of a home where they might earn their living in peace and the while serve God according to His word and the example of their ancestors. But now five young men of Zauchtenthal definitely resolved to bring about the resuscitation of the Unitas Fratrum, should it please God to use them for this purpose. They were all sons of well-to-do parents, who knew that they ran a serious risk, and at best would reduce themselves to poverty by the step. They were David Nitschmann, a weaver, known later as the Syndic, a most useful agent of the Moravian Church in after years as a negotiator with various governments; David Nitschmann, a carpenter, to whom Bishop Daniel Ernest Jablonski transmitted the episcopate, a man of unflagging zeal and identified with the commencement of the missions amongst the heathen; Melchior Zeisberger, a pioneer in America, and the father of the apostle of the Delawares; John Töltschig, a leader in the establishment of the Moravian Church in the north of England and in Ireland; and David Nitschmann, the Martyr, an elder of the congregation at Herrnhut at the time of its baptism with the Spirit, and destined to witness a good confession by a martyr's death in the prison at Olmütz, on April 15, 1729. On the first of May, 1724, Töltschig's father, the village burgess, summoned these five comrades before him, and strictly enjoining their holding of religious services, gave them what he deemed soundly appropriate advice—to act as became their lively youth, frequent the taverns, and take part in dances and jollifications. Any attempt at emigration on their part would be dealt with severely. Decisive action was their reply. At ten o'clock on the night of May 2 they slipped out of Zauchtenthal and abandoned all their possessions and prospects. When fairly outside the place, they knelt down and commended it and their relatives to the mercy of God. Then they raised the hymn sung by Bohemian-Moravian Brethren when going into exile:

> " Selig ist der Tag, da ich muss scheiden,
> Mein liebes Vaterland muss meiden
> Und mich begeben in das Elend."

It was their deliberate and brave purpose to proceed to Lissa, the old Polish center of their fathers' Church, and there labor for its renewal. But at Jaegerndorf, south-east of Neisse, the roads forked, one way leading to Upper Lusatia. Here they resolved, before proceeding to Lissa, to pay a visit to Christian David. Reaching Nieder-Wiese on May 9, they received distinguished kindness from Pastor Schwedler. After praying the Lord's Prayer with them, he addressed them in words that now seem almost prophetic, and thrilled their very souls by his praise of the steadfastness of their forefathers. Thence he had them conducted to Friedersdorf with a letter to Baron von Schweinitz, whose treatment of them was very considerate, and who furthered them on their way to his kinsman, Captain von Schweinitz of Nieder-Leube. He in turn gave them guides to Berthesldorf, with a letter of recommendation to Pastor Rothe.

Here they arrived in the morning of the 12th of May, and were at first received very coldly by Rothe. But when he discovered that they were from good families and had actually given up all for Christ's sake, he became very friendly and tendered them his sincere sympathy. Afterwards he had them conducted to Herrnhut to the Neissers, who welcomed them with great joy. However their own feelings were those of disappointment. The grain in the fields seemed poor and instead of a place where a town of some size was being laid out, as Christian David's enthusiasm had led them to expect, they saw only a poor collection of modest houses.

It so happened that at three o'clock that very afternoon the corner-stone of the college which the associated brethren were erecting was to be laid. The five strangers were presented to Zinzendorf previous to the service; but Pastor Schwedler's letter did not insure them a cordial welcome. On the contrary, they felt keenly that the Count was not concerned in them. Soon afterwards the service commenced. In the course of it the Count delivered a powerful address, setting forth the purpose of the new building. His sentiments of utter devotion and absolute submission to God's will deeply impressed the five young Moravians. One expression in particular filled them with holy awe, his wish that God would put hindrances in the way or soon bring the project to naught, if it should not prove conducive to His glory. The heart-affecting prayer which Baron de Watteville offered, kneeling on the corner-stone, crowned the impressions of the hour. They felt that it was the purpose of Providence that they should cast in their lot with Herrnhut, and not proceed to Lissa.

The building whose corner-stone was laid amidst such peculiar circumstances served as a college for young noblemen for only one year and a half. Then it became an orphanage, and its large hall was used as the first place of worship for the people of Herrnhut. The hand of God is very evident in the failure of the plans of Zinzendorf and his associates, and their being rendered undesignedly subordinate to the renewal of the Unitas Fratrum.

CHAPTER IV.

THE DEVELOPMENT OF HERRNHUT, AND THE RESUSCITATION OF
THE MORAVIAN CHURCH MADE POSSIBLE THROUGH
THE BAPTISM OF THE SPIRIT.

For the present Zinzendorf gave his chief attention to other affairs than those of the Moravian exiles. Every effort was put forth to carry out the plans which he had formed with De Watteville, Rothe and Schaeffer. In Dresden Superintendent Löscher tolerated Zinzendorf's services in his own apartments. But when the Ebersdorf press, established after the prohibitory decree stopped negotiations with Ludwig at Pirna, began to issue Zinzendorf's *"Dresdener Socrates,"* a caustic weekly sheet which first appeared on November 1st, 1725, it made such a sensation that the third number was confiscated by the order of the consistory. However the inhibition was only temporary, and it reached a thirty-second number in December, 1726. From the same press an edition of the Bible appeared in 1725. Rothe's fervent eloquence attracted crowds from the surrounding country, and necessitated an enlargement of the church at Berthelsdorf. De Watteville had general oversight of the affairs of the college and of an orphanage for girls near the *Schloss* at Berthelsdorf. Schaefer's private meetings at Görlitz, however, aroused the opposition of other ministers. Nor did Rothe's efforts remain unchallenged; for in 1725, when the people from the neighboring estates manifested special interest by their attendance in large numbers, various noblemen sought to prohibit their retainers from going thither. But Zinzendorf had friends as well as enemies in the Saxon Cabinet, and a decision was secured annulling any and all such inhibitions. In fact the very purpose of those hostile to the four friends was thwarted by the accompanying order from the Saxon Cabinet, that its decision must be announced from the pulpits. Significant also was the cor-

respondence carried on by the Count, because destined hereafter to open the way for the Moravian Church in various
directions.   Prince Charles of Denmark (Canstein's benefactor), Countess von Schaumberg-Lippe, Count Schönberg-
Lichtenstein, several of the Reuss family, Count Promnitz of
Sorau, and others, were in touch with his efforts to further his
Pietistic undertakings.   With Cardinal Noailles he maintained
an exchange of letters, and through him sought to be of service to the Gallican Church.   As a means of this he translated
and published Arndt's *Wahres Christenthum*, which had proved
a blessing in the churches of Germany for more than a century.   Their mutual friend, De Watteville, carried the work to
the Cardinal, who received it with satisfaction.   But the chancellor of France forbade its circulation, and Zinzendorf had to
turn over the entire edition to a bookseller in Amsterdam,
Van Woesberge.

In the summer of 1724 Zinzendorf had paid a visit to Halle.
He went full of enthusiasm for its men, considering himself
their disciple, imitator and co-laborer.   He wished to report
to them the progress of his projects.   Anton rejoiced in the
light that was being kindled among the Lusatian hills, but
Francke would have been better pleased had Berthelsdorf been
distinctly tributary to Halle.   The visit resulted in the very
opposite of that for which it had been designed.   Hostility to
Zinzendorf and jealousy of his influence began to characterize
Halle.

But whilst the Count was occupied with his own projects,
the movement from Moravia to Herrnhut grew in force.
Nitschmanns, Hickels, Quitts, Webers, Fischers, Beyers and
others, some of them rich in their old homes, most of them in
comfortable circumstances, and all of them self-impoverished
by their willing exile for Christ's sake, made escape from spiritual bondage.   By May, 1725 there were ninety of these
refugees at Herrnhut.   Some of them had made thrilling
experiences.   Not a few had very narrowly escaped apprehension.   Some had made their way out of prison in a marvelous fashion.   For example, Christian Jaeschke was a
wealthy inhabitant of Sehlen, and had the prospect of being
made burgomaster.   When he felt the power of the Gospel he
at first tried to serve the Lord in secret, but soon found it
uncomfortable to try to serve God and Mammon.   Hence he

wrote to Augustine Neisser, to learn the prospects for new-comers at Herrnhut. The reply caused a violent struggle of conscience; but faith emerged victorious. At any cost he would seek Herrnhut. He and his family, seven souls in all, began the journey on a moonlight night. To their consternation a thick fog arose, and they lost their way. When at last they emerged into a familiar locality, behold! they had come back to their old neighborhood, and were in Zauchtenthal. Here they found lodging with David Schneider. When afterwards they learnt that the police had been following them in the night, and that the fog had saved them from being apprehended, their gratitude was great. Setting out on the following night, they made good their escape and in time reached their destination, though enduring great hardships by the way. After the flight of David Nitschmann, the weaver, his father was arrested and confined in the tower of the castle. One day he found a rope hanging out of a window. By means of this he escaped. His wife was arrested, but sang a hymn of Gospel trust in the presence of the magistrate, was dismissed and fled. Though they had no preconcerted plan, they were providentially brought together on the way to Herrnhut. David Nitschmann, the wheelwright, and David Schneider were thrown into prison and were chained. One day they found that through some negligence their chains had not been locked and that the doors of the castle had been left open. In broad daylight they walked out, went to Schneider's house, where they took refreshment, and then set out for Herrnhut. David Hickel was sent after them. Because he did not succeed in finding them he was accused of having abetted their flight, and was placed in a dungeon without food for three days and two nights. At last scraps of meat, meant for the dogs, were given to him, and he was taken to a room above ground. From this room he escaped by walking out between the guards when their backs were turned. He took time to bid farewell to his friends whilst passing through the village, and yet reached Herrnhut in safety. David Quitt was in the habit of conducting religious services in his own house. For this he was heavily fined. Later because he was suspected of intending to emigrate he was cast into a cold and filthy dungeon and had to pay an additional one hundred thaler before being released. After this, when he had given lodging to a visitor from Herrnhut, his house was

4

searched, but the man had already gone.　Next night Quitt fled with his family, taking nothing with them but the clothes they wore.　In a neigboring village they were stopped by several Roman Catholics, who prepared to send them back.　Quitt cast himself on their mercy, telling them what he had already endured.　Compassion wrought their release and even secured them aid.　David Weber and Thomas Fischer long lay in prison for their profession of evangelical faith.　Finally they were condemned to the galleys.　To escape this cruel fate they risked a leap from a lofty window of their prison, accomplished it in safety, and fled with their families.　Andrew Beyer, of Kunwalde, had been in confinement for more than a year, and had remained steadfast in spite of tortures.　Now he was condemned to lie in chains in a subterranean dungeon.　His companion for conscience sake was David Fritsch.　Early in the morning of the day during which the stern sentence was to be carried out Fritsch happened to push against the door of their cell, which was usually secured by a heavy chain drawn across it on the outside.　This had been imperfectly fastened, and fell to the ground.　Seeing no guards when they peered out, the two walked forth unhindered, and with their families set out for Herrnhut.　On their way through Moravia some armed men, conjectured to have been robbers, seized them, and one placed his sword at Beyer's breast, but the pitiful entreaties of the fugitives prevailed and they were released.

Not all indeed were so fortunate.　For example, David Nitschmann, henceforth to be known as the Martyr, having started for Moravia in disguise, in order to visit his father, was recognized and apprehended, and languished in prison in Kremsir.

Nor was every one who came to Herrnhut from Moravia as a matter of course allowed to remain there.　On his arrival he was brought before a justice, and compelled to give a reason for his presence.　Was he moved by anything else than a desire to serve Christ freely, he was given a letter of recommendation to his former feudal lord and dismissed with the advice to return, possibly with money in his pocket for the journey, furnished by Zinzendorf.　In no case were inducements thrown out on the Count's part to attract refugees.　Christian David's visits to his fatherland, whither he went ten times in all, were in fact contrary to Zinzendorf's expressed desires.

Yet the tide of emigration continued. Therefore in August, 1726, Zinzendorf undertook a journey to Kremsir, in order to arrive at some agreement with the imperial authorities in regard to this delicate matter, despite the risk involved in placing himself in the power of these officials. But the interview with Cardinal von Schrattenbach, Bishop of Olmütz, and with his brother, Count Otto, an officer in the imperial service, proved ineffectual. When he based his arguments upon the right of emigration granted to Protestant subjects by the terms of the Peace of Westphalia, he received a polite hearing, nothing more. When he asked for the liberation of Nitschmann, or at least to be permitted to see him, a downright refusal followed. Moreover it was well that he did not prolong his own stay in the city for more than twelve hours, for the rapidity of his movements alone saved him from the pursuit which these gentlemen instituted.

Emigrations continued in spite of Austrian watchfulness and notwithstanding the scruples of the young Saxon Count. It was natural, too, that the fervent religious life of those who had shown that they considered freedom of conscience the most precious thing, should attract others than Moravians. This, in conjunction with the fame attending the preaching of Rothe, began to draw one and another from the immediate vicinity and from various parts of Germany. As early as 1725 Frederick Kühnel, a linen-weaver from the neighboring village of Oberoderwitz, had built himself a house near those of the Moravians, and thus introduced into the place a valuable industry. Another industry was brought by the brothers Martin and Leonard Dober, Swabians, of Austrian extraction, who had been led to Saxony during their "*Wanderjahre*" as potters by the fact that their uncle was a maker of artistic ware in the capital. Diversified occupations and the reputation for thoroughness acquired by Herrnhut began to give promise of prosperity.

But with the variety of religious sentiments now represented in the place, troubles arose. Some of the people were practically Lutherans, others Calvinists, whilst a number of the Moravians, under the lead of the five young men who desired the resuscitation of the Unitas Fratrum as a *sine qua non* of their remaining in Herrnhut, urged the adoption of its principles and practices. Moreover individuals who adhered in part to one or another confession, clung to their own peculiar views. Their standing in relation to the parish of Berthelsdorf was also undefined, and antagonism arose between the members of the *ecclesiola* there and the people of Herrnhut who resisted all efforts to bring them into its membership. Nor had any rules and regulations been formulated for the government of the inner life of Herrnhut. Sectarianism and separatism threatened to wreck the welfare of the new settlement. Many kept aloof from the administration of the word and the sacraments. The trouble was intensified towards the close of 1726 by the arrival of a company of Schwenkfelder from Silesia. These were descendants of the followers of Caspar Schwenkfeld, a Silesian noble contemporary with Luther, who had in the main embraced the evangelical faith but had disagreed with the Reformer respecting the Lord's Supper, holding peculiar views of his own. They had been oppressed by the Lutherans, especially in 1590 and 1650, and had been exposed to great hardships through the machinations of the Jesuits in 1719. Now a number of families had cast themselves for a time on the benevolence of the Count, most of them residing at Berthelsdorf.

Zinzendorf himself was very much worried by the outlook. Francke had cautioned him regarding the separatistic tendencies of Herrnhut in 1725. Early in 1727 he therefore sought and obtained indefinite leave of absence from his official duties, that he might devote himself to the people on his estate. Upon removing thither and discovering that Rothe had lost the confidence of the Moravians, he made himself responsible for their spiritual welfare as catechist. To most successfully discharge the duties of this office, he made his home at Herrnhut on the twenty-first of April, and entrusting his business matters wholly to his wife and De Watteville, gave his entire time and attention to the task of correcting existing evils. He now labored earnestly with individuals, seeking to converse closely and searchingly with every inhabitant of the place. It became evident to him that a problem requiring solution, was how to accede to the desire of the Moravians to have the disciplinary features of their ancient church preserved to them, and at the same time maintain the connection with the parish organization. Even if he had at this time desired to resuscitate the Unitas Fratrum pure and simple, the laws of the state would not have allowed it; nor was he at present contemplating anything of this sort. In fact the peculiar relation of Herrnhut to the State Church for some time to come and Zinzendorf's later effort to have it both a Moravian congregation and a part of the State Church gave a peculiar tendency to the development of the Unitas Fratrum for many decades. Moreover his relation to Herrnhut in civil affairs complicated his endeavors as an individual. He had not only accorded the Moravians a refuge, but was their feudal lord.

He next consulted with Rothe, Christian David, Marche—the last named now his legal adviser—and with the most influential of the Moravians, for the drawing up of statutes which should regulate the communal life of Herrnhut, special consideration being given to what the Moravians represented to be the traditional discipline of the old Unitas Fratrum. The result was, that on May 12th forty-two statutes relating to Christian walk and conduct, together with certain prohibitions and injunctions setting forth their relation to Zinzendorf as their feudal lord, were publicly accepted by all the people of Herrnhut, and each individual gave the Count his right hand in token of solemn purpose to abide by the compact. On the same day twelve "elders" were chosen to have spiritual supervision, four of whom, after the time honored usage of the Bohemian Brethren, were by lot singled out as "chief elders"—Christian David, George Nitschmann, Melchior Nitschmann and Christopher Hoffmann. Night watchmen, inspectors of public works, watchers by the sick, almoners of the poor, etc., were subsequently chosen. To promote personal growth in grace and spiritual fellowship, "*Bunden*," that is, "bands" or "classes," were instituted, small associations of those who had spiritual affinity for each other. These had frequent conferences for prayers and the interchange of personal experience. During the subsequent weeks the conferences of Zinzendorf with the elders as well as the gatherings of these several companies and the Sunday services were marked by signs of a deep undercurrent of spiritual interest. Melchior Zeisberger, George Schmidt, Melchior Nitschmann, David Tanneberger, Frederick Böhnisch, Leonard and Martin Dober, Augustine Neisser and others, entered into a special covenant to meet frequently for mutual edification, and gave special study to the first Epistle of St. John.

From July 22 to August 4, Zinzendorf was absent on a visit to Baron Gersdorf at Hartmannsdorf. Shortly before he had received a copy of Comenius' *Ratio Disciplinae*, a work with which he was up to this time wholly unfamiliar. He was amazed at the substantial agreement of the statutes of May 12th with the discipline of the Unitas Fratrum as set forth by Comenius—itself a proof of the purity of the tradition respecting the ways of their fathers preserved amongst the "Hidden Seed" in Moravia, and a token of the vitality of that "Seed." When he communicated to the assembled people his German version of the *Ratio Disciplinae* on his return in August, it caused a profound sensation. He himself now for the first time began to think seriously that the resuscitation of the Unity of the Brethren might be providentially intended through the establishment of the colony of Moravians at Herrnhut.

The varied experiences of this memorable year culminated in a realization of the presence of the Lord and a baptism of His Spirit in connection with the celebration of the Holy Communion at Berthelsdorf on Wednesday, August 13th.

The day began with a short address on the Holy Communion by Rothe at Herrnhut. It was at his invitation that the special celebration was about to take place, the first opportunity of this kind since a better state of feeling had been restored, and he desired to be a guest at the Lord's table with his people. At the parish church in Berthelsdorf the service opened with the hymn:

> " Entbinde mich, mein Gott,"
> " Deliver me, my God, from all that's now enchaining."

Then Pastor Rothe administered the rite of confirmation to two Moravian candidates with a blessing that was truly apostolic. A most earnest discourse followed. During the singing of another hymn:

> " Hier legt mein Sinn sich vor Dir nieder,"
> " My soul before Thee prostrate lies,"

the congregation knelt, and then the Count offered the public confession amidst the penitent tears of many. He interceded for a true union of hearts, a freedom from any sort of schism and from offense to those that were without, for the solid and unshaken foundation in the blood and cross of Christ, for the establishing of their brethren and the many hundreds of awakened persons in other places who had wandered into by-paths, and finally for a blessing upon two of the elders who were absent, Christian David and Melchior Nitschmann, away on a visit to fellow Moravian exiles at Sorau in Hungary. Three other fervent prayers followed. The absolution was pronounced by Pastor John Luke Süss, of Hennersdorf, who administered the elements. The hearts of those who partook were filled with peace and joy in the Holy Ghost in a manner they had never experienced before, and they were drawn to one another in loving union. In short, they received a veritable baptism of the Spirit, though the full significance of the day was only later completely realized. Montgomery describes the transactions of this spiritual birthday of the resuscitated Brethren's Church in appreciative verse:

"They walked with God in peace and love,
　　But failed with one another;
While sternly for the faith they strove,
　　Brother fell out with brother;
But He in Whom they put their trust,
　　Who knew their frames, that they were dust,
Pitied and healed their weakness.

He found them in His House of prayer,
　　With one accord assembled,
And so revealed His presence there,
　　They wept for joy and trembled;
One cup they drank, one bread they brake,
　　One baptism shared, one language spake,
Forgiving and forgiven.

Then forth they went, with tongues of flame,
　　In one blest theme delighting,
The love of Jesus and His Name
　　God's children all uniting!
That love, our theme and watchword still;
　　That law of love may we fulfill,
And love as we are loved."

It is remarkable, that on the same day and at the same hour Christian David and Melchior Nitschmann, at Sablat near Sorau, felt an overpowering impulse to pray for their brethren at Herrnhut, and on their return at once asked what had transpired just at that time.

CHAPTER V.

Herrnhut for some years remained an integral part of the parish of Berthelsdorf, and yet gradually developed communal, liturgical and doctrinal features of its own, practically complete by the year 1732; and in 1756 an absolute separation took place, a legally binding agreement to this effect being concluded in 1758 between the patron of Herrnhut and the ecclesiastical authorities of the older community. The resuscitation of the Unitas Fratrum as such could take place only after a formative period of transition. Several features of the revival in the latter half of 1727 are however of significance in their influence upon future regulations of the church.

One was the awakening amongst the children, fostered by the Count and by the teachers, Krumpe at Berthelsdorf and Rohleder at Herrnhut. Among the first to be affected were Susanna, the eleven-year-old daughter of Frederick Kühnel, Anna, the sister of Melchior Nitschmann, Rosina Fischer and Julia Quitt. Soon religious interest touched the boys also. Boys and girls delighted in hours of prayer, and young though they were obtained assurance of personal salvation, which led them to pledge their lives to the service of Christ.

Another feature was the institution of the "Hourly Intercession," called forth by the dangers that threatened the settlement, some of them arising in connection with the revival amongst the children. For Rothe did not remain on the best terms with Herrnhut, and when Kühnel disapproved of his daughter's intimacy with her awakened Moravian associates, sided with him and in his public utterances began to display an ultra-Lutheran tendency. Halle's position became positively hostile. Zinzendorf's own relatives, his half-brother and his aunt Henrietta, cooled towards him and then antagonized his work.

It was reported from Dresden that the crushing of Herrnhut had been determined. Lords of adjacent domains prohibited attendance at the services in Herrnhut. When Jacob Neisser and Gottlob Wried went to a neighboring place to hold a meeting, the latter was arrested and lodged in prison at Zittau. All this convinced of the need of unintermitted prayer in behalf of Herrnhut. On the 27th of August the time from midnight to midnight was divided amongst twenty-four men and the same number of women, in such a manner that each one of them should consecutively spend an hour in intercession, the hours being assigned by lot.

Various other unique characteristics began to distinguish the life of Herrnhut. Modifications in the internal and communal arrangements were made at various times, especially in 1728; yet the following distinctive features obtained more or less permanence:

The idea of a theocratic republic prevailed, in so far as it was permitted by the laws of the land and by the requirements of feudal suzerainty which Zinzendorf was not at liberty to wholly resign.

A town meeting and a church council regulated secular and religious affairs. A communal court of justice similar to the *collegium judicum* of the old Unitas Fratrum had the general oversight of business and trade and arbitrated when disagreements arose; its members were Frederick de Watteville, Tobias Friederich, Zinzendorf's *Kapellmeister*, a certain Bezold and Michael Linner. At the head of the community in both civil and ecclesiastical relations stood Zinzendorf, with De Watteville as his chief assistant in business matters. The spiritual oversight was committed to the elders, whose number varied from time to time, there being finally only one "chief elder" with one or more assistants, not lording it over others, but aiming to serve them and intercede for their welfare. Martin Linner and Leonard Dober were noteworthy incumbents of this office, the former choosing alike in winter and in summer to sleep on a bare board so as not to differ from the poorest of his brethren. Augustine Neisser, Martin Dober, David Nitschmann, the future bishop, Melchior Nitschmann, John Gottlob Klemm and Martin Rohleder, men distinguished for ability to edify by public speech, were commissioned to conduct the public services at Herrnhut, though the occasions of worship and the sacra-

ments still took the people to Berthelsdorf. Zinzendorf frequently occupied the speaker's desk. Provision for a thorough
culture of spiritual life was made by the subdivision of the congregation into the "bands" or "classes" according to sex and
spiritual affinity, each "band" choosing its own leader. These
"bands" were not identical with the "choirs" of a later date.
It is true that in 1728 those of the unmarried men who were
living in homes where the heads of the families were likely to
be absent much of the time on account of work, in order to
avoid all occasion for reproach moved into one house where
they lived by themselves, and on May 14th, 1730, Anna Nitschmann and seventeen single women covenanted together to have
their entire life and all its relationships, even thoughts of marriage, subordinated to the service of Christ; but it does not
appear that there existed at this time any systematic division
of the entire congregation according to sex and condition in
life, with all that the "choir system" entailed. The subordination of the family life to the "choir" regulations took place only
after Zinzendorf had developed the theological conceptions
which he deduced from the truth that the perfect life of Christ as
well as His sufferings and death avail for man's salvation. As
yet "band meetings," with their opportunity for free utterance of
personal experience, were voluntary associations for the culture of Christian life, though the transition to the later "choir-
meetings" was anticipated in the brief addresses of Zinzendorf
to the different "bands" (*Viertel Stunden*) on Sunday afternoons.
The first germs of his thought that the merits of Christ are to
be applied in a mysterious manner to the various relations of
sex and age appear in a hymn, "*Auf Mariä Verkündigung*,"
which he wrote in July, 1729. Time must be allowed for the
development of this conception, and for the change from voluntary connection with a "band" into compulsory membership in
a "choir;" so that the "choir system" as such is not to be associated with Herrnhut in these years. In its complete development it belongs rather to the Wetteravian era.

But in addition to the frequent meetings of the "bands" other
and ample provision was made for the religious life of Herrnhut. Daily services were held soon after dawn, with a similar
brief season of devotions for the aged and infirm at 8.30, and
a service for the children at 10. On Sunday the sermon which
has been preached by Rothe at Berthelsdorf, was repeated at

Herrnhut in the afternoon by Zinzendorf or by some other layman for the benefit of those who had been unable to proceed to the parish church. Gradually visitors from the surrounding country frequented this service, which thus obtained the name of *Fremdenstunde*, whilst in contrast the evening service was known as the *Gemeinstunde*, it being especially designed to edify those who were assured of their relationship to the Saviour. In the spring of the year 1728, the so-called *Bettag* or *Gemeintag* was instituted. This was a monthly festival, mainly set apart for the reading of reports or letters from Christian friends, but later especially from missionaries in various fields of labor. Numerous services were held. The occasion awakened much enthusiasm and fostered the missionary spirit.

Marriages and baptisms were conducted in a simple and unostentatious manner, Rothe always officiating. In 1730 baptisms were transferred to Herrnhut. In the same year the celebrated "Hutberg" cemetery was laid out. No outward show of mourning in dress was allowed; for the departed had "gone home." In 1732 the celebration of Easter morning in the open air took place for the first time. In 1733 the midnight watch-meeting, on New Year's Eve, was introduced.

The celebration of the Holy Communion was attended with great solemnity, and various preparatory services were customary. At first the sacrament was enjoyed only four times a year, but in 1731 a monthly communion was instituted, the participants still proceeding to Berthelsdorf. Later a transfer was made to Herrnhut, Rothe officiating as before. Theologically the Brethren refrained from attempts to explain the words of institution, the principles of their spiritual forefathers prevailing in this respect. The words of Christ were accepted in all simplicity, without subjecting them to any human interpretation. The chief care remained that all the members should worthily partake. To this end private examination was enjoined on all. The elders and their helpers conversed singly with each individual. If any one was found not to be in the proper frame of mind, he was advised to remain away from the Lord's table. After having enjoyed the sacrament at Berthelsdorf, the communicants assembled in the chapel at Herrnhut, being seated according to sex; then during the singing of a hymn which treated of brotherly love, the kiss of peace was given. Candidates for admission to the Lord's Supper prior to confirmation not only received a careful instruction in the doctrines of religion, but were also privately counseled by the elders and trained in all spiritual things.

Lovefeasts, based on the ἀγάπαι of the primitive church (Jude v. 12), were originally of a private character. On days of special significance, or on Sunday evenings, or in connection with weddings, they were held at Zinzendorf's house, and only a small company participated. The elders also had their love-feasts amongst themselves. At such times the service con-sisted of singing, conversation, and religious narratives. Usually water and bread were served, or water only.

The washing of feet, *Pedelavium*, in imitation of Christ's example, recorded in John 13, originally occurred in single instances only, on the arrival of distinguished friends or breth-ren at Herrnhut, according to 1 Timothy 5:10. The usage was not general, nor did it form a part of the ritual. Never-theless Rothe took great offense at it, claiming that it would tend to sectarianism and depreciation of the value of the sacra-ments.

The "Text-book" originated in 1728. In the early part of this year Zinzendorf delivered addresses in the daily singing meet-ings, either on a text of Scripture, or on a stanza from a hymn. On the 3d of May he recommended the stanza constituting his theme as the *Losung*, or watchword, for the congrega-tion on the following day. This usage was continued every evening, and a copy of the watchwords was preserved. Towards the end of the year and early in the next, Zinzendorf, with the assistance of the elders, made a collection of Scripture texts. This collection was completed on June 29. Out of it an elder drew a text at the evening service. On the follow-ing morning this text was made known in every house in Herrnhut as the word for the day. A brief exhortation might be added. The same usage was continued in 1730. In 1731, however, a collection of texts was printed for the first time. Since then this devotional manual has been issued every year.

Yet another marked feature of the inner life of Herrnhut was the frequent recourse to the guidance of the lot when in perplexity. It was employed in the selection of the first elders in 1727, but whether it was used officially in other cases prior to 1728 does not appear. Then it was introduced as a customary mode of deciding questions in church councils and conferences. In July, 1732, it was employed in regard to the proposed marriage of John Töltschig and Julia Haberland, and after 1733 its voluntary use in connection with marriages became frequent.

From the very nature of the case a community of zealous Christians like the people of Herrnhut—by the year 1730 fifty-six of them had borne chains for Christ's sake—could not remain isolated, the more so on account of Zinzendorf's rank and his previous extensive correspondence with friends of the Pietistic movement. Already in September, 1727, with the prayers of the congregation, David Nitschmann, the Syndic, and John Nitschmann were dispatched to Copenhagen, where they were most kindly received by Prince Charles and Princess Hedwig Sophia, by Chamberlain von Pless and Baron Sohlenthal. They returned with a manuscript account of Hans Egede's work in Greenland. Andrew Beyer and Gottlieb Wried were sent to Prince Christian Ernest of Saalfeld and to Professor Buddaeus of Jena. During this visit Beyer made a deep impression upon Augustus Gottlieb Spangenberg, a student at Jena, and the connection was formed from which sprang an association of members of the University who were in sympathy with Herrnhut, many of whom later entered the Moravian ministry. Buddaeus sent a letter of cordial greetings by the hands of the messengers. Zinzendorf himself visited Thuringia during the same year, with several of the Moravians as his companions. Christian David and David Nitschmann, his fellow-craftsman, itinerated in Austrian territory. Andrew Beyer next went to Teschen in Silesia. Augustine Neisser visited Sorau in Hungary. Melchior Nitschmann and George Schmidt, penetrating into Moravia, were arrested and imprisoned, Nitschmann to die and Schmidt to meditate for years in a dungeon as a preparation for missionary work in Africa. Wenceslaus Neisser, John Töltschig and David Nitschmann, the Syndic, proceeding to England in order to form a connection with the Society for the Propagation of Christian Knowledge, failed in their purpose, but were kindly received by the Countess Lippe-Schaumberg, a lady of the court who belonged to Zinzendorf's circle of friends, and at least indirectly gave the initiative to the work of the Moravian Church in Britain. Melchior Zeisberger was dispatched to Stockholm. Christian David and Timothy Fiedler, in 1729, proceeding by way of Berlin, where they visited Bishop Daniel Ernest Jablonski, one of the two surviving bishops of the Unitas Fratrum, went to Riga and Reval, and were later followed by David Nitschmann, the Syndic—a prelude to extensive activity in the Baltic Provinces. Others went to Switzerland, by way of Tübingen, and thence visited the Westerwalde and Wetteravia, and Zinzendorf himself journeyed to Berleburg, and repeatedly to Jena, where he organized the Christian union of the students.

Meantime Herrnhut grew and the immigrations from Moravia continued. In 1731 seventy-four refugees arrived. But the gradual separation from the parish of Berthelsdorf and the State Church was not to be accomplised without inner friction as well as antagonism from outside. At least two specially formidable crises arose.

During Zinzendorf's absence in the summer of 1728, Rothe and other Lutheran ministers of the neighborhood persuaded Christian David and some of the elders to give up the name and regulations of the Brethren's Church, and to amalgamate entirely and absolutely with the State Church. It was plausibly asserted that by taking such a step their true catholicity would be increased, and that not only would they themselves escape all persecution, but also prevent persecutions from being brought upon evangelical believers in Austrian territory, whom the Roman Catholics identified with them. The stanchest and most influential of the Moravians were at the time absent on journeys. By most of those who happened to be at home the new idea was favorably received, though others vigorously opposed it. Christian David and Andrew Beyer were dispatched to Zinzendorf at Jena to tell him of the proposal. He and the Moravians who were with him protested against it. They sent a letter to Herrnhut embodying their objections, and another was drawn up by Spangenberg, and signed by one hundred and two students and professors, beseeching the people of Herrnhut not to cast away the legacy received from their fathers. Zinzendorf added a positive refusal to consent to it, with a reminder of his rights as feudal lord. He foresaw that the true Moravians would instantly leave Herrnhut, break away altogether from the State Church, and thus be deprived of Christian liberty. Besides he considered an attempt to avoid persecution unworthy. On his return the scheme fell through.

But in the beginning of the year 1731 Zinzendorf himself proposed and earnestly advocated the very thing which he had so vigorously antagonized. Probably he was influenced by the dissatisfaction with regard to the developments at Herrnhut, expressed by those of his opponents whose piety he respected. This new crisis was far more perilous than the former. The man who by force of personal character and circumstances stood at the head of the community now advocated the change. On the 7th of January the subject was laid before the church council. It met with strenuous opposition from the Moravians. Finally it was agreed that the whole matter should be referred there and then to the decision of the lot. Two tickets were prepared. On one of them stood, "Brethren, stand fast, and hold the traditions which ye have been taught," 2 Thess. 2:15. On the other was written, "To them that are without law, as without law," 1 Cor. 9:21. All being ready, Zinzendorf's son, Christian Renatus, a young lad, was called in, and drew one of the tickets. It was the former. Zinzendorf's implicit faith in the lot led him at once to yield. He was more and more persuaded that God had some special purpose with Herrnhut.

But now the ever growing opposition from outside assumed serious proportions. This was in part owing to the continued immigrations from Moravia, and in part owing to the dissatisfaction of neighboring clergymen and of the leading Pietists at Halle. Formal accusations were laid before the Saxon court, both by Zinzendorf's personal enemies on the ground that he was a dangerous man, and by the Austrian government on the allegation that he was enticing its subjects to remove to his estates. He therefore asked for a judicial investigation. This was granted. From January 19 to 22, 1732, the Prefect of Görlitz, Baron George Ernest von Gersdorf, by royal commission thoroughly examined into the affairs of Herrnhut. Emigrants from twenty-three places were questioned concerning their migration. The result was a most favorable report. Government took no action, however, until August of the following year; but in March Zinzendorf asked for permission to resign his office in the service of the State, and obtained his request. The further reception of refugees from Bohemia and Moravia was next prohibited. Nor did the intrigues of

the Count's enemies cease. They sought to have him imprisoned in the fortress of Königstein, but failed. Yet there were
indications that they would achieve his banishment. He therefore anticipated the decree by carrying into full effect the transfer of his estates to his wife, and especially of those acquired
since their marriage. In November, 1732, an order was received from the Saxon Court, directing him to alienate his
property. Fortunately the decree came too late. Had his
estates passed into hostile or even unsympathetic hands, the
Moravians at Herrnhut would undoubtedly have been dis-
persed.

CHAPTER VI.

THE FIRST DECADE OF THE FOREIGN MISSIONS.

Of the various affiliations effected by Count Zinzendorf that with the Danish court was destined to be of first and most immediate significance. That the man who in youth established his "Order of the Mustard Seed" had been observant of movements for the evangelization of the world is apparent from the fact that when David and John Nitschmann were sent in 1727 to Prince Charles, the brother of Frederick the Fourth, at Copenhagen, they had instructions to inquire whether the Brethren could be of service in connection with the undertaking of the Lutheran missionary, Hans Egede, in Greenland. Since 1708 this large-hearted servant of Christ had devoted himself to an effort in behalf of descendants of the ancient Norse settlers on the east coast of that dreary land, whom he hoped to find and lead to a knowledge of the truth. When at last he was able to make his way thither, in 1721, disappointment was inevitable, for no such people could be discovered. But his attention had been turned to the Eskimos, and to them he heroically ministered for their bodily diseases, though as yet he could not find the key to unlock their hearts. The Danish king seconded his project with an attempt to found a colony of soldiers and traders, but the results had been inadequate. Nor was this the only manifestation of the sympathy of the Danish court with the promotion of vital religion. Its well-known attitude in religious affairs had long awakened in Zinzendorf a desire to enter the service of this pronouncedly Christian government, and at that to become a court preacher, if it could be brought about without a surrender of conscientious convictions. Ever since the death of his grandmother, in 1726, this had been a cherished purpose. He as yet by no means proposed to confine his energies to the interests of the

5

Moravians, considering himself *Ein freier Knecht des Herrn*—a
free volunteer in the service of Christ.

In October, 1730, Frederick the Fourth died.   The accession of Christian the Sixth, whose coronation was appointed
for the following May, seemed to offer a favorable opportunity
to the Count, ready as he was to surrender his Saxon office.
On April 25th he therefore set out, with David Nitschmann,
the future bishop, and two other Moravians as his companions.
The visit in Copenhagen was a protracted one.   Having previously been on a footing of intimacy with several members of
the court, he was received with distinguished kindness.   In
token of sympathy with his zeal in the service of God, the king
decorated him with the Order of the Danebrog, in June.   But
his wish for some office was not gratified.

Yet this failure, like several failures of Zinzendorf's plans
during these years in connection with affairs beyond the horizon of the Moravians, became pregnant in results for Herrnhut.
Two widely separated Macedonian cries met with a response
in consequence.   On the one hand the Count learnt to his
sorrow that the royal policy with regard to Greenland had
been reversed and the soldiers and artisans recalled.   He also
met two Eskimos from whom he heard that Egede's efforts
were on the verge of failure, and that he sorely needed help.
On the other hand, Anthony, the negro body servant of Count
Laurwig, described most pathetically the dark moral and intellectual and religious condition of the slaves in the Danish West
Indies.   These things led him to plan forthwith for missions
in Greenland and Lapland, and in Africa and America.   He
requested and received permission to take Anthony with him
to Herrnhut.

Herrnhut had been providentially prepared for this visit.
Already in 1644 or 1645 Comenius in his *Judicum duplex de
regula fidei* had set forth the truth that the evangelization of
the heathen is an imperative obligation for a living church, and
had planned the translation of the Scriptures into the Turkish
as preparatory to the propagation of the faith in Moslem lands.
And the spiritual sons of Comenius had already been vouchsafed a recognition of the duty of evangelization as binding
upon them.   On the 10th of February, 1728, a memorable day
of prayer had been observed in Herrnhut.   Zinzendorf and his
brethren had conferred together in addresses interspersed with

hymns and prayers, how they might venture upon some worthy undertaking for God. Distant lands had been named to be won for Him—Turkey and Africa, Greenland and Lapland. "But it is impossible to find a way thither," some had said. Zinzendorf had replied, "The Lord can and will give grace and strength for this." His reply and child-like faith had so inspired all, that on the following day twenty-six unmarried brethren had come together, with a view to prepare to answer the call of the Lord when it came to them. The missionary purpose was already there, and needed only the external occasion to change it to the missionary deed. This occasion was now to be furnished.

"On the 23d of July," says Spangenberg, "the day after the Count returned to Herrnhut, he reported, in the meeting then held, what he had heard in Copenhagen with regard to the wretched state of the negroes. By the grace of God, his words produced such an effect upon Leonard Dober, that he there and then resolved to offer himself as a missionary to these poor enslaved races. The same resolution was formed at the same time by another of the Brethren, Tobias Leopold; but though they were intimate friends, they said nothing to each other on the subject till they had spread the matter before the Lord. After an almost sleepless night, Leonard Dober opened the Bible, on the morning of July 24, to seek for some direction from above, and his eye fell upon Deut. 32:47, 'It is not a vain thing for you; because it is your life; and through this thing ye shall prolong your days in the land, whither ye go over Jordan to possess it.' The words greatly strengthened him. He then communicated his thougths to Leopold, by whom they were warmly reciprocated. They then knelt together before God, and told Him the desire of their hearts. On the 25th of July Leopold wrote to the Count, and informed him that he and Dober felt impelled to go and preach to the negroes. That evening their letter was read in the singing-meeting, without any mention of names. On the 29th the negro Anthony arrived from Copenhagen, and a short time afterwards gave his own account, in one of the meetings of the Brethren, of the deplorable condition of the black population in the West Indies. But he stated it as his belief that it would be impossible for a missionary to reach these poor creatures in any other way than by becoming a slave himself,

for their toils were so incessant and exhausting that there was
no opportunity of instructing them, except when they were at
work."

This prospect did not deter Dober or Leopold, but rather
confirmed them in their resolution. The matter being then
referred to the church council, it was decided by lot that
Dober should go to the West Indies, but that Leopold should
remain a while longer in Herrnhut. Even before Anthony had
made his personal appeal, the example of the two friends
affected their companions so powerfully that two others, Mat·
thew Stach and Frederick Böhnisch, offered to go to Greenland. But in the case of each and all Zinzendorf deemed it
wise to delay their actual departure, that their fitness might be
thoroughly tested. It was therefore not until August 21,
1732, that Dober, now twenty-six years of age, set out for
Copenhagen on foot, with David Nitschmann, the carpenter,
nine years his senior, as his companion. They had each one
ducat, and had also three thaler in common—their sole resources for a journey of several thousand miles. Wherever
they came, as they proceeded via Wernigerode and Hansberg,
ridicule or dissuasion formed their welcome, with the sole exception of the cordial encouragement received from Countess
Stollberg-Wernigerode. Nevertheless they remained firm, and
at Copenhagen Counts Reuss and Blum were won by this determined front, and becoming their advocates at the court, rendered various services in furtherance of their project. Thus
at last, on October 8, 1732, they set sail, Nitschmann having
secured work as ship's carpenter, and reached St. Thomas on
December 13.

The island had been in the possession of Denmark for sixty-
six years. When Erik Smidt, of the good ship *De Endracht*,
took possession of it in the name of his Majesty Frederick the
Third, he found about a dozen English and Dutch families on its
soil. As early as 1680 there were fifty tobacco plantations, and
slaves were already employed. The poor Caribs were dwind-
ling away into extinction, leaving a few carvings on rocks at
Rif Bay and scanty celts to tell the meager story of their ownership of the Virgin Islands. Christian the Fifth, in accordance
with the sentiment of his times, directly encouraged the importation of African slave labor by establishing forts on the Gold
Coast and ordering ships thither to secure negroes for St.

Thomas. By 1732, thanks to the trade in tobacco, St. Thomas had become a flourishing port. Its houses of brick, one story in height, paved with tiles and whitewashed in the interior, were arranged along one long street, conforming to the shape of the bay, and along two shorter streets, near the handsome factory of the Danish Company, and were occupied chiefly by the families of numerous Huguenot refugees. A fort served to assert the majesty of the Danish flag. The well-tilled, though small, estates in the interior produced indigo, sugar-cane, manioc, millet, sweet potatoes, and all kinds of fruit and herbs, in addition to tobacco.

Long before the arrival of Dober and Nitschmann provision had been made for the religious welfare of the colonists. Indeed Jorgen Iwersen, who became the first governor in 1672, was a martinet in every relationship of life. Under his regime every inhabitant was obliged to attend service every Sunday in Christiansfort at drum-beat, under penalty of twenty pounds of tobacco. He who worked or allowed his men to work on the Lord's day was liable to a fine of fifty pounds of tobacco. But for the spiritual care and enlightenment of the blacks nothing was done. The type of religion dominant amongst the whites was distinguished by narrow intolerance and a comfortable belief in one's own predestined inheritance of heaven together with a large measure of indifference as to the predestination of any other man. In fact the poor slaves had hitherto supposed that to rejoice in a Saviour was a perquisite of their masters, while obeahism and fetishism were sufficiently good for them. Great was their delight when on the third Sunday in Advent, 1732, the Moravian missionaries commenced their labors with the message, "The poor have the gospel preached to them."

Dober and Nitschmann were at first the guests of a planter who received them into his house on the strength of a letter of recommendation. Anna and Abraham, the sister and brother of Anthony, made easy their approach to the slaves. For four months Nitschmann supported his companion and himself by working at his craft. But it had not been intended that he should remain permanently. In April, 1733, he therefore returned to Europe. Dober for a time found himself in great straits. As a potter he could gain no employment. Governor Gardelin then kindly offered him the position of steward of his household, and so saved him from the worst distress. But this occupation left too little leisure for his more important work. Hence next year he cut loose from this assured means of livelihood, and earned a precarious living as a watchman in town and on the cotton-plantations, content, nevertheless, since now he could devote far more attenttion to the negroes.

To be thus identified with the blacks at this time made heavy demands upon moral courage. It involved social ostracism as a matter of course, possibly even something worse. For the little island of St. John, only four miles away and under the same jurisdiction, was the scene of terrible events. Colonized only in 1716, its slave population so outnumbered the whites that the most stringent regulations had been framed to keep the former in subjection born of abject fear. Amongst the provisions of this awful code were the following: "The leader of runaway slaves shall be pinched three times with a red-hot iron, and then hung. Each other runaway slave shall lose one leg, or if the owner pardon him, shall lose one ear and receive one hundred and fifty stripes. Any slave being aware of the intention of others to run away and not giving information, shall be burned in the forehead and receive one hundred stripes. Slaves who steal to the value of four rix-dollars shall be pinched and hung; less than four rix-dollars, shall be branded and receive one hundred and fifty stripes. A slave who lifts his hand to strike a white person, or threaten him with violence, shall be pinched and hung, should the white person demand it; if not, shall lose his right hand. A slave meeting a white person, shall step aside and wait until he passes; if not, he may be flogged. No estate slave shall be in town after drum-beat; otherwise he shall be put in the fort and flogged." On the 13th of November, 1733, a sanguinary insurrection broke out. Except on one estate, where an old Englishman, assisted by fugitive planters who had gathered around him, fought off the insurgents, only one white man survived, a surgeon who was spared on condition of attending to wounded slaves. It required the aid of French soldiers from Martinique before the military force in St. Thomas could quell the rebellion. Even then, when the last three hundred insurgents had been surrounded, they preferred suicide to surrender. The general sentiment of the colonists was therefore scarcely favorable to the undertaking of Dober.

The more rejoiced was he when in June, 1734, Tobias Leopold and seventeen others arrived, some of whom were to continue the work which he had commenced, and others to colonize and evangelize St. Croix at the solicitation of Chamberlain von Pless. He himself was under orders to return to Europe, to assume the office of chief elder, rendered vacant by the death of Martin Linner. With him sailed an orphan, Carmel Oly, the first fruits of his work, whose freedom had been bought, and who was baptized next year at Ebersdorf, receiving the name Joshua.

St. Croix had been acquired from France only the year before. Its soil was more fertile than that of St. Thomas; but it had been practically abandoned in 1720, owing to successive droughts. Dense jungles and undergrowth had encroached upon the former plantations. Denmark contemplated sending thither slave labor, and in anticipation welcomed missionary colonists. But they had arrived in no proper condition to face the strain of life in the tropics. Their voyage had been unduly prolonged and had been attended with severe hardship. They had sailed from Stettin on November 12, 1733, and had been seven months on the way, having been driven by storms into the harbor of Tremmesand, in Norway, and compelled to winter there. The cabin assigned to them, though eighteen in number, bad been but ten feet square, so overcrowded was the vessel. Water almost failed during the latter part of the voyage. Several succumbed to yellow fever before they passed from St. Thomas to St. Croix. By the end of the following January eight of the eighteen, including Leopold, had died. In February eleven persons set out from Herrnhut to reënforce them, and Dr. Grottausen, of Copenhagen, also volunteered. But the mortality continued—the physician being the first to fall, and then four others of the new comers within two months. During the years 1725 and 1726 most of the survivors returned home in a miserable plight, three of them suffering shipwreck en route. The last survivor in December, 1736, passed over to St. Thomas to join Frederick Martin, who had been in charge of the mission there since March. He and his assistant, Bönike, had met with great success amongst Dober's catechumens. Their hearers sometimes numbered two hundred.

They themselves not yet being ordained, could not administer baptism to their converts. Augustus Gottlieb Spangenberg, for some time past active as an evangelist amongst the Germans of Pennsylvania, had therefore been sent thither in September, and on the 30th of the month had baptized Andrew, Paul and Nathaniel, who became the nucleus of the first mission congregation in the West Indies. The opposition of white planters continued to be exceedingly bitter, the more so because the lives of many of them were a reproach to the gospel. And the opposition deepened when in August, 1727, with the assistance of a friendly planter an estate was purchased for the mission, known as Posaunenberg—later New Herrnhut. In fact they might have succeeded in their design to crush the work, had it not been for the providential arrival of Count Zinzendorf, in accordance with a plan of visitation formed quite independently of knowledge of trouble other than that caused by fevers, scarcity of provisions and hindrances of a general nature. On the one hand he wished to obtain personal insight into the work of the mission; on the other hand he desired to silence the calumnies of certain persons, who said that he did not scruple to send his brethren to pestilential climates but was afraid to go thither himself. On approaching the island in the latter part of January, 1739, the thought of the terrible death-rate amongst the missionaries hitherto led him to say to one of his companions, George Weber, a Moravian by birth, "Suppose that the brethren are no longer here; what shall we do in that case?" Weber's instant reply was, "In that case we are here." The calm steadfastness of the man, so characteristic of the Moravian witness-spirit, evoked this comment from the astonished Count, *"Gens aeterna, diese Maehren"* ("An indestructible race, these Moravians").

He found the missionaries suffering unjust imprisonment in most wretched quarters. The case had been this. The Reformed clergyman, Borm, according to his own statement, had taken upon himself to examine some of the converted negroes. They were not willing to answer his captious questions. He therefore instigated the Common Council to petition the Governor to prohibit the Brethren from baptizing their converts, and to compel a certain missionary, whose marriage had been performed by Martin, to have the ceremony repeated by a clergyman of the State Church. The Governor had too much confidence in the Brethren to be drawn into the scheme. Then their foes raised up the false charge of a robbery, from which the Brethren were required to clear themselves by oath. This they had not been willing to do, all taking of oaths being contrary to their conscientious convictions. Zinzendorf's indignation was excessive, on learning these facts. He at once waited upon the Governor with a demand for their immediate release. It was granted next day, with an apology for what had happened.

The visiting brethren were astonished at the extent of the work and its success. About eight hundred blacks were under the influence of the gospel. Daily, in the evening, the converts assembled for worship, and Zinzendorf himself frequently addressed them. After his farewell address at Posaunenberg they forgot prudence in their religious enthusiasm, and some of them sought to accompany him to town, contrary to regulations. This offered an excuse to their enemies, to set upon them and then attack the mission station. The missionaries were with Zinzendorf, and so escaped personal harm by their absence. But much damage was done to the property. Notwithstanding the Governor's expression of his disapproval of the riotous outrage, when a protest was lodged the missionaries later experienced personal ill-treatment, so that it was necessary to retreat to the woods in order to hold services, and to station sentries against a sudden attack. But on Zinzendorf's return to Europe his personal representations, together with petitions from influential friends, secured from the Danish crown concessions practically guaranteeing liberty of worship.

Not long after a sad catastrophe threw a shadow over the work. Theodore Feder and Christian Gottlieb Israel, after having been ordained for service here, set sail from Texel on November 17, 1739. On January 17 their vessel struck on a reef near Tortola. The sailors took to their boat, and left the missionaries to their fate. Feder, hoping to swim ashore, let himself down from the ship and perished before the eyes of his companion, whose calm farewell sounded forth in imperishable faith, "Depart, my brother, in peace." For hours he clung to the wreck, sustaining his confidence with hymns. At last he was rescued by people from the shore, and was hospitably cared for. A month later he joined Frederick Martin, and during the same year with George Weber and his wife moved to St. Croix, to recommence the mission on that island. Their first converts were baptized in 1744, though land for the first mission station was not acquired until 1755—Friedensthal.

The year 1741 was signalized by the extension of the work to St. John, when a pious overseer, Jens Rasmus, requested the Brethren in St. Thomas to preach statedly to the negroes in his charge. Baptisms took place in 1745, but a resident missionary was not stationed there until 1754, when John Brucker removed to Bethania, an estate purchased in 1749.

But Greenland had not been forgotten.

On April 10, 1733, the good ship *Caritas* left Copenhagen with three missionaries on board—Matthew and Christian Stach, cousins, and Christian David. They knew so little of its climatic and other conditions that they had spoken of felling trees for the erection of their house; but no hindrance could deter men of their stamp, whether realized or unimagined. Fair weather was succeeded by a violent storm as they neared Greenland, and the drift-ice swept around threateningly; but comfort was found in the Daily Word at debarkation, "The peace of God, which passeth all understanding, shall keep your hearts and minds through Christ Jesus." Egede's reception of them, thanks to a cordial letter of recommendation from Chamberlain von Pless, was warmly affectionate. About a mile away from his colony they selected a site for their home, and built a hut of stones and sod, after the fashion of the natives.

What a land they had come to! Does it properly belong to America or to Europe? Only a narrow strait separates it from the western continent; but its geological formation and its fauna are rather European. Perhaps it is no true land, but only a vast congeries of islands cemented together by eternal ice and snow. Drake called it "The Land of Desolation." Here and there grow a few small bushes, but no real forests. Huge snow-capped cliffs, black where the earth crops through, enormous glaciers and deep-cut fjords, with a few ptarmigan to give life, are its scenes of beauty. Glacier after glacier launches icebergs with the thunder of heavy artillery. The interior is a "Sahara of snow and ice." Here and there a patch of brown earth, perhaps; the elevation gradually rising to mountainous table-land, but all ice and snow, desolation reigning in unrivaled and unchallenged security. Animal life, like that of man, keeps close to the coast, and at that mostly to the west coast. Such a thing as a climate the land can be said to possess only by courtesy. For long months darkness is the guest of cold. But then the aurora, shining and quivering and flashing—the heathen native thought this was caused by the spirits of his dead playing a game of ball up yonder with a walrus-skull—and the doubly brilliant stars take pity on the unfortunates whom the sun has forsaken. In the brief summer, indeed, willow bushes and stunted birches burst out into green along the coast, and grass and berries and poppies and moss for a time break the monotony of white; but it is a silent solitude, save for the sea-fowl. Land animals do not flourish. The icy earth becomes a tomb for seeds cast into it by the stranger who experiments. It is from the sea that the Greenlander gets his chief supplies of food. But the seals, and walrus, and the dolphins, the porpoises, and herrings, and perchance a giant whale, the prize of his harpoon, afford him the heat-giving sustenance which his northern latitude requires.

The Greenlander—"Innuit," man, emphatically man, he calls himself; Europeans with less narrowed standard of comparison have dubbed him "Eskimo," eater of raw flesh—in person is short, inclined to be stout, somewhat flat-nosed. His small black eyes sparkle merrily, for he is fond of a joke. He is an excellent mimic, quickly scrapes acquaintance with a stranger, finds out his weak points and lets them be seen. A slight moustache may adorn his face, but whiskers and beard will be scanty. The skin, if it appears at all through the layer of dirt, normal in the case of the uncivilized heathen, is brownish, yet not so dark that a rosy cheek will not show. He arranges his dress to suit the climate, his clothing being of furs, with trowsers tucked into skin-boots, and his shirt having a hood that can be drawn over the head. As a heathen his half-underground house is in a state of utter filth, he himself having no aversion to dirt or to noisome smells. Inclined to be indolent, overeating is one of his great weaknesses, provided his hunt has been a success. Extremely superstitious, and peopling earth and air and water with evil spirits, he is at the mercy of shrewd witch-doctors, the *angekoks*. Of morality he has not an overplus.

Perhaps two thousand such natives lived in the immediate vicinity of New Herrnhut, as the spot was named where the missionaries built; but they at first confined their intercourse with the newcomers to attempts at begging or stealing. For the missionaries the barrier of language was long in the way—·a most difficult agglutinative type of speech. Nor could Egede render much assistance, for his knowledge of German was as limited as was theirs of Scandinavian. Moreover, unfortunate misunderstandings between him and Christian David arose from doctrinal discussions, so that the Moravians after a while became completely isolated. Then disasters began to follow in quick succession. Their boat drifted out to sea. Success in fishing and hunting was meager. If better housed now in a wooden dwelling, the materials for which had been brought from Denmark, the scanty fare which they could secure had to be won by laborious spinning of flax for the Danish traders, and before long that means of livelihood also failed. Then came the dreadful small-pox, introduced by a native who had visited Denmark. Two or three thousand Eskimos of the west coast were swept away by it, and though the kind attentions of the missionaries broke down the wall of prejudice in a measure, no heart was touched by the gospel. Later, scurvy partially disabled the missionaries themselves, who at this juncture owed much to Egede's kindness. Yet they labored on as best they could, endeavoring to teach the Ten Commandments and the Lord's Prayer to those who would listen—often only to be laughed at for their pains.

Their numbers were recruited, in 1734, by the arrival of Frederick Böhnisch and John Beck. But the failure of supplies from Europe, and the scarcity of wild fowl, with the unwillingness of the people to come to their assistance, again reduced teem to sore extremities. Shell-fish and raw sea-weed became their diet for days, and had it not been for the piety of a heathen, Ippegau, on a visit from his home, forty leagues away, the mission might have come to a tragic end.

Nevertheless, at a conference held in March, 1735, though their lives were at the time threatened by hostile savages, they determined that John Beck and Matthew Stach should remain in Greenland for the rest of their days, in spite of the fruitlessness of the mission, and that Christian Stach should advocate the cause of the mission when temporarily absent in Europe. Christian David had been sent only to help to establish the work, not to remain permanently. Next Egede, whose devoted wife had died, returned to Denmark, but there for some years trained men for the Danish mission in Greenland. In that year also the Moravian mission family was augmented by the arrival of Stach's mother, and his two sisters, Rosina and Anna, who subsequently married John Beck and Frederick Böhnisch.* Not until May 7, 1736, did any Greenlander even make inquiry concerning divine truth; and the first convert, Mangek, was a stranger whom the persecutions of his countrymen rendered unstable.

On June 2, 1738, Kajarnak, a man on a visit from the south, was struck with the story of the agony in Gethsemane and on the Cross, and eagerly drank in the words of salvation preached to him by John Beck in response to his questionings, called forth by the missionary's reading from a translation of the New Testament at which he was engaged. In a voice that trembled with emotion he asked, "How is that? Tell me that again; for I, too, would fain be saved." His baptism, with the name Samuel, and that of his wife Anna, his son Matthew and his daughter Aima, followed on Easter Sunday, 1739. But then Satan raged. Kajarnak's brother-in-law was murdered and his own life endangered. He had to leave New Herrnhut for the south. Yet he remained true to Christ for the brief remainder of his life, and testified of Him to his countrymen. Carried off by consumption in 1741, his last message to the missionaries was full of comfort, "I was the first of my countrymen who found the Lord, and I shall be the first of them to go to Him."

The harvest had commenced. Soon Arbalik, baptized Simon, took Kajarnak's place. A visit paid by Bishop Andrew Grasmann to New Herrnhut in the spring of 1740, and a visit of Matthew Stach to Europe, whence he returned in 1741, both proved influential in causing the missionaries to change the

* Descendants of Anna Stach have continued in mission service in unbroken line. After the death of Frederick Böhnisch she was married to John Zacharias, and with him labored in Greenland from 1765 to 1784. Their daughter, Anna Benigna, in turn married John Godfrey Gorke, and served in the same country from 1792 to 1825. Their daughter, Henrietta, went to Labrador in 1819 as the wife of John Lundberg, and served many years, dying at Herrnhut in 1881. Their son, John Eugene Lundberg, was one of the first missionaries on the Moskito Coast, where he labored for thirty-three years. His daughter, soon after his death in 1881, went to the Moskito Coast as the wife of Augustus Hermann Conrad Berckenhagen, dying there in 1860, whilst her brother, Paul Eugene Lundberg, entered mission service in Labrador in 1884, where he is still active.

type of their preaching, and make it less legal, more Christo-
centric, and with more pronounced insistence upon the possibility of joyful assurance of personal salvation. In spite of the
active hostility of the medicine men, the number of converts
now rapidly increased. The chapel was found to be too small
for the congregation of about 200, that was wont to assemble
in 1745. John Beck, on furlough in Europe, at a Synod held
at Zeist, pleaded for better accommodations. The missionary
ship, *Irene*, was commissioned to convey to Greenland a frame
church in sections, and Christian David was sent to assist in
its erection. What feelings this apostolic man must have had,
when on October 28 John Beck consecrated this building in the
presence of three hundred interested Greenlanders!

For ordinary Christians the West Indies and Greenland
would have afforded sufficient scope for pent-up missionary
zeal. Not so with the inspired men and women of Herrnhut.
On March 7, 1735, George Piesch, George Berwig and Christian von Larisch left for Surinam. Spangenberg had arranged
with the Dutch Surinam Company the terms upon which the
Brethren, with whom he had been fully identified for about two
years, might make a settlement in that country. Their primary
purpose was a preliminary tour of exploration with a view to a
later settlement. Whilst thus engaged Larisch died. The
others fulfilled their commission; and this led to the starting of
the mission which was placed on a permanent basis in 1745.

Coincident with the preparation for the mission in Greenland, the attention of Zinzendorf and the Brethren had been
drawn to the religious destitution of the Lapps. But their
missionaries, after setting out, learnt that a Danish mission
had been begun amongst these people in Norway. Consequently Andrew Grasmann, Daniel Schneider and John Nitschmann, junior, were instructed to go to the Lapps in Sweden.
Spending the winter of 1734 in Stockholm, they proceeded to
Tornea in the spring of the following year, and thence made
their way inland. Contrary to expectation, they found the
people under at least nominal supervision of the State Church,
and therefore withdrew.

The call to the next undertaking came in 1736, a year of distress for Zinzendorf; but it was nevertheless undertaken. It
came from two Reformed pastors in Amsterdam, Van Alphen
and De Bruyn. They had been much moved by the distressing

account given by Ziegenbalg and Plütschau, the founders of the mission in Tranquebar, respecting the condition of the Hottentots at the Cape of Good Hope, where they had touched on their voyage to India. Though the Dutch East India Company had sent an expedition in 1652 under Van Kiebeek to seize the Cape as a base of supplies for their fleet en route to the Orient, and though refugee Huguenots had flocked thither after the revocation of the Edict of Nantes, the natives had been made to lead a sad life. Hottentots and Bushmen, both undersized non-negroid races, the former naturally indolent, living in low dome-shaped kraals, shiftless and untidy, yet removed from the very lowest of savages, being herdsmen rather than mere hunters, with a kinship to the Malays, if high cheekbones, oblique eyes, thin beards and dull yellow complexion be sure signs, or to the old Egyptians, if their speech, rich in consonants and admitting pronominal suffixes, afford a correct index of affinity; the latter more energetic, but having not yet reached the pastoral stage, living by the chase—such as they were they had been treated by Dutch and Huguenots as merely superior animals. They were called *schepsels*—things, not persons, creations of Satan, perhaps. To hunt them down, like so many jackals, was deemed no crime. To enslave them was akin to conferring a favor. But the slaves were not taught the religion of their masters.

As soon as the call reached Herrnhut, George Schmidt, who although only twenty-seven years of age was of vigorous and forceful faith and had spent six years in an Austrian prison for conscience sake, volunteered promptly, and was ready to start for Holland within a week, to acquire Dutch prior to sailing. Zinzendorf joined him a few days later, and prepared the way in Holland. Through the intervention of Isaak Lelong, and the Burgomaster of Amsterdam, Van den Bempen, and Admiral Schryver and Rath van Rumswinkel, the "Council of Seventeen," granted Schmidt permission to sail to the Cape. He left on March 17 and reached Cape Town on July 9, 1737. At first he settled amongst the Hottentots in Zoetemelksvallei, on the Zondereind River, not far from a military post of the Trading Company. But in April of the next year, owing to the bad influence of this post, it seemed wise to remove three hours' journey farther. Now a secluded valley was selected, known as Baviaanskloof. Here he gathered a school numbering about fifty. Besides the white Sergeant, Kampen, two natives, Africo and Kybodo, who had accompanied him from Cape Town, and one Willem, were soon won for Christ. Whilst on a visit to Cape Town, in June, 1738, to his delight Schmidt met David Nitschmann, the Syndic, and Dr. Eller, missionaries of the Brethren's Church on their way to Ceylon. They brought him news of most serious opposition which had broken out in Holland. Domine Kulenkamp's *Hirtenbrief*, *i. e.*, pastoral letter, which had aroused such deep animosity against the Moravians there, was soon circulated in the colony also, and Schmidt began to feel the effects. Still he persevered, and baptized his first convert, Willem, on March 31, 1742. Within a month four other Hottentots were baptized. The Reformed pastors in Cape Town were provoked at this, denying the validity of Schmidt's orders, acting as he did only by written commission, sent for two of the Hottentots, catechised them, and sent them back to Schmidt with a good testimonial. In August, 1743, Schmidt himself was summoned to Holland to report and await decision as to the validity of his proceedings. He left behind a congregation of forty-seven Hottentots, had been the means of leading thirty-nine whites to Christ, and bore with him complimentary testimonials from Sergeant Martinssen, the commander of the neighboring post, from Captain Rhenius, and from Governor Söllengebel. He reached Texel on June 17, 1744. But when, next year, Zinzendorf asked permission for his return, although the request was seconded by various persons of influence, it was refused.

Whilst Schmidt was laboring to overcome the prejudices of whites and reach heathen hearts at the southern end of the continent, another undertaking was inaugurated on the west coast of Africa. In Copenhagen in the year 1735 Zinzendorf met a mulatto from the Guinea Coast, Christian Jacob Protten, who had been taken to Denmark against his will, and had there become a Christian and had studied theology. This man returned to Herrnhut with him, and next year volunteered to go to his own people at Fort George de la Mina, the headquarters of the Dutch traders, known also as Delmian or Elmina. The offer was accepted. With him volunteered Henry Huckoff, a native of Moravia. Armed with a letter to the Governor, they sailed from Holland. But whilst they were endeavoring to establish a school near Delmina, Huckoff died of fever, on June 17, 1737. Protten, who seems to have been unsuited to the work, and who was in danger of being apprehended as a runaway slave, met with no success, and was recalled in 1741.

Yet another African land was to be the depository of a missionary's heroism. Abraham Ehrenfried Richter was in early life a prosperous merchant of Stralsund. After Zinzendorf's stay in that city in 1734 he joined the Brethren, and was engaged in evangelistic labor in western Germany and amongst the Germans of London. Whilst passing through Amsterdam on his return from that city, he made the acquaintance of Admiral Schryver, who described to him the religious destitution of the Christian slaves in Algeria. With him to realize their need was equivalent to a call to minister to them. The authorities of the church approved of his determination, and he set out via Marseilles in the latter part of the year 1739, arriving at Algiers on February 11, 1740. Letters of recommendation from Holland to the Dutch Consul Paravicini led this official to obtain the consent of the Dey to his becoming the religious teacher of the Christian slaves. In March the plague broke out amongst them, but Richter fearlessly continued his ministrations. In consequence he himself fell a victim on July 10, lamented by many, Consul Paravicini testifying his esteem in a report dispatched soon afterwards.

In 1737 and 1738 Andrew Grasmann, Daniel Schneider, and Michael Miksch attempted to evangelize in Russia, especially amongst the Samoyedes and other heathen tribes on the shores of the Arctic Ocean. For this purpose they journeyed by way of Reval to Archangel, but were arrested on the charge of being Swedish spies. After an imprisonment of five weeks in solitary confinement, they were sent to St. Petersburg under escort of three soldiers. On the way two of these guards broke through the ice whilst crossing a frozen lake, and were rescued by their prisoners. Their innocence having been established by an examination at St. Petersburg, they were returned to Germany by sea via Lübeck, with the statement that their services were not at present needed.

According to Zinzendorf's plans Schmidt's labor at the Cape was to have served as a link with Ceylon. Ceylon might become the door to the East Indies, and a chain of connections might thence be established with missions in Mongolia and Per-

6

sia. Such was the comprehensive nature of his designs. In 1740, therefore, the missionaries whom Schmidt met in Cape Town, inaugurated a mission in Ceylon, then a Dutch possession. At first the Governor, Von Imhoff, and Wetzelius, the senior clergyman of the colony, lent their countenance, friends were gained, and at Mogurugampelle converts began to be won. But the prejudices aroused by the *Hirtenbrief* completely changed the aspect of affairs, and although Wetzelius stood by the Brethren in a few months the work had to be relinquished on account of the persistent opposition of the colonial authorities and the other representatives of the Dutch clergy, at the very time when it had begun to prosper. Thus hampered in Ceylon, Nitschmann and Eller desired to cross over to the Malabar Islands, but this the Governor forbade, stigmatizing them as heretics whose work was not to be tolerated.

This period was also distinguished by the inception of a mission among the Indians and Negroes of the American Colonies in 1735 and 1738; a work directly linked with the founding of the Moravian Church in America.

The significance of this world-wide missionary movement, in connection with the extensive itinerations in European lands appears, when it is borne in mind that the entire congregation at Herrnhut in 1732 numbered only about six hundred, and that many of its members were very poor, that the means of transportation and the maintenance of communications were excessively meager, and the difficulties in the way prodigious. It is significant also that the majority of the missionary pioneers were Moravians by birth. It was the "witness spirit" brought from lands of persecution and martyrdom, that gave impetus to the movement. Indeed in August, 1733, the people of Herrnhut were divided into two classes, former members of the evangelical church who might stay at home, and the descendants of the Bohemian-Moravian Brethren, who were expected to furnish men willing to become "pilgrims" or heralds of the church of God throughout the world.

CHAPTER VII.

THE TRANSFER OF THE EPISCOPATE, AND THE BANISHMENT OF COUNT ZINZENDORF.

In gradually identifying himself with the Moravian exiles at Herrnhut, it was far from Zinzendorf's purpose to establish an independent religious body. Nor did he in the event call into being an ecclesiastical body *de novo*. Yet the result of his evangelistic labors and those of his associates was more than a congeries of *ecclesiolae* in *ecclesiis*. Zinzendorf did not mean to be identified with a *dc facto* ecclesiastical organization distinct from the confessional churches. Nevertheless to his instrumentality more than to that of any other man must be ascribed the emergence from its dormant state of what had long ago been a distinct church, and its further differentiation from other churches; and though he was not the founder of a mere sect, if the obloquy of schism is to be considered inseparable from that term, he was almost in spite of himself and undesignedly on his part the resuscitator of an ancient Protestant church. His own plans were continually thwarted by Providence, until the prayer of Comenius received an answer. This is one of the wonderful things of God, which gleams forth from the story of Herrnhut.

Zinzendorf's personal desire and inner call to enter the Christian ministry, noticeable during his student-years, appear never to have left him, but to have been deepened by the experiences of 1727 and the following years. After the arrival of Spangenberg at Herrnhut in April, 1733, and Oettinger, of Tübingen, in June, he pursued a course of systematic study under these theologians. But it was one thing to fit himself for, and quite another thing for a nobleman to be admitted to, the ordinary ministry. Even apart from the excessive eccentricity which would be supposed to attach to the taking of such a step by a man of rank, he had more than one Haman at the court in Dresden, who would interfere. In some other country he might possibly hope for less prejudiced treatment. Hence when Abraham Ehrenfried Richter, still a merchant of Stralsund, wrote to Herrnhut to secure a private tutor for his motherless children, by Spangenberg's advice Zinzendorf responded in person, employing one of his titles, Von Freydek, as a screen for his actual personality. The day after his arrival in Stralsund, at the end of March, 1734, he disclosed his name and the object of his coming to Dr. Langemack, who with Dr. Sibeth had been commissioned to act as examining commissioner for the university of Greifswald in the case of candidates for the ministry. By the invitation of the former he thereupon preached for the first time, in Stralsund, on April 11. The formal examination in all points of Christian doctrine followed in the latter part of the month. On the 26th the examiners gave him a complete certificate of orthodoxy from the Lutheran standpoint, expressly excepting and granting as non-essential certain details of church discipline not contained in the articles of faith. He now notified Superintendent Löscher of his purpose to enter upon the spiritual office. In December he journeyed to Tübingen, and on the 18th presented a formal application to the theological faculty of the university, requesting recognition as a Lutheran minister. This faculty in April of the preceding year had published its judgment respecting the doctrinal standpoint, discipline and ritual of the congregation at Herrnhut, and whilst recognizing its substantial harmony with the Evangelical Lutheran Church in doctrine, had approved of the retention by the Moravians of the heirloom of discipline and ritual received from their fathers, and characteristic of the Unitas Fratrum for upwards of three hundred years. Zinzendorf's request was now granted, Chancellor Pfaff replying in the name of the faculty and quoting precedent for the assumption of the clerical calling by a man of rank. On the fourth Sunday in Advent he therefore preached in the cathedral and in the church of St. Thomas, in Tübingen, and thus publicly entered the ministry. It was not his purpose, however, to be bound to the service of any one congregation, but rather to exercise ministerial functions after the fashion of the abbés of the French Church.

For the parish of Herrnhut, alienated as it was from Rothe, he also had plans. During the winter of 1732 to 1733 it had been his endeavor to secure as its pastor Magister Steinhofer, of Tübingen, a man whose previous visit to Herrnhut had brought him into warm sympathy with its life. The call proved not unwelcome, and the faculty of the university gave its approval. But the Saxon government interposed such qualifications and restrictions that the negotiations came to nothing, and Steinhofer before long became court preacher at Ebersdorf. Failing in this, and the need of a fully recognized ministry, becoming apparent in connection with the success of the missions amongst the heathen, Zinzendorf tried another plan. Spangenberg was sent by him to Würtemberg to treat with Duke Charles Augustus and his cabinet and consistory for permission to restore, at his own expense, the ruined Protestant cloister of St. George in the Black Forest. This would have carried with it Zinzendorf's consecration as a prelate of Würtemberg. Having gained this, he proposed to establish in the cloister of St. George a theological seminary to supply the needs of the widening work of the Brethren. But the reply to the request was unfavorable. Had it been granted, or had Steinhofer come to Herrnhut, the probability is that the Unitas Fratrum would not have been organically resuscitated, since Lutheran orders would have been imposed upon Herrnhut and its affiliations.

But something had to be done. The return of Dober from St. Thomas with the converted negro boy pressed home the necessity of supplying the missionaries with such ordination as would qualify them in the sight of other Christians and in the opinion of governors and courts of justice to administer the sacraments and perform other ministerial functions. Quite naturally the Moravians bethought themselves of their fathers' episcopate, and according to their custom they sought the guidance of the Lord by the use of the lot. An affirmative answer was received. Then David Nitschmann, the carpenter, one of the elders of Herrnhut, was also selected in the same manner as the one of their number who should receive consecration—a man well qualified for the office by the gravity and reliability of his character, his spiritual gifts, sound judgment and considerable experience in the work of an evangelist at home and abroad.

The episcopate of the Unitas Fratrum was at this time represented by Daniel Ernest Jablonski, the grandson of Comenius

and at this time court preacher in Berlin, and Christian Sitkovius at Thorn, Superintendent of the united Reformed and
Brethren's congregations in Poland. With the former Zinzendorf had been in correspondence since 1729, and the aged bishop
had manifested a deep interest in Herrnhut. Of his own accord
already in 1734 he had proposed to consecrate one of the
Brethren a bishop. This offer Zinzendorf now requested him to
carry out. He readily consented, the more so because he knew
Nitschmann favorably. Sitkovius signified his written approval,
and accordingly Jablonski consecrated David Nitschmann a
bishop of the Unitas Fratrum in Berlin, on March 13, 1735, in
the presence of Janik and Wenceslaus Zlatnik, two members of
the Bohemian Church of that city, the transaction being preceded by a thorough examination of the candidate. The following certificate of consecration sets forth Bishop Jablonski's
conception of the purpose of the consecration:

"In the Name of the Blessed Triune God, to Whom be honor
and glory for ever and ever, Amen!

"Inasmuch as it seemed good to the eternal and wonderful
God, to permit His faithful confessors, the Bohemian-Moravian
Brethren, to fall into such evil circumstances, that many of them
were forced to forsake their native land and to seek other
places, where they could serve their God with freedom of conscience, and confess His truth; therefore it has come to pass
that some of them are scattered in the northern portions of
Europe, and others even in America, both on the continent and
the islands there; but this all-wise God put it into the heart of
the noble-born Count of the Empire, Sir Louis Nicholas, Count
of Zinzendorff and Pottendorff, to receive as a father such
Bohemian-Moravian Brethren in their dispersion, and to care
for their bodily and spiritual welfare, especially also for the
maintenance of their venerable ancient Christian church statutes
and discipline; in accordance with all this with the knowledge
and approval of the congregation he also piously resolved to
have the Rev. Mr. David Nitschmann, who was one of the first
of the Moravian witnesses in America, who had ventured all
things in trust in God, and to whom the Lord had given the
first fruits of the heathen, in accordance with the ancient Moravian rites ordained a Senior and Superintendent of this and all
future colonies, in all their congregations and for all their ministers.

DAVID NITSCHMANN.

"Therefore I, the undersigned, in accordance with this properly presented request, as Elder, Senior and Episcopus of the Bohemian-Moravian Brethren in Great Poland, with the knowl-edge and consent of my colleague in Great Poland, Sir Senior Christian Sitkovius, did ordain the afore-mentioned Mr. David Nitschmann, on March 13, 1735, in the name of God, according to our Christian custom, with imposition of hands and prayer, a Senior of the afore-mentioned congregations, and endowed him with full authority to perform the visitations called for by his office, to ordain the pastors and church servants of those congregations, and to take upon himself all those functions which belong to a Senior and Antistes of the Church. May the dear Saviour, to Whose service he has devoted himself, abide with him most sensibly, endow him with courage and strength, accompany his apostolic office with rich blessing to the glory of God, and to the salvation of many souls; in order that he may bear much fruit in God's vineyard, and that his reward may be great in eternity.

"I myself have written the above, signed it, sealed it with the seal of our Church. So given at Berlin, June 14, 1737.

DANIEL ERNST JABLONSKI,

[SEAL.]

Royal Elder Court Chaplain, Consistory and Church Councillor—as Elder Senior and Antistes of the Bohemian-Moravian Brethren in Great Poland. *Manu propria.*"

In the judgment of Zinzendorf the episcopate which had thus been transferred was intended merely for the foreign missions, and was not in any way to separate Herrnhut from the Lutheran Church, or to be significant of independent organization. Yet just these things necessarily resulted. The first ordination performed by Nitschmann was that of John George Waiblinger, not a missionary, but minister-elect of the settlement at Pilgerruh, in Schleswig, July 29, 1735; nor did he afterwards confine his exercise of episcopate functions to the supervision of missions and the ordination of missionaries.

Meantime Zinzendorf's own entrance upon holy orders had alienated the King of Denmark, and most of his own relatives considered it a breach of propriety. The virulence of his enemies was also increasing. Amongst these were now to be reckoned Anthon and the younger Francke at Halle, Court

Preacher Marperger at Dresden, Chaplain Winkler at Ebersdorf, Magister Urlsberger at Augsburg, Court Preacher Ziegenhagen in London, of the clergy; Count von Brühl at Dresden,
Baron Huldenberg of Neukirch, Count Christian Ernest of
Stollberg-Wernigerode, and his own aunt Henrietta, of the
nobility. Frederick Augustus, "The Strong," had died, February 1, 1733, and had been succeeded by his son Frederick
Augustus the Third, who was open to the influence of the foes
of Zinzendorf, and was in general easily swayed by favorites.
In 1735 Baron Huldenberg complained that many of the people
of his estates had been so attracted by the religious institutions of Herrnhut as to become vassals of Zinzendorf by removal thither.   This concrete accusation induced the Saxon
government to issue a decree of banishment against Zinzendorf
on March 20, 1736, without according him any opportunity of
defence. He and his wife were at the time absent in Holland
with a number of fellow-workers, in the interests of the missions in Dutch colonies, and planning a settlement on the
estates of the Baroness of Ysselstein.   On his way back to
Saxony he was met at Cassel by David Nitschmann with the
harsh edict. He took it calmly, although the outlook was dark,
for the previous harvests had been very poor and money was
scanty. "It mattered not at all," he said; "in any case he would
not have been able to live at Herrnhut for the next ten years,
since he had intended to move about from place to place engaged in work for the Lord."   Accordingly he went on to
Ebersdorf, whilst the Countess proceeded to Herrnhut.

Now was the golden opportunity for crushing out the Moravian settlement. Its foes ·secured the appointment of a new
commission to examine into its affairs—men by no means
prejudiced in its favor, two nobles and two divines, Captain von
Löben, Chamberlain von Holzendorf, Superintendent Dr. Valentine Löscher, and Dr. Heidenreich, a member of the Consistory at Dresden. From May 9 to May 18 this commission
thoroughly investigated all the peculiarities of Herrnhut.
Its report was as favorable as that of the first commission; and
the Saxon government declared that as long as the Brethren
remained faithful to the Augsburg Confession they might retain
their own constitution and discipline. Yet the Count was not
recalled, nor was he given a trial and with it an opportunity
to clear himself of all charges. In this respect the whole pro-

ceeding was most arbitrary and unjust. Yet the act of persecution had an effect the very opposite of what his enemies had
hoped. Zinzendorf's banishment served to spread the Moravian Church throughout the world.

He was literally without definite plans, determining to be led
by God. Having spent a month at Ebersdorf, he proceeded
to Frankfort-on-the-Main, and was well received. To the
east lay a region known as the Wetterau (Wetteravia), about
fifteen quadrant miles in extent and with forty thousand inhabitants, between the Taunus Mountains and the Vogelgebirge
and watered by the river Wetter. The lords of this principality, Counts Ysenburg, were deeply in debt, and for this reason welcomed all manner of settlers and allowed all manner
of religious views to find expression amongst their subjects.
They were now anxious to secure a people who had by this
time acquired a reputation for thrift, that their estates might
be improved. Count Ysenburg-Wächtersbach therefore offered
Zinzendorf the use of the Ronneburg, a half-ruined castle dat-
ing back to the Middle Ages. It was a wild and forbidding
place. Fifty-six families of Jews and gypsies lived around and
in the out-buildings. Christian David, indefatigable itinerant
and accustomed as he was to the rude accommodations of
Greenland, thought it unfit to live in. Yet Zinzendorf accepted
the offer, in view of the field of labor which it presented. On
June 17, 1736, he commenced his evangelistic activity here,
preaching on the gospel for the day, the parable of the Lost
Sheep. Next he began schools for the poor of the neighborhood; and to put a stop to their habit of begging, distributed
amongst them bread and money for clothes. But his motives
even here were misunderstood, and eventually efforts were
put forth to stop his preaching, so that he had to explain himself to Count Ysenburg.

Here at the Ronneburg an institution was inaugurated which
exercised a most important influence upon the development of
the Brethren's Church for the remainder of Zinzendorf's life.
This was the so-called *Pilgergemeine* or *Pilgerhaus*—"The
Congregation of Pilgrims." This body stood at the head of
affairs during the years of his banishment. In his view it was
a union of men and women whose mission it was to proclaim
the Saviour in the whole world, and who therefore itinerated
from place to place in accordance with the needs of the cause.

Its arrangements were peculiar. Its members were appointed by Zinzendorf from time to time, probably always with the approval of the lot; but there were frequent changes. One or more might be sent on distant missions in Europe or among the heathen. The organization itself frequently changed its headquarters as the needs of the church demanded. Sometimes it was in Wetteravia, then in Berlin, again in Holland, then in England, etc. There was a common housekeeping. No one received a salary. Whoever had money of his own used it for his own support. Otherwise the money needed came from the income of Zinzendorf's estates, or through gifts and loans from friends in Holland and elsewhere. Lady Zinzendorf stood at the head of the financial department, assisted by Frederick de Watteville and Jonas Paulus Weiss, a former merchant of Nuremberg, who in casting in his lot with the Brethren had contributed a large portion of his means. Daily religious services were participated in by the members of this body, for it was regarded as constituting a little congregation, and the peculiarities of Moravian ritual were observed. Besides Zinzendorf and his wife the most prominent members in the early days were Christian David, John de Watteville, Leonard Dober, John Nitschmann, Wenceslaus Neisser and Samuel Lieberkühn. In 1747 the so-called *Diarium der Hütten*, afterwards known as the *Diarium des Jüngerhauses*, was begun, the *Pilgergemeine* being called the *Jüngerhaus* after Zinzendorf's return from banishment. This diary was a complete account of what Zinzendorf and his coadjutors did from day to day, and contained also verbatim reports of all the discourses he delivered and copies of all the reports received from every mission in Christian and heathen lands. No part of it was printed, but the whole was written and multiplied in a number of manuscript copies sent to all parts of the world, wherever the Brethren were established. In order to render this work of writing possible, the so-called *Schreiber-Collegium* was instituted, a body of copyists who devoted nearly all their time to transcribing the diary and the many letters which were received.

Zinzendorf's first stay at the Ronneburg was only brief. On July 26 he set out by way of Jena, Magdeburg, Berlin and Königsberg for Livonia, where Christian David and Timothy Fiedler had been followed by other Moravian evangelists. Since 1721 this country had belonged to Russia. The privileged classes were mainly Germans, Lutherans amongst whom the Spenerian revival had been influential for good. Amongst the masses of the people—Letts in the south and Finnish Esthonians in the north—relics of actual heathenism survived, faith in witchcraft and in magic blended with a surface acceptance of the Roman Catholic or Greek type of Christianity, and there were no schools. Herr von Bohn of Nerva and other persons of rank had solicited a visit from the Count, desiring his aid in their attempts to relieve the religious poverty of the land. He arrived in Riga on September 8. Whilst in Livonia he was entertained chiefly by Lady von Hallart, m. n. von Bülow, the widow of General Louis Nicholas von Hallert, a Polish-Saxon who had entered Russian service in 1721. This lady desired him to furnish her with a chaplain, and with tutors for a teachers' institute at Wolmar, her home. Five brethren were therefore sent hither. In Reval Zinzendorf founded a society in fellowship with the Moravians, and adopting their methods for the cure and care of souls. Its officers were Lutheran pastors, Mickwitz, Vierorth and Gutsleff. The society in 1741 developed into a congregation of the Brethren's Church, whose members indeed continued to partake of the communion in the cathedral once in each quarter year. Though this congregation failed of permanence, largely because of persecution, the extensive *Diaspora* which was also the fruit of Zinzendorf's visit continues to the present day. Another result was the formation of a Bible Society, the Count opening a subscription list for the printing of the Bible in the Livonian dialect for the benefit of the peasantry. The volume was issued at Königsberg in 1739, for one ruble and a half, bound.

From Memel on his way home, he wrote to Frederick William the First of Prussia, asking permission to make some efforts for the spiritual welfare of the refugees from Salzburg who had found an asylum in his dominions and especially along the Baltic. On his arrival in Berlin Jablonski handed him an autograph letter from the king, inviting him to his hunting lodge at Wusterhausen, where the court was then assembled. He had heard so many things against Zinzendorf that he was desirous of judging him from personal acquaintance. His observations during this three days' visit brought the shrewd monarch to the conclusion that the Count's only fault was that he wished to be pious although a nobleman. He therefore

espoused his part and further advised him to have himself consecrated a bishop of the Brethren's Church. This suggestion
was taken into serious consideration by Zinzendorf, on consultation with Jablonski. But he requested as a condition that
the Lutheran deans at Berlin might make a searching preliminary investigation into his orthodoxy. Drs. Reinbeck, Roloff,
Jablonski and Kampstädt were accordingly ordered to undertake an examination of this nature. The Count placed the
requisite documents in their hands and having intimated to
them also where they might find the accusations that had been
published against him, desired them to prosecute their investigation at their convenience.

On his return to Wetteravia the first Synod of the resuscitated Unity was held in the castle of Marienborn, another estate
which was leased from the Counts Ysenburg. One of the chief
subjects of discussion in this gathering, from December 6 to
December 9, 1736, was the importance of the episcopate as giving the Brethren's Church a distinct and independent position.
At its close Zinzendorf proceeded to Holland, where many
friends had been won in Amsterdam, and on January 9 visited
Heerendyk in the Barony of Ysselstein, to inspect the commencement of the buildings of the future settlement which had
been designed as a fitting-out place for missionaries and as a
center of influence in Holland. Thence he crossed to England,
his four-fold business being to consult with the trustees of the
Colony of Georgia with regard to the Moravian settlement
begun recently in Savannah, to do evangelistic work amongst
the Germans of London, to confer with Archbishop Potter of
Canterbury respecting the Moravian episcopate, and to seek
a revival of the "Order of the Grain of Mustard Seed." His
Grace was most friendly, repeatedly acknowledging the validity
of Moravian orders, furnishing an open letter of recommendation for the Moravian colonists in Georgia, and urging Zinzendorf to accept consecration at the hands of Jablonski.

Encouraged by his conversation, the Count at length determined to take the decisive step. He therefore went to Berlin
in April, where the investigating divines had arrived at a satisfactory conclusion. Then on May 20, 1737, he was consecrated by Jablonski and Nitschmann, in the presence of several
members of the old Bohemian congregation, Sitkovius also
consenting to the transaction. This was a most important step

in the direction of independence, which was almost forced upon Zinzendorf, that the Moravians might not be driven from Herrn-hut, but have an acknowledged standing as members of a recognized church. The King of Prussia, Bishop Sitkovius and Archbishop Potter sent him letters of congratulation.

CHAPTER VIII.

THE BEGINNINGS OF THE MORAVIAN CHURCH IN AMERICA.

On April 4, 1733, an edict of banishment was proclaimed against the Schwenkfelder refugees living in the circuit of Görlitz. Four men representing thirty families, one hundred and eighty souls, interceded with Count Zinzendorf, whose benevolence they had experienced these several years, to secure for them a home in Georgia, known to have been recently carved by royal letters patent out of the Carolina grant between the Savannah and Altamaha, in accordance with the plans of General James Oglethorpe, that it might serve as an asylum for insolvent debtors and for persons fleeing from religious persecution. Zinzendorf corresponded with Herr von Pfeil, the ambassador of Würtemberg, at Regensburg, who acted as German agent for the Trustees of the new colony. A favorable reply was received. A grant of land was promised to the Schwenkfelder, and a free passage thither. The English authorities were glad to receive accessions of Protestants as a bulwark against threatened encroachments of the Spaniards of Florida and the French of Louisiana upon the colonies of the southern Atlantic seaboard. So the Schwenkfelder left Berthelsdorf on May 26, 1734, led by George Wiegner, and accompanied at their own request by a Moravian evangelist, George Böhnisch. Whilst on their way, however, in Holland they changed their plans, and selected the older colony of Pennsylvania as their destination, having been offered a free passage thither.

The Schwenkfelder thus failing to avail themselves of the opportunity in Georgia, the plan was now conceived of securing land for the Brethren there, that they might have a place of refuge in case of similar banishment, and might commence missions amongst the Creeks and Cherokees. Spangenberg was sent to London to prepare the way, and had numerous

interviews with General Oglethorpe and with Vernon, the secretary of the Trustees. A grant of five hundred acres on the
Ogeechee was secured for the projected colony, and the negotiator himself received a present of fifty acres, a part of the
site of the present city of Savannah. Throughout the negotiations the fixed antagonism of court-preacher Ziegenhagen had
to be steadily encountered—one of the various instances of the
obstructive tactics of the Hallensian party against anything
and everything identified with Herrnhut. Under the guidance
of David Nitschmann, the Syndic, John Töltschig, Anthony
Seifferth, Godfrey Haberecht, Gotthard Demuth, Peter Rose,
Michael Haberland, Frederick Seidel, and George Waschke
joined Spangenberg in London, and with him set sail for Georgia on February 6, 1734.

They reached Savannah on April 17. On the land granted
to Spangenberg a cabin was built. Fields were cleared and
planted, and the prospects for the first crop were very good.
But with the warm weather sickness broke out, and the work
was especially hindered by the fact that the one of their number who best understood farming was ill. Spangenberg one
day knelt by his bedside, and having offered a fervent prayer
turned to the man and said, "My brother, get up from this bed,
and consider yourself well." The man actually was able to rise
and go to his work again.

Before long a school for Indian children was established on
the island of Irene, about five miles above the town.

The colony was increased by the arrival of twenty additional
Moravians under the leadership of Bishop Nitschmann, on
February 7, 1736. In the same vessel with them came Governor Oglethorpe, John and Charles Wesley, Benjamin Ingham
and Charles Delamotte. John Wesley had received an appointment as minister of the Anglican Church in Savannah. He
and his companions became intimately acquainted with the
Moravians during the voyage, and he in particular was deeply
impressed by their calm fearlessness during a severe storm on
January 25. It taught him that they had a peace in believing,
to which he was a stranger. During his stay in Savannah,
then a town of about two thousand souls, he was on terms of
close intimacy with the Brethren. With Spangenberg he had
several conversations about the possibility of a personal assurance of salvation, doctrine as yet novel to him, and about

Herrnhut. Soon after his arrival, namely, on February 28, Bishop Nitschmann ordained Anthony Seifferth as pastor of the Moravian congregation, now fully organized. In his journal he describes its solemn simplicity as carrying him back in thought to the days of the apostles. He was also very much interested in the missions of the Brethren amongst the Indians of whom Tomotschatschi was chief, and thought of himself learning their language, in order to coöperate in the noble effort.

On March 15 Spangenberg left for Pennsylvania, in order to take the place of Böhnisch. Governor Oglethorpe gave him a warm letter of recommendation to Thomas Penn. After a stormy voyage from Charlestown to New York he arrived at Wiegner's farm in the Schippack on April 4. In September he visited St. Thomas in place of Bishop Nitschmann, organized the first congregation of converts, and then returned to Pennsylvania, to be active in evangelistic labor there until October, 1739.

In connection with the colony in Georgia a mission amongst the slaves in South Carolina was also projected, and met with the approval of the Archbishop of Canterbury. Peter Böhler, a young man of twenty-six, an ex-student of Jena, received the appointment to begin this enterprise. His ordination, on December 15, 1737, was Zinzendorf's first exercise of episcopal functions. On his way to America in the early part of 1738 he spent some time in England, a period critical in the spiritual experience of the Wesleys, who were aided by him to the clear apprehension of the truth as it is in Jesus and to personal assurance of salvation—a visit also of prime importance in connection with the commencement of the Brethren's Church in England. Arriving at Savannah on October 15, 1738, Böhler shortly afterwards began a mission at Purysburg, in South Carolina, a German settlement founded in 1733. In this effort he was assisted by his friend George Schulius and by young David Zeisberger. Every Sunday they preached to the German inhabitants of the town, and in the week visited the negroes in the vicinity and instructed them in the gospel. But when the warm weather came Böhler fell ill, and was brought to the point of death. He had not fully recovered when Schulius took sick, and after eighteen days died, July 24, 1739. Amidst many privations, faithfully nursed by young Zeisberger, Böhler continued at his post, until the difficulties in which the Spanish War involved his brethren at Savannah constrained him to remove to that place. Even prior to this the Moravian colony in Georgia was in a languishing condition. It had dwindled from thirty persons to twelve in consequences of disagreements as well as the political disturbances. Some of the settlers had died, others had returned to Europe, and others had gone to Pennsylvania independently. When the Spaniards of Florida prepared to invade Georgia, and the Moravians were required to take up arms in its defense, a conflict of duties had arisen, for like the Friends they were then non-combatants. Finally, when only five men and one woman and one boy remained, they determined to go to Pennsylvania.

On New Year's Day, 1740, George Whitefield arrived in Georgia for the second time. At Savannah great crowds flocked to hear him, and extraordinary scenes of excitement followed. It was the commencement of the "Great Awakening." When about to leave for Pennsylvania he offered Böhler and his friends a passage on board his sloop. This offer they gladly accepted, and sailing from Savannah on April 13 arrived in Philadelphia on the 25th. In Georgia and Carolina they had made several warm friends, some of whom followed them later to Pennsylvania and became identified with the work of the church—John Brownfield, James Burnside, Henry F. Beck and Abraham Büninger amongst the rest. They had expected to find both Spangenberg and Bishop Nitschmann in Pennsylvania, and were greatly disappointed to learn that the former had left and that the latter had not yet arrived.

When on the point of dispersing Böhler kept them together and found employment for them, deeming it their duty to await the arrival of Bishop Nitschmann, who had been commissioned by a synod at Marienborn in November of the previous year to lead a colony to Pennsylvania, in consequence of Spangenberg's representations.

George Whitefield, with the aid of William Seward, of London, had purchased five thousand acres of land in the Forks of the Delaware, the present Northampton County, in order to erect a school for negroes and to found a village for Englishmen in danger from the harsh laws against insolvent debtors. Since a number of the Moravians were carpenters, he offered to engage them to do all the carpenter work and

7

desired Böhler to superintend the entire erection of the projected building. This offer was acepted. After a toilsome
journey of three days on foot into the Indian country south
of the Blue Mountains the company of seven men, two women
and two boys reached Nazareth, as Whitefield had named his
tract, on May 30, and held their first religious service there
under a noble oak. Two days later the commissioners sent by
Whitefield marked off the spot where the house was to be
built, on a gentle hill commanding a noble view of rolling forests to the distant valley of the Delaware eastward. Having
put up a log-house for themselves, the Moravians began to
build Whitefield's school. But in November they were placed
in a position of jeopardy. When Böhler went to Philadelphia
to report to his employer in November, the latter led the conversation into a discussion of controverted points of doctrine,
predestination amongst the rest. Unable to make Böhler yield
the Moravians' position of free grace, and stirred up as he
already was by the prejudices of the Irish Presbyterians who
were the Moravians' nearest neighbors, he gave way to an
unworthy fit of temper, and ordered Böhler and his people to
leave his land forthwith. But this was out of the question, as
winter was at hand. The friendly interposition of Justice Nathaniel Irish, of Saucon, the agent of William Allen from whom
Whitefield had made his purchase, secured a temporary stay of
the sentence. Providentially, too, Andrew Eschenbach, who
had been sent by Zinzendorf to labor amongst the Germans of
Pennsylvania and had arrived in October, had brought word
that he would soon be followed by Bishop Nitschmann and a
company of Brethren.

This party now came in the nick of time, the latter part of
December, 1740. Besides the bishop it consisted of his uncle,
old "Father Nitschmann," of Zauchtenthal, and his daughter,
Anna, the former leader of the single women of Herrnhut, Mrs.
Molther, whose husband was at present active in London, and
Christian Frölich, appointed a missionary to the Indians. Having entered into negotiations with various other persons, the
bishop finally purchased five hundred acres at the junction of
the Lehigh and the Monocacy from William Allen, through
Justice Irish. Before this purchase had been actually consummated the Moravians on Whitefield's tract, taking it for granted
that the land on the Lehigh would be bought, began to fell tim-

ber where Bethlehem now stands. In the early spring of 1741 a log-house was completed, and in it lived the founders of Bethlehem. Anna Nitschmann and Mrs. Molther went to Oley to assist Eschenbach. Bishop Nitschmann was at the head of the colony, Böhler having been recalled to Europe. On his way thither, whilst passing through New York, he became acquainted with the Noble and Horsefield families, an acquaintance which led to the founding of the Moravian Church in that city.

CHAPTER IX.

THE BEGINNINGS OF THE MORAVIAN CHURCH IN ENGLAND.

In the early summer of 1728, in order to form connection with the Society for the Promoting of Christian Knowledge, Zinzendorf sent Wenceslaus Neisser, John Töltschig and David Nitschmann, the Syndic, to England. He counted on the kind offices of Countess Lippe-Schaumberg, a lady of the court with whom he had been in correspondence, to obtain an introduction for them to officials of the University of Oxford. Leaving Herrnhut on June 7, and traveling by way of Jena, they received from Dr. Buddaeus a letter of recommendation to Court preacher Ziegenhagen. As in the case of many of the early Moravian itinerants and messengers, their funds for the journey consisted of faith rather than coin of the realm. Twenty-seven shillings formed the sum total of their resources. Hence extreme privation was endured. In Rotterdam they almost perished from starvation, and lacked a lodging place, being content to spend one night on the city wall. In their extremity one of the three was about to sell himself for a period of years for labor in the East Indies in the service of the Dutch East India Company, when means of transport to Harwich were provided through the good offices of a compassionate stranger. But after their reaching London their errand failed of success, largely through the hostility of Ziegenhagen, whom the Hellensians had prejudiced. Such was the first contact of the resuscitated Moravian Church with Britain.

Somewhat more significant, and productive of future consequences, was the visit of Spangenberg to London from December 28, 1734, to February 3, 1735. Not only did he accomplish his mission of preparing the way for the colonists destined for Georgia, but he also formed the acquaintance of Mr. Weinanz, a Dutch merchant at whose house Böhler later met John Wesley. Moreover, the meetings of a devotional character which were maintained by the prospective colonists on their arrival in London were attended by pious fellow country-men resident in the city.

The next contact of the Brethren with England was in connection with the setting out of the second company for Georgia, under Bishop Nitschmann. They sailed in the same ship with the Wesleys and arrived at Savannah on February 7, 1737.

It was whilst this ship with its important freight of souls was yet being tossed on the high seas, that Count Zinzendorf, with Wenceslaus Neisser, arrived in London, towards the end of January. He wished to confer with the Trustees of Georgia respecting the Moravian colony, a task which was materially lightened by the opportune arrival of Andrew Dober with letters thence. Incidentally moreover his seeking counsel from Archbishop Potter of Canterbury in regard to his own consecration as a bishop of the Brethren's Church led to the proposal that the Brethren should undertake a mission amongst the negro slaves in South Carolina, a mission to which Peter Böhler was subsequently called. During his stay in London the devotions of his household were attended by a number of Germans, presumably the same who had been attracted to the meetings of the colonists whilst en route. Amongst them Zinzendorf now organized a "society" of which Andrew Ostroem and John Frederick Hintz were the chief officers. On March 6 he left for Rotterdam.

Early next year Peter Böhler arrived, and with his arrival the more definite influence of the Moravian Church in the ecclesiastical life of Britain began. Nor was there the less need in Britain than on the Continent for the wholesome introduction of the fervid and cheerful piety and the realization of personal assurance which characterized the Brethren's theology and life. The cold intellectualism of Tillotson, paramount in the best circles, was having its legitimate effect in repressing religious spontaneity. The swing of the pendulum from the fanaticism typical of England in the middle of the seventeenth century to the reckless license of the Restoration had begun to incline towards external adherence to accredited dogmas in combination with a disrelish for vital godliness. The wretchedness of the masses was as lamentable as their ignorant superstition. Drunkenness and debauchery were too common not to be palliated. Profanity was the vice of both sexes and all classes.

Gross brutality entailed slight reproach. Numbers regarded
highway robbery as the trade of a gentleman. The courts of
justice suffered notoriously from bribery. Charities were
openly perverted or despoiled. The prisons for criminals and
for debtors had not yet felt the efforts of a Howard. A
"Society for the Reformation of Manners" had been formed,
but even its members laid more stress on church attendance
and other formalities than on heart religion. In his narrative
of the awakening in England, James Hutton, who became so
prominent in the establishment of the Moravian Church in England, and whose father had opened his own house to the meetings of one of these societies—counterparts of Spener's *ecclesiolae*—testifies with regard to it, that the majority of the members were "altogether slumbering or dead souls, who cared for
nothing but their comfort in this world, and as they had once
joined this connection they were willing to continue in this respectable pastime on Sunday evenings, by which at a small expense they could enjoy the pleasure, and fancy themselves better than the rest of the world who did not do the like." Thus
it had continued until towards the end of the year 1729, when
several students at Oxford—John Wesley, a graduate, Charles,
his brother, George Whitefield, Benjamin Ingham, John Gambold, and others, about one dozen in all—covenanted to live
piously and seek the one thing needful through a weekly celebration of the Holy Communion, the common study of the
Greek New Testament, stated observance of fasting, regular
hours for private devotions, the visitation of the sick, of the
poor, and of prisoners, and the instruction of neglected children.
Laying great stress upon a systematic regulation of their time,
they had been sneered at as "Methodists." But with all their
holy desires they did not as yet apprehend the possibility of an
assurance of salvation through faith in the meritorious life and
death of Jesus Christ.

On the very day of his arrival in London, February 7, 1738,
Peter Böhler made the acquaintance of John Wesley, meeting
him at his lodgings, the home of Weinanz, whither he came
with a letter from Töltschig, whom he had left in Georgia. He
had landed only on the first of the month. It was destined
to be a meeting fraught with momentous consequences. Here
are two ardent young men, scholarly, deeply in earnest. The
one has lately returned from his attempt at mission work, con-

PETER BÖHLER.

scious of failure, and conscious that deep down he lacks something, the possession of which would have averted failure. He
is burning with ardor to serve his Lord and his own generation,
a very knight errant of the gospel, yet not himself in the light
as to fundamentals. The other is nine years the junior of his
new English acquaintance, and has been ordained a few weeks
since, with a commission to cross to the western world. His
cheerful, open countenance invites confidence. There is a poise
of calm and peace which the senior lacks, for all his advantage
of years and experience. As zealous as he of doing with his
might what his hand finds to do, Böhler is more free from
anxiety respecting the leading of the Lord. Whilst they converse
together through the medium of Latin, it is natural that their
very similarity and dissimilarity should mutually attract. With
Böhler are Schulius, who is to accompany him to America, and
Abraham Ehrenfried Richter and Wenceslaus Neisser, whom
Zinzendorf has sent to maintain the connection with the pious
Germans of London, previously gathered by him into a society.
Wesley is staying at the house of a young book-seller, James
Hutton, in Nettleton Court, Aldersgate Street.

Just how the time was spent and what transpired during the
next ten days, is not ascertainable from any existing records,
and yet is very open to conjecture, from the fact that Wesley
was Hutton's guest. This earnest young man had made the
acquaintance of the Wesleys whilst on a visit to some of his former school-fellows at the university in the days when the "Holy
Club" at Oxford was bearing reproach and fitting its members
for future service. Of kindred mind with them, Hutton had
invited them to stop at his father's house when next they came
to the city. This had happened when they were about to proceed to Georgia in 1735, under the auspices of the "Society for
the Propagation of the Gospel in Foreign Parts." During this
visit the preaching and example of John Wesley had made a
deep impression on the heart of Hutton. He accompanied the
Wesleys to their ship, and made the acquaintance of Bishop
Nitschmann and the second party of Moravians destined for
Georgia, being favorably drawn to them by their apostolic
devotion and unfailing cheerfulness. At the expiration of his
apprenticeship Hutton had commenced business as a book-
seller on his own account, and had a society meet at his house
for mutual edification week by week. Maintaining his corre-

spondence with Wesley, he read the diary of the voyage to a number of people. That Wesley should now introduce Böhler to Hutton was therefore natural. And that Böhler should preach in Latin to various affiliated "societies," Hutton or Viney, one of the Oxford Methodists, serving as interpreter, was also natural. The account of the calm faith of his Brethren during the storm at sea would have prepossessed a number in his favor. His presentation of a living Christ and free grace for the sake of His love manifested in His sacrificial death, fell like seed into fallow soil that had been well harrowed by legalism. On February 17 Böhler accepts an invitation to proceed to Oxford with Wesley. Soon the acquaintance of John Gambold, the young rector of Stanton Harcourt, an associate of Wesley's student days, and like him a deeply earnest seeker after peace, is made, and to him Böhler is early privileged to act the part of Priscilla and Aquila towards Apollos. John Wesley returns to London on the 20th, but Böhler remains. On the 22d he addresses a gathering of students, and proves helpful to some. Charles Wesley is now taken seriously ill, and Böhler whilst nursing him is drawn into a relation of peculiar intimacy, and is privileged to lead him into the light. By March 5 John Wesley is convinced that he himself has been resting on a false ground. He has several close conversations with Böhler in the latter part of April. The other Moravians add the testimony of their own experience, that it is possible to gain assurance of acceptance with God. Böhler's exposition of the Pauline doctrine of justification by faith at last removes the lingering mists from John Wesley's mind, and after Böhler on May 4 leaves London for Southampton, to embark for America, he can on May 24 write triumphantly giving him assurance that he has found peace. Meantime Hutton has also made the great experience.

Already on May 1 Böhler and Wesley had drawn up statutes for the first society of the Brethren, which met at the house of Hutton, until its accommodations proved too small, when it removed to the chapel, 32 Fetter Lane, known as the Great Meeting House, or Bradbury's Meeting House. Shortly afterwards Hutton wrote a letter to Zinzendorf, signed by fourteen members of the society, asking that on his return from America Böhler be retained as their pastor in England.

John Wesley now for a time seemed likely to altogether cast in his lot with the Moravians. On June 13, together with Ingham and Töltschig, who had returned from Georgia, he sailed for Rotterdam, thence to proceed up the Rhine to visit Zinzendorf in Wetteravia. At Marienborn Ingham was permitted to participate in the celebration of the Lord's supper with the congregation, but the request of Wesley was not granted, on the ground of his being a *homo perturbatus*. Nevertheless he does not appear to have been incensed at the refusal. For at Weimar, when asked by the Duke, why he was going to Herrnhut, he replied, "To see the place where the Christians live." At Halle the views of the younger Francke respecting Zinzendorf were not accepted by him without reserve. In Herrnhut he heard Christian David preach four times to his edification, and had various personal interviews with him. Ingham for his part was wholly charmed with all he witnessed. But his companion mingled admiration with questioning; for on his return to England he endeavored to disconnect Hutton and his society from the Moravians, though without effect. As yet indeed the differences of conception were not clearly formulated. On January 1, 1739, the two Wesleys, Whitefield, Ingham, Kinchin, and Hutchins were all able to heartily participate in a lovefeast at Fetter Lane, remarkable for enthusiastic unity. And it was with the cordial approval of the Fetter Lane Society that John Wesley in April acceded to Whitefield's request to proceed to Bristol. Now began his wonderful career of open-air preaching. At this time Hutton and Viney left for Germany, to strengthen the bonds which linked them with the Brethren. On their return they brought back Töltschig, who was commissioned to visit awakened persons in England. It was the end of October before they reached London. At this very juncture Spangenberg returned from Pennsylvania. Previous to the arrival of any of these, however, Molther, who had received a call to Pennsylvania, reached London and learnt that no vessel was likely to sail before the middle of the following January. He naturally attached himself to the Fetter Lane Society. When John Wesley returned to London at the beginning of November the two found themselves compelled to disagree. To Wesley, Philip Henry Molther, who appears to have been inclined to quietism, seemed to underrate the value of the means of grace, since he recommended inquirers simply to be still, and wait till they received the gift of justifying faith, meantime abstaining from the means of grace, and especially from the Lord's supper. Furthermore, Molther would not admit that there are degrees and grades of faith. To Molther, Wesley seemed to teach what bordered on justification by works, and to be in antagonism with scripture in affirming the possibility of complete sanctification—sinless perfection. Differences now grew apace. Wesley charged the Moravians with antinomianism, and they regarded him as perverting the doctrine of salvation through grace without merit. The disagreement came to a head on July 20, when John Wesley withdrew from Fetter Lane, having already in June organized those who were of his way of thinking. Thus arose the Foundry Society in Moorfields. For a season bitterness was felt. But the estrangement was not permanent. Even during Wesley's lifetime it was mutually recognized that each body had its own specific destiny to fulfill.

Meanwhile Spangenberg and Molther had made a deep impression on many in London; and Ingham and Delamotte, who were closely connected with the Brethren (though the former never took a radical step like that of Gambold, but refrained from severing his connection with the Established Church) with Töltschig were rewarded by becoming instrumental in promoting a mighty revival of religion in Yorkshire. In April, 1741, Spangenberg, who had been absent from England for a time, but had returned to labor here at the request of Hutton and his associates, organized in London the "Society for the Furtherance of the Gospel," which for about twelve years did exceedingly valuable work in promoting both home and foreign missions. Then suffering a decline, it was reorganized in 1766 by its original founder. Its first committee, or board of managers, were Hutton, George Stonehouse, vicar of Islington, Ockershausen, Bray, Adam von Marschall and William Holland. During the spring of this year, and especially in May, repeated efforts were made by Spangenberg to effect a union with Wesley. His pardon was asked for wrong things said of him by some members of the Fetter Lane Society. On May 12 Wesley relented so far as to participate in a lovefeast at Fetter Lane, but organic reunion was not to be effected. Gradually the influence of the Brethren widened nevertheless. During this same year Schlicht visited Dummer, Kinchin's parish in Hampshire. Chapman, Rice and Knight in turn followed him; and Gussenbauer organized a society at Buttermere, in Wiltshire. In Bedford the Rogers and Okely families began to come into connection with the Moravians. Ipswich was visited by Ostroem. A connection was established with Cornwall. The first English hymn-book was ready by November 24, a translation published as a private undertaking. By May, 1742, there were twenty German laborers engaged in the work of the church in England. Yet the first congregation was not formally established in England until November 10, 1742, when Spangenberg organized the Fetter Lane congregation with a membership of seventy-two. License therefor was obtained from Doctors' Commons on September 7, under the designation "Moravian Brethren, formerly of the English Communion."

CHAPTER X.

THE WORK AND WANDERINGS OF THE BANISHED COUNT.

That the banishment of Zinzendorf had no dampening effect upon his ardor, was abundantly manifested from the very first. On his return to Wetteravia from his first visit to the King of Prussia, and prior to his consecration as a bishop, he convoked the first synod of the resuscitated Brethren's Church at Marienborn, in December, 1736. Not only was the significance of the Moravian Episcopate discussed, but various business was transacted which was closely connected with the spread of the influence of the church. Throughout the early part of the year negotiations had been on foot for the establishment of a settlement in Holstein, near Odesloff, five German miles from Hamburg and two and a half from Lübeck. The consent of the King of Denmark had been granted in November, and thus Pilgerruh came into existence. This undertaking indeed shriveled into nothing in a few years, largely because the reigning Duke insisted that its people should strictly adhere to the Confession of Augsburg and be independent of Zinzendorf and Herrnhut. Heerendyk, in the Barony of Ysselstein in Holland was also in process of establishment; and although it also failed of permanence, it resulted in the settlement at Zeist in 1746. The important operations in Livonia received due attention from the synod, and it was arranged to send additional catechists thither. An evangelistic tour amongst the Cevennes was planned for De Watteville. Similar operations in Scandinavia were projected. In consequence the Swedish *Diaspora* soon attained important proportions. Pastors Quandt at Urbs, Suter at Camb, and Meder at Randen manifested active sympathy. Negotiations for the purchase of the Ronneburg were set on foot, as a result of which in a few years Herrnhaag was founded, a second Herrnhut, and after the lease of Marienborn had been renewed in 1738 this twin congregation in Wetteravia also grew in importance. Mission work in Surinam and Pennsylvania was discussed.

Next month, with the removal of young Christian Renatus Zinzendorf to Jena, in order to prosecute his studies under escort of John Nitschmann, the sympathetic tie which had for years linked many of the students of its university to the life and aims of the Brethren was strengthened, and a student-congregation resulted that became of great significance in later years, inasmuch as after the expulsion of this band of sympathizers in April, 1739, a number of them entered the theological seminary of the Moravian Church at Herrnhaag under Polycarp Müller and Layritz, and about sixty in time served in its ministry.

After Zinzendorf's consecration, thanks to the pressure which Field Marshall von Nazmer brought to bear upon Count Brühl, the minister of King Augustus, he was privileged to spend a portion of the year 1737 at Herrnhut, and for a time there seemed to be some slight prospect of a revocation of the edict of banishment. But when he found it impossible to agree to conditions which would have practically involved self-incrimination, the King remained obdurate, and in July issued a stringent decree against conventicles, designed to strike a blow at the special institutions of Herrnhut. Zinzendorf's renewed request for a judicial investigation at which he might receive a hearing was refused, and in March, 1738, a sentence of perpetual banishment was pronounced. For the next ten years the existence of Herrnhut remained in uncertainty, and its religious life stood quite isolated in Saxony. Rothe, no longer in sympathy with the Brethren, had left Berthelsdorf during the previous year. Zinzendorf himself set out from Herrnhut for Wetteravia on December 4, arriving there ten days later. On the sixteenth of the month he performed his first episcopal function, the ordination of Peter Böhler. But before the year was ended the Count visited Berlin, by way of Jena and Halle. Whilst at the former city he became acquainted with a young man destined to become his principal assistant, and to be bound to him by a special tie. This was John Michael Langguth, the son of the Lutheran pastor of Walschleben, now just of age. He shortly afterwards attached himself to Zinzendorf personally, becoming his private secretary. Seven years later he was adopted by Frederick de Watteville, whose only child had died, and was later by letters patent created a baron of the German Empire. He married Zinzendorf's eldest daughter, Benigna.

During the first three months of 1738, spent in Berlin, the Count delivered two series of sermons which attracted large numbers and drew public attention to him and his cause. The one was addressed to women, and constituted an exposition of the Lord's Prayer; the other, to men, was based on the second article of Luther's *Erklärungen*. Taken down by Langguth as delivered, and published soon afterwards, the *Berliner Reden* incited a considerable number of persons to desire fellowship with the Brethren. A society was accordingly organized, which later became the nucleus of a congregation. Meanwhile the Berlin congregation of Bohemians was growing, and similarly developed into the Rixdorf organization. During this visit the friendship with King Frederick William was strengthened. Furthermore the Count's entrance upon a distant field was determined upon—America, a plan the advisability of which became the more apparent after Töltschig reported to him in August at Marienborn with regard to the progress of affairs in the Moravian colony in Georgia. During a conference held in October it was, furthermore, decided that this American tour, to be made by way of St. Thomas, should include Pennsylvania in addition to the southern colony.

From the latter part of May to the latter part of October, with the exception of brief intervals, Zinzendorf's residence was in Wetteravia, where Herrnhaag was increasing in importance. Thence he proceeded to Amsterdam in hopes of finding a ship for the immediate voyage to St. Thomas. In this he was disappointed. It was the 21st of December before anchor was weighed. Yet the delay was opportune. At this very juncture a publication came out under the title of a pastoral letter— *Hirtenbrief*—in which the Brethren and Zinzendorf in particular ticular were pilloried, as perverters of the faith. The era of polemical tractates against the Brethren had commenced. Already various pastors and university professors in Utrecht and Groningen had attacked the church, and in October De Watteville had endeavored to clear away the fog by publishing an explanation of the purposes of the Brethren in Holland. The particular polemic now causing trouble had been issued by Dr. Kulenkamp, of the Classis of Amsterdam, though Francis de Bruyn and another clergyman had protested against its publication. He declared that Zinzendorf and his associates were not to be identified with the Bohemian-Moravian Brethren, who were worthy of all honor, but were mere sentimental mystics, neither good Lutherans nor good Reformed. Zinzendorf now published a reply. Nor did the affair prevent the organization of the society in Amsterdam on a permanent basis on November 24, Jacob Schellinger, Grasmann and Catharine Beuning being prominent amongst its officers.

At length Zinzendorf put to sea. The account of the voyage and the providential opportuneness of his arrival at St. Thomas belong to the history of the missions. The visit was brief, and circumstances interfered with the projected voyage to the American continent. Reaching Dover on his return on April 20, a hasty visit was made to London and to Oxford, which appears, however, to have been without special significance for the work of the Brethren's Church in England. In Holland he found that the pastoral letter had aroused bitter opposition and had poisoned the minds of many; but the Brethren at Heerendyk and in Amsterdam were not dispirited thereby. It was the first of June when he returned to Marienborn. The whole visit had been accomplished in a marvellously short time for that era. Now when he resumed the thread of European activity, indefatigable diligence was displayed in spite of the ill health which had resulted from the stay in the tropics. A synod was convened at Ebersdorf from June 9 to 16; then came a journey to Württemberg, with many public addresses. A serious attack of fever temporarily interrupted active labor. As soon as recovery was complete the supervision of all manner of projected missions at home and abroad, for example the missions to Algiers, Ceylon and to the Indians of New York, and the development of the theological seminary and oversight of the spiritual life of the Wetteravian congregations afforded abundant labor. In the middle of December, accompanied by De Watteville, the Count proceeded to Switzerland via Basel. Montmirail was their objective point. The old Baron de Watteville was now favorably disposed. In Berne also a number of awakened persons manifested sympathy. From June 12 to 20 a synod met at Gotha, the tendency of whose transactions was to lay emphasis on the independence of the Moravian Church as a distinct ecclesiastical organization. The publication of the first catechism of the resuscitated Unity was authorized. Yet the calling of the Brethren's Church was still conceived to be especially to act as a leaven amongst other bodies, and hence the term *Diaspora* was now adopted. The Count himself was if anything more than ever enamored of his function to promote Christ's kingdom as a free servant of the Lord, and spoke of resigning his episcopal office, especially in connection with his plans for personal activity in Pennsylvania. Now, too, it was determined to send Bishop Nitschmann to that colony with a band of evangelists, and Polycarp Müller, formerly director of the *gymnasium* at Zittau, was chosen and consecrated a bishop to supply the vacancy which would thus be created in the European work of the church.

Another synod was convened at Marienborn from December 5 to 31, 1740. Its sessions were largely devoted to a discussion of the doctrinal standpoint of the Brethren's Church, though important details of administration were also arranged, for example, that Bishop Müller's position in Wetteravia, including his having charge of the archives and church publications, and an extensive manuscript correspondence, as well as his oversight of the church schools and of the theological seminary, should resemble that of the presiding bishop of old at Jungbunzlau. Yet with all these arrangements, characteristic of distinct churchliness, plans for the activity of the Brethren according to the conception of "inner missions" were so largely present that they have usually been allowed to overshadow the former almost to the degree of causing them to be ignored. At the close of this synod, on December 31, 1740, Leonard Dober had asked to be relieved of his chief-eldership, and soon afterwards Zinzendorf desired to lay down his office of general-warden. After the latter, with his chief associates, had spent a season of evangelistic labor in Switzerland, with headquarters in Geneva, experiencing bitter opposition from Pastor Leger, but gaining many friends, the Castle of Montmirail henceforth becoming a center of *Diaspora* activity in French Switzerland, the fifth general synod was convened at Marienborn to consider the resignations. Neither was accepted; but Zinzendorf resigned his episcopal functions for the time being—not his episcopal character, which was apprehended to be indelible—in view of his intended labors in Pennsylvania, where he wished to promote the cause of true religion and vital Christianity not primarily as a Moravian bishop but as an unhampered servant of God. John Nitschmann was elected to the vacancy, and consecrated by Zinzendorf and Müller on July 22. Further, Leonard Dober received assistance by the appointment of Jacob Till as vice-elder; and it was resolved to convene a "synodical conference" in London, the membership of which should be determined by the lot, in order to make provision for the direction of affairs during the absence of the Count in America. Dober's immediate field was to be mission work amongst the Jews of Amsterdam, while his brother Martin and Arvid Gradin were sent to Upsala, for evangelistic labor in Sweden and Norway, where they were aided by the friendly approval of the Archbishop of Stockholm after their real purposes became known and won appreciation. Gradin had already been employed in distant service. In March, 1740, with Frederick Cossart, it had been his endeavor on the commission of Zinzendorf to open negotiations with the Greek Church, through personal interviews with the Patriarch of Constantinople. But the months spent in the Orient had been in vain.

The "synodical conference", constituted of ten persons prominent in the activities of the church—Zinzendorf, his wife, his daughter Benigna, Leonard Dober, Anna Maria Lawatsch who was "general elderess" in place of Anna Nitschmann now in America, Frederick de Watteville, Rosina wife of Bishop David Nitschmann, about to follow her husband to Pennsylvania, David Nitschmann the Syndic, and Spangenberg and his wife—convened in London in Zinzendorf's apartments on September 11, 1741. He was about to sail for America on the 28th. Although this convention is known as a synodical conference, it really took the place of the sixth general synod. Its chief object was to provide for the administration of affairs during the absence of Zinzendorf. The idea prevailed that Leonard Dober would consent to remain "chief elder" and in addition take on himself the Count's duties as "general warden." But instead, he was firm in resigning his office and in declining the added duties, being sustained in his decision by the lot. In drafting a reply to Dober, the conference submitted each paragraph to the lot in like manner. Now those present found themselves in perplexity. Various Brethren were nominated as Dober's successor; but the lot negatived each. It was at this juncture that on

8

a sudden the idea presented itself simultaneously to every mind, "The Saviour shall be our Chief Elder." One of the members opened the Text-book for the new year at these two passages:— "I stand at the door and knock," Rev. 3: 20, and "Thus saith the Lord, the Holy One of Israel, and His Maker, Ask of me things to come concerning my sons, and concerning the work of my hands command ye me," Is. 45:11. At the same time it appeared that the text for the day was, "The glory of the Lord came into the house," Ezek. 43:4. Full of enthusiastic faith as to the meaning of these passages, the confernce now submitted the following question to the Lord by lot, "*Ob dies nun so viel zu bedeuten habe, dass der Heiland das Amt selbst ubernehmen wolle*"—"Whether this signified that the Saviour would Himself undertake the office." The answer of the lot was now affirmative. In the simplicity of faith the members of the conference regarded it as an answer direct from the Lord Himself, the chief eldership was abrogated, and Grasmann and Till were chosen as special elders for Herrnhut and Herrnhaag. Thus ensued "a powerful experience, in the Unity of the Brethren, that Jesus is the Chief Shepherd and Head of His Church."

It would appear that prior to November 13 this occurrence was not made known to the congregations, but merely to the "elders' conferences." The former were only informed that something extraordinary had transpired. When all was disclosed on November 13, special feeling was manifested by young and old. Meanwhile, in place of Zinzendorf as "general warden" the so-called "General Conference" was established, consisting of Bishops Müller and John Nitschmann, Frederick de Watteville, and other prominent leaders.

Such in brief is the story of this unique transaction, which exercised great influence upon the after-history of the Brethren's Church. There exists no formal journal of the conference held in London. Sources for the narrative are:—1. Short declarations in regard to this subject by Count Zinzendorf, Jonas Paulus Weiss, and an unknown writer. 2. A collection of documents by David Nitschmann, 1741-1759. 3. The diaries of Herrnhut and Herrnhaag, giving an account of the celebration of November 13. 4. The most important printed source, because it comes from an eye witness, is Spangenberg's *Leben Zinzendorf*, p. 1350, etc. (See also Memorial Days, 208-222, Cröger's *Geschichte*, p. 416; Burkardt's *Zinzendorf und die Brudergemeine*, p. 87-95;

"Forscher's" *Was ist die Wahrheit?* p. 15, etc., and the Synodal Journal of 1857).

Confessedly the subject is involved in difficulties. The following considerations have been urged by conservative writers:

1. The details of the proceedings of the "synodical conference" on September 16 are not fully known.

2. These proceedings took place amidst an extraordinary manifestation of emotional religion.

3. Hence the principal occurrence itself, the making-over to Jesus of the office of chief elder was not, properly speaking, an objective act, but a subjective feeling in the hearts of the members.

4. When the enthusiasm of the moment had passed away, it is very likely that different brethren understood the actual result of their experience in a somewhat different way.

5. The elder's office had been originally an office of intercession, and was not in any wise connected with the government of the church. But now the idea of government was added to it. This led to the notion of a theocracy. By some it was openly said that the Brethren's Church constituted the chosen people of the New Testament, that Christ had made a special covenant with it, and that he governed it immediately by the lot. At the present time the objectionable idea of a theocracy no longer obtains; but the term, "The Government of the Saviour in the Brethren's Church" is still used. What is meant by this term is clearly set forth in the Results of the General Synod of 1899 pp. 51 to 56, and especially in the following paragraphs:—

"We speak of the 'Elder's Office of the Saviour' in the Brethren' Church; we call Him the 'Elder' of our Church. We imply thereby nothing else than Christ's office as Shepherd and King in His Church, as attested in Holy Scripture. We declare, however, thereby at the same time, that Christ exercises this office in our Brethren's Church in a particular manner, corresponding with its purpose and its requirements, after He had brought our Church to a consciousness of its great poverty and need, and thereby to a child-like faith in His sovereignty—to the full and conscious appropriation of this blessing.

"Something similar takes place in the experience of individual believers. Though all that which Christ purposes to be to His own exists for each one, yet He often gives possession of Him-

self to individuals in a particular manner in one or the other respect, as they desire to possess themselves of the gift in faith,
and according to the peculiarity of mind and soul bestowed by
God on each, or the particular conditions of the outer and inner
life into which the Lord leads them.   For the Saviour gives to
each believer that which he particularly needs.   And what we
thus observe in the case of individuals may also take place in
whole religious communions in proportion to the measure in
which they really constitute a community and are capable of
making common experiences.

"Accordingly the Saviour has led our Brethren's Church in a
particular manner to experience and believingly to appropriate
the blessing of His office of Shepherd.   He prepared the Church
for this from the beginning, by teaching it not only in faith to
lay hold of His work of atonement, but also to keep Himself in
view—His own person, at once, human and divine—and to
maintain cordial and confidential intercourse with Him as with
a friend and brother.   He then showed the Church how
greatly it stood in need of Him as its only Shepherd and Elder.
He permitted the human leaders entirely to despair of their own
ability to control the constantly-expanding Church, and to deal
with the dangers which beset it.   He deprived the Church of all
external support, and permitted it to experience hostile attacks
from all sides.   At the same time He committed to it a work
which far exceeded its strength and means.   And when He had
thus brought His servants to the complete recognition of their
own weakness and inability, and when in this their perplexity
they fervently besought Him to take them under His own
charge, He heard and answered according to His promise
their united prayer, and manifested Himself to them as willing
to be their All."

6. Unfortunately assumptions were made in the early times
in connection with September 16, for which there is no warrant
in Scripture—abuses characteristic of the "Time of Sifting," but
long ago completely repudiated.

7. In the year 1841, the centenary of the conference in London, certain individual ministers in Germany, in connection with
the celebration of November 13, were carried to extremes of enthusiasm, and entangled in phraseology began again to speak
in objectionable terms about the eldership.   This led gradually, in the years 1855, 1856, and 1857, to a thorough discussion

of the whole subject in the *Fraternal Messenger*, in England, and in the *Moravian* in America, in a pamphlet written by Bishop Benade, and in "Forscher's" *Was ist die Wahrheit?* The American and English Brethren and their representatives in the mission fields for the most part stood out stoutly against everything unscriptural.

8. The practical gain which abides from the experience of the men of 1741, and remains a heritage of their spiritual sons, may be summed up thus: By this experience the Moravian Church was saved from a spiritual popedom. Personal daily fellowship with the personal Saviour is one of the essentials of the Moravian conception of religious life. The headship of Jesus in the church contains in it truths of first moment for the denomination as such. It finally carries with it the Moravian conception of the ministry, viz., that ministers are absolutely the propert of Christ, unreservedly consecrated to His service. All forms of labor done for Him and as unto Him are therefore equally honorable.

CHAPTER XI.

ZINZENDORF IN PENNSYLVANIA.

When the tract on the Lehigh was purchased, the Blue Mountains and the Susquehanna practically formed the northern and western boundaries of the Proprietaries' domains actually occupied by settlers. Trackless and unbroken primeval forests for the most part dominated the territory beyond, save where here and there around Indian villages corn waved in the summer and orchards rejoiced in their russet glow in autumn. Even south of the Blue Mountains the original masters of the woods and streams were reluctant to abandon what the settlers gained by the cunning of the "Walking Purchase." Narrow though these limits were, and meager as was the population, roughly estimated at about three hundred thousand, of whom perhaps one third were Germans, a number of nationalities and all shades of thought and creed were represented. When William Penn in 1681 had received from King Charles the territory of the Delaware from the 39th to the 42d degree north and 5 degrees to the west of the river, he had expressly determined to constitute it a refuge for the down-trodden and oppressed of all lands. In particular his visits to the Rhine-lands had drawn forth his sympathies towards those who had been impoverished by the devastations of the Thirty Years' War, or had failed to participate in the benefits of recognition by the signatories to the peace of Westphalia. Beginning with the band of emigrants led by Francis Daniel Pastorius in 1683 under the auspices of the Frankfort Land Company, thousands had responded who despaired of prosperity in their European homes owing to the almost incessant wars of the Continent, or restive under vexatious governmental interference in matters of conscience and religion. Some came directly up the waterway of the Delaware, others drifted to the land of promise after a period of unsatisfactory attempts at colonization elsewhere, especially along the Hudson and its tributaries.

By the second quarter of the eighteenth century the religious condition of the Germans was deplorable. Lack of adequate ministerial supplies and absence of regular channels of connection with recognized ecclesiastical authorities in Europe had combined with the reaction against the formalism and oppression of state churches to produce something akin to religious anarchy. Irreligion and indifference to all forms of public worship prevailed to an alarming extent. Whilst it is true that many Mennonites, Dunkers, Lutherans and Reformed from the Palatinate, and Schwenkfelder from Silesia and Saxony, had originally emigrated for conscience sake, a larger number had been influenced by other motives. Of the few ministers who came out with the emigrants the most had died; some had returned. To English clergymen the Germans would not have recourse. Thousands who had been nominal members of the church in the fatherland were now without worship, and had little or no desire for it. There were heads of families who had never been baptized and who had received scanty if any religious training. Their children were brought up in a similar manner. Sectaries of all sorts could gather something of a following for the most extravagant notions. There were hermits along the Wissahickon and Protestant monks and nuns at Ephrata. The organized German Lutheran parishes were only three or four in number, and even these were without pastors much of the time. Though the Swedes along the Delaware were somewhat better off, the supply of ministers was inadequate in their case also. Nor was the condition of the Reformed congregations much superior. In neither case was there the co-operative action of a synod or any systematic provision for general oversight. Even had the few congregations of these two churches been regularly supplied, they would have been quite inadequate to the care of the large German population. Besides various separatists formed a feature of the religious complexion of the colony, men who had few fixed principles in common save a general agreement to disagree with each other and to oppose all churchly forms of worship and all recognized confessions. It had become a proverbial expression, that a man who was utterly indifferent to revealed religion belonged to "The Pennsylvania Church."

Spangenberg during his three years of evangelization in the colony became deeply impressed with the demands of the situation. He came in contact with men of all shades of opinion and fraternized with all who sincerely desired the common good. For men were to be found even among the deplorable confusion and destitution of the times, who could rise above the narrow bounds of denominationalism and plan for an improvement. One outcome of his activity and that of similarly minded men was the formation of an association to amend the religious condition of the Germans. It was known as "The Associated Brethren of Schippack," and to it belonged men of various creeds. Leading spirits were: Henry Frey, Christian Weber, Jost Schmidt, Henry Antes, George Stiefel, William and Andrew Frey, Abraham Wagner, John Bertolet, Francis Ritter, William Pott, John Bechtel, John Adam Gruber, and George Bensel. They met every month in order to consult concerning remedies for the spiritual destitution of the land, and their conferences were continued until 1740.

Spangenberg's report of his observations suggested a two-fold work amongst the colonists as awaiting the Brethren, the preaching of the gospel to the nominal but unchurched adherents of a half forgotten faith and to the thousands who were utterly ignorant, and the establishment of schools, educational facilities being practically non-existent amongst the colonists in the interior. And it also sounded a call to mission work amongst the Indians. After a detailed description of the religious condition of the nominal adherents of the two chief confessions and of the separatists, he wrote: "Thus there is now a two-fold work for the Brethren who shall go thither in pursuance of the Lord's will: the gospel may be preached to many thousands who know nothing of it, or who have an indescribable hunger for it; and the awakened who are desirous for fellowship must be gathered into congregations. And this is not the work for one man, but for many. Moreover there are the Indians, who do not willingly dwell near the Europeans; for them it may be that the hour of grace has sounded. And in the whole country there are few schools, and there is almost no one who makes the youth his concern. One may indeed see signs of a waking up here and there in the land; and it is often not otherwise than if a wind from the Lord was passing through the entire land and bringing all into movement and the spirit of inquiry. But since the affair is so extensive every one considers himself lacking in ability to take it in hand. Perhaps the hand of the Lord is in this." This report led to the sending of Bishop Nitschmann's colony of evangelists, and to the appointment of Christian Henry Rauch to commence a mission amongst the Indians. And it caused the Brethren to pay special attention to educational work as soon as they obtained a foothold in the colony.

Zinzendorf himself was stirred with a noble ambition, namely, to effect an evangelical alliance of German Protestants in Pennsylvania, irrespective of creed. That he might not be hampered by prejudice against denominationalism, he had preliminarily resigned his powers as a bishop of the Moravian Church at the synod held at Marienborn in July, 1741. Whilst he held the episcopal character to be inalienable, he thought he could differentiate from it the prerogative of active use of episcopal powers. Apart from his Moravian consecration as a bishop, he felt entitled to exercise the functions of a recognized clergyman in virtue of his admission to orders by the faculty of Tübingen in December, 1734. At this time, moreover, no central ecclesiastical authority in any church in Europe had jurisdiction in Pennsylvania with the right to either endorse or prohibit labor of this sort on his part. Furthermore, in order that his rank might not be obtruded and prove a hindrance, it was his purpose from his very arrival in Pennsylvania (a fact publicly acknowledged before the Governor in May) to be known as Louis von Thürnstein, and not as Count von Zinzendorf, for the nonce making use of a subordinate family name to which he was entitled, and which he had already employed with the cognizance of German civil authorities when traveling to Riga in 1736. With it all it was not his desire to advance the Brethren's Church as such. It does not appear that he himself as yet fully recognized that by the logic of events the Brethren's Church did constitute a distinct ecclesiastical body.

With the stimulating experiences of September 16 in London still in mind and filled with his lofty purpose, Zinzendorf arrived in Philadelphia on December 10, 1741, having landed in New York. On the 24th Governor Thomas addressed to him a letter of cordial welcome, expressive of satisfaction at his purpose to supply the Germans of the Province with preaching. He received the letter at the little settlement on the Lehigh, where he spent Christmas, and gave the place its significant name, Bethlehem, in connection with the celebration of the Christmas Eve vigils. On December 30 he returned to Germantown, lodging with John Bechtel, a licensed preacher amongst the Reformed. He had previously made the acquaintance of Henry Antes, who on the fifteenth of the month had issued a call for a general conference of German Christians of every name to meet in Germantown. This had been preceded by John Adam Gruber's call to union amongst the awakened in Pennsylvania, issued in 1736, and was directly in accord with his own plans, though it was a fruit of the deliberations of the "Associated Brethren of Schippack."

Zinzendorf attended this gathering, which met in the house of Theobald Endten, in Germantown, and over which Antes presided. It reminded him of the "Consensus Sendomiriensis." He threw himself into the movement with all his energies, and naturally by the force of his strong personality and rank and educational advantages exercised a marked influence at this and the similar conferences which followed, and which were known as "The Pennsylvania Synods of the Congregation of God in the Spirit." Very few of the Moravians were present until the seventh session, in June. Only two of them were amongst those who officially attested the journal of the first session, John Martin Mack, of Bethlehem, and Augustine Neisser, of Germantown. At first the outlook for organic Christian union was very bright. Every German denomination in Pennsylvania—none of them being as yet organized for itself—was representd amongst the more than one hundred members who constituted the first four synods. It seemed as though the confessional lines of Europe might not necessarily reappear in Pennsylvania. Provision was made to supply unchurched neighborhoods with preachers and school-masters, and to fill vacancies where congregations desired. Though Zinzendorf had been meantime chosen as president, the men so appointed were by no means regarded as Moravians, but were classified according to their original connection. A federation of the churches seemed at one time to be achieved. Seven of these synods met before the middle of the year: at Germantown, January 1; in George Hübner's house at Falckner's Swamp, January 14; at Oley in the house of John de Türck, February 10; at Mr. Ashmead's in Germantown, March 10; in the Reformed

Church in Germantown, April 16, and in Philadelphia, May 6 and June 1. But after the fourth synod the Lutherans, Reformed and Moravians alone were left. If anything, denominational differences were intensified, and the separatists were confirmed in their hostility to churchly organization. Yet although the project proved an abortive failure, being more than a century in advance of the age, there was in its conception much that is worthy of admiration.

But Zinzendorf did not confine his activity to the furtherance of efforts at union. In judging of his undertakings, it must be remembered that religious affairs were in an abnormal state amongst the Germans.

The Lutheran congregation of Philadelphia, which dated back to about 1730, and which worshiped in a barn on Arch Street adapted to the uses of religion and rented in common with the Reformed, had been without a pastor for several years. Nor was there any prospect of obtaining one. Negotiations with Court Preacher Ziegenhagen in London and with Halle had been suspended owing to the inability of the congregation to pledge a definite and adequate salary in cash. The warden (*Vorsteher*) of the congregation in January, 1742, in his official capacity requested Zinzendorf to fill their pulpit. He consented to do this only after learning that Pastor Boehm, of the Reformed congregation, who lived at a distance and preached only every fourth Sunday, had no objection to interpose. In February a deputation of the officers of the Lutheran congregation requested Zinzendorf to administer the Holy Communion to them. He deferred his reply for a while, so as to give them time to reconsider their request; and then on Palm Sunday conducted preparatory services, and on Easter Sunday administered the sacrament according to the Lutheran ritual. A few days later the congregation gave him a call to become their pastor. Again he desired the people to duly consider their request, and also propounded various questions, amongst the rest whether they were unanimous, etc. Receiving an affirmative reply to these inquiries, and having himself previously learned from Ziegenhagen that there was no prospect of a pastor being sent, he finally accepted the call on May 26, with the understanding that he was to receive no salary. That he might not be hampered in his wider work, he stipulated that Christopher Pyrlaeus, formerly student of theology in Leipsic, should

be his assistant. The Reformed then also desired his ministrations; and a spirit of union began to manifest itself amongst
the Germans of the city, until on July 29, during the observance of the Lutheran worship, some disorderly persons rushed
in, and expelling Pyrlaeus and his hearers, took possesion of
the building in the name of the Reformed. To prevent further
hostilities Zinzendorf erected another church at his own ex-
pence. This was on Race Street, and was used by the Lutherans and by the English Moravians who had arrived in Philadelphia early in June as part of the "First Sea Congregation."
Further disagreements followed as the result of the avowed
efforts to destroy Zinzendorf's influence, put forth by Henry
Melchior Mühlenberg, the father of Lutheranism in Pennsylvania, after his arrival in November. He had previously been
superintendent of the orphanage at Hennersdorf maintained
by Henrietta von Gersdorf, the aunt of Zinzendorf, who was
estranged from him. Want of funds for this establishment in
1741 had led him to Halle, where Francke begged him to supply the urgent need of a Lutheran minister in Pennsylvania.
On Zinzendorf's part it was quite natural not to recognize that
Halle had any jurisdiction over Lutherans in Pennsylvania.
On Mühlenberg's part it was as natural not to appreciate Zinzendorf's scheme of Christian union, and to fail to understand
how a man who had been consecrated a bishop of the Moravian
Church could at the same time retain orders in the Lutheran
Church. Both were mortals, and liable to err. Both were
men of God, and have long since learnt to see eye to eye; and
both divisions of the church which they planted in Pennsylvania had a providential work to perform in America.

In the latter half of the year Zinzendorf made three tours in
the Indian country. The first of these, July 24 to August 7,
was to the region beyond the Blue Mountains. The most important event in connection with this journey was an interview
with the deputies of the Six Nations at the house of Conrad
Weisser, the interpreter for the government, at Heidelberg.
These Indians were on their way back from an interview with
Governor Thomas, at which an important subject of negotiations had been the persistent stay of the Delawares within the
"Forks" south of the Blue Mountains, on land which was to
have been vacated in accordance with the terms of the "Walking Purchase." Zinzendorf, as the head of the Moravian

Church, now ratified a covenant of friendship with these Indians, securing permission for the Brethren to pass to and from and sojourn within the domains of the great Iroquois confederation as friends and not as strangers. Thus a door was opened amongst the most influential tribes of the Atlantic slope.

The second journey was to Shekomeko, in Dutchess County, New York. At this place a mission had been established in 1740. Christian Henry Rauch had arrived in response to the appeal of Spangenberg, and had accompanied certain Mohicans from the seaport to their home about twenty-five miles east of the Hudson, on the borders of Connecticut and near Stissik Mountain. In spite of the danger from their knives and tomahawks when intoxicated, he had persevered, and had the gratification of baptizing the first three converts at the Pennsylvania Synod at Oley in February, 1742. Zinzendorf, on August 22, now organized a congregation at Shekomeko, consisting of ten Indian converts; and he also perfected arrangements for serving the white settlers of the vicinity with the gospel.

The third journey, September 24 to November 9, was from Bethlehem to Shamokin, now Sunbury, and the Wyoming Valley. It has been thought that his was the first party of white people to view this gem of Pennsylvania scenery. As a missionary tour this journey was of little result, chiefly owing to the notorious Madame Montour, whose services were required as interpreter. It was attended with many adventures and dangers. On one occasion, whilst Zinzendorf was stooping over some papers spread out upon the ground, two spreading adders passed over his person without injuring him; but this did not prevent the Indians from attempting the murderous attack which they had planned, as fable states. The treacherous design was hindered by the providential arrival of Conrad Weisser.

Though Zinzendorf's effort at a union of denominations in Pennsylvania failed, he was directly and indirectly instrumental in establishing the Moravian Church in America in a manner which he had not previously designed. Just before the session of the "Pennsylvania Synod" in Philadelphia in June, fifty-seven Moravians arrived in that city from Europe, a company known as the "First Sea Congregation" from their having been organized as such and maintaining stated worship and church discipline during the long voyage. Peter Böhler was in charge.

The majority of these persons settled at Bethlehem, the English members being destined for Nazareth, which had recently been bought from Whitefield. A congregation was formally organized at Bethlehem by Zinzendorf on June 25. As a result of the acquaintances which he formed, congregations were also later established at Hebron, Heidelberg, Oley, Lancaster and York. Schools were founded at Germantown and at Oley.

In November of this year the first form of government for the Moravian Church in America was devised, viz., Bishop Nitschmann was to superintend the Indian mission, and Peter Böhler to be the President of the Pennsylvania Synod, with Seifferth as his assistant. A final meeting was held with the leading members of the Synod at the Ridge, near Philadelphia, when arrangements were made for future convocations. Then Zinzendorf dedicated the new church in Philadelphia, January 1, 1743, and set sail from New York on the 9th in the ship *James*, which he had chartered, Captain Garrison commanding. His return to Europe was hastened by the news respecting the policy of denominational extension pursued by the governing board, a radical departure from his own ideas.

CHAPTER XII.

THE GROWTH OF THE CHURCH ON THE CONTINENT, FROM THE
SYNODICAL CONFERENCE IN LONDON TO THE REVERSAL
OF THE DECREE OF ZINZENDORF'S EXILE.

With Zinzendorf's setting sail for America it became more evident that two inherently contradictory purposes were actuating the operations of the Unity.   On the one hand men like the Nitschmanns, the Neissers, the Dobers and Polycarp Müller were at one in laboring for the natural extension of the Unity as one of the ecclesiastical organizations of Christendom.   The securing of the episcopate, even though it had been originally conceived as of value first and foremost for the missions amongst the heathen, gave natural justification to their hopes. On the other hand the great leader of the Unity believed the chief calling of the resuscitated church to be not self-propagation, but the infusion of a vital leaven into the confessional churches by the promotion of vital religion in the lives of individual members of these churches who should not detach themselves from the fellowship of the ecclesiastical bodies in which they had been born even though they became affiliated with the Brethren. If anywhere "settlement congregations" were established, they were to be only strategic points around which a wide ramification of *Diaspora* circles might be maintained in efficient operation.   But it may be doubted whether the representatives of the old Unity had ever regarded with complete satisfaction this subordination of their ecclesiastical independence.   When therefore an opportunity arose for the extension of the Unity as such, they naturally deemed it their duty not to fly in the face of providence by declining to enter the opening doors. Thus, for example, they in December, 1741, welcomed overtures from awakened Bohemians of Lusatia, who next August founded Nisky, with the consent of their patron Sigismund Augustus von Gersdorf, lord of Trebus.

The industry and thrift of the people of Herrnhut were now attracting attention, and had come to the notice amongst the rest of the shrewd King of Prussia, Frederick the Great, who was not the man to submit to the outworn trammels of the Peace of Westphalia, even though unable to appreciate Herrnhut after the fashion of his father. When the Peace of Breslau, in June, 1742, secured to him Silesia as the fruit of the campaigns of Olmütz and Glatz, he held out special inducements to the Moravians to settle in his newly acquired dominions. On their part the negotiations were conducted by David Nitschmann, the Syndic, Wenceslaus Neisser and Count Balthasar von Pomnitz, a young Silesian noble and one time Saxon colonel of cavalry, whose valet had been instrumental in his conversion and had directed him to Herrnhut during the previous year. The terms of the concession granted by the Prussian king distinctly recognized the Moravian Church as an independent church with an episcopal constitution, and granted its members liberty of conscience in Silesia, though a proselyting propaganda was prohibited. A second concession, in 1746, secured by Abraham von Gersdorf, permitted the reception of persons who asked admission to the Moravian Church of their own free will and without the pressure of external constraint. At this juncture moreover the accession of another Silesian noble proved of importance, Ernest Julius von Seidlitz, of Ober Peilau, near Reichenbach. Born in 1695, he had been led to a satisfying knowledge of Christ by his pastor, Benjamin Linder, and making the acquaintance of Christian David in 1727, had been drawn to Herrnhut. Imprisoned on account of religion by the Austrian authorities in 1739, he had endured persecution for a year and a half, until Frederick the Great's invasion set him free, his family meanwhile having found safety at Herrnhut, whither he himself went when Frederick's success was no longer doubtful. On his return to Peilau he had taken with him various brethren, with the result that incipient congregations had been gathered by them at Krausche, Peilau and Rossnitz, Wenceslaus Neisser, Martin Dober and Samuel Lieberkühn being especially active in the work. On one of his estates he now commenced to establish a "settlement," known as Gnadenfrei; and it was speedily followed by the founding of Gnadenberg near Breslau. The prospects for extension in Silesia soon afforded so much encouragement that Bishop

Müller removed from Wetteravia to Peilau, in order to give his personal supervision to the activity, and with his removal that of the college and seminary was also involved. Martin Dober estimated that in 1742 about four thousand persons in Silesia were in fellowship with the Brethren. Moreover Count von Promnitz purchased from Count Gustavus Gotter the domain of Neudietendorf, near Gotha, in Thuringia, with the view to found a settlement there, since in this vicinity there had long been appreciative friends, at Jena, Gotha, Erfurth, Meiningen, etc. Early in February, 1742, Bishop John Nitschmann had conferred with the friends in Jena and Gotha, and a congregation had been organized in the latter town in July. Hence the offer of the Count was peculiarly opportune. The members of the congregation in Gotha removed to the vacant houses at Neudietendorf, and a memorial was addressed to the Duke of Gotha, requesting religious liberty for the Brethren, endorsed by Counts Promnitz and Gotter.

The news of all these transactions made a disagreeable impression upon Zinzendorf, and he hastened to return from America. In the middle of February, 1743, he reached London. Detained here for a month by a visit to the important center of operations in Yorkshire and having his final interview with John Wesley, he sent in advance an indignant protest against the assumptions of the General Conference, and wrote to the Duke of Gotha in order to interpose before the concessions had been granted to Neudietendorf, disavowing any part in the steps that had been taken in connection with the founding of this settlement, and affirming that the only kind of settlement which could be planted there in fellowship with Herrnhut must be one whose religious life was based strictly upon the Confession of Augsburg. On the fourth of April he met a number of members of the General Conference in Amsterdam, and entered into a preliminary discussion of their transactions during his absence. According to his view the operations of the board ought to have been confined to existing enterprises. His own office of "general warden," which he had desired to resign, had not been accepted previous to his departure to America. Therefore he should have been consulted before any alteration in aims had been avowed. Besides he found various of the undertakings of a sort likely to involve in complications, and could not approve of the manner in which things had been

9

done. Promnitz also met him in Amsterdam, and although he rejoiced in the accession of the young and generous noble, it seemed to him inappropriate that negotiations of so much importance had been entrusted to one who was but a novice in the affairs of the Brethren.

After a sojourn of some months in Wetteravia, Zinzendorf joined issue with his co-workers clearly and distinctly at a synod held at Hirschberg, near Ebersdorf, from June 30 to July 12, 1743. Till, Grasmann, Polycarp Müller, Bishop John Nitschmann, Abraham von Gersdorf, Martin Dober, Jonas Paulus Weiss, Frederick de Watteville, David Nitschmann the Syndic, and Hutton were amongst the most important of the leaders of the church who were present. Zinzendorf protested against the policy and transactions of the General Conference and declared its powers abrogated. His co-workers surrendered unconditionally, overcome as they were by the sense of what they owed to him and by a realization of his personal sacrifices. The place of the germinant directing board was taken by offices vague in their functions and prerogatives, adapted less to the churchly phase of development than to the work of "inner missions;" devotion to an independent form of ecclesiastical activity was to be avoided, and Zinzendorf was requested to effect a rearrangement of the privileges secured in Silesia with a view to this change in policy. Moreover, on the 20th of the following November the leading men presented to him a formal document clothing him with unlimited powers of management and oversight, as *Advocatus et Ordinarius Fratrum*, that is, absolute general administrator and executive, responsible to no synod or conference. Thus the monarchial principle was allowed to temporarily displace the conferential principle characteristic of the Unity of the Brethren from the earliest days. The church was now liable to a far graver danger than had been avoided by the abrogation of the "chief eldership." Nor can the unfortunate occurrences of the decade be wholly disassociated from the consequences of this complete reversal of the traditional policy of the church. Providentially so far as externals were concerned the efforts of Zinzendorf to have the concessions which had been secured by the General Conference judged null and void by the State authorities were overruled. In Berlin Frederick the Great refused to place the Brethren in Silesia under the surveillance of the Lutheran consistories, nor would he consent to make a new examination into their doctrinal status, being personally indifferent as to matters of faith, but very much alive to the advantage of securing the industrial advantages likely to accrue from "settlements" of the Brethren in Silesia. In fact, the Count was reminded that he himself had already passed a satisfactory examination before divines in Berlin, and a royal intimation was given that it would be agreeable to have the Brethren form an additional settlement in Neusalz. He effected a reversal of plans only in the case of Neudietendorf, which to the present occupies an anomalous position with regard to the appointment, installation and responsibility of its pastors.

Whilst it is useless to speculate what might have been, had the spirit of firmness, characteristic of Herrnhut in January, 1731, dominated the men of the synod of Hirschberg, it is of interest to note the numbers of those who were reported as in close fellowship with the Brethren at this time. They are as follows: Herrnhut, 750; Heerendyk, 30; Montmirail, 10; Marienborn, 150; Herrnhaag, 400; the Ronneburg, 100; *Arbeiter aus der Gemeine, i. e.*, evangelists, 700; Lusatia, 1,700; Saxony, 100; Bohemia, 300; Silesia, 2,000; Wetteravia, 200; Holland, 300; Sweden, 100; Württemberg, 200; Augsburg, 20; Franconia, 300; Thuringia, 500; Iceland, 1; Voigtland, 200; Berlin, 100; Magdeburg and Pommerania, 300; Holstein and Jutland, 500; St. Petersburg, 2; Denmark, 500; Sweden, 520; Livonia, 7,000; London, 300; Lamb's Inn, 100; Yorkshire, 1,200; Scotland, 4; Isle of Man, 1; Pennsylvania, 300; Georgia, 12; New York, 53; Hungary and Transylvania, 57; Greenland, 20; Cape of Good Hope, 30; Ceylon, 5; Berbice and Surinam, 27; St. Thomas, 300; St. Croix and St. John, 3; North America, 45; total, 20,974.

But the unlimited and unquestioned sway of one man was of even more significance from the fact that the influence of Zinzendorf's personality and individual temperament now inevitably left its impress upon the inner life and spirit of the Unity, at times even swaying and carrying away the more independent thinkers. This is of importance because the external conflict of conceptions before described had its counterpart in the inner life of the church. The old Moravian element and the Pietistic element had already displayed marked and most important divergencies; and now the ultra Pietistic element was temporarily to become dominant in a hurtful fashion. In

Wetteravia in particular the theological concept of the true humanity as well as the true divinity of Jesus Christ was coming to the forefront, fostered especially by John de Watteville. Laying hold of some of the bold figures of speech characteristic of Zinzendorf's terminology, and combining these with the fundamental conception of the meritorious effects of the life of Christ for the body and soul of men, the thought of His example and of His having passed from infancy to mature manhood was brought to bear with modifying effect upon the "bands" or "classes" which had existed since 1727, and new regulations for the "choirs" were adopted. The latter flourished especially in Wetteravia, and were introduced into Herrnhut during a visit of Langguth from February 28, 1741, to August, 1742. Whereas the motto of the Moravians in Herrnhut had been *Streiterschaft für den Herrn,* and warriorship and the "witness spirit" the governing traits, now the ideal was to be an imitator of the God-man in the pure manhood of His soul and body, and to be receptive of the mysterious efficacy of His chaste purity; in the "choirs" of young men and women much was made of an absence of personal will as to one's future condition of life whether as a celibate or as a head of a family, leaving that to the leading of the Lord; and thus it was that the use of the lot in connection with marriages became general.

Now the spirit of the age and the conditions of the mental environment of Wetteravia were such that any departure in the direction of sentimentalism carried with it elements of danger. Pseudo Pietism had many representatives in the vicinity of Frankfort. Mysticism and sectarian fanaticism had attached to themselves many devotees. The followers of Rock, Hochmann and Dippel and kindred souls had given the Pietism of western Germany a questionable tinge. The Berleburg Bible had accustomed many devout minds, possessed of religiousness rather than discrimination, to find mystical suggestions in all manner of descriptive or narrative portions of the Scriptures. In Switzerland devout but injudicious Lutz was revealing the sickly emotional features of exaggerated Pietism in "flowery and not always tasteful language." The Brugglers were indulging in prophecies. Oettinger, the "Magus of the South," once Zinzendorf's instructor for a brief time at Herrnhut, from excess of zeal against the rationalistic tendency was erring in the opposite direction, sinking into theosophy in his endeavor to combine natural and spiritual things, and aiming to present spiritual truths in a concrete, vivid, sensuous fashion. Literature, French and German alike, smacked of the sentimental with a touch of bombast. Pietistic poetry in general inclined to the painting of sensuous pictures, and a dallying with the Saviour, and the habitual use of endearing diminutives, such as "little dove," "little sheep," "little lamb," etc. With the accession of considerable numbers of Pietists from Frankfort and Jena and their vicinity, the mode of thought in vogue in Wetteravia in connection with the drift of the age therefore involved ominous features, especially since Zinzendorf was a man of impulse and feeling, rather than a logically systematic theologian. In point of fact time was soon to demonstrate that the Moravian Church was as little able to disregard the general current of thought around it as any other division of Christendom, and that it must suffer from drifting too near the danger point. The most wonderful feature of its experience was its rapid and complete return to Scriptural sobriety.

After the synod of Hirschberg a brief period of residence in Berlin followed, during which Zinzendorf entered into his unsuccessful negotiations with the Prussian authorities for the revocation of the concessions. Then came a visit to Count Promnitz at his castle of Burau, in Silesia, and an inspection of the beginnings of Gnadenfrei, near Peilau, and Gnadenberg, near Gross Krausche, and also of Neusalz and Niesky—the visit in addition giving an opportunity for interviews with the leaders of affairs at Herrnhut, whither the decree of banishment made it impossible for him to go as yet. To Burau where these conferences were held, came also John Michael Langguth and Spangenberg, to consult about the procedure to America of the "Second Sea Congregation" of a hundred and thirty-three persons. The consecration of Frederick de Watteville and of John de Watteville as bishops also took place during this period, the former at Burau, the latter in the castle at Peilau.

Then came a boldly conceived and resolutely attempted journey to Russia, with a few companions, one of whom was his own youthful son, Christian Renatus.

Various circumstances impelled the Count to take this step. Three Brethren, Conrad Lange, Zatharias Hirschel and Michael Kund, who had been dispatched as missionaries to Mongolia, *via* the Russian Empire, had been arrested and imprisoned at

St. Petersburg. Nor were they destined to obtain freedom until 1747. Moreover, Arvid Gradin, who had been sent in June to lay before the Holy Synod a letter setting forth the affairs of the Unity and its relationship to the Greek Church, had received the same treatment. In addition to this, the extensive evangelistic and educational activity of the Brethren in Livonia had been developing in such a way as to cause friction since Zinzendorf's visit to that country in 1736. The institute at Wolmar for the training of catechists, of which Lady von Hallart was patroness, had assumed large proportions. Its students were now about seventy in number. The evangelists had acquired a mastery of the Lettish language, and were reaching masses of people. An extensive revival of religion amongst the peasantry had resulted. Coupled with it was a not unnatural effort to introduce the characteristic discipline of the Moravian Church, a measure welcomed, moreover, by some of the Lutheran clergymen, though it was contrary to the instructions of Zinzendorf as conflicting with his conception of the service which the evangelists were to render. And it had aroused others of the clergy to enter complaints against the Brethren as a dangerous sect, and request the interference of the civil authorities. To this form of activity on the part of the Moravians the Count now wished to put a stop.

Arriving at Riga, he desired a pass to St. Petersburg, in order to proceed thither and lay before the Empress Elizabeth in person the affairs of the Brethren. But the Governor, Field Marshall Count Laski, instead lodged him and his companions in the citadel, on December 23, and confiscated his books and papers—an act which he indeed afterwards recognized as a real kindness, being meant to save him from the worse treatment sure to be meted out at the capital in case he should have passed onwards. The appeal for an investigation now addressed to her majesty brought for a reply an order to quit Russian territory forthwith. Under an escort of soldiers he was shown the way to the Prussian frontier, leaving the citadel on January 12, 1744.

Another sojourn in Silesia now followed. On the way thither the news of the death of Count Promnitz from small-pox, at Erbach in Franconia, reached him, an event which temporarily interfered with the building of Gnadenfrei and Neudietendorf. Despite the danger thereby incurred, furtive visits were twice made to Herrnhut, and on April 22 he set out for Wetteravia, where he arrived on May 1.   For a season the center of the Unity was to be here, and the spirit of the twin congregations of Herrnhaag and Marienborn, in distinction from that of the Saxon mother congregation, should be temporarily dominant.

At the former place eight hides of land had been bought for about $6,000 in 1738, and soon a brethren's-house and a sisters'-house had been erected, the means for building first having been furnished by John de Watteville. Next year the theological seminary was located here.   In 1740 the first place of worship and an orphanage had been completed, and a school for girls soon followed.   In 1743 a new contract had been drawn up with the ruling family, whereby the estates of Lenstadt and Dilsheim were leased for thirty-three years for upwards of $75,000.   A new place of worship had recently been commenced and also a residence for the Count, known as the Lichtenberg. At the foot of a hill crowned by the old castle of the Ronneburg, there clustered close together about a central square the well-built, substantial houses of the architectural type which characterized Moravian masonry in the middle of the eighteenth century.   Carefully tilled fields and a park-like garden, designed after the vogue of the old regime in France, and the unique Moravian *Gottesacker* lay between the town and the meadows of neighboring estates.

Two hours' walk southwest from Büdingen, and near the frontier of Cassel, in a pleasant valley bordered by wooded hills, lay Marienborn, once the seat of a Cistercian nunnery, but since the year 1588 the site of a stately castle.   Here schools for the education of the children of the church had been founded. Since 1742 the castle and the estate together with the domain of Eckartshaus had been leased for thirty years, and next year the *Schlosskapelle* had similarly come into the possession of the Brethren.   At Marienborn, where the Count now made his home, for a time reunited to his family, and having many of the most prominent servants of the church about him, a synod had been summoned to meet on May 15.   Such an influx of temporary residents resulted that it was deemed wise to remove the students, noteworthy amongst whom were John Frederick Cammerhof, Theophilus Schumann, David Cranz, John Adam Schmidt and Ernest Lewis Schlicht, to the neighboring castle of Lindheim, the home of the Von Schrautenbach family, now residents of Herrnhut, their son Louis, Zinzendorf's future biographer, being an inmate of the seminary.

It was the period of Marienborn's prosperity. The eloquent Albert Anthony Vierorth, erstwhile cathedral preacher at Reval, whence he had been dismissed in consequence of the rescript of December 12, 1743, was about to become chaplain at the castle. Bishop Müller was presiding over the seminary and the publication house. All was being carried on upon an enthusiastic and dashing scale. Two purposes predominated, the desire to avoid sectarian proselytism, but to serve as a link of union for true believers of various confessional schools, and to shun a mere intellectual and dead adhesion to the formulated standards of Christian doctrine. The joy of consecrated religious life became an uppermost thought. To be a sinner saved by grace should be counted a soul-stirring privilege. Something of a disdain of the strict Moravian discipline also entered into the spirit of the day. This savored too much of legalism, it was thought. Hence the judicious statutes and regulations promotive of sober godliness at Herrnhut since May 12, 1727, had never been introduced in Wetteravia. Sinners conscious of their justification in Christ had no need of these artificial restraints.

But with it all there was something unsound in the tendencies of the place and times, though the men and women excelled in unfeigned sincerity of devotion, unquestioned purity of purpose, amazing zeal and honest diligence of life. In the first place, the financial basis of operations was questionable, from the standpoint of safety. Most of the Wetteravian lands were held only on a limited lease, and the valuable improvements placed upon them might be alienated without remedy—as occurred in the event. Too much depended upon the good faith and favor of the Counts of Büdingen. Moreover, the establishments here and elsewhere and the spread of the missionary enterprises were costing vast sums, exceeding the resources of the Count, who was on principle opposed to laying fixed assessments upon or asking stated contributions from members of the church. Dutch friends like Beuning, Schellinger and Decknatel were unwisely kind with their moneyed assistance, and thus helped to swell the credit system. The first mentioned was already a creditor to the amount of upwards of $150,000. And the revenues from these estates were in proportion inconsiderable.

A change had also taken place in Zinzendorf himself. The flood of controversial tractates directed against him and his endeavors had not been without effect; the continued success of his enterprises in spite of bitterest opposition had tended to cause him to estimate the criticism at possibly less than its worth, and to fail to fully learn from it those lessons of self-restraint and self-discipline, which a wise man seeks to learn from the judgment of adversaries. His experiences in Pennsylvania and at Hirschberg seem to have rendered him apt to pay less attention than formerly to the adverse opinions of others. A fondness for solitary meditation increased. He became a man living more by himself, more self-contained, more reserved, less approachable, and having intercourse with his coadjutors as a rule chiefly in formal conferences, associating himself with younger men, with the natural result that they deferred to his judgment or at least hesitated to speak to him as freely as men of his own age might have spoken. In consequence, things might transpire about him, concerning which he had not the intimate acquaintance which characterized his residence at Herrnhut in 1727.

During the synod of Marienborn, from May 12 to June 15, and succeeding gatherings which followed in quick succession, Zinzendorf developed his idea of the so-called *Tropen*, a term derived from the Greek τρόποι πειδείας —methods of training. It was this conception, in a more or less nebulous form, perhaps, that had been underlying his efforts at church union in Pennsylvania, and his unwillingness to see the denominational ecclesiasticism of the Moravians advanced in Europe. He believed that the evangelical churches were essentially one, and that in each of the Christian churches, even the ultra-montane Roman Catholic and the Gallican, there reposed a peculiar gift for training souls according to its own special method. Hence there is a Lutheran, a Reformed and a Moravian "trope," in the Unity of the Brethren, according to which souls are educated for eternity in conformity with the peculiar tendencies of each church. In itself alone no one church has the exclusively correct method; that which is eternally true and absolutely correct is the *Original Religion des Heilands*. This is taken up in differently modified types by the different churches. Within the Unity of the Brethren there is room for the various "tropes," each of which is to have its recognized leader as such (later he wished to distinguish even a Methodist "trope"); and therefore it seemed to him desirable to discourage the use of the epithet "Moravian" as applied to the whole Unity.

After this synod Zinzendorf proceeded to Holland, partly on mission business connected with Schmidt's return from Africa, and partly with a view to the founding and development of a settlement-congregation at Zeist.

During the administration of affairs by the General Conference, whilst the Count was absent in America, Baron Abraham von Gersdorf had endeavored to secure from the States General liberty of operations in Holland for the Brethren; and from February to April, 1742, Amsterdam had been the seat of the Conference. At the synod of Hirschberg Zinzendorf had reported that a barony in the Province of Ysselstein belonging to Count Nassau, a son of King William III, was for sale for 200,000 florins. The purchase was promoted by wealthy friends of the Brethren in Holland, the Schellingers, Matthias Beuning, Cornelius van Laer and Jan Verbeek in particular. It included a castle, which had been a residence of Louis XIV of France in 1672, together with the adjoining village, beautified by noble avenues of beech trees. In 1745 Frederick Wenceslaus Neisser had been sent to take charge and prepare for the reception of the Count and his coadjutors. Hither they came in April, 1746; and hither came also Count Henry 29th Reuss from Ebersdorf, with Magister Steinhofer, to arrange for a closer union of Ebersdorf with the Brethren—finally consummated in December. Special attention was paid to missionary business at the ensuing Synod held in the castle in May, and amongst the rest it was determined to have a ship built for the use of the church, manned and officered by members, to be employed in connection with missionary undertakings and for the transportation of Moravian colonists. In the event the snow *Irene* was acquired, having Captain Garrison as commander, and Cook as first mate, with seven of the Brethren as sailors. The business of the synod also included a consideration of the various orders of the ministry; and the subordinate orders of acolytes and deaconesses and sundry offices, like that of *Senior Civilis*, which had obtained in the Unitas Fratrum were reintroduced, though the essential functions of their incumbents were not entirely the same as in the olden time.

After the synod of Zeist the rapid development of the work of the Brethren in England rendered it desirable to prepare the way for some authoritative definition of the relationship of their movement to the Established Church. Hence the Count crossed the channel with a number of his chief associates and held several conferences in London with prominent representatives of the British activity. Opportunity was besides afforded for conversation with Governor Thomas Penn with regard to various matters of importance relating to the settlements in the colony under his jurisdiction. Returning by way of Holland, in November, after a visit to Ebersdorf, the Count early in the year 1747 took possession of the house newly erected for him at Herrnhaag. He was not, however, to remain here permanently.

The steady advance in external prosperity which attended the thrift and industry of Herrnhut, the enviable reputation which its people had acquired for morality and good citizenship, the fame of the rapidly developing establishments in Wetteravia, and the idea that Zinzendorf's influence could command the use of large financial means, had all been conspiring to gradually moderate the hostility of the Saxon government. Policy dictated a qualifying of the adverse opinion hitherto held with respect to the operations of the exiled nobleman, whose philanthropy assumed a different aspect in the eyes of statesmen now that it seemed to be productive of valuable industries and desirable resources. The king himself was more leniently disposed, since he had recently passed through Herrnhut and had personally made himself acquainted with its affairs. At a time, therefore, when the general public had little expectation of such a thing, intimation was given to the Count that he might revisit Saxony. Of this permission he was quick to avail himself, and arrived at Herrnhut on September 16, 1747. An interview with Count Hennicke, the Saxon minister in Leipzig, followed next month, which resulted in his majesty's sending the exiled Count an autographic revocation of the edict of banishment. Next summer a new commission, appointed by royal authority, consisting of eight members, five laymen and three clergymen, came to Herrnhut. The doctrines, the discipline, the episcopate and the civico-religious regulations of the Brethren, as well as their relationship to the evangelical church were scrutinized very searchingly in the course of an investigation that lasted from

July 29 to August 12. The consequences were most favorable. As a first result, the government of Saxony desired to lease to the Brethren the castle and royal estate of Barby, on the Elbe, a proposal which was accepted, and in November of this same year the theological seminary was removed thither. As a second result, a royal decree in September, 1749, granted the Brethren full liberty of conscience and of worship and ritual in Upper Lusatia and on the estate of Barby in recognition of their substantial adherence to the tenets of the Confession of Augsburg.

Before the completion of these negotiations, important transactions of a similar nature had been in process in London, in connection with the determination of the status of the Moravians in Britain and its colonies. Hence after a brief visit to Wetteravia, Zinzendorf in the latter part of September, 1748, proceeded to Holland whence he made his way to England, landing at Harwich on January 1.

But in the midst of all these indications of external prosperity, and especially since September, 1745, the Wetteravian spirit had been manifesting itself within the church in a most unfortunate manner, and was about to bear most unfortunate fruits, none being more distressed than Zinzendorf himself when the culmination was reached. "It seemed as though the church had gone to sleep and was dreaming a bad dream." The defamatory pamphlets which continued to be directed against him had excited in him a scorn of his opponents, and he gave less concern than ever whether or not he shocked men by paradoxical statements and mystic ideas. Moreover, his intellectual disposition was such that when a figure of speech captivated him, he had a tendency to carry it to extremes, and build about a metaphor a system of theology. These conceptions he embodied in hymns and liturgies, especially with reference to the concept of the Trinity. The sober doctrine of the atonement which had hitherto prevailed, was distorted by a sentimental and extravagant emphasizing of the physical wounds of Christ. The "choir system" was exaggerated and the protests of men of the old Moravian stamp, whose exaltation of the churchly conception of discipline the adherents of the newer ideas termed Pharisaic, were of no avail. Moreover, Pietistic enthusiasts who had flocked to Herrnhaag and Marienborn from the vicinity of Frankfort and others from Livonia, coming as they did with a predilection for morbid sentimentalism, carried the conceptions germinal in these paradoxical utterances of the Count to extremes of which he in his absence from western Germany had little or no knowledge. Naturally the friendship of some half admirers was now alienated, and weapons were placed in the hands of the antagonists of the Brethren. Tübingen withdrew its favor. Bengel declared that this was no longer the old Moravian Church. Drs. Hofmann, Fröreisen, Benner, Volk and especially Fresenius found profitable material for hostile tracts and volumes. But finally, early in 1749, Zinzendorf's eyes were opened by some of his coadjutors. Christian David, Steinhofer, Godfrey Clemens, Molther, Spangenberg, and the Neissers had been repeatdly raising voices of opposition and warning. When the Count really understood the character and extent of the fanaticism, his indignation was great. He blamed his own son, Christian Renatus, most severely, and summoned him to England.

In February, 1749, Zinzendorf wrote a letter to the erring churches, in which he sternly pointed out the sinfulness of the excesses into which they had been betrayed, and furthermore sent his son-in-law, John de Watteville, to visit these churches, and to put a stop to everything anti-scriptural. The most important point in connection with the whole case is the absolute return of the Brethren to simplicity and a scriptural form of thought. No other church has passed through an experience parallel to this. It has well been said, "Such fanaticism followed by so complete a victory, shows how firmly and fully the church was founded on the Rock of Ages."

Nothing tended so much to sober the minds of the Brethren as the troubles which broke out in Wetteravia about this time. The government became unfriendly to them. In October, 1749, on the death of Count Casimir of Büdingen, his son and successor Gustav Friedrich, a royal chamberlain at Copenhagen, under the influence of his agent, Councillor Brauer, sought to take advantage of the inhabitants of Marienborn and Herrnhaag, in connection with the necessity for the renewal of the lease of the former place and the taking of the oath of allegiance on the part of the people of both settlements. Ignoring the favorable terms of the contract entered into in 1743, which was to have run for thirty years, Brauer skilfully planned the terms so that if necessary they might be exiled on the alleged ground of disloyalty in temporal matters, and thus the appearance of religious persecution be avoided. Amongst the rest he required them to abjure all subordination to Zinzendorf and the other leaders of their church, with the purpose of diverting them to one of the recognized confessional churches. To this they objected. Then they were told that they would have to emigrate within three years and abandon their homes and improvements, if they remained obstinate. This was a mere threat. The authorties of Büdingen never thought it possible that they would actually relinquish two such flourishing towns as Marienborn and Herrnhaag, built by their own labor and at their own expense.

But after appealing in vain to the terms of the contract of 1743, they decided to a man to do this very thing rather than give up their church—and this heroism ought not to be forgotten by any who would indulge in a cheap sneer at their previous temporary excesses of religious sentimentalism. It should be remembered that these were the men who were willing to go at short notice to the four corners of the world to herald Christ. Every continent except Australia was a mission field for them, at a time before ever a Carey was known. Theirs was a manifestation of that same spirit of fidelity, which shone out in the old days of exile during the Counter-Reformation, in the voyage of the Puritan Pilgrim Fathers, in the exodus from France after the revocation of the Edict of Nantes, in the emigration of the Salzburger and the flight from the Kuhländel to Herrnhut. It fully atoned for previous aberrations. Let those who would laugh at them, first earn the right to do so by manifesting a spirit of equal devotion to Christ.

In 1750 the emigration began, and in three years the Wetteravian settlements were deserted, save that a handful of workers remained at Marienborn to maintain a *Diaspora* activity until 1773. Nearly three thousand members of the church had lived there. Many came to America; some went to Barby, others to Zeist, and others—a contingent of French-speaking Brethren originally from Switzerland—to the recently commenced settlement at Neuwied on the Rhine. The harsh measure of tyrannous oppression naturally entailed heavy financial losses upon the Moravian Church—and proved a piece of utterly foolish statesmanship as far as the Counts of Büdingen were concerned; but it administered a most excellent tonic of providential discipline to the Brethren themselves, and revived the manly spirit so characteristic of the refugees of 1722-1727. Moreover, the dross of fanaticism was completely sublimated and eliminated by this fire of persecution. The complete disappearance of the extravagances of the "Time of Sifting," with the suppression of hymnals and liturgies which had been instrumental in promoting it, followed as a fortunate consequence.

CHAPTER XIII.

PROGRESS IN GREAT BRITAIN, TO THE RECOGNITION BY ACT OF
PARLIAMENT.

Although the establishment of the congregation in Fetter
Lane in London, by Spangenberg, in November, 1742, marked
the formal inception of the work of the Moravian Church in
Great Britain, the evangelistic activity of various men during
previous years, at first quite distinct but then more or less identified with the Moravian movement, must be regarded as inter-
linked with the efforts of the Brethren.   Prominent amongst
those who thus consciously or unconsciously prepared the way
for the Moravians were Benjamin Ingham and John Cennick.
The former remained within the communion of the Established
Church, but throughout his life served his various parishes in
a spirit kindred to that which animated the friends with whom
at one time he came into a very close touch.   The great life-
work of the latter was performed by commission of the Unitas
Fratrum itself.

Cennick is generally supposed to have been of Bohemian extraction, the family name having been originally Kunik, possibly one of the numerous families of refugees that found asylum
in England after the disastrous battle of the White Mountain.
Certain it is that his grandfather, a clothier, had espoused the
faith of Fox, and had suffered imprisonment for religion's sake.
The future evangelist was born at Reading in 1718. Deeply
convicted of sin whilst in London at Easter, 1735, he found
peace in September, 1737. A perusal of Whitefield's Journal in
the latter part of the following year drew him to seek association with men of his stamp. Undeterred by the ordinary requirements of etiquette, he hunted out the ardent seeker for
souls whom he had admired at a distance, and soon after his
kindly reception by him made the acquaintance also of the
Wesleys and Hutchins. In June, 1739, Whitefield's offer of a

position as school-master for the children of colliers at Kingswood was gladly accepted. Here it was that Cennick first attempted to preach, addressing a gathering of from four to five hundred colliers under a sycamore tree. In these zealous efforts Wesley gave him special encouragement, perceiving his native endowments and zeal. About Christmas, 1740, Cennick, however, separated from the Wesleys, and itinerated more or less independently in Wiltshire, or in company with Harris. In 1741 Whitefield gave him charge of his society in Moorfields, London, and again there followed a period of itinerancy in the southwest of England. In June of the next year he sought the fellowship of the Brethren at Fetter Lane, and in 1745 finally became fully identified with them. His labors in Somerset and Wiltshire had been truly apostolic. Through visits of Töltschig, Böhler and Spangenberg the societies formed in Bristol and at Kingswood and Tytherton were developed into congregations of the Moravian Church. That his itinerancy had been no child's play, so degraded was the state of morals and religion in the rural districts, is evident from his description of what Harris and he experienced in June, 1741. His diary reads thus:

"Went with Rev. Howell Harris to Swindon, and the Vale of the White Horse. A large company assembled in the grove. We sang and prayed, but were hindered from preaching by a mob, who made a noise, played instruments among the people and fired guns so near our faces that Mr. Harris and myself were black with the powder. We were not affrighted, but opened our breasts and said, 'We are ready to lay down our lives for the gospel, and would not resist if the guns were leveled at our hearts.' They flung dust from the road over us, and played an engine upon us, filled us with stinking water from the ditch, until we were like men in the pillory. While they vented their rage on Brother Harris I spoke to the people, and when they turned the engine upon me he preached. They kept on till the engine was spoiled, and then threw buckets of water over us. We endured their spite and malice upwards of an hour, a spectacle of shame and derision." The account continues:

"This persecution did not originate amongst the people, but wicked men were hired to insult and abuse us. *Gentlemen* furnished them with the guns, halberd and engine, telling them to use us as bad as they could, only not to kill us. He was present on horseback, well-pleased and laughing heartily. They

10

dressed up two images, calling the one 'Cennick' and the other 'Harris,' marched them up and down, and publicly burned them, amidst the shouts and buffoonery of the mob.

"Next day they visited the house of Mr. Lawrence, broke his windows, cut and wounded four of his family and knocked down his daughter. If singing were heard in his house, or a minister supposed to be there, they would raise a riot about it. The mob was next encouraged to pull it down, and had actually commenced the work when a violent storm which burst over the town, accompanied with thunder and lightning, so terrified them that they were obliged to desist. An oak in the field of their unrelenting persecutor was riven to pieces and scattered about. This was noticed by the people when they saw what followed.

"On preaching being appointed again at Stratton, near Swindon, the leader of the former mob got a butcher to save all the blood he could, in readiness to play it out of the engine and give us blood enough, he said, 'because Cennick preached the blood of Jesus Christ cleanseth from all sin.' But God interfered, and struck with particular judgments the author of this plot and his associates at once and the same time. J—— and T—— and K—— and B—— all bled at the nose, and some at the mouth, with little or no intermission. One had fits and never recovered his faculties. Another bled so profusely that he died in ten days.

"On their flight from Stratton, the mob, which had been posted on each side of the road for nearly two miles, beat them like dogs with whips and sticks, cursing and swearing that they would butcher them. The proud man who was at the bottom of all this cruel treatment now rejoiced that he had given them enough to drive them from Stratton. But God was watching his conduct, and soon visited him with judgment. A few days after, while riding the same horse on which he sat when cheering the mob at White Horse Vale, his servant, who had been cleaning a gun, fired it off as his master rode into the court; the horse started—the rider fell off to the ground—death followed—and where is he?"

In the southwest of England during the forties additional evangelists were Schlicht, Francis Okely—a graduate of Oxford—Horne, Syms, Brampton, Heckewelder—the father of the future missionary in America—Münster, Cooke, Parminter, Heim, Schultze and Hutton.

Meanwhile, however, Ingham and Delamotte were meeting with such success among the rough colliers of Yorkshire that they asked assistance, and Töltschig joined them. In 1740 they could report upwards of fifty societies whose members met regularly for mutual edification. A corps of evangelists was organized by the Brethren in London, and Smith House, a large farm in the parish of Halifax, was rented for their accommodation. Here on May 26 Töltschig, Viney, Piesch and Gussenbauer were installed as the leaders in charge of affairs in the north. Soon after Ingham, with the consent of those whom he had been serving, formally turned over his work to the Brethren, and by the end of 1743 forty-seven recognized preaching-places were supplied by them. Over each of the five districts into which the Yorkshire work was sub-divided experienced brethren were in charge; Spangenberg, at Smith House; Ockershausen, at Mirfield; Gussenbauer, at Pudsey; Töltschig and Piesch, at Great Horton; Brown, at Holbeck. In the scope of their activity they included also evangelization in Lancashire, Derbyshire and Cheshire, where David Taylor itinerated and filled appointments at various points. In the latter part of 1743 a very critical state of affairs arose in the north, during the temporary absence of Spangenberg in Germany. That the proceedings of the synod of Hirschberg should have given offense in various quarters is not to be altogether wondered at. Richard Viney, since June warden of the Yorkshire congregations, utilized this dissatisfaction to create differences between the English and German officials of the church. His chief pretext was found in what he declared to be the unscriptural use of the lot, and the arbitrary dominion of Zinzendorf and the *Pilgergemeine*. Spangenberg's return in October, on his way to Pennsylvania, sufficed to heal the breach. Viney in the following spring went over to the Wesleys; but in their societies also his restless discontent and religious vagaries became a source of trouble.

The Bedford group formed another circle of operations—in the Midlands, where again Ingham and Delamotte were pioneers. Peculiar interest attaches to this beginning in the town hallowed by the memory of the stalwart Christian heroism of the saintly author of the *Pilgrim's Progress*. "In 1738 the small-pox raged so fearfully here, that sixty to seventy persons died in one week, and the then clergyman of St. Paul's Church, the Rev. Jacob Rogers"—himself later to worthily follow in Bunyan's footsteps, and when appointed to clear himself from the aspersions of high-churchmen who denounced and condemned his connection with the evangelicals, to sturdily preach to the bishop and clergy in convocation assembled, on the text Isaiah 56: 10—"sent for Ingham, his University chum, as he was a very earnest preacher, and the latter took Brother Delamotte with him. Shortly afterwards Brother Francis Okely, B. A., who had spent some years in Germany, returned to England, and it appears that through him Mr. Rogers became intimately acquainted with the Brethren. Hutton was sent later on to Bedford, as also Brown, Knolton, Bowers and Schlicht. In 1742, there were in Bedford forty, and in the twenty-two villages round that had been visited, one hundred and fourteen awakened souls. Rogers and Okely requested that Bedford should be made a 'station' of the Brethren's Church, and in the same year Brother Heckewelder was sent here as minister."

It is with the names of these Anglican clergymen, Ingham and Rogers, that the commencement of Ockbrook in Derbyshire, is also to be associated. In the course of their zealous pilgrimage from place to place for the purpose of promoting true Christianity, on one occasion a sermon preached by the latter at the Market Cross in Nottingham, in 1739, made a deep impression on Isaac Frearson, the owner of the land on which Ockbrook now stands. Upon his invitation Rogers, who had meanwhile joined the Brethren, preached now and again at his home, and the number of those who profited was so considerable that Töltschig in 1740 and 1741 organized societies here and in Nottingham.

In addition to the widely ramified evangelism, in which more than twenty German and Moravian brethren were engaged, besides a considerable number of Englishmen, as in Germany and America provision was early made for educational undertakings. The commencement was a school at Broadoaks, in Essex, in a mansion formerly belonging to Wyseman Clagett, Esq., whose widow, like himself, had attained assurance through the instructions of the Brethren. This was now leased, and the children of the London members formed the nucleus of the scholars. When in 1745 Mary, the daughter of Sir John Crispe,

Bart., a wealthy member of the Moravian Church who placed large means at its disposal, offered her estate at Buttermere in Wiltshire for its uses, the boys were removed thither from Broadoaks, until 1748, when a further migration took place to Yorkshire in connection with the formation of the chief settlement in the north.

Spangenberg's period of administration closing in 1743, the brothers Dober took his place, and were in turn succeeded from 1746-1752 by Peter Böhler as superintendent of the British activity, seconded by John Gambold, erstwhile rector of Stanton Harcourt, whose first charge amongst the Brethren had been the management of the school at Broadoaks, but whose chief sphere was the London pastorate, from 1744 1768. At this time Fetter Lane was not the only meeting place in the metropolis. Affiliated societies met at Wapping, Hampstead, Kensington and at a couple of other points. In 1747, for example, the London Brethren accepted the use of a large Baptist house of worship near Little Moorfields, where Böhler preached for two years, and where appointments were met until 1757.

The history of these years is also that of the gradual separation of the work of the Brethren from that of the Methodists. In spite of the efforts of Spangenberg and others to reëstablish an organic connection, each was to have its own peculiar field of labor. The final parting of the ways took place in the early spring of 1743, on Zinzendorf's return from America. Hutton had succeeded in securing a conference between him and John Wesley for the express purpose of ending the rupture, if possible. They met in Gray's Inn Gardens, then a public promenade. To the man whose Pietistic training had inclined him to emphasize the vital power of regenerating grace as a divine influence which must be passively received, Wesley's view of the coöperation of the human with the divine, manifested in active striving after holiness and Christian perfection and the furtherance of sanctification by active use of the means of grace, appeared to be a covert form of Pharisaic legalism. They parted unable to agree concerning truths they honestly deemed fundamental.

With Whitefield also Zinzendorf renounced all connection, owing to his doctrine of reprobation.

What the Methodists had been to the miners of Cornwall and around Bristol, Cennick and his coadjutors now became to the poor Protestant population in the north of Ireland, powerful preachers in cottages and in the open fields to thousands. It was in June, 1746, that Cennick commenced his labors in the sister-isle. The doctrine of the Cross was an offense to many, and more than once he had to flee from violence. Yet the society which he formed in Dublin increased to more than five hundred members. In August he visited Ballymena, in County Antrim, and delivered his first sermon in a private house. It made such an impression that he had to preach thrice that day, the last time in the open air, so that the crowd who thronged the place of meeting might be able to hear. At least two thousand persons listened to him. When the sermon was ended a gentleman, accompanied by two servants on horseback, dashed through the crowd and beat him about the face and head with his whip, so that he was with difficulty rescued by sympathizing hearers. Even so he was compelled to return to Dublin. Later he came again and was assisted by other ministers, like Cossart, Bryselius and Schlicht. Every four weeks they were accustomed to meet and consult at Gloonen. From Ireland Cennick went to Wales, where he labored with much blessing. Töltschig followed him in February, 1748, as superintendent of the Brethren's work in Ireland.

On June 2, 1748, an important event in the history of the work in Yorkshire was the consecration of the congregation-house on Lamb's Hill (1744-49), to which the name of Grace Hall (1749-63) was given. This was the beginning of the settlement in future called Fulneck—a name of two-fold appropriateness, first as a memorial of Comenius, who had commended the Unity to the care of the Anglican Church, and then as an adaptation of the ancient name by which the property had been known, the Falneck, Fal'nake or Fallen-oak estate. In 1749 a society was organized in the city of Leominster, a fruit of the labors of Wesley and Cennick. In January of this year Count Zinzendorf visited England once more, and convened a provincial conference in London. Among other things the establishment of "choir houses" in the English congregation was agreed upon. On June 22 the Count set out for Yorkshire with his son Christian Renatus. His company, visiting Ingham at Aberford on the way, arrived at Lamb's Hill on June 30, and remained there for about four weeks. He was much pleased with the beautiful site and complete designs for the new settlement on the gently sloping hillside opposite the noble woods of Tong Hall, with the purling twin streams of the trout-denized Tong Beck between, a settlement which was to rival Herrnhut and Herrnhaag and Marienborn. Every Sunday preaching was held in seven places of worship in the neighborhood, and private meetings in eleven others during the week, attended in all by about three thousand persons.

But the most important result of the visit of Count Zinzendorf to England at this time proceeded from his negotiations with the English government. Preparations for this weighty affair had been in progress for several years, and the incentive was of yet more remote date. As far back as 1740 the windows of Fetter Lane Chapel had been broken by rioters. The hostile demonstrations at the house of Brother Bowes, in Little Britain, London, in December, 1743, had necessitated a suspension of the services there. In the north their enemies had endeavored to arouse popular prejudice against the Brethren by slanderously asserting that they were secret Papists and adherents of the Young Pretender. In March, 1745, the superintendent at Broadoaks was tendered a visit by a crowd rampant with bumptious loyalty, threatening dire vengeance; but the civil reception accorded them by Brother Metcalf and the sight of a Bible and a Book of Common Prayer in close proximity and in a place of honor upon his parlor table appeased their wrath. In the western world the Assembly of New York in 1744 had adopted repressive legislation directed against the Moravian missionaries amongst the Indians, and in consequence Post and Zeisberger had been arrested. At the time of the Scotch invasion, in common with numerous civil and religious bodies, the Brethren had presented an address to King George, assuring him of their attachment to the House of Hanover and to the Protestant faith, and the representations made by Abraham von Gersdorf to the Archbishop of Canterbury and to Prime Minister Lord Granville and to the Board of Trade and Plantations had been productive of an earnest recommendation of the Brethren to the authorities of New York; but the exact status of the church was still undefined. By force of circumstances, rather than from a settled policy the organization of congregations in distinction from mere societies had been brought about, through the procuring of licenses from local magistrates, in self-defence against mob violence. In 1747, thanks to the friendly advocacy of General Oglethorpe in the House of Commons and of Lords Dublin and Sydenham in the Upper Chamber, Parliament had granted the Moravian Brethren a dispensation from the oath of fealty, which was a condition of naturalization in Pennsylvania, and thus placed them on the same footing with the Friends.

All these things increased the desirability of having their legal position in England clearly defined. Hence in December, 1748, Abraham von Gersdorf, Louis von Schrautenbach, Charles von Schachmann and David Nitschmann, the Syndic, were empowered to conduct negotiations, and for this purpose landed at Harwich on January 1, 1749, and proceeded to London, where Count Zinzendorf had previously secured a house in Bloomsbury Square. The court party and the ministry were opposed. But the arrival of the *Irene* on January 11, with one hundred and fifty colonists destined for Pennsylvania and several Eskimo converts from Greenland, excited general interest. A Parliamentary committee of investigation was secured, consisting of fifty members, chiefly through the activity of Horace Walpole, and to this committee evidence was submitted by Zinzendorf, whose researches were assisted especially by Henry Cossart. The chief positions substantiated thereby were the following: that this church is of ancient Eastern origin; that the Brethren have been known widely for twenty or thirty years as the descendants of the old Bohemian-Moravian Church, but also in fellowship with the adherents of the Confessions of Augsburg and Berne; that this church had been acknowledged by King Edward VI, and by King George I, and had been recognized by the primate under George II, in 1737; and that its true ecclesiastical name is the Unitas Fratrum. One hundred and thirty-five documents were offered in substantiation of these points. A bill drawn up in accordance with these facts and reported favorably by the committee, passed its third reading in the House of Commons on April 16, and though at one time its fate seemed doubtful in the House of Lords, where objection was chiefly raised against the powers of Zinzendorf as a foreigner, by virtue of his position as *Ordinarius et Advocatus Fratrum*, after being championed by Lord Halifax, Lords Carteret, Granville, Chesterfield, Argyle, Prince Frederick of Wales and the Bishop of Worcester, it was sanctioned by the Upper House on May 12, and received the royal signature on

June 6. By this act the Moravian Church was recognized as a Protestant Episcopal Church, and its members formally granted full liberty of conscience and worship throughout Britain and its dependencies; and the position of its ministers and of Zinzendorf in particular became one of immediate prominence and honor. Friendly relations were established with a number of prelates, especially with Sherlock of London and Wilson of Sodor and Man, and with the Archbishop of Canterbury, and the Primate of Ireland.

CHAPTER XIV.

BETHLEHEM AND NAZARETH AS JOINT CENTERS OF EVANGELISTIC
ACTIVITY. 1742-1748.

In June, 1742, one hundred and twenty persons who constituted the congregation at Bethlehem had subscribed to rules and regulations unique in character, conceived with the definite purpose of furthering what the Brethren believed to be their distinct mission in America. At the basis lay a classification of the members into two sets, one portion devoting themselves to missions and to education, the other laboring to support these heralds and teachers. On July 15 ten itinerants were sent out—Leonard Schnell, Gottlieb Petzold, George Kaske, Christopher Heine, Frederick Post, Gottlieb Enter, Joseph Shaw, John Okely, Reinhard Ronner and Philip Meurer. It was enjoined upon them not to interfere with the affairs of other ministers and to abstain from religious controversy, but to attempt to bring the unchurched colonists to a saving knowledge of Jesus Christ. From time to time they reported at headquarters and received new fields of labor. Compensation was neither sought nor desired at the hands of those for whom they labored. Their own brethren provided the frugal support with which they were content. Private dwellings, barns, school-houses and sometimes one or another of the few humble log or stone churches that existed in the interior of the colony, gave opportunity for their audiences to gather. As their work assumed distinctness and circles of persons here and there became definitely identified with them, the labors of the itinerants were followed by house-to-house care of souls on the part of "visitors" who practically did the work of pastors. Nor were the needs of the young overlooked. By the year 1746 at least fifteen schools were supplied with teachers. Often a married couple was placed in charge, for even when children were not fed and housed outright, a mid-day meal had to be given, especially in winter, owing to the scattered condition of the sparse population.

In it all the primary aim was not to advance the interests of the Moravian Church as such. The idea of union dominated. The work was unselfish and disinterested to a degree. The tendency was to repel rather than to solicit additions to the membership of the particular denomination whose energies were so zealously bent to the general good. Even evangelists themselves, who in Europe had been led through the agency of Moravians to deeper heart-religion and having identified themselves with some settlement were now heralds for the Brethren in the woods of Pennsylvania, did not conceive that they had broken off from fellowship with the adherents of the confession of faith to which they had been previously attached. They labored side by side with the distinctively Moravian element, were subject to the same regulations, observed the ritual of the Moravians and were completely at one with them, but did not understand this identification as incompatible with membership in the Lutheran or Reformed or Anglican Churches, as the case might be. No denomination was organized in the colonies as yet, and the furtherance of vital religion not of denominationalism was the aim of the evangelists. Hence there could be fundamental agreement among men who had made similar heart-experience in heralding the all-sufficient atonement of the God-man, the Saviour Jesus Christ, and proclaiming justification and assurance through faith in His meritorious life and death. Though the previous training and nationalty of the evangelists differed, Germans, Swiss, Swedes, Welsh, Scotch, English and Moravians were as one. Former Lutherans, like Meurer, Büttner, Schnell, Bryzelius, Petzold, Roseen, Reutz, Reinke, Meinung, Kaska and Soelle, and erstwhile Reformed, like Lischy, Bechtel, Brandmüller and Rauch, and ex-Anglicans or dissenters, like Shaw, Powell, Bruce, Okely, Rice, Yarrel, Utley, Thorpe and Gambold, as the years passed were scarcely to be distinguished from the old Moravian stock—Seifferth, Seidel, George and Joseph Neisser, Jacob Till, Paul Schneider, Paul Münster and Anthony Lawatsch.

Throughout the land these fervent self-denying heralds awakened a great hunger for the Word of God. Through their agency the "Great Awakening" of 1740-1742 under the agency of Whitefield, Jonathan Edwards, Gilbert Tennant, Jonathan

Parsons, Benjamin Pomeroy, Joseph Bellamy and others, had its counterpart amongst the German settlers though the outward signs of intense conviction may not have been so startling. Indeed the two movements had met when the "First Sea Congregation" touched at New Haven in the spring of 1742. Thirty-one localities were centers of itineracy, each with its group of preaching places around it, by the year 1748. The more important were Germantown, Philadelphia, Lancaster, York, Donegal, Heidelberg, Quitopehilla (later Hebron and finally Lebanon), Warwick (Lititz), Oley, Allemaengel, Maguntschi (Emmaus), Salisbury, Falckner's Swamp, the Trappe, Mahanatawny, Neshaminy and Dansbury in Pennsylvania; Manocacy (Graceham), in Maryland; Maurice River, Racoon, Penn's Neck, Oldman's Creek, Pawlin's Kill, Walpack and Brunswick in Jersey; Staten Island and Long Island; Newport, Rhode Island; Broadbay, Maine; and Canajoharie, New York. Nathanael Seidel and Eric Westmann in the winter of 1747 journeyed west of the Susquehanna. In Maryland and Virginia many listened with profit to Schnell and Gottschalk, and held to the Brethren notwithstanding the adverse proclamation of the governor of the latter colony. In spite of it, moreover, Spangenberg and Reutz renewed the attempt to be useful here in 1748. Jasper Payne and Christian Frölich, after visiting the negroes of Maryland and Virginia, in 1748 made a tour through New England, going beyond Boston. Nor were these devoted itinerants wont to consult the condition of the weather or of the roads, or to have regard to the season of the year when setting out upon their toilsome foot-journeys sometimes of hundreds of miles in extent and of months' duration.

In the latter part of October, 1744, Spangenberg, consecrated a bishop at Marienborn on the 15th of June, came to take charge of the entire field of operations in America, relieving Böhler, who returned to Europe. It was an exceedingly wide sphere, embracing the most diversified duties. But adding as he did to the indefatigable industry and system of an efficient administrator and shrewd man of affairs the sound judgment of a thorough theologian and the quenchless zeal of a pioneer missionary, by his unflinching aderence to what he conceived to be right and his unaffected sincerity and active sympathy he well earned the cognomen by which he was affectionately and familiarly known, "Brother Joseph," protector and director as he was of his brethren in a strange land, who concealed a warmth of heart beneath a sometimes severe exterior. In addition to the supervision of the itineracy, he superintended the missions amongst the Indians, and to a considerable extent also made provision for the work in the West Indies and in Surinam. Besides he directed the economic life and enterprises of the settlements at Nazareth and Bethlehem, and presided over all the undertakings controlled by the "Pennsylvania Synod."

The Indian mission alone made heavy demands upon his time and care. Difficulties characteristic of efforts for the aborigines in every decade of American history annoyed and hampered it.

Rauch's commencement of operations had given omen of a fine future. Landing in New York, a young man of twenty-two, on July 16, 1740, he had unexpectedly met Frederick Martin, on a visit from St. Thomas, who introduced him to Christian friends. Certain Mohicans having business with the Governor and acquainted with the Dutch language, permitted him to go with them on their return home to Shekomeko, which he reached on August 16. Results were not long delayed. Wasamapa, the fourth of his converts, and previously a drunken ruffian, thus described his mode of preaching: "Brethren, I have been a heathen, and have grown old among the heathen; therefore I know how the heathen think. Once a preacher came and began to explain that there was a God. We answered, 'Dost thou think us so ignorant as not to know that? Go to the place whence thou camest!' Then another preacher came and began to teach us, and to say, 'You must not steal, nor lie, nor get drunk, and so forth.' We answered: 'Thou fool, dost thou think that we do not know that? Learn first thyself, and then teach the people to whom thou belongest, to leave off these things; for who steal or lie, or who are more drunken than thine own people?" And thus we dismissed him. After some time Brother Christian Henry Rauch came into my tent, and sat down by me. He spoke to me nearly as follows: 'I come to you in the name of the Lord of heaven and earth; He sends to let you know that He will make you happy and deliver you from this misery in which you lie at present. To this end He became a man and gave His life a ransom for man, and shed His blood for him.' When he had finished his discourse, he lay down upon a board, fatigued by the journey, and fell into a sound sleep. I then thought: 'What kind of a man is this? There he lies and sleeps; I might kill him and throw him out into the road, and who would regard it? But this gives him no concern.' However I could not forget his words. They constantly recurred to my mind. Even when I was asleep, I dreamt of that blood which Christ shed for us. I found this to be something different from what I had ever heard, and I interpreted Cristian Henry's words to the other Indians. Thus through the Grace of God, an awakening took place amongst us. I say, therefore, brethren, preach Christ our Saviour and His sufferings and death, if you will have your words to gain entrance amongst the heathen."

Soon after the organization of the congregation at Shekomeko the power of the gospel made itself felt in the neighboring villages of Pachgatgoch and Wechquadnach. The fame of the changed life of Wasamapa, formerly fierce as a savage bear, now lamb-like, brought Indians to Shekomeko from places more than a day's journey distant. Example preached effectively. Soon the thirst for truth made it imperative that Rauch should receive assistance. Gottlob Büttner, John Martin Mack, Pyrlaeus and Senseman, the two latter married men, came to extend operations into Connecticut. At Potatik whites as well as Indians attended Mack's preaching; at Pachgatgoch Büttner was gladdened by numerous conversions of savages. Next Rauch visited the vicinity of Albany, Schoharie and Canajoharie; and Pyrlaeus, who had previously spent three months with Conrad Weisser studying Indian dialects, with his wife removed into the Iroquois country to perfect his knowledge of their speech. By the end of the year 1743 Shekomeko alone reckoned sixty-three baptized Indians.

But next spring the opposition of unscrupulous whites came to a head. Liquor-sellers in particular, whose occupation was seriously affected by the progress of the gospel amongst the Indians, stirred up false reports, and circulated the story that the Moravians were Papists in disguise and secret emissaries of the French in Canada. When required to clear themselves by oaths of allegiance to King George they begged to be excused from this because contrary to their conscientious convictions, but declared their willingness to solemnly affirm what was demanded. But the Assembly in September made the oath of allegiance obligatory, and also imposed a license on "vagrant preachers, Moravians or disguised Papists," on pain of a fine of forty pounds and six months' imprisonment, with expulsion from the colony on repetition of the offense. In consequence of this, when Frederick Post and David Zeisberger went to Canajoharie, to learn the Maqua language, they were arrested and brought to New York on February 22, 1745, and on refusing to take any oath suffered in jail for seven weeks, until Governor Thomas, of Pennsylvania, interposed in their behalf.

This attitude of the authorities of New York caused the Brethren in Bethlehem to determine on a removal of the mission to the interior of Pennsylvania, beyond the settlements of the colonists; and in order to secure the assent of the great confederacy of the Six Nations then dominant on the Atlantic slope, Bishop Spangenberg, with the missionaries Zeisberger and Schebosch and the interpreter Conrad Weisser undertook an arduous and perilous journey to Onondaga, the chief town of the Iroquois league. The treaty made with Zinzendorf three years before was solemnly renewed, and permission granted for a settlement at Wyoming on the Susquehanna. But contrary to expectations the converts at Shekomeko declined to remove until compelled by their hostile white neighbors. And the French rendered Wyoming unsafe. Therefore after a temporary stay of the converted Indians near Bethlehem, they were settled on a tract of land beyond the Blue Mountains, beside the Mahoni where it adds its tribute of waters to the Lehigh. This land had been purchased for the founding of a Christian village, and here in 1746 the mission church and a circle of dwellings arose, receiving the name of Gnadenhütten. Governor Thomas lent his approval to the undertaking, and it is stated that by the year 1748 the number of converts in the care of the mission reached the respectable total of five hundred.

During the years 1746 to 1748 an outpost was also established at Shamokin (Sunbury) by Martin Mack, Joseph Powell, John Hagen and Anthony Schmidt, at the request of Chief Shikelimy.

Evangelistic and missionary activity so extensive, and carried on by settlements which together did not number more than six hundred people, could have been maintained by no ordinary methods. Capacity to support this work is explained by the adoption of a religico-communal system of life, which was, however, not based upon communistic convictions as usually under-

stood by political economists. These arrangemets arose gradually, and took special form after 1744. They were not adopted
with the design of retaining them permanently, or from the
notion that they were the ideal for normal Christian society.
They were rather conceived with a view to develop as quickly
as possible the resources of the new settlement in a manner
coördinate with the utmost employment of the latent power of
the congregation for evangelism. Partly from lack of house-
room in the beginning, and partly from the necessity of self-
dependence in relation to the church in Europe at the commencement of pioneer life, the family as an institution was made
secondary to the requirements of the congregation. This tendency was strengthened by the choir-system which coincident
with the colonization in Pennsylvania began throughout the
Unity to take the place of more customary provisions for the
close care and cure of souls. A community of labor rather than
of property, coupled with an extreme application of the division
of the members according to age, sex and condition in life as
married or single, each choir living apart, was fundamental.
He who had property retained it if he chose; but all placed
their time, talents and labor at the disposal of the church. No
private enterprises were carried on. Every business and manufacture, and all real estate belonged to the church. Every
branch of industry came under the supervision of committees
responsible to a board of direction, the *Aufseher Collegium*, of
which Spangenberg was chairman. The result was the establishment and successful prosecution of at least thirty-two industries, apart from a number of farms, by the year 1747. The
duties of each person were assigned to him by the central committee of managers, who made a study of his capacities. In
return each person received the necessaries of life and a home.
With all its defects, chief of which was its overlooking the fact
that the family is a divine institution even more ancient than
the church, this "Economy" in its day served its purpose remarkably. No town in the interior of Pennsylvania could at
this time so efficiently minister to the varied wants of travelers
or of neighboring settlers. About fifty evangelists and ministers were supported, and about fifteen schools maintained, and
the traveling expenses provided for missionaries to the West
Indies and Surinam. Instead of requiring grants from Europe
as a missionary province of the church, after the financial em-

barrassments in Germany, Holland and England in the fifties Pennsylvania could send money to help to make good the losses. And, not least, a race of men and women was nurtured who did not count their lives dear, but held themselves in readiness for any arduous undertaking that would further the kingdom of Christ. Spangenberg testified that, when word reached Bethlehem concerning the death of the missionaries on St. Thomas, if he had called for volunteers, twenty or thirty would have been willing to set out at once for that pestilential spot.

Religion and the spirit of devotion dominated the life of the two settlements. Frequent assemblies for daily prayer, on the part of single choirs, or of the entire congregation, were characteristic features. Church discipline was carefully administered. The adoption of municipal and ecclesiastical regulations, though referred to the church council, was often decided by the lot. Offices were filled in a similar manner. The function of even the night-watchmen was not only to insure security, but also to promote piety; they announced the hours by singing hymns as they made their rounds.

Associated with Spangenberg and his wife, and after 1747 with his chief assistant, Bishop Christian Frederick Cammerhof, were especially the following: Adolphus Meyer, David Bischoff, Nathanael Seidel, Matthew Schropp, George Neisser, Anthony Lawatsch, and last but not least Henry Antes, who for several years fully identified himself with the Moravian Church. Jasper Payne and John Brownfield, formerly secretary to Governor Oglethorpe, were the book-keepers; and Abraham Boemper and Timothy Horsefield, and later Henry van Vleck acted as financial agents in New York. So active was the trade with Europe and so considerable the stream of emigrants that for a decade after 1746 the missionary ship *Irene* was busily employed going backwards and forwards between New York and European ports in the interests of the church.

11

CHAPTER XV.

With the formal recognition of the Unitas Fratrum by the government of England, London assumed new importance for the Brethren. For several years it served as the center of their operations. That Zinzendorf himself regarded London somewhat in this manner is evident from the elaborate plans which he now adopted for an extensive establishment, worthy of the dignity of the *Advocatus et Ordinarius* of the Unity, now that it had attained a favored standing in Britain and the colonies. In April, 1750, the ancient mansion of the ducal family of Ancaster in Chelsea, once the home of Sir Thomas Moore, was leased for a long term of years, with the adjoining Beaufort grounds and gardens. Chelsea was at this time a pleasant western suburb, and a terrace led from Lindsey House, as this mansion was named, to the steps whence a barge might push off for a journey on the waterway. Under the supervision of Zinzendorf's kinsman, Count Sigismund Augustus von Gersdorf, the newly acquired property received alterations in accordance with the architectural taste of the age, a clergy-house and chapel were erected, the grounds laid out, a cemetery planned, and rows of houses projected in a series of hollow squares after the fashion of the continental settlement congregations, roomy accommodations being designed for the members of the various choirs. As thus planned the place received the name of Sharon. Not all the designs were carried out in connection with it. The improvements which were made cost 75,000 thaler. But in twenty-one years this fine property had to be alienated, the chapel, clergy-house and burial-ground alone being retained. This was one of the consequences of the financial distress which swept down like a devastating storm immediately after the enforced exodus from Wetteravia.

For an understanding of these troubles it is necessary to review the past.

During the period from 1722 to 1736, that is, from the founding of Herrnhut to Zinzendorf's banishment, the sphere of the Brethren's activity was mainly limited to Herrnhut and the itinerations at home and the incipient missions abroad. The Count's property was encumbered for one quarter of its value when he acquired it. The emigrants at first possessed only their hands, their skill, their diligence and their good-will. Both parties contributed their all to the advancement of the common cause, and were strong in faith. Gradually the cutlery, linen-weaving, pottery and farming of the people prospered, and the rent which they paid their patron for their lands and houses became a considerable sum. At the time of the merging of the Count's evangelistic interests with the future of the Moravian Church, the Countess paid off the friends who had been parties to the covenant of 1724, and in 1728 the extensive family establishment was made to include provision for those Brethren who were employed in the Lord's service as evangelists. Thus began in a germinal way the *Gemein-Diakonie*, or financial system for the enterprises of the church in which no distinction was made between the accounts of the Zinzendorf family and those which involved the purely disinterested enterprises of religion, though the accounts of Herrnhut as a congregation and as a commune were kept separate from this common reckoning. Sometimes friends sent contributions, sometimes small sums were collected for the equipment of the heralds; but as a rule they set out with very scanty supplies, relying mainly on faith. Meantime the Count regarded the obligations of the church as his own.

Providentially just before Zinzendorf's exile a wealthy Labadist in Holland, Matthias Beuning, urged the Count to fund all his obligations at a lower rate of interest than was customary in Saxony, he himself offering to advance the money out of regard for the Count's zeal for the cause of Christ. His loan of 20,000 florins was most opportune. After Pilgerruh, Heerendyk, Herrnhaag and Marienborn were projected, the same friend, and other Dutch sympathizers, Jacob Schellinger, Van Alpen and Decknatel, advanced additional money on easy terms, whilst Lelong helped to provide supplies for the mission in Greenland. During the Count's absence in America Lady

Zinzendorf, and Jonas Paulus Weiss, a former merchant of Nuremberg who had joined the church, and Jacob Schellinger came to the assistance of the General Diaconate, each contributing two-thirds of their property. Now Jonas Paulus Weiss became identified with the financial management. It appears that he had contributed 40,000 thaler and Schellinger 90,000 florins. The establishments in Wetteravia and the settlements which were now projected in Silesia and at Neudietendorf involved very considerable outlays. Though Spangenberg in England and the General Conference in Germany encouraged liberality on the part of members and friends, nothing was systematized, so as to secure an income of a definite amount. Hence when the functions of the Conference were suspended and Zinzendorf assumed absolute control after the synod of Hirschberg, a very critical state of things had arisen, the indebtedness being estimated at 300,000 florins. Yet such was the enthusiastic spirit of the day, faith being carried to extremes in connection with the extravagances of the "Time of Sifting," that there followed further expansion and the assumption of new obligations, without sufficient guarantees to cover them. Indeed, the synods paid practically no attention to the subject of finances.

In 1747 Zinzendorf purchased the estate of Hennersdorf. Negotiations with Parliament in England involved outlay, owing to the lordly state which it was deemed necessary to assume in order to make a favorable impression in London. The lease of Barby added to the complications. The choir establishments sought their individual interests rather than those of the entire Unity. The crash in Wetteravia came, very heavy losses being the consequence of expulsion from the properties which the Brethren had rendered valuable by extensive improvements. Colonization expeditions were costly. Lindsey House and Fulneck and other English establishments demanded great financial resources. The journeys of the *Pilgergemeine* were expensive. The creditors in Holland began to become restive on account of the dilatory manner in which the interest was paid by Frederick Wenceslaus Neisser, the financial manager of the church in that country. Well it was the undertakings of the Brethren in America and in Livonia were self-sustaining. A pity it was that British needs were merged into the general finances of the church in 1747, since here wealthy members and friends, like Dinah Raymond von Layrisch and Mary Crispe Stonehouse were willing to assist, and the introduction of a system of stated collections for the defrayal of current expenes, like that in vogue in the Methodist societies, seems to have been contemplated at one time. In 1748 a conference was held in Amsterdam in reference to the financial situation; but no radical measure was taken. Apparently it was difficult for Zinzendorf to tear himself away from his special forte, the upbuilding of the spiritual inner life, and concentrate his powers upon the details of finance in a systematic manner; and yet such was the constitution of the church at this time, that he alone was vested with power to shape definitely the financial policy. Even though others may here and there have perceived the critical features of the situation, they could do little to remedy it, authority not being in their hands. On the Count's return to London, in 1751, Hutton, Cossart and Gambold expressed their fears that the complicated state of affairs must end in bankruptcy; but to one of Zinzendorf's ardent temperament to entertain this thought seemed akin to lack of faith. Temporary relief was rendered by a wealthy dyer, a Mr. Hockel, who though not a member of the church, in 1752 undertook to pay the pressing claims of certain creditors. Money was also raised by James Charlesworth, warden of the choir of unmarried men at Fulneck, whose superior financial ability in the management of an extensive cloth-manufacture, carried on in Yorkshire for the benefit of the church, had developed a trade with Portugal and Russia.

In the midst of these perplexities the shadow of a sore affliction fell upon Zinzendorf. On February 27 of this year a hemorrhage disclosed the weakness of his son's constitution. Christian Renatus was only twenty-five years of age, the third child of his parents. The raw winds of spring and the heavy atmosphere of London aggravated his trouble. But the end came with unexpected suddenness on May 28. His father was absent, preaching at Mile End, and the parting blessing was given by his former tutor, Bishop John Nitschmann. Tenderly his companions took the body by boat to Chelsea on the first of June. In May of the previous year his father had spoken of sending him to Pennsylvania, but then he could not be spared from his duties amongst the young men. In person Christian Renatus von Zinzendorf was of slight build, in temperament mild and affectionate, with a leaning to the meditative and emotional in religion.   He was called home before his powers had fully matured; but that he might have become a worthy successor of his father as a writer of religious poetry, had he been spared, is borne out by the superior sentiment of his hymns of the Passion which gave promise of rich poetic gifts.   His

> " My Redeemer, overwhelmed with anguish
> Went to Olivet for me."

will be cherished wherever the Moravian Church makes its way.

By the end of the year Count Zinzendorf realized the precarious financial situation of the church.   Instead of trying to screen himself by any expedient, or repudiating the obligations as those of the organization but not his personal affair, he magnanimously offered security for ten thousand pounds of the English indebtedness.   Soon it was evident that thirty thousand would be needed.   About a month afterwards the climax of emergency arrived.   A Portugese Jew, Jacob Gomez Serra, the banking correspondent of the Brethren, went into bankruptcy, and through him £67,621 were lost.   The Count was in imminent danger of the debtor's prison.   But providentially the solicitor of the Brethren, Mr. Heaton, and their friend alderman Hankey obtained temporary security and pacified most of the creditors to the degree of granting an extension of time.

But the year which followed was full of care.   Already in January the confidence of the Dutch creditors was shaken.   On the fourth of May Whitefield came out in an open "Expostulatory Letter" to Zinzendorf, in which he violently attacked the character of the Count and his Brethren, representing that he and his Germans had used their British adherents and were making tools of them for their own purposes, and would get them into prison for debt.   A financial conference was held from August 27 to September 25, Leonard Dober presiding. A triple board of general administration was projected, one part to meet the obligations of the debt, another to maintain existing undertakings, and a third for new enterprises.   Nicholas de Watteville became steward of the Unity in London, Cornelius van Laer was given charge of the finances in Holland, and Count Henry the 28th Reuss, with John Frederick Köber as his assistant took charge of the German accounts.

Providential interpositions were repeatedly recognized.   Zinzendorf's own unselfish conduct became the best apology overagainst unfriendly pamphleteers, and went far towards restoring confidence.   In March, 1754, Mary Stonehouse bequeathed her estates of Buttermere in Wiltshire and Dornford in Oxfordshire to the church.   Dinah von Layrisch and her husband offered 40,000 thaler.   The Von Damnitz, Von Schachmann and Von Wiedebach families in Saxony and the Van Laer family and Jan Verbeek in Holland proved friends in need.   Abraham Dürninger of Herrnhut and the Yorkshire industries of the Church together brought aid to the amount of two thousand pounds.   Count von Gersdorf, Prefect of Lusatia, who had died in 1751, had left his estates nominally to Baron Henry von Zczschwitz, but practically to the church.   These became available in 1753, and although not unencumbered and at first regarded as precarious property, in time became a source of revenue.

What however helped as much as anything else to tide over the difficulty, was the boundless faith and unshrinking confidence in the mission of the Unity at this time manifested by its leaders.   The mission to the negroes of Jamaica was undertaken in 1754, the purchase of the one hundred thousand acre tract in North Carolina as a center for missions and the seat of an exclusive settlement was negotiated, and additional missionaries were sent to Greenland and to Surinam in this year. So the storm clouds began to scatter in the English sky.

But the crisis in the Dutch affairs had yet to be met.   Here the purely financial matters were entangled in personal animosities, connected with partisan spirit centering about a former pastor of Heerendyk, Petsch by name.   In November, 1752, he and his adherents in the place had declared Heerendyk an independent congregation.   In 1754 they withdrew from the settlement.   He seems to have spurred on Beuning and Decknatel to institute lawsuits.   The Schellingers and others vacillated.   What aggravated the situation was the fact that the Classis of Amserdam had decided against the doctrinal position of the Brethren, though the Synod of Utrecht withheld its verdict.   When Zinzendorf arrived at Zeist on March 31, on his way to Germany, the worst was threatened.   A conference with the chief creditors on April 10 proved fruitless.   But on the death of Beuning his widow quashed the suit which he had instituted.   A favorable opportunity was at length offered for a representative of the Brethren, Frederick Henry Goldschmidt von Guldenberg, formerly a captain in the Dutch army and now a member at Zeist, to open negotiations. The less wealthy creditors were paid in full, and the others consented to a refunding of their claims at three per cent. The total amount reached the considerable sum of 287,000 florins.

This favorable issue was largely owing to the deliberations of a synod held at Taubenheim, an estate in Upper Lusatia belonging to Baron von Zezschwitz. Fifteen of the leaders of the Church constituted this important gathering. A three-fold task was before them: to devise plans to raise interest and ultimately pay off the debt; to provide support for the servants of the church, and to supply the means for new undertakings. John Frederick Köber, formerly a jurist in the service of Prefect von Gersdorf, and since 1747 a member of the church, who henceforth should exert a most wholesome influence in its administrative affairs, strenuously urged the separation of the debt of the church, the accounts of the *Jüngerhaus*, that is, of the work of the church in its undertakings at large, and the accounts of the Zinzendorf family. A method by which this might be accomplished was sketched out, but was not carried into effect. It was decided that, if possible, every member should be led to recognize a personal obligation to contribute to the extinction of the debt. The revenues of the various estates were estimated to annually fall short of the interest of the debt in England and Holland alone by 4,000 thaler. Every effort was to be made to secure the acceptance of notes at three per cent. on the part of the creditors.

The germs of the future constitutional government of the church also lay in the transactions of the synod of Taubenheim. Since 1750 collegiate government had been in vogue in Silesia, affairs there being in charge of Leonard Dober, Waiblinger, Von Seidlitz, and Louis von Schrautenbach. In the spring of 1752 a sort of cabinet had been organized in London, to act as Zinzendorf's board of advisers for the administration of the church as a whole. Of this cabinet Baron Abraham von Gersdorf had been Treasurer; James Hutton, Secretary; Cossart, Agent of the Count in Britain; and the Syndic Nitschmann, Baron Sigismund von Gersdorf and Frederick von Marschall, Councillors. Later Jonas Paulus Weiss, and during his stay in England, Spangenberg had been also associated with them. But the powers of this cabinet were merely advisory, and were wholly subordinate to Zinzendorf's own judgment. Now at Taubenheim a "Board of Administrators" was appointed for the management of all business connected with the indebtedness and with the estates—still responsible, it is true, to the Count, and not to the church, and yet very largely acting independently. Its members were: Von Damnitz, President; Von Zezschwitz, Vice-President; Von Seidlitz, Von Lüdecke, Von Schachmann and Köber; with Weinel and John Gotthold Wollin as Secretaries. Though this proved to be only a temporary arrangement, it marked a return to the Unity of some of the extraordinary powers conferred upon and accepted by the Count after the synod of Hirschberg. It was significant as an approach to conferential government, formerly so characteristic of the Unitas Fratrum, and destined to be again the fundamental feature of its constitutional development.

Thus two blessings in disguise came as an accompaniment of the financial embarrassments succeeding upon and not unconnected with the heedlessness of the Wetteravian period. The one was absolute return to sober scriptural thought and ritual, accellerated by the sharp discipline of anxiety. The other was the escape from the dangers sooner or later inevitably attendant upon irresponsible one-man power, in another way than at the cost of a disagreeable and unseemly rupture with the magnanimous nobleman to whom the Brethren were so deeply indebted.

CHAPTER XVI.

ZINZENDORF'S EVENTIDE.

On June 4, 1755, Count Zinzendorf returned to Herrnhut with the acknowledged aim of reëstablishing the importance of the mother congregation in relation to the life and activity of the Unity. Henceforth the interests of the entire organization should be furthered by him from the place where the various agencies for good had taken their rise. His reception was a worthy one. Between rows of children dressed in white and singing songs of welcome he passed on to a service of praise in the thronged church. It was a lovefeast indeed. How much reason for praise had not he and those who welcomed him in spite of all the vicissitudes of the years of his exile. Herrnhut itself had greatly improved. Stone houses displaced the former structures of wood. Abraham Dürninger's masterly management since 1747 had spread the connections of Herrnhut's manufactures far and wide—to Holland, Spain and Portugal. His business in general merchandise was highly remunerative. His yarn and linen factory had won an enviable reputation. Two years ago he had established on the Petersbach the first chintz and cotton factory in Saxony. Thrift had been accompanied by public improvements. Nor was the happiness of the situation confined to the Count's relationship to the prospering town and to the people whom he regarded as Brethren, not retainers. The bitter antagonism of neighboring gentry and clergy had given place to an appreciation of Herrnhut and its institutions and the aims of its patron. Baron Huldenberg of Neukirch, a main agent in his former banishment, now visited him in company with his pastor, Charles Rudolph Reichel, and acknowledged the wrong of which he had formerly been guilty. Neukirch became a rallying-point for the Lusatian *Diaspora*. Now also the second of a series of conferences with pastors and candidates for the ministry in the State Church was held at

Herrnhut for the purpose of mutual edification, counsel and exhortation.

The first of these conferences, hereafter in session annually and destined to become an important factor in the religious life of the neighborhood, had been planned in connection with the *Diaspora* in Upper Lusatia and had convened on Whitsunday of the previous year. Pastor Groh of Berthelsdorf, Charles Rudolf Reichel of Neukirch, John Frederick Reichel of Taubenheim, Michaelis of Hermsdorf near Görlitz, Löwe of Hermsdorf near Meissen, Benade of Milkel, and Franz of Klix had been the chief participants, with Frederick and John de Watteville as the representatives of the Brethren. It had been agreed to unite with the Brethren in their simple method of proclaiming justification through faith in the merits of the life and death of Jesus Christ, and to keep in touch with the Unity by communicating the *Gemein-Nachrichten* to awakened souls, and by convening quarter-yearly at Herrnhut. Bands of such who were in sympathy were to be statedly visited by suitable Brethren from Herrnhut, and services held; but all this without any separation from the Lutheran Church. Widespread awakenings resulted.

Meanwhile the administrative arrangements projected at Taubenheim began to go into effect, Zinzendorf with the *Jungerhaus* —accommodated at Berthelsdorf—having supervision of the inner life and spiritual activity of the church, whilst Count Reuss and Köber and their associates administered the finances.

Educational affairs now attracted Zinzendorf's attention. In 1754 a college had been commenced by Clemens at Barby in connection with the theological seminary. At Hennersdorf the *Catharinenhof* purchased in 1747 had been remodeled and was occupied as an academy under Layritz, with more than one hundred and fifty pupils. The castle, known as the *Friedburg*, housed one hundred and six others under Vierorth. In consequence of changes planned by the Count, by October, 1756, the scholars of the *Catharinenhof* were transferred to Barby, and the curriculum of the college improved in order to increase its efficiency as a school of preparation for the seminary. It was recognized that the church could no longer count upon obtaining its ministers from the universities, but must educate its own men. Hither the library of Count von Gersdorf had been removed, becoming the nucleus of the archives of the Unity, and here also a publication house was now established, where with the assitsance of Clemens a new edition of the various works of Zinzendorf should be published.   In Herrnhut a flourishing school for girls and in Niesky a school for boys already existed. In this year an additional school for boys was opened at Neuwied, for the benefit of the Swiss *Diaspora*.

From May 27 to June 8, 1756, a general synod was in session at Herrnhut, to which special importance attaches.   Sixty-three brethren and nine sisters constituted its membership.   The Continental and British congregations were represented by delegates duly empowered to act in their name.   In his opening address Zinzendorf laid stress upon the necessity of so developing the constitution of the church as to make provision for the independence of the collegiate governing board, the convocation of synods constituted by the votes of the membership of the church, and for meeting the financial requirements of administration by stated contributions.   It seemed that the time had come when a theocratic republic would be at length inauguarated, especially since Köber and Sigismund von Gersdorf strenuously urged that attention be centered upon the needful legislation.   But a mournful loss interrupted the proceedings.

On June 19 the death of Lady Zinzendorf was announced. She had scarcely been herself since the death of her son, Christian Renatus; and her life of unremitting toil and anxiety in behalf of the church had worn upon her.   From the first she had entered with all her soul into her husband's projects.   For twenty-three years she had managed their property, leaving him free to devote himself to his chosen work.   Simplicity, absence of affectation, sympathy, uniform poise of disposition, less inclination to speak than to listen, with affability and fondness for social intercourse, excellent judgment, quick insight, strong force of character and self sacrificing willingness to undergo and endure labors and hardships—had been the traits which had endeared her to all sorts and conditions of people.   Her loss was the more startling since her illness lasted only ten days. She was laid to rest on the Hutberg on the 25th in the presence of two thousand persons, twenty-four ministers serving as pallbearers, and John Nitschmann, jr., praying the burial litany at the grave.

Her death had an influence upon the transactions of the synod.   Though a complete review of the operations of the church was had, and its finances inquired into, the formulation of a constitution was postponed, save that the "Board of Administrators" was changed to a "Board of Directors" responsible to the church, not to Zinzendorf. He had himself expressed his conviction of the necessity of preparing for collegiate government by giving utterance to these words, when the startling news of his wife's departure reached him: "No one departs before the Lord wills it, and when the loss can be endured. I shall also depart and—there will be improvement. For this the conferences exist, and they will remain permanently." The functions of the new Board of Directors were still limited to affairs of business, oversight of the inner life and spiritual activity remaining in the hands of the Count and his immediate associates.

In preparation for the synod a conference of former exiles from Moravia and Bohemia had been held, which appointed a special committee to prepare lists of all emigrants, including those who had found a home in Berlin and Rixdorf or in America, with the dates of their flight and accounts of their experiences. Thus most important materials for future history were gathered and preserved. The conference also formulated a memorial to be addressed to the synod with regard to the retention of the distinctly Moravian tenets respecting declination of judicial oaths, the holding of political offices, amassing of wealth, bearing of arms, etc., and urged the importance of the ancient discipline. This memorial the synod received very favorably. John de Watteville gave it as his opinion that it was the duty of the church to perpetuate the distinctively Moravian characteristics. Clemens considered the Moravian episcopate to be especially valuable for the welfare of the missions. Köber declared that the malice of the world demands that we maintain our ecclesiastical rights inherited from the Moravian Church. As a practical result of this consensus of views Andrew Grasmann, since 1751 pastor of the Bohemian congregation in Berlin, was consecrated a bishop at Herrnhut on July 5 by Bishops John de Watteville, Leonard Dober and John Nitschmann, sr.

His wife's death now began to have an effect upon the habits of Count Zinzendorf, who was no longer his former energetic self. He became more and more morbidly fond of seclusion. Instead of the wonderful regularity and systematic dispatch of business which had been so characteristic of him in the past, the secret of his prodigious capacity for work, he gave himself up to periods of listless inaction; then to overtake his duties he spent whole nights in writing, and so disordered his already impaired health. Noting this and fearing for the worst, his friends persuaded him about a year later to marry Anna Nitschmann—June 27, 1757. It was a private, morganatic marriage, the ceremony being performed in the castle at Berthelsdorf, and not conferring upon her the title of Countess.

In the preceding December Count Frederick Christian, his elder brother, had died at his estate of Garveiwitz near Dresden. Less inclined than ever for worldly honors and proposing to devote himself absolutely to the service of the church, our Count abdicated his position in the empire as head of the house of Zinzendorf in favor of his nephew Louis, a diplomat in the service of Austria, his renunciation being dated on the day of his second marriage.

In September, with a large company of co-workers, he commenced a tour of preaching and visitation. Ebersdorf, Barby, Wetteravia, Basel, Montmirail, Lausanne and Geneva were scenes of his activity. The return journey was by way of Schaffhausen through Swabia and Franconia. It was no pleasure trip and occupied five months. The severe weather and the rough roads made demands on his powers of endurance, and undermined his strength.

Meantime several congregations on the Continent had been in the midst of dangers since the outbreak of the Seven Years' War. The Saxon and Silesian settlements were in the very thick of war's alarms. For two months Herrnhut was the headquarters of a Prussian division and for six months Prussian troops were in the vicinity. During the battle of Lowositz the thunder of the cannons could be plainly heard. On February 23, 1757, about two thousand Prussians were quartered there, costing the settlement five hundred thaler. Before the battle of Hochkirch Herrnhut was full of troops. One day two thousand pounds of bread had to be supplied to the Austrians, and at another time Austrian hussars pillaged the Brethren's House. But on the whole Herrnhut fared well. Special consideration was shown for the religious character of the place. Officers of high rank in both armies were willing to furnish military protection. An enormous trade sprang up, to meet the requirements of the troops. In a couple of days in August,

1758, for example, the Dürninger establishment sold goods to the value of two thousand thaler. Notwithstanding the fact that the fields were ravaged and great anxiety prevailed, Herrnhut was far more fortunate than neighboring towns; and when the new church was dedicated on August 13, 1757, thirteen hundred communicants could partake of the Lord's Supper without molestation.

Kleinwelke, where awakenings amongst the Wends dated back to 1730, and where a church had been dedicated on July 2, 1758, became a refuge for plundered people of the vicinity after Hochkirch; but Neusalz experienced the bitterness of war's distress to the full, being plundered and totally destroyed by the Russians on September 24 and 25, 1759. From their blazing homes its people fled to Gnadenberg.

Nevertheless, on the whole the Seven Years' War proved a blessing in disguise. A large number of princes, generals and diplomats visited Herrnhut and the other settlements; and personal observation and intercourse on their part did more to remove prejudices than could have been accomplished by many apologetic writings. Esteem and respect took the place of hostility or contempt.

After his visit to Switzerland Zinzendorf more and more confined his personal activity to Herrnhut and the neighboring congregations. Indeed, his only considerable absence was for a visit to Heerendyk, where he met Beck from Greenland and Schumann from Surinam. Sickness again and again gave intimations that his usefulness was nearing its end. When conferring with his Brethren it was noticeable that he was losing his powers of concentration and attention. He frequently lapsed into reminiscences. It became evident that he was no longer indispensable to the church. It was firmly founded, and his presence might hinder progress in the direction of self-development. Hence the Lord called His servant home at the right time. He fell asleep on May 9, 1760, after a brief but painful attack of catarrhal fever. His end was very peaceful, a falling into gentle slumber, whilst his son-in-law, John de Watteville, uttered the Old Testament benediction. His last words that could be understood were *"Ich werde wohl heimgehen."* His second wife followed him on the 21st of the month. All that was mortal of him they laid aside the Countess in the center of the Hutberg. More than two thousand members of the church which Providence had destined him to resuscitate walked in the funeral procession. Vast crowds had viewed the coffin previously and a detachment of imperial guards had been sent from Zittau to maintain order, had that been necessary. John de Watteville delivered the discourse, and John Nitschmann, jr., as pastor of Herrnhut again officiated at the grave.

Being but a man, Count Zinzendorf had his faults. They were those that grew out of his temperament. But his extraordinary virtues and signal devotion to Christ so completely overshadow them that a worthy estimate requires that they be ignored. The very mistakes which he made arose from an excess of zeal in unfaltering adherence to his life-purpose. He realized the true object of earthly existence, the glory of God and the enjoyment of fellowship with Him whom to know is life eternal; and his service was His servant's passion. Zinzendorf was worthy of a place in Germany's Walhalla. It was he more than any other one man who providentially became the founder of Protestant missions; for he preëminently served his own and succeeding generations by recalling Christendom to a sense of its obligation to carry out the last command of the Lord Jesus Christ. Nor did the significance of his place in history end with this. Humanly speaking, the Moravian Church as an ecclesiastical body, resuscitated by his utter self-sacrifice, owed him a debt which it could never repay. This church was, however, privileged to perpetuate what was best in the Pietistic movement, and to serve as a handmaiden holding the torch of vital Christianity for the rekindling of churches whose warmth and light had been almost choked by the miasma of Rationalism.

BENJAMIN LA TROBE.

CHAPTER XVII.

BRITISH AFFAIRS FROM THE RECOGNITION BY PARLIAMENT TO
ZINZENDORF'S DEATH.

Whilst the Count was absent on the Continent from July,
1750, to August, 1751, Peter Böhler held the reins of leadership. It was a year of progress; the financial storms had not
yet broken over the Unity.

In Ireland, especially, the first enthusiasm was ripening into
speedy fruitage. Dublin, where Cennick had commenced his
preaching in June, 1745, with Benjamin La Trobe as his indefatigable coadjutor, had become a permanent center of activity in May, 1748, with the opening of a hall for purposes of
worship on Bishop street, capable of accommodating four hundred people. Though the old weapons of mob violence had
been directed against Cennick and his assistants, Cossart,
Thomas, Knight and Smith, there had been a rapid increase in
the membership of the society adhering to the Brethren.
Böhler, with the assistance of Heine, therefore formally organized a hundred of the three hundred members of the society
into a congregation in full connection with the Unitas Fratrum.
William Horne was given pastoral charge, to be succeeded in
1752 by Laurence Nyberg, whilom Lutheran minister in Lancaster, Pennsylvania, who had joined the Brethren there in
connection with the effort at Christian union undertaken by the
"Pennsylvania Synod."

Meantime the itineracy in the north of Ireland was gradually
widening its scope. By 1752, with the assistance of La Trobe,
Svms, Caries, Cooke, Wade, Knight, Brampton, Pugh, Brown,
Thorne, Hill and Watson, Cennick was awakening a dead Pres-
byterianism and enlightening superstitious followers of Rome
in Counties Cavan, Monaghan, Armagh, Down, Antrim, Derry,
and Tyrone. Gloonen, a few miles northeast of Lough Beg;
Ballinderry, east of the southern end of Lough Neagh and

about eight miles west of Lisburn; Drumargan, near Rich Hill, and a few miles southeast of Armagh; and Cootehill, on the Analee River, and on the borders of Monaghan and Cavan, were the chief centers of the itineracy at this time. That there was a famine of gospel-preaching, and that the people hungered for the Word of God appears from the thronging of vast audiences to listen to the Brethren. Their wayside, open-air services were often attended by more than a thousand persons; and by the middle of the decade under consideration preaching-appointments existed at from fifty-five to sixty places. Moreover, permanence began to be sought by the erection of places of worship and ministers' houses. At Gloonen, for example, a chapel was consecrated on November 25, 1750, where Pugh and his family had been living since May, and where Caries and Syms as well as Cennick now joined him. The next years witnessed the erection of chapels at Grogan, Lisnamarra, Cootehill, Kilkeel, Derryscallop, Ballinderry and Ballymena, though in several instances the insecure terms of possession, owing to the short period of the lease of the land, later necessitated a removal to a settlement in the vicinity. This was the case with Grogan, the congregation here being ultimately merged into that at Ballinderry, and also with Lisnamarra, whose people removed to Gracehill in 1767.

Characteristic of the general service rendered to the cause of public morality by the Brethren, whose effective presentation of the gospel of free grace was laying hold of the hearts of hundreds, and especially important on account of its future permanent results, had been the visit paid by Cennick to Ballinderry, in County Antrim, in October, 1750. The neighborhood was notorious for the careless, reckless depravity of the masses. Here cock-fighting, gambling and dissolute living found abundant patronage. Services at first being held in private houses, the throng of auditors soon became so great that recourse was had to a cock-pit or the open air. The Spirit of God moved mightily upon the hearts of some of the former champions of vice. A society was formed, and the erection of a church being desired, an acre of waste land including and about the above-mentioned cock-pit was leased. At times as many as fifty men gave their labor for the erection of the place of worship. It was consecrated by Cennick on Christmas Day (Old Style), 1751, its dimensions being 63x42 feet. When Böhler visited the place next year he expressed his signal satisfaction, and described the awakening as the most considerable which had taken place in the north of Ireland under Cennick's ministrations. The usual audiences averaged five hundred persons and more than filled the place of worship.

It would have been a marvel, however, had nothing occurred to ruffle the peaceful progress of affairs. In the same year disharmony, somewhat akin to the former manifestations in Yorkshire, in which Viney had figured prominently, began to manifest itself in Dublin, the dissatisfaction being directed against the liturgical forms which were being introduced. Hence in 1753 Töltschig was sent to assist La Trobe in allaying the trouble, and have general oversight of the operations in Ireland. His reputation for cautious prudence soon justified the appointment. The erection of a new place of worship on Bishop street, and its consecration at the end of November, 1754, followed. A school for girls had been commenced in the capital in 1753, and establishments for the two unmarried choirs set in order in 1752.

In England also large auditories attended the preaching of the Brethren's itinerants at the commencement of the decade. Ockbrook attained new importance on September 24, 1750, through the formal organization of a congregation there by Bishop Böhler, the consecration of the church taking place on April 5, 1752. Henceforth it became the center of operations in Derby, Nottingham and Leicestershire. The year 1751 was signalized, moreover, by the erection of church-edifices at Gomersal in Yorkshire, Dukinfield in Cheshire, and in Bedford; the opening of a hall for purposes of worship at Haverfordwest in Wales; the special impetus given to the Leominster District by Cennick, Thorne, Syms and others; the development of the Wiltshire group by Francis Okely, Schlicht, Parminter, Cooke and Münster; and by the securing of a house at Mirfield in Yorkshire for stated services.

When in May, 1752, a British synod was convened at Ingatestone Hall, it was reported that in London the commencement of financial difficulties was causing some defections, but that in Yorkshire the people were streaming to the Brethren.

As yet the religious movement in which the Brethren's agency was chiefly prominent appeared to be still in a formative state. Whether the members of the various societies organized by them should be regarded as members of the Unitas Fratrum or not was a question left open until the succeeding synod. It was, however, resolved to introduce the use of the Moravian Litany in connection with the stated preaching services, and a desire was expressed that a hymn-book be published for the use of the English Brethren, Schlicht having previously compiled a collection. The two synods of the year 1754, in May and in November, formally recognized the fact that the work had assumed such proportions that its distinct denominational character must be admitted, and drew the line of demarkation between the "societies" and "congregations" in full fellowship with the Unitas Fratrum, on the basis of the administration of the sacraments in the latter. General regulations and local statutes and a brotherly agreement, as the bond uniting the members of the local organizations as such and cementing their union with the entire church, were also formulated. At the synod in November, moreover, Kingswood and Bristol were admitted into the circle of the congregations. John Gambold was elected a bishop of the Unity, and received consecration at the hands of Bishops John de Watteville, Leonard Dober and John Nitschmann. Whilst his immediate sphere of activity was not changed, in addition to his pastorate in London, and his participation in the general oversight, Bishop Gambold also devoted his time and talents to literary labors in behalf of the Moravian Church in Britain.

Meanwhile Count Zinzendorf had engaged in an important tour of inspection, from June 28 to August 22. Proceeding first to the west, and visiting Wiltshire, Bath and Bristol, by way of Bedford and the Midlands, he sought the flourishing sphere of activity in Yorkshire. Here upwards of four thousand persons were now members of the societies affiliated with the Brethren, and more than seventy preaching-places were regularly supplied. At Fulneck between eighty and ninety persons occupied the choir houses. This settlement, in addition to the various trades carried on in these establishments, was the center of the cloth-weaving industry commenced for the church in 1745 by James Charlesworth, the warden, unfortunately a source of entanglement through Gomez Serra, but now a means of employment for a large number of members. The rocky hill-side and swampy valley began to assume an aspect of bloom and fruitage and pleasant shade. In the previous year the church boarding schools, which have since spread the fame of Fulneck throughout the United Kingdom, had begun their career of signal usefulness. And now through Charlesworth, the Count on August 10 effected a settlement with Ingham, the former owner of the property. In short, the visit to the Yorkshire "plan," by its robust enthusiasm and sturdy vigor, must have exceedingly comforted the Count, hedged in with distress as he now was. Here he saw an English counterpart of Herrnhut.

Next year, in accordance with the decisions of the synod, the societies at Bristol and Kingswood were formally organized as congregations, in January and May, respectively. In April Pudsey, Gomersal, Wyke and Dukinfield were added to the list. The last named became the center of operations in Cheshire and Lancashire, and for a period the fervent and able preaching of Francis Okely here and at his eight other preaching-places drew large audiences, hearers coming from the towns of Ashton, Stockport and Manchester, and becoming in turn the nuclei of new beginnings in their own vicinity. So, too, in the immediately ensuing years George Traneker labored with signal acceptance as Gussenbauer's successor at Fulneck. Similarly also, from Ockbrook Ockerhausen and after 1757 Münster and Parminter ministered to inquiring souls at Eaton, Nottingham, Belper, Codnor, Matlock, Wolverhampton, Sheffield, Duffield, Dale and a number of other towns and villages. The financial distresses had not shattered the confidence reposed in the Brethren by the people of the north, however disastrously the effect may have been felt in London. The more gratifying must this have been in the face of the most unfraternal efforts put forth by Whitefield, amongst the other controversial opponents in England, to discredit the Brethren. Friends like Lord Granville and the Bishops of London and Worcester had, indeed, counseled that the unworthy and slanderous attack be left to fall without reply by the weight of its own contemptible rancor. Yet, being accompanied by other screeds of a similar nature from various pens, the wonder had been that the appeal to narrow national prejudices had not been more effective. As it was, it may be questioned whether it did not work unfavorably upon the mind of Whitefield's former associate, the brilliant Cennick, whose career was cut short by fever all too soon, at London, on July 4, 1755, only thirty-seven years of age.

With the removal of Zinzendorf and the *Jüngerhaus* from London to the Continent, in March, 1755, Frederick von Marschall and Benjamin La Trobe and Peter Böhler stood at the head of affairs in the British Province, with Töltschig as their associate in Ireland. Böhler's tour of visitation, now undertaken, disclosed a good spirit. Special interest was manifested in Bedford in support of the mission recently begun in Jamaica. Haverfordwest, in Wales, requested recognition as a congregation. The Yorkshire evangelistic efforts were reported to be flourishing under Traneker's direction and the industrial undertakings gave like promise under Charlesworth.

But overagainst all this, and overagainst the encouraging liberality of the English members of the Unity, who had contributed about $25,000 towards the liquidation of the church's debts by the year 1757, it began to become apparent that as an organization the Unity in England was in danger of drifting into isolation, not being in touch with other churches of the land, but becoming more and more closely connected with the Brethren in Germany. Apparently the demands of national life and the requirements of national characteristics were not taken into account by the leaders of the Unity. In June, 1759, for example, when Bishop Gambold wrote to Count Zinzendorf with regard to overtures made by the Rev. Howell Harris, expressive of a desire to promote some sort of mutual understanding, and, if possible, union of activity and operations between the Brethren and the Methodists, the Count expressed his complete disapproval. On the other hand, it may be questioned whether the new *Choreinrichtungen*, with regard to which the Count entertained particular desires, were calculated to promote the work of the Unity in Britain.

Meantime, in Ireland Töltschig's conservatively progressive administration had been bearing good fruits. Cross Hills, Kilwarlin, Glenavy, Ballinderry, Artrea and Drumargan had been the scenes of special expansion and preparations for permanence, through the formation of congregations and the erection of churches. Drumargan, in Armagh, permanently organized in October, 1757, had been intended for a complete "settlement." In addition to the place of worship and the minister's house, establishments for the choirs were provided, and till towards the end of the century the place was maintained with fluctuating fortunes. More fortunate, on the other hand, was the transfer of the congregation at Gloonen, where the short lease of the property rendered all hope of permanence nugatory, to the town of Ballykennedy, not far away. Here in December, 1758, two hundred acres were secured by Horne, as representative of the Brethren, from Charles O'Neill on perpetual lease. On November 7, 1760, with the completion of houses for the choirs, the settlement was consecrated, and received the name of Gracehill. This congregation became the Fulneck of Ireland, and here for many years Horne labored with marked acceptance. Its well-known schools belong, however, to a later period.

CHAPTER XVIII.

With strenuous perseverance the ideal of Christian union continued to be pursued by the Brethren in America for almost six years after the arrival of Mühlenberg made it plain to some of themselves as well as to other thoughtful observers of the religious life of the colonists, that the denominational lines of Europe must have their counterpart in America. They could not forever hold out against the logic of events. They might gather representatives of all sorts of faiths for common deliberation in behalf of unchurched colonists and heathen Indians, twelve denominations being recognized, for example, amongst the members of the "Pennsylvania Synod" convened in the court-house at Lancaster in 1745. They might record resolutions that Bethlehem was to be regarded not as a denominational settlement, but as the home of a missionary society; and that the congregations which were organized and supplied with ministers and school-masters as a result of the "Pennsylvania Synods" were to be considered as attached to no denomination. In point of fact, however, in spite of their purposes they could not prevent the synods from assuming a distinctively Moravian cast. The so-called undenominational congregations inevitably became Moravian, even though contrary to the intention of the leaders of the Moravian Church. The very ministers who exercised greatest influence in the "Pennsylvania Synods," although theoretically classified into denominational consistories subordinate to the confederated body, as a matter of fact were actually and in reality Moravians; for their former associates repudiated them and ceased to have fellowship with them. Hence they themselves finally realized the necessity of abandoning the pleasing hope of federated denominational coöperation.

This abandonment of the original design and the adoption of arrangements for the distinct organization of the Brethren's

Church as such were the chief transactions of a synod held at Bethlehem in October, 1748, in connection with an official visit on the part of Bishop John de Watteville, who unfortunately at this time leaned to the religious romanticism typical of the Wetteravian era, already represented in America by Cammerhof. The influence of the unhealthy spirit of the temporary fanaticism is undeniably apparent in connection with the transactions of the synod, when the extravagant idea that "we are the visible body of the Lord" was suffered to be promulgated. It was announced that the denominational regulations adopted in recent years by the synods in Germany must obtain in the congregations in America which wished to be regarded as in fellowship with the Brethren. The chief test was a recognition of the doctrine that the Lord Jesus Christ is the Head of the Church and Chief Elder of the Brethren's Church in particular. During the ensuing weeks De Watteville visited the principal scenes of the recent evangelistic activity. The names of those who were willing to subscribe to the distinctive tenet in connection with celebrating the Lord's supper as members of the church were finally communicated at a purely denominational synod held in Bethlehem in January, 1749. In thirty-one localities, exclusive of the missions amongst the Indians, Moravian congregations were accordingly organized. These were situated in seven of the thirteen colonies, though the majority were in Pennsylvania.

Spangenberg was retired from his position of chief-executive, Bishop John Nitschmann, sr., taking his place. But the change did not last long. On the death of his chief assistant, Cammerhof, from consumption contracted by exposure during a journey to the Iroquois capital, Onondaga, Nitschmann was recalled to Europe, and the man was restored who had made the sphere so peculiarly his own. With him as a colleague having special supervision of the activity in Lancaster, Berks, Lebanon and York Counties, in Pennsylvania, and in Maryland, came Bishop Matthew Hehl, an alumnus of Tübingen, who had been in charge of the schools at Herrnhut for a number of years. Their partnership was to be more congenial than the former one with Cammerhof. They arrived at New York on December 4. Whatever had been the cause of his removal from office, Brother "Joseph" was now himself again. A synod, convened on the 22d, gave him opportunity to take up the thread of

affairs. A visitation of the mission stations in the Indian country followed. Work was before him in connection with the settlement congregations which might have taxed the most skillful
administrator. To the delicate task of removing the traces and
effects of the "Time of Sifting" was added the arduous responsibility of supervising externals in the most economical and yet
advantageous manner; for the catastrophe in Wetteravia and
the financial embarrassment of the church in Europe necessitated the most complete self-support in America. Moreover,
provision must be made for the reception of large companies of
new colonists.

Scarcely were affairs adjusted when an expedition involving
considerable hardship and some danger loomed up. In con-.
nection with the British negotiations of 1749 Lord Granville,
the Speaker of the House of Commons, had offered at reasonable terms a tract of land owned by him in North Carolina. A
three-fold purpose swayed Zinzendorf and his associates in entertaining thoughts of purchase: evangelization amongst the
colonists, missionary efforts amongst the Cherokees, Catawbas,
Creeks and Chickasaws, and the acquirement of a large territory wherein the Brethren might exercise undisputed sway and
live according to conscience with no fear of disturbance. In
the heart of this territory of one hundred thousand acres a town
was to be laid out, houses built for the members of the various
choirs, and also a training-school for ministers and missionaries and the residences of the members of the executive board.
Around this town the land was to be parcelled out to farmers
who were members of the church. Instead of being deterred
by the financial straits, the leaders believed that a bold and conspicuous operation like this would aid in restoring credit.

Accordingly on August 25, 1752, Spangenberg, with his old
friend Antes, now indeed no longer a Moravian, Timothy Horsfield, Joseph Müller, Herman Lösch and John Merk, set out
from Bethlehem on horseback. On September 10 they reached
Edenton, North Carolina, where they consulted with the agent
of Lord Granville. In company with the surveyor of the
province the explorers next rode to the Catawba via the Indian
town of Tuscaroras. Attacks of fever greatly hampered their
progress. In fact, Horsfield had to be left with Müller to take
care of him, at the house of an acquaintance. Two hunters
were now engaged, to supply them with food; and thus in the

JAMES HUTTON.

latter part of October they reached the vicinity of the Catawba, about two hundred and forty miles from Edenton. Not finding suitable land in the western mountains of North Carolina, they retraced their steps eastward towards the Yadkin valley, and at last met with rolling and well-watered woodland. The surveys were completed on January 13, 1753. In May Spangenberg reported to Zinzendorf in London, and strongly advocated the purchase of the territory. Terms were therefore negotiated with Mr. Childs, the agent of Lord Granville. The title was vested for the church in James Hutton, Secretary of the Unity in England, in trust, the purchase-money being largely raised by subscription amongst members and friends of the church in that country. Governor Dupp, of North Carolina, under instructions from Lord Granville, recognized Wachovia, as the territory was named after Austrian lands belonging to the Zinzendorf family, to be the Brethren's special diocese.

Meantime, whilst Spangenberg was still in England, colonists, chiefly unmarried men, left Bethlehem for the south, Bernard Adam Grube, a friend of John de Watteville from boyhood, going as their minister, Jacob Lösch as warden, and John Martin Kalberlahn as surgeon and physician. The rest followed trades needful for pioneer life in the wilds. They reached their destination on November 17, 1753, and commenced the village of Bethabara, in the present Forsyth County. Next spring Grube was recalled to Bethlehem, and John Jacob Fries, a former student of theology at Copenhagen and lately professor in the seminary at Barby, succeeded him as spiritual adviser. Soon afterwards Peter Böhler also arrived and gave the place its name, significant of its temporary nature, and a declaration that the purpose to found a central town had not been abandoned. Gradually numbers were increased, so that at the close of 1756 the new settlement had sixty-five inhabitants.

In the year of Spangenberg's return from making his report, 1754, a similar task was undertaken in Lancaster County, Pennsylvania, near the old preaching station of Warwick. In August George Klein for a nominal consideration transferred to the church his farm of nearly five hundred acres as the site of a settlement, which should be Bishop Hehl's place of residence in accordance with the plans of a recent synod. It received the name of Lititz in June of the next year at the suggestion of Zinzendorf, to perpetuate the memory of the original home of the Unity.

Meantime the older settlements were steadily developing their resources and industries, and were receiving repeated accessions from Europe. Companies of colonists came under the lead of Lawatsch and Töltschig in 1752; of Böhler in 1753, he taking Spangenberg's place whilst abroad reporting concerning Carolina; of Spangenberg, when returning in 1754; of Nathanael Seidel and Böhler in 1754, and of Louis Weiss and Gottlieb Petzold in 1755.

New tracts of land were steadily acquired, roads were constructed, and the untamed wilderness yielded to the touch of man. The missions on the northern and southern continents and on the islands were diligently prosecuted.

But a time of severe test was approaching. Peaceful Bethlehem was to be drawn into the turbulence of the contest between England and France for supremacy in America. The treaty of Aix-la-Chapelle had been of practical significance here only as suited the governors and military commanders of the various provinces. On the St. Lawrence and in the valley of the Ohio French inroads caused continual alarms. Fort Le Boeuf had been the subject of diplomatic remonstrance on the part of Governor Dunwiddie of Virginia and the occasion of Washington's first services to his country. Colonel Fry's advance in the spring of 1754 had marked the commencement of actual hostilities. Fort Du' Quesne had been completed at the junction of the Allegheny and Monongahela Rivers. Against it Braddock had been sent by the crown. Large bodies of Indians had made common cause with the French. The dress parade of the magnificently self-confident but stubbornly indocile regulars had merged into demoralization and slaughter and rout beneath the crack of unseen savage guns in the rank density of the walnut forest on that fatal July 9, and Braddock lay buried at Great Meadows.

An immediate effect was the outbreak of repeated atrocities along the western frontier of Pennsylvania. The settlements in the valley of the Susquehanna were devastated by tomahawk and torch. Then massacres along the Swatara and along the line of the Blue Mountains spread the alarm. On November 24 the worst fears were realized at the Gnadenhütten mission station on the Mahoni. As evening shadows lengthened and the occupants of the mission-house were gathered for their frugal evening meal, the dreaded war-whoops suddenly rang out and the reports of fire-arms reëchoed among the hills. When the startled men and women darted from the lower story to the room above, and barricaded its entrance, fire was applied to the house. Those who fled from the flames by leaping from the windows were pierced by bullets or slashed by tomahawks. Out of fifteen only four persons escaped to tell the manner of their companion's martyrdom. When the Indian converts in their village across the Lehigh, less than a mile away, gathered around their teachers and offered at once to make reprisals on the enemy, they were restrained by the reminder that they were the servants of the Prince of Peace. Scattering to the woods, they and their teachers gradually reassembled at Bethlehem. The raiders soon left only ashes and charred fragments to tell where once the church and school and dwellings had stood. For more than a year the "brown hearts" were harbored by their brethren at Bethlehem. Then in view of the apparent hopelessness of peace, they commenced to build a new village, known as Nain, up the river about a mile from Bethlehem, and a second village, Wechquadnach, beyond the Blue Mountains, on a tributary of the Lehigh.

Dreadful as were the experiences of that 24th of November on the Mahoni, they did not take the Brethren wholly by surprise; for on the 12th a letter had been received from the missionary post at Wyoming, and Schmick and Frey, from Shamokin, had made deposition before a notary with regard to the facts that had come under their observation. The same day the Brethren at Bethlehem had also put on record their sentiments: "If it must be so, it is better that a Brother should die at his post than to withdraw and have a single soul thus suffer loss." In accordance with this sentiment John Gattermeyer, one of the victims of the massacre, had not hesitated to accept a call to the point of danger only seven days before he gained the martyr's crown.

Now the settlements themselves were seriously threatened. No precaution could be deemed superfluous. At Bethlehem a regular system of patrol and sentry-duty was at once established. The children from the other affiliated places were gathered into a house central in location and easily defensible. The women of the more exposed villages were also removed to Beth-

lehem. In a few weeks the town was surrounded with a substantial stockade, and two swivel-guns mounted. Laborers in
the fields were attended by armed guards. Should a skulking
hostile be discovered the pickets had orders to shoot at once—
but to aim only at the spy's limbs, to frighten him off, not to
kill him. Fugitive settlers of various faiths and nationalities
streamed from the surrounding country into the Moravian
towns, as to cities of refuge, by December 19, 187 being welcomed in Nazareth alone. On the 30th it was reported that
1100 Indians and French were on their way to attack Bethlehem
and Nazareth on New Year's Day. Though the number had
been exaggerated, on that day three assaults were made—near
Gnadenhütten upon a small body of colonial troops, at the "Irish
Settlement" and near Christianspring. Yet when on January 5
volunteers were called for in order to take a letter to the Shawnese war-chief, Paxnous, whose wife was a convert of the mission, ten men stepped forth. That the fearlessness and good
faith of the Moravians in the Forks of the Delaware had due
moral effect upon the savages appears from their declaration,
"If the Great God were not the God of the Brethren, we should
have made an end of the whites."

Franklin, on visiting Bethlehem, was surprised to find the
place in so good a state of defense, and to perceive the methodic
way in which these non-combatants kept watch and ward. Yet
it ought not to have been difficult for a philosopher to discriminate between professional participation in military operations
of an aggressive character and preparation for self-defense
against savages in order that bloodshed might be averted by the
very thoroughness of the preparation. Moreover the people of
Bethlehem did not in the last resort place their hopes in the use
of arms. "In the present state of affairs the Saviour is our best
reliance, they declared just after the massacre on the Mahoni.
Nor did He put them to shame. Though the hostiles encamped
within six miles of Nazareth, the settlements escaped the necessity of putting their precautionary measures to the test of an
actual encounter.

Meanwhile they had their enemies amongst a class of whites
whose opportunity for ill-gotten gains they had marred. Slanderously denounced as in league with the French and Indians,
on the strength of a forged letter which was alleged to have been
intercepted on its way to Quebec, they had been exposed to the

opprobrium of the public in the newspapers of the day. In Jersey public proclamation had been made with beat of drum, that Bethlehem and its filials must be razed to the ground and its people slain. Nor did even the ruin of a flourishing mission and the loss of lives wholly dissipate the angry spirit. But the Brethren were also the object of special enmity on the part of the Indians who had donned the war paint, because the influence of the missionaries baffled their endeavor to secure the alliance of the converted Delawares. Teedyeuscung, the leader of the hostiles, as one of their renegade converts in particular bore them no good-will. Yet in July, 1756, and in October, 1758, when this redoubtable warrior met Governors Morris and Dennis at Easton to treat for peace in the name of the Delawares, the Brethren proved of decided service in furthering negotiations. And in 1758 the missionary Post, as agent of the government, lent valuable aid in allaying hostility and in promoting the security of the frontier, in conncetion with his journey to the Ohio.

During the same years the southern settlement, Bethabara, experienced the inconveniences of Indian war. Surrounded by a stockade, the place became known to other settlers as the "Dutch Fort." Thither likewise many refugees found their way from the open country, many of them later to seek permanent fellowship with those who received them in so friendly and Christian a spirit. For their accommodation another settlement was begun in the vicinity. It received the name of Bethania.

Nowhere was joy more universal than in the Moravian villages when the year 1759 ushered in an era of peace. This was particularly the case at Nain. Prosperity in every respect characterized its life. It became the center of attraction for large numbers of wondering heathen, and thus the influence of the gospel spread mightily. Amongst the rest there came from Wyalusing on the Susquehanna a notable medicine-man, and chief of the Muncies, Papunhank. In his own ignorant way he had been endeavoring to inculcate morality. As a sincere seeker after truth he now yielded to the power of Christ, and though not yet baptized returned home changed in heart, to testify of salvation. The growth of Nain led to the purchase of fourteen hundred acres beyond the Blue Mountains, and the missionary Gottlob Senseman removed thither in April, 1760, with thirty baptized Indians. So Wechquetank arose. Hither came Papunhank with his wife and thirty-three followers in search of more light.

Meanwhile the future prince of American missionaries, David Zeisberger, was engaged in diligent literary labor, to secure permanence for the results and to render future help to beginners in the work. His Iroquois Grammar and Iroquois-German Dictionary, for which materials had been collected at Onondaga, belong to this period.

The news of the death of Count Zinzendorf reached Pennsylvania on August 22, 1760. Radical changes followed. Spangenberg was needed in Europe, and Böhler followed him two years after, in 1762. To Bishop Nathanael Seidel and Frederick William von Marschall were assigned the superintendence of the spiritual and temporal affairs respectively.

The abolition of the "Economy" also took place. Whilst the gradual working out of the alterations therein involved required time, June 20, 1762, may be regarded as the date of the inception of the new order of affairs.

The ownership of land belonging to the church in a number of instances was transferred to individuals, and in other instances the rules governing its use were affected. The original purchases in Pennsylvania had been made in the name of various agents who had transferred the title to Spangenberg, Henry Antes and David Nitschmann, as "Joint Tenants." In the year 1751 a nominal sale had been effected, by which Nitschmann had become the sole proprietor, who had given a written pledge that he would administer the property to the best of his ability for the good of the church, and in no sense for personal ends. On his death, in 1759, his executors, Spangenberg and Böhler, sold the estates to Bishop Seidel, who had been designated by the church as the next proprietor, and who assumed all the debts and encumbrances on the same in lieu of purchase-money. On the abrogation of the "Economy" members who desired to do so bought or leased from the church on their personal account what they wished of the land and of the stock and fixtures of the various industries, and now did business for themselves personally and in their own names. Yet until 1771 neither the individual settlements as such, nor the American division of the church as a whole, owned land or property. This was managed and business enterprises were still carried on,

(FATHER) DAVID NITSCHMANN.

for the benefit of the Unity at large, as a part of the financial system under the final control of the directing board in Germany, which apointed its various agents in America. Thus a most intricate system of accounts arose, and the unfortunate tendency was confirmed, which regarded the congregations in America as mere outposts of the organization whose vital center was on the continent of Europe. In consequence the natural development of the American Moravian Church was much hampered.

CHAPTER XIX.

For ardent imaginative minds the Orient has ever possessed
fascination. To this fascination Zinzendorf was no stranger.
Under his leadership the synod of Ebersdorf in 1739 devoted
particular attention to the East. Prospective missions in Ethi-
opia, on the Madras coast of India, in China, in Persia, in Constantinople, and in Wallachia, were discussed. Gradin's journey to Constantinople in 1740, to renew the ancient fellowship
between the Unitas Fratrum and the Greek Church, was intended as a step towards Oriental missions. It resulted in little
more than a polite exchange of compliments. A severe check
was received when Russia's welcome to Lange, Hirschel and
Kund, who were on their way to China and Mongolia, took the
form of close imprisonment. But in 1747, almost coincident
with the removal of their fetters, Christian Frederick William
Hocker, a physician, and John Rüffer, a surgeon, went forth
as misionaries to the Guebres, in Eastern Persia, the supposed
descendants of the Magi. Joining a caravan that set out from
the coast of Syria for Bagdad, the two intrepid doctors made
their way to Ispahan by the end of November. But they found
it impossible to penetrate farther. Twice they had been plundered by Kurdish robbers, and Hocker had been severely
wounded. Now they learnt that most of the Guebres had been
massacred or exiled, so that their journey was rendered pur-
poseless. Hence, in June, 1748, they retraced their steps by
way of Bagdad, Aleppo and Damietta. A third attack of robbers had to be endured. At Damietta Rüffer succumbed to the
hardships experienced, July 26, 1749. Hocker reached the
home church on February 8, 1750.

Undeterred by what he had encountered, in 1752 he returned
to Egypt with the intention of proceeding to the Copts of Abys-

sinia.   Promises of various kinds had been made by a certain
Count D'Esneval, who was in the service of the Negus, and
claimed to be empowered to secure skilled European colonists.
In Cairo Hocker supported himself by his profession, and made
use of the time to familiarize himself with Arabic.   His representations procured a firman from the Grand Vizier and a letter
of recommendation from the Coptic Patriarch, Mark, to the
Coptic Metropolitan of Abyssinia; but political disturbances
prevented the projected journey.   Hence he returned to Europe
in 1755.

Next year, however, he once more established himself in
Cairo, together with George Pilder, a young student of theology.   The mission in Abyssinia was still their goal.   Circumstances detained them in Egypt till October, 1758, when passage was taken in an Arab vessel sailing on the Red Sea.
Wrecked on the island of Hassani, they with difficulty made
the coast of Arabia at Dschidda, not far from Mecca, but lost
their valuable medical supplies.   This necessitated a return to
Cairo for a new outfit, a journey which was accomplished amid
all sorts of perils.   Both were taken seriously sick, so that Pilder left for home at once, and Hocker followed in 1761.

Eight years afterwards the indefatigable Hocker once more
sought Egypt, this time with two companions, John Henry
Danke and John Antes.   To proceed to Abyssinia was impossible, owing to the revolution headed by the Mameluke commander, Ali Bey.   Hocker practiced his profession, and Antes
gained a livelihood as a clock-maker.   To preach to the Mohammedans involved a risk of the death penalty.   But a commencement was made at a translation of the Bible.   Danke pushed
on to a Coptic settlement at Benesse, four days' journey up
the Nile, where he labored with considerable acceptance till his
death, in 1772.   His successor was H. G. Winiger, whose services amongst the Copts at Cairo and Benesse continued till
the misison was abandoned.   Hocker died in 1782.   The harsh
treatment meted out to the missionaries by various officials, and
especially to Antes, who was fearfully bastinadoed by a cruel
and avaricious bey in the hope of thus securing money, and
absolute inhibition of labor amongst Mohammedans finally
caused the synod of that year to order a withdrawal from this
field.

The commencement of another mission in the East took its inception from a very different quarter. In the latter part of February, 1758, the attention of Count Zinzendorf was directed towards Iceland by an article which appeared in an Erlangen newspaper. He wrote to the King of Denmark, suggesting the planting of a Moravian colony on that island. Count von Moltke, President of the Danish East Indian Company, replied that whilst Iceland did not offer a suitable field for activity, in the East Indies it was otherwise, and that the King would favor a mission on the Nicobar Islands. Here the Danish Company had established itself two years earlier. Upon Zinzendorf's entertaining this suggestion favorably, and requesting permission to found a station on the main-land, at Tranquebar, as a base for the mission proper, his desire was granted and religious liberty was promised. Accordingly on August 3, 1759, a circular was issued to the church, calling for men and means for the projected undertaking. Liberal responses were received, Herrnhut alone contributing two thousand thaler. Fourteen unmarried men were selected, with George F. Stahlmann as their leader. Two students of theology, Adam Volker and Christian Butler, were to do specific missionary work, whilst the rest, eleven of whom were artisans representing various trades, were charged with the maintenance of the enterprise. They reached Tranquebar on July 2, 1760, and after purchasing a tract of cultivated land and a dwelling in the vicinity of the town, henceforth named Brüdergarten, they settled down to self-support by the cultivation of rice and the prosecution of their trades. Next year a second colony came, consisting of a number of families under the leadership of N. A. Jaeschke, formerly active in Wallachia. But he and his wife soon succumbed to the fatal climate, a factor sadly prominent in the history of this mission.

Nor were these the only new attempts, notwithstanding the financial stringency. Scarcely had Greenland begun to actually yield returns when its neighbor across Davis Straits attracted the attention of the Brethren. The triangular peninsula to which the name of Labrador, "Land that may be cultivated," had been given in cynical derision, had offered even fewer inducements to colonization. A peculiarly dreary region it surely was and is. Stones and boulders, varying in diameter from one to twenty feet, cover much of its surface. In winter the mercury may remain for a considerable period thirty degrees below zero, and may run down to seventy. Fruit trees are not. Here and there in protected valleys scrubby pines and birches and aspen-poplars venture to put forth an apology for timber. Mosses and grasses and bright flowers take advantage of the short warm summer; but in severity the climate excells even that of Greenland. The very deer and bears and wolves and foxes have a hard time of it, for the snow sometimes lies fifteen feet deep. Human life depends chiefly on the catch of cod-fish and salmon and seal. The Eskimos of this coast bore a worse reputation than the heathen Greenlanders for treachery, superstition and savage ferocity. Though Cabot had touched here in 1497 no English churchman had looked on them as possible trophies for Christ. In 1520 France founded a western Brest; but the aborigines were not baptized. In 1669 the Hudson's Bay Company received from Charles II liberal grants in these parts; but the fur-traders cared little enough for demonstrative Christianity at any time, and nothing at all for missionating. Money-making was their business. It needed another kind of man to be interested in the souls of these uncouth heathen. He was at last found in the mate of a Dutch ship, John Christian Erhardt, who in 1741, in the course of one of his voyages, had come into contact with Frederick Martin. The missionary to the negroes brought the knowledge of personal salvation to the sailor. When his avocation took him into northern latitudes he visited New Herrnhut, and writes to Germany, "I have an amazing affection for those northern countries, and for Indians and other barbarians, and it would be the source of the greatest joy if the Saviour would discover to me that He has chosen me and would make me fit for this service." De Watteville encourages Erhardt's desire; but the Hudson's Bay Company will hear of no such thing as preaching to Eskimos near their establishments.

In the fall of 1751 Matthew Stach, with Lawrence Drachart, a former Lutheran minister in Greenland who had recently entered the service of the Brethren's Church, reports concerning the mission in that country, and urges similar work in Labrador, suggesting that trade be combined with evangelization. But this proposition does not meet with the approval of Count Zinzendorf. Merchants who are members of the London congregation, however, adopt the idea, and in 1752 fit out a ship

for trade and possible colonization on the coast of Labrador,
James Nisbet being especially active in promoting the undertaking. Erhardt and several other Brethren take passage in
her, and on July 31 reach their destination, entering a fine bay
which they call Nisbet's Haven. Here four prospective missionaries land and prepare to build a house, naming the place
Hopedale. Then Erhardt sails northward. But when he and
five others put off unarmed in a small boat to do business with
the natives, their goods prove an incentive to murder. Their
boat never returns; only mutilated remains tell the tragic story
of treacherous crime. Short-handed as he now is, the captain
forthwith returns to Hopedale, and represents to the four missionaries that it is impossible for him to safely navigate his
ship home without their aid. They must therefore reluctantly
abandon their enterprise.

Meanwhile the status of the mission in the West Indies had
decidedly improved. Success had gradually altered public
opinion in relation to it. Since 1751 its management had devolved upon Bishop Spangenberg at Bethlehem, with Seidel as
his assistant. The latter visited St. Thomas in 1753, and made
provision for the systematic development of the enterprise by
the appointment of twenty-four national-helpers. Within a
few years land was purchased for settlement congregations.
Nisky in St. Thomas, Friedensthal in St. Croix, and Bethany
in St. John. The appointment of resident missonaries in the
latter islands, Ohneberg in St. Croix, and Brucker in St. John—
1751 and 1754—was attended with gratifying results forthwith.
But the purchase of land inaugurated a policy of doubtful legiti-
macy and expediency. Taking the institution of slavery as
they found it, the missionaries at first made no protest against
it as such, but sought to mitigate its evils by securing their
converts as laborers on the mission estates. That in the end
this militated against successful spiritual labor, by leading to a
not unnatural suspicion of the disinterestedness of those who
were at the same time task-masters and religious teachers, is
not to be wondered at. On the other hand the faithful and
blameless conduct of the mission-negroes during an insurrection of the slaves at Christmas, 1759, testified to the genuine-
ness of their conversion and to their affection for the Brethren
who had rescued them from the brutality of conscienceless overseers.

Prior to this the good influence of the missionaries upon the morals of the slaves drew favorable attention to their work, and caused its extension to the English Islands. Soon after the passage of the Act of Parliament in 1749 overtures came to Zinzendorf to establish missionary settlements in Jamaica from a Miss Edwin, of London, a friend of Mrs. Stonehouse. But nothing could be done at this time. It was the era of deepest financial embarrassment.

That Jamaica was well worthy of their attention, and offered an attractive field for philanthropic effort, they fully realized. Well-wooded, fertile and watered by countless rivulets, the "Isle of Springs" was the most important of the British possessions in the West Indies. Discovered by Columbus in 1494, it had been wrested from the Spanish in 1655 by Cromwell's expedition under Admiral Penn and General Venables. Before the end of the century it was beginning to export vast quantities of sugar, and Port Royal, the rendezvous of the Buccaneers, was known as "the finest town in the West Indies and the richest spot in the universe," till the awful catastrophe of June 7, 1690, involved all except two hundred of its three thousand houses and by far the larger portion of its inhabitants in sudden destruction. This had led to the settlement of Kingston. With its thousands of slaves Jamaica before and since that time had proved no exception to other West Indian islands in regard to servile insurrections. From time to time many blacks escaped to the fastnesses of the mountains rising from two thousand or two thousand five hundred feet above sea level, and by the beginning of the eighteenth century had massed together in such numbers as to establish a veritable town on one of the highest points. To reduce this fastness of the Maroons, as they were called, had taxed the military strength of the island in 1734; and despite its destruction they had rallied under their able leader, one Cudjoe, so effectively as to dictate terms to the government and compel the latter to have recourse to conciliation rather than force. In 1738 a treaty of peace had been made with them, according to the terms of which two thousand five hundred acres of land were assigned to them in different parts of the island, and perfect freedom was granted to them and to their posterity. "Captain Cudjoe" was confirmed as their chief commander, with two white superintendents as their advisers, and they were required to aid the government in repelling invasions and in suppressing rebellions. But notwithstanding this recognition of the legal status of a large portion of the blacks, and the increase of the stipends of the clergy of the Established Church, in 1707, because of their being "required to instruct all free persons of color and slaves who may be willing to be baptized and informed in the tenets of the Christian religion," it does not appear that any systematic missionary work had been undertaken.

In February, 1754, two members of the church in England, Barham and Foster, who owned plantations in Jamaica, asked for the appointment of missionaries to instruct their four hundred slaves. Zinzendorf was apprehensive that circumstances would not allow of a new venture at this time, but gave his consent when Zacharias George Caries volunteered to go and the two proprietors promised their support. With two companions Caries set out in October. Foster and Barham made good their word, providing generously and presenting a plot of ground for the benefit of the mission, named Carmel. Other planters encouraged the missionaries and urged their people to give heed to them. Additional missionaries soon followed, amongst the rest Christian Henry Rauch from America, later superintendent of the field. Numbers were baptized. Emmaus was added to Carmel, and outposts were established at the Bogue, Island and Mesopotamia, three other plantations. But differences of judgment amongst the missionaries respecting the length of probation advisable prior to the admission of converts to church fellowship disturbed the harmony of the workers and seriously affected the confidence of the negroes.

Meantime in 1756 the missionaries on St. Thomas commissioned Samuel Isles to investigate the prospects in Antigua. Well received by the governor and by a number of the planters, he met with speedy success, his first convert being baptized next year. In 1760 a piece of ground in the outskirts of St. Johns was purchased and a permanent base of operations secured.

The year 1754, "the colonial year," as it has been distinctively termed by Moravian writers, was of significance also for the mission in Surinam. The exploratory tour of the year 1735 had not imparted favorable impressions. Low-lying, swampy land, the boat or canoe affording the best means of travel up the numerous rivers, soil fabulously fertile but also malaria-breeding, the climate one of intensest heat, requiring Europeans to seek absolute rest during the mid-day hours—these were the chief features reported from Surinam. Arawack, Warrow and other Indian tribes and free Bush Negroes and negro slaves constituted the bulk of the population. Discovered by Columbus in 1498, the country has received Dutch settlers as early as 1580, and slaves have been introduced in 1621. Since 1669 it has been continuously the property of Holland.

A patriarchal, but utterly heathenish life was that of its Indians, treachery and implacable thirst for revenge rendering futile any attempt at stable tribal organization. Characteristic of this life was the "avenging of blood." "If an Indian die, the sorcerer decides whether the evil spirit or a human enemy has killed him. If a man be supposed to have poisoned the deceased, a caldron containing water and the leaves of a certain plant is placed on the fire until the water boils. The side of the caldron on which the water first froths over indicates the direction from which the murderer has come, and the sorcerer now names the place and person. The nearest male relative of the deceased then sets out to take vengeance. Until this be done he may neither eat nor speak. For days, and even for weeks, he may lie in wait for his unsuspecting victim, until an opportunity presents itself of shooting him in the back with a poisoned arrow. If the unfortunate man fall down dead, the murderer buries him in the bush, returns to the place on the third night, thrusts a pointed stick into the ground so as to pierce the corpse lying beneath, pulls the stick out again, licks the blood which adheres to it, and goes home contented and proud. If the sorcerer, however, has named a woman or a child as the murderer, vengeance must be executed in another way. The innocent victim is surprised in a lonely place, and thrown to the ground. After the woman's mouth has been forced open the teeth of a poisonous snake are pressed into her tongue. The victim of this outrage is now allowed to run home, for before she reaches home her tongue will be so inflamed and swollen that she will not be able to name her murderer. Usually death soon follows. Thus no Indian is sure of his life, and all are under the power of the sorcerer, who is able at any time to contrive the death of an enemy by naming him to the avenger of blood as the murderer of his deceased relative."

After the return of the explorers, in response to the offer of a welcome on a plantation on the Rio de Berbice by a gentleman of Amsterdam, Christopher Daehne and John Güttner had been sent thither in 1738. At first regarded askance by the planters, they had established Pilgerhut about one hundred miles inland. In 1739 Dr. Frederick Regnier and his wife found their way to Paramaribo, and through the friendly offices of Abraham Boemper, who later removed to America and idenfied himself with the church, commenced a mission which began to excite interest especially amongst the Jews of the city. But the civil and ecclesiastical authorities manifested such hostility that a removal became necessary, and a small plantation was secured on the Cottica, to be in turn relinquished in 1745, when part of the working force was transferred to Pilgerhut. Here the first convert was baptized in March, 1748, an old woman, and so great was the impression which this made that by June the number of those baptized rose to thirty-nine.

New life had been already inspired by the arrival of Theophilus Solomon Schumann, a friend of Cammerhof and his counterpart in soul and zeal. Formerly a tutor in the Protestant cloister at Klosterbergen in Saxony, he readily acquired the language which had proved so difficult to his predecessors, translated portions of the Scriptures into the Arawack, and prepared lexical and grammatical helps for his associates. But in 1750 the operations of the missionaries were more than ever thwarted by hostile whites, who conceived that the conversion and enlightenment of the Indians would be prejudicial to trade. Efforts were made to arbitrarily enroll the Christian Indians on the military lists of the colony. Military duties and the taking of oaths were to be forced upon the missionaries. Notwithstanding the unrest thus occasioned, by the end of 1756 Pilgerhut numbered two hundred and thirty-nine baptized persons.

Now in 1754 the countenance of the authorities was secured by Daehne and Ralfs at Paramaribo. Seidel and Schumann also obtained concessions for the founding of mission colonies, and two years later Captain Garrison, of the *Irene*, was sent to take possession of these tracts in the name of the church. Sharon was commenced on the Saramacca by Schumann and others, and Daehne founded Ephraim on the Corentyne.

Daehne's sole companion was one Christopher, a baptized

negro from Pilgerhut, who deserted him. For two years he lived a life of utter solitude, danger and hardship.

"One evening he had lain down in the dark to rest in his hammock, when a large serpent fell upon him from a lath of the roof, twined itself twice and then three times round his neck, drawing itself all the time closer together. He thought his end had come, and wrote on the table with chalk, 'A serpent has killed me,' that his brethren might not think the Indians had murdered him. Suddenly the promise of our Saviour to His disciples occurred to his mind, 'They shall take up serpents, and it shall not hurt them.' Relying upon this, he sought with all his might to free himself from the serpent's embrace, and was so vehement in his efforts that he tore off a part of the skin of his face. He did not know whither he had flung the reptile in the darkness, but was soon peacefully asleep in his hammock.

"Often in the evenings he heard the roar of a jaguar, which crept stealthily around his hut. He kindled a fire to frighten away the unwelcome visitor, but even when the flames died out he remained fearless. Then again, one day, while gathering wood for fuel, he was stung by the black ants, and was rendered insensible. These ants are an inch in length, and as poisonous as the serpents.

"Another time fifty blood-thirsty Indians with iron hatchets and wooden swords surrounded his hut, bent on executing their long cherished design of murdering the white man. Daehne, however, went out to them, and told them of his God, who had sent him to them, and of God's love to them. The result was that the Indians gave him some of their provisions and promised to come again soon, in order to hear more from him. While yet living alone, he fell ill and lay in his hut, stricken with a severe fever, but was saved by the timely arrival of Schumann. Even in his sickness he did not feel lonely. 'In all my need and bodily weakness my dear Saviour helped me through, and sweetened everything that was bitter,' he wrote to his brethren.

"After two years Daehne had the pleasure of seeing Indians settle down at Ephraim, and in this way a small Christian congregation sprang up around his hut. Of the two years which had elapsed he said: 'I have hitherto lived alone with my dear Saviour, and done what I could, with a contented and happy heart. The Saviour comforted me so powerfully by His presence in this lonely place that I spent very happy times.'"

Finally he was relieved by the arrival of three Brethren, and was transferred to Sharon on the Saramacca.

But now a period of retrogression ensued. In 1758 Schumann lost his wife, and circumstances connected with the mission rendered it necessary for him to visit Europe. On his return to Pilgerhut in 1760, he found the state of affairs completely changed. The missionary who was to have taken his place had been unable to find a ship in which to proceed to Surinam. The converts had been left without the enjoyment of the sacraments and the discipline had been sadly relaxed. Epidemics had carried off as many as forty persons in one year. Raids of hostile Bush Negroes had entailed heavy losses. In consequence a large portion of the congregation had scattered. The rest were quite dispirited. Finally, in addition to all this, Schumann himself fell a victim to the prevalent disease, October 6, 1760. Only forty years of age, he had personally baptized about four hundred Indians. Well did he deserve the designation of "apostle of the Arawacks." With his sudden death the mission was thrown into a deplorable state.

CHAPTER XX.

THE THEOLOGY OF THE ZINZENDORFIAN ERA.

In the formative years of childhood Zinzendorf was subjected to the influences of Pietism, and Pietistic thought ruled his environment at Halle. Yet the years at Wittenberg also exercised a determinative influence. In his case the antagonism of the divergent schools of evangelical faith issued into a blending of Pietistic ethical practice and aspirations after practical reform in the sphere of religion with the theoretic habit of thought characteristic of the older Lutheran theology. Nevertheless his was not a Lutheranism unaffected and unchanged by personal temperament and experience. What he lived through vitally transmuted and materially altered his religious views, and the Moravian aversion to a strict definition of dogmas posited in technical terminology found in him a sympathetic appreciation. In turn his master-mind impressed upon his associates and coadjutors his personal apprehension of the essentials of religion and of the most effective mode of their presentation; hence the theology of the Brethren's Church in the Zinzendorfian era was more completely identical with the theology of Zinzendorf than is the theology of a church as a rule identical with that of any one of its writers or leaders.

Any fair presentation of the essentials of the Zinzendorfian theology must take into account the fact, that their purpose and character give to his several writings very varied value as sources. Some, like the *Berliner Reden*, evidently placed well matured and permanently apprehended thought before the wider public in lasting form. Others, fugitive religious poems and hymns of emotion, addresses and tractates occasioned by temporary states of feeling, or controversial or apologetic pamphlets, were not of lasting significance—were later possibly repudiated by their author. These last possess little or no true value as a means of ascertaining his underlying and permanent theological conceptions. Amongst the writings of importance, in addition to the *Berliner Reden*, mention may be made of the following: *Sonderbare Gespräche eines Reisenden über Wahrheiten der Religion,* published in Leipsic at Easter, 1739; *Versuch zu einer abermaligen Uebersetzung des Neuen Testamentes aus dem Griechischen, Büdingen,* autumn of 1739; and *Probe eines Lehrbüchleins für die so-genannten Brüdergemeinen,* a catechism authorized by the synod of Gotha, July, 1740. Of his hymns without doubt the most significant, as setting forth his own doctrinal position, and personal experience was his *Christi Blut und Gerechtigkeit,* written on the West Indian island of St. Eustace, in 1739, originally in thirty-three strophes, twenty being still in use in the German and twelve in the English version. It has ever deservedly remained a favorite in the Brethren's Church.

Hallensian Pietism early lost the allegiance of Zinzendorf, who was compelled to reject its claims to correctly present scriptural and experimental theology. His own Christian development could not be harmonized with its theories. At the basis of the revival of 1727 lay not so much the Pietistic conception of the struggle of repentance, which issues into peace from the terrors of an accusing conscience with the conviction that the wrath of a just and angry God has been appeased, but rather the conception of the grace of the Son of God, whereby personal fellowship with Him and unfeigned following of Him are made possible and acceptance with God is realized. The universal necessity of a painful struggle of repentance (*Busskampf*) was not conceded. In fact, uniformity of method could not be ascribed to the operations of divine grace. The *Busskampf* and the *Durchbruch,* on which the Hallensians laid such stress, were felt to be out of place where in spite of sin the love of God had been a gentle but persistently regnant force in a life from childhood. Personal relationship to Jesus, through whatever providential leading it might be attained, was conceived to be more important, bringing with it assurance and peace. Penitence denotes not anguish and distress under conviction of sin and the felt wrath of God, but a change of mind, heart, disposition and life's purpose, whereby one emerges into the enjoyment of the divine sonship. To earnestly yearn after the mind of Christ and an acquirement of the Christ-life, is a more sound evidence of conversion, than to be driven to a painful discriminaton between things lawful and unlawful, and to a shunning of the latter from a dread of the punishment of sin.

In the year 1734 Zinzendorf's Biblical studies led him to an exaltation of the person of the historic Christ, as of central importance, and to a special appreciation of the vicarious atonement in particular. He was impressed with the significance of the word λύτρον (a ransom) and its kindred derivatives (e. g. Matt. 20: 28, Mark 10: 45, Luke 24: 21, Titus 2: 14, 1 Peter 1:18, Heb. 9:12). In consequence the person of Christ henceforth became central in his theology and in his preaching and in the preaching of his brethren. But the language of Scripture, of experience and of feeling, rather than the terminology of scientific theology was employed, with an absence of dogmatic theories of substitutionalism. Indeed the term "redemption" was favorite rather than "atonement." That the death of Christ has the value of a complete deliverance from the punishment for sin, so far as man is concerned—the sinner being no more regarded as a sinner in God's sight; that the objective act of redemption carries with it for the believer the right to subjectively appropriate forgiveness of sin; that both the act of redemption and the act of pardon have their ground in the all-availing merits of the life, sufferings and death of Christ; that God the Holy Ghost works in a believer the conviction that his sins are forgiven and therewith fashions in his heart a new purpose in life—the new birth, a momentary act—whence springs an inclination towards and a desire for sanctification; that growth in grace follows as a consequence and result of regeneration; these became the chief themes of Zinzendorfian and Moravian preaching in the succeeding years.

In the *Berliner Reden* of 1738 the following tenets appear chararacteristic: the essential and eternal divinity and at the same time the true and essential humanity of Christ; the merits of the slaughtered Lamb of God for the forgiveness of sins and for the salvation of poor sinners; their privilege of obtaining grace to conquer sin; the truth that Jesus is everything and man less than nothing—not a hindrance, but a stimulus to sanctification. The death on the cross from one standpoint is the depth of the humiliation (κένωσις) but from another standpoint is the acme of his glorification.

The synod held at Marienborn in December, 1740, has received from Moravian historians the distinctive appellation of the *Lehrsynode*. It gave formal sanction to the conceptions and expressions which had become characteristic of the Brethren and their heralds in home and heathen lands, familiar by this time alike to their friends and their antagonists through sermons, addresses, hymns and published writings. The very kernel of doctrine was held to be the forgiveness of sins through the blood of Christ. Faith is a firm assurance which is wholly the work of God. This assurance manifests itself to a believer first of all in a conviction of his helpless sinful state. Then follows absolution. Before the gospel can savingly reach a soul, that soul must be made poor in spirit and must see that in itself it is worthless and helpless. Then it is capable of receiving the message that the Lamb of God has died for it. The foolishness of the gospel of the cross consists in this, that it was needful for the Son of God to shed his blood for us, if men were to be helped. Thereby all philosophizing is put to shame. The blood of Jesus is in the first place the ransom ($\lambda \acute{v} \tau \rho o v$) paid for the redemption of men. Since Satan brought to the cross the Son of God, His Lord and God, who was innocent, mankind is taken out of his power. In the second place, the blood of Christ is the satisfaction for the justice of God, for God must have punished man, if he remained under the power of the devil. In the third place, the blood of Christ has physically tinged the world of nature, and has affected something supernatural for it. It should be noted in passing that these conceptions do not appear to have been permanent or to have been insisted upon strenuously. "So soon as one obtains grace, faith and love enter the heart, and one first of all feels love; one loves Him whom one has not seen. The difference between the Brethren's standpoint and that of the Tübingen theologians lies in the fact that the former set forth as the one essential the blood and the merits of the Lamb of God, whilst the latter lay stress on other truths in addition. The difference between the Brethren and the Hallensians lies in the fact that the latter seek to obtain grace by pious following of Christ, while the former begin with the obtaining of grace. Unlike the Lutherans we, however, construct no confession of faith, which may not later be altered. We desire to retain freedom, that the Saviour may from time to time enlighten our teaching." Thus the men of 1740 expressed themselves. This freedom from all purely authoritative definition of doctrine brought with it not only that the Brethren did not make issues out of matters of secondary importance, but also that they endeavored to come to their reading of the Scriptures with minds unaffected by dogmatic prejudices, in order that both the word and the spirit of the Bible might be apprehended.

That the synodical conference in London in September, 1741, with its far reaching subjective experience of the chief eldership of the Saviour, should have powerfully influenced Zinzendorf's conception of the church, is what might well have been expected. More than ever for that daily close fellowship of the individual believer with the Saviour, which gave the key-note to his apprehension of the state of grace, he now sought to find some correspondent relationship in the life of the church and of its congregations as units. Emphasis was laid upon the immediate leading of the Saviour as the head of His church. Amongst the various confessional denominations the Brethren's Unity was held to occupy the position of the church of Philadelphia in the Apocalypse. The direct decision of the lot and the indication of the will of the great Head of the church through this means, came to be considered a special privilege of the Unity. Within the Unity itself various modes of apprehending saving truth (the *Tropen*) were to be equally encouraged, as of use in leading to the Saviour men of varied disposition and fundamental habits of thought, and as a means to evangelical union amongst the denominations. The religious tolerance to be found in the settlements of the Brethren in virtue of a recognition of the *Tropen* rendered them "free cities" for those who otherwise might be unable to elsewhere discover a place where they could enjoy true fellowship. Here the basis of union consisted less in uniformity of theological conception but rather in a community of ethico-religious convictions and practice, based upon unity of apprehension of the one thing needful.

Therewith, moreover, was connected the conception of the true humanity of Christ, very-man as well as very-God, who in passing through each stage from infancy to maturity sanctified human life in all its progress from the cradle to the grave, and gave to each believer in each period of his career the example of faultless conduct and spotless purity. For the Brethren's characteristic method of the care and cure of souls through the "choir system" this idea acquired special importance, being

14

second only to the realization of the atoning merits of the Lord's life, sufferings and death.

The "Period of Sifting," with its figurative theory of the Trinity and its exaggeration of the material efficacy of the blood of Christ, furnished no permanent contribution to the theology of the Brethren's Church, thoroughly repudiated as its main features were by Zinzendorf himself and its peculiar liturgies suppressed from 1750 to 1756.

When he emerged from the fantasies of the later forties Zinzendorf did not so much return to an emphasizing of the doctrine of redemption, as it had been presented just before the Wetteravian era. The recalling of the Unity to the rock-foundation became rather the special task of Spangenberg and Clemens. The tendency of Zinzendorf himself, though completely purged from the aberrations of the past, rather inclined to a contemplation of the person of Christ than to a presentation of soteriology in its usual aspects. He was convinced that "religion does not root itself in knowledge, but in the feeling of love, in a belief of that which one loves," as he expressed it. But complete love demands a *person* as its object. For Zinzendorf now as ever this personal object of love was the Saviour; his religion, constant fellowship with Him. He declared, "The Saviour, the God-man, and atoner, is the object of religion; the essential manifestation of religion is loving fellowship with Him," at one time described as "intercourse with Him," at another time as "His blessed presence," "*Seine liebe Nähe.*" Henceforth, from 1756 to the end of his life, "*Seine liebe Nähe*" became a favorite thought with Zinzendorf. In this conception and in the merits of the humanity of the Saviour for body and soul he discovered the ground for efforts in regard to the inner life of a Christian, the while he admitted the need of our Lord's moral precepts, and especially those of the Sermon on the Mount. And as a corollary to the tenet, that the fundamentals of religion lie in daily fellowship with the Saviour, he deduced the privilege of true union of believers, to be exemplified in the "*Diaspora.*"

Originality of thought and expression markedly distinguished Zinzendorf, and in various respects he was undoubtedly a pioneer in the realm of theology, especialy in his Christo-centric presentation of the truths essential to salvation. Summarized in brief, his characteristic tenets, tenets maintained with fairly steadfast consistency from first to last, were the following: the presentation of Christ as God, with an acceptance of all the consequences of this presentation, amongst the rest prayer directly to Christ; the sacrifice of the God-man on the cross, as the complete atonement for the sins of the world, so that through faith, which is the gift of grace, it is possible for the believer to obtain firm and well-grounded though humble assurance of his acceptance with God; the subjective condition of this assurance, and an essential to salvation, being the regeneration of the believer through the power of the Holy Ghost, whilst the mode of this divine work can not be predicated in any case, God dealing with each as seemeth Him best, and for the man the fact of his regeneration being of importance rather than the manner in which it was effected in and for him; the continuance of his conflict with depravity so long as life lasts, he remaining sadly conscious that he is a sinner, dependent on the mercy of God, though the issue, which is wholly of grace and as such a divine work, is assured to the believer; the privilege of personal daily fellowship with the Lord Jesus in spite of realized unworthiness and personal sinfulness; the obligation and privilege of following the guidance and leading of the Lord, the chief elder and bishop of souls, the good shepherd, to whom both the welfare of the individual Christian and the prosperity and progress of the church are a care; and the significance of His perfect humanity and spotless human life as an example to all classes and conditions of believers and sanctifying all the relationships of life into which they are brought by His leading.

In various details the terminology of Zinzendorf became obsolete in the course of years. But from the Zinzendorfian era the Brethren's Church still enjoys the heritage of a precious heirloom, a theology Johannean rather than Pauline in its dominant characteristics, the love of God in Christ being basic—not His sovereignty, nor His justice, the person of the Redeemer being central, not the attributes of the Godhead.

CHAPTER XXI.

THE POSITION OF THE UNITAS FRATRUM AT THE DEATH OF
ZINZENDORF.

By the act of Parliament in 1749 the representatives of the Unity in Great Britain and Ireland and in the colonies passed from the status of unorganized foreign evangelicals without rights under English law, and dependent upon royal toleration in the occupancy of an undefined position, to that of recognized liberty of operations as adherents of an old Protestant Episcopal Church. One point was not definitely settled, the right of the Unitas Fratrum as a whole and of its local organizations to hold property with corporate powers.

In other lands the situation varied. In Saxony its members were regarded as constituting the Evangelical *Bruder-Gemeine*, adhering to the Confession of Augsburg, but enjoying liberty of ritual and discipline. The exact measure of their privileges depended upon the tolerance of individual lords of domain and did not rest upon a fundamental concession on the part of the government. And although the Saxon congregations practically enjoyed all the freedom of life and worship which they desired, the officials of the country ignored the management of the Unity as a whole and the connection with foreign congregations, as things extraneous to the national constitution.

In Prussia, and especially in Silesia, on the other hand, where the rescripts of 1742, 1743 and 1746 had conferred special privileges upon the "Moravian Church" and its settlements, such as independence of consistories, and the freedom of alien Brethren from military service, they were not recognized as adherents of the Confession of Augsburg. As defined by the Codex Fridericianus, their position was rather that of members of a tolerated sect. Unpleasant consequences had resulted from this—expulsion from Rossnitz in 1749 in the face of the concession of 1746, and a series of pesterings on the part of sub-officials who annoyed the three Silesian settlements.

As to the three other German congregations—Ebersdorf rested only on the concession of 1745, which had in reality been granted to an organization now extinct and which the decrees of 1751 had rendered only partly relevant; Neudietendorf based its existence on nothing more explicit than the good-will of the lord of the manor; Neuwied enjoyed more certainty in view of its concession and supplementary decrees, to secure which had been amongst the later endeavors of Zinzendorf, unwilling as he was to leave any conditions that might permit a repetition of the Wetteravian inequity.

With Holland and Denmark negotiations had been necessary for the conduct of the missions in Surinam, Greenland and the West and East Indies. Relationships had to be established both with trading companies and with the governments. At first active coöperation or at least warm favor, then a secret placing of hindrances in the way and endeavors to thwart the work, and even open opposition had been characteristic of these bodies. At present their attitude was one of toleration on certain conditions.

With regard to the position of the Unity in relationship to the three great divisions of the Protestant Church, the question of essential agreement or of practical separatism had been passed upon by the faculty of Tübingen in 1733 in a manner favorable to Herrnhut. The ultra-orthodox party in Germany and the Hallensian Pietists took another view of the case, the latter being especially aroused by Spangenberg's transfer of allegiance to Herrnhut after the breach had begun to manifest itself, and by the outspoken adherence to the Moravian episcopate at the first synod of Marienborn. The spread of operations to Holland had awakened a storm of opposition from the Reformed, on account of the Brethren's strong repudiation of the doctrine of Reprobation. After Zinzendorf's Christology departed from the customary method of presentation, during his absence in America the *Bedenken* of the Theological Faculty of Halle, drawn up by Dr. Baumgarten, sought to offset the former favorable judgment of Tübingen, and refused to recognize that the Brethren's doctrinal and governmental standpoint possessed essential affiliation to that of the Evangelical Church. The Prussian edict, granting the Brethren independence of the consistorial authorities in connection with the establishment of the Silesian settlements, gave countenance to the Hallensian view. Moreover, the Faculty of Tübingen revoked its former decision, owing to the excesses of the Wetteravian era. It seemed as though the ecclesiastical character of the Unitas Fratrum would be thoroughly discredited by continental Protestantism, and that it must sink into the category of a schismatic sect. But just at this juncture the investigations by the Anglican authorities reached a favorable issue. Then Saxony acknowledged the kinship of the Moravians to the adherents of the Augsburg Confession. They themselves manifested sufficient soundness to cast off the excrescences of the Wetteravian era, and to show that these had been in truth extraneous to their essential faith. Since 1750 the relationship of the Unitas Fratrum to the chief divisions of the Evangelical Church had been a subject with which the Brethren had busied themselves but little. They were content to leave it to the less partial and more intelligent decision of futurity.

Meantime their disinterested activity for the promotion of spiritual life had been very widely exerted. In the year 1756 it was estimated that about seventeen thousand persons, belonging to other communions, were identified with the *Diaspora* societies in the German Empire alone. Lusatia, Dresden, Magdeburg, Pommerania, Brunswick, Hanover, Westphalia and Holstein were centers of this activity. In Copenhagen a society had existed in spite of royal disfavor since 1731. Thence connections had spread to Fünen, Jutland, Norway, Sweden. The South German, Swiss and French phases of the work had attained importance. In and about Basel one thousand persons were affiliated. In the Grisons there were many sympathizers. Hutton had been at Lausanne since 1756, and had established an institute to train men for work among the French. He was in friendly connection with M. Court, of the Languedoc Seminary, and with Paul Rabaud of Nismes. At Montpellier and Bordeaux the Brethren were active. The earlier and widely extended field of operations in the Baltic Provinces had passed through a period of special trial in 1743, in consequence of the fanaticism of Biefer and others. Hostility had been aroused and repressive edicts had inhibited the work. Yet with the repudiation of ultra-emotionalism, by the adoption of a more subdued and sober method quiet good was being accomplished in spite of restrictions.

Thus the Unity at the death of its resuscitator, although not fully assured as to permanence in certain territories, had achieved a position of significant influence, its actual importance being measurable not merely by the number of those who publicly avowed themselves its constituents, but rather by the widespread agencies which it brought to bear upon the spirit and principles of a far larger number of such who continued to remain outward adherents of the principal confessional churches.

CHAPTER XXII.

PROVISIONAL ARRANGEMENTS FOR SUPERVISION, AND THE AFFAIRS
OF THE CHURCH ON THE CONTINENT, TO THE
CONSTITUTIONAL SYNOD OF 1769.

The leaders of the church who had been present at the funeral
of Zinzendorf met two weeks later at Herrnhut to determine
upon some provisional administration of its affairs. Amongst
them were Bishop John de Watteville, the Counts Reuss, Jonas
Paulus Weiss, Frederick de Watteville, Layritz, Köber, Leonard
Dober, Bishops Grasmann and John Nitschmann, John Nitschmann, jr., Vierorth, Peistel, Anderson, Von Seidlitz, Waiblinger,
Töltschig, Von Marschall and Seidel, representative men,
although not specially commissioned to act in the church's name
in the emergency. They concluded to adhere to existing arrangements as far as practicable. Hence as the various con-
ferrees returned to their distant posts, an advisory committee
was formed by residuary process, consisting of the five members
of the former directing board, together with John de Watteville.
The abrogation of the *Jüngerhaus* was determined, and Spangenberg was to take a seat in the *ad interim* conference.   In
the event he practically became the leader.   His wholesome
theological standpoint and his marked executive ability served
as a complement for Köber's courageous and sound financial
management and prevented disintegration.   It was demonstrated that the Lord had further employment for the Unitas
Fratrum. The predictions of its enemies failed of fulfillment.
The Unitas Fratrum as an organic factor in the ecclesiastical
life of the age was found to be not wholly dependent upon the
personality and generous liberality of its resuscitator.   The
concept of the *tropes* did not afford lines of cleavage, nor facili-
tate the amalgamation of the various congregations with the
national churches of the lands in which the Brethren had been

active. These and the *Diaspora* societies were yet to minister to the inner life of Protestant Christendom.

But the larger movements of the age severely tested the organization which Zinzendorf had rebuilt. The terrible and resultful Seven Years' War, which was to establish a dual leadership in Germany, emancipate and anew nationalize German intellectual life, practically give the exclusive possession of North America to the English race, prepare for the independence of the thirteen colonies, and also hasten the alienation of the populace of France from the monarchy, was still at its height. From the summer of 1760 to its close it proved particularly exhausting to the Silesian and Saxon congregations. Financial cares increased. Not more than three-fifths of the interest on the debt could be raised by contributions. On the other hand, complaint arose regarding luxurious living where the abnormal local prosperity of war times made its appearance. Unity of purpose and devotion to the interests of the church were weakened.

With the approval of the advisory committee John de Watteville therefore undertook an extended official visit—Niesky, Kleinwelke, Barby, Zeist, England. After inspecting the British congregations and convening a provincial synod, he returned to Hernhut by way of Zeist, Neuwied and Ebersdorf. His helpful and conciliatory disposition, as contrasted with the endowment of an ability to organize, rendered it natural that he had been assigned to this duty. Yet in effect it hastened a crisis which led to the adoption of a more definite polity. Certain Brethren became apprehensive of an autocratic primacy, a dominance of the individual in the administration of affairs. Moved by this apprehension, Köber on January 21, 1762, addressed to the members of the advisory conference a letter containing certain reflections upon the supervision of the Unity, in which he declared that the authority and power formerly vested in Zinzendorf ought not to be committed to any one person. It should rather be a function of the general synod, which ought to be convoked as soon as possible. The complete absence of ulterior designs from the mind of De Watteville was demonstrated by the fraternal manner in which he received this communication. He himself shared Köber's views. Now the arrival of Spangenberg from America proved opportune. His ripe years (he was fifty-eight), his placid but strongly masculine disposition, his candor, his wisdom, his executive ability and knowledge of affairs and his deep experimental piety all rendered him peculiarly the man to harmonize differences of view and diversities of gifts amongst his associates. Possessing neither the ultra-practical bent of Köber nor the one-sided tendency to religious sentimentality to which De Watteville leaned, he combined in his own person the distinctive excellencies of them both.

Foremost amongst the tasks which confronted the *Enge Conferenz* as the *ad interim* board of management had been named since May, 1762—its members being besides Spangenberg, the De Wattevilles, Köber, Abraham von Gersdorf, Leonard Dober, Grasmann, David Nitschmann, the Syndic, Weiss and Layritz—was that of defining the financial relationship between the church and the heirs of Zinzendorf. But discussion and the appeal to the lot in connection therewith caused a temporary retention of the existing state of affairs. In addition to providing for the interest on the debt, about ten housand thaler were required for the general obligations of the church. Hence it was determined that half of the revenues of the estates should be annually applied to the general needs, including the meeting of the accounts of the Zinzendorf family, the support of the laborers of the church and the payment of pensions.

At length the critically important synod convened in the castle of Marienborn on July 2, 1764. In was constituted of the members of the previous board of management, the lords of domain of several estates where settlements had been formed in accordance with special concessions, the representatives of various congregations explicitly authorized to act in their name, and a number of specially appointed brethren—ninety in all. The chair was occupied in turn by John de Watteville, Spangenberg, Leonard Dober and Frederick de Watteville.

At the outset apparently irreconcilable diversities of opinion came to the surface. Attaching strenuous importance as they did to what they believed to be the guidance of the Lord through the use of the lot, this divergence of views led the members to believe that He desired to convey a special message to the Brethren's Church at this time. Accordingly a committee was appointed from the expressed opinions of whose members twelve concise declarations were formulated and submitted *seriatim* to the approval or disapproval of the lot. In this manner a series of sentences came before the synod, which were taken to be the message of the Head of the church to His servants at this juncture. They made a deep and lasting impression. In them the ministers were rebuked for seeking their own and striving too much to carry out their own personal ideas in the management of the Unity and in the life of the congregations. The spirit of worldly-mindedness and an undue pursuit of riches and temporal prosperity were uncovered. Searchings of heart were called forth, that were productive of confession and resulted in a very brotherly spirit of reconsecration.

Being thus inwardly prepared, they then proceeded to frame a constitution on the basis of a theocratic republic. The Brethren's Church is to be regarded as a Unity in all its parts, governed by a general synod, in the intervals of whose meeting an executive board elected by the synod and responsible to it shall superintend affairs. To this board the local boards of each congregation are subordinated. As first chosen the *Directorium* or *Directory*, as it was entitled, consisted of John de Watteville, Spangenberg, Leonard Dober, David Nitschmann the Syndic, Böhler, Waiblinger, Christian Gregor and Wenceslaus Neisser. Besides there was to be a *Board of Syndics* to take charge of negotiations with governments and the civil status of the settlements, and a *Unity's Warden's Board* to manage the finances of the church.

The consideration of the financial question presented peculiar perplexities. Zinzendorf had left four heirs; three daughters, Benigna, the wife of John de Watteville, Agnes and Elizabeth, and Count Reuss, the nephew of his wife. In law these were now the owners of the estates of Berthelsdorf and Hennersdorf; but at the same time it was undeniable that these properties had been pledged for the debts of the church. Both the heirs of the Count and the leaders of the Brethren now displayed a noble spirit. The former were quite willing to allow the old methods to continue, and to permit the estates to be used as hitherto. The latter desired to end if possible their utter obligation to the Zinzendorf family and solve the intricate questions involved. The final outcome of the negotiations was that a capital of $90,000 was paid out, half to Count Reuss and half to the daughters of Zinzendorf, and the church became the owner of the estates, assuming all the indebtedness that had been contracted by the former owner for the advancement of Christ's cause. Of personal debts he had none. It was undoubtedly a great act of sacrifice on the part of the daughters of Zinzendorf in particular, who thus relinquished the hope that their posterity would ever come into possession of their noble paternal domain. The debt on the other hand amounted to $773,162.

The synod had meant well and had acted according to its best judgment; but in the event it was found to have devised a very complicated piece of machinery for the general management of the Unity. The relative rights, powers, functions and responsibilities of the three boards had not been clearly defined. Their spheres of business at times overlapped. Moreover the peculiar relationship of certain members of the *Directorium* to their colleagues in virtue of their having seats in the two secondary or coördinate conferences, was calculated to furnish opportunity for misunderstanding. Layritz, Gregor and Neisser belonged both to the *Directorium* and to the *Unity's Warden's Board*; Frederick de Watteville had a vote in the *Directorium* and in the *Board of Syndics*. Each of the three conferences was also hampered by the fact that it was constituted of both resident and non-resident members, the latter in some instances being scarcely more than correspondents. Among the members of the *Directorium* Nitschmann and Waiblinger were general supervisors in Holland and Silesia. The Board of Syndics had seven members in Herrnhut, three in other German congregations, two in England and North America. The Unity's Warden's Board reckoned seven absentees in addition to eleven residents. And finally absences on special commissions sometimes lasted for months. Hence the test of time taught the need of simplifying this unwieldy contrivance.

Nevertheless men are of more consequence than machinery, and an unskillfully designed mode of operation if thoroughly employed will disclose more valuable results than a most carefully adjusted code of regulations left to attain achievements merely by its inherent excellence. Fortunately here were men of rich endowments and sincerely desirous to obtain the Lord's guidance that they might work out His will. Their ranks indeed did not remain unbroken. Leonard Dober, whose unfeigned and unobtrusive consecration, clear perception and calmly judicial spirit had long been recognized and prized, died on April 1, 1766. He was in his sixty-first year. He was followed on July 3 by Baron Ernest Julius von Seidlitz, the patron

of the Silesian congregations since 1742. Shortly before his
death he had purchased the estate of Paulowitzka, near Kosel,
and had offered it as a settlement for Moravians. This offer
was not the only one in Silesia. Herr von Heyde, who had
recently joined the church, offered to the Board of Syndics for
a similar purpose land at Habendorf, near Gnadenfrei and
Reichenbach. But his plan could not be entertained owing to
an imperfect guarantee of civil rights. With Paulowitzka it
went otherwise. Families moved thither from Rossnitz, where
adverse circumstances had counteracted the conceded privileges,
and an endeavor was made to secure a transfer of the concession from Rossnitz to the new locality. But the reply from
Berlin did not correspond to the expectations of the Brethren.
Hence the only alternative was to establish at this new center,
named Gnadenfeld, in the midst of a Polish Roman Catholic
people, a country congregation whose regulations bore some
resemblance to those of contemporaneous country charges in
America.

With the conclusion of the war a period of growth and prosperity had dawned for the Silesian and Prussian work. In Rixdorf a new church had been built in 1761, and Grasmann contemplated the extension of activity amongst Bohemians. At a
Silesian Provincial Synod in 1765 it had been decided not to
employ here the *Diaspora* plan with reference to those who desired fellowship with the Unity, but to receive them into full
membership, a step favored by the members of the *Directorium*
who were present and by Spangenberg in particular. Gnadenfrei grew, and the numbers attracted by the preaching of
Clemens reached such proportions that a new church had to be
built. Although financial difficulties attended the restoration
of the Brethren's quarter in Neusalz, it was steadily prosecuted.
Gnadenberg, however, still felt the stress of bitter opposition.

In Saxony a new settlement was commenced, Gnadau, three
miles distant from Barby, in the direction of Magdeburg. Impetus thereto was given by the flourishing condition of the
numerous *Diaspora* circles of the district and by the renewal of
the lease of the Barby estate.

For the Lusatian congregations and especially for Herrnhut
an era of prosperity had dawned. Its industries had acquired
an enviable reputation, and after the visit of Joseph II, in June,
1766, the Saxon court manifestated decided favor. Yet causes

for apprehension were not absent. The very prosperity disclosed, if it did not incite, a tendency towards independence of the "choir" establishments each for itself, to the loss of a spirit of coöperation with the entire financial and industrial life of the Unity.

The western congregations also shared in the general prosperity. Neuwied schools were attracting attention, and Zeist enjoyed the countenance of the Statthalter of Holland and of King Christian VII of Denmark.

But in one quarter disappointment was experienced. During and after the synod a hope had been entertained that the congregation at Herrnhaag might be renewed. Köber had been in negotiation with Councillor Brauer, the adviser of the Counts von Büdingen, and had secured from him an acknowledgment that the contract of 1743 was still valid, and that in consequence the church was entitled to compensation for losses entailed by the expulsion of the Brethren from Wetteravia. Yet in the name of his principals Brauer had declined to negotiate with the Directory as such on the ground that the sway of this board over the members of a settlement congregation, alleged by him to be as absolute as that of Zinzendorf formerly, was incompatible with their fealty to the feudal authorities. Meantime, in the year 1765, Count Gustavus Frederick von Büdingen had dismissed Brauer from his service, and was understood to have given some intimation of a desire to see the abandoned Wetteravian settlement reoccupied. Neisser and Loretz were therefore appointed special commissioners to represent the Directory in this business, and received assistance from Privy Councillor George von Spangenberg, the Bishop's brother, and Frederick Charles von Moser, faithful friends of the Unity and well acquainted with the circumstances. In spite of Brauer's active opposition, exerted through another channel, a scheme for a new contract was drawn up on the basis of that of 1743. But before a conclusion was reached Count Gustavus Frederick died, and his brother, Lewis Casimir, who succeeded him, broke off the negotiations, influenced by his wife, a member of the unfriendly family of Wernigerode. The rest of the story of the Wetteravian connection is soon told. In 1773 the land and buildings of Herrnhaag were sold to a clergyman named Agricola. About the same time the lease of Marienborn expired and the few members of the church who had been living there moved away. Before this, however, it became the seat of another and a very important general synod.

To this period belongs the publication of Cranz's *Historie von Grönland*, which appeared in 1765. The author had been sent to make investigations on the spot. His simple and unaffectedly direct style, the intrinsic interest of the unique transactions his work recorded, and its demonstration of the power of the gospel amongst the most unenlightened savages, won for it such general recognition that a second edition was demanded within five years, and it has since been translated into Dutch, English and Swedish.

Now also the first systematic attempt to collect and arrange the archives of the church was made by a special committee— Abraham von Gersdorf, Peter Böhler, Charles Frederick Reichel, Otto William Hasse and Eric von Ranzau. The castle at Zeist was the scene of their labors, begun in the summer of 1765. Hither the most important documents had been brought from Lusatia and from Lindsey House.

The mortuary record of the period includes the deaths of several prominent personages. The venerable Judith Nitschmann, the mother of David Nitschmann the Syndic, herself the granddaughter of Martin Schneider of Zauchtenthal, the contemporary of Comenius, fell asleep in Herrnhut in 1765, in her ninety-third year. At Frankfort-on-the-Main that indefatigable herald of the church, Conrad Lange, ended his wanderings in 1767. During his thirty-four years of activity he had visited Holstein, Holland, Wetteravia, Brandenburg, Thuringia, Alsace, Württemberg, Franconia, Poland, and Russia—in the last instance en route for China. In 1768 Christian Godfrey Marche died at Herrnhut, for whose modest beginnings his words of cheer and those of Heitz had been so helpful. He was now an aged sire of seventy-four winters. There was a peculiar fitness in his spending the evening of his life, since 1763, in the town which had arisen in accordance with the expectations of his faith.

CHAPTER XXIII.

THE COLONY OF THE VOLGA. 1762-1765.

Observation of the actual life of the Moravians in their villages during the Seven Years' War had been potent in removing prejudices; it also led to the extension of their activity within the bounds of the Russian Empire on the invitation of the Czarina herself. This involved a reversal of the jealous exclusivism of the Russian authorities, exemplified in the imprisonment in St. Petersburg of two friendly Livonian pastors, Gutsleff and Hölterhof and two agents of *Diaspora* activity, the Brethren Fritsche and Krügelstein, in 1749. On the death of the first named the rest had been banished to Kasan, Hölterhof alone receiving his liberty in 1762, after his companions had also died.

The chief agent in the initiatory steps which now secured a welcome, was General Zacharias von Czernitscheff, who had learnt to personally esteem Moravian integrity and thrift during the course of his campaigns. At his request, towards the close of the reign of the Empress Elizabeth his brother Ivan, a dignitary of the Empire, had sent an invitation to the Conference at Herrnhut soliciting the establishment of a Moravian settlement on his estate near Moscow, but no guarantee of governmental toleration could be given. In 1762 Catherine II seized the reins of power from her husband, Peter III, whose assassination followed. Though the overthrow of the Holsteiner had been accomplished by her adroit flattery of Russian prejudices, she had the wisdom to perceive that the civilization of the people over whom she ruled, and with regard to whom Peter the Great had recently said, "We have to do with barbarians who are digging the grave of humanity," required to be furthered by a liberal patronage of culture and industry through an infusion of foreign blood. Colonization must be encouraged on a large scale, liberty of conscience and of ritual limited only by the inhibition of proselytism, and freedom from taxation and military service promised for a number of years.

After the appearance of the Ukase which announced this complete alteration of Russian policy in December 1762, Count Czernitscheff renewed his proposals to the authorities at Herrnhut. But they still demurred, renewing their conditions of acceptance—thorough investigation and approval of the doctrines and usages of the Unity by an imperial commission, with explicit authorization to colonize. This brought to Herrnhut in September, 1763, Councilor Von Köhler by command of the Czarina, and on his return Layritz and Loretz accompanied him to complete the negotiations.

Catharine was very gracious. She assured that the Moravian colonists should enjoy all necessary civil and religious privileges. A commission of investigation had already been appointed, consisting of Count Orloff and Demetrius Archbishop of Novgorod. The selection of just these men was in itself a token of favor, promising fair treatment. The latter reported to the Holy Synod so favorably that it recognized the Unitas Fratrum as an ancient and legitimate church, possessed of regulations and discipline after the pattern of primitive Christianity. But at the same time this prelate in private and the synod in its official utterances gave the Brethren to understand, that they must not reckon on ever obtaining permission to conduct operations amongst members of the Greek Church or to gain proselytes therefrom. In as much as they entertained no such purpose, the warning seemed inapposite. When, however, the deputies brought forward the question of missions to the heathen Kalmucks, much though Russia desired to profit by the introduction of industries, difficulties arose. Avoidance of a direct reply on the part of the archbishop was followed by a refusal of further interviews, and finally it became known that the clergy had urgently represented to the Czarina the necessity of inserting a clause in the concession, prohibiting the establishment of missions amongst her heathen subjects. This threatened to bring negotiations to an abrupt end, for the Brethren declared that on such terms the Moravian Church could not avail itself of the promised liberties. The government, however, was not satisfied to let the affair drop, but endeavored to mediate between the ecclesiastics and the representatives of the Unity. The latter at last had to content them-

15

selves with the equivocal verbal declaration "that the Brethren need fear no prevention of their converting the heathen. On the contrary it would be acceptable to her majesty, if all her heathen subjects should become Christians."

On February 11, 1764, old style, an edict was published, communicating the favorable decision of the Holy Synod, and granting permission to members of the Unitas Fratrum to freely colonize in any part of the Russian Empire, with complete liberty of conscience and religion, including dispensation from all judicial oaths except that of fealty. Furthermore the Czarina stated that she would take them under her own special protection. In a farewell audience she personally intimated that it would give her satisfaction to have the proposed colony settle in the Province of Astrakhan.

The consideration of this important report was referred to the general synod. This body took favorable action, it having been ascertained that Kalmucks were to be found in Astrakhan, and it being thought that this might become a strategic point for missions amongst the Turks and other Mohammedans. Five Brethren were selected as pioneers, with Daniel Henry Fick as their leader and pastor. Peter Conrad Fries was dispatched to St. Petersburg, to conduct further negotiations according to necessity. A native of Montbéliard, whilst pastor of the neighboring Héricourt he had become acquainted with Zinzendorf's writings and so had been drawn to the Brethren's Church. Of late the *Diaspora* in and around Geneva had been his field. His companion in the present instances was Eric Westmann, a man of considerable experience in outlying posts, after 1746 an itinerant in Pennsylvania and New Jersey, in 1749 a missionary on the island of St. Thomas, and in 1750 again active in America. From the primeval forests and primitive settlements along the Delaware and the glades and swamps of New Sweden, it was a considerable remove to the banks of the Volga. But in this wide sweep of activity he was a typical servant of the church. Nor were his wanderings to cease on the eastern frontier of Europe. Five years hence he should be sent as missionary to Guinea. But at present his practical knowledge of the needs of colonists is to be at the service of Fries in making purchases for the pioneers, and after accompanying them to their destination, he will report to the directing board.

It was not until the end of March, 1767, that all points of difference between the government that desired them for purely industrial reasons and the colonists who had the good of souls in view, were finally adjusted. At last on the 27th Catharine appended her signature to the charter which actually conferred the long debated concessions and privileges. These included the right to establish houses in St. Petersburg and Moscow as agencies; and in them also the ritual of the Brethren might legally be observed as in private chapels.

The pioneers had arrived in St. Petersburg by way of Lübeck and the Baltic in June, 1765. They were Daniel Henry Fick, Christian Frederick Rabel, Nils Hoy, Louis Brodberg, and Jacob Brey, Scandinavians, Germans and Swiss. Brodberg alone understood the Russian language. He had been born at Tobolsk, the son of a Swedish prisoner of war. Even his knowledge was scanty. With them, when they left the capital at midnight on June 26, journeyed Westmann, as temporary warden, and Charles Hussy as interpreter. Other companions were Christian Busch, a member of the church, but appointed assistant to the Lutheran pastor Neubauer in Astrakhan, and Abraham Louis Brandt, to whose facile industry in the portraiture of many of the leaders of the Unity in his day Herrnhut still testifies a generous indebtedness, now appointed special agent in Astrakhan itself. Sympathetic Von Köhler also went part of the way. So with seventeen horses distributed amongst their seven wagons, they experienced all the discomforts of characteristically bad roads, dust, vermin and accidents to axles and wheels and harness, until the tedious stretch of country to Nijni Novgorod had been covered, the weariness being indeed broken by a brief halt and the experience of fraternal hospitality at the hands of Hölterhof at Moscow. A vessel was now chartered. Laden with baggage and the dismantled wagons, it left the wharf at Novgorod on July 19. And thus they made Saratov, having landed at Kazan to visit the graves of Krügelstein and Fritsche and arrange for their fitting preservation. From Saratov a troop of ten Cossacks, with officers who were to survey the grant of land, escorted them to Zarizin, where they arrived on August 12. Finally, on the 15th, their toilsome wanderings came to an end with the selection of a site for the future town on the Sarpa, a small stream tributary to the mighty Volga.

The features of the landscape corresponded very little to their preconceptions or to the anticipations created by the descriptions given them at the capital. The very volume of the great river and its steep banks would deter from any attempt to utilize it for irrigation or the driving of mills. Though an island in its midst was wooded, forests like those with which Westmann had become familiar in Pennsylvania were altogether wanting. The land was almost treeless, and near the river was rent into ravines by the annual inundations caused by the melting snows. The herds of the Kalmucks roamed at large over the steppes which their owners rendered insecure. The prospect for successful cultivation was poor. Nevertheless with prayer and faith the Brethren commenced the onerous task of securing a home in the wilderness. The governor of the province ordered about 8,000 acres to be surveyed on their side of the river, and added to their domain about 1,000 acres on the island. On September 3 the foundations of the first house were solemnly laid, amidst prayers for the guardian care and blessing of the Almighty, and thus Sarepta, designed as a city of the true God amongst the heathen, began to be. So isolated was the position of the six foreigners that first winter, that the government made good its promise of protection by assigning them a guard of seven soldiers. Westmann meantime returned to Germany to report; but Brandt had found little to do as agent at Astrakhan, and therefore joined his Brethren in the humble house beside the Sarpa.

CHAPTER XXIV.

THE AFFAIRS OF THE UNITY IN BRITAIN AND IRELAND, FROM THE
DEATH OF ZINZENDORF TO THE SYNOD OF 1769.

In general three features characterize the activity of the Unity
in Britain during the years under review. On the one hand,
attention is being paid to the consolidation of the work previously commenced, and there is a tendency to centralize in the
various settlement-congregations, modeled after the pattern of
a German *Ortsgemeine*. In the second place, the working out
of the financial resolutions of the synod of 1764, in their bearing upon the personal responsibility of members for the debt
of the church, and in their effect upon the title to the properties of the Unity and of the congregations, presented problems
the adjustment of which required time and delicate consideration. In the third place, efforts at extension were not abandoned, Ireland and Scotland and Wales being each the theater
of new activities.

Although the British Province was represented at the synod
of 1764 by seven of its leading men, the congregations themselves are now somewhat inclined to demur at those of its resolutions which implied an individual responsibility for the general
indebtedness of the Unity. And the requirements of English
law must be met in connection with the titles to church property. Hence a provincial synod and two provincial conferences
of the ministers without lay delegates are convoked in this
period; visitations are made by John de Watteville, by Peter
Böhler, and by David Nitschmann, the Syndic. Benjamin La
Trobe, in London, meantime exercises an oversight over the
provincial finances. Moreover, for a period of three months
the *Directorium* transfers its seat to Lindsey House, to aid in
the solution of the problems involved—as well as to advise with
the resuscitated Society for the Furtherance of the Gospel concerning a new attempt at missions in Labrador.

In Wales the society for some time affiliated with the Brethren in Haverfordwest was now elevated into a congregation, its ministers maintaining a large number of preaching-places. Here Bishop Gambold spent his years of retirement from 1768 until his death in 1771, undertaking an extensive tour throughout the principality, and drawing audiences so numerous that often the meetings had to be held in the open air. Himself a Welshman, born at Puncheston in 1711, and having taught school at Haverfordwest from 1722 to 1724, after surrendering his living at Stanton-Harcourt, when he left the Anglican Church for conscience sake, it was natural that he rejoiced in thus using his sonorous mother-tongue for the promotion of the gospel. But it was only for a brief period. His native climate had been recommended as a possible means of relief from a dropsical malady. This carried him off in the sixty-first year of his age—a saintly man of God whose gentle piety endeared him to his Brethren, even as his learning was valuable to their cause. One of his recent services had been the editing of a hymnal to take the place of the collection issued in 1754.

In Ireland, Gracehill rejoiced in the consecration of its place of worship in 1765; and the transfer from Gloonen was completed, Anthony Seifferth being pastor. The activity at Lisnamarra, owing to the impossibility of acquiring title to land, was in time similarly transferred to the vicinity of Ballymaguigan, where more than a hundred acres of land were obtained on perpetual lease, and the settlement of Gracefield rejoiced in the consecration of its church in 1769. At Cootehill a congregation was recognized as a unit in the Brethren's household of faith in 1765, Bishops Gambold and De Watteville and Benjamin La Trobe lending impressiveness to the occasion by their joint presence.

But the course of events in these Irish congregations was not always smooth. The people had to contend with the evils of poverty, and malicious neighbors frequently exposed them to severe trials. During the months of October and November, 1768, for instance, the congregation at Ballinderry suffered considerably. The hurling of stones by a hostile mob into the houses of members, the breaking in of doors and the firing of bullets through the windows, even in hours of worship, testified to the intensity of bigoted ignorance.

JOHN GAMBOLD.

The year 1765 was noteworthy for the beginning of work in Scotland. Ever since 1743 the Brethren had enjoyed the esteem of gentlemen of prominence in that country, who had solicited their services, and a few years later an offer of land for a settlement had been made by the Duke of Argyle. Unfortunately circumstances had prevented its acceptance. Now, however, a commencement was made from the north of Ireland, in response to requests presented to the general synod by members of the church, who had removed to North Britain from the sister isle. The evangelist dispatched was John Caldwell, of Presbyterian extraction, whose conversion had been brought about through the instrumentality of Cennick in 1755, when in his twenty-second year. Since then extensive itineracies had developed his natural gifts for public speech. Crossing to Portpatrick, he proceeded on foot to the town of Ayr, where he commenced daily services in his lodging. The room proving far too small, his friends fitted up a large malt-kiln as a place of worship; but the very first time it was used it also proved inadequate, and he was forced to take to open-air preaching. Invited to other places, he soon had preached in twenty-seven towns, and had thousands of people amongst his hearers. This state of things could not last very long; but in the town of Ayr a permanent society was formed and a chapel built, in 1768. Later another was built in the neighboring town of Irvine, and ministers of the Brethren's Church went on evangelistic tours to Glasgow, Dumfries, Edinburg, and other cities, preaching in chapels, private houses, or in the fields, as opportunity offered.

CHAPTER XXV.

THE ADOPTION OF A PERMANENT CONSTITUTION AND THE FORMU-
LATION OF THE DOCTRINAL POSITION OF THE CHURCH
AT THE SYNODS OF MARIENBORN AND
BARBY, 1769 AND 1775.

One hundred and eighteen persons met in the castle of
Marienborn to constitute the eighteenth general synod. Preparatory gatherings had been held in Silesia, Saxony and Pennsylvania, and contributed to the recognition of the representative principle, whilst they added weight to the authority of the
legislation of the present assembly. Bishop John de Watteville
opened its sessions. Bishop Spangenberg was chosen president, and the election was confirmed by the lot.

The reports of the three executive boards disclosed certain
ill-advised features in the existing methods of administration.
Furthermore, the general financial situation gave cause for
serious apprehension.

Early in the proceedings a deep impression was produced by
the communication of a farewell letter from the venerable Frederick de Watteville, who was lying ill at Herrnhut expecting his
end. He drew attention to the misuses which he regarded as
blameworthy in connection with the indifferent appreciation
both of the Holy Communion and of the rite of Foot-washing,
disregard of the Hourly Intercession, the falling into abeyance
of the former office of exhorter or reprover, the predominance
of the mechanical over the spiritual in the liturgical services of
the church, the faulty appreciation and misuse of the lot, the
effeminate training received by the children, and the haste which
marked the transaction of business at conferences and synods,
instead of a patient waiting until the mind of the Lord should
be made clear.

Spangenberg insisted that it was first of all necessary to consider, as in the presence of the Lord, what was hindering His

blessing from resting upon the church; this was ere long acknowledged to be mutual mistrust. Much plain speaking followed, and mutual confessions were induced. Resolution to maintain the integrity of the church was the outcome.

After business of importance in connection with the missions had been dispatched, and provision made for sending reënforcements to Egypt and to the Guinea Coast, earnest and prolonged attention was given to the formulation of rules to regulate the use of the lot. Its origin was traced to Zinzendorf's custom already in his youth, and to its employment at Herrnhut in order to fill various offices in the congregation during the formative years 1727 and 1728, with the purpose of ascertaining and following the Saviour's will rather than relying upon the wise counsel of any man. Its Scriptural warrant was declared to be found in Acts 1:26. Its special utility lay in a recognition of human inefficiency and in the unanimity of conviction arrived at through attaining certainty as to providential leading. That the Lord must rule His church through this means was not claimed, but only that He does thus manifest His will. When resorted to, the manner of employing the lot, *i. e.*, with two ballots, a positive and a negative, or with three, a positive, a negative, and a blank, had differed from time to time. Definite rules were now adopted. Spangenberg, indeed, at a later session, when the revision of the minutes was in hand, declared that for his part he questioned whether recourse to the lot were not better abrogated, since it seemed to remain an apple of contention, because they were not yet all clear upon what its certainty rested. "This," he said, "did not depend upon the method employed, but upon the faithful heart of Jesus."

By a natural step methods of practical edification were next considered. Systematic reading of the entire New Testament and of selected portions of the Old at the public services, was carefully planned. Weekly catechetical instruction was recommended. Provision was made for the revision of the Liturgy. Spangenberg was encouraged to continue his preparation of a life of Zinzendorf. It was determined that certain of the writings of the Count should be suffered to go out of print—a reaction towards more exact churchliness.

In connection with affairs of constitution and finance, Köber proved the leading spirit. The hard force of circumstances, he

urged, rather than Zinzendorfian views and methods must dictate the policy. Briefly summarized, the transactions assumed
the following form: Out of the three separate boards which
had previously exercised joint and sometimes conflicting oversight according to the proposal of John Frederick Reichel a
new executive board, the Unity's Elders' Conference, was
formed with three departments, distinct and yet related. Its
membership was as follows: the *Aufseher Collegium*, Abraham
von Gersdorf, Köber and Count Henry 28th Reuss; the *Helfer
Collegium*, Spangenberg, John de Watteville, Christian Gregor
and John Frederick Reichel; the *Diener Collegium*, Loretz, Layritz, Frederick Wenceslaus Neisser, John Christian Quandt,
Böhler and Van Laer. Its seat until 1771 was at Hennersdorf,
then at Barby.

The principle was laid down that the members of the church
were morally bound to personally and individually stand for the
debt—a declaration which afterwards aroused great opposition,
as involving the exercise of an unwarranted right over the property of the individual. The establishment of a sinking fund
was determined upon. Otherwise the financial measures mainly
aimed at retrenchment. If a minister could support himself in
part or wholly by work aside of his ministerial duties, he was
expected to do so. The church schools, wherever practicable,
were to be changed into parochial day schools, to lessen the
cost. The study of law and of medicine should cease in the college and in the seminary. Henceforth the resources of the
Unity should not be invested in industries prosecuted in the
congregations. These were to be acquired by the local organizations, or better yet by members in their private capacity.
Each congregation must make provision for its own necessary
expenses, including the salaries of ministers in its service. The
governing board of the Unity was to exercise rather an advisory
than a mandatory power over the congregations in local affairs,
and the church council, consisting of all adult male communicants, came into greater prominence. Nevertheless, whilst the
united theocratic republic thus assumed some of the features
of a more loosely compacted federation, the influence of coun-
terbalancing centralization was felt in the constitution of the
Unity's Elders' Conference, and in its relationship to the execu-
tives of the divisions of the church in Britain and America.
These became only "Helpers" of the governing board, ap-

pointed by it and responsible to it and not to the churches over which they exercised supervision. The current business of the missions and of the management of the schools continued to be transacted by a Mission Committee of three at Herrnhut and by six Trustees of the schools at Barby, Niesky and Herrnhut.

Six years later, at the general synod of Barby, this legislation was supplemented, and the tendency to centralization was intensified. The minister of a congregation was declared the agent and representative of the Unity's Elders' Conference, rather than the executive of the local organization. Membership in the church council was restricted to a portion of the communicants, to whom alone should pertain the right to elect the elders and trustees. A bishop should not ex-officio be clothed with executive power, but was rather to be regarded as "an elder appointed by the synod to ordain ministers of the church." Selection of candidates for ordination was declared to be a function of the Unity's Elders' Conference, which body should also possess the prerogative of selecting men for episcopal consecration in cases of necessity and with the approval of the lot. In respect to finances the accounts of the separate congregations and "choirs" were placed in closer connection with the governing board. It was held that the latter could require the wealthier organizations to assist the poorer, and that any surplus accruing to an individual organization which was not really needed for its own affairs should be regarded as the property of the whole church. All local financial officials were made responsible to the governing board, under obligation to transmit yearly reports of their transactions.

A direct effect of this legislation was that in all three divisions of the church extension at home received less attention. Aggressive energies were reserved for the field of foreign missions. Apart from the leavening influence of the *Diaspora* and the widely extended educational undertakings through which thousands received religious impressions that bore choice fruit in other churches and in which some of the future leaders of religious thought in Europe received their dominant impulses, one purpose became increasingly characteristic, viz., the effort to cultivate the unalloyed simplicity of unfeigned Christian discipleship in the quiet and sanctified retreats of the "settlements," where religion was the all-absorbing topic and the chief factor in life. A Moravian "settlement" normally consisted of a village all of whose inhabitants were adherents of the Moravian Church, permanent residence or the acquirement of property therein by others not being permitted. Its spiritual affairs were superintended by an elders' conference of which the minister (*Gemeinhelfer*) was chairman, and of which all the other ordained servants of the church resident in the place and the women who had the oversight of their sex, were members. The communal government was vested in a warden with whom were associated the members of the *Aufseher Collegium*, a committee elected by the church council. Matters of primary importance were referred to the decision of the church council, a larger body of male communicants. The inn, a general store, a mill, a smithy, a tannery and possibly other industries were managed for the "settlement" as part of the property of the church. Establishments known respectively as the widows', brethren's, and sisters' houses, where members of these "choirs" prosecuted trades for the benefit of the establishment, and in return received a home and the necessaries of life, were each superintended by a chaplain or *Pfleger* in spiritual and a warden or *Vorsteher* in secular affairs. Daily services were held in the chapels of these houses, and each evening of the week as well as on the Lord's Day the entire population of the "settlement" met for worship in the church, the liturgical forms and usages being characterized by a rich variety and pleasing simplicity. That many a soul thus found calm solace and happy vital assurance amid the deadening influences of a steadily encroaching Rationalism is made plain by abundant testimony.

The truly catholic breadth of liberality in non-essentials, the while adherence to fundamentals was required, which enabled men and women of very different temperament thus intimately to associate and labor together to mutually promote culture of Christian character, was further secured by the deliberations of the synod of 1775. Consistent refusal to arbitrarily bind the conscience of all members by the formulation of a detailed creed remained fundamental. But the following essentials, to be understood in the language of Scripture, were postuated:

1. The doctrine of the universal depravity of man; that there is no health in man, and that since the Fall he has no power to save himself.

2. The doctrine of the divinity of Christ; that God, the Creator of all things, was manifest in the flesh and reconciled us to

Himself; that He is before all things and that by Him all things consist.

3. The doctrine of the atonement and satisfaction made for us by Jesus Christ; that he was delivered for our offences and raised again for our justification, and that by His merits alone we receive freely the forgiveness of sin, and sanctification in soul and body.

4. The doctrine of the Holy Spirit and the operations of his grace; that it is He who worketh in us conviction of sin, faith in Jesus and pureness of heart.

5. The doctrine of the fruits of faith; that faith must evidence itself by willing obedience to the commandments of God, from love and gratitude to Him.

It was further recognized as of the utmost importance with respect to doctrine and practice, that the person of Jesus, as God and Man, should be placed in the center, His vicarious redemption being the characteristic and dominant tenet of the Brethren's theology.   The idea of personal communion with the Saviour was to be the key-note in the teaching of the church and should sound through all non-essential differences of religious views.

CHAPTER XXVI.

THE ESTABLISHMENT OF THE MISSION IN LABRADOR, 1764-1776.

Undeterred by the disastrous ending of Erhardt's endeavor, the Brethren did not abandon Labrador.   In 1764 Jens Haven, a Dane who had served at Lichtenfels in Greenland long enough to acquire the Eskimo, through the favor of Sir Hugh Palliser, Governor of Newfoundland, secured passage via St. Johns, and by his employment of their familiar dress and speech disarmed the hostile suspicions of the natives of Labrador, so as to prepare the way for a permanent mission.   In the following year, accompanied by Drachart, he made a more extensive reconnaissance, penetrating a considerable distance into the interior.   But at this juncture affairs of state called a halt.

As a special agency for the prosecution of missions in Labrador the church looked to the Society for the Furtherance of the Gospel, established in London by Spangenberg in 1741, though now in a somewhat dormant state.   On March 10, 1766, a revision of its statutes took place, the officers being James Hutton, Chairman, Thomas Knight, Treasurer, and William Oxley, Secretary.   The revived society then undertook the publication of a translation of Cranz's History of Greenland, that interest might be awakened and prejudices removed.

In the autumn of 1767 turmoil in Labrador itself hastened the founding of the mission.   Sundry Eskimos made a raid on the few settlements along the southern coast.   During their attempt to steal boats in the vicinity of a fort in Charles Bay several natives were killed and three women and six children taken prisoners.   Some of these prisoners were detained in Newfoundland; but Palliser brought to England one of the women and two boys, one of them a bright lad named Karpik, twelve years old.   Brief as had been the intercourse of Haven and Drachart with the people of the coast, it was remarked that the woman recited a prayer which Drachart had taught.   Karpik was therefore entrusted to the care of the Society for the Furtherance of the Gospel, and was placed in Fulneck School. He made a creditable progress in primary branches and manifested a receptive religious mind. But next year he died from small-pox, having been prepared for his end by baptism at his own request. Mikak, his mother, had meantime become an object of curious and compassionate interest to a number of persons of rank, and joined her solicitations to those of the Brethren for the requisite legal sanction of a missionary and trading enterprise. At last, on May 3, 1769, an order of Privy Council with royal approval sanctioned the undertaking, and granted to the Society for the Furtherance of the Gospel one hundred thousand acres on the coast of Labrador as might be selected. It was the desire of the church to establish four stations and to acquire a tract of equal dimensions at each place in order to insure unhampered operations.

Sanction of government having been obtained, in this same year it was determined to purchase a ship for Labrador service, at a cost of one thousand pounds, to be divided into one hundred shares of ten pounds each. Twenty-three Brethren, the majority being members of the Society for the Furtherance of the Gospel, took shares. These Brethren were to be the proprietors of the ship, and were to elect a committee to act for them. Profit from this ship over and above five per cent. clear to the proprietors should be paid into the Society for the Furtherance of the Gospel. All business connected with the ship was to be in the hands of the "Ship Committee." The Society for the Furtherance of the Gospel was to pay the "Ship Committee" for the passage of missionaries and the freight of their goods. All trading was to be done by a member of the Church in the employ of the "Ship Committee." It was to be quite independent of the mission proper.

In March, 1770, a small brig, the *Jersey Packet*, was purchased. On May 2 a lovefeast in Fetter Lane Chapel constituted the farewell of the church to the pioneers of the gospel in Labrador. With the members of the missionary society were present the missionaries proper, Drachart, Haven and Stephen Jensen; John Thorton, from Fulneck, apointed trader with the natives; John Glew, from Haverfordwest, mate of the vessel; Theobald Frech, Daniel Peters and Wynstrauch, from Zeist, carpenters and sailors; and Alexander Campbell and Robert Gilroy of

London, landsmen, and the wives of three of the party. Six additional sailors and the captain, Francis Mugford, not members of the church, completed the number of those about to sail. On Saturday morning, May 5, anchor was weighed and the ship dropped down the Thames for the adventurous voyage to the chartless coast of Labrador. Her instructions included provision for morning and evening prayers in the cabin and services for all on board on the Lord's Day.

The voyage was tedious and in its latter part hazardous. Storms drove the brig to seek shelter in bays whose rocks and shallows were unknown and at whose entrance bergs and floes offered a threatening barricade. At length on August 10 a landing was effected. The natives were disposed to welcome the strangers. Mikak's return resplendent in the glory of European finery made a profound impression. The spot was about one hundred and eighty miles north of Ehrardt's Hopedale of 1752. Friendly intercourse was soon established, and the new settlement was called Nain.

That the authorities at home might keep in touch with Labrador and that a comprehensive policy for the prosecution of the mission in the immediate future might be wisely adopted, in 1773 Layritz was commissioned by the Unity's Elders' Conference to pay an official visit. Proceeding by way of Newfoundland, his reception by the natives confirmed the reports of their friendliness and impressibility. He spent the short summer at the mission, and on his return to Barby the establishment of two additional stations, to the north and to the south, was sanctioned. The tour of exploration northwards, in 1774, cost the lives of two missionaries. During the return voyage, after they had already experienced many thrilling escapes and had endured many hardships, their vessel ran on a reef in the night and began to go to pieces. At dawn they took to the boat. This too was dashed on the rocks. Brasen and Lehmann were drowned. Haven and Lister and the sailors barely saved themselves by swimming to spray-swept ledge, whence they escaped only on the fourth day after patching up their boat. With a favoring wind they were at last towed to Nain by a native in his kayak. When the foaming sea gave up the poor bodies of Brasen and Lehmann, they were laid to rest side by side at Nain.

In the summer of 1775 Haven and Jensen as a fruit of this exploration occupied Okak, about one hundred and fifty miles north of Nain, purchasing land from the Eskimos. Here the coast is grandly rugged, abounding in precipitous fjords. Okak itself—"The Tongue"—is situated on a hilly island, which for nearly half the year is practically part of the mainland, for the broad straits are bridged by thick ice. Though the landscape is barren of verdure, noble mountain ranges stretch away to the north. Not far off rises the bold island of Cape Mugford, its seaward face "a perpendicular precipice of about two thousand feet, with white base and a middle strata of black blocks surmounted by castellated cliffs."

Both at Nain and at Okak the progress of the work though requiring patience encouraged the missionaries. The natives' habit of scattering on the approach of winter gave the usages of ancient heathenism opportunity to reassert themselves at a distance from the stations. But when the notorious *angekok* Kingminguse received baptism at Nain on February 17, 1776, choosing for himself the name of Peter, hope began to burn brightly. Amongst the early converts was also Mikak. Removing to the south soon after her baptism, she seemed to relapse into heathenism, her husband, Tuglavina, being an *angekok*, a shrewd leader of his people in violence, and a man of uncommon physical frame and hardihood. On one occasion "when Tuglavina, at the head of a party of Eskimos, returned the first time from Chateau Bay, having furnished himself with a sloop of two masts, European arms, and many other accoutrements, he stepped unexpectedly into the Mission-house and into Brother Haven's room, dressed in an old officer's uniform, with a bob-wig and a huge laced hat, a sword at his side, and altogether in the habit of a European officer, uttering several threats and boasting of his valiant deeds in the south, Brother Haven, looking sternly at him, exclaimed, 'What, are you Tuglavina? Depart this minute. I have nothing to say to you in this dress. Put on your old Eskimo furs and then return. Behave like a sober Eskimo, and I'll answer your speech.' Tuglavina instantly left the room, as if thunderstruck; and without reflecting on the degrading appearance he must make before his own countrymen in putting off his boasted ornaments, returned to the missionaries, dressed in the plain Eskimo fashion. They then very seriously reproved him for the wicked practices and the murders of which he had been guilty, and for inveigling so many of the baptized to follow him to the south, where he had seduced them into all manner of heathenish abominations. During this address Tuglavina grew pale, 'trembled exceedingly, confessed himself an abominable sinner; but said that he must sin, for the devil forced him to it and he could not help himself. This gave the missionary a desirable opportunity of preaching to him Jesus as an Almighty Saviour. Such opportunities became more frequent in the following years; and he often shed tears when confessing his wicked deeds, which contrary to the general practice of the Eskimos, he never denied. In the sequel he became more attentive to the gospel," eventually submitted to its power, and died in the faith.

By the year 1781 at Okak alone there were thirty-eight baptized Eskimos and ten catechumens.

CHAPTER XXVII.

Upon the newly created executive devolved the difficult task of carrying into effect those resolutions of the recent synod which proposed to rehabilitate the finances by retrenchment of expenditure and increase of capital. It was no light duty, since sectional feeling and an exaltation of local interests were manifested in Germany, whilst in England complaint was made that the spiritual life of the Unity was being neglected for the sake of improving the financial situation. Contributions for the general cause came in very slowly.

Various plans were proposed. In imitation of Wesley's method, by which the class leaders collected weekly subscriptions from the members, a Brother Skinner, of London, suggested the gathering of weekly contributions throughout the entire church to meet the interest and pay off the debt in ten years; but this seemed insufficient in the magnitude of the present emergency. At length it was determined that the debt be divided amongst the various congregations. In Germany and especially in Herrnhut the scheme was received with dissatisfaction, though Spangenberg labored unintermittently with pen and voice, in public and in private, to promote larger disinterestedness. Then Cornelius van Laer in the name of the Zeist congregation proposed that instead of dividing the capital amount of the indebtedness between the congregations, each local organization should annually obligate itself for a share of the interest. But the unwillingness to assume anything like fixed obligations remained, despite the fact that Layritz, Böhler and Count Reuss labored with the local boards. So urgent became the perplexity that Spangenberg and Reichel were next appointed to interview every member of the Herrnhut congregation, and thus if possible break the front of opposition, re-kindle enthusiasm for the cause and remove the religious indif-ference of which illiberality was a fruit. But not even this ex-treme measure at once afforded help. Then came the astound-ing and disheartening news of a heavy loss through a defalca-tion in Neuwied. The warden and another brother had gone into lottery speculations with money belonging to the church, and had thus used 60,000 florins. The members at Neuwied keenly felt the consequent disgrace, and were resolved to re-trieve everything by their united efforts, working in extra hours until the money had been restored.

It was under these disheartening circumstances that the jubilee of the founding of Herrnhut was celebrated. The Lord overruled this occasion for good. A better spirit was to obtain the upper hand, through the loyalty of the unmarried women. On September 2 twenty of their number addressed a letter to the church. In this they recognized the debt to be their debt, so long as it was not divided amongst the congregations, and pledged themselves to do all in their power to pay it, poor though the most of them were and dependent upon their own labor for support. They said: "After weighing how we might be able in proportion to our slender means to contribute some-thing towards lessening the debt of the Unity, i. e., our own debt, we agreed cheerfully to sacrifice and dispose of all un-necessary articles, such as gold and silver plate, watches, snuff-boxes, rings, trinkets and jewelry of every kind for the pur-pose of establishing a sinking fund, on condition that not only the church at Herrnhut, but all the members of the church everywhere, rich and poor, old and young, assent to this pro-posal. This agreement, however, is not binding on those indi-viduals who can contribute in other ways. Therefore, dearest brethren and sisters, let us not delay, but united in love, as one person, let us take the work in hand with courage and faith, either in the manner proposed now or in any other which may be deemed more eligible, and let us not be the last to show love and faithfulness to our Lord and His cause." The letter pro-duced a deep and wide sensation. The people of Herrnhut entered into generous rivalry who should be foremost with willing gifts, and in less than a year their contributions amounted to $17,000. The impulse was felt also in the other congregations; so that by September, 1775, a capital of $220,000 had been raised. Better yet, the spirit of narrow local selfishness was quenched.

Nevertheless it was often a test of faith for Köber, and for Quandt, his successor in office, to maintain courage at times when payments had to be made and no money seemed to be forthcoming. On one occasion a note for 1,500 thaler had almost matured. Only one day of grace was left. Quandt retired with a very anxious heart. Next morning, in spite of himself, there would come into his head the lines of the well-known hymn:

> "Thu' auf den Mund zum Lobe dein,
> Bereit das Herz zur Andacht fein,
> Den Glauben mehr, stärk den Vertand,
> Dass uns dein Nam' werd wohl bekannt."

He went to the post-office, and found there a letter with a draft exactly covering the amount needed. At another time, in Barby, he was utterly heart-sick over a payment of more than 100,000 thaler, which had to be made at the following Easter. He had studied his accounts carefully and long, and made all the combinations which suggested themselves to an expert financier; but this evening, near the end of 1772, it seemed impossible to find any way out of the difficulty. In the midst of this anxiety the night-watchman was heard singing:

> " Was kränkst du dich in deinem Sinn
> Und grämst dich Tag und Nacht?
> Nimm deine Noth und wirf sie hin
> Auf dem Der dich gemacht."

He writes, "Heartily ashamed of my unbelief, I instantly put away my accounts, and retired to bed full of hope. And lo! very soon I found that the Lord had taken my great trouble on Himself. For I received intelligence that a suit which had been pending for ten years had been decided in favor of the church, which was to receive 145,000 florins for the improvements which it had made on the domain of Marienborn."

Additional resources were derived from the legacy of Abraham Dürninger, who at his death, February 13, 1773, devised his extensive establishment jointly to the local congregation and the church as a whole. The sale of Lindsey House and of Heerendyk in 1774 brought in needed capital.

During these years steps were taken to found a congregation in Denmark. In 1771 the government invited the Brethren to form a settlement within the German domains of his majesty Christian VII, who had been favorably disposed through a visit to Zeist. The proposal was welcome on account of the extensive *Diaspora* associations in Schleswig and Holstein, and because of the advantages which might accrue to the missions in Danish colonies. Preliminarily, however, the repeal of certain unfavorable edicts of Christian VI was requested, with the guarantee of all religious and civil rights. The king readily assented, promising his special protection, and his Minister, Count Struensee, gave assurances of personal satisfaction. Next the Brethren appointed John Praetorius, son of the Minister of Justice, their agent in Denmark. An unoccupied royal domain named Tyrstruphof, between Hadersleben and Colding in Schleswig, was therefore purchased. Building operations commenced in 1773 and the place received the name of Christiansfeld. Schools for both sexes were established, and soon prospered exceedingly.

Meantime movements were taking place which threatened disaster to another recent settlement. Under Pugatcheff, the pseudo Peter III, a rebellion of the Cossacks of the Don for a time put an end to law and order in the region around Astrakhan. During the summer of 1774 they took the city of Saratov. A Russian army, setting forth from Zarizin, was cut to pieces at Praleika. The news of this defeat reached Sarepta on August 17, Old Style. The commandant at Zarizin sent word that he could in no way guard the settlement, and urged all its people to flee in haste. It was therefore resolved to send all the women and children with a number of the married men to Astrakhan; and the same evening one hundred and ten persons commenced the journey in twelve boats. These had been secured with greatest difficulty, since two of Pugatcheff's Cossaks had appeared at the Volga and warned the Russian fishermen against lending any assistance to the people of Sarepta. Sixty-five Brethren remained under the leadership of Daniel Fick, the warden, to pack and remove as many of their effects as possible. Soon the Kalmucks of the vicinity began to present a hostile front, and to cast longing eyes upon the cattle of the settlement, which were with difficulty saved from them and driven off. Then they began to plunder the sister settlement of Schönbrunn and the unoccupied houses of Sarepta itself. At length the rebels closed in on Zarizin, and from Sarepta the smoke of its suburbs could plainly be seen. On the evening of August 21 the news came that Pugatcheff, having burned Zarizin, was on his way to Sarepta. Meeting for the last time in their house of worship, the fugitives thanked the Lord for His past mercies, and commended themselves to His care, whilst they pledged to one another that they would not separate in their flight. At sunset they left in fourteen wagons. Those who were so fortunate as to possess horses believed that they might easily have escaped, had they not determined to remain with those who had only oxen, and share their fate. But this very disinterestedness proved to be providential. In their good fortune they lost their way in the darkness, and so avoided a company of fifty Cossacks whom Pugatcheff had ordered to search for them and when found to put them to the sword. On August 29 they reached Janaitefka, where they remained until General Michelson defeated and scattered the rebels. Thereupon four Brethren went back to Sarepta, where they found the houses standing, but stripped to the bare walls, and in many cases defiled by having been used as stables. The rest of the fugitives returned in the month of September. One of the first occurrences after the reoccupation was a service of thanksgiving for the unexpected preservation. When the news of this trying experience reached the other congregations, brotherly sympathy practically demonstrated that the bonds connecting the various parts of the Unity were more than flimsy sentiment. Liberal contributions poured in upon Sarepta. An official visit from Gregor and his wife further served to acquaint the churches with the condition of its affairs, and to give the Brethren at the outpost assurance of adequate aid.

Consolidation of existing work, rather than entrance into new fields, now became the order of the day, though in a certain quarter hopes were at one time entertained of a distinct advance. A new concession received from Frederick the Great in 1781 in favor of the Silesian field proved of particular advantage for the upbuilding of Gnadenfeld, and suggested the idea that from this point the Unity might be of service in the homeland of Moravia. The Edict of Toleration published by Joseph II of Austria in the same year, coupled with the arrival of delegates from the Protestants of Zauchtenthal, gave rise to the hope of reviving the Unity in her ancient seats. But it soon appeared that the Edict allowed of an interpretation which robbed it of value for those who wished to adhere to the discipline of Blahoslav and Comenius. Persons who desired to enjoy the privilege of worshiping in any other mode than that authorized by Rome were required to declare formally to what church they adhered. In this connection the Lutherans and the Reformed were recognized, but by a special decree Bohemian and Moravian Brethren were excluded from the benefits of the Edict. Nothing, therefore, came of the fact that one hundred and fifty thousand persons in Bohemia and Moravia indicated their preference to be considered adherents of the Unitas Fratrum.

From August 1 to October 22, 1782, the twentieth general synod was in session in the castle at Berthelsdorf. Spangenberg presided. Special attention was paid to the *Diaspora* activity. The financial outlook was found to be gradually assuming a more encouraging aspect. A number of communications were presented with regard to the curtailment of the use of the lot, desired in various quarters. Its employment in reference to questions of property was therefore abrogated, but in reference to the marriage of members no change was made. Synod formally ordered that confirmation be insisted upon as a rite to be universally observed preparatory to the first enjoyment of the Holy Communion. Overagainst the spread of Rationalism it was determined to adhere the more faithfully to the language of Scripture.

In the course of years the altered attitude of the theological world towards the Brethren was becoming apparent. The Seminary at Barby enjoyed friendly visits from professors of Halle and Wittenberg; and an active correspondence was exchanged with Leipsic, Wittenberg, Halle, Jena, Tübingen, Giessen, Göttingen, Erlangen and Helmstädt. The former tone of controversy had given place to one of esteem and approval on the part of conservative theologians, manifested in the reception accorded to several of the publications now issued with official sanction—notably Spangenberg's *Idea Fidei Fratrum*, Gregor's Hymn-book and Lieberkühn's Catechism.

Spangenberg's work was intended to place before the ministers and members of the church a scheme of Christian doctrine expressed in biblical language, and to present to its friends a vindication of its scriptural catholicity. Its twenty-four sections set forth the essentials of sound Protestant theology free from one-sided confessionalism. The love of God in Christ is its central theme. The terminology of technical theology gives place to plain biblical language that makes for edification. In the exposition of the sacraments the traditional union-stand-point of the Moravian Church is consistently maintained. The *Idea Fidei* appeared in 1779, and at once won favor amongst clergy and laity beyond as well as within the bounds of the Unity. Struensee, the Danish Minister of religion, wrote of it: "Its contents correspond with my conceptions. I have showed it to various pastors, and all have expressed their satisfaction with it. A famous philosopher at one of the universities in a letter complains to me about the modern theology and adds: 'I even now prefer to read Spangenberg's *Idea*. Of a certainty our posterity must get back their theology from the Moravian Brethren.'" Meeting with a rapid sale, the work won friends for the Brethren in many lands, and effectually removed from them any previously existing suspicions of heterodox faith. In the course of time it was translated into English, Danish, French, Swedish, Dutch, Bohemian and Polish.

Of its companion work, Gregor's Hymn-book, Burkhardt in his *Brüdergemeine* says: "Its author, who had become a member of the Unity in his twentieth year, had grasped its spirit with clearness and warmth, and embodied it in both his music and his hymns. His task was necessitated by the character of the church's life, and its completion supplied a pressing want. The Unity had possessed its own hymn-book since 1735. The hymnal of that year had given expression to the spirit then animating the church. Later it had been enlarged by a number of appendices, each of which in its day reflected the changing characteristics of the Unity. The excrescences of the forties had also found a voice in these appendices, though many a hymn of permanent worth had been also bound up with them. The cautious sobriety of the fifties had renounced the extrava-gant hymnology and prohibited its employment. Zinzendorf while in London had undertaken to provide a new hymnal chastened in tone, which had appeared there in 1753 and 1754. But its bulk rendered it a historical collection of sacred songs, rather than a practically serviceable hymn-book. Moreover, the process of correction had not proceeded with sufficiently far-reaching method. Hence for use in public devotions a compend had appeared under the title *Gesang des Reigens von Saron.* It contained only hymns of Moravian origin, and being in its turn increased by the addition of appendices, served in a most unsatisfactory manner until 1778. A new hymnal was therefore now an absolute and unavoidable necessity. Gregor however accomplished his task so excellently that it remained in use in the churches for a hundred years. He added to the Brethren's own hymns selections that were the collective treasure of evangelical Christians, after the model of the hymnbook of 1735. The whole collection was massed into sixty groups with reference to the festivals of the Christian year and the needs of the religious life. Its year of publication was 1778, and a tune-book by the same author followed in 1784. Both were treasured in the congregations and amongst the *Diaspora* from generation to generation."

The twenty-first general synod convened on June 1, 1789, in Herrnhut. A new departure lay in the fact that the British delegates presented themselves without having been confirmed by lot. Gregor became president, the previous election of Spangenberg having been negatived by the lot. From the outset it was apparent that great differences of opinion existed with reference to the retention and employment of this usage of the church. Great difficulties had arisen in the way of enforcing marriage by lot in the town and country congregations. Hence synod resolved that although the usage should be retained in the "settlements," exceptions might be allowed in the other congregations, such cases to be decided by the local conference in conjunction with the governing conference of the Province. On the mission fields the institution had been introduced only in Greenland, and here it was now to be abolished.

The affairs of the missions were given special prominence. Bishop John Frederick Reichel had little of encouragement to report as a result of his recent visit to the East Indies. Yet indirectly his long journey was to give the initiatve to work elsewhere. During his stay at the Cape of Good Hope he had heard how the Hottentots cherished the memory of George Schmidt. Now it was resolved to open negotiations with the Dutch East Indian Company. Operations were to be begun also on the West Indian island of Tobago. The missions were found to have assumed such proportions, that it was determined to add a fourth department to the Unity's Elders' Conference, to be specifically charged with the superintendence. This board was to reside permanently at Berthelsdorf. As now constituted it consisted of the following: *Missions Departement*, Liebisch, Reichel and Verbeek; *Helfer Departement*, Gregor, Risler, Briant; *Diener und Vorsteher Departement*, Count Henry 28th Reuss, De Watteville, Spangenberg and Sternberg; *Aufseher Departement*, Loretz, Quandt and J. F. Kölbing. Although the general financial situation had improved, a debt of 40,000 thaler was reported in the mission accounts. In a few days, however, 15,000 were received, 10,000 being the gift of Count Reuss. Arrangements were made for issuing quarterly reports of the work for the information of friends of the Brethren's Church in Britain; and thus *Periodical Accounts Relating to Moravian Missions*, probably the oldest periodical devoted wholly to the dissemination of intelligence concerning Protestant missions, came into being. Finally, in order to withdraw candidates for church service from the influence of neighboring universities, tainted with the poison of Rationalism, synod ordered the transfer of the seminary from Barby to Niesky and of the college to Barby.

Special attention was now being paid to two forms of Christian usefulness, the *Diaspora* activity and the schools of the church. The former had reached its zenith. On November 1, 1785, a convention of forty-four of the ministers who were employed in this field assembled at Herrnhut. Fundamental principles for the conduct of the work were formulated and carefully considered instructions drawn up, that the possibility of proselytism might be removed and the wisest means of promoting the culture of Christian character amongst the members of the State Churches employed. The field of operations was divided into twenty districts: 1. Lusatia, centering about Herrnhut, Niesky and Kleinwelke. 2. Silesia, around Gnadenfrei, Gnadenberg, Gnadenfeld and Neusalz. 3. Brandenburg, near Berlin, and Potsdam, in Priegnitz and Altmark. 4. Pommerania, in the vicinity of Stettin, Rügen and Mecklenburg. 5. In East Prussia, Königsberg, Danzig, Elbing, to the borders of Lithuania. 6. The Gnadau district, *i. e.*, Magdeburg, Halberstadt, Altmark, the Harz. 7. Brunswick and Hanover. 8. The Neudietendorf District, *i. e.*, Thuringia. 9. The Ebersdorf District, *i. e.*, Voigtland, the Erzgebirge, Franconia, Upper Palatinate and the Vogelsgebirge. 10. The Neuwied District, the

Palatinate, Wetteravia, etc. 11. The Niederheim District,
Berg, Cleves, etc. 12. The South German, *i. e.*, Württemberg
and Alsace. 13. The Holstein District; Hamburg, Altona and
vicinity. 14. Denmark; Schleswig, Fünen, Copenhagen and
Christiansfeld. 15. Norway; Christiania, Drammen and Ber-
gen. 16. Sweden; Stockholm and Gothenburg. 19. Switzerland; Montmirail, Basel, Berne, Zürich and the Grisons.
20. Holland. The societies in the last two districts only were
amongst the Reformed, the remainder being amongst Lutherans. In the very nature of the case the main results of this
unselfish and unpretentious nurture of spiritual life did not
come to the surface. But, as Burkhardt says, "by means of a
thousand larger and smaller channels of influence, by means
of itinerant preaching and house-to-house visitation, and not
least of all through the circulation of the publications of the
Brethren, true life, warm heart life of living faith, was infused
into the church, and apprehension of the personal fellowship
of the forgiven sinner with the Saviour imparted as a more
precious possession than the mere maintenance of a coldly correct faith of intellect overagainst Rationalism." Intercourse
with the Brethren served as a safeguard for many who wished
to be preserved from having their faith undermined by the
fashionable unbelief of the times, or from being satisfied with
a merely surface appearance of Christian life, the external garb
of a dead supernaturalism. Moreover, whenever revivals of
religion arose beyond their immediate affiliations, as in the
nineties in Württemberg and in the Netz- and Warthe-bruch,
the Brethren gladly lent a hand to serve the awakened with their
counsel and the teaching of their own experience.

In the educational field the leading characteristic was the
hearty acceptance of this trust as carrying with it a responsibility second only to that of the missions themselves. Recognition of this special opportunity to helpfully influence the age
had been connected with the stringency of the post-Zinzendorfian era. Up to the year 1769 provision had been made for
the education of the children of all members of the settlement-
congregations. Gradually the cost was found too heavy to be
carried without some change. The synod of 1769 therefore
ordered the abandonment of the large schools as undertakings
for which the Unity as such was responsible, and relegated the
education of the children to the individual settlements, each

AUGUSTUS GOTTLIEB SPANGENBERG.

being expected to make local provision for its own young people. Only the children of those who were employed in the undertakings of the Unity remained in the schools belonging to the Church as a whole, their education being regarded as part of the compensation due to the parents and as a necessity in the case of those who labored in foreign parts or who were liable to removal from one sphere of activity to another at shortest notice. In order to lighten the financial burden various congregations threw open their parochial schools to the children of others than members, making provision for board as well as tuition. This process of development marked the years 1776-1782. For sons of friends a college was founded at Uhyst on the Spree in 1784. It attained to particular eminence in the years from 1787 to 1791. Baron Peter von Hohenthal, Vice-President of the Upper Consistory at Dresden, accepted the position of President. The beginning, like most beginnings, was attended with difficulty. But after a change in personnel, when at Easter, 1787, John Hartley, Renatus Frueauff and John Christlieb Mahler, gifted teachers, joined forces in its behalf, the change for the better speedily followed.

Meantime the old leaders were one by one passing away. In 1775, Waiblinger; in 1776, Godfrey Clemens; in 1777, Count Dohna, the husband of Agnes von Zinzendorf; Frederick de Watteville, Cranz, Lieberkühn, Frederick Wenceslaus Neisser and Count Sigismund Augustus von Gersdorf; in 1778, John Henry von Zezschwitz; in 1779, David Nitschmann the Syndic and Jonas Paulus Weiss; in 1781, Melchior Zeisberger; in 1783, John Nitschmann, jr., and Grasmann; in 1785, Henry von Bruyningk and George Schmidt; in 1786, John Frederick Köber; in 1788, Anthony von Lüdecke, Paul Eugene Layritz and John de Watteville—entered into their rest. An event which aroused liveliest sympathy throughout the church was the departure of Spangenberg at Berthelsdorf, 88 years of age, on September 18, 1792. The last time he officiated at a public service had been in connection with the festival of November 13 at Herrnhut, the fiftieth anniversary of the experiences of the synodical conference in London. On that occasion he delivered an address full of feeling and power, although he had to be led to the place from which he spoke. He had spent sixty years of labor for the Unity, to which he had rendered services second only to those of Zinzendorf.

CHAPTER XXVIII.

Periods of transition are not usually characterized by prominent evidences of advance. Rearrangement and readjustment
imply a staying of those forces which condition visible progres-
sion, though the while there may be unseen gatherings of ac-
cumulated resources that shall burst forth with all the greater
vigor after favorable conditions shall have at last secured for
them a less hampered working out of their destiny. With the
gradual abrogation of the essential features of the "Economy,"
the Brethren's Church in America was entering upon a period
of transition which was to last for upwards of a century; for
until exclusivism had been completely put aside it remained of
necessity something of an exotic on American soil. Not that
growth was wholly absent; but what growth there was lacked
system and design.

In the period immediately following the return of Spangenberg and Böhler to Europe Bishops Seidel and Hehl, together
with Von Marschall as general warden, were charged with the
leadership. Seidel's career had given him wide experience.
Born at Lauban in Silesia, in 1718, he had fled to Herrnhut on
reaching his majority, and had come to Pennsylvania as a member of the "First Sea Congregation." Active as an itinerant
evangelist, he had assisted also in the Indian mission. From
Massachusetts to Maryland, and from Long Island to the junction of the west and north branches of the Susquehanna, he
had journeyed on foot, carrying the gospel to all sorts and conditions of men. Besides making visits to Europe on business
of the church, he had twice inspected the work in the West
Indies, had participated in the Moravian colonization of North
Carolina, and had been one of three to visit the Governor of
Surinam and negotiate for a renewal of temporarily suspended

operations there. His wife, Anna Joanna Piesch, the niece of Anna Nitschmann, had formerly enjoyed intimate association with Count Zinzendorf and the circle of his immediate coadjutors. Marschall, born near Dresden in 1721, had been destined for the military profession, his father being commandant of the garrison at Stolpe and later of the important fortress of Königstein, the key to the upper Elbe. Whilst a student at Leipsic he had been attracted to the Brethren's Church. His fields of service had been in Holland and in England, where his business ability had been displayed in helping to disentangle the imperilled finances.

One of the features of the American activity was the inauguration of a church academy. In 1755 and 1756 a spacious stone building, known as "Nazareth Hall," had been erected at Nazareth as a manor house for Count Zinzendorf, whose return to America was then expected. Since 1759 it had been devoted to educational purposes. Of this school Francis Lembke became principal in 1763. A student at Strasburg and Jena, he had been appointed a professor in the *gymnasium* of the former city in 1735. Resigning in 1746 in order to unite with the Brethren, he had occupied various posts in Germany and England previous to coming to America in 1754. Most gratifying results attended his first efforts in connection with the school, its pupils at one time numbering one hundred and six. But the financial straits of the church necessitated its suspension in 1779.

Other obstacles thwarted both educational and evangelistic activity. The representatives of high contracting powers might solemnly meet and negotiate terms of peace in Europe, but their signatures to the stipulations at Paris did not necessarily quiet the perturbations of the western world. Pontiac had been dreaming of the utter extinction or expulsion of the English, and his designs should be checked by no treaty to which his allies, the French, were committed. In May, 1763, the rising of the red-men, which was to have swept from Detroit to the ocean, began with the siege of that frontier fortress by the wily Ottawa in person. Though the staunchness of Gladwyn foiled him, Sandusky, Fort St. Joseph, Fort Miami, Michilimackinac, Presqu' Isle, and Fort Venango fell into the hands of the savages, and Fort Pitt was beleagured. Many of the settlements of Western Pennsylvania were ravaged. Bouquet's expedition, sent to cover the western border of the colony, encountered desperate foes, and only after well-nigh repeating Braddock's experience reached Fort Pitt with relief. Now the exasperated frontiersmen of the Susquehanna resorted to bloody retaliation, directing their fury against the friendly and civilized tribesmen near the settlements, and the massacre of the Conestoga Indians stained the annals of Pennsylvania. Prior to this the colonial authorities had entertained fears for the Moravian Indians at Nain and Wechquetank. Dreading a counterpart of the Conestoga massacre at their villages, Governor Penn had therefore already ordered the Moravian Indians to be removed to Philadelphia for safety, together with their missionaries, Zeisberger, Grube, Schmick and Roth. Excitement ran high in the city. Members of the Society of Friends setting aside their peace principles in the conflict of duties, took arms to defend their charges against whom the frontiersmen swore vengeance. For a time the lives of the missionaries and of their converts appeared to be in serious danger. But actual strife was providentially averted, though the arrangements for their sustenance at Province Island, the summer-quarantine of the port, were distressingly inadequate, and the evidences of insecurity and of possible inability to protect them led to an attempt to remove them to New York. Thither they proceeded under escort. But when Perth Amboy was reached they were stopped by a peremptory inhibition of further advance, and had to retrace their weary steps. Returned to Philadelphia, the barracks were assigned as their quarters. Now came a rumor that men from Lancaster and Reading were marching on the capital, bent on having the lives of the Moravian Indians. Philadelphia surged with excitement, a large part of the people sympathizing with the Paxton party. Again blows were averted by the determined position of the Governor and his associates, backed by the sober treaty-respecting majority. But terrible distress was experienced by the Indians and their teachers in their cramped quarters and from the unnatural mode of life. Confinement enfeebled them. Dysentery and small-pox broke out. From January, 1764, to March, 1765, fifty-six victims of barrack life were laid in the Potter's Field.

For the American branch of the church the year 1765 was further rendered noteworthy by a visit of David Nitschmann the Syndic, as representative of the directing board in Germany.

One of his first duties was to convene a synod at Bethlehem, May 30 to June 4, characterized by the enthusiasm with which the thirty-three ministers and fourteen lay delegates—one of them an Indian—received his report of the transactions of the synod of 1764. Recent awakenings were also reported as attendant upon the itinerations in Jersey and in New England. At Newport, Rhode Island, where a congregation had been organized in 1758, in conection with the transit of missionaries to the West Indies, a new church had been built. At Broadbay, in Maine, George Soelle had effected an organization in 1762, consisting chiefly of Germans from the Palatinate acquainted with the Brethren in their old home. But the most important advance had been the founding of the central town in Wachovia. Marschall had been dispatched to take charge of affairs there in 1763, and had platted the town next spring, giving it the name Salem according to the wish of Zinzendorf. Salem was destined to be the Bethlehem of North Carolina, and speedily assumed fair proportions through the influx of colonists from Europe. Marschall's associate in the management of affairs here was John Ettwein, who also devoted himself to evangelistic labors, itinerating as far south as Georgia.

From October 20 to 23, 1768, a synod was in session at Lititz, at which Bishop Hehl presided. It became notable as the last convention of a legislative body in the American division of the church under the arrangements of the old constitution. Owing to the principles of centralization, adopted at Marienborn in the following year, eighty-one years were to pass before an American synod should convene.

Changes in connection with the holding of title to congregation property also ensued. In 1770 Christian Gregor, John Loretz and Hans Christian Alexander von Schweinitz were commissioned to visit the American congregations in order to carry into effect the resolutions which had been adopted. Von Schweinitz had been appointed administrator of the property in America which belonged to the Unitas Fratrum as such, and at the same time was to be the representative of the governing board in the American executive committee, known by various titles since the abrogation of the Economy and last of all as the *Oeconomats Conferenz*. A settlement was to be effected between the American estates belonging to the Unity as a whole and the property of the individual congregations. The nego-

17

tiations were protracted through the next five years. Typical of the agreements was that with the congregation at Bethlehem, in accordance with which it acquired from the Unity almost four thousand acres of land and the houses and business concerns yet belonging to the church by assuming $87,000 of the debt of the Unity, and by agreeing to pay annually a certain sum towards the defrayal of the joint expenses of the American branch of the church, included in what was now known as the American Sustentation Diacony.

In 1771 the three commissioners visited Wachovia, dissolved the local Economy, and organized an executive committee distinct from that in Pennsylvania. Thus a transfer of titles was providentially effected just before the storm of war broke, and serious complications were averted.

In both divisions of the American field attempts at extension also preceded the outbreak of hostilities. In the latter part of November, 1774, the site for a settlement was surveyed not far from the present town of Oxford, in New Jersey, on land purchased from Samuel Green, a member of the church who had previously offered it as a gift. At first known as Greenland, its name was soon changed to Hope. During the years 1773 and 1775 Friedberg and Friedland were commenced in Wachovia. To these new clearings in the sunny South-land the Broadbay members moved practically as one united body, glad to leave the bleak ruggedness of Maine. On the invitation of Mr. Knox, Under-Secretary of State in London, in 1774 Lewis Müller and John George Wagner were sent to his estate at Knoxborough in Georgia to attempt to renew missionary labor in harmony with the first purpose of the Brethren in coming to America. Early next year Andrew Brösing from Wachovia joined them in their effort to bring the gospel to the slaves, and preaching was commenced at the neighboring estate of Silkhope also. But Müller died of fever in November, and the incipient conflicts of the struggle for national independence rendered the situation hopeless. Brösing returned to Wachovia and Wagner to England.

The Indian mission in the North was acquiring new importance. At the end of the Pontiac War there was no reason why the Moravian Indians should not be released from their virtual imprisonment in Philadelphia. But whither should they go? Public opinion in its exasperated state would not discriminate in favor of these Christianized Delawares. The government felt obliged to insist on their removal beyond the territory long ago ceded to the colony. Nain and Wechquetank must be permanently abandned. The Indians themselves desired to secure new homes in the wilderness at such a remove from the whites as might promise immunity from future encroachments. At this juncture Papunhank who had been baptized by Zeisberger in 1763, proposed that, government permitting, the entire band of converts should proceed with him to his sheltered little valley where the Wyalusing leaps dashing and foaming to join the mighty Susquehanna. The proposal won the consent of all concerned. Early in April, 1765, eighty-three persons, including a few from the once flourishing Pachgatgoch, a mission that never really recovered from the effects of the war, though its existence was protracted till 1770, set out from Bethlehem for their new home. David Zeisberger and John Jacob Schmick accompanied them. The toilsome and perilous march across the mountains and through the unbroken and often swampy wilderness occupied five weary weeks. For food dependence had to be placed largely upon the finding of game, and sometimes the supply almost failed. Roads had to be made and streams bridged. A woman and a boy succumbed to the hardships of the exodus. Permission to occupy the site of the old village was obtained from the Iroquois of Cayuga who claimed the valley of the Susquehanna to this point, Zeisberger's adoption into their nation being a powerful plea. At a slight remove from the former site a permanent town was platted, and named *Friedenshütten* (Tents of Peace), outpost of the Prince of Peace amongst the warring tribes of savages and a refuge for the "brown hearts" who had roved so long against their own desire. In September, 1776, Zeisberger was compelled to proceed with Senseman to Onondaga, in order to avert a threatened disavowal of the grant of the Cayugas on the part of the Iroquois council. He was eminently successful. The council distinctly recognized and approved of the purposes of the missionaries. He himself was invited to become a respected resident at the Indian capital, as in former days. But the church found itself unable to reënter upon missions amongst the powerful confederation of the Six Nations, and Zeisberger's activity was to be henceforth confined to the Delawares.

Meanwhile John Roth, a Brandenburger in his fortieth year, had been sent to assist Schmick at Friedenshütten. Their labors as those of Zeisberger previously, were richly blessed. The settlement itself was an admirable object lesson of the thrift and industry which accompanied the civilizing power of the gospel, and at the same time seeds of truth were scattered in many a direction by the impressions made upon frequent visitors from many tribes, for the place lay on the main trail from the Iroquois towns to the Indians of the south. In 1769 Roth and his wife removed to Schechschiquanink, a Delaware town twenty-four miles to the north and on the opposite bank of the river. From this filial Friedenshütten received accessions, and here Roth won a number of converts. John George Jungmann, once a hearer of Eschenbach at Oley, and his wife, a daughter of Büttner of Shekomeko, filled the vacancy at Wyalusing.

Zeisberger had been assigned pioneer work. With Anthony, the Mohican, and Papunhank he had set out for the forests of the present Venango County. Goschgoschünk, a Muncie town, founded only two years before, was their objective. Its reputation was extremely unsavory even amongst the heathen, past whose scanty lodges they had to thread their way. Some of its braves had figured in the massacre on the Mahoni in 1755. His first address at this spot was a thrilling experience. In the long council-hall of bark the ruddy glow of the central fires lit up dusky faces that gleamed with hate. But the power of the truth, and the eloquence of the veteran missionary, more than the equal of the average Delaware orator in his own sonorous tongue, commanded attention, and secured immunity. On his return next year trophies were won for the gospel. Yet the place proved a veritable stronghold of Satan. Though the medicine man who had been loudest in his opposition, Wagonmen, suffered his lodge to be converted into a church when an attempt was made to found a mission, the wily fellow was far from having experienced a change of heart, and in time resumed open hostility. Gradually the people divided into a Christian and a heathen party. Life became so unbearable for the converts, that in 1769 a new site was selected for their village three miles above, at Lawmakhannek, on the eastern bank of the river Allegheny.

Now an invitation came through Glikkikan, a sachem renowned for sagacity and eloquence, hitherto a champion of heathenism, but recently impressed by what he had heard on a visit to Goschgoschünk. In the name of the supreme chief of the Wolf clan of the Delawares, Packanke, he promised the missionary and his converts land at Kaskaskunk, at the junction of the Shenango and the Mahoni, for their exclusive and undisturbed possession. The invitation was accepted. In April, 1770, the journey was made in fifteen canoes by way of the Allegheny, the Ohio and the Beaver, and Friedensstädt was founded on the last named river. Now the triumph of the gospel was signalized by the accession of certain of the former heathen party from Goschgoschünk whose wickedness had become a reproach even to their own people, and by the conversion of Glikkikan himself. Veteran warrior though he was, this rebutter of the Jesuits in former days, who had baffled Post and whose native gability had been counted upon as a main stay of the heathen, sobbed like a child, when the love of Christ touched his proud heart. Unflinchingly he not only bore the passionate reproaches of his chief, Packanke, but even interposed to avert from the white teachers the wrath of the old Wolf. Next spring Zeisberger with several Indians, Glikkikan included, by invitation visited the Delawares of the Tuscarawas River in Ohio and preached before their council in the home of Netawatwes (King Newcomer), the recognized head of the nation.

By June, 1771, Friedenshütten numbered one hundred members. But troubles were at hand. Though the Iroquois had solemnly ratified the grant of land on the Wyalusing, at the treaty of Fort Stanwix, in November, 1768, they had sold it to Pennsylvania. John Penn had recognized the validity of the verbal grant to the mission and its Indians, and instructed his surveyors to run no lines within five miles of Friendenshütten. But an artful Delaware, Job Chilloway, to whom the government was under obligation for sundry services in the Pontiac War, represented to the authorities that he had been empowered by the Moravian Indians to ask for a survey of Wyalusing, to secure their rights. Hence the tenure of the land threatened to involve disputes. At this juncture an invitation from the Grand Council of the Delawares in the Tuscarawas Valley, that their Christian brothers should come and occupy lands in Ohio, accompanied as it was with the assurance that these should

never be "sold under their feet to the white people," was gratefully accepted. Zeisberger recommended the removal thither of
all the converts from Pennsylvania. To this the western station also assented. Netawatwes proposed as a site "The Big
Spring" beside the Tuscarawas.

John Heckewelder, whose acquaintance with the Delawares
dated from his residence with Post near the present Bolivar in
Stark County, Ohio, in 1762, was appointed to coöperate with
Zeisberger and his colleagues. This reënforcement left the
veteran free to lead an advance party to the Tuscarawas in the
spring of 1772, to prepare for the arrival of the main body. The
luxuriance of the forests and the rich fertility of the bottom-
lands as well as the copious gush of water from the "Big
Spring" delighted the first comers. Late in the summer Zeisberger returned to Friedensstädt and welcomed the people from
the Susquehanna, two hundred and four souls who arrived in
two companies under the leadership of Bishop Ettwein and
Roth respectively. Then leaving Roth in charge of Friedensstädt, they made their way to their new home to which they
gave the fitting name of *Schönbrunn* ("Beautiful Spring"). Next
year the converts on the Beaver also took the western trail. A
second station was commenced about ten miles down the valley, designed originally for the remnant of the Mohican congregations. Later it received the name of Gnadenhütten, to
perpetuate the memory of the spot on the Mahoni, rendered
sacred by the martyrdom of missionaries. Four years from
the removal to the west a third station was begun in the present
Coshocton County, and named *Lichtenau* (Meadow of Light);
but was abandoned three years later owing to its being in the
track of incessant war-parties. In its place Salem was commenced, five miles below Gnadenhütten.

Now the mission seemed to have been at last placed on a
permanent basis. Netawatwes came out on the side of Christianity. Numerous bands of Indians from all parts visited the
Christian settlements. Its influence spreading far and wide,
the mission promised to achieve a mighty change amongst the
"People of the wandering eye and the roving foot." The church
at Schönbrunn, although able to accommodate five hundred persons, often proved too small. The six missionaries whose devoted lives were as powerfully eloquent a testimony as their
words, found abundant opportunity to offer the gift of grace.

Civilization advanced. Several hundred acres were under cultivation. Large herds of cattle were maintained. Non-combatant principles were an inseparble part of the religion of the converts. It seemed as though the true solution of the Indian problem was to enjoy an opportunity of being demonstrated to the world. But, alas! cruel war again obstructed the chariot of the Prince of Peace.

CHAPTER XXIX.

That some confusion of conceptions should have followed the
formative synod of 1769, with its leaning to centralization in the
general administration of the Unity's polity, was not unnatural.
When the skepticism of Bolingbroke and Hume, filtering
through the ranks of the educated, and affecting only too many
of the clergy of the establishment with an indifference to the
Thirty-nine Articles, summoned every organization possessed
of vital Christianity to contend earnestly for the faith once delivered to the saints, and come to the rescue of the masses, men
like Hutton, La Trobe, Okely and Seifferth perceived no reason why the Brethren in Britain should not multiply their organizations as occasion and opportunity might offer. On the
other hand, upon the members of the Unity's Elders' Conference the practical problem of indebtedness, which some of the
British would have answered by a reference to Matthew 6:33,
was pressing so sorely that they discountenanced too rapid an
extension of the work. Furthermore, accustomed to the legal
limitations that had been thrown around the continental activity, and laying stress upon the importance of Christian unity,
viewing the Unitas Fratrum not so much as a distinct church
as a federation of members of various churches, they insisted
that the evangelistic activity in Britain and Ireland must proceed on lines parallel to those of the continental *Diaspora*. For
their part, too, they were also not wholly satisfied with the manner and measure of effort put forth in England for the extin-
guishment of the Unity's indebtedness. The situation involved
easy possibilities of disharmony. In the end, indeed, loyalty
to the Unity prevailed over every other consideration. But
in the effort to avoid denominationalism the Unity's Elders'
Conference in pursuance of a natural interpretation of the **legislation** of the synod, by an insistence upon the subordination of

the life and activity of the church in all its parts unintentionally prevented a development of the Unity in conformity with national traits and circumstances and impressed the cast of a foreign body upon the Brethren's Church in Britain and in America, with denominationalism and the crippling of energies as a result.

Nevertheless the vigorous evangelistic activity of the British Brethren continued. More than forty preaching-places were served in Scotland from the center at Ayr, Wade and Caries being the chief evangelists. The latter, although a foreigner, had been for years associated with Cennick in Ireland, and had been active in the "Cheshire Plan," and this previous experience together with his natural gifts as a speaker fitted him to be a successor of Caldwell. In Yorkshire, Lancashire, Cheshire and Derby vigorous prosecution of the itinerancy was still the order of the day. In the Midlands a noteworthy advance was made by Francis Okely, in laying the corner-stone of a place of worship at Northampton, on August 31, 1769. Here a small society was organized with filials at the neighboring towns of Culworth, Eydon and Towcester.

To remove mutual misunderstandings and promote closer connection with the work in Britain, Count Reuss and then Peter Böhler were temporarily transferred to England in 1772 and 1773.

A providential instrument as he had been in the conversion of John Wesley, it must have been a source of gratification to Böhler that the estrangement of the Brethren and the Methodists was waning away. In its place had come something of the true fellowship which was to be expected from the community of interests between the two bodies overagainst the unbelief and worldliness which were still only too prevalent throughout society at large. The two Wesleys had laid aside their old ill-will, and Bishop Gambold and Benjamin La Trobe had visited and addressed the theological seminary at Trevecca, in charge of Howell Harris, Cennick's former coadjutor, and now of Lady Huntingdon's connection, to mutual satisfaction.

Böhler's activity was now drawing to an end. On April 20, 1773, whilst preparing to conduct a service in Fetter Lane, a sudden stroke became his summons, and he died on the 27th. He was in his sixty-third year.

In the Irish congregations, hampered by straightened circumstances and keenly feeling the animosity of neighbors, Count Reuss found much opportunity to give counsel. In Dublin a step forward was taken in the securing of a second place of worship, on Stafford Street, in 1769. But lack of encouragement in results led to its abandonment in 1777, when all effort was concentrated at Bishop Street. During the insurrection of the *Hearts of Steel*, a turbulent outbreak against absentee landlordism, Gracehill was in special danger. A party of these rebels approached the settlement and held their nocturnal meetings in its immediate vicinity. In 1772 they made a sudden attack upon the place. Surrounding the home of the unmarried men, they fired at the windows and demanded arms. Observing a light in one of the rooms, they poured their shots in and wounded a brother in the face. Thence they proceeded to the chapel and tried to open the windows with their bayonets. The warden of the congregation, Daniel Gottwald, opened the door and asked them what they wanted. Pointing a gun at him, the leader of the rebels said: "You have taken away the land from its former possessors, and we are come to lay everything waste with fire and sword and drive you away. But as you are a man of some consideration, whose opinion has much weight, we thought it right first to acquaint you with our intention." The reply of the warden and his promise to procure for them within a fortnight a document from Dublin, proving that the land had been legally purchased by the Brethren and all demands of its former occupier satisfied, secured from the captain a pledge of delay. Then the rebels proceeded to the establishment of the unmarried women. A furious altercation ensued between them and their captain, because he would not consent to their proposed attack. At last he succeeded in dissuading them, and they departed without doing any further damage. Gottwald's letter to the Brethrens' minister in Dublin was presented to Lord O'Neill, the proprietor of the land, and he laid it before Parliament. Effective measures for quelling the insurrection were soon adopted, and tranquility was restored to the land.

CHAPTER XXX.

THE CHURCH IN AMERICA FROM 1775 TO 1792.

Scarcely had the Moravians in America accustomed themselves to the new regulations introduced by Gregor, Loretz and Von Schweinitz, when mutterings of approaching strife were heard. The signal lights flashed from the steeple of the Old North Church. Lexington, Concord and Bunker Hill proclaimed to the world that a war and no mere riot was on the hands of the ministers of King George. At the beginning of the contest the majority of the Brethren entertained conservative sentiments or refused to take sides. Non-combatants from conscientious convictions, they had no special interest in the principle "No taxation without representation;" *Magna Charta* had no deep significance to the great majority of them, of other than English birth; in their former homes *Habeas Corpus* was unknown; they had personally received no wrongs from government; rather in 1749 and since Britain had laid them under tribute of gratitude; and above all this they were citizens of the world in so true a sense and to such a degree through their readiness to follow their Master's commission, that it seemed to them of comparatively little moment under what civil authorities they lived. Wherever they found themselves in the pursuit of their calling they endeavored to lead a quiet and peaceable life in obedience to the laws and in submission to the powers providentially holding sway. To meddle in politics of any sort was foreign to their disposition. After a time they did come to perceive and accept the independence of the colonies as a providential development of affairs, and farseeing men like Von Schweinitz appreciated and espoused the colonists' position at a very early stage.

One immediate effect of the outbreak of hostilities was the cessation of evangelistic itineracies. Communication between the congregations became very difficult and uncertain. After the alliance with France serious inconvenience also arose from the difficulty of corresponding with the authorities of the church in Europe. Von Marschall, who had been sent as a delegate to the synod of 1775, could not return until 1778. No Americans could participate in the synod of 1782. Heavy losses were sustained by members of the church in Philadelphia, New York, Staten Island and Newport, many of whom abandoned their homes, and fled to secluded districts.

The burden of administration fell mainly upon John Ettwein, the assistant of Bishop Seidel, owing to the latter's advanced age. Born on June 29, 1721, at Freundenstadt, in Württemberg, he had joined the church in 1739 at Marienborn, and had served in various capacities. In 1750 he had been sent to England, and was called to Pennsylvania in the spring of 1754. From 1758 to 1766 his field of labor had been in the south, Since then he had stood at the side of Seidel in Bethlehem. Although a Tory at first, his sturdy honesty, fearless courage, Christian self-abnegation, and strong native good sense, Moravian Franklin that he was, now secured him the friendship and esteem of a number of the leaders of the patriots—Henry Laurens, Samuel Adams, John Hancock and George Washington in particular. From intercourse with him these men learnt to appreciate the standpoint of the Brethren, and to perceive that there was no unwillingness to bear a full share of taxation and other burdens, and to minister to the wounded and suffering, even though conscientious scruples stood in the way of actual shouldering of arms.

From December 3, 1776, to March 27, 1777, and from September, 1777, to June, 1778, the General Hospital of the American Army was established in Bethlehem; and from December 19, 1777, to August 28, 1778, Lititz rendered similar services. From August, 1777, to March, 1778, Hessian prisoners of war were confined in the Hebron church. In the Bethlehem hospital, where the mortality was very high owing to contagious fevers, Ettwein served as volunteer chaplain. Lafayette was nursed in a private home in this settlement after the Battle of Brandywine. In February, 1777, Bethlehem became the depot of the military stores of the American army, and it was found that vey few towns in the interior could supply all manner of needs so adequately from home manufactures, thanks to the de-

Etwein Episc

velopment of very diversified industries during the period of the Economy.

But the peculiar position in which they were placed by their principles involved the Brethren in many difficulties and brought on them a heavy financial burden. With their repugnance to oaths, for them the Test Act of 1777 filled the air with storms. At one time there was reason to fear that their refusal might jeopardize the title to their properties. Accordingly in 1778 Ettwein presented petitions to Congress when in session at York, and to the Assembly of Pennsylvania at Lancaster, asking to have the Moravians excepted from its requirements. Only after several weeks of further effort in Philadelphia in 1779 he at last won his object. But the Act had already occasioned great distress. For example, on April 4, 1778, twelve members of the Emmaus congregation were imprisoned at Easton, and were kept on bread and water till the 29th because they refused to take the oath; and in September thirteen others repeated the experience.

Conscientious scruples with respect to military service called for further pecuniary sacrifices. When the Brethren in Northampton County were notified by due process of law that unless all men above sixteen years of age presented themselves at Easton on a certain day for military duty, they would be taxed three pounds three shillings for each man between the ages of sixteen and fifty, they resolved to pay the tax rather than do military duty. At one time the fines thus imposed upon seven amounted to two hundred and ninety-four pounds. At another time eight men were mulcted to the sum of four hundred and one pounds. Not all the Brethren appreciated the need of resisting such arguments. Towards the close of the war certain Brethren went to Easton to be enrolled without the consent of their authorities, and were severely reprimanded and in several cases excluded from membership. But as time wore on the sentiments of the younger men underwent a marked change, and by them the new order of things was accepted with satisfaction. Similar experiences were made in the South, where Moravian lands narrowly escaped confiscation, and much anxiety was lived through especially just before and after the Battle of Guilford Court-house.

Meantime, notwithstanding the unsettled state of the country, the development of inner congregational life required attention. With a pass secured from the British authorities that might insure freedom from molestation at sea, and with letters of recommendation to Franklin from his old friends Hutton and Spangenberg that the journey on land might not be prohibited after a prosperous voyage, Bishop Reichel reached Bethlehem in April, 1779, commissioned to adjust the American affairs of the church to the enactments of the synod of 1775, and to give comfort and counsel to his Brethren. On August 5 he convened a conference of ministers at Lititz, at which his work was mapped out. The very fact that it was a conference of ministers, and not a synod constituted of ministers and representative of the congregations as had hitherto invariably obtained in the American branch of the church, was in itself suggestive. The era of centralization had already begun, and it could scarcely have been inaugurated at a time less propitious for the future of the Moravian Church in America. "No taxation without representation" had been the rallying cry of the colonies now emerging into sovereign statehood. The fateful experiences of the period of strife had taught the entire population, even sections of it most removed from active participation in politics, that a world of meaning lay in that principle. Home rule, from the town-meeting up, was seen to be fundamental to American life. Could a worse time have been chosen for limiting to the clergy the right of even authoritatively discussing church methods, and for constraining even their action to accommodate itself to a mold that had been rigidly framed in a land where circumstances differed *toto coelo*, and framed, too, without the consent of men who were now to live according to these regulations? Had Ettwein and his associates received a freedom of operation even measurably corresponding to that enjoyed by Asbury and Coke, or Seabury and White and Provoost, the future of the Moravian Church in America would have assumed a different form. But just at the time when the Methodist and Protestant Episcopalian Churches were making provision for natural activity and expansion, the tendency to ultra-centralization in the Moravian Church caused it to ignore the boundless opportunities in America which carried with them proportionate responsibilities. What was in accordance with the mode and spirit of the settlement congregations in European lands, that lacked absolute liberty of religion, was taken to be in and of itself the supreme object of all efforts under any and every set of conditions. As in England, the scrupulous endeavor to secure only an unquestionably regenerate membership, coupled with the notion that the choir-system and the regulations of the settlement-congregations were exclusively the wisest methods unvaryingly to be applied for the attainment of this desired end, caused an ignoring of the bearing of the parable of the talents upon a church in its relationship to a land still scantily supplied with a gospel-ministry. Subjective, introspective, quietistic devotion to the culture of their own spiritual life appears to have distorted the Brethren's apprehension of the great commission, which demands a beginning at Jerusalem, however loyal men may be in reference to the claims of the regions beyond. In fact they now passed to the extreme of repudiating any purpose to organize new congregations. They decided that "in no sense shall the societies of awakened persons affiliated as the fruit of the former extensive itinerations be regarded as preparatory to the organization of congregations, and that membership in these societies does not at all carry with it communicant membership or preparation for it." They carefully explained that these people have been grouped into societies, "because their attachment to the Brethren had caused their exclusion from the communions of which they had been formerly adherents. Our Brethren have therefore refrained from administering the sacraments amongst them." Had this conception of the church's calling prevailed during the previous forty years, Bethlehem, Nazareth and the congregations in Wachovia would have been almost the only congregations in America. If the other organizations were legitimate, their very existence should have shown the falsity of the theory now to dominate the life of the church in America for half a century.

After this conference at Lititz, Bishop Reichel at great personal inconvenience visited almost all the scenes of the church's activity, North and South, David Zeisberger moreover coming to Bethlehem to report to him concerning the missions in Ohio. Then in April, 1781, he convened a second conference of ministers to sum up for them the impressions of his visit. The most important transaction was the adoption of the Brotherly Agreement as a fundamental bond of union incorporated into the statutes of the various congregations.

With' the death of Bishop Seidel on May 12, 1782, the responsible leadership more than ever devolved upon Ettwein, the finances being administered by Von Schweinitz. In August Bishop Graff died at Salem. Hehl, the only surviving representative of the Moravian episcopate in America, was now in his seventy-eighth year. Ettwein's consecration, which naturally followed, was delayed until the arrival of Bishop John de Watteville in 1784, on an official visit to America. He and his wife experienced the perils of the deep when on their way. "They took ship at Amsterdam and put to sea on September 27, 1783. In the beginning of November, when off the coast of America, a series of storms set in which made it impossible to reach New York. They beat about in utter helplessness, provisions and water began to fail, most of the sails were torn, the principal anchor was lost, and the ship itself very much strained. In January of 1784 they steered for the West Indies. Watteville and his wife lived for weeks on hard biscuits and beer. The supply of water was entirely exhausted, until a copious rain replenished their casks. About the middle of February they at last reached the West Indies; but in the night of the 17th the vessel struck a reef off the island of Barbuda and was lost. The passengers and crew took to the boats. In descending Bishop de Watteville missed his hold and fell into the sea. He was rescued by two sailors with great difficulty. After many escapes the entire ship's company reached the land. The Governor of Barbuda took Bishop de Watteville and the Countess into his own house and showed them great kindness. They had been on ship-board one hundred and forty-four days, and had suffered intensely. In the European and American churches great anxiety prevailed on their account, and many believed that they were lost. They remained in the West Indies for several months and then sailed to the United States, where they arrived in safety, reaching Bethlehem on June 2."

Bishop de Watteville's stay in America lasted three years. His duties were responsible and delicate. He was commissioned to communicate to the American congregations an account of the transactions of the synod of 1782. It had been the more unfortunate that it was not possible for American delegates to be present, because complaint had been made of the lack of church-spirit in the American congregations from an official point of view. From an American point of view in the present century, it appears unfortunate, however, that just at the present juncture this synod more than ever encouraged painfully repressive confinement of effort to the development of a quietist type of piety amongst the members of the exclusive settlements by the most minute regulations. Even the town and country congregations were, if possible, to be constrained into conformity with the details of rigidly regulated life and ritual which characterized the settlements. Recourse was to be had to the decision of the lot not only in connection with the marriage of members, but also in deciding applications for communicant membership, and in various other contingencies. The support of the work of the church was derived from the proceeds of business enterprises carried on for its benefit, rather than from the voluntary gifts of the people.*

---

* Glimpses at the characteristic features of life in a number of congregations, afforded by the records of the conference of ministers at Lititz in 1790 illustrate the effects of this policy. In connection with Graceham there are 150 souls, of whom only sixty are communicants. Lancaster, with 330 persons in connection, has only seventy-two communicants. Brother Meder, of Philadelphia, has a membership of 176, but only 38 communicants. He reports that the English services are well attended, but there is no increase in membership. The *Sprechen* — obligatory visits paid by the members individually to the pastor at stated intervals for close and searching religious conversation—are not the success that might be desired. Very few of the Society members comply with this requirement. At Oldmanscreek, in Jersey, Brother Franz Böhler reports a lack of *Gemeinverstand*. Few children attend the school. The Society does not grow. He has 168 members, only thirty-seven of whom are communicants. There is a preaching-place midway between his charge and Philadelphia, which is occasionally served by Brother Meder and himself. Brother Möhring, of Staten Island, has to report that his people will not come to the *Sprechen*, especially not the Society members. The occurrence of disorders at funerals on the Island is lamented. They are too often made the occasion for social festivity. He stands in fraternal relationship to the Episcopalians and Methodists of the vicinity. He has 120 members, of whom twenty are communicants. Concerning Gnadenhütten, on the Mahoning, Brother Schmidt must deplore that the choir-services are not attended. Amongst the seventy-two persons in his charge there are thirty-one communicants. Brother Roth, of Emmaus, can give his congregation the credit of approaching most closely to the norm of an *Ortsgemeine* (settlement-congregation). The people living near together, daily services can be maintained. He has 144 members, seventy-four being children. The communicants number fifty-one. Schoeneck, begun in 1762, is not yet wholly detached from Nazareth, and is still under the supervision of the elders' conference of that settlement. Brother Ellert Coortsen, however, is schoolmaster and has pastoral oversight there. Preaching is had only at intervals, the people generally attending the Nazareth church. The choir regulations are in good condition. As to the Society members much can not be said—*etwas schlecht*. Of the 144 members only sixty-six

18

Yet if there seems to be failure to grasp the opportunities of the times and a lack of adaptation to the needs and spirit of the land, there are tokens of life in some directions. The rapid advancement of Nazareth Hall Academy for boys, reopened in 1785 by Charles Gotthold Reichel, who with his family had arrived from Germany in the preceding year, and the even greater growth of the Seminary for Young Ladies at Bethlehem under John Andrew Huebener, necessitating a new building in 1789, are very noteworthy.

Moreover the year 1787 was marked by the resuscitation at Bethlehem of the old missionary society of 1745, under the title of "The Society for Propagating the Gospel among the Heathen." Its first meeting was held September 21, Ettwein being President, Hans Christian Alexander von Schweinitz, Treasurer, and Jacob Van Vleck Secretary, with a total membership of ninety-three. In his address at a general meeting of the society, held on November 1, Bishop Ettwein defined its object in substance as follows: "Every member of the Brethren's Unity is bound to take part in furthering the missionary work of the church; but those who join this association pledge themselves in a particular manner to do all within their power to further Christ's kingdom among the heathen nations, and confess before the world that they love the whole human race and take a deep interest in the eternal salvation of such as still sit in the darkness of heathenism." A charter was obtained from the Assembly of Pennsylvania and signed by the Governor on February

---

are communicants. But there are fifty-eight children, a feature which gives the school special importance. At Hebron the attendance at preaching is reported to be good; but in other respects the work is not in a satisfactory condition. The communicants number only twenty-four, although there is a total membership of ninety-six. Heidelberg is being served from Hebron, but the results of a recent awakening lead the people to desire a pastor of their own. He may also serve as schoolmaster. Here there are fifty-six in church connection, sixteen being communicants. At York, where Brother Reinke labors, services are well attended, especially funerals. The school is small, for the children live at distances. The Society decreases. Good relations are maintained with the Lutherans and the Reformed. The total membership is 155, and the communicants number thirty-eight. At Bethel Brother Reizenbach is pastor. He has a large school. The *Sprechen* have been abandoned by him, and pastoral visits take their place. He ministers to 110 persons, of whom twenty-three are communicants. Brother Schweishaupt. of Mountjoy (Donegal) has to complain of a weak congregational life. He does not see much good resulting from the *Sprechen*. The school is poorly attended. He has seventy-seven members.

27, 1788. Ettwein communicated to General Washington that organization had been effected, and enclosed a copy of the rules and a manuscript of his own on the manners, customs and languages of the Indians. The reply, under date of May 2, 1788, was in keeping with his Christian and courteous character. It reads as follows:

"Dear Sir:—I have received your obliging letter of March 28, inclosing a copy of some remarks on the customs, languages, etc., of the Indians, and a printed pamphlet containing the stated rules of a Society for Propagating the Gospel among the Heathen; for which tokens of polite attention and kind remembrance I must beg you to accept my best thanks.

"So far as I am able of judging, the principles upon which the Society is founded, and the rules laid down for its government, appear to be well calculated to promote so laudable and arduous an undertaking; and you will permit me to add that if an event so long and so ardently desired as that of converting the Indians to Christianity can be effected, the Society at Bethlehem bids fair to be a very considerable part in it.

"With sentiments of esteem, I am your most obedient, humble servant,
GEO. WASHINGTON."

The resuscitation of this missionary society was an act of brave faith; for the Christian Indian villages whose prosperity it delighted the veteran Zeisberger to be able to describe to Bishop Reichel, were now heaps of charred ruins, and the entire mission was at a low ebb. Soon after the conclusion of peace a petition had been addressed to Congress, asking for an indemnity, inasmuch as these flourishing settlements had been destroyed by American militia. "On May 19, 1785, Congress passed an act reserving the sites of these settlements together with as much land as Mr. Hutchins, the Geographer of the United States, might see fit, for the benefit of the Christian Indians and their children forever......Ten years, however, passed by before the survey could be completed. This was owing in part to the death of Mr. Hutchins, but chiefly to the distracted state of the Indian country and the hostility which the tribes manifested towards the United States. So bitter did this feeling grow and so alarming were the outbreaks that the remnant of the Christian Indians, after wandering from place to place, was at last constrained to seek refuge in Canada."

The tragic fate of the Christian Indian villages on the Tuscarawas must now be briefly recounted.

Dwelling directly in track of marauding parties roaming between the British frontier post of Detroit and the American fort at Pittsburgh, the very neutrality and peace principles of the six missionary families and their converts drew down upon them the enmity and suspicions of the rangers attached to either side. There had been foreshadowings of trouble as far back as 1777. Zeisberger's influence in the councils of the Iroquois and Delawares, ever exerted in behalf of peace, had held in check savage warriors, who otherwise would have swooped down on the frontier settlements, throwing the weight of their hatchets into the scale when the fate of the colonists still hung in the balance. Delaware chiefs had resolutely returned the war-belt which the Hurons of Lake Erie had sent, and had thrust aside their plausible persuasions to despoil those who had gradually ousted them from the ancient hunting-grounds. The mutterings of trouble had later caused the temporary abandonment of Gnadenhütten, and Lichtenau had been permanently given up, its place being taken by Salem. Yet both Americans and British viewed the mission askance; the latter because to their influence was ascribed the only restraint, which prevented large masses of Delawares from enlisting under the standard of King George, the former from unfounded prejudice and suspicion that the mission stations harbored red-skins in British pay, and formed the rendezvous of raiders. Despite all apprehensions, however, the missionaries faithfully kept their posts, and the internal condition of the congregations was a source of satisfaction. Amidst war's alarms the dusky converts, some of whom had formerly achieved a name as warriors, zealously pursued the arts of peace, and meadow and orchard and field responded to their industry.

On August 10, 1781, there appeared at Salem one hundred and fifty men—Indians and whites—under British officers and bearing the British flag. Soon their number was increased to three hundred. After many councils had been held by the members of this war-party, whose mutual disagreements alone saved the missionaries and their converts from a cruel death, all were made unresisting prisoners on September 4. The mission-houses were plundered. On the 11th the sad exodus of the entire population of the Christian Indian villages commenced. Five thousand bushels of almost ripe but unharvested corn were left behind, as well as garden produce and poultry and all property save what could be transported by the prisoners on pack-horses or in canoes. Valuable manuscripts were also involved in the general loss. At the Sandusky their captors deserted them on October 1, in the midst of an utter wilderness, with no other provisions than the cattle they had driven before them. Soon there came a summons to the missionaries to proceed to Detroit for trial as American spies. Though no armed guard compelled obedience, they responded, relying on their innocence. The trial took place on November 9, Major de Peyster, the commandant presiding. British fairness insured the verdict—a complete acquittal. But the disaster to the mission could not be compensated for by courteous words, even though formal permission was given to the missionaries to return and without hindrance renew their spiritual calling.

This was a dreadful winter for the refugees on the Sandusky. Starvation was not far off. A pint of corn a day was the allowance for each member of the missionary family, and in the extreme cold the suffering was very great. The heathen around them gloried in the distress of teachers and converts, and even threatened to take the lives of the missionaries, when an attempt was made to erect a chapel. At length in despair a party of about one hundred and fifty Christian Indians obtained permission from their savage neighbors to return to the Tuscarawas Valley and secure whatever of their corn of the previous year might still remain unspoiled.

This band soon experienced the terrible consequences of American distrust. These Christian red-men who had consistently refused to take up arms in self-defense, were unjustly charged by American frontiersmen with various outrages and massacres that had enraged and terrified the border-settlements during this winter, and in particular with the horrible murder of the family of William Wallace. About ninety men under the command of Colonel David Williamson had set out from the settlements on the Monongahela, determined to wreak vengeance for this dastardly crime.

The Moravian Indians, after completing their delayed harvest, had intended to begin their return journey to Sandusky on March 7, having succeeded beyond expectations in gathering their belated aftermath. It was on the evening before this appointed day that the Americans arrived in the immediate vicinity. They were hospitably entertained without a suspicion of mistrust on the part of the Christian red-men, who seem to have been wholly ignorant of even the fact of the massacres which had occasioned the expedition. Indeed the Salem Indians came to Gnadenhütten to voluntarily place themselves under the protection of Colonel Williamson, whom they regarded as their deilverer from troubles originating in Detroit. In cold blood, on the morning of the 8th, ninety Christian and six heathen Indians, who were visitors—none of them striking a blow in self-defense—fell in what were aptly named the "slaughter-houses," meeting their faith with noble resignation. Five of them had been serving acceptably as assistant missionaries. The pious exhortations of Abraham, the Mohican, prepared his companions for martyrdom. Only two lads escaped to tell the tidings. Providentially, however, the full completion of the atrocious designs of the militia was frustrated. The Schönbrunn Indians received warning in time and fled to the Sandusky.

On their arrival they found that Zeisberger and his companions had again been summoned to Detroit by Major De Peyster, on false accusation of an Indian chief whose warlike schemes they had formerly thwarted. The new charge was that of aiding the Americans by corresponding with Pittsburgh. As a matter of course, they were cleared. The sympathetic commandant, however, counseled a removal from debatable territory. His advice was followed. The remnant of the scattered converts by way of Lake St. Clair sought a home in the Chippeway country in Michigan, and founded New Gnadenhütten in what is now Macomb County, where they remained four years. Their longing for the old homes in the Tuscarawas Valley, and the setting apart of the reservation by Congress in response to the petition of Ettwein and others after peace had been restored, led a party of one hundred and seventeen to set out from the Chippeway land. But they halted at the Cuyahoga, for it seemed madness to proceed while American sentiment remained intensely hostile to the Indian race. Here Pilgerruh was founded. In 1787 New Salem on the Petquotting—the Huron River of Ohio, emptying into Lake Erie—took the place of this temporary refuge, and bloomed into speedy prosperity. But political complications and the disturbed state of the Northwest Territory in 1790 rendered its permanence very improbable. Next year threats of a repetition of the massacre came from Indians who were banded against the United States, with the overt intention of thus compelling the Christians to don the war-paint against the whites. This at length constrained Zeisberger and his associates to remove with some of their converts to Canadian territory. Accordingly in April, 1792, he proceeded with Senseman and Edwards and the whole congregation to the French River—later called the Thames—and about eighty miles from its mouth and on the right bank founded the Christian Indian village of Fairfield amidst the Muncies and Chippeways. Thus at last and at so great sacrifice permanence was secured.

CHAPTER XXXI.

Amid all changes in methods of administration at home and in spite of perplexities in the financial situation, the church ever regarded the missions amongst the heathen as its chief calling. Diligence and persistence characterized their prosecution. Hence at the synod of 1789 about 14,000 members were reported in the West Indies and about 18,000 in connection with the other mission fields.

In Greenland the fifties had been an era of steady progress, though cares were not lacking. The winter of 1752 to 1753 was terribly cold. Storms raged, famine threatened, and an epidemic carried off sixty of the four hundred members, amongst them several of the most skillful hunters and fishermen. Nevertheless, when a few years later tidings reached Greenland of the destruction of Gnadenhütten on the Mahoni, the Eskimos testified to their sympathy by offerings of skins and blubber for those who had been rendered homeless.

About ninety miles south. from New Herrnhut Matthew Stach in 1758 founded a second station, Lichtenfels, on an island in a fjord three miles from the open sea. In a few years two hundred converted Eskimos formed a village around him, whilst the numbers at New Herrnhut rose to five hundred and forty. It was a time of powerful awakening. The people trembled with emotion. Some hurried away in haste as soon as a service was over, in a vain endeavor to shake off their impressions and ran as though pursued; but found no peace till self-surrender had been made.

In 1763 Frederick Böhnisch died, the first of the missionaries in Greenland to be called home. Matthew Stach, who had prepared a brief Eskimo grammar and lexicon, retired in 1771, and spent his last days at Bethabara in North Carolina. John

Beck, in 1770, had the satisfaction of welcoming two of his sons at New Herrnhut, and cried out, "Now I may depart in peace, for my prayer has been heard, and I see my sons here at my post." They had come out with Martin Godfrey Sternberg, who had been officially commissioned to visit Greenland, in order to amend regulations that were the outgrowth of the extravagancies of the forties at home. In consequence of this visit Christopher Michael Königseer, hitherto warden at Gnadenberg, was sent to superintend operations.

In 1774 the plan of establishing a third station, Lichtenau, on the island of Onartok, about four hundred miles south of New Herrnhut, was carried out by John Sörensen. It was he who at Marienborn, in 1746, when Zinzendorf asked him, "Will you set out to-morrow for Greenland?" replied "Yes, if I can get from the shoemaker a pair of boots he is making for me." Having set out on that morrow, he had been in service in Greenland ever since. Lichtenau blossomed out with speedy success. By the winter of 1775 to 1776 nearly two hundred persons had established homes adjacent to the mission house, and in a few years the baptized numbered one hundred and five.

Königseer's trained mind and linguistic abilities were now pressed into service for the translation of the New Testament, Beck lending him the aid of his long familiarity with the Eskimo tongue. An Eskimo Hymn-book and a Summary of Christian Doctrine were also undertaken and were printed at Barby in 1785. Portions of the New Testament and of the *Idea Fidei Fratrum*, and a grammar and dictionary in manuscript were also fruits of Königseer's industry.

In 1776 certain regulations were introduced by the Danish trading company, which proved detrimental to the mission under existing methods. In order to possibly increase the volume of trade in peltries, the Greenlanders were required to scatter along the coast, and were not permitted to dwell in settlements of any size. This dispersion of the people inevitably detracted from the steady and continuous influence of Christian usages and institutions. Nor did the expedient of appointing assistants, to minister to groups of natives at a distance from each station, compensate.

Then followed another fatal epidemic. From April to August, 1782, one hundred and twenty-five perished in New Herrnhut alone, amongst whom were a number of valued native assistants. Königseer himself was absent at this time in Germany. After his return he was spared but three years more, dying in 1786, in the sixty-fourth year of his age. He was succeeded in the superintendence by Jasper Brodersen, well qualified to take up the philologian's mantle. Historical portions of the Old Testament and part of the Prophecies of Isaiah and hymns in the Greenland language were the fruit of his leisure. But in 1792 he was compelled by a shattered constitution to return to a temperate climate. With him came Sörensen, after forty-eight years in the Arctic.

In Labrador, where Samuel Liebisch took general charge in 1775, although Okak was established in 1776 and Hopedale in 1782, progress was slow. The year 1782 was rendered memorable by a remarkable providential deliverance. Liebisch and William Turner set out from Nain for Okak on March 11 in a dog sleigh. Their route lay across the frozen sea. Though the distance was one hundred and fifty miles, and for a considerable part of the way they had to pass over very deep water, preferable on account of the smoothness of the ice, under the favorable atmospheric conditions of their start no special anxiety was entertained. But in the afternoon there were indications of a coming storm. The heaving of the restless ocean could be felt under its icy covering. By evening the wind had become a gale that whirled the snow with blinding violence. The undulations of the vast sheet of ice, several yards thick, began to impede progress. Soon the ice commenced to burst with the sound of heavy ordnance. Only with the greatest difficulty, and in the very nick of time, did the travelers make the shore. Scarcely had they effected a landing, when the ice for miles along the coast broke up with the violence of the storm amid terrific noise. The Eskimo companions of the missionaries built a snow house on the beach. Thankful for this refuge in the piercing cold, they had but settled down to rest, when Liebisch, who could not sleep owing to a painfully sore throat and the howling of the storm outside, perceived that salt water was trickling through the roof. Hastily digging a passage through the side of the house, they were hardly at a safe distance, when a mighty wave carried away their abandoned resting place. A hole cut into a snowbank was their sole resource till morning. Their scanty supply of provisions had to be carefully eked out for several days in a new snow-hut. On the 13th the storm abated, but the sea was absolutely clear of ice, and it was impossible to proceed or to return. Not until twelve oclock on the night of the 17th did they at last succeed in once more making their starting-place, Nain, grateful for the marvellous protection of God.

At Hopedale the outlook was at first exceedingly discouraging. An eagerness to be taught had been displayed by the natives; "but in their words and demeanor the evil influence of intercourse with dissolute European traders living farther south was painfully evident. The majority seemed to care more for the advantage of the ship's annual visit and the accommodation of the trade than for the blessing of Christian training and instruction. The traders put forth every effort to keep the Eskimos away from missionaries, and with only too great success. Articles of food and luxury, and especially intoxicating liquors, were offered as an almost irresistible bribe, and once entangled in the snares of these men, the poor Eskimos were made use of with diabolical skill and malice to tempt their countrymen to their destruction. The evil influence spread to all three stations, and considerable numbers from each made their way to the south. A spirit of indifference and levity became generally diffused, and much opposition and defiance were shown to their teachers. While boldly demanding in a season of scarcity to be supported by the mission, they took all the produce of the chase to the southlanders, so that the ship returned with scarcely any cargo, and serious apprehension arose as to the pecuniary means for continuing the mission. Exhortations and remonstrances of the missionaries had little or no effect; an admirable letter from the pen of the venerable Bishop Spangenberg, which touched the hearts of many, only sufficed to check them a while in their evil course. The missionaries were by no means inclined to lay this decline wholly to the charge of the natives; they deplored their own ignorance and inexperience, and blamed themselves for many mistakes made in the treatment of individuals, for too hastily admitting to membership people who had strong religious convictions and cherished many good desires and resolutions in regard to conversion, but who were really not solidly awakened. 'We are working in a kind of twilight,' they wrote. 'Many a time were we made anxious by the duplicity and relapses into sin of the baptized, and our Saviour knows best what distress and perplexity were thereby occasioned to us, little as we were able, with all our care and watchfulness, to prevent what we so greatly deplored.'" Drachart and Haven were both spared the experience of the worst of this time of trial. The former died at Nain in 1778. The latter retired to Europe in 1784, Liebisch having preceded him by one year, appointed a member of the governing board of the church. For a brief period Christian Lister and then Christian Lewis Rose served as superintendent.

In the Danish West Indies, on the other hand, a rapid increase in the number of converts was now a marked feature. In the year 1771 Nisky became an independent station, and Friedensberg at the western end of St. Croix was similarly equipped. Yet the great naval war between the European powers interrupted connections with home, and all intercourse with English lands was prohibited in 1760. Scarcity of provisions followed, being enhanced by protracted drought. In 1765 losses were suffered by the burning of a mission house on St. Croix and the destruction of the church on St. John by a storm. The night of August 31, 1772, became memorable for years through the ravages of a hurricane which caused much damage on all three islands, but especially on St. Croix. Friedensberg mission house suffered severely, and the entire station of Friedensthal was obliterated, the missionaries and their families barely saving their lives by taking refuge in cellars. General scarcity, famine, sickness and wide-spread mortality ensued. But the blessings of adversity became manifest in the turning of hearts to the things which can not be shaken. When the Friedensthal church was rebuilt its auditories numbered a thousand, and baptisms added to the number of believers month by month. The presentation of land on St. John by Commandant Von Malleville of St. Thomas made possible the founding of Emmaus, as a companion station to Bethany in 1782. During the fifty years of the mission in the Danish West Indies, 8,833 adults and 2,974 children had been baptized. One hundred and twenty-seven members of missionary families had entered into rest, including children.

In 1784 valuable service was rendered the mission by an official visit on the part of John Loretz. He promoted the development of systematic division of spiritual labor and the establishment of a local conference of supervision. Martin Mack had died on June 9, having barely overlived the arrival of his successor, Schaukirch from America. Native assistants were now more widely utilized, especially for the instruction of candidates and for the administration of discipline. Prominent amongst these Cornelius, a freed-man, gifted with unusual native ability, and deeply devout, lived to the advanced age of eighty-four, and served the mission most acceptably for forty-seven years. "He spoke Danish, Dutch, English and German, enjoyed universal respect among all ranks, and was so diligent and successful in his trade as a mason that he had been able to purchase the freedom of himself and his family. His unwearied faithfulness in visiting day and night the negroes on the scattered plantations led great numbers of the poor slaves to gratefully regard him as their spiritual father, while his clear and persuasive preaching attracted men of rank and education, who heard him with pleasure and profit."

The translation of portions of Scripture and of the Harmony of the Four Evangelists and of the Summary of Christian Doctrine into Negro-English and the printing of a Negro-English Hymn-book also materially facilitated the work and provided for its permanence.

In the English islands the feature of periodicity prevailed, eras of advance and retrogression alternating.

In Antigua, Isles died at his post in 1764, having barely accomplished the organization of the native church. The small congregation was reduced to sore straights by the time his successor, Peter Brown, arrived from Pennsylvania, in 1769, to become the second founder of this mission. A native of the Palatinate, he had served chiefly as a teacher in America, but ever betrayed his German birth in his speech. It was not, therefore, in virtue of the graces of rhetoric that his ministry became distinguished for signal fruitfulness. Devoted fidelity and unconquerable love were his best gifts. Visiting the despised blacks in their huts and taking advantage of the mid-day rest in the fields, by his loving sympathy he showed himself a brother or a father. Benjamin Brookshaw from Fulneck, in England, who joined him in 1771, proved a most acceptable coadjutor, when former assistants had to leave on account of the failure of their health. But he was granted less than two years of activity; and when Brown's wife also died, soon after, the outlook was very trying. Then Fulneck furnished another colleague, John Meder, a Livonian by birth. Native assistants were judiciously employed. Ground for a second station was purchased in 1774 at Bailyhill, near the town of Falmouth (exchanged in 1782 for Gracehill, as more convenient). Samuel Watson, a man of eminent gifts, became Brown's colleague in 1776. "In 1791 Brown had to retire from the scene of his twenty years' faithful, humble, but apostolic service, thoroughly worn out in it; and in the following year Watson died, in his forty-ninth year, and was followed to the grave by two thousand persons of all classes and colors. The number in charge of the Brethren had grown between the years 1769 and 1792 from 14 to 7,400; of these the majority were baptized."

One of the crosses inevitably to be endured so long as slavery lasted, was the removal of converts to islands devoid of gospel privileges. The more ready, therefore, were the Brethren to respond, when John Gardiner, a prominent solicitor and planter in the neighboring island of St. Kitts, requested missionaries for the instruction of his slaves. In 1777 Gottwald and Birkby were sent. Mr. Gardiner's kind offices secured for them the countenance and assistance of the governor. Preaching was commenced at Basseterre and at Palmetto Point, the estate of their earliest benefactor, and when Gottwald's failing health compelled retirement in 1787, the congregation numbered about one hundred persons. Schneller and Reichel, who were next associated, carried the work forward with even greater rapidity. The former alone statedly visited about fifty plantations, and by the close of the century the Moravian negroes numbered more than two thousand. Moravians and Methodists, in hearty fellowship, had effected a change in the character of the slave population.

The year 1765 witnessed an attempt in Barbadoes, the pioneers being John Wood and Andrew Rittmansberger; but the death of the latter within a month after landing utterly disheartened the former. Brookshaw's effort in 1767 was more propitious. All alone he manfully supported himself by handicraft in apostolic fashion, and staunchly held his ground for some months till joined by Bennet. Bennet died in 1772, and only one missionary was left, Brookshaw having been transferred to Antigua. Then sore trial was occasioned by a terrific hurricane on October 10, 1780, known for a hundred years as "the great storm." Scarcely a house was left standing. The mission property was utterly destroyed. Several thousand persons perished. Semi-famine followed. Masterless slaves took to the woods. Outlaws threatened life and possessions. When John Montgomery, the father of the poet, arrived in 1784, he found only fourteen communicants. Though his able ministrations for a time infused new hope, they were cut off by death in 1791, after a brief intermission of labor caused by his attempt to inaugurate a mission in Tobago.

The incentive to this undertaking, in 1787, had come from a planter named Hamilton, who had known the Brethren in London and Barbadoes. "Count Dillon, the French governor at this time, had learnt to value the missionary labors of the Brethren when holding a similar position in St. Kitts, and at once gave full approval of the effort, welcoming Montgomery with much kindness. In the upper circle of society, too, a favorable view was taken of the projected mission. Meetings were held, and the negroes joyously welcomed the gospel-message. Montgomery returned to Barbadoes with a report which was very hopeful for good results for a missionary effort in Tobago. But men were so scarce, and the requirements of the rapidly growing mission elsewhere so multiplied that it was not till 1790 that the first missionary could be sent in the person of Montgomery. His work was begun with great vigor, but was sadly hindered by a formidable outbreak of soldiers and people on receipt of the tidings of the French Revolution, by a disastrous hurricane a month or two later, and the failing health of his wife, which ended in her happy departure before the year closed. In March of the following year Montgomery had to return to Barbadoes, with his health completely shattered, and there in the month of July his brief missionary career was terminated by his death. For eight years no attempt was made to renew the mission, not entirely on account of the great drain on all the available resources of the church in other fields of labor, but partly on account of the uncertain political circumstances of the land."

In Jamaica, the gift of the Carmel estate proved a Greek present. It represented a policy, to say the least, as erroneous as the former attempt to colonize in St. Croix. This was still the era of experiment in missions, and the privilege of being taught by the blunders of others was denied the Brethren. Yet the era of decline which followed the return of Caries to Ireland was made good by the advance during Frederick Schlegel's all too brief service of six years, terminated by his death in 1770. Next came a period of prolonged fruitlessness. Discouraging relapses into paganism occurred. The superstition of the Africans appeared to be well-nigh ineradicable. Not that men of zeal and ability were lacking. Samuel Church, Nathaniel Brown, Joseph Jackson and Thomas Ellis were gifted and labored indefatigably. But the system which identified them with the management of an estate worked by slave-labor was a dead weight about their necks. Besides the malarial influences of Carmel compelled too frequent changes in personnel. In seventy years it demanded twenty-four missionary graves, and twenty additional deaths elsewhere completed the fatal lists. The wonder is, that men like Christian Lister, after a transfer from the totally different climate of Labrador, could hold out for nearly fourteen years in the face of every distress. By the year 1804 the baptisms in Jamaica numbered only 938.

At the time of Schumann's death, the brimming marsh-land of Surinam was occupied by the Brethren at four points—Pilgerhut on the Berbice, Ephraim on the Corentyne, Sharon on the Saramacca and Paramaribo, the capital. The last, slow in assuming its proportions, was to arrive at highest importance, while the Indian mission dwindled away.

The Bush Negroes, runaway slaves who had taken refuge in remote swampy forests and whose liberty was conceded by government in 1764 after the failure of a resort to force, regarded the Indian tribes with fixed animosity. When the blacks of Copename in 1761 made a raid against the villages on the Saramacca, the people from Sharon scattered in flight. Next year the Negroes of Berbice rose in arms, and in 1763 caused the flight of the missionaries and their converts from Pilgerhut. Schumann's translations and other linguistic works perished in the ashes of the station. The same fate overtook Ephraim. The Indian mission threatened to wholly disappear in the flames of the servile rebellion. With the restoration of peace in 1764 Sharon was however reoccupied, and Hope arose in place of Ephraim. But Sharon was again abandoned in 1779, owing to repeated alarms from the turbulence of the Bush-Negroes, oft-recurring fevers, and the failure of the cassava plantations, the chief source of food. Nor did the pious wishes enshrined in the name of the companion station long enjoy fruition, although in 1783 its membership numbered 186. The nomadic tendency of the Indians, with their proneness to intoxication, in addition to pestilence and war, perpetually interposed obstacles, though signal instances of the power of grace were not lacking.

Meantime the mission amongst the black population became more important. Coincident with the establishment of peace, the colonial authorities asked that missionaries be sent to the camps of the Bush-Negroes. Rudolph Stoll and Thomas Jones, under the guidance of the aged Daehne, penetrated into the interior, where the atmosphere is that of "a hothouse and vapor-bath combined." Early in 1766 they reached Senthea Creek, after a most toilsome and dangerous journey by boat. Here a chief named Abini, vaguely feeling that they were sent by a divine power, rendered what poor aid he could. Their home was a wretched hut. Food was scanty. The deadly climate established its claims. In a few weeks Jones succumbed to fever. Daehne returned to his Indians, but Stoll faithfully kept his solitary post. Two years later Abini, his protector, fell in war with a neighboring tribe. His son, Arabi, endeavored to maintain the friendly relations; but deep-seated hostility gleamed forth, incited by his grandmother, a bigoted adherent of the old superstitions. In the face of undisguised hate, Stoll opened a school with a handful of children, one of whom, Grego, in adult life became a very serviceable assistant of the missionaries. In 1769 Christopher Kersten and his wife came from Paramaribo to second Stoll's efforts. Arabi was baptized on January 6, 1771, and shot the alligator worshiped by his people. Slowly a congregation was gathered, and in 1773 a settlement was formed at Bambey, some miles nearer the city, with again a removal in 1786. Kersten was called away to become superintendent of the entire field, and when Stoll brought his bride to the lonely village in the bush, she died from fever in a few months. He himself soon followed her to the grave, having spent eleven years of heroic effort in the tangled pestilential forests. His memory is yet cherished by the blacks who lovingly revere "Brother Rudolph." Missionary after missionary endeavored to occupy the post; but health invariably gave way. No European could long endure life in the tropical swamps. Arabi remained faithful; but at the close of the century New Bambey could not count fifty converts.

In Paramaribo it was otherwise. Christian Cupido, the first convert, was won in 1776. Within one month of his baptism

19

seven other baptisms followed. A church was built two years
later. Though some planters were bitterly hostile, the governor
and other people of influence countenanced the undertaking.
In 1785 the government offered the mission a piece of land
conveniently situated for visits to several important estates
and Sommelsdyk was established. When Kersten was succeeded by Samuel Wagner, in 1789, the Paramaribo congregation numbered about 250 souls. If the day of great things had
not yet dawned, foundations had been successfully laid, and the
indications of a hopeful future were here. Moreover a pledge
for the stability of the mission was given in 1793 by the formation of the *Zendinggenootschap der Broedergemeente* in the congregation at Zeist in Holland, which was to make the support of
the Brethren's missions in Dutch colonies its special object.

Less happy were the fortunes of the mission in the East
Indies. Halle regarded with disfavor the presence of missionaries from Herrnhut in close proximity to its own heralds.
Using their influence at Copenhagen, the Hallensian authorities insisted that the Brethren must occupy the Nicobar Islands,
as originally designed. Correspondence between the governing
board of the church and the Danish government, with visits
to the Danish capital, occupied several years. At length, in
1768, Denmark established a military and trading post on the
island of Nancawery, and six Brethren were sent thither. Two
died soon after their arrival. Next year more colonists followed. But in a few years the entire colonial project came to
nothing from the terrible mortality. Yet the four Brethren
manfully remained, without any regular means of correspondence with Tranquebar, unable to have satisfactory intercourse
with the natives owing to the barrier of the language, often in
great straits on account of the unproductiveness of the soil, and
frequently in ill health. Nevertheless nothing else than permanent occupation of the post was contemplated. Breaches in
the ranks were filled from Tranquebar. But although the first
convert, Kutti, was baptized on January 6, 1774, on the whole
the station remained a fruitless one, and the drain on men
and means was excessive. Tranquebar also proved a place
most costly in precious lives. The relations with the Hallensian
missionaries improved, but the rewards of missionary endeavor were scanty. With the success of Schwarz in the English colonies an invitation came to the Brethren from the Dan-

ish Company to initiate missionary labors at Serampore in Bengal. The call was welcomed, and John Grasmann was sent thither in 1777. Seven years later, at the suggestion of a Mr. Livius in England, James La Trobe, a cousin of Benjamin, was dispatched to Patna.

The various discouraging features of the mission now determined the Unity's Elders' Conference to undertake a thorough investigation of its condition and prospects. Bishop John Frederick Reichel was charged with this important duty. With him voyaged Christian Lewis Schumann and others who were to remain in the event of the continuance of the undertaking. For five months, June to October, 1786, Reichel thoroughly looked into the state of affairs and had frequent conferences with the missionaries, the two Brethren from Bengal being present. It was decided to abandon all the outposts. This took effect for Patna at once, for the Nicobar Islands and Serampore later, 1788-1791. At Tranquebar changes were made, in the hope of a more successful prosecution of the work. La Trobe returned with Reichel, and their stay at Capetown in January and February, 1787, led up to the renewal of the mission in Cape Colony, abandoned fifty years ago. Finally in 1795, after long hesitation, the Unity's Elders' Conference determined upon complete withdrawal from the East Indies. Forty out of the seventy who were sent thither by the church had found their graves at the scene of their unsuccessful endeavors.

CHAPTER XXXII.

THE RENEWAL OF THE MISSION IN CAPE COLONY, 1792.

Schmidt's attempt to evangelize the Hottentots never altogether passed out of the scope of the church's plans. In 1748 a member of the Herrnhaag congregation named John Martin Schwälber, who had formerly served for five years as an official of the Dutch East India Company at the Cape, volunteered to go in his place, at his own costs, and was permitted. He apparently reached Baviaanskloof in safety, and died there during an epidemic prior to 1756. The little congregation held together for some time, but after the death of Africo and Willem, about 1756, the rest scattered, and the wilderness returned where once fields and gardens bloomed.

When on June 16, 1789, in connection with his report concerning the East Indian mission Bishop Reichel communicated to the synod the results of his observations in Cape Colony, and held out hopes of the timeliness of an attempt to renew the mission there, keen interest was aroused. Circumstances were propitious. Governor Van der Graff was understood to be favorably disposed. The purposes and character of the church were better known. The prejudices of former days had been dissipated. Ranzau and Rothe, the Provincial Helpers in Holland, together with Reichel were therefore instructed to open negotiations with the Directors of the Dutch East India Company to secure permission for the resumption of missionary operations. A successful issue was delayed only by the revolutionary movements in Holland.

In the summer of 1792 Henry Marsveld of Gouda in Holland, Daniel Schwinn of Erbach in the Odenwald and John Christian Kühnel of Herrnhut were dispatched to Africa. Trained mechanics, and aged respectively 47, 42 and 30 years—unmarried—they were men admirably adapted for pioneer work, qualified to win the Hottentots for civilization as well as for Christian life. Ordained at Herrnhut, they left the Texel in the *Little Dove*—"*Z'Duyfje*"—on July 11 and reached Cape Town on November 21. Cheered by the manifestation of considerable sympathy, though their undertaking was scouted in other quarters, on December 20 they left for the interior in a twelve-ox wagon in company with "Baas" Martin Teunessen, the "inspector" of the district around Baviaanskloof. Here the government had donated as the site for the new mission the spot hallowed by the memories of Schmidt's in-gatherings. The place itself was first visited on Christmas Eve, the three new-comers being meanwhile the guests of the "inspector," who had received instructions to protect them and their work and to render them all reasonable assistance. Remains of Schmidt's house, traces of his garden, and especially a large pear-tree beneath whose shade services were now temporarily held, served as reminders that the former attempt had not been given up for lack of fruitfulness. The tenacious hold of the faith which Schmidt had engrafted was also disclosed by the joy of one of his converts, Magdalene, an old woman of eighty, who now came forward with Anna-like rejoicings at the answer to her prayers, and produced her Dutch Bible carefully wrapped in a sheep-skin, whilst she gave proofs that its passages were not wholly unfamiliar to her.

In accordance with the instructions of his superiors, Teunessen rendered welcome aid. When certain of the natives became suspicious that the kindness of the missionaries was to be explained on the ground of ulterior designs, possibly a scheme to kidnap them for slavery in Holland, he dispelled these fears, saying: "Government has sent these men to instruct you, and if you are willing to learn, to teach you what is good, and baptize you. Then you will be Christians as well as the farmers, and they dare not hurt you. The Governor loves you, and has therefore sent teachers to you, charging me to bring them to you. If they were not good men he would not have recommended them to me; nor would I have brought them to you." In March a school was commenced with twenty-five adults and children. Practical instruction in the herding of cattle, agriculture and gardening supplemented lessons from the books.

But storm-clouds gathered. The policy introduced by Holland in its dealings with the colony had been wholly unworthy of an enlightened Protestant state possessed of commercial experience. Partly by contracts and partly by force, the Hottentot natives had been gradually deprived of their lands and pushed into the interior. Many had been enslaved. The Boers had been narrowed down in agricultural operations by governmental restriction of the crops which they were permitted to grow, by heavy taxation and the discouragement of manufactures. All this was engendering an ugly spirit amongst them. On the one hand they ached for independence, and abortive insurrections broke out; and on the other hand the natives were made to feel that the natural kindliness of the Dutch heart was departing. A group of colonists professed tenets which included a determination to hold as slaves all Hottentots or Bushmen who could be captured, and to compel all natives born on an estate to work without pay until twenty-one years of age. Scanty scruples meanwhile existed against defrauding or debauching them. These Boers beheld with alarm the improvement which was noticeable in the people whom the Moravian missionaries had taken in charge. Resisting the solicitations of drink, these Hottentots began to insist on the rights of intelligent manhood. They were enjoying school privileges, whilst the colonists had none. Their labor would become too costly. Even Teunessen for a time yielded to the pressure of prejudiced opposition. "The Moravians must withdraw to the Bush-country"—such was the demand. Some possibly cast a longing eye on the improvements at Baviaanskloof. Nor could the colonial government render the protection which it might have furnished under ordinary circumstances, for it was beginning to cope with open rebellion, the echo of the excitement caused in Holland by the revolution in France.

The story of the bell, narrated graphically in Schneider's account of the founding of the mission, furnishes an illustration of the shameless opposition now experienced. In April, 1793, clever Kühnel fashioned a rude makeshift, a home-made article that could be designated a bell only by a stretch of courtesy. It served, indeed, to proclaim the hour of worship by giving out a sound never heard before. It also served to stimulate the benefactions of friends in Cape Town, by moving them to pity; so that in October an actual bell was presented, which had previously done service on a farm. Great rejoicing greeted its advent at Baviaanskloof. So shapely a thing with so fine a tone was a complete novelty to the Hottentot population. Their joy and the satisfaction of the missionaries culminated when a few days later it was elevated on a suitable campanile of timber, where it could take pleasure in waking the echoes of the neighboring hills. But alas! the harmless proclaimer of the hours of religious devotion soon became the intolerable disturber of the peace! The clergyman of Stellenbosch lodged a complaint with the government on the ground that this impertinent bell annoyed him and was an offense to his conscience. Its tones broke in upon his peace. Yet he lived two days' journey distant! His weighty representations moved government to require Teunessen to place an injunction upon the pestiferous bell. So the instrument which had been judged wholly harmless when it was employed to give notice of the hours of labor and of refreshment and rest, as was customary on many of the farms, dare no longer sound; for its invitation to worship—that was quite another thing. The justification of this injunction moreover sheds a curious light upon the prevalent conception of Christian comity. The Lutheran Church in Cape Town was not permitted to enjoy the use of a bell; still less therefore might the mission in Baviaanskloof. So the poor bell hung its silenced head in shame for its own uselessness, until an official named Brand visited the settlement in December. To him the missionaries made earnest representations and pictured the necessity of a bell for the proper conduct of their work. He perceived the reasonableness of the plea and promised help. Nay, he even ventured to do more than this. Temporarily the ringing might be sanctioned. On his return to the capital he laid the matter in all form before the governor and before a commissioner of the Dutch East India Company, who happened to be there. At last in the latter part of December a document officially signed and sealed reached Teunessen, removing the injunction from the bell. Yet this was not the end of the affair. Next month when Marsveld visited the city, he was amazed to receive a new inhibition, and at that from the lips of the official whose friendly representations had achieved so much. Again the injunction was justified by the alleged annoyance given by the penetrating tones of this wonderful bell, so disturbing to the folk of Stellenbosch, two days' journey away! True, it was added that quite too many complaints had been heard in reference to the work of the Brethren. All the representations of the missionary were to no purpose. The poor bell remained silent until March 19, 1798, when English rule brought about a rescript in favor of the patient servant of the native congregation. No wonder the thankful Hottentots went to the sea-shore, a day and a half distant by wagon, and brought thence three loads of shell-fish, that lime might be burnt, to build a belfry of stone, whence the victorious bell might henceforth peal forth freely.

Meanwhile opposition manifested itself in ways not so harm-less. When on September 30, 1794, Schwinn in a personal in-terview with the governor sought permission for the erection of a church, the rude reply was, "Not so much as a pig-sty shall be built. Everything must remain as it is." Teunessen actu-ally forbade the building of a stall for goats! Commissioners came from Cape Town and ordered the Hottentots to remove their herds from the neighborhood. Only a few cattle might be retained for use as beef. Henceforth every native must first obtain written permission from a Boer, prior to his settling at Baviaanskloof. Then a paper was circulated amongst the Nationalists, with three thousand signatures. Its main points were the expulsion of the missionaries, the practical enslave-ment of the Hottentots, and the complete enslavement of the Bushmen. Next it was reported that a certain semi-bandit named Pisani with a lawless company was on his way to destroy the mission. These fellows the Nationalists themselves, how-ever, arrested and threw into the citadel at Cape Town. At last the climax was reached in August, 1795, when the British fleet, sent to support the authority of the Prince of Orange, took possession of Cape Colony in his name.

Marsveld waited upon the British authorities, Generals Clarke and Craig, and received assurance of protection. Let him and his Brethren continue to prosecute their benevolent work. In February, 1796, the destruction of the mission at one blow was plotted by its enemies. But due notice of the danger having been given by Teunessen, the malicious scheme came to naught. The village about the mission now grew apace. A church was built. Five hundred inhabitants centered around it. A vineyard of two thousand vines was under cultivation. The herding of sheep had been introduced. A grist mill had been built. A cutlery had been founded; for Kühnel had been a journeyman in the establishment at Herrnhut originated by the

Neissers. And as years passed the prejudices of the more thoughtful of the Boers gave way. They discovered that Baviaanskloof contributed to their wants, and that a reliable, conscientious and intelligent Moravian convert, even if paid reasonable wages, was a more profitable employe than a drunken, pilfering, ignorant savage, though practically an unpaid slave.

In 1797 John Philip Kohrhammer of Gnadau was appointed superintendent of the mission, and with his wife arrived next spring. The gradual increase in the number of inhabitants, more than 1,200 according to a census taken in January, 1799, required the erection of a larger church. The missionaries planned according to their faith, and on January 9, 1800, a building accommodating fifteen hundred persons was consecrated—an object of interest to settlers far and wide and of astonishment to the savages. Aged Magdalena survived to see this pledge of greater things; for she fell asleep just one week prior to the dedication, "having probably attained the age of nearly one hundred years."

New missionaries were now sent, and Christian Louis Rose, formerly of Labrador, in turn became superintendent. In externals the converts were prospering from the produce of their fields and orchards and gardens and the increase of their herds. The disposition of the neighboring proprietors, and especially of Teunessen, had become friendly. The change of the name of the station from Baviaanskloof to *Genadendal* (Vale of Grace), being made as it was at the suggestion of the Dutch governor Jansen on the restoration of the colony to Holland after the Peace of Amiens, testified that the value of missionary effort had won recognition.

CHAPTER XXXIII.

With the advent to power of the "Ministry of the sansculottes" unhappy Louis XVI in the spring of 1792 had been compelled to declare war against Francis II of Austria. From that time till the Treaty of Lunéville the tornado of strife raged with scarcely any intermission and the whole of Europe became involved.   Existing institutions of every kind were severely tested.   Scattered through various lands the congregations of the Brethren's Church inevitably suffered.   Communications were interrupted.   Direct losses of property were endured and the oppressive burden of requisitions felt, wherever the track of conflict passed.   The demoralizing consequences of war upon honest toil, and its effect upon the intellectual spirit of the age, the unrest and disquiet engendered, with a disinclination for the ordinary round of duties—all these were keenly felt.

Berthelsdorf was now the seat of the Unity's administrative board.   Since the death of Spangenberg Jeremiah Risler, John Frederick Reichel and Christian Gregor, all of them bishops and men of parts, were leaders.   The actual vacancy caused by the death of Spangenberg was filled in October, 1793, by Christian Geisler, hitherto warden of various congregations.

Valuable services were rendered by John Frederick William Kölbing, the man on whom most especially Köber's mantle had fallen.   With him as financiers were associated two men like himself originally trained for the law, Godfrey Goldman and Frederick William Schober.   The office of Provincial Helper in Upper Lusatia had ceased with Layritz.   In Silesia Carl Sigismund von Seidlitz held the corresponding position till 1801, when it also fell into abeyance.

During this period the hand of death worked a number of changes in the board. On May 10, 1797, Count Henry 28th Reuss, the nephew of Count Zinzendorf, since 1789 the President of the Conference, died at Herrnhut. Esteemed and prized in wide circles beyond the bounds of the Unity, he had been an ornament of the church, whose necessities he had several times met out of his private means. The death of Martin Godfrey Sternberg on July 5 of the next year and that of Bishop Loretz on July 23, created other vacancies. Shortly before, Hans Christian Alexander von Schweinitz arrived from America, to take the place of Count Reuss; and now Jacob Christopher Duvernoy and Charles Forestier made good the other places. Upon these men and their associates fell the task of devising ways and means to pilot the church through the difficulties and dangers of these anxious years.

Providentially not all the groups of congregations were alike exposed to molestation. At first the Saxon settlements escaped. In 1790 the peace of the Silesian congregations had been threatened from the massing of a Prussian army on the Austrian frontier, till the convention of Reichenbach united these two kingdoms against France. Central Germany still enjoyed the sweets of peace, and Neudietendorf was a refuge for those who fled from the western settlements. But Neuwied and Zeist suffered.

In 1795 the climax of trouble was reached. French intrigues in Poland, stimulating Kosiusko's revolt, had drawn away the attention of the two German powers to the east, and compelled them to rest content with defensive operations along the Rhine. In April Frederick William had signed a separate treaty of peace at Basel. France was to retain the Prussian territories on the left bank, with the understanding that at the close of the war some compensation should be awarded on the eastern side of the river. But although the North German states were recognized as neutral in virtue of their alliance with Prussia, when Pichegru and Jourdan received orders to cross the Rhine, the fire of hostilities neared Neuwied. The conflict burst out afresh in its very vicinity. To prevent the crossing of the Rhine by the republicans the Austrian forces erected batteries at the upper end of the town, close to the Brethren's quarter. On the 13th the French on the opposite heights of Weissenthurm opened a brisk cannonade, which was answered by the imperialists. On the 27th a heavy artillery duel raged, the French having taken possession of a small island in the Rhine. Shot and shell poured through the streets of the town. Many houses were injured, and an extensive manufactory was set on fire. All of the inhabitants who could do so fled. Most of those who remained took refuge in their cellars. A shell burst just before the house of the pastor, Christian Frederick Gregor, jr., pieces flying through the window into the very room where his wife and children were sitting, but without injuring any of them. As soon as there was a lull in the firing, flight from the place became universal. By the foresight and promptitude of the Principal, Hillmer, the pupils of the boys' school were provided for in the castle of Montrepos, about five miles distant. Two weeks of suspense passed. Then news came that the French had effected a crossing at Düsseldorf. The imperialists withdrew and the French occupied the town, but committed no excesses. With the growth of their numbers, however, their conduct grew worse, and plundering became the order of the day. On October 19 they evacuated the town, but entrenched in its immediate vicinity. An attack by imperial riflemen once more drew the fire of their batteries on the place, and when they withdrew, the French rushed in and commenced an indiscriminate rifling of the houses. A street fight followed. But now an armistice was arranged at the instance of the governor of Neuwied by one of the Brethren, and although the theater of war once more drifted into the neighborhood next year, and several skirmishes took place, Neuwied itself was declared a neutral town.

Zeist, like Neuwied, felt the direct effects of war, especially during Pichegru's invasion. Yet in the midst of these times of trial the organization of its active missionary society was effected. In the early part of 1795 the settlement was occupied alternately by the British and the French. In spite of apprehensions entertained in advance, distinguished consideration was shown by Pichegru and Moreau. Although no supplies were allowed to be sent from the town of Utrecht to the country, a measure rigorously enforced and a cause of much distress, a special exception was made in favor of Zeist. With the establishment of the Batavian Republic in May, 1795, faithful adherents of the old order were put to much inconvenience. The ministers of the congregations in Amsterdam, Haarlem and particularly in Zeist could be exempted from the universal conscription only by the payment of considerable sums. The new regulations respecting the local administration of justice, the increased taxation and the interruption of the channels of trade involved annoyances. Nevertheless in Amsterdam the small congregation in 1795 ventured to purchase as a new house of worship a stately edifice on the Kaisersgraat.

In the Scandinavian field Christiansfeld enjoyed peace and a blessing rested upon its educational institutions, its industries and its inner life. At Copenhagen and Altona, in Jutland and Fünen, and in the Duchies of Schleswig and Holstein, the itinerations of the Brethren were of special significance during this period. The Scandinavian *Diaspora* flourished. Christiania and Drammen in Norway had their resident ministers. Stockholm, Gothenburg, Carlscrona and Uddewalla were centers of influence, and the translation of Spangenberg's *Idea* was accorded a wide welcome. Yet all was prosecuted on the basis of the *Diaspora* only; for negotiations carried on for the church by Ulric Roslin with the Diet at Stockholm, in 1786 and 1788, to secure permission for a settlement in Sweden, had failed.

In Livonia and Esthonia, the extensive range and wide ramifications of societies in connection with the Brethren were such that when Quandt, in 1793, on the occasion of an official visit, convened assemblies of the ministers of the church and their assistants, as many as three hundred gathered for one of the conferences.

Sarepta was prospering, though the mission amongst the Tartars which was to have had this settlement as a base of operations was hemmed in by adverse circumstances.

As far back as January, 1797, the Unity's Elders' Conference had felt the desirability of convening a general synod on account of the altered conditions of operation here and there introduced by the French Revolution. But by the decision of the lot it was postponed until 1801, a date at one time apparently impracticable, but eventually rendered possible by the armistice of Lunéville.

CHAPTER XXXIV.

THE BRITISH PROVINCE AT THE CLOSE OF THE EIGHTEENTH CENTURY.

Since the year 1789 the Provincial oversight in England had been entrusted to Cornelius Renatus Van Laer; after 1791 to Gotthold Wollin; then from 1792 to 1800 to Thomas Moore, with Ignatius La Trobe as a colleague after he succeeded to Hutton's office of *Secretarius Unitatis in Anglia*. On the death of Abraham Taylor in 1790, Bishop Schaukirch, erstwhile active in America and then in the West Indies, was associated with William Horne, until he sought retirement, in the Irish supervision, to be succeeded in turn by Steinhauer in 1797.

Death thinned the ranks of the generation which had personally known the beginnings in England. Among these fathers, James Hutton fell asleep at the advanced age of eighty, on May 3, 1795—a man of limitless charity, whose later life was "literally spent in going about doing good," and withal a man of more than ordinary endowments, strong common sense, and quickness of feeling and apprehension, one of the founders of the Unity in Britain. He had been preceded in 1794 by Francis Okley, the energetic and eloquent minister of the Northampton congregation.

The bond of fellowship connecting the British with the Continental Province was strengthened by an official visit paid in the summer of 1795 by Bishop Liebisch. His first attention was given to the affairs of the church in London, difficulties having arisen in connection with the management of the mission in Labrador between the Society for the Furtherance of the Gospel and that portion of it known as the "Ship Committee," the mercantile association charged with the trade and transportation. These disagreements were about a decade old, and some feeling had been engendered, the Brethren Edmonds and Hurlock maintaining the rights of the narrower circle, not from self-interest, but from a conviction of justice as they regarded it. Unable to reach or promote any definite conclusion immediately, the visitor had to pass on to other duties. But in 1797 the "Ship Committee" was abrogated, and the entire financial management of everything connected with the mission was relegated to the Society. After visiting a number of congregations on his way thither, Liebisch was present at a provincial conference in session at Fulneck from September 30 to October 13. Its significance would doubtless have proved the more eventful, had not the propositions agreed upon been invalid until referred to the Unity's Elders' Conference for approval and confirmation—as in the case of ministerial conferences held during the same general period of the Church's history in America. How the natural development of the church, in an age when national characteristics were clear-cut and distinct, was to be promoted by such a method is difficult to understand; and it certainly is open to question, whether the unity and uniformity which it was desired in this way to conserve, were worth all that was inevitably sacrificed. For example, when John Hartley, Steinhauer's able successor in the directorship of the schools at Fulneck, wished to attempt a plan of supplementing the curriculum of the boys' school with collegiate studies, and so provide the preparatory education of the future ministers of the Province, who should then receive practical training as assistants of various ministers, whilst residing in their homes after the olden fashion of the Unity of the Brethren in its ancient seats—a plan which would remove the necessity of having recourse to the schools in Germany—the entire project received official condemnation as "impracticable," "*unausführbar.*"

From Fulneck Liebisch traveled through the west of England and Wales. Carnarvorn, Langharn and Carmarthen, as well as Haverfordwest were now centers of activity in the Principality. Intimate association with earnest ministers of other churches was found to be characteristic of this district. The same trait also appeared in Ireland, especially in Dublin, where Christian Gottlieb Hüffel, active here from 1791 to 1798, in June of 1795 formed a union with nine ministers akin to that of the annual conferences of pastors at Herrnhut. But for the Irish division of the Moravian Church a period of retrogression had commenced. Probably no portion of the British Empire was suffering more from the almost incessant strife of the European powers, even as it had felt the consequences of war with the American colonies. Business was stagnant, and this reacted upon every avenue of life. Great distress prevailed; misrule was not unknown. Church life felt the effects. Arva had been given up in 1790, and Drumargan in 1794. The use of Bally-mena chapel had been discontinued in 1790. At Kilwarlin the numbers were decreasing at such a rate that it was only a question of time when it would sink to the condition of an out-station served from Gracehill and Ballinderry. One bright spot indeed appeared, the newly projected enterprise at Clifden; but it should rapidly decline. In 1788 Mr. Edward Burton, an influential landed proprietor near Ennis, in County Clare, had solicited the services of the Brethren on his estate at Cifden Hall and in the vicinity, and the impressions received by John Worthington, pastor in Dublin, on investigation of the prospects, had led to the sending first of Lewis West, and then of Collis as permanent pastor. With the work at Clifden he had associated activity at Crossard, where a church and parsonage being built, he in 1794 made his home. But the rebellion of 1798, following upon the transfer of Collis to the English field in 1796, and compelling Mr. Burton and other friends to flee from the vicinity, the property was sold.

From Ireland, Liebisch made his way to Scotland in the spring of 1796. Arran and Galloway had been repeatedly sought out of late by the Brethren's indefatigable itinerants, amongst whom Thomas Almond proved himself zealous to imitate the good example of Caldwell and Wade and Caries in former times. But no permanent results came of these efforts, though continued through several years, and Irvine itself, the filial of Ayr, should pass into extinction because of the removal of the members elsewhere.

Although the proposal of Hartley with reference to the founding of an institution for ministerial education had failed of approval, the conference of 1795 had not been altogether unattended with outward results in the widening of the work. In the central counties Bedford, where the foundation stone of a new place of worship was laid in 1795, and whose pastors served some eight preaching-places in addition to that in St. Peter's parish, had for years been fruitful by means of itineracies far and near, especially throughout the rural districts. About forty miles distant, for example, in Northamptonshire, and served also from the county-seat, in the cluster of villages formed by Culworth, Eydon and Woodford, there had gradually gathered an increasingly numerous company of men and women attached to the Brethren's Church. The "society" plan of serving them had been tried since 1792, but without affording complete satisfaction to these friends themselves, whose leader was William Hunt, a yeoman of Woodford. To the conference convened at Fulneck they accordingly sent a petition to be organized into a regular congregation, and this transpired at Woodford on September 25, 1796.

It was during this period also that the usefulness of the Yorkshire Brethren reached forth to Doncaster, and to Kirby-Lonsdale among the hills of Westmoreland. The first visit to the latter place had been paid in 1789, though no actual organization was formed here, the service rendered being the promotion of life within the parish church. About eight miles away, however, within the Yorkshire borders, where the Swale begins to gather its tribute of waters to swell the stream of the Yorkshire Ouse, an Independent minister, Edward Stillman, in his youth a member of the Moravian Society at Bristol, with his flock came into recognized fellowship with the Brethren, the first contact taking place in 1794, through a visit thither of a minister from Fulneck. The union was the more naturally effected since Keld had been one of the scenes of Ingham's activity, whom the people held in blessed remembrance.

During this period also energies were directed towards the educational sphere, boarding-schools being established in 1796 at Fairfield (for girls, and six years later for boys), in 1792 at Gomersal and Dukinfield, in 1794 at Wyke, and in 1799 at Ockbrook, the last four being the church's contribution to the education of Englishwomen, whilst for their Irish sisters Steinhauer commenced to put forth similar exertions at Gracehill in 1798. The last school was favored with rapid prosperity, thanks to the special talents of its founder and the general esteem in which the Brethren were held. But its foundation was laid in unpropitious times.

Since 1791, in part a fruit of reaction from the terrorizing of the *Peep o' Day Boys*, and stimulated also by the successful development of the French Revolution, the *United Irishmen* had been secretly compounding rebellion. Under the leadership of

20

Wolfe Tone, and misled by the hopes of a French landing at Killala, the turbulent discontent assumed the proportions of an open insurrection in 1798. With the example of the Jacobin fury before them, and maddened by their own sense of wrongs, the patriots allowed gross brutalities to disgrace their cause and contribute to its defeat. Though Wexford was the chief theater of actual warfare, the rising assumed ominous proportions in Ulster also, and for a time the vicinity of Gracehill threatened to be the scene of a conflict between the royal army and that of the rebels. During the week from the third to the tenth of June apprehensions rose to a climax. For three days the settlment was in the hands of the insurgents, who had overpowered the troops at Randalstown and at Ballymena. Happily no actual violence was endured, though life and property had been held at a cheap rate elsewhere, and loud threats were uttered against the Moravians. The worst was averted through the rapid desertion of their standards by several thousand rebels at Ballymena, on receiving news of the downfall of their cause elsewhere, the most determined only maintaining an unequal contest hereafter by recourse to outlawry. Having served as a place of refuge for loyalists of the vicinity, Gracehill was exposed to the vengeance of desperate irreconcilables, whose excesses and depredations still rendered life unsafe, and for some time it was necessary to maintain semi-martial regulations at night. Patrols and pickets kept watch and ward. As late as the Christmas season of 1799 the outlaws created alarm, and until public tranquility was restored church work was at a disadvantage.

CHAPTER XXXV.

THE CHURCH IN AMERICA DURING THE YEARS PRECEDING THE
SYNOD OF 1801.

More than ever the dearth of ministers and the need of an institution in America for the preparation of candidates became apparent. From time to time there arrived from abroad men for the service of the congregations or of the schools, but it was difficult for them to adjust themselves to the new surroundings; and the leaders were beginning to feel the weight of years. This was especially the case after the recall of Von Schweinitz to Germany. Bishop Ettwein no longer possessed the physical vitality which had rendered possible the extensive itinerations of his prime and on November 5, 1798 his chief assistant since 1790, John Augustus Klingsohr, died. Bishop John Andrew Hübner served as successor of Hehl. John Gebhard Cunow was administrator in place of Von Schweinitz. Marschall, like Ettwein in the eventide of life, received as his special assistant Frederick von Schweinitz, his own grandson and the son of the former administrator.

Under Jacob Van Vleck, its Principal from 1790 to 1800, the Seminary for Young Ladies at Bethlehem enjoyed prosperity. Higher education for women had few exponents as yet. In the summer of 1797 the Principal was compelled to address a circular to patrons, explaining the impossibility of considering new applications for admission for one year and a half to come, so many were on the list. The catalogue of the three hundred and sixty-five pupils, entered during this term, contains the names of many well-known and influential families. A grand-niece of President Washington and names like Sumpter, Huger, Alston, Bayard, Heister, Addison, Butler, Bleeker, Lansing, Livingston and Roosevelt testify to the national reputation now enjoyed. Nazareth Hall, until 1802 in charge of its resuscitator, Charles Gotthold Reichel, also flourished, though its numbers were not equal to those of the sister institution in Bethlehem.   Its tutors were secured from among men classically trained in the schools of the church in Germany.

Amongst the features of life in the congregations the following deserve notice. Christianspring, west of Nazareth, which from its inception had been occupied by unmarried men only, in the early part of the year 1796 ceased to have this distinctive character.   Indeed the choir establishments, and especially those of the single men, were all in a backward condition.   Nor did the settlement at Hope in New Jersey flourish.   When the call of Von Schweinitz to become a member of the Unity's Elders' Conference reached Pennsylvania, it gave rise to a thorough discussion of the American situation previous to his departure for Europe, and the probable abandonment of Hope in the near future was then recognized.   Situated at a distance from centers of population, off the lines of travel and commerce, and in a neighborhood at that time insalubrious, it lacked the natural elements of success.

Efforts to be of service beyond the bounds of the organized congregations were not altogether wanting.   In 1794 stated appointments north of the Blue Mountains were met from Nazareth and Schoeneck, and the Brethren at Lititz preached monthly at an outpost in Earl Township, and in 1798 at Hempfield.   On Staten Island, in 1792, the pastor strove to evangelize the colored people.   But chief energies were directed towards the missions amongst the Indians.

Fairfield in Ontario soon became a prosperous home for the wanderers, and the missionaries won an excellent reputation amongst the settlers.   To them Michael Jung preached fortnightly at a place seven miles distant, and other colonists forty miles away also desired the services of the Brethren.   By the year 1798 quite a tract was under cultivation, wheat as well as Indian corn being grown.   The industry of the converts, it was admitted, lowered the cost of some of the necessaries of life at Detroit.   The great Northwestern Fur Company each year as a rule purchased about 2,000 bushels of corn and a large number of cattle at Fairfield.   The annual output of maple sugar was estimated at 5,000 pounds.   The Christian Indians supplied canoes for all the neighboring settlements.   Their manufacture of baskets and mats, etc., was in great demand, and found a ready sale. Yet the resumption of communications with Bethlehem, and the news of the reservation by Congress of the lands along the Tuscarawas created a feeling of special satisfaction. The hearts of many were at home across the border. In spite of the prosperity that blessed them on the Thames, there were those who were ready to accompany the venerable missionary, Zeisberger, when he announced that the time had come for a re-occupation of their former fields in Ohio. This announcement could not be made until 1797, for until that year the unsettled state of the Northwest had prevented the surveying of the land. This having been effected by General Putnam, the Surveyor General of the United States, in conjunction with John Heckewelder and William Henry, as representatives of the church, in the latter part of May, 1798, John Heckewelder and William Edwards left Fairfield with five Indian brethren to make the needful preparations for the reception of the returning colony. In August Zeisberger and his wife, with Benjamin Mortimer, who had recently entered the service of the mission, once more sought the scenes along the Tuscarawas, and brought with them seven Indian families, thirty-three souls, to form the nucleus of the resuscitated mission. The new village was established about half an hour's walk from the site of Schönbrunn, on the opposite bank of the river, and farther down the stream. It received the name of Goshen. By the end of the year 1799 it numbered fifty Indian inhabitants, forty-six of whom had been baptized.

It was evident that not all the land granted on the Tuscarawas could be occupied by the Christian Indians in person. Hence the Society for Propagating the Gospel as their trustee, in 1796 invited members of the church to remove to Ohio and occupy lands on the Gnadenhütten and Salem tracts, whose rental was to be used exclusively for the benefit of the converts. A ready response came from Gnadenhütten on the Mahoni, it being understood that the church would supply the colonists with a minister and establish a store, the surrounding country being practically a wilderness. Thus in the spring and summer of 1799 a new congregation came into existence. Amidst great hardships, the road having frequently to be cut through the forest after leaving Georgetown, the nearest settlement, to allow of the passage of wagons and cattle, the pioneers had made their way from Pittsburgh. Bush, Peter, Hotel, Greer, War-

ner, Walton, Rhodes, Davis, Edmunds and Chitty are the names
that figure amongst those who braved the toil of a life in the
wilderness.   Heckewelder was appointed the agent of the
society, empowered to grant leases.   David Peter had charge
of the store,   Louis Hübner, of Lancaster, became pastor in
1800, Mortimer from Goshen previously ministering to the little
company, who numbered at the close of the year before only
twenty-five souls.   New accessions doubled the number in the
first year of the new century.

Nor was this the only enterprise projected by the society.
In the year 1790 there arrived at Philadelphia three deputies
of the Senecas, asking that teachers be sent to their people, who
were desirous of adopting civilized usages.   Various gentlemen
of influence considered this an opportunity for the Brethren;
and on January 6, 1791, Governor Mifflin invited Bishop
Ettwein to meet the Indians.   Whilst in Philadelphia Ettwein
learnt that the Legislature of Pennsylvania had determined to
grant 70,000 acres of unreclaimed land as a source of revenue
for the establishment of schools and institutions of learning.
In the name of the society he therefore applied for a tract situated on Lake Erie, to be used in defraying the expense of securing teachers for the Indians.   The petition was favorably received, and an act was passed granting the society 5,000 acres
for this purpose.   This grant was surveyed in 1794 by John
Heckewelder and Jacob Eyerly for the church, in two tracts,
one lying along the Conneaught and reaching to Lake Erie, and
the other on the French Creek, not far from Presqu' Isle; and
to these lands 985 acres were added, in part purchased from the
State and in part a donation.   That on the Conneaught received
the name of "Hospitality" and the other "Good Luck;" but settlers came forward very slowly.

In the year 1782, when the converts on the Tuscarawas had
been taken captive to the Sandusky, some of their number had
escaped westwards to the White River, a tributary of the
Wabash.   Here a portion of the Delaware and Nanticoke tribes
now had their home.   In 1799 William Henry Gelelemend (Kilbuck) sent a message from Goshen to this portion of his people
through a chief named Hakinkpomagu, who paid a visit to the
Tuscarawas in May, announcing the return of himself and his
Christian companions to their old homes, and inviting the Delawares of the White River to come frequently to Goshen and

receive the gospel. This established a connection between them and the missionaries, and in April, 1800, a messenger arrived from the council of the Delawares at Woapikamikunk, as their town was called, with an invitation to send teachers thither. In response John Peter Kluge, formerly a missionary in Surinam, and Abraham Luckenbach, a teacher at Nazareth Hall, received the call, and proceeding from Bethlehem in October, arrived at Goshen on November 18. The project met the entire approval of Zeisberger. During their four months' stay in order to familiarize themselves with the language under his direction, two Indian Brethren, Charles Henry and Jacob Pemaholend, went in advance to announce their coming to Chief Packanghill. Land was promised at Woapikamikunk, the assurance was given that no rum-seller or drunken person should be allowed to annoy them, and that they should labor unhindered.

Accordingly on February 24, 1801, the missionaries, accompanied by Joshua, a native helper, as interpreter and nine other persons, left for the Wabash in canoes, via the Muskingum, the Ohio and the Miami. On their arrival many privations were at first endured owing to scantiness of provisions, and fevers prostrated them. The house of the missionaries was on an elevated spot between nine populous Indian towns. In March, 1802, two Indian women were baptized as the first converts, and the moving thither of Christian Indians from the former settlements caused a little village of ten houses to spring up around the church. Other baptisms followed, so that by the close of the year the congregation counted twenty-three souls.

Meantime two of the veterans of the Indian Mission entered into their rest, Gottlob Senseman at Fairfield on January 4, 1800, and William Edwards at Goshen on October 8, 1801. The place of Senseman was filled by Christian Frederick Denke of Nazareth, who now came to assist Michael Jung and Sebastian Oppelt. Soon their united endeavors reached out towards an extension of the mission. Being joined in 1801 by John Schnall, it was possible to commence activity amongst the Chippeway villages on the Jongquahamik.

The original intention of the settlement of the Brethren in Georgia had never passed wholly out of mind. Missions amongst the Cherokees, Catawbas, Chickasaws and Creeks had been repeatedly planned. John Hagen's visit to the Cherokees in 1740 and Ettwein's negotiations with their chiefs at Betha-

bara in the sixties failed of permanent results chiefly because
of the unsettled state of the country. In 1783 Martin Schneider
had visited Cherokee towns on the Tennessee River, but strife
between the colonists and the Indians had once more inter-
vened. In 1799 and 1800 journeys of exploration were undertaken with encouraging results by Abraham Steiner and Frederick Christian von Schweinitz, of Salem. Through the kind
offices of Captain Butler, of the U. S. army, they were enabled
to arrange preliminaries for a mission at Tellico Block-house
on September 23, 1800, at a great council of from three to four
thousand Indians. In April of the following year Steiner and
Gottlieb Byhan set out to found the mission. The spot they
selected they named Spring-place (now the county-seat of Murray County, Georgia). At first the intricacies of the Cherokee
language and the lack of an interpreter presented great difficulties; but slowly a Christian congregation was successfully
gathered and the life of the people as a whole was savingly influenced.

CHAPTER XXXVI.

THE GENERAL SYNOD OF 1801.

Throughout the church great, if somewhat vague, expectations attended the preparations for the first synod in the new century. Hope awaits a new era with the turn of each century, even though no intelligent reason assures that the imperfections of the past, and the imperfections only, will be left behind. Besides a sunny gleam of peace now lit up skies long dark with war clouds. Yet what transpired might have taught the thoughtful that the hopes were not substantial. The conviction was current, that the lay element should be given a voice in the discussions of the synod. But it was regarded with apprehension by the authorities, the more so because the demand was voiced in Herrnhut itself, in a letter addressed on September 20, 1800, to the Unity's Elders' Conference by a lawyer named Riegelmann. Then towards Christmas John Jacob Fischer, who had arrived from Surinam, began to rather freely criticise the methods of management and alleged arbitrary dealings of certain officials, and in February, 1801, by paper entitled "Considerations with respect to our Constitution" turned his criticism into a public attack. He received the *consilium abeundi*, and in response to his appeal for legal redress, Minister von Burgsdorf suggested the propriety of his withdrawal to Württemberg, his native state, since Saxony did not care to harbor "revolutionary spirits." Meantime Riegelmann, who did not identify himself with Fischer's personalities, was elected one of the delegates of the Herrnhut congregation. How sedulously care was taken on the other hand to curb the agitations of "revolutionary spirits," will appear from the fact, that when this deputy-elect asked for copies of the "Results" of the synods of 1764 and 1769, with the view to a more intelligent discharge of the functions assigned to him, he was refused his request, *"weil kein Privat-*

mann einen Synodal Verlass in Händen haben dürfe." Apparently
the French Revolution and the enormities perpetrated in the
name of liberty, fraternity and equality, had associated the
stigma of Jacobism with every attempted emendation of existing institutions and regulations. By arbitrary repression of
expression of opinion the unimportant outworks of church
policy must be defended, lest the fall of the citadel of the faith
itself should follow. A vague fear of revolutionary purposes
created disinclination to distinguish between essentials and
non-essentials. Burkhardt thus accounts for the disappointing
features of the situation: "On both sides, on the part of the
leaders of the Unity and within the congregations themselves,
the requisite conditions were not forthcoming. An aspira-
tion after larger independence and freedom from tutelage permeated a wide circle in the congregations. The civil and communal features stood out in antithesis to the spiritual ties which
cemented together the Unity. But the aim of the strivings was
confused and unclear, without an understanding of the special
calling of the Unity. Those who presented themselves as leaders, Jurist Riegelmann, now living in Herrnhut in the capacity
of a private citizen, and the former superintendent of Hope in
Surinam, John Jacob Fischer, who had been dismissed from
mission service, lacked the earnest spirit of a conviction resting upon the conscience. But on the other side, amongst the
leaders in the Unity's Elders' Conference and in the conferences
of the individual congregations, there failed a comprehensive
understanding of the mission divinely appointed to meet the
needs of the age. Spangenberg's benign yet so far-seeing spirit
was missing. It was felt that the task of the synod in its guidance of the church would be best fulfilled by a strict conservation of external forms and regulations, the heritage of former
days, together with an external repression of all movements
and strivings of a contrary sort. By sheer force this policy was
carried forward to victory; but not to the true profit of the
church or the real promotion of its inner life. This character
of the synod of 1801 moreover remained firmly imprinted on the
following period, from 1801 to 1818. In many respects there
was a retrogression in the spirit of the Unity during the first
two decades of the century, and all strivings to attain a freer
attitude over against customary usages were suppressed by
recourse to more or less external means."

The news of the occurrences at Herrnhut had spread to the other congregations, and aroused considerable apprehension and tension of spirit. In the political world also the air was charged with portentious possibilities of disturbance. On March 23 the Czar, Paul I, of Russia had been assassinated, the violent outcome of a conspiracy of nobles made desperately venturesome by the universal discontent throughout his empire. Britain, regarding the Armed Neutrality as tantamount to a declaration of war, had sent Nelson into the Baltic, and on April 2 the bombardment of Copenhagen had compelled the Danes to withdraw from the league against the isolated foe of France. Kleber's assassination by a Moslem fanatic had shaken the power of the Republican forces in Egypt, and their discomfiture had been completed by Abercromby. The news of Menou's capitulation could not be far off. Amid such pregnant events the influence of the times refused to be ignored.

The composition of the synod predisposed its deliverances in the interests of ultraconservatism, championed by the weighty influence of the venerable Godfrey Cunow. The chief speakers were the most elderly men who had participated in all synods since 1764. Out of forty-five members only two represented the unofficial lay element.

Bishop Risler was chosen President. A review of the Results (*Verlass*) of the Synod of 1789 directed the course of the discussions. No material changes were made in the statement of doctrine. In connection with the ritual and worship no important alterations were suggested, except that in future the "Praying bands" in the congregations—the outcome of the "Hourly Intercession" of former days—should be restricted to those of the members who were chosen each quarter-year by lot. The idea was promulgated that the actual kernel of the church consists of a faithful band within each congregation—*Das treue Teil der Gemeine*. With questionable accuracy this notion was supposed to be identical with what Zinzendorf sought to convey by a similar expression as far back as 1731. Yet the lessons of the past should have taught that any attempt to discriminate and fix by regulations divisions that might promote the idea of an inner circle of the elect in contrast to the rest of the membership, would hardly promote unity, vitalize the religious life of the whole, and insure the normal growth of the entire church. The expression $\tau\acute{\epsilon}\lambda\epsilon\iota o\iota$, employed in Philippians 3:15 and Hebrews 5:14, by reference to which the notion was defended, had no sharply defined portion of the apostolic church in view. As Plitt truly observes, "the present conception involved the narrowing down of the Zinzendorfian idea of the Brethren's Unity as a '*Gemeine Gottes im Geiste*,' and that of Spangenberg as a 'living Church of Christ,' to a fragment within the Unity." This formal recognition of a "faithful part" within the church was calculated to further depress its life, being tantamount to a confession of weakness and ill-health with an implied recognition of inability to cope with the situation; for an organization usually falls below its ideal rather than outreaches it. The more hopeful plan would have been to hold out to the entire organization the possibility of outdoing even the best era in its past.

With all the leaning to conservatism, it was admitted that the plumbline of the exclusive settlements could not be longer applied to all the congregations and that even in the settlements the determination of the membership of the church council by lot must give place to an election. Various congregations in England and Ireland asked that freedom be granted in respect to the use of the lot in connection with marriages. The discussion became especially lively when Riegelmann read his *promemoria* in favor of liberty. Hegner, the successor of Cranz as church historian, supported him. John Christian Geissler opposed. John Frederick Reichel advanced objections to any change. Cunow recommended adherence to the most definite rules for the settlement congregations—"our entire constitution necessitates that in them no marriage shall be contracted without the approval of the lot." This opinion prevailed. It was a victory dearly bought, as the sequel of declining numbers shows. A usage which had come into existence gradually and without legislation, by the voluntary assent of those concerned, the incorporation of which in the regulations since 1764 was justifiable only on the ground of the previous voluntary practice, was now insisted upon as a *sine qua non* of membership in the congregations proper.

Earnest discussion was aroused in connection with the organization of the "choirs" by an inquiry into the condition of the establishment of the unmarried men at Herrnhut. As in other congregations, it no longer served as a worthy training school for missionary candidates. The old severe simplicity had departed. Undue attention to refinement of tastes, a love of pleasure, a relaxing of discipline and a decline of thoroughness and masterly execution in handicraft could be lamented. The establishment was becoming rather a joint lodging-house than a religico-industrial institution. Synod resolved to insist upon external rules for this and the kindred institutions with more rigid strictness than ever—a futile panacea for the amendment of inner life, especially since with the altering conditions of the world of labor these establishments were outliving their usefulness.

Financially the church had been prospering in spite of the war, not so much on account of liberal contributions as by reason of extraordinary sources of income, the proceeds of annuities and the sale of certain estates in 1798, inherited from one of the Gersdorfs. At the opening of the synod only $54,000 of indebtedness remained. On July 12 Strümpfler, one of the representatives of the Herrnhut congregation and a director of the Dürninger establishment, assumed this remainder in the name of his firm. Yet the financial outlook was not altogether rosy. Bishop Gregor dampened the general exultation by drawing attention to the fact that the debts of the individual congregations were formidable, and had been increasing since the last synod. Moreover, the general sustentation account of the Unity and that of its schools still needed liberal support.

Of the former members of the governing board Briant now retired from active service, and Kölbing became warden of Herrnhut. Their places were taken by Goldmann and Bishop John Andrew Hübner.

Finally Christian Solomon Dober of Gnadenfrei, Gotthold Reichel, Thomas Moore and Traugott Benade, Provincial Helpers in Wachovia, England and Ireland, were consecrated bishops; and Von Forestier, Von Schweinitz and Christian Ignatius La Trobe were solemnly set apart as *Seniores Civiles.*

CHAPTER XXXVII.

THE CONGREGATIONS ON THE CONTINENT OF EUROPE DURING THE
NAPOLEONIC ERA.

On November 6, 1801, Bishop Gregor suddenly passed away, overtaken by a stroke at the door of his dwelling. His place in the Unity's Elders' Conference was taken next spring by Godfrey Cunow, hitherto professor in the seminary, who soon acquired a dominant influence. In 1808 he was consecrated a bishop at Herrnhut by Bishops Reichel, Liebisch and Hübner, and three years later became President of the Conference. "He viewed affairs mainly from the external historical standpoint, and conceived that a remedy could be found for every faulty circumstance primarily by the application of external means. It was difficult for him to appreciate the views of others. Hence he emphasized his own opinions strenuously and gave them effect with strongly developed self-consciousness. He meant to be faithful to the best interests of the Unity, but he apparently had too little appreciation of the innermost being of a man and of the heart's needs. Hence his activity lacked the right spiritual influence and therewith the deeper blessing." Such is Burkhardt's analysis.

However the sole blame for the retrogression characterizing this period cannot justly be laid at the door of any one man. The spirit of the times must be taken into account. It was a transitional epoch, when modern institutions were emerging amid the storms of war. With the unsettling of principles that had held unquestioned sway for centuries in civil and political life, when moreover it seemed impossible to predict what precise changes would attain stability, the conservative men who stood at the helm in their bewilderment could not discern the currents amid which the Unity was drifting. Heavy financial losses and prolonged moral and industrial depression predisposed many to fear and expect the worst. There was an excuse for pessimism in Germany in the era of Austerlitz and Jena and Wagram.

Before the flimsy texture of the peace of Lunéville had given way Hans Christian Alexander von Schweinitz died, February 26, 1802. His place was taken by Niels Amtrup, since 1798 accounting treasurer of the board.

During the portentous period when the First Consul seized the imperial crown and his ambition to pose as the modern Charlemagne unmade and created dynasties, a new settlement was being founded. In response to a petition addressed to the synod of 1801, Goldmann had been sent to Stuttgart in December, 1802, to open negotiations. The Duke of Württemberg was favorable, but certain of his officials demurred at the desired freedom from military service and the enjoyment of religious liberty. In May, 1805, events took a new turn. A favorable conclusion was reached, and arrangements were made for the purchase of certain estates near Villingen, in a mountain district with the typical features of Black Forest scenery, about forty miles from Stuttgart, but the outbreak of the war put a stop to any actual commencement.

With fearful rapidity the "grand army" of France was hurled down the valley of the Danube. The capitulation of Ulm, October 20, followed by the awful carnage of the "battle of the three emperors" at Austerlitz on December 2, made it impossible for Talleyrand to dictate humiliating terms to the Austrian envoys. Now Napoleon began to find thrones for the members of his family. "The Confederation of the Rhine" was proclaimed in July, 1806, that a line of dependent states might serve as a defensive barrier for France on the east. "The Holy Roman Empire" was abolished. Now, too late, Prussia became the active champion of German liberties. Proud in the memories of her great Frederick, she was over-confident of her ability to wrestle a fall with the Gallic Hercules. The double defeat of Jena and Auerstädt shattered these patriotic expectations.

In connection with the operations of this disastrous campaign several of the congregations experienced the horrors of war. When Brunswick retired to Magdeburg, Barby and Gnadau suffered from their proximity. "To Barby the Saxon General Von Zezschwitz retreated with about six thousand men. He was pursued by the French, who took possession of the town and, notwithstanding the neutrality granted to Saxony, plundered and in a most shameless manner ill-treated the inhabitants. Generals Murat, Bernadotte and other persons belonging to the staff lodged in the castle, and were provided for by the warden of the congregation. A depredatory party set a house near the church on fire, for the purpose of plundering with greater secrecy. Some of them forced their way into the kitchen of the college, but were prevented from committing any excesses, a guard being procured, who kept off the marauders. The students rendered essential service in helping to extinguish fires. All the other inhabitants that were able were put in requisition by the French, to assist at the ferries across the Elbe and the Saale. During this season of terror a thousand dragoons were quartered a day and a night at Gnadau. The smallness of the settlement rendered this burden so much the more oppressive. Twenty, thirty, and even sixty men and their horses were billeted on private houses, and four hundred privates, besides officers, took up their quarters in the Brethren's House. This night cost the Brethren nearly $1,000, not reckoning the value of property lost by individuals. The farm of Döben, belonging to the settlement, was plundered of sixteen horses, all the grain and hay, the linen and clothes of the farmer, besides $700 in ready money."

Other circumstances were also operated against Barby. The lease of the manor farm, which had been a source of profit, had expired in 1801. Electoral Saxony was willing to renew the lease, but at a higher rate—at least 20,000 thaler in place of the former 18,000. Whilst the authorities of the church were hesitating, a certain Mr. Dietze came forward with proposals even more favorable to the government. Hence only the castle and the land immediately connected with it, held by hereditary feehold, remained to the church. This involved the maintenance of an expensive establishment without due resources. At this juncture, in May, 1805, Christian Theodore Zembsch, the president of the college for fifty-five years, resigned on account of failing powers. His former colleague, Cunow, advocated a retransfer of the institution to Niesky. To this the Unity's Elders' Conference agreed in 1807. But the course of public events caused the withdrawal to be even more radical in its nature than was at first contemplated.

The interview of the emperors on the raft in mid-stream at Tilsit narrowed the territory of Prussia to about one-half of what Frederick William III had inherited, and the Kingdom of Westphalia was given to Napoleon's youngest brother, Jerome. Barby lay within the new realm. Most of its people removed to Gnadau. With the college the archives and various scientific collections had been transferred to Niesky. The printing establishment was closed, and the book-store transferred to Gnadau. The castle and its subsidiary buildings stood empty. In the early spring of 1808 Goldmann had appeared before the French authorities at Cassel to solicit a retention of the special concessions. The answer was equivocal, except that relief from military service could be enjoyed only by the purchase of substitutes. Thoroughly discouraged, the authorities of the church now offered the castle of Barby, exclusive of the farm of Doben, to the astonished Dietze on very easy terms. He gladly closed with the offer. On May 6, 1809, the property was surrendered; and to Christian Gottlieb Hüffel, since 1804 preacher at the castle, but now member-elect of the Unity's Elders' Conference, was assigned the sorrowful duty of conducting the farewell service, on August 20. "The surrender of this memorable spot aroused throughout the Brethren's Church a universal feeling of deepest regret. Even the French-Westphalian Prefect at Magdeburg said: 'Why was that necessary? We would have protected the Brethren, and no harm would have come to them!'" Time endorses this verdict. The abandonment of Barby was not an absolute necessity. Had patient endurance held out for less than a decade, Barby might again have become a source of strength. But the castle around which hallowed memories clustered now became a magazine for grain and wool! The chapel was turned into the office of the French ruler of the district, and later became a tax-office, and finally a sugar-factory!

Meantime the new settlement in the Black Forest slowly assumed proportions. It had first been proposed to call the place Nain. But the King of Württemberg preferred to stand sponsor to a "Königsfeld." During the years 1806 and 1807 the most necessary edifices were erected. The civil authorities desired the establishment of pretentious business and manufacturing concerns under Moravian auspices, but the risks of the times precluded large ventures. As yet the church did not feel

21

free to urgently solicit the removal thither of *Diaspora* members. Who could tell what new combinations might result from the next turn of the political kaleidoscope? Nor did the hesiancy of the church lack justification. The terms of the Peace of Pressburg were too hard for Austria. In connection with the new delimitations of territory in South Germany, consequent upon Wagram, the portion of the Black Forest to which Königsfeld belonged was now assigned to Baden. Fortunately the new ruler was disposed to ratify existing concessions.

Whilst Barby and Gnadau had been specially affected by the operations of the campaign of Jena, other settlements had also been caused to severely feel the stress of the times. Billetings of troops and quarterings of various officials at Christiansfeld, the passage of several thousand Prussian troops through Neudietendorf, Prussian and Saxon and French bivouacs in turn at Ebersdorf—about 20,000 of Napoleon's men, with their leader himslf and twenty of his staff being accommodated there for several days in October, 1806—the occasional interruption of the peace at Herrnhut, Niesky and Kleinwelke, together with their being very heavily mulcted to furnish the sinews of war, requisitions laid upon the Silesian congregations in 1806 and 1807, and the humiliation of Berlin in 1807 and 1808; all these experiences taxed the resources of the church and interfered with its life and usefulness. That the brief period of rest which followed the treaty of Vienna was thankfully received, may well be understood. But it was of very short duration. Napoleon's insatiable ambition hurried him into one of the greatest crimes of his life, on which retribution waited, and the slumbering national consciousness of Germany awoke like the arousing of a giant to become an instrument in his downfall. The dynastic idea led the "Man of destiny" to wring from a pliant senate and a specially constituted ecclesiastical council a decree of separation from his wife. Then the Austrian marriage formed the prelude to the disastrous invasion of Russia, and the War of Liberation followed.

During the operations in Saxony several congregations were dangerously exposed. In February and March of 1813 the hospital of the Saxon army passed through Herrnhut, and large requisitions were made. After the battle of Lützen more than seven hundred wounded were cared for in the Brethren's House alone. Throughout the spring and summer numerous bodies of either army were quartered in the settlement, Blücher at one time making it his headquarters, and the Emperor of Russia visiting it on April 21. But although the burdens were sufficiently heavy, no actual conflict occurred at this time in the immediate vicinity.

During March, April and May, Niesky was laid under requisition to supply troops with provisions, at times almost daily; the Cossacks signalized themselves by their extortions. After the battle of Bautzen several hundred wounded were nursed here. At Kleinwelke the nearness of the conflict caused intense anxiety. Only three miles from Bautzen, its destruction at one time seemed inevitable. "May 15 was a very heavy day. The rumor of the retreat of the allies was confirmed. The roads were thronged with artillery and ammunition wagons and troops of every description, which exposed our place to imminent danger. In the afternoon the vanguard of the French, after a victorious attack at Gausig and Goede, advanced under a heavy cannonade on Salz Foertgen, only a mile distant, and planted a battery on a neighboring hill. The balls whistled through the air, and many fell in the fields close to the settlement. Terrified by this scene, many of the sisters resolved on immediate flight, hastily bundled up some clothes and provisions, and retired into the chapel to await the issue.

"Scarcely had they entered this sanctuary when two men belonging to a plundering party, exasperated by the delay, pursued the warden of the congregation into his house, adjoining the chapel. He fortunately escaped through a window. Meeting his wife on the stairs, they robbed her, forced their way into the parlor and burst open the bureau. But before they could secure their booty two brethren succeeded in seizing one of them and breaking the sword of the other.

"This and some similar occurrences induced the elders of the congregation to have the sick and infirm conveyed to Radibor, three miles distant, where they were kindly received by the Roman Catholic priest. A large company of sisters and some families went the next day to the same village, passing without being molested through the Russian and Prussian outposts. They were comfortably accommodated by Lady Von Boese.

"They were not long gone before the French occupied a hill, called the Wiewalze, close to the settlement, placing their foreposts up to our very houses. Several officers came to procure provisions, followed by great numbers of soldiers, complaining of oppressive want, not having tasted bread for four days. They dug up potatoes and turnips and ate them raw with the greatest avidity. Fifty and more at one time rushed into one house and seized all the victuals they could find. We now became seriously afraid of a general plunder, especially when observing the settlement surrounded by a bivouac of twenty thousand men, and at but a short distance an army of nearly two hundred thousand, occupying a line twenty-four miles in length. A great part of the wood belonging to the village of Welke was cut down, our garden fences, and even our out-buildings were demolished to serve as materials for erecting tents. It was a fearful sight to see four thousand men walking silently through our place at night, laden with straw they had collected in the neighboring villages. In the midst of this danger a circumstance occurred, which at any other time would have appeared an intolerable burden, but now proved a real benefit. The whole staff of the French army, commanded by General Bertrand, consisting of twenty-two generals and above two hundred officers, was quartered upon us, though our settlement does not contain forty houses. The officers behaved handsomely, and were ready by day and by night to do their utmost to quell disturbances.

"On the 17th the danger increased..... The large camp-fires, kindled in the bivouac and before our very doors, increased our danger. We attributed it solely to the protection of God that our houses were not reduced to ashes, for our predatory guests examined houses, barns, hay-lofts and cellars with lighted candles and firebrands. A report was spread that the two armies would halt and come to an engagement here.

"Cut off from all supplies, in the center of a camp surrounding us on all sides, we were in fear of soon being in want of necessaries. On the 19th at noon Bonaparte suddenly made his appearance, and rode with incredible speed along the line of his troops, which extended many miles, examining the disposition, and giving orders. He was received with enthusiasm by the soldiers, who seemed to forget all their hardships as soon as they saw him.

"A continuous and heavy cannonade from the direction of Konigswertha commenced, and ended in Marshall Ney's corps joining the main army, which completed the plan for battle.

All was terror and confusion. A division of Württembergers and the whole corps of the Duke of Tarentum passed through our settlement. Some Brethren who served as guides to these troops were in imminent danger of their lives, being sometimes in the thickest of the fight; yet they all escaped without receiving the slightest hurt. The camp near our place was in part evacuated; but Napoleon and a numerous staff remained there till after midnight. Columns of troops were marching across our fruitful fields, and treading down the young and promising corn.

"In the forenoon of the 20th we heard distant firing, but in our immediate vicinity there was a dead silence. Quite unexpectedly a cannonade, dreadful beyond description, commenced at noon, about three miles from us. The ground trembled, the windows shook, and the very air was agitated. This was the commencement of the bloody battle of Bautzen. We could distinctly see the firing of the cannon, the movements of the regiments and every change in the position of the combatants. In the evening we heard the French had gained the day. Had they been defeated and obliged to retreat, the batteries behind our place must have reduced it to a heap of ashes, as had been the fate of other villages, the flames and smoke of which filled the air."

Kleinwelke had then to accommodate two thousand sick and wounded soldiers. After the removal of the hospital strolling marauders gave annoyance till the beginning of June.

On May 23 Gnadenberg, in the line of the retreat of the allied army, was alarmed by reports of the approach of the French, and most of the people fled. The vanguard entered next day, and about thirty thousand troops passed through in forty-eight hours. The place was given up to plunder for several days. On the promulgation of the armistice quarters were required for one thousand men. In the preliminary movements of the next campaign on August 16 it was the scene of a contest between the French and the Russians, during which much damage was done to property, and another clash of arms occurred nearby on the 21st. After the second action the French troops wrought furious havoc.

Though threatened with distress from the proximity of the Prussian and Russian camps of 200,000 men during the armistice, the headquarters being only five or six miles away, Gnadenfrei escaped serious damage. Both sovereigns and various persons of rank honored this settlement with visits.

Finally the crowning contest of October 16 to 19, the great battle of the nations at Leipsic, and the two days' engagement at Hanau, October 30 and 31, turned the scales permanently against the French. Brilliant strategy and desperate courage could not avert the entrance of the allies into Paris. Abdication, exile at Elba, the landing at Cannes, and the "Hundred Days," with Ligny, Quatre-Bras and Waterloo, and St. Helena closed the tragic drama of empire. At last there was peace.

Its advent gladdened exhausted Europe, and the Brethren's congregations had as great cause for thankfulness as any. Apart from the demoralizing effects of incessant war, various settlements had been seriously affected by the stagnation in manufacture and trade, as well as by the direct losses and burdensome requisitions. Many private families were impoverished. Rixdorf had so declined that in 1811 it had been combined with Berlin. Sarepta had lost heavily by the destruction of its house in Moscow during the great conflagration. In 1815 the debts of the congregations as such were estimated at a total of $112,500.

Meanwhile death had been active in the church. On November 22, 1808, Jacob Christopher Duvernoy, a member of the governing board since 1797, passed away. On November 17, 1809, the John Frederick Reichel, one of the most distinguished figures of the post-Zinzendorfian period, followed him into rest. The next to be taken was Bishop Samuel Liebisch, on December 3, and on the 26th of the same month their colleague Bishop John Andrew Hübner also died. Then in 1811 Frederick Rudolph de Watteville and Bishop Jeremiah Risler were called home, on January 11 and August 23. The former, the husband of Elizabeth, youngest daughter of Count Zinzendorf, who died on February 17, 1807, had been a member of the Conference since 1785, and since 1798 the chairman of its financial department, his sound judgment, ripe experience and even temperament being most valuable in recent years. With his death the title to the Zinzendorfian estates passed to two unmarried ladies, as proprietors for the church, Countess Charlotte von Einsiedel and Henrietta von Tschirsky. Bishop John Godfrey Cunow now became President of the Unity's Elders' Conference, and Bishops Dober of Gnadenfrei and George Henry Loskiel of

Pennsylvania were chosen to fill the vacancies, Richter, Wied of Surinam, and Fabricius of Zeist having previously obtained seats in the board. But Loskiel, for a season detained in America, soon answered a most imperative summons, and ended his career in the western world. Nor was his place supplied before the meeting of the next synod, as little as was that of Charles von Forestier, deposed in 1812, or that of Geissler, who died in 1815. From that year the Conference was constituted of but ten members.

As a result of the negotiations of the "Holy Alliance" Prussia's territory was augmented, and now Niesky, Gnadau and Neuwied came under Prussian dominion. Though Frederick William III refused to remit military service, considered by him a duty inseparable from citizenship, assurance was given of his protection and favor. A similar mark of esteem came from Czar Alexander. Unsolicited, on October 17, 1817, he published an edict, granting the Brethren and their *Diaspora* circles privileges in Livonia and Esthonia. These manifestations of regard, and the new spirit of hopefulness imparted to Germany by the peace purchased at so costly a price, were not without a good effect. As a contribution to the forces influencing religious thought, and as a counterpart in Germany of the *Periodical Accounts* in Britain, "*Beiträge zur Erbauung aus der Brüder-Gemeine*," edited by Christian Frederick Stückelberger, were issued in 1817 and 1818. Nevertheless exclusivism and isolation had gained the day, as contrasted with the flexibility, universality and syncretism of the Zinzendorfian period. New affiliations were deprecated and shunned rather than sought, and opportunities even in the *Diaspora* activity were lost, with the exception of the field in the Baltic Provinces. Contraction rather than expansion was characteristic, if the field of foreign missions be left out of the count.

CHAPTER XXXVIII.

The era introduced by the synod of 1801 was noteworthy in Britain for increasing interest in foreign missions, for the founding of the British and Foreign Bible Society in 1804, and zeal for better Sabbath observance. It was also a period rendered anxious by excessive taxation, a consequence of the wars, by depression in commerce, manufacture and trade, by riots directed against the introduction of improved machinery, by agrarian distress, and by agitation for the reform of the "Poor Laws." Within the sphere of the Moravian Church itself it was a time rendered memorable by the manifestation of kindly interest in the missions of the church on the part of members of other households of faith.

As far back as the disastrous campaigns of the continental war and especially after 1812 and 1813, when the losses sustained by the church appealed to the sympathy of all friends, the benevolence of liberal Christian people in England contributed to relieve the most pressing necessities thus occasioned. Meanwhile the stated issue of the *Periodical Accounts* had been enlarging the circle of friends. At length a number took steps to secure the permanence and enlargement of the assistance which they rendered to the missionary cause. Thus on December 12, 1817, "The London Association in Aid of the Missions of the United Brethren" came into existence, destined to become a very important factor in the history of Moravian Missions. In the first year its contributions amounted to more than $3,350.

Presenting as it does a spectacle almost unique, a combination of numbers of Christians of every name for the stated support of evangelization amongst the heathen carried on by one division of the church as such, and so affording ever since its establishment a noble illustration of Christian union, the following extracts from its annual report for 1818 are of special value, setting forth as they do the motives and designs of its founders:

"When the conflicting armies overran Germany their (Moravian) settlements were intruded upon and utterly impoverished; other sources from whence their missions derived their largest supplies were destroyed in that unhappy country which was the chief seat of their church. Hence an appeal became necessary to the benevolence of other Christians; for on one hand a vast debt was incurred, and on the other there was an increasing demand upon the church to supply the necessities of the many missionaries laboring in the different stations, and to provide for those who, from age or infirmity, were becoming incapable of further exertion; and also for their children, for whom they could not make provision themselves, having expended all their time, their strength, their life, upon the work of the mission.

"The appeal was made at length, and it was not made in vain. By various contributions the debt was so diminished at the close of the last year that it was supposed not to exceed (at that time) the sum of five thousand pounds, although when complete accounts were collected from their widely scattered settlements (each of which bears a part in the supply of necessaries for the missions), this estimate was discovered to have fallen very far short of the fact.

"It was under the impression made by this appeal that the *London Association* was formed. Its object was to excite the attention of Christians of every denomination, to labors, so valuable, standing so much in need of support; and to gather their willing contributions. In prosecuting this object your committee have felt the importance of observing caution and delicacy, lest they should seem officiously to interfere with the concerns of the United Brethren's Church, or take any steps which might wound the feelings of its members, or present it under a false character to the world. It became, therefore, a fundamental principle with them, that the whole should be conducted with as much privacy as possible, that no interference whatever should take place in anything relating to the proceedings of the United Brethren; nor any documents be printed without the full concurrence of their Society for the Furthering of the Gospel among the Heathen. On this principle they have uniformly proceeded and have recommended the same in case any association for a similar purpose may be formed in union with them, as the only ground on which they can coöperate. For the assistance of such friends of the cause as may wish to associate for the above purpose, an outline of the necessary rules is added.

Rules of the London Association, in Aid of the Missions of the United Brethren.

"I. All persons subscribing annually one guinea, or collecting sixpence per week, shall be members of this Association.

"II. Benefactors of ten guineas and upwards, and ministers making congregational collections to the amount of twenty guineas, and executors paying bequests of fifty pounds, shall be life-members.

"III. The Committee shall consist of all ministers who are members, and of twenty others to be chosen out of the lay-members of the Association annually in the month of October, who shall hold their meetings on the second Friday of each alternate month, which shall be open to the attendance of any member of the Association; three members of the Committee attending shall constitute a quorum, and it shall be in the power of the Committee to meet more frequently, if judged expedient by them.

"IV. That the whole of the Funds obtained (after deducting incidental expenses), shall be remitted to the Conductors of the Missions of the Church of the United Brethren, commonly called Moravians.

"V. All members shall receive, *gratis*, a copy of the Periodical reports of the Missions of the United Brethren."

Circumstances rather than the previous formulation of a settled policy led to the second feature of the life of the church in Britain during this period. Napoleon's decrees of Milan and Berlin rendered intercourse between the Continent and Britain exceedingly uncertain. Communications between the governing board in Berthelsdorf and their assistants in England, as well as the rare instances of personal intercourse, were under the necessity of utilizing a costly and circuitous route via Copenhagen and Gothenburg. Hence a measure of independence followed, Thomas Moore and William Foster being Provincial Helpers in England with Hartley as their colleague in Ireland.

A seminary for the training of candidates for the ministry was opened at Fulneck, October 12, 1808, with Henry Steinhauer as principal—a measure approved by Verbeek and Forestier when on their return from America.

Often it was impossible for the British Provincial Helpers to consult with the Conference in Saxony previous to filling a ministerial appointment. Hence larger discretionary powers were assumed.

Under Reichel as director, the two schools at Fulneck enjoyed especial prosperity. Wellhouse (Mirfield) founded in 1801 for boys, Bedford in the same year for girls, Ockbrook in 1813 for boys, testified to a vigorous prosecution of the educational movement in England; and Gracefield school for girls and Gracehill school for boys, both founded in 1805, were the fruit of similar endeavor in the sister isle.

Congregational life fluctuated. In 1806 Baildon, eight miles away, across the Aire and perched on the cliffs at the edge of the heather-clad solitudes of Rumbles Moor stretching across to the valley of the Wharfe, an outpost of Pudsey in the old days of itineracy before Fulneck had arisen, received a place of worship, and ten years afterwards became a distinct congregation. Manchester chapel had been abandoned in 1800, but preaching was commenced at Greenside, as an outstation of Fairfield, in 1807 —to be given up in 1809, because the place of worship could no longer be had. In 1811 Pudsey was combined with Fulneck. In the Midlands a permanent advance was made. About a dozen miles north of Bedford, in the midst of rural quaintness and simplicity, rise the magnificent trees of Kimbolton Park, dominated by the towers of Kimbolton Castle, famous for its melancholy association with the first unfortunate queen of Henry VIII. Just beyond the Bedfordshire border of the park is the little village of Pertenhall. Here John King Martyn, first curate, then rector of the parish, afterwards minister and finally bishop of the Moravian Church, warmly evangelical in his principles, was at this time in sympathy with the work of the Brethren. In his house, "the little House on the Hill," the first religious service under Moravian auspices in this vicinity was held on August 19, 1809. Out of it a congregation came into existence, obtaining its first place of worship in 1823, and in time several filials were organized. From Woodford, in the vigor of its youth, branched out Priors Marston, the first place of worship being consecrated by Bishop Traneker on September 26, 1806; Culworth, near by, consecrated its chapel on November 15, 1809. In the south of England, the society at Plymouth, whose beginnings had resulted from Caldwell's itineracies in 1768 after his return from Scotland, in May, 1805, was organized by Bishop Moore into a regular congregation with Ralph Shufflebotham as its pastor. Pendine chapel, in Wales, was dedicated by Moore in the autumn of 1812.

Ireland's distress from the effects of repeated insurrections and the consequence of the wars did not cease with the Act of Union. All the energy of a man like Hartley was needed to merely hold existing enterprises. When he could write in his diary, in 1805, respecting the chapel at Ballymena, "It held 300, and was sold for a trifle," this man of aggressive vigor must have felt many a thorn in his side. He and his associates were not the men to merely fold their hands and lament the lost opportunities of the past; but his early death, in his fiftieth year, on June 27, 1811, proved a serious loss. Traugott Benade was called in his place to Gracehill. Though Kilkeel, amidst the mountains of Mourne, was abandoned in 1817, the home missionary spirit was vigorously manifested with Gracehill as a center of activity.

Thirty preaching-places were statedly served by the itinerants in 1815. Old affiliations were revived, and former connections renewed. At Grange a chapel was built. But all this vigorous revival of the old spirit was unattended with results commensurate with the amount of energy expended.

CHAPTER XXXIX.

THE CHURCH IN AMERICA DURING THE OPENING YEARS OF THE
NINETEENTH CENTURY.

Bishop Ettwein died at Bethlehem on January 2, 1802, and
Frederick William von Marschall at Salem on February 11.
Bishop George Henry Loskiel, the son of a Lutheran clergyman
in Courland, who had been educated at Barby and had held
various positions in the church in Germany since 1765, was
placed at the head of affairs in the North. His chief colleague
was John Gebhard Cunow. In the South, Bishop Charles Gotthold Reichel and Christian Lewis Benzien and Simon Peter
were the Provincial Helpers, all men of European birth and
training.

Soon after the arrival of Loskiel a conference of ministers,
thirty-six in number, was convened at Bethlehem. Remaining
in session from October 8 to 30, 1802, it reviewed the various
phases of life in the congregations. Placid absence of desire
for a far-reaching policy centered attention upon the adjustment of arrangements to meet the regulations of the Unity as
such. Yet two important measures were adopted, one of local
the other of general significance. The first was the erection of
a new and for existing conditions an immense church at Bethlehem. The second was the establishment of a theological seminary, advocated especially by Benzien. By the incessant wars
of recent times communication with Europe, and with it reliance upon the European institutions of the church for a supply
of ministers, had been rendered precarious. The actual execution of the plan was delayed until the arrival of Charles von
Forestier and John Renatus Verbeek, commissioned by the
Unity's Elders' Conference to pay an official visit in 1806. By
them, on October 3, 1807, Ernest Lewis Hazelius and John
Christian Bechler were inducted as professors in the theological
seminary organized in modest proportions in connection with

the school for boys at Nazareth. Humble though the beginnings were, the actual founding of a divinity school involved an important preparatory step in the direction of provincial independence. A school for girls and young women was founded at Salem in 1804, and a new building was completed for the similar institution at Lititz, begun in 1794.

But the period was one of retrogression. In the cities and in the South the transition from German to English was attended with the perplexities that must be faced by every bilingual church. The country congregations in the North suffered through the removal of members to larger centers of population and the lack of provision to follow them up. In Pennsylvania Donegal, and in New Jersey Hope and Woolwich were abandoned. Gnadenthal, Christianspring and Friedensthal were merged into Nazareth. The people of Gnadenhütten on the Mahoni had removed to Beersheba, across the river from the new Gnadenhütten in Ohio. Of new enterprises mention can be made only of Sharon, near Goshen, in Ohio, in 1815, begun through the efforts of Jacob Blickensderfer. The hampering regulations which obtained, and especially the excessive recourse to the lot repelled rather than attracted new members.

In 1811 Bishop Loskiel, recalled to Europe by the Unity's Elders' Conference, retired from his American office, but did not at once leave Bethlehem. Next year he received an appointment as a member of the Conference, but was unable to set out on account of the war and his own declining health. After a protracted illness, he died at Bethlehem on April 9, 1814. His memory is perpetuated by his history of the missions amongst the Indians.

Charles Gotthold Reichel had been transferred from the South, and was President of the Helpers' Conference until 1817. Bishop John Herbst, who filled the corresponding position at Salem, was succeeded by Jacob Van Vleck, consecrated a bishop at Bethlehem on May 2, 1815.

At length in 1817 premonitions of a new era appeared. Conferences were convened to discuss changes requisite to the health and prosperity of the American congregations. That at Bethlehem on June 9 consisted of twelve ministers and thirteen delegates of the "settlement" congregations. Bishop Reichel presided. Practical unanimity of views was disclosed. On June 21 a recess was taken until August 4. In the interval the

Provincial Helpers and three official representatives from Bethlehem and Nazareth met the pastors and eleven delegates of the remaining churches in the North. At Salem a similar gathering had been in session in May.

When the requests of the conference of the settlement congregations are considered, they appear to scarcely warrant the judgment pronounced upon them in Europe: *"In den Nordamerikanischen Gemeinen eine nationale Freiheitsliebe, Unlust an willkührlichen Verfassungseinrichtungen, Lust alles abzuschaffen, und neues einzurichten."* The following were the main amendments sought: the abolition of the *Sprechen*; abrogation of the inhibition of military service; release of the President of the Helpers' Conference from the duties of any other office; empowerment of the Helpers' Conference to make appointments without previous consultation with the Unity's Elders' Conference, with the proviso that existing rights of appeal to the highest board shall not thereby be annulled; pastors to be no longer connected with the oversight of the temporal affairs of a congregation, whose committee shall be elected without recourse to the lot; the congregation-council to be composed of all male communicants of legal age and in good and regular standing; the abrogation of the use of the lot in connection with applications for membership, in connection with marriage, and in connection with the appointment of American delegates to the general synod; the guaranteeing that at least one member in the Unity's Elders' Conference shall be personally acquainted with the American congregations. Though dealing with non-essentials rather than essentials, these requests exerted a decided influence upon the general synod summoned for June of the next year.

During the opening years of the century the Indian missions were prosecuted with vigor. But the bright outlook on the White River was speedily darkened. Upon the death of the chief who had been their friend and protector, and after the deposition of his similarly disposed successor, the missionaries had to encounter all the opposition and all the machinations of rum-sellers and other foes of the gospel, who with the medicine-men stirred up the latent hostility of the heathen. During the year 1805 they became aware that their lives were in actual danger. A certain Shawnese stranger who had ingratiated himself amongst the tribe, claimed that he could detect the arts of those who practiced witchcraft and poisoning; hidden mysteries were open to him. A council was called before which those whom he accused should be compelled by torture to make confession, recalcitrants to receive the blows of war-hatchets and then be burnt. The first to be accused before the hellish assembly was old chief Tettepachsit. He had nothing to acknowledge. So the inquisitors fastened him by cords to two posts and began to roast him at a slow fire. Agony forced from his blistering lips a lie of despair—that he kept poison in the house of Joshua, the missionaries' interpreter. On March 13, 1806, seven painted Indians dragged Joshua from the mission by main force. The converts had fled; some were compelled to abet the malicious cruelty. When confronted with the prisoner, Tettepachsit admitted that he had accused him only to pacify his torturers, and declared that Joshua was innocent. The Shawnese asserted that although Joshua had no poison, he had a familiar spirit by whose means he destroyed other Indians. On the evening of the 16th word reached the missionaries, that an aged convert named Caritas had been burnt. Next day a howling mob, with blackened faces dragged old Tettepachsit to the mission, lit a huge fire, and wounding him on the head with a hatchet, cast him alive into the flames, the while they diverted themselves with the convulsions and cries of the miserable victim. The flames of his pyre kindled the grass and brush nearby and filled the mission with the smoke. Around the missionaries the frenzied furies danced. Several hundred miles from friends, and agonized by the probable fate of Joshua, they expected the worst. Then the murderers burst into their dwelling and demanded bread and tobacco. Giving these, they interceded for Joshua, but to no effect. That same day the martyr, enduring torture by the aid of prayer, perished in the flames. For a time Kluge and his wife and Luckenbach maintained their post amid days and nights of terror. At last it was made clear to them that duty no longer demanded a useless risk. With great difficulty they made their escape, and after many hardships found refuge in the settlements on the Tuscarawas. Perforce the western mission was abandoned.

In the autumn of 1803 Bishop Loskiel paid an official visit to Goshen, and a renewal of the mission at New Salem was resolved upon. Accordingly Oppelt and John Benjamin Haven proceeded to the Petquotting early in 1804. But a sad reverse

DAVID ZEISBERGER.

was again experienced. Drunkenness amongst the Indians was industriously promoted by traders and by unscrupulous white settlers, in order to take advantage of them when intoxicated. The damaging consequences of this solicitation, successfully pursued especially when the people were scattered through the maple forests for the manufacture of sugar, were very far-reaching. The carousals begat a spirit of heathenish repudiation of all restraint. Inner corruption began to work what external persecution alone could never have effected.

This was the case both at Goshen and the Chippeway mission. The latter proved a failure. All these distressing features became a source of deep grief to the aged Zeisberger. His end was fast approaching. At the age of eighty-seven, and after a most remarkable career of sixty-two years of missionary service, he was called to rest and reward on November 17, 1808. During these years of toil he had itinerated amongst his "brown hearts" in Massachusetts, Connecticut, New York, Pennsylvania, Ohio, Michigan and Canada. Mohicans, Wampanoags, Nanticokes, Shawnese, Chippeways, Ottawas, Wyandots, Unamis, Unalachtgos, Muncies, Onondagas,.Cayugas and Senecas had been the recipients of his message. He was fluent in the Delaware, Mohawk and Onondaga tongues, and was familiar with many other Indian dialects. The translation of the Bible and of the Moravian Hymn-book and Liturgy into the Delaware, the compilation of a German-Delaware lexicon, and the composition of Onondaga and Delaware grammars formed only a part of his literary labors. He had led hundreds of savages to live a consistent Christian life. By his counsels the Delawares had been restrained from yielding to the solicitations of Indians in British pay, when the fate of the Colonies was uncertain. Sad it is, that his mighty energy, signal ability and unquenchable devotion were so largely neutralized by the folly, the selfishness and the sin of white men.

The War of 1812 broke in upon the charming pastoral life at Fairfield in Canada, and caused the cessation of the work on the Sandusky. When Detroit was occupied by the American army under General Harrison, it was perceived that Fairfield would soon be untenable. But whilst arrangements were being made to abandon the place, the church was transformed into a British hospital, in which seventy wounded were at once received. On October 3, 1813, General Proctor announced his

22

intention to fortify the place. The Indian congregation had meanwhile taken to the woods. On the 5th the Battle of the Thames was fought about two miles away. It was now charged, though the proofs did not accompany the charge, that some of the Fairfield Indians had been implicated in a massacre on the Raisin, and the victorious American general, mistaking the character of the place, gave the mission to pillage and the flames. Not a house was left standing. Michael Jung, old and infirm, accompanied by Schnall, and their families, toiled back to Bethlehem heart-broken, and Denke, the third missionary, wandered with the scattered converts in the woods, putting up temporary homes now here, now there. Attacked and plundered by Kickapoo and Shawnese bands, he was cut off from communications with his brethren for a couple of years. Not till the close of the war did the converts dare to return with him to Fairfield. In 1815 it was rebuilt on the opposite bank of the Thames, and soon numbered about thirty houses, with one hundred and twenty Christian and forty-seven heathen inhabitants.

Meantime Goshen had seen its best days. Steadily the natural increase of the white population and the enlargement of the land under cultivation, with the ensuing competition in primitive industries, rendered the conditions of life more and more unfavorable for the Indians. Therefore New Fairfield became the Christian Indians' Mecca.

In the South on the other hand satisfactory progress was being made by the new mission. In 1807 its extension into the country of the Creeks was attempted. Karsten Petersen and John Christian Burghardt set out from Salem for Flint River, near Milledgeville. John F. Holland joined them as an assistant in 1810. But five years afterwards this post was given up. In the Cherokee mission several changes had taken place. Steiner had returned, and Jacob Wohlfarth, his successor, had died in 1807. John Gambold had gone out in 1805. A school had been early established at Springplace, and the mission was solidly advancing. With regard to the Christian Cherokees it could be reported: "The men are altogether of the first respectability in the nation, and as such, during the late embassy to Washington, have done honor not only to the Gospel but to the capacity and good sense of the aborigines." Disinterested testimony was further borne by the Abbé de Serra, in his account of his tour in the United States, as follows: "Judge of my surprise, in the midst of the wilderness, to find a botanic garden, not indeed like that at Paris, or yours at Kew; but a botanic garden, containing many exotic and medicinal plants, the professor, Mrs. Gambold, describing them by their Linnean names. Your missionaries here taught me more of the nature of the manner of promulgating civilization and religion in the early ages by the missionaries from Rome, than all the ponderous volumes which I have read on the subject. I there saw the sons of a Cherokee Regulus learning their lesson, and reading their New Testament in the morning, and drawing and painting in the afternoon, though, to be sure, in a very Cherokee style; and assisting Mrs. Gambold in her household work or Mr. Gambold in planting corn. Precisely so in the forests of Germany or France, a Clovis or a Bertha laid aside their crowns, and studied in the hut of a St. Martin or another missionary."

CHAPTER XL.

An era of general war is never favorable to missionary operations. Now the blockade of continental ports by British naval
squadrons, exchange of cannon shots with privateers, and in
several cases actual capture, had to be taken into account when
men were sent forth. All ordinary means of intercourse with
distant colonies sometimes failed. Colonies exchanged masters, and therewith the legal status of the church was altered and
new requirements had to be complied with. Financial losses
were frequent.

In Greenland the missionaries received reminders of the rigor
of the region. The age of adventure had not passed. During
the intensely cold weather of three months of the year 1793
through lack of even their usual unsatisfactory source of fuel,
drift-wood and scrubby brush, the missionaries were reduced to
the train-oil lamps of the natives as a source of heat. On June
10, 1794, two missionaries left New Herrnhut for a neighboring
island, where they hoped to procure wood but were shut in by
the ice. For almost one month they found it impossible to make
their way home, nor could provisions be brought to them. After
encountering many dangers and supporting life by catching fish,
they at last reached home on July 8. In 1798 Jacob Beck and
his wife after a long and stormy voyage from Copenhagen, had
a narrow escape from the ice whilst on the way from Friederich-
shaab at Lichtenau. John George Grillich left Julianenhaab for
Copenhagen on October 4, 1798. When only fairly out to sea,
the ship had to put back on account of the ice. Two weeks later
another attempt was made to set sail; but after five weeks of
hopeless tacking hither and thither, was again driven back by
the ice, this time in a damaged condition. In February, 1799,

another attempt was made to put to sea, but from the 18th to the 25th the ice completely shut in the ship, after she had barely missed shipwreck on a sunken reef. Now the captain gave orders for her abandonment. A weary march over the ice followed. Two nights were spent without shelter, and water was to be had only by melting snow. Scarcely was the desolate shore of Greenland reached, when a terrific storm arose. Not until October 29, and after many adventures did Grillich reach Copenhagen. In 1804 and 1805 these experiences were practically repeated by Christian David Rudolph and his wife.

The conflict between Denmark and Britain, until the blockade was relieved in 1811, meant peculiar distress. In 1808 the British government, indeed, in a spirit of true humanity fitted out two ships for Greenland. But the larger of these was lost in the ice, and was the one destined for the portion of the country where the Moravian stations were situated. Flour became very scarce. Tobacco, the common medium of exchange, and powder and shot were quite exhausted. In May, 1811, Henry Menzel wrote: "No ships arrived in Greenland last year. We have therefore not received any provisions from Europe, nor does it appear that we should receive any this year; and if not, there is little prospect for us left, but that we must die of famine and distress of mind; for no European can subsist on what the Greenlanders eat, without bread. The consequences soon appear in a dysentery which carries the patient off in a short time....For these three years past we have not received any seeds, and this year we can sow nothing in our gardens." The very clothing of the missionaries began to give out. But at last, on August 16, 1812, to their intense relief the Danish ship *Freden* arrived with goods of all kinds sufficient to meet all needs for two years. It had been sent from London by the Society for the Furtherance of the Gospel, a license having been procured which permitted a Danish vessel to proceed from Copenhagen via Leith for the express purpose of relieving the mission.

John Conrad Kleinschmidt who had now completed nineteen years of service in Greenland, and had recently lost his wife, took advantage of this opportunity to return to Europe with his children and the widowed sister Walder. They set sail on September 2. On the 29th the *Freden* was struck by lightning during a tremendous storm. The bolt killed one of the sailors and stunned another. For three days and two nights the ship

drove helplessly before the wind. For a week the whole company were put on a short allowance of water. Leith was at last
reached on November 10. In two weeks Kleinschmidt's youngest child died from the hardships experienced. Nevertheless
after his furlough this hero was ready to go back to Greenland.

John Godfrey Gorke, detained for a while in Europe by the
war, in March, 1813, left Copenhagen with his family and two
other missionaries to return to his former sphere of labor. The
Danish vessel in which they sailed, the *Hvalfisken*, had been duly
licensed by the British to carry provisions to the dreary land
of bergs. With the messengers to Greenland there voyaged
also a party of missionaries destined for the West Indies via
England. In mid-channel between Denmark and Norway Captain Cathcart of the *Alexandria* frigate brought the Danish vessel to, and pronounced the license invalid. Not till April 5
were they permitted to weigh anchor for Leith. Five weary
weeks were required for the passage from the Scotch port to
Greenland. Then their Captain, Lindber, contrary to agreement, instead of landing them at Lichtenfels or New Herrnhut, where there was every facility for unloading, carried them
to Godhaven on Disco Bay. Thence they had to coast back
about 600 miles to New Herrnhut, from which station Kleinschmidt and his wife had yet another 500 miles in an *umiak* before making Lichtenau. Twice during the four months of
voyaging along the rocky and dangerous coast, did the delicate
Europan woman faint from fatigue.

In 1817 John Frederick Kranich, returning for a visit at home
after twelve years of work, was lost at sea, the ship foundering
with all on board.

Such were some of the episodes which gave variety to the
often monotonous round of missionary toil in Greenland. But
it was undertaken none the less willingly, nor did it go without
reward. The population in the districts about the older stations had become nominally Christian. Lichtenau alone afforded opportunity for contact with utterly pagan barbarians.
Here baptisms repeatedly occurred. Meantime Jasper Brodersen besides translating portions of the Scriptures comenced to
render into the Eskimo the liturgies of the church, which were
preliminarily printed at New Herrnhut. Henry Menzel translated a short compendium of the Bible for children. This
the Society for the Furtherance of the Gospel undertook to

print. Kleinschmidt was commissioned to prepare a version of the New Testament, with the publication of which the British and Foreign Bible Society made itself chargeable.

Until the turn of the century Labrador sorely tested faith and patience. The total number of Eskimos who had made their homes at the three stations was only 228. Occasionally the heathen were hostile. Sometimes supplies almost failed. But with the new century there came a reward to the fidelity of Benjamin Kohlmeister and his associates. The awakening began at Hopedale in 1804. Its nature marked its origin as from above. The conversion of two wild young fellows, Siksigak and Kapik, the latter as notorious as was Tuglavina formerly, made a deep impression on their countrymen. They had gone from Nain to Hopedale with the deliberate intention of causing trouble, but came back changed men, exhorting their countrymen to repent and turn to Christ. The revival necessitated the building of a new church. By 1818 six hundred people now made the mission stations their homes. As in the case of Greenland, Labrador also enjoyed the assistance of the Society for the Furtherance of the Gospel and of the British and Foreign Bible Society for the creation of an Eskimo literature.

Success encouraged a desire to widen the work. But although Kohlmeister explored the coast as far as Cape Chudleigh and the Ungava country, plans were strangely thwarted. On the one hand the force of missionaries was diminished by a peculiar accident. On the other hand the Hudson's Bay Company interposed objections. The former hindrance transpired as follows. As usual the missionary ship proceeded to Labrador in the summer of 1816. For more than a month after drift ice was reached, it could not make port. The floes extended two hundred miles out from land. But at length Okak was reached on August 29. Supplies were landed. Then the *Jemima* for three weeks lay a helpless prisoner of the Frost King. By dint of skillful efforts Nain was made on September 22. Here John George Kmoch, John Körner and Thomas Christensen, together with the wife of the first, boarded the vessel to proceed to Hopedale. But instead they made port in the Thames on October 28. For on the very day of sailing a tremendous snowstorm followed by a gale carried them out to sea, and no exertions of Captain Frazer served to bring his ship to the third station. During the night of the 9th disaster threatened.

Twisted by the violent blows of the storm-lashed waves, the larboard side of the vessel opened its seams, and water gushed in; but the overruling power of God averted loss. It was August 7, 1817, however before Kmoch and his wife and Körner concluded their trip to Hopedale, begun almost a year before.

The course of the mission in the West Indies is now intimately connected with the movement for the abolition of slavery. The pens of Clarkson and Ramsay had already stimulated and reënforced the voices of Wilberforce and Sharp, and in 1788 the Crown had appointed a committee of Privy Council to make inquiry concerning the slave-trade. Wilberforce had made his first motion for a committee of the whole House of Commons on this question, and during the years 1790 and 1791 evidence was taken. Meantime the outbreak of the Revolution in Paris had direct bearing upon the issue in the French colonies. In 1791 the National Convention passed a decree giving to the mulattos all the rights of French citizens. The plantation slaves became infected with a determination that the principles enunciated in the Declaration of the Rights of Man should be extended to themselves. Slave insurrections broke out in Hayti, Martinique and in the British colony of Dominica. In 1793 the abolition of slavery in Hayti was proclaimed, and made possible the enormities of Toussaint l'Ouverture and Dessalines. These events prejudiced sentiment in Britain. In Denmark the necessity for progressive action became apparent. So long as Denmark preserved neutrality, her colonies, and especially St. Thomas with its capacious harbor, became the rendezvous for commerce under every flag. Refugee capitalists and adventurers from the other Antilles and all parts of the Spanish Main sought out the Danish islands. All the more likely was the slave trade to flourish there, and all the more open would her slave population be to the influence of insurrectionary movements in progress elsewhere. Most urgent representations were accordingly made to the home government respecting the dangers that threatened. This situation of affairs led the King of Denmark on May 16, 1792, to issue a royal order, that the traffic in slaves should cease in Danish possessions from the end of the year 1802. At the same time and in the years immediately following, repeated requests were addressed to the Unity's Elders' Conference by Minister Schimmelmann and Countess von Reventlow in the name of land-owners on St.

Croix that the Brethren would widen the scope of their undertakings, and in particular assume the religious and civil education of the children of the slaves. With all good will, the trust could not be accepted in the measure intended by the proposers. The times were hard. Long continued drought, following a season of general sickness, lasted for four years. Scarcely any vegetation was to be seen, except the foliage of the large trees. In St. Croix drinking water was sold at a considerable price. Scarcity of provisions added its distressing features to those produced by the prostration of industry, complicated by the monetary confusion in America since the trade of these islands was chiefly with the States. Planters in their financial embarrassment frequently separated parents and children, husbands and wives, selling them wherever purchasers could be secured. Thus members of the church were scattered to Porto Rico, Tortola and St. Domingo. Moreover an awful tornado on August 12 and 13, 1793, long left its memory impressed upon St. Thomas and St. John. The church at Bethany collapsed in utter ruin, and the missionaries barely escaped with their lives. Most of the people lost houses, stores, provisions and cattle, and many men and women and children perished. The church at Emmaus remained standing, but the surrounding settlement was destroyed. The smaller buildings at New Herrnhut and Nisky were demolished. Not a plantation on St. Thomas but suffered. Forty ships were driven ashore. John Gottlieb Mücke, superintendent since 1791, had his burden of cares made heavy indeed.

These circumstances brought John Renatus Verbeek to the islands, to minister comfort in the name of the home congregations. Three months from April, 1797, he closely inspected each station. Then he proceeded to St. Kitts. Here progress had been made. Large accessions were the rule. The mission enjoyed general esteem.

Steady progress also characterized Antigua. Moravian blacks were selected for positions of responsibility, owing to their well-attested reliability and fidelity. In 1796 land for a third station had been acquired at the sea-shore. It received the name of Gracebay.

In Barbados Adam Haman and John Montgomery had begun to reap after years of patience, but the disadvantage of operations with Bunkershill, so remote from Bridgetown, as the center, had become apparent. Hence in 1794 eleven acres had been acquired in the vicinity of the capital, and named Sharon. Verbeek returned to Herrnhut in August, 1798.

Though greatly encouraged by his active sympathy and wise counsel, the missionaries on the Antilles were to realize, however, that difficulties were not over. In March, 1801, St. Thomas surrendered to a powerful British fleet. The remaining Danish islands speedily followed this example. The requisition of the mission buildings at Friedensberg for a hospital followed in April. With an intermission of a few years Britain kept control of the three islands until 1815. But with all the uncertainty of the times a new station was begun on St. Croix, Friedensfeld, central in its location. Characteristic of the conditions of the period were the experiences of John Gottlieb Ramsch and John Samuel Schaerf, who had been detained in company with the missionaries to Greenland on the *Hvalfisken* in the spring of 1813. Having sailed from Portsmouth in November, they were rapidly nearing their destination, when on January 10, 1814, their ship was chased by a vessel of superior size flying the American colors. It proved a privateer of fourteen guns. Though the Englishman mounted only six, decks were cleared for action. The missionaries went below and betook themselves to earnest prayer. The chase was stern. Not until half past seven in the evening was the American close enough to exchange shots. The fight was stubbornly continued through the night. Thrice the privateer tried to board the merchantman. But although one hundred and twenty assailants were met by only twenty-two, soon after daybreak the aggressor drew off. The English ship was so badly damaged that it was fortunate she could make St. Thomas next noon. One of her men had been killed and eleven wounded. The sequel is found in the diary of Friedensberg for 1819. In March a captain from Philadelphia who was known to the missionaries brought a fellow captain of similarly pronounced Christian character to visit the Brethren. After a while it developed in the course of conversation that the latter, Captain Boyle of Baltimore, had commanded the American ship in the fight. When Sister Ramsch now described to him the earnestness of the intercessions of the missionaries during the hours of conflict and suspense, he confessed that at the time the escape of the English vessel had been a mystery to him. He had later

learnt that her passengers were missionaries, and the whole episode had providentially served to lead him from rough habits
and a life of indifference to religion. In fact it had been the
means of his conversion.

Meantime on the English islands progress was being made.
As soon as Tobago came again into the secure possession of
Britain, Carl Schirmer was sent to the slaves on the Hamilton
estate, and in 1800 John Church became his efficient coadjutor.
The Antigua mission grew apace, in spite of frequent deaths
of missionaries from fever. Gracebay was transferred from its
old site to Manchineel Hill, in 1811, and Newfield was begun in
1817, the membership having grown to seven thousand. Barbados remained a field of more modest proportions. St. Kitts
severely felt the vicissitudes of the war. Provisions rose to
famine prices. In the spring of 1805 the French fleet anchored
in Basseterre harbor, and for a time the Union Jack had to give
place to the Tricolor. This delayed the establishment of Bethesda until 1819. About two thousand persons were in charge
of the missionaries here at this time. Jamaica also knew its
deep anxieties, from its proximity to St. Domingo. David
Taylor, Christian Lister, superintendent since 1790, Christopher
Herbst, John Bowen, Philip Howell, Nathanael Brown, Joseph
Jackson and Thomas Ellis were the chief missionaries during
the closing decades of the century. Early in the new century
the proprietors of various plantations placed halls on their estates at the disposal of the missionaries, and in 1815 Thomas
Ward began Irwin Hill, near Montego Bay.

In Surinam the arrival of John Jacob Fischer from Barby in
1789 imparted a new spirit at Hope on the Corentyne. Endowed with unusual linguistic ability, he acquired the Arawack
so as to preach within a few months, and in addition to the
possession of executive gifts he was also blessed with strong
physical powers. By his persuasion, the Indians removed to a
more fertile spot on the Aulibissi creek, in the vicinity of the
old station, where the mission was reëstablished in 1793. Plantations of coffee, bananas and cotton soon rewarded the diligence of the converts, and a neat village surrounded the church.
Mat-weaving and the manufacture of hammocks and the preparation of lumber formed an additional means of support, the
products being taken to Berbice. Before long a mission boat
was regularly employed to carry these goods to market. The

voyage back and forth was sometimes attended with a spice of danger, Fischer and John Peter Kluge suffering shipwreck in August, 1795, and the latter being captured by an English privateer in 1796.

But alas, the glory of Hope with its three hundred people was nipped in the bud. Small-pox broke out in 1800. More than twenty died within six months. Fear stimulated the reassertion of the Indians' disposition to rove, and missionaries rather encouraged the hiving of their swarm, in order the more thoroughly to influence numerous Arawack and Carib villages. By April the majority wished to be transferred to Aporo, seven hours' distant, but their teachers remained at Hope, visiting the filial at stated intervals. Aporo never prospered. Hope itself soon met with a sore calamity. At two o'clock in the afternoon of August 18, 1806, the cry of "fire" suddenly rang out. Built as the houses were of logs, plastered externally or weather-boarded, and having lath and plaster partitions, ceiled with planks and thatched with large leaves in the Indian manner, the school, the mission-house, the homes of individual missionary families and those of the converts quickly succumbed to the flames leaping like lightning from roof to roof. The entire village was reduced to smoking embers. Stores of various kinds, tools and implements, the tackle and rigging of the mission-boat, and the very orange trees whose shade had been so pleasant, were destroyed; books, clothing, some gunpowder and two barrels of flour, and the charred walls of the church— this was all the devouring element had spared. The fire was of incendiary origin and two years later the place had to be abandoned owing to the hostility of the heathen. Yet the ground was not yielded without an effort. In September, 1811, Thomas Langballe and his wife came from Paramaribo in order to renew the work. They found a desolate solitude. Where formerly the house and gardens of the mission had stood, rank tropical vegetation had taken possession; Hope had become the home of screaming parrots and the hiding place of reptiles. Yet the memory of better days survived. Langballe and his wife met seventy-seven of its former Indians, and were assured that nearly two hundred were still living. A desire was also expressed for the renewal of the mission. Therefore in the following year Genth and Hafa were sent from Paramaribo to the Corentyne. Three miles from Hope they found an Indian house prepared for their reception by Barzillai, one of the converts. Neither fevers nor the toil of clearing the dense forest would have daunted them. But the indifference of the Indians themselves finally caused them to turn to others who prized the message more highly, the slaves on the plantations.

For under John Wied this mission made vigorous strides forward. Appointed superintendent in 1790, he had been accompanied on his voyage out by Bishop Samuel Liebisch, whose official visit had materially systematized methods of work through the creation of a local board of supervision. Notwithstanding the interruption of communications owing to the war between Holland and England, flour at one time rising in cost to 150 florins per barrel; notwithstanding the repeated deaths of men and women from fever (when Liebisch visited Paramaribo fifteen missionaries already lay at rest in the little cemetery in the Brethren's quarter); and in spite of the fetishism in the very blood of the people, the congregation in the city now advanced rapidly, numbering seven hundred and fifteen in 1815. At the price of several lives New Bambey had been maintained, but in 1813 the mission in the wilderness had to be abandoned. So, too, the opposition of the planters compelled a cessation of operations at Sommelsdyk with its one hundred and fifty converts in 1818.

After the restoration of Cape Colony to the Dutch, Governor Jansen was very sedulous in developing a corps of Hottentot auxiliaries for defence against future invaders. The fame of Baviaanskloof had spread by this time, and its people had so won a name for steadiness, that rascally natives were wont to palm themselves off as inhabitants of the place in order to better secure positions in the service of the Dutch planters, and the missionaries issued certificates as a protection against imposters. Now Moravian Hottentots were particularly in demand as non-commissioned officers of this militia. Next John Philip Kohrhammer was appointed chaplain, but his chaplaincy came to a sudden termination in January, 1806. On the fourth of the month sixty men-of-war flying the British flag entered the roads. After a furious cannonade throughout the eighth, the invaders made good their landing. On the twenty-first Cape Colony once more became a British possession. On June 29 the new Governor honored Genadendal with a visit, and expressed his delight at what he saw. Pursuing Jansen's policy with regard to the enlistment of natives, however, General Baird unwittingly hampered the mission. Baird's successor, Lord Caledon, similarly appreciating the humanitarian aspects of the undertaking, suggested a new center of influence, at Groenekloof, near the sea, forty miles from Cape Town on the high road to Saldhanha Bay. Kohrhammer and John Henry Schmidt left Genadendal to inaugurate the new mission in March, 1808. By the end of the year about one hundred natives had established permanent homes in its vicinity.

Here in 1811 Schmidt made a thrilling experience. Packs of wolves constantly ravaged the flocks of the mission. Hence in August Schmidt and Bonatz organized a wolf hunt. They soon wounded one beast, but he managed to get away. Wearied with fruitless searchings, the chase was at last abandoned. Suddenly a shout apprized them that their people thought they had discovered the beast in a thicket. Schmidt gave his horse to a Hottentot and returned, gun in hand. One of the dogs plunged into the dense brush and started—not the wolf, but a tiger! (*Felis serval.*) The natives, except one, fled. Like a flash the tiger springs on this Hottentot, and has him beneath his body in such a way that Schmidt cannot shoot for fear of injuring the man. Soon the tiger turns on the missionary, whose gun is useless at such close quarters. But he wards off its cruel jaws with his uplifted arm. They snap upon his elbow. Then he grasps the tiger's fore-foot with one hand and with the other clutches its throat. It is a wrestle for life or death. At last the beast is thrown, and the missionary plants his knee on its body, the while he keeps his grip on its throat. His companion, Philip, can render no aid, all blinded as he is from his own wounds. But their cries bring the others. One of them points his gun under Schmidt's arm, and shoots the struggling tiger through the heart. Poor Schmidt has been dreadfully lacerated, and suffers extreme pain. Upon removal home, fever sets in. Happily the treatment of a physician is successful. Philip also rallies from his injuries and the shock of the attack.

The first of the three pioneers of the resuscitated mission to be removed by death was John Christian Kühnel, on April 20, 1810. He departed in the midst of usefulness, deeply mourned. But the workmen could safely pass to their reward now; their work was well established. Genadendal could soon count one thousand souls.

CHAPTER XLI.

THE GENERAL SYNOD OF 1818.

The second general synod in the nineteenth century was opened on June 1, 1818, by Bishop John Godfrey Cunow, who presided. It continued in session until the end of August. Younger men than usual were present in considerable numbers.

A searching and thorough examination into the entire structure of the Unity—doctrine, practice, ritual, constitution, administration, missions, social and economic life, finances, etc.—was entered upon with loyal enthusiasm and undoubtedly high purpose. This is to be conceded, even though compromises of doubtful utility resulted. To prepare for the discussions the second session was devoted to the reading of a declaration of fundamental propositions concerning the character and calling of the Brethren's Unity, which should be regarded as the standard. This paper had been previously drawn up by Bishop Cunow at the request of his colleagues, and had been approved by them. Synod in its turn also accepted the positions thus set forth, and testified to the practical unanimity of its members in respect to essentials.

Debate developed sharp differences of opinion concerning the use of the lot. It was fully understood, however, that the government of the Lord Jesus did not stand or fall with the employment of the lot, the latter being a subordinate affair of the external associated life of the Unity. Synod decided that when recourse to the lot was had in determining appointments to office the blank, third, lot should not henceforth be employed, but that the alternative should ever be stated after the fashion of the apostolic lot—"Which of the two." Nor should it be obligatory, when clearness and certainty of decision could be reached without its guidance. As to the decision of the lot in connection with proposed marriages, it was plain that the old order could not be maintained contrary to the wishes of the people. Yet there seemed to be no sufficient reason why the usage should be abolished where objections had not been raised. Therefore for the European settlement-congregations it should still be the rule; for the town and country congregations in Europe and for the American congregations liberty to dispense with it was granted. But when the news of this legislation reached the European settlements (and the synod had made this possible through the circulation of a weekly report of its proceedings) great dissatisfaction arose, notably in Herrnhut. Petitions came in, often contradictory in their purport. After a reconsideration synod empowered the Unity's Eders' Conference to give a new decision for the European settlements; and in 1819 this body extended the rule of freedom to all except ministers and missionaries of the church.

When reviewing the religious life of the congregations, zeal for the promotion of vital godliness distinguished the synod, whatever may have been the real value of plans adopted. Confessedly the former conception of a "faithful kernel" within the congregations had failed to achieve what had been desired and hoped. Now Bishop Cunow came forward with a new plan, according to which a distinction should be made between those who were only outwardly connected with a congregation and those who truly belonged to its inner fellowship. His plan was adopted. In brief it was as follows: The Unity of the Brethren is constituted of two concentric circles of associated members. The more external may be called the Brethren's Church. Into this enter the children of Moravian parents by birth, baptism and confirmation. Into this are also received those who from outside make application for membership. For the members of this outer circle four celebrations of the Lord's Supper shall be arranged annually. But within this circle there shall now be also a closer covenant fellowship—*ein engerer Bund*— the actual and essential congregation. An indispensable qualification for admission to this circle is an outspoken, earnest religious disposition. He who be received into it must declare his desire, and submit to the decision of the lot. In this inner circle the Holy Communion shall be celebrated every four weeks. Its members alone shall be admitted to the church council and the committee—*Aufseher Collegium.* Besides these two classes of persons, people who do not belong to the church may also dwell in a "settlement" on signing a declaration that they will do nothing contrary to the rules and regulations. In the event this legislation proved hurtful. It ministered to spiritual pride and a false sense of security and religious sloth, to be able to lay to the soul the flattering unction that one had been pointed out by the lot as one of the elect. Therewith it was only too difficult not to despise those who failed of attaining this privilege and the implied endorsement.

The doctrinal position of the church remained unaltered, save that a fifth article was added to the four already enunciated, viz., confession of faith that the work of the Spirit is made manifest in the fruits of a godly life.

In connection with the ritual, besides the distinction between the monthly and the quarterly communion an inner fellowship of prayer—*engere Betergesellschaft*—was projected for members of the inner circle, apparently a substitute for the "hourly intercession" of former days. Perpetuation of the rite of footwashing, which had been falling into abeyance for some time, was referred to each local elders' conference, action tantamount to abrogation.

A step forward was taken in the matter of church publications, by authorizing the bi-monthly issue of selections from the *Gemein Nachrichten*. They were arranged according to a threefold classification; first, reports from the mission fields and sermons and addresses; second, reports of the *Prediger Conferenzen*, memoirs and addresses and sermons; and third, reports of the congregations and *Diaspora* posts. The first of these were now to be printed; the second and third should continue to circulate in manuscript as heretofore. During recent years the educational activity had received a powerful impetus. Twenty-five church schools had been founded since the beginning of the century. In all about twelve hundred children of non-Moravian parentage were now entrusted to the care of the church. Synod therefore made public declaration of the fact that the Brethren's church regarded the educational sphere as a distinct and weighty trust. A special department of the Unity's Elder's Conference was charged with educational oversight. This involved a reconstruction of the board, henceforth to have three sub-divisions—the Department of Pastoral Oversight and Education, the Department of Missions and the Department of Finance. Considerable discussion was evoked by the status of

23

the joint college and seminary at Niesky. Experience had taught that the union of these two institutions was undesirable. Now one phase of sentiment, championed by Christian Frederick Ramftler, since 1803 stationed in England, urged the abolition of the seminary, and advocated the preparation of future ministers for their pastoral duties by having them serve, like the acolytes of the old Unity, as assistants to pastors who should receive them into their families and personally supervise their studies. On the other hand Frederick Lewis Kölbing vigorously contended for the maintenance of the seminary, as essential to the existence of the church. His views prevailed. It was resolved to leave the college at Niesky, and when Röntgen of Gnadenfeld suggested the Brethren's House of his settlement as a possible home for the seminary, its removal thither was decided upon. Here in a quiet *Ortsgemeine*, in the seclusion of rural life, it was thought a theological equipment might be acquired with the least distraction. Fortunately for the church the right man for the work of reconstructing this important institution was at hand. This was John Plitt, at present principal of the school at Neuwied. His biblical studies and systematic theology, and not least his researches in the history of the church, were to mark the beginning of a new era, imbuing his students as he did with a more philosophic understanding of, and a more ardent devotion to, the essentials of the mission of the Unitas Fratrum.

The finances of the church occasioned grave anxiety. Whilst the joint undertakings of the Unity as a whole were prosperous, serious losses had been suffered through fire at Hennersdorf in 1814, and in connection with the abandonment of Hope, New Jersey. Contributions showed a marked falling off; but the returns from the Unity's estates, money obtained by the sale of lands in Wachovia, and the earnings of the Dürninger establishment had combined to place a surplus at disposal amounting to 170,000 thaler. On the other hand the treasuries of the individual congregations in many cases were embarrassed. The net indebtedness of all taken together amounted to 660,000 thaler. On the principle of "one for all and all for one" the surplus was therefore divided pro rata amongst the congregations as a contribution towards the liquidation of the debts. These were to be funded. Since the fraternal principle had tended to foster an inclination of local authorities to lean on the general resources, it was urged that the spirit of self-dependence be fostered, and the communal and churchly accounts were to be separated; for the latter only were the local organizations under any circumstances to look for help from the general treasury.

Finally, the Unity's Elders' Conference was reconstituted: the Department of Pastoral Oversight and Education, John Renatus Verbeek, Bishop Herman Richter and Frederick Lewis Kölbing; the Department of Missions, Bishop Godfrey Cunow, Bishop Wilhardus Fabricius and Gottlieb Martin Schneider; the Department of Finance, John Frederick William Kölbing, Niels Amtrup, John Wied and John Henry Zäslein. Bishop Cunow became President of the new board.

CHAPTER XLII.

The removal of the theological seminary to Gnadenfeld was effected in September, 1818. Eight students bade farewell to Niesky and in company with one of their instructors, Adam William Braht, commenced the journey to the distant settlement on the Polish border, where the reopening took place on the 25th amid misgivings on the part of some who regarded the change, in part in the interests of economy, as equivalent to a banishment of the most important educational institution of the church to an environment, Polish and Roman Catholic, that would scarcely compensate for the absence of worldly distractions. Meagerly supplied with a teaching force—for at first Braht was the only assistant of Plitt—its indebtedness to the latter becomes all the more apparent. Then Braht's health failed, and he was replaced by Christian William Matthiesen. The curriculum crystallized into a two years' course in Exegesis, Dogmatics, Paedagogics and Didactics, Introduction to the Old Testament, Church History, History of the Unitas Fratrum, Applied Mathematics, Physics, Natural History, Physiology and Encyclopaedia—entirely too diversified a range of studies for any two men. Yet as the reward of seven years' toil, during which he contended for an ideal against adverse circumstances, Plitt could back upon his didactic labors with the satisfaction of one who knew that he had laid deep and solid foundations for the future. Meantime the college remained at Niesky, with John Stengörd in charge, his duties being later divided between Charles Frederick Schordan and Theodore Dober, the former becoming President and the latter Dean.

In the year 1820 another removal ordered by the synod was effected, the transfer of the archives from Niesky to the *Herrschaftshaus* at Herrnhut, the collection being placed in charge of Frederick Louis Kölbing. As a fruit of his researches, and as a preparation for a worthy celebration of the centenary of the resuscitation of the Unity, the *Gedenktage der alten und der erneuerten Brüderkirche* appeared at Gnadau in 1821. Next year an English translation "The Memorial Days of the Ancient and of the Renewed Brethren's Church" made the work accessible in Britain and America.

In quick succession the church was called upon to mourn several of her well-tried leaders. The first to be called home was the venerable John Renatus Verbeek, on July 13, 1820. From 1782 to 1789 a secretary to the mission board, he had been a member of the Unity's Elders' Conference ever since the latter year, and had been eminent from the talent for affairs which he inherited from his father, Peter Verbeek. The next was Bishop Hermann Richter, who resigned about six months later, feeling incapacitated by the effects of a stroke from which he never fully recovered. He died on March 19, 1821. The vacancies were filled by Bishop John Baptist von Albertini, Schleiermacher's friend and a gifted pulpit orator and a poet of no mean quality, and Samuel Christlieb Reichel, hitherto a secretary to the Conference. On March 20, 1822, there passed away the venerable form of one who linked the church of the new century to that of the Zinzendorfian era, John Christian Quandt, eighty-eight years of age, fifty-four of which had been actively spent in the service of the church. With Köber he had helped to pilot her through the worst financial storms. From 1769 to 1818 he had been a member of the governing board.

Herrnhut's centenary anniversary aroused enthusiasm more than local. In the mother-congregation itself the celebration lasted for three days, an immense concourse of people being in attendance, including representatives from England. In contrast to the expressions of sympathetic appreciation of the services rendered by the Unitas Fratrum, which at this time voiced the estimate of divines of various confessions, there were, however, those who sought to mar the very rejoicings of the Unity by a renewal of the attacks which had been the peculiarity of a past age, and which it had been reasonable to hope had been buried amid forgotten issues of that past. Strikingly characteristic, on the other hand, was the change in the source of these newer antagonistic writings. No longer, as in Zinzendorf's day, did they originate with men who alleged the unchurchliness of the Unity, but rather with those who championed the rationalistic school, to which the Unity had become offensive as a repository of pure Scriptural simplicity of doctrine and as the promoter of spiritual life within the church. This was especially the case in Switzerland, where sundry controversial articles appeared in theological journals. In two instances purely personal motives were at work. A certain John Hansen, a former member of the Christiansfeld congregation, published a tract entitled, *"Kann die herrnhutische Gemeine eine wahrhaft Evangelisch Christliche genannt werden?"* Dr. Luther of Dietendorf replied. Hansen wrote again, in 1823, *"Ein ernsthaftes Wort wider die Herrnhuter,"* but made public retraction in 1827. The other hostile writer was Charles Limmer, a deposed preacher of Saratov, whose attack was entitled, *"Meine Verfolgung in Russland, eine actenmässige Darstellung der jesuitisch herrnhutischen Umtriebe des Doctor Ignatius Fessler und seine Verbundeten."* A brief exposure of the falsehoods herein set forth was published by the Unity's Elders' Conference in the *Hamburger Correspondent* in 1823, and in the same year a thorough exposure of the pasquinade of Limmer appeared from the pen of Paul Pesarorius, Vice-President of the General Consistory in Russia. On the other hand a number of publications calculated to place the Unity in a correct light before the public were now issued: e. g., *"Kurzgefasste Nachricht von der Brüdergemeine,"* fifth edition, completely revised; *"Haupt Inhalt der Lehre Jesu Christi,"* by Jacob Plitt—both in 1822; and in 1823 the new edition of the Liturgy by Garve.

Of more consequence than the libellous controversial publications just referred to were the manifestations of active opposition to the *Diaspora* in certain quarters. At the instigation of the Greek Church party, Palucci, Governor of Livonia, issued a decree prohibiting the Brethren's services. In Canton Zürich the dislike of orthodoxy for the Pietism of the Krüdener-Haldane-Malan adherents, whom their opponents nicknamed "Momiers," bore upon everything that might be thought to resemble conventicles. In South Germany similar restraints were felt not only from distaste for the simple Biblical standpoint of the Brethren, but also from a dread of all private assemblages in an age when the spirit of revolution was abroad and political troubles were brewing. In Thuringia and Brunswick the latter cause placed hindrances in the way, and in Hanover the services were disallowed. But as the breach widened between the rationalisic and evangelical parties in state churches, the fraternal feeling between the latter and the Brethren widened and deepened. Practical proofs of this became evident in the financial assistance rendered to the missions.

From its comparative repose the Unity was awakened in the summer of 1823 by the news of a catastrophe which aroused sympathy everywhere. Sarepta was the scene of distress. It had been an exceptionally hot and dry summer. The Sarpa almost ceased to flow. The wooden houses of the town had become dry as tinder. Suddenly at noon, on August 9, the alarm bell rang. One of the rear buildings in the densest part of the town was on fire. It swept onward with awful rapidity. The rescue of valuables left an insufficient force of men to fight the flames. They burnt on till in the night. When the sun rose next day two-thirds of the town had been destroyed, thirty-seven buildings—dwellings, stores and factories—amongst the finest in the place, and about one hundred and sixty houses of a secondary sort. More than three hundred people were homeless. The complete subdual of the fire consumed upwards of a week, and for two weeks there prevailed keen anxiety, till a heavy rain put an end to care. Freewill offerings came in, not only from Germany, but also from England and from America, the congregation in New York, for example, contributing more than one thousand dollars.

Deaths again broke the circle of the Conference. On December 30, 1823, the long career of William Frederick Kölbing suddenly closed. Half a year later, on July 30, after a protracted decline Bishop Cunow passed away. Bishop Albertini now became President, the vacancies not being filled, since the synod was soon to convene. Prior to it two other departures thinned the lessening ranks. On January 11, 1825, Bishop Fabricius died, and on April 5 John Henry Zäslein.

When on May 24 the general synod assembled at Herrnhut, Frederick Louis Kölbing presided. The general tone was conservative. The condition of the church aroused well-founded apprehensions. The total membership showed a net decrease of 1200 members since the synod of 1818. The distinction between the membership at large and an inner circle had been wholly detrimental, and was therefore now abolished. As to the choir establishments, their universal maintenance was felt to be open to criticism, and it was agreed that whilst the time had not come for their compulsory abrogation, they might be quietly suffered to die out as local conditions required. Whilst the indebtedness reported at the previous synod had been reduced by 33,207 thaler, no less than 36,000 of the income had been derived by the sale of land in Wachovia. To continue to alienate property merely that interest might be met and the capital debt slightly reduced would be suicidal. The creation of a sinking fund was therefore devised. Marriage by lot should be obligatory only in the case of missionaries. Although the synod of 1818 had contemplated the abandonment of the grade of *Senior Civilis,* the unique position of Louis David de Schweinitz as administrator of the Unity's property in Pennsylvania and proprietor of its estates in North Carolina in addition to the fact that he had already served as the responsible negotiator for the Society for Propagating the Gospel in the retrocession of the lands in Ohio to the government of the United States, caused a revival of this grade in his person. In the event his became the distinction of being the last to be so appointed. The Unity's Elders' Conference, as reconstructed, consisted of the following: the Department of Education and of the Pastoral office, Bishop Albertini, the President of the entire board, together with Frederick Louis Kölbing and Peter Frederick Curie; the Department of Missions, Bishop Schneider, John Wied and John Beck Holmes; the Department of Finance, Christlieb Reichel, Niels Amtrup and John Daniel Römer.

Bishop Holmes did not find it practicable to remove to Herrnhut, but in January, 1726, was constrained by the state of his wife's health to tender his resignation. In his place Bishop Hüffel, President of the Conference in Bethlehem, was summoned to membership in the Mission Board. Before returning to resume labors in which he had shared prior to 1818, he was commissioned to officially visit the West Indies—St. Croix, St. Thomas, St. John, St. Kitts, Antigua and Barbados—and landing in England early in October on his way to the Continent, forged a valuable link of personal acquaintance with the members of the British Conference at Ockbrook. Prior to his arrival in Germany, viz., on June 4, 1827, Niels Amtrup, a member of the Department of Finance since 1802, passed away. It was not deemed necessary to order an election. The financial division of the governing board was simply reduced to correspond with the two other divisions.

In more than one respect it was a critical age, and the gloomy prognostications of several at the recent synod seemed to be justified. Yet the gloom was the darkness that precedes dawn, and here and there glimmerings of light shimmered on the horizon. But for the time the outlook was sufficiently troubled. The communal life of the settlements presented perplexities in relation to externals. In 1828 there was a wide-spread failure of crops. The complications involved in adjusting circumstances to the new methods of manufacture and commerce had their effects upon economic conditions, members more and more numerously moving away for a livelihood. Sometimes the inner life of the communities was disturbed; notably at Neuwied and among the *Diaspora* societies of the Palatinate in 1829, when a certain fanatic named Kaufholz attacked the standpoint of the Brethren respecting the doctrine of sanctification, and drew after himself some who were deluded by his professions of attained holiness—to learn the dearly bought lesson, repeatedly demonstrated in the history of the church universal, that what is begun in the spirit may end in the flesh and may necessitate police suppression.

Nevertheless the influence of men like Albertini and Kölbing and Plitt was silently working like a leaven amongst those of a younger generation. Their apprehension of the ideal of the Unity's historic significance and calling together with the influence of their personality should prove exceedingly germinant. Moreover, a deep spirit of earnest desire that the days of old should be renewed, and prayers for a revival of the positive and joyous assurance of personal acceptance with God, characteristic of the fathers, in short for a rebaptism of the Spirit, had been promoted by the celebration of a three-fold centenary of even greater significance than that which preceded the late synod. The first was the centenary of the festival of the Thirteenth of August. As became its character, it was a day of quiet heart-searchings and renewals of personal vows in all the congregations. Closely connected with this was the centennial jubilee for the children, on the 17th. In connection with the centenary of the "Hourly Intercession" the Cup of Covenant gave opportunity to anew pledge personal fidelity and to strengthen the bonds of brotherhood in a manner which had long since ceased to be employed. At the same time the very anniversary pointed to the spirit of prayer as both the right means and the best indication of a renewal of the inner life of the church.

In the providence of God manifestations of a better spirit before long characterized the chief institutions of learning. The fearful ravages of cholera in Russia, where the mortality in some districts rose to fifty per cent., and in the border districts, in 1830 led to the temporary removal of the students from Gnadenfeld to Herrnhut. Cranz accompanied them, but the services of members of the Conference were drawn upon in the emergency. Plitt lectured on Systematic Theology and the History of the Moravian Church, and Curie on the Sciences. Plitt's lectures in particular kindled enthusiasm. A new life began to animate the future servants of the church. With the return to Gnadenfeld William Kölbing took the place of Cranz, called elsewhere, and proved to be the man for the place.

The year 1832 began an epoch in the history of the college, with the appointment of Frederick Emanuel Kleinschmidt as Dean. Deeply religious, unshaken in his Biblical faith, strenuously insisting upon the necessity of regeneration, he held up before the teaching force of the institution a lofty scholastic and religious aim. Exact and wise and discriminating discipline, together with an emphatic insistence on the need of constant fellowship of prayer, gradually achieved far-reaching results through the formative influence exerted upon the lives of those now pursuing classical study preparatory to service in the church.

The man to whose preëminent personality and noble aims much of the coming improvement would hereafter be traced, whose soul-stirring addresses, especially in connection with centenary celebrations had inspired younger men with the highest ideals, was not permitted Simeon-like to enjoy personal sight of that to which his labors had been particularly directed. Bishop Albertini died of pectoral fever, on December 6, 1831. He was in his sixty-third year, and had been born at Neuwied shortly after his father had removed thither from the Grisons. Educated in the schools of the church, his native talents had been early discovered and employed first as an instructor and then as a pastor. Since 1820 he had been a member of the Unity's Elders' Conference, and since 1824 its President. Burkhardt discriminatingly analyses his source of power thus: "A man of far-reaching and everywhere blessed influence, in

JOHN BAPTIST von ALBERTINI.

whatever sphere he was engaged, and most of all during the last decade of his life. A man of deeds, of affairs, he was not—and as little a man of scientific theology, although at one time an instructor in the theological seminary. His forte lay, if we may say so, in the characteristics of his personality. By virtue of his disposition and the culture of his Christian life his influence went forth as a teacher of the young, as a pastor, as a preacher, as a leader of the church. He had once been the soul of that circle of younger ministers who had formed an un-historic ideal conception of Zinzendorf and of the church, and had lived in this world of their fancy. But through this very thing he had riveted himself and his companions to the church in a whole-souled fashion, at a time when there had been a lack of apprehension of its distinctive theology, and of a scientific understanding of its history. For him and his friends it had been a means of carrying them over in safety to the new era in which they could serve the church with unreserved devotion and a consciousness of power. When in looking back upon Schleiermacher's departure from the seminary, to whom he had been bound by the ties of youthful friendship, he himself once said that the Son of Man in Gethsemane had held him to the Unity, he in those words discloses his own inner position very clearly. By his sermons and his sacred poems he edified many; but everywhere had chiefly wrought through his winsome personality, permeated by the love of Christ. With this is connected the characteristic that he gave his whole soul to and left the impress of his entire being upon every office to which he was appointed—and these were very varied—and in each sphere disclosed faculties and traits requisite thereto which had not before been recognized in him. As Zinzendorf and Spangenberg in the past, he in association with similarly minded brethren led up to the new era of the church. His memory should ever be cherished amongst us."

Bishop Römer had already entered into his rest on May 9, 1831. Charles William Just and Jacob Levin Reichel now took the places rendered vacant in the governing board, and John Christian Breutel was also elected to the Department of Finance. Thus the conference was once more constituted of ten members.

For the *Diaspora* these were years of varying fortunes. A request was received from about one hundred and twenty-seven

families of German emigrants from the Palatinate who had settled in the vicinity of Neusulzfeld, in Poland, that they be
served with the gospel. In the spring of 1829 Charles Frederick Domke, engaged in the *Diaspora* service about Gnadenberg, was dispatched in response and the church rejoiced to learn
of the prospect that its usefulness might be renewed in a land
associated with the names of the fathers. But the spread of
cholera and the revolutionary uprisings which in November,
1830, echoed the strife of July in Paris, interfered for a while.

In the Baltic Provinces the Unity was brought into a critical condition from other causes. Here it was estimated that
in the year 1834 more than forty-five thousand persons belonged to *Diaspora* societies. An imperial edict of April 29 confirmed the previously existing liberty of operation, but with the
serious limitation that the national assistants should henceforth
be permitted only to read from the Bible and from writings approved by the consistories—a sign of the increasing hostility
of the Lutheran clergy. Next year the German agents of the
Unity were placed under similar restrictions. This hostility
had also necessitated the closing of the College at Hennersdorf in 1832, since it had drawn most of its students from
Livonia, and of late Russian influence restrained them from
seeking an education among the Brethren.

The Swiss field suffered from the contests between the aristo-
cratic oligarchies and the democratic party which aimed at the
abolition of class privileges that had been revived by the Congress of Vienna—especially in Basel, when the division of the
Canton into Stadt Basel and Landschaft Basel was devised as
the basis of peace; for of the twenty-eight pastors who were
forcibly ousted from their parishes in consequence, no less than
sixteen had been affiliated with the Brethren. In Cantons Bern
and Aargau on the other hand the work spread. In Silesia obstacles seemed about to be put in the way by a royal decree primarily aimed at separatists and ultra-confessional Lutherans,
but if construed rigidly likely to prohibit the meetings of the
Diaspora as conventicles. But representations which were
made by the church secured a gracious interpretation of the
edict and exempted the societies from all annoyance. Less
successful was the appeal to the Hanoverian authorities. In
Saxony the new constitution, wrested by liberalism's threatening movements, confirmed the old privileges for the settle-

ments, save that freedom from military service was no longer to be vouchsafed.

Meantime a wholly new center of usefulness was disclosed. After several preliminary visits in the Department of the Somme, John Mentha of Zeist at the invitation of pastor Cadoret removed permanently to Vadencourt near Amiens in the summer of 1834, and hopes were entertained that the church would find a providential sphere amongst the people of northern France.

The year 1835 drew attention to the centenary of the transfer of the episcopate from the ancient to the resuscitated Unity, and kindled additional reminiscences which should inspire to loyalty. Valuable researches prosecuted by Frederick Louis Kölbing preparatory to the anniversary were embodied in a monograph now given to the public under the title *Nachricht von dem Anfange der bischöflichen Ordination in der erneuerten evangelischen Brüderkirche*. Bishop Frederick Benjamin Reichel had died on January 16. It was appropriate that Kölbing himself, who had been President of the Unity's Elders' Conference since the death of Albertini, should now receive consecration. This transpired at Herrnhut on March 13, 1835.

CHAPTER XLIII.

Bishops Moore and Foster were the representatives of the governing board of the Unity in England at the beginning of the trying period of reaction which followed the great war and ushered in the struggle for multiform readjustments and innumerable reforms. When wide-spread distress fell alike upon the agricultural and commercial interests, it was inevitable that the organizations of the Brethren should be affected and that choir-establishments could scarcely be maintained.

In the Bedford district, however, signs of progress peep forth in three localities. At Stow, in August, 1818, Elijah Peacock instituted services. In 1822 a similar beginning was made at the neighboring village of Kimbolton, and a chapel consecrated in August of the following year. John King Martyn, dissatisfied with the lack of provision for promoting vital godliness in his former environment, together with a considerable number of his parishioners came over wholly into the membership of the Brethren's Church, and served as minister here for fourteen years. Meantime the congregation at Pertenhall was formally organized in April, 1825.

Bishop Thomas Moore died in 1823, and his former colleague Bishop Foster found himself face to face with grave responsibilities, requiring sound judgment and delicate handling. In addition to the economic perplexities of the times, well calculated to give rise to misunderstandings, party spirit was rife in Gracehill—so much so that a visit from a representative of the Unity's Elders' Conference was deemed necessary. Wied was selected for this duty, and in company with Foster in 1823 paid a protracted visit to the scene of trouble, happily succeeding in allaying it. On his return in the early part of 1824 he extended his tour to Fulneck, Fairfield, Bristol, Kingsword, Bath, Tytherton and London.

For some time, especially at the Synod of 1818, a desire for a regularly organized conferential government of deputies of the governing board of the entire Unity had found expression in England. It was deemed wise to meet this desire at the present time. With Bishop Foster were therefore associated as Provincial Helpers, having residence in the same place and acting conjointly and conferentially, James Liley and Frank Mallalieu. The former was a pupil of Hartley, and a man of similar disposition and aims. He had seen service especially in Gracehill and Fairfield. The latter had been a corn-merchant in Manchester, and was of particular usefulness in connection with financial affairs. The first session of the new conference was held at Bedford, its seat, on April 24, 1824. Next year, in accordance with the decision of the synod, a transfer was effected to Ockbrook.

Despite the anxieties of the times two other efforts at advance can be chronicled, the one closely connected with an endeavor to further develop the distinctive life of the Province as such. This was the establishment of a theological seminary in the now almost vacant Brethren's House at Fulneck, with Samuel Rogers as chief instructor, and Charles Reichel, as general director, he being at this time at the head of the other schools of the settlement. It was maintained, however, only until 1828. Then candidates for service in Britain again sought their preparation in the institutions of the church at Niesky and Gnadenfeld, and not infrequently commenced their active career with a period of employment as teachers in the schools on the Continent.

The other new beginning was the founding of a congregation in the vicinity of Manchester, near Oldham. As far back as 1772 ministers of the Brethren's Church had been in the habit of visiting and preaching at Greenacres, and their ministrations there had been attended by visitors from Oldham and Lees. At intervals, from 1784 on, preaching in private houses at Lees had been maintained until 1800. Now in the year 1823 John Lees, a member of the Fairfield congregation, arranged a spacious room at Clarkesfield in a manner appropriate to divine worship. This met with such encouraging response, that at the joint expense of himself and two of his brothers, Mr. Lees erected a place of worship here in the following year, and at his own cost provided also two school rooms, the furnishing of all being supplied by other members of the church. In August, 1825, Liley consecrated the new chapel. John Smith became the first resident minister in 1827. A preaching place was established as a filial at Lees, and in 1836 the congregation at Clarkesfield, which had received the name of Salem, was fully and formally organized, Cornelius West, who had succeeded Smith in 1829, being the pastor. From Fairfield, too, preaching was begun and maintained at Glossop Bridge in 1827.

In 1824 a provincial conference met at Fairfield and was attended by thirty Brethren (June 3 to July 15). Frederick William Foster presided. The members of the church were reported to be decreasing, the congregations with few exceptions were yearly diminishing, and some spoke of living to witness the extinction of the Brethren's Unity in the British Province. As against this impression the growth of foreign mission work, and the spread of educational activities at home were emphasized. The theological seminary had only just been instituted. The continuance of the use of the lot in general was approved, but a diversity of opinion existed as to the marriage of ministers by lot, and a representation on this subject was made to the forthcoming general synod. The spirit of the conference was essentially conservative. The choir regulations were upheld as preventive of irregularities, the choir houses as a means of blessing, and *Diaconies* as indispensable. In regard to finance, it was stated that in several congregations the salary allowed to the ministers was wholly inadequate to the most necessary requirements. Many had, in consequence, to supplement their income by teaching or by business. This state of things led to the institution of "the Ministers' Fund," the rules of which were now ordered to be printed. Efforts on behalf of the foreign missions are encouraged. Home work is depressed. Kilkeel and Cootehill and Kilwarlin are without ministers; the last has been in this condition for upwards of thirty years.

Liley died on March 2, 1827, fifty-four years of age, and Samuel Frederick Church, pastor at Ockbrook, became his successor in the Helpers' Conference.

In Ireland the spirit and aims of Hartley had been taken up by John Carey, of Dublin, who was connected with the "City Mission." Beautiful Cootehill, in County Cavan, his native place, was the first object of his laudable endeavors. Visiting here in 1826, he found that the congregation as an organization had passed out of existence, though a number of old members were still living, and the aroma of Moravian teaching still lingered lovingly in memory. The buildings had some of them been alienated, and all were in a more or less ruined condition. With zeal and earnestness he rekindled in the scattered remnant a desire to renew the days of old, and brought affairs to such a pass that John Willey was appointed pastor. In 1830, during another visit, he could write, "It is with surprise and astonishment that I contemplate the wonderful improvement that has taken place. The whole of the buildings in thorough repair, the walks and gardens are elegantly laid out, and my heart rejoices at the sound of redeeming love once more heard among these verdant meads." He could write also of the presence of about sixty persons at divine worship, of a Sunday-school of about one hundred children, of two boarding-schools, and of a general spirit of hopeful energy.

The year 1829 was marked by the organization of a Society for the Propagation of the Gospel in Ireland. Under the guidance of a committee at Gracehill, Scripture-readers were to be employed to itinerate and do evangelistic work. One of the fruits of this organized concentration of the missionary zeal which had been centering about Gracehill ever since the days of Hartley, and which was evidenced by the maintenance of stated services at quite a large circle of preaching-places, is to be found in the resuscitation of the work in the fishing village of Kilkeel among the mountains of Mourne. So highly was appreciation accorded to the labors of the Scripture-reader who was sent thither in 1829, that two years later John Sutcliffe was stationed here as home missionary.

A romantic interest attaches to another rebuilding of an ancient home. Kilwarlin, in County Down, had known no resident minister since 1798, though it had not been wholly deserted by the ministers in Gracehill. In 1834 it received aid in an unlooked for way. In 1826 family prayers, conducted in his absence one day by a lady friend of the proprietor in the Bilton Hotel in Dublin, happened to be attended amongst the rest by Sir William Eden and his companion, Basil Patras Zula, a Greek chief, who had escaped from beleagured Missolonghi, and had found his way with the British nobleman via Smyrna and London to the Irish capital. The lady was a member of the Moravian Church, and presented the strangers afterwards

24

with a small volume giving its history. Its origination from oriental sources attracted the attention of the Greek patriot. He attended the Baptist Street church, was savingly converted, and joined its membership. After visits to London, and a residence in Gracehill in 1828 devoted to study, he prepared systematically to enter the ministry under the guidance of the Dublin pastor. Marrying the lady who had been his first instructor in the truth, he in 1834 gave all the energy of his fiery nature and the wealth of his talents to the rebuilding of ruined Kilwarlin. Church and minister's house were reërected, and the former consecrated in March, 1835. Large audiences gathered. Schools were established. The friendly coöperation of the Marquis of Downshire, the owner of the land in the vicinity, was secured. Reorganization of the congregation was fully effected in March, 1837; and in ten years from Zula's coming, the membership had grown from a paltry remnant of six to two hundred and fifty-one.

In connection with Ireland the literary work of John Holmes, minister in Dublin, deserves to be mentioned. In 1818 he published the first account in English of the Moravian Missions. The work was entitled *"Historical Sketches of the Missions of the United Brethren."* A few years later he issued his *"History of the Protestant Church of the United Brethren,"* Vol. 1 in 1825, Vol. 2 in 1830. For a long period these books remained standard works.

Meantime for at least one congregation in England there had been a period of great anxiety. The intense excitement which had attended the discussions of the Reform Bill in 1831 had found vent here and there in connection with the discontent of the agricultural laborers in the burning of hay-ricks and the smashing of machinery, turbulence far less formidable than the almost contemporaneous revolutionary movement on the Continent. After the prorogation of Parliament the excitement deepened. Riots occurred at Derby and Nottingham. But in Bristol the madness of the scum of that seaport for two days in October held the lives and property of the people in jeopardy, breaking open the jails, and firing public buildings and private dwellings—with the accompaniment of intoxication usual at such times. Yet through the mercy of a kind Providence the church on Maudlin Street was unharmed.

Next year rewards of the Bristol pastor's consecrated enterprise were to be amply apparent. Since 1824 Charles Frederick Ramftler had been stationed at this post, "filling it with his pervading energy," and blessing it with the ripe fruit of his experienced ability. Within easy reach of Bristol, on the banks of the picturesque Wye, beyond Tintern, was a village devoid of any place of worship, being an ultra-parochial district. This was Brockweir, once a thriving and populous center of shipbuilding, when its calkers' mallets rang on the sides of East Indiamen, slowly attaining completion in its two rival dock-yards, but now sparsely inhabited and somewhat in decay. Though without any church or chapel it had seven public houses, and its reputation was not the best. In March, 1832, Ramftler had visited the place at the invitation of some pious people of the vicinity, and had established divine worship. Through his endeavors Lewis West was secured as resident minister. The Bristol congregation stood by their pastor nobly, and a small but neat chapel was built in 1833. A marked revival of religion followed, and in time the congregation grew to number one hundred and twenty members. The laying of the corner-stone of the Brockweir chapel on October 15, 1832, was indeed one of the last public services of Ramftler. In ill health already, delicate in constitution, and more or less of an invalid for several years, he closed his career on October 25, fifty-two years of age. Though foreign-born his had been a prominent figure in the ministry of the Brethren in England during the first three decades of the century.

On March 14, 1831, Frank Mallalieu died, and was succeeded by Samuel Rudolph Reichel, of Bath. On April 12, 1832, the venerable Bishop Foster, in his seventy-fifth year, entered into his rest. Charles Augustus Pohlman was appointed in his place.

Preparatory to the synod of the following year, a Provincial conference was convened at Fulneck on July 1, 1835, and remained in session until the 18th. Bishop Holmes was President. Thirty-six members were present, of whom seven were delegates of congregations. As regards the internal and spiritual state of the church, the reports were cheering. There was a general spirit of prayer in the congregations, as in the other churches of the country, an increasing interest in the foreign mission work, and a willingness to give financial support to the church. Peace and love prevailed in the Province as a whole. The state of the congregation at Gracehill, however, gave cause for anxiety, and a letter of exhortation was addressed to its members. It was decided that the church as such could not and should not interfere in politics, but as individuals the members should carry the spirit of the church into all political duties which they discharged. Trades Unions and Orange Lodges were held to be injurious. The statistics of the last ten years were as follows:

	COMMUNICANTS.	RECEIVED MEMBERS.	TOTAL, including children.
1824.	2596	2062	4673
1834.	2698	1831	5000

Archbishop Whately's wish for a settlement of the Brethren on his estate in Wicklow could not be entertained, because it aimed chiefly at colonization. The chief causes impeding extension at home were want of time on the part of the ministers and want of money. The Sunday-schools are not alluded to in the abstract of the minutes. Self-preservation seems to have a strong hold on the feeling of the conference. The idea of "guarding" against the admission of "improper persons" into the church is prominent. The missionary idea for home activities seems to be entirely lost sight of. It is not a question of gaining new blood so much as of training the old blood. There were fourteen church schools in the Province, in which about fifty Brethren and Sisters were employed. It is stated that an abundant blessing rested on the schools. The question of establishing a theological college in Dublin was negatived. A similar decision was reached in reference to a missionary college in the British Province. In regard to finance the British Province drew far more money from Germany for superannuated ministers and for distressed *Diaconies* than the amount contributed by it to these two purposes. The "Provincial Expenses Account" was instituted with one hundred shares, to be divided among all the congregations, the excess above one hundred shares to constitute a reserve fund.

CHAPTER XLIV.

THE CHURCH IN AMERICA, FROM 1818 TO 1836.

For the American congregations one of the results of the synod of 1818 was the appointment of Bishop Hüffel as President of the Helpers' Conference in the North. At first his colleagues were John Gebhard Cunow, the administrator of the Unity's property in Pennsylvania, John Frederick Früauff, Emmanuel Randthaler and Andrew Benade, the pastors of the Bethlehem, Nazareth and Lititz congregations respectively. In 1822 Cunow returned to Germany, to succeed Verbeek in the care of the Sustentation, and then Louis David de Schweinitz, who had come from the South during the previous year to become minister at Bethlehem and principal of the school for girls, followed Cunow as administrator and ex-officio member of the Conference. To the board was also added Thomas Langballe, whom ill-health had compelled to leave Surinam in April, 1821, after years of most efficient service. But he died on February 13, 1826. Benade was consecrated a bishop at Lititz on September 15, 1822, by Bishops Hüffel and Jacob Van Vleck, being appointed to succeed the latter, since 1812 President of the Southern Conference, now retiring on account of age. Theodore Shultz, the new administrator in the South, and Christian Frederick Schaaf, the surviving member of the old Conference, constituted the new Southern executive together with Benade, and continued in office until 1829. Meantime in 1825 John Christian Bechler and Charles Frederick Seidel were added to the Northern board. With Hüffel's appointment to the Unity's Elders' Conference, the presidency in the North was assigned to John Daniel Anders, hitherto in Berlin, and consecrated a bishop at Herrnhut on September 16, 1827, by Bishops Albertini, Wied and Curie. Bishop Benade, becoming pastor at Lititz in 1829, also entered the Northern Conference, and Bechler was transferred to the South in his place.

Beneath the surface during these years the slow but sure disintegration of the "exclusive system" was preparing the way for and necessitating the changes which should characterize the middle of the century. The era of home missions was dawning.

In April, 1830, the Provincial Helpers' Conference in Bethlehem received letters from thir colleagues in the South, calling attention to the religious needs of certain Brethren whom the general impulse of removal westward had drawn to the primeval forests and virgin soil of the then frontier. Since 1825 a number of Moravians from North Carolina had settled in what later became Bartholomew County, Indiana. In November a warm-hearted Brother who had been actively engaged in the Sunday-school and in evangelistic labors, and had been licensed to preach, Martin Hauser, a native of Salem, joined them for the purpose of gathering the scattered families into a congregation. Land was still to be had at Congress rates. A tract of one hundred and sixty acres on Haw Creek had been selected and entered at Indianapolis from his own means. But the country was covered with forest, and had not even a cabin or dug-out upon it. A clearing had to be made, roads opened, a farm begun and his family provided for. Hardships customary in pioneer life had been endured in the rude cabin of logs in which the winter had been passed. Health had suffered from exposure. Were the Brethren at Bethlehem able to lend any aid, lest the enterprise be nipped in the bud?

Had a deaf ear been turned at this time, it is likely that church extension would have perished stillborn, and the Moravian Church in America might have gradually shrivelled into a sect interesting chiefly if not exclusively to the antiquarian.

At this juncture Louis David de Schweinitz as administrator advanced the money necessary to purchase land for church purposes, an agreement having been entered into on January 2, 1830, by Martin Hauser, Daniel Ziegler, John Essex, Samuel Rominger and Joseph Spaugh, that they and their families would become the nucleus of a congregation. The first services were held at Goshen, as this settlement was first named—later Hope—on June 17, though as yet the primitive structure of logs was without a roof, leafy boughs being interlaced overhead to form a screen from the sun. Thirty-three persons participated. Such was the primeval condition of the country, that deer wandered in numbers under the spreading beech trees, and at noon, during the intermission between the services, one too inquisitive denizen of the forest was killed.

Just one year later a congregaton was formally organized by Louis David de Schweinitz, who had been sent out to examine into the prospects. Additional colonists came from North Carolina, and in 1833 Hauser received ordination at the hands of Bishop Anders at Bethlehem.

Another rootlet of the tree of church extension was fixed among the hills of eastern New York. Forty and more miles northeast of Albany, in Washington County, almost on the line of Vermont, and watered by a rapid brook emptying into the Battenkill, lies a secluded valley nestling amongst picturesque hills, at this time only partly cleared and partly covered with a growth of beech and birch and maple and ash and oak. It had been named by its first proprietors Camden Valley in honor of the famous British statesman from whom they received it by letters patent. Here in 1770 Abraham Büninger, at the close of his career as a missionary in the West Indies and amongst the Indians, had retired to spend his declining days. Some of his descendants had since removed to the city of New York and were prominent members of the Moravian church there, now in the pastoral charge of the beloved and eloquent William Henry Van Vleck. Occasional sermons delivered in the small school house had hitherto constituted all the gospel privileges enjoyed by the people of this valley, no denomination having organized a congregation. The people were poor, the conditions for agriculture being unfavorable, and very diversified religious views were represented in the sparse community.

Under these circumstances the members of the Bininger family who had remained in the valley expresesd a desire that the Moravian Church should supply their spiritual needs. After preliminary visits by Van Vleck and Jacob Bininger of New York in 1830 and 1831, application was made to the authorities at Bethlehem for the services of a resident minister. After a visit of investigation by Louis David de Schweinitz, Charles A. Blech, assistant minister in New York, was sent late in December, 1832, and commenced to statedly preach at Camden Valley, meeting appointments also at Sandgate in Vermont and at "The Mills" on the Battenkill, two neighboring communities. Gradually a congregation was gathered, and on September 29, 1834, a church consecrated by Bishop Anders. Soon there were about one hundred and thirty stated hearers. Although this undertaking did not prove a permanent success, chiefly because of internal disagreements, it also contributed to the movement for a change in the policy of the church in America.

In November, 1834, a third new center of operations was occupied. In the year 1820 a considerable number of German emigrants, many of them from Baden, had settled in the flats beside the Wallenpaupack, in "The Beechwoods," then a region as wild as it was mountainous in the southern part of Wayne County bordering on Pike County, Pennsylvania. Being without religious privileges and acquainted with the Moravian Church in their European home, they made application to Bethlehem for a pastor. Emmanuel Rondthaler of Nazareth was commissioned to inquire into the state of affairs. He organized a society in fellowship with the Moravian Church. By the end of 1837 a church edifice was erected, and the settlement became known as Hopedale. Its first pastor was George Ferdinand Troeger, who had come to America in 1819 and had served in Ohio.

Meantime at Salem, on November 11, 1855, the United Brethren's Home Missionary Society of North Carolina was organized. This was in consequence of the visits which had been paid to the destitute mountains of what is now West Virginia by Vanaman N. Zevilly. From his evangelistic activity sprang the congregation of Mount-Bethel.

But before these incipient projects had any of them passed the experimental stage, a most serious loss was experienced in the death of the man who had lent his energetic countenance to two of them. On February 8, 1834, at the comparatively early age of fifty-four, Louis David de Schweinitz entered into his rest. Representative as he was of the newer school of Moravian ministers, enthusiastically appreciative of the distinctive characteristics of his church, he had been identified with everything that had pointed to progress in America in recent years, and foresaw that radical changes were at hand. Distinguished for his scientific attainments and having won recognition as a botanist amongst European and American specialists, his services to the church as a financial manager had been

LOUIS DAVID DE SCHWEINITZ.

preëminent at the synod of 1825 and during his long period of administration, twenty-five years in all. The Conference in Germany appointed as his successor Philip Henry Goepp, formerly professor at Gnadenfeld, and of late a secretary to the governing board. He was destined to participate in the changes which his predecessor had foreseen.

For the missions amongst the Indians these were momentous years. With the increase of white settlers in the Tuscarawas Valley, Goshen had been suffering a steady decline. One by one its Indian families removed to localities where game was more plentiful and where the outrages of border ruffians need not be dreaded. For years the care of the reservation on the Tuscarawas had been a costly burden to the Society for Propagating the Gospel as trustees for the converts. Now that missionary work was at an end, retrocession to the government was not only inevitable, but would afford a relief. At the general meeting of the Society in 1822 it was reported that fully $32,000 had been expended over and above all income from the land. Negotiations were therefore set on foot which resulted in the retrocession of the reservation to the United States in April, 1824. The Christian Indians were to receive a per capita annuity of $400 or a new grant of 24,000 acres. This retrocession involved the abandonment of Beersheba, but Gnadenhütten was laid out in town lots by an agent of the government. Not that missionary interest and activity ceased. The first official periodical of the American Church was just in the days of its palmy youth—The *Missionary Intelligencer*, a quarterly devoted to the furtherance of the foreign missions, and issued since January, 1822, by the Provincial Helpers' Conference. In June, 1823, to stimulate new interest in the mission amongst the Cherokees, with the consent of the parent society the Society of the United Brethren in North Carolina for the Furtherance of the Gospel was organized by southern members of the Society for Propagating the Gospel. Moreover, a legacy of Godfrey Haga, a member of the Moravian Church in Philadelphia and of the missionary society, in 1825 placed the directors of this society in the position of trustees of a fund of about $200,000 for the benefit of the American Indian missions of the church.

Shortly before the negotiations for the retrocession of the Tuscarawas reservation had been effected, one of the most dis-

tinguished veterans of the mission passed away.   This was John
Gottlieb Ernestus Heckewelder, who died at Bethlehem on January 31, 1823, almost eighty years of age.   Of old Moravian
stock, he was born at Bedford in England in 1743, and had
come to Pennsylvania in 1754.   In 1762 he had been Post's
companion in the adventurous journey to the Ohio, and had
labored for years as missionary in Pennsylvania, Ohio and Michigan.   In 1788 he had been appointed agent in Ohio for the
Society for Propagating the Gospel.   Twice he had served as
United States commissioner for negotiating peace with Indian
tribes; once with General Rufus Putman at Vincennes, Indiana,
in 1792, and next near Niagara with General Lincoln, Colonel
Pickering and Beverly Randolph.   Since 1810 literary labors
had occupied the years of his retirement at Bethlehem, represented by his three chief works, *An Account of the History, Manners and Customs of the Indian Nations who once inhabited Pennsylvania and the neighboring States; A Narrative of the Missions
of the United Brethren among the Delaware and Mohegan Indians;*
and *Names which the Lenni-Lenape or Delaware Indians gave to the
Rivers, Streams and Localities,* etc.

Meantime the Cherokee mission was prospering.   In June,
1821, Gambold, replaced at the first station by Renatus Smith,
formerly of the Canadian mission, commenced a second station
about thirty miles distant, at Oochgelogy, in Gordon County.
It soon became a success.   Here as at Springplace the young
converts manifested a desire for more advanced education.
Already in 1818 three young Cherokees from Springplace had
appeared at Salem on their way to study in the mission institute at Cornwall, Conn., and Gambold could write of five
others who had preceded them.   Ambition for assimilation with
the whites was very evident amongst the people of the upper
towns, though the tribesmen of the lower lands had begun their
movement westwards, having received from government an
extensive tract on the Arkansas and White Rivers in exchange
for their ancestral homes.   Their brethren who remained in
Georgia on the other hand were making rapid progress.   The
English language had gained precedence as the tongue in which
their national records were kept.   Hunting had been largely
exchanged for agriculture.   Agricultural implements, mills,
machinery for cleaning cotton, etc., had been introduced.

A powerful revival of religion characterized the winter of 1824-25. In the two succeeding years their own national written constitution was developed, Abraham Hicks, a member of the Moravian Church, becoming the recognized head of his people. Dying in 1828, he was succeeded by his brother, Christian Renatus Hicks. But dangers were gathering and interrupted this pleasing progress. Disregarding the solemn treaties with the general government in 1785, 1791, 1798, etc., the state of Georgia sought to extend her jurisdiction over the 8,000 square miles of Cherokee country. During and after 1827 especially repressive measures were passed by the state legislature. This naturally accellerated the tide of migration to the West. Next the state of Georgia directed its attack against the missionaries. The notorious case of Samuel Austin Worcester outraged the religious sentiment of the country. But President Jackson for party reasons declined to enforce the decision of Chief Justice Marshall of the Supreme Court of the United States, that the law of Georgia under which he had been condemned was unconstitutional. The noble missionary of the American Board had to sit in jail like a felon for fifteen months. All whites had been ordered to vacate the Cherokee country by March, 1831, except officials appointed by the United States or by Georgia. The compulsory withdrawal of all the Moravian missionaries followed, Gottlieb Byhan alone excepted, who resolved to remain at Springplace in reliance of his position as post-master. His arrest but speedy release followed. The other missionaries had found a temporary home with Captain McNair, across the border of Tennessee, about fifteen miles distant, his wife being a member of the church. For continuing to visit his members, Henry G. Clauder, who had been in the field since 1829, was arrested on March 21 by Georgia Guards. But their commander upon investigation permitted him to continue his ministrations, on condition that after due notice had been given he should finally leave the country within ten days. Such notice came in July, coupled with a threat of imprisonment in case it was not heeded. Hence he returned to Salem with his family.

During the months of uncertainty services were meanwhile maintained at Oochgelogy by Hicks and Christian David Wattee, the native assistants. At the end of the year Byhan sought release from his appointment as post-master, and Clauder received it in his place. During 1832 the state of Georgia divided the Cherokee country amongst white people by lottery. The mission property at Oochgelogy was taken from the church and seized by strangers. On New Year's Day, 1833, three families compelled Clauder to give up one-half of the mission house at Springplace, and a few days later an alleged agent of the government of Georgia appeared, drove away the former intruders, and ignoring the United States post-mastership, ordered the missionaries off the premises. In the course of a few years Springplace became a county-seat, and the Moravian church was turned into a court-house.

Again McNair accorded the homeless missionaries a friendly welcome and provided a temporary center for missionary work, placing a house and a plot of ground at their disposal. Here the mission school was once more opened by Miss Ruede, and a number of Indian communicants, heads of families, moving into the neighborhood, it seemed as though a renewal of the ruthlessly disrupted work might possibly be made in Tennessee.

During 1834 about one thousand Cherokees moved to Arkansas Territory, and in the years following dissentions began to deepen as to the policy which the remainder ought to pursue. In 1837 the compulsory removal of the main body of the people at length took place. United States troops under General Scott facilitated the transportation, and served as a guard both for the territory through which the emigration took place and for the exiles whom they transported. Thirteen thousand were thus conveyed during the autumn of this year, amongst whom was the division of the tribe to which the Moravian missionaries had ministered. Chief John Ross, or Kroweskowee, the head of the nation, attached to the Moravian Church by various ties, could give no assurance that missionaries would be permitted to settle with their converts in the new homes, so great a mistrust of the whites had been aroused in the Indian mind by the perfidy of the recent past.

Meantime the mission at New Fairfied enjoyed a steady career of usefulness, though frequent changes in the force of missionaries were necessary. John Schnall died at his post of duty in September, 1819, having been identified with the mission since 1801. Abraham Luckenbach came from Goshen to assume charge. He had already served as a missionary amongst the Indians for nineteen years, and was to be the leading spirit at New Fairfield for another period of twenty-four years, with various assistants from time to time.

In the year 1833 C. J. La Trobe of London, who visited the reservation in the course of his travels in America, described the tract as distinguished for the richness of its alluvial soil and its luxuriant growth of sugar maple, white pine and oak. He pictures the settlement as formed of "one principal street of rude log cottages, at some distance apart from each other, stretching across an open space, flanked by wheat fields, and almost surrounded by a bend of the river." About six hundred acres were under cultivation.

But soon an eventful change took place, partly on account of repeated encroachments of white settlers notwithstanding the fact that the reservation had been granted in perpetuity. In the early summer of the very next year after La Trobe's visit, three reliable Indian brethren, Abraham, Augustus and Noah, were sent to make reconnaissance in the United States territory west of the Mississippi, near the head waters of the White River. Returning in the latter part of October, they reported that they had not reached the intended objective, but had visited the Delawares about three hundred and thirty miles northwest of St. Louis, from whom they met a reception that could not be called cordial. This report at first had dampened the spirit of migration. Yet from time to time the project was renewed, and was finally carried out in 1837. Meantime the winter of 1835-36 was marked by a deep revival of religion, and at the close of the latter year the congregation numbered two hundred and eighty-two persons.

CHAPTER XLV.

THE MISSIONS FROM 1818 TO 1836.

On the restoration of peace in Europe communication with Greenland via Copenhagen could again be regularly maintained. The obstacles were only those which nature placed by fencing in the inhospitable coast with ice blinks and bergs, as when Frederick Christian Kranich was lost at sea in 1824, and in the same year a company of missionaries encountered ten dreadful gales in succession during their outward voyage, the vessel at times becoming unmanageable from the freezing of the rigging and sails, and being severely damaged off Staatenhuk.

Kleinschmidt's translation of the New Testament was printed by the British and Foreign Society, the first copies being received in Greenland in July, 1823. The translator unweariedly continued literary labors until his death on December 11, 1832. Parts of the Old Testament, and a Greenland Grammar were his additional memorial.

For some time an extension of operations southwards had been desired, to reach the heathen with whom contact had been possible only when they visited their favorite herring fishery five miles from Lichtenau. Narkasamia, near the promontory of Staatenhuk, was selected, and in 1824 Kleinschmidt and his wife, John Conrad Bauss and his wife, with John Arnold de Fries and Martin William Popp, made a commencement. For twelve weeks tent-life had to be endured amid storms, and the exchange effected on October 17, was only to a sod hut of narrow dimensions. In a space 28 feet by 12 the six missionaries had to live as best they could. Owing to the uncertainties of transportation the frame of their permanent dwelling did not reach them until June of 1828. Moreover, the log hut which was erected but not completed in 1825 to replace the sod hut, was almost blown over during a storm early in November. This led to a removal across the Königsbach, a salmon stream to the north, and beyond it the permanent station was established. Popp meanwhile so suffered from rheumatic fever, that he returned to Europe in 1826. Though traces of ancient buildings, relics of the former Norse settlers, were discovered, the new site also had its disadvantages. No harbor afforded a landing for the trading vessels. One of the very features which had led to its selection, the supply of brushwood that promised to afford fuel, proved inadequate after a considerable number of Eskimo families had been attracted to the place, and dependence had to be put upon imported coals, brought from Julianenhaab. Nevertheless for missionary purposes Friedrichsthal was admirably situated. Umiak after umiak of heathen South and East Greenlanders came to the place. The work of evangelization progressed with marked rapidity. On September 2, 1824, the first convert, Samuel Ivenak, was baptized. By the end of 1825 two hundred and fifty Greenlanders were living here.

When the centenary of the Greenland mission was celebrated, January 19, 1833, he total membership of the mission was 1,808 souls. During the century one hundred and two missionaries had served—some of them for remarkably long periods: John Beck, 43 years; his son Jacob, 52; John Sörensen, 47; John Fliegel, 41; John Gorke, 44; John Grillich, still in service, 46 years; and Conrad Kleinschmidt, almost 40 years. Four missionaries had lost their lives at sea, Daniel Schneider in 1742; the widowed Sister Königseer and Christian Heinze in 1786, and Frederick Kranich in 1824.

In Labrador the mission was being steadily developed. As in the case of Greenland, the British and Foreign Bible Society assisted by printing various portions of the Scriptures in the dialect of Labrador—the Epistles and the Apocalypse, Genesis, etc. Seven hundred hymns, translations by Traugott Martin and George Schneider, were printed by the Society for the Furtherance of the Gospel, and reached Labrador in 1825.

For a number of years it had been desired that the arm of the mission might reach out helpfully towards the heathen of the northern stretches of the coast. In the spring of 1828 the missionaries at Okak commenced to prepare building materials for this projected extension of operations. Permission was received from the British government to found a fourth station, coupled with the use of the coast for missionary operations as far as the 59th degree of north latitude. At length in 1829 the bay of Kangertluksoak was selected by Sturmann and John Christian Beck, and in April of the following year Beck and Jonathan Mentzel set out for this place sixty miles distant from Okak, and on dog sleds conveyed thither the framework of a house. Every circumstance conspired to favor the enterprise. Kmoch could declare that in all the thirty-three years of his experience he had never known a better condition of the ice-encrusted well-packed snow to have been maintained for so long a period. Though one hundred and five journeys in all were made by the faithful dogs, rarely did it require more than one day to cover the sixty miles between the two places! By July 8 the frame was erected and by the 21st protected with weather-boarding. Next day—the programme could not have been better carried out if previously arranged—the *Harmony* dropped anchor in the bay, and with her a sister ship, the *Oliver*, chartered to bring special stores and building materials for the new station, named Hebron. The entire season was so favorable that Lundberg, the superintendent, reports a journey from Nain to Okak, ninety miles apart, accomplished by his dogs in one day!

But fair seasons and mild winds are the exception in Labrador. In contrast with this dovetailing of plans, the voyage of the *Harmony* in 1836 was one of the most memorable she ever made. Two hundred miles off the coast she met drift ice in treacherous masses of great thickness, often concealed by a covering of water too shallow for a ship, and threatening her safety from the heaving of the ground-swells. Only by letting down fenders of tow or "cable junk" was serious injury averted from the vessel. For eight days she remained embedded in the ice, with not a drop of water in sight. Hopedale harbor had been clear of ice only two days when she entered it on August 4—a providential circumstance its being free, otherwise in the narrow and rocky channels destruction would have been inevitable. During her return voyage a storm raged on September 26, when a heavy sea carried away her skiff hanging astern, stove the cabin windows, swamped the cabin, washed away the binnacle and cook house, broke the wheel and nearly killed the man beside it. Five days later she rescued nine men from a wreck after they had been reduced to the last extremity of famine and exposure, one man dying on the following night. For the marvellous protection of the Lord all through the series of years from the founding of the mission a sense of gratitude was deepened in the hearts of its friends, when the events of this voyage became known.

Steady progress and advance in the number of stations and in the widening of educational activities now characterized the work in the West Indies. On the Danish islands the favor of royalty was experienced in connection with a rescript of December 24, 1830, which put the operations of the Brethren on the same footing with those of the State Church, and the valuable regard of the local government and of the planters continued to be enjoyed. On the English islands a new feature was introduced by the increased activity of the Anglican Church and its development of a more thorough organization through the appointment of bishops for two dioceses with their seats in Jamaica and Barbados. Here, too, the premonitions of emancipation were accompanied with more or less grave disturbances. As so frequently, the turbulence of the forces of nature had also to be taken into account, severe tornados marking several of the years and increasing the financial burdens of the work. Most alarming of all was that of August 10 and 11, 1831, on Barbados. The church at Sharon was completely wrecked and the mission-house damaged, whilst church and mission-house at Mount Tabor were left in complete ruin, the missionaries Zippel and wife, with their son escaping as by a miracle. This last calamity called forth liberal gifts in England and America for the rebuilding of the stations.

Various experiences demonstrated the fact that travel by sea was not yet unattended with dangers. In June, 1820, Christian Glöckler and his wife, together with Sister Schärf and seven children of different missionary families on their way to school, took passage for Germany. On July 15 altogether unexpectedly Glöckler's wife was carried off by a malignant fever of which the mate of the ship had previously died. A sailor in the vigor of young manhood was next seized, and was also committed to the deep. Then through the perversity of a self-willed pilot the night of August 16 found them stranded on the coast of Holland. Taking to the boats, and abandoning all their effects, unprovisioned, with nothing but their lives and the clothing that had been hastily donned, the passengers and the ship's company with difficulty made the island of Ter Schilling. Here the burgomaster set an example of Christian benevolence.

The castaways were kindly cared for and furthered on their way. In May of 1823 a thrilling experience was made by William Eberman and his wife, newly appointed to St. Croix. They set sail from Philadelphia. When only one hundred miles out, a sudden squall threw the ship on her beam ends. Sister Eberman was in her cabin at the time. Water was rapidly pouring in, and she was imprisoned. With difficulty a hole was cut through the deck with axes. When the rescuers reached her, they found the water already up to her neck. Nothing daunted, however, the brave missionary couple proceeded by a later opportunity, ready to endure hardness for Christ Jesus.

At the close of the year 1834, after a little more than one hundred years of labor, the missions on the Danish islands numbered 10,321 members—in St. Thomas, 1,998; St. Croix, 6,682; St. John, 1,641.

In Jamaica a new era had begun. Carmel's pestilential site was exchanged for the romantic slopes of the Mayday Hills. Here the attention of Louis Stobwasser, when on an official visit, was attracted to the prospects for an opening by the gathering of negroes around Samuel Hoch who had retired to the uplands for the sake of health. Situated as his retreat was near the summit of a high mountain, the torrid heat of the lowlands was never known; and yet it never became so cold that fire was needed. The blue of the sun-lit sea feasted the eye in the distance. To the south the savannah, pasture land interspersed with shady groves, formed the foreground of a magnificent view. Westward the Santa Cruz mountains, about ten miles away and studded with coffee plantations, rose beyond a plain covered with guinea grass, woodland and well-tilled fields. To the northwest undulating tracts, hill after hill, stretched out to meet the horizon. Well might the spot elicit its name—Fairfield. Stobwasser having disposed of the property at Carmel, acquired land here for a mission, and John Ellis, lately transferred from Antigua to superintend the work in Jamaica, undertook the establishment of operations. A church was dedicated on January 15, 1826. Irwin Hill was meanwhile doing well, and a new church could soon be consecrated there, to be speedily followed by New Carmel, Fulneck and Bethlehem—all by the end of the year 1831, whilst a new attempt was also made at Mesopotamia.

And now came the anxieties and the opportunities of the transition period leading to complete emancipation. For a quarter of a century the importation of blacks from Africa had been inhibited. But a slave population of six hundred thousand existed on the islands under the British flag. The long labors of Wilberforce and Buxton at last ripened in the decree that slavery should be abolished through the payment of twenty millions sterling as compensation to the proprietors. This legislation of 1833 was preceded by various premonitions of trouble, notably in Antigua in 1831 and in Jamaica in 1833. As far back as 1823 there had been friction between the Assembly of the latter island and the home government, the points especially at issue being the abrogation of Sunday markets, the cessation of the practice of carrying a whip in the field and the exemption of women from all forms of corporal punishment. Sentiment was aroused to such an extent that there were threats of transferring the allegiance of Jamaica to the United States, or even of aiming at independence. The excitement reached the slaves themselves. Agitators persuaded them, that if they did not now strive for freedom, emancipation would be forever lost. A rebellion broke out on December 28, 1831. The military speedily crushed it; but property had been destroyed to the value of $3,334,885. A number of clergymen of various churches were arrested and tried by martial law, and acquitted, on the charge of inciting the slaves to rebellion. The animosity of some slave-holders towards those who were trying to ameliorate the spiritual condition of the blacks caused the destruction of Wesleyan and Baptist churches in the parishes of St. Ann, Trelawny and St. James, whilst personal insults and injuries were suffered by the missionaries.

During this time of excitement Henry Gottlieb Pfeiffer, the Moravian missionary at New Eden, was seized, and taken to Mandeville by a lieutenant with a squad of thirty men. Explicit charges were not forthcoming. Trial by courtmartial was set for January 15, 1832, one week hence. In vain did John Ellis endeavor to secure a copy of the indictment. Knowledge in advance respecting the exact form of the accusation was withheld from prisoner. Verbal testimony for the defense was ruled out, written evidence alone being admitted. Legal assistance was refused, though he had only imperfect knowledge of the English language and still less acquaintance with English legal procedure. Against him two women and two men were produced. Verbal evidence in accusation was in order. Justice seemed suspended. The principal witness for the prosecution was brought from prison to the court, and had not sat under the preaching of Pfeiffer for two years. Moreover he was soon afterwards shot as an active agent in the insurrection. The other male witness was more than suspected of having perjured himself in connection with the trial. One of the women had been excluded from church fellowship six years previously for adultery, and had not been seen in the church of late; nevertheless she proposed to testify concerning the pulpit utterances of the minister. The evidence offered by the other woman was to the effect that he had publicly incited the negroes to rebellion in his address to them at Christmas—an absurdity on the face of it, since in the audience on that occasion were persons who were slaveholders. Inevitably acquittal followed. But amid the wrought-up feelings of the times the week had been one of deepest anxiety for poor Pfeiffer.

Freedom was not delayed by the disturbances. By Act of Parliament on and after the first of August, 1834, slavery became impossible throughout the British colonies. An apprenticeship of four or six years, according to the class of employment, was however inaugurated, to prevent evils that might have come from too hastily overturning the existing order of affairs. No less than 311,070 of the inhabitants of Jamaica were affected by this beneficent legislation. Meanwhile very few Moravian negroes had been implicated in the late disturbances, even to the extent of abandoning their work for a few days. Not one member was convicted of an act of violence—not even in congregations like New Carmel, New Fulneck, Mesopotamia, Malvern and Beaufort, near to the chief scenes of rebellion. Whole properties where the Brethren had been privileged to preach, remained perfectly quiet, though incendiary fires were blazing within a few miles of them. In some cases Moravian "native helpers" were entrusted with and guarded their master's property, when he himself had to flee.

In anticipation of complete emancipation special attention was now given to the work of education. By March, 1834, no less than twenty-six Moravian schools were in operation.

In spite of all apprehensions Emancipation Day, August 1, 1834, a public holiday by Act of Assembly, was spent by the liberated multitudes in a manner worthy of its significance. The thankful people thronged the churches, and with devout hallelujahs ascribed their deliverance to Almighty God. The religious life of the people was deepened by their great experience. All the mission stations felt the impetus of the change. Churches had to be enlarged or new structures built. A great desire for instruction arose, though superstitions and obeahism did not die in a day. At the end of the year 1835 the total membership on the island was 8,521, an increase of 1,339 in twelve months.

In the eastern English islands a similar advance took place. During the year 1819 six hundred and seventy-two adults were baptized in Antigua. St. Johns budded out into new congregations, Newfield in 1819 and Cedar Hall in 1822. When Christian Frederick Richter died in September, 1825, he could rejoice in the knowledge that his labors had not been in vain. Joseph Newby followed him as superintendent, to be succeeded in turn by Bennet Harvey in 1831. At the close of the year 1835 the mission counted 10,654 members, a gain of about three thousand in less than twenty years.

In St. Kitts Bethesda was consecrated in 1821 and Bethel was commenced in 1831, and during the period a net increase of about one thousand souls brought the membership to 3,168.

In Barbados, where John Taylor was superintendent, Sharon was the only congregation at the commencement of the period, with a membership of from two to three hundred. Tabor was placed at the disposal of the mission by the Haynes family of Bellmount in 1826—on a beautiful elevation commanding a fine view out to sea and in the midst of a populous neighborhood that supported fifty sugar mills. Both stations speedily arose from their ruins after the storm of 1831, and a wide-spread revival of religion followed. In May, 1835, the dedication of a third church, on Roebuck Street, in Bridgetown, was Taylor's last achievement, before yellow fever, fatal to ten West Indian missionaries at this time, brought his fruitful labors to an end. The Barbados mission, exclusive of Bridgetown, for which returns are not at hand, had increased to 1,441 members.

In 1826 at the repeated solicitations of members of the Hamilton family, who had sought to promote the establishment of a mission there in Montgomery's day, a renewed attempt was made on the island of Tobago by Peter Ricksecker from Pennsylvania. The station at its dedication two years later received the name of Montgomery. Very frequent changes in the missionary force on this island were necessitated by its unhealthy climate; but at the end of the year 1835 the new station numbered 309 members.

At the opening of the period operations in the colony of Surinam were practically confined to the capital and a few estates whose managers permitted occasional visits of missionaries. In January, 1821, a great conflagration swept away four hundred buildings in Paramaribo, exclusive of those on side or rear streets. The roaring torrent of flame came seething across to the very edge of the Brethren's quarter, and for twenty-four hours seemed irresistible. Their prayers were heard in its being averted from the church. The deliverance was so signal, that following as it did on the heels of a great mortality from small-pox, very many were led to seriously inquire the way of salvation, and before the end of the year ninety-six adults were baptized.

New estates now began to be thrown open—by 1826 six, thirteen during the following year, and ninety within a decade. It was impossible to pay as close attention to the slaves as was desired, for they were compelled to stay within the limits of the estates to which they belonged, and during the early part of this period only five missionary couples were stationed in the capital. But the effort was made to visit each estate at intervals of about eight weeks. Intercourse was had by water up the rivers, the boats and boatmen for the regular round of visits being provided through the Dutch Society for the Promotion of Christian Knowledge amongst the Negroes of Surinam, founded in 1828. This same society manifested its appreciation of the missionaries' labors by defraying about half the cost of the new church which the increase of membership in Paramaribo now rendered necessary. Commenced in July, 1827, its dimensions 95 by 60 feet, it was built over and around the old church in such a manner that the regular round of the services was not interrupted while its walls arose. The governor of the colony lent his countenance and personal financial aid. The reputation of the Brethren was also shown by the transfer to them of the spiritual care of the prisoners and slaves in the fort of New Amsterdam and the suburb of Zeelandia (Combe), with

CHRISTIAN IGNATIUS LA TROBE.

the evident desire of thus contributing to prepare the black population for emancipation.

Though the Harmony of the Four Evangelists, translated into Negro-English, had been published in 1821, as yet no portion of the Bible itself had been printed for circulation amongst the negroes of Surinam, few of them hitherto being able to read. The New Testament in this mongrel tongue existed in manuscript. Now the British and Foreign Bible Society judged that the time had come to place it in the hands of the people. The mission naturally felt the good effects of this beneficence; for even where older persons could not themselves read, it often happened that their children could do this service for them. Paramaribo could now report 2,133 members, and about 400 were in addition scattered among the plantations, whilst Charlottenburg on the Cottica, about thirty miles to the east of the city, was founded in 1835 as a center of operations for about eighty estates.

During the official visit of Christian Ignatius La Trobe, the Secretary of the Society for the Furtherance of the Gospel, who landed on Christmas Eve, 1815, a number of proposals had been received for the commencement of new missions in Cape Colony. One of these was accepted. Though within the colony, it was to furnish a basis of work amongst the Kaffirs, being situated on the White River, a tributary of the Sunday, about four hundred miles east of Capetown, in the Uitenhagen district.

On February 15, 1818, John Henry Schmidt, who was to superintend its establishment, set out from Groenekloof (Mamre), with his wife and John Frederick Hoffman and Godfrey Hornig. At Genadendal they were joined by the widowed Sister Kohrhammer. Their destination was reached on April 17; and several families of Hottentots from Genadendal, the nucleus of Enon, as the new place was named, set to work with them to clear away the mimosa bushes, prepare the ground for cultivation and erect temporary homes. Scarcely was the work opening up, when the border territory was plunged into all the horrors of a war of rival savages, T'Gaika and Stambe. On February 9, 1819, a band of Kaffirs suddenly rushed from neighboring wood and made off with two hundred and thirty-five head of cattle belonging to the Enon. Until March 7 the mission, isolated, and with the nearest neighbors a day's journey distant, was in expectation of the worst. Guards were set day and night, and their vigilance alone averted an actual attack. Food became very scarce. But at last the colonial forces pushed the raiders back across the border. Yet a second invasion followed, and the mission was reluctantly abandoned by the advice of the colonial authorities, after nine Hottentot Christians had fallen under the Kaffirs' assegais whilst defending their herds. At Uitenhagen suitable quarters were appointed, and the utmost kindness was experienced at the hands of Colonel Cuyler. In October, peace being concluded, John Peter Hallbeck, now superintendent of the entire mission, led the return. Desolation marked the track of the African warriors. Blackened ruins showed where houses had once stood. Orchards and gardens had been ruthlessly destroyed. Yet it was a comfort to know that their one hundred and fifty-five Hottentots were resolved to stand by the missionaries at any risk and with them reërect their Christian village.

About this time another product of Hottentot diligence was a standing refutation of the slander that the Hottentot was and must remain one of the laziest of men. Across the Zonderend at Genadendal under missionary supervision, they built by voluntary labor a bridge one hundred and fifty feet in length, wide enough for ox-teams, and resting on five massive piers. No such structure existed in the entire colony, and its completion made a sensation. But efforts at improvement suffered a check through a general failure of the wheat harvest in 1820 and 1821. The price rose to five times the normal figure. During the early part of 1822 at Genadendal alone three hundred recipients of charity were on the hands of Hallbeck. Fortunately the yield of fruit this year was unusually large, Schmidt's famous tree in its old age bearing fifteen sacks of pears.

In 1823 Michael Peterleitner and his wife took charge of a hospital for lepers recently established by government in a romantic valley under the shadow of the Tower of Babel mountain not far from the sea coast and Cape Town. Christian Hottentots were amongst the earliest inmates, and the steward of Hemel en Aarde, as the place was called, was a native convert, the first instance of one of his people receiving a position of trust other than that of a non-commissioned officer in a Hottentot regiment. Here the manifest blessing of God rested upon the self-denying labors of the missionary couple. When their teacher died suddenly from apoplexy, whilst in the act of administering baptism on Easter Monday, 1829, he was mourned as a father. John Christian Tietze became his successor.

Meantime in 1824 a fourth station was begun, Elim, about forty miles southeast of Genadendal. Now sundry innuendos appeared in public prints at Cape Town, an anonymous writer who shielded his personality under the pseudonym of "Rusticus" alleging that the missionaries were not disinterested in their efforts to promote the material welfare of the natives. As so often under similar circumstances, when the accused secured an official investigation their complete vindication followed, and with it came an unqualified expression of the confidence of government in their aims and methods. Indeed, Lord Somerset, the Governor, in 1827 gave special publicity to his sympathy. On the northeast frontier a Tambookie chieftain named Bowana had requested that missionaries be sent his people. The London Missionary Society, the Glasgow Missionary Society and the Wesleyans had already founded missions in Kaffraria. Yet it pleased the Governor to solicit from Hallbeck the services of the Moravian Church. He himself, with John Fritsch and several natives undertook an exploration of Bowana's territory— no pleasure jaunt in the cold of a South African winter. On June 27 snow-drifts several feet high had to be passed. On the night of the 29th Hallbeck's wagon stuck in the river Tarka, and his wet clothing was frozen stiff. Along the Oskrall and the Klippaat rivers Bowana pointed out land eligible for a mission. In February, 1828, Lemmertz, Hoffmann and Fritsch, with twenty-odd Hottentots and Wilhelmina Stompjes, a Christian Tambookie Kaffir woman, set out for permanent occupation of Shiloh, as the new station was to be named. But mission work on the Klipplaat had to encounter many obstacles. Bowana found objection after objection when it came to the question of building, notwithstanding his fine speeches of the year before. His Tambookies were stolidly indifferent. Then knavish Fetkanna raiders swooped down on the cattle. Locusts ravaged the gardens. In 1829 Mapasa, a son of Bowana, led fifty armed men to the mission with a view to massacre the very people whom his father had invited. Had it not been for Wilhelmina, the fate of the strangers had been sealed. She was at work helping her husband, the gardener of the mission, when her countrymen marched in, bedecked with gaudy crane feathers and lavishly smeared paint. The war dress told her quick glance the murderous intent of the young chief. Although Kaffir etiquette expected silence on the part of a woman in an assembly of men, she boldly pushed in amongst the gleaming assegais, and with all the fervid eloquence of a righteously indignant woman dared Mapasa to his face. With reproaches for his treachery, she energetically bade him begone. Somewhere beneath his war paint the young African possessed a conscience, and this conscience the honest fidelity of Wilhelmina touched. He gave orders to withdraw, and next day sent an apology for having caused alarm.

Now a change for the better set in. Early in the next year the baptism of the first converts took place, one of them the future mother of John Nakin, hereafter to grace the record as consecrated native minister. By December, 1835, Adolphus Bonatz preached to 340 Tambookies in addition to his 162 Hottentots, and the former could enjoy the Church Litany and the history of our Lord's passion and death in their own tongue. Tambookies stooped to agriculture, and old prejudices were breaking down.

Meanwhile at Genadendal a remarkable revival of religion blessed the year 1833. When slavery was abolished, on December 1, 1834, the mission in the Colony had reached a membership of 2,386.

In all the missionaries of the Moravian Church now had 51,000 souls in their recognized care.

CHAPTER XLVI.

THE GENERAL SYNOD OF 1836.

When the general synod of 1836 convened in Herrnhut on May 30, the revolutionary movements of the thirties were over. On the surface there lay a treacherous calm. The theory of government which dispensed alike with popular interference and with popular criticism, seemed to have enthroned itself especially amid the multitude of states which constituted the loosely-knit confederation of the Germanic peoples. The tendency of the age to the average observer appeared to be fully set towards conservatism, and this affected the gathering of representatives of the church. It needed the vision of a seer to discern the vast convulsions of many a populace which only twelve years hence should bring on throes of revolution more significant than any yet chronicled in the century. And it needed scarcely less prophetic foresight to anticipate a correspondent upheaval in the life of the Moravian Church within the next twenty years. The conservation of the old and established, identified as it was with the accepted conception of what was supposed to be the acme of the Unity's healthiest inner state, formed the standard for strivings and endeavors. Bishop Curie presided.

A thorough discussion of the doctrinal standpoint and of the constitution of the Unity left everything unchanged. The need of having all appointments to office confirmed by the lot was strenuously affirmed. Yet in connection with the ritual certain minor concessions to the spirit of the age seemed inevitable. The "Kiss of Peace" may give place to "the Right Hand of Fellowship" at the celebration of the Lord's Supper, where the former no longer tends to edification; and whilst the personal interview of every member with the spiritual leaders of the several choirs is still recognized as the most desirable mode of procedure in preparation for the enjoyment of this sacra-

ment, it is admitted that in various congregations insurmount-
able difficulties are in the way; in such cases pastoral visits must
be the substitute.

From June 12 to 22 the general sessions of the synod yielded
to the deliberations of the Committee on Finance, presided over by Samuel Christlieb Reichel. Its report presented
a state of affairs indicative of careful management. The general finances of· the church and of the diaconies of the several
congregations seemed to have materially improved during the
past eleven years. The capital of the sinking fund for the ex-
tinguishment of the debt had been almost doubled by donations,
legacies and careful investments.

A similarly encouraging outlook could be presented by the
Committee on Foreign Missions, whose sessions were held from
July 14 to 19, under the leadership of Bishop Curie. Notwithstanding the marked growth of the work in recent years, the
accounts showed a small surplus, so liberally had friends as well
as members of the church come forward to the support of the
work.

The thirty-nine schools in various lands were reported to be
in a flourishing condition on the whole. Discussion was again
had with reference to the advisability of removing the seminary from Gnadenfeld, and the Unity's Elders' Conference was
requested to give this important matter its most thorough and
earnest consideration at the first opportunity. If practicable,
the removal was recommended for the next autumn. On the
other hand synod expressed an unwillingness to authorize the
establishment of a distinctive institution for the training of
missionaries. It regarded the "Brethren's Houses" and teacherships in the various schools as the best forms of preparation.

The election of the Unity's Elders' Conference resulted as
follows: the Department of Finance, Samuel Christlieb Reichel,
John Ballein and Christian William Matthiesen; the Depart-
ment of Missions, Bishops Wied and Anders and John Christian
Breutel; the Department of Education and the Pastoral Office,
Bishops Kölbing and Curie and Frederick Renatus Frueauff.
Bishop Kölbing was reëlected President. Peter La Trobe was
appointed *Secretarius Unitatis in Anglia*, and Count Henry 55th
Reuss, *Advocatus*. John Plitt was clothed with the office of
Archivist at Herrnhut.

CHAPTER XLVII.

THE CHURCH ON THE CONTINENT OF EUROPE, FROM 1836 TO 1857.

That the men responsible for the administration of affairs vigorously endeavored to discharge their obligations as intelligently as possible during the years which preceded the constitutional changes must be conceded. If they failed to wholly satisfy those whose interests they served, it was from the inadequacy of the system itself. Indefatigable activity was displayed in connection with official visits. The circle of officials at Berthelsdorf was rarely complete. Often the visits covered a considerable time. With it all, frequent changes in the personnel of the Conference made it difficult to maintain continuity in office, important under existing regulations. On December 13, 1840, Bishop Kölbing died. Bishop Curie was chosen President, and John Martin Nitschmann filled the vacancy in the board. Then Bishop Wied was called home, on March 7, 1844. He had been engaged in the work of the church for more than half a century, twenty years as superintendent of the mission in Surinam, and since 1811 a member of the governing board. John Gottlieb Hermann, born at Niesky in 1789, but identified with the American congregations since 1817, and since 1836 a member of the Helpers' Conference at Bethlehem, was transferred to Berthelsdorf. Next year, 1845, Bishop Anders retired owing to failing health, and died on November 5, 1847. His successor was Christian Frederick Benjamin Gregor.

Since the close of the Zinzendorfian era the Moravian Church had been led to consider that it had providentially received a three-fold calling—to energetically labor for the unevangelized heathen and especially for such whom others passed by, to serve as a leaven imparting vital faith and promoting simple godliness amongst members of state churches without requiring them to withdraw allegiance from the confession with which they had been familiar from childhood, and to promote the avowedly Christian education of the young in order to win them early for Christ and implant the principles of active Christian character, whilst avoiding proselytism. The second phase of activity was now to receive a fatal blow. This was the arbitrary repression of the *Diaspora* in Livonia by the hand of irresponsible imperial power guided by evangelical bigotry.

Deeply taught by the far-reaching consequences of the Napoleonic wars, Czar Alexander I of Russia profoundly desired to promote heart religion amongst his subjects. He himself had come under the influence of the writings of Madame Von Krüdener and Jung Stilling. His visit to Herrnhut in 1813 and the favorable testimony of others had disposed him to appreciate the work of the Brethren in various parts of his empire. At least two of his trusted advisers, Prince Galitzin and Count later Prince Lieven, shared with him this high regard for the Moravian Church—the latter to such an extent that he was sometimes sneeringly called "the Moravian." Accordingly the ukase of 1817 had placed the *Diaspora* in the Baltic Provinces on a very favorable footing, even though complete religious liberty was not granted. Amongst the rest it declared: "We permit the above members of the Brethren's Church, in accordance with previous practice, for the spiritual welfare and salvation of the Livonians, Esthonians and others who desire it, to erect and establish prayer-halls in the cities, villages and hamlets, and to hold them under their supervision, with the consent of the owner of the landed property and the knowledge of the civil authorities—and this without hindrance. All who desire are at liberty to assemble in these prayer-halls, in accordance with existing usage, at hours other than those set apart for the stated services of the churches, provided it be in time free from the obligation to labor. These meetings for prayer, for the reading of the Holy Scriptures and for instruction in morality, shall stand under the supervision and direction of the elders and members of the Brethren's Church." This favorable edict contributed in a marked degree to the progress of the *Diaspora* in the Russian Empire. But this very prosperity aroused feelings of hostility. In the year 1832 Czar Nicholas granted a new constitution to the Lutheran Church within his dominions. In his case there was a lack of the personally favorable disposition in relation to the Brethren which had distinguished his predecessor. His entire character inclined him to fixedly regulated and sharply defined relationships in church and state—witness his codification of the laws of Russia in 1830. This offered an opportunity which the theologians at Dorpat and the ultra Lutheran clergy were not slow to utilize. First the right of the Brethren to deliver free addresses was challenged, and such an interpretation was sought for the language of the edict of Alexander I as would limit them to the reading of sermons or other compositions previously approved by the consistories. Then the effort was made to interfere with the services of Russian-born subjects who had been appointed the "national assistants" of the German laborers. And finally in 1840 the blow fell. An edict was secured placing the supervision of the prayer-halls of the Moravian *Diaspora* in the Baltic Provinces under the Lutheran consistories. It was further expressly stipulated that the spiritual exercises should be confined to the reading of the Scriptures without any comment, and to the singing of hymns and the offering of fixed forms of prayer which had been examined and approved by the consistories. The administration of the sacraments was prohibited. The labors of the Germans appointed to this work must be confined to the places where they resided; they were not to itinerate.

One immediate effect of this diplomatic stroke on the part of the hostile evangelical clergy was that out of two hundred and fifty-five prayer-halls only twelve practically remained under control of the Brethren, and even these with hampering conditions. Had the edict been enforced literally and without exceptions, the end of the *Diaspora* in the Baltic Provinces would have come. At best an uncertain, crippled existence was maintained.

In pleasing contrast to the oppressive treatment of Russia several occurrences marked the truer esteem in which the church was held elsewhere. In 1841 King Frederick William III of Prussia decreed that the title to its estates in his dominions might be held by the Unity's Elders' Conference as a corporate body. The nominal proprietorship of individuals could therefore come to an end. Similar concessions were granted in Saxony in 1844. To these concessions was attached the stipulation that the Conference should receive a power of attorney from the general synod of the Unity authorizing it to hold its trust in the name of the church; and in order that the synod might be in a position to confer power of this nature and in a manner recognized as legal by the Saxon Government, the further condition was implied, that the synod itself should be constituted of representatives whose credentials should be attested in accordance with the law of the various lands whence they came. All this contributed to the movement for constitutional change now proceeding within the Unity itself.

Another token of regard on the part of others was manifested in connection with the resuscitation of the episcopate for the so-called *"Unitäts-gemeinden"* in Prussian Posen. These were five congregations which constituted the remnant of the once flourishing Polish Province of the Unitas Fratrum. After the second destruction of Lissa, during the closing years of the seventeenth and the opening years of the eighteenth century, what remained of the Brethren's Church in Poland, Hungary, Transylvania and Silesia had gradually been amalgamated with other evangelical bodies, and in particular with the Reformed Church, yielding to the tendency set in motion by the Union Synod of Sendomir. In 1817 the King of Prussia had achieved a further amalgamation by combining the Lutherans and Reformed of his dominions into the *Unirte Kirche*. Yet these five *"Unitäts-gemeinden"* of Posen amid all changes maintained the seniorate or episcopate which they had received from the Unitas Fratrum—a succession of ten bishops since the days of David Cassius. They were the churches at Posen, Lissa, Lasswitz, Waschke and Orzeszkowo, and formed part of the State Church of the Province of Posen, being officially designated *"Diocese Posen II."* Their bishop or "Senior" was *ex-officio* a member of the royal consistory of the province. The five congregations unitedly possessed the remnant of a church fund known as the *"Unitäts-fond,"* and enjoyed the right of electing their "Senior." They had their annual district synod and an annual convention of pastors. Otherwise they were distinguished from the rest of the congregations under the royal consistory only by certain peculiarities of ritual and of church judicature preserved from former days.

In the year 1841 Samuel David Hanke, their bishop, died without consecrating a successor. Doctor Siedler was elected to this office in Posen in January, 1843. At the suggestion of King Frederick William III of Prussia, and with the cordial consent of the Prussian cabinet, he sought consecration from the bishops of the Unity at Berthelsdorf. This was willingly imparted at Herrnhut on June 16, 1844, by Bishop Curie, assisted by Bishops Levin Reichel and John Martin Nitschmann; and thus the resuscitated Unity was anew connected with representatives of the church of the forefathers.

Meantime for the inner life of the European congregations significant events were transpiring. The wholesome and searching influence of Frederick Emanuel Kleinschmidt upon the student-life of the church during his term of office as co-principal of the college at Niesky from 1832 to 1839 was followed for a year and a half by the even deeper effect of his sermons and expository lectures as co-pastor. Meantime on the foundations which he had laid in the college other earnest men—notably Ernest Reichel and Gustavus Tietzen—continued to build. The truth, that personal experience of the new birth is an indispensable condition of all efforts to do what is pleasing to God, and the corollary, that unqualified conscientiousness in the fulfillment of duties must be the consequence and sign of the experience of the new birth, became germinal ideas. The students were in a peculiar receptive state, when the centenary of the experiences commemorated by the entire Unity on November 13, 1841, drew the thoughts of all to an examination of their personal relationship to Christ. This coincided with the return of the sons of Prince Reuss-Stohnsdorf from their father's death-bed, deeply affected. The Lord poured down His grace in rich measure. A true revival of religion characterized the life of the students in the days and weeks following the festival. It became the joy of their instructors to lead them to assurance. Most helpful was the influence of Tietzen. By the grace of God the awakening was preserved from every taint of the fanciful or fanatic. In the simplicity of faith forgiveness was accepted. Peace and joy were calmly received. Desire for and appreciation of fellowship in prayer were manifested. Yet all the wholesome spirited traits of young manhood remained. But conversation was well guarded. Conscientious fulfillment of duties and industrious use of opportunities displaced the usual weaknesses and foibles of student days.

The peculiar significance of this renewal of spiritual life and earnest purpose just here is readily apparent. Here, alike in the circle of instructors and officers and in that of the taught, were many who should hereafter carry far the influence of these indelible experiences by their service of the church in the pastorate, in charge of administrative activities, in the *Diaspora*, in the foreign field. By those who remained in the ranks of the laity a similar apprehension of her mission was spread through the membership of the congregations. Together with the centenary celebration of 1822 this revival served to mark a new epoch.

Gravest complications were however at hand before the new life could develop new forms and regulations more suited to its needs than the old and outlived. Years of scarcity from floods or other natural causes, deepened the popular discontent and furnished opportunities for political agitators. High prices began to rule already in the spring of 1845. The Rhine overflowed its banks at Neuwied in March, so that the water stood several feet deep on the floor of the church, lacking only three feet of the high-water mark of 1784. Then came a poor harvest, general, not merely local. The scarcity was not relieved next year, for another poor harvest followed. Not even did the wide-spread distress cease in 1847. Instead of driving the people to take refuge in God, a rank crop of infidelity sprang like a fungus growth from the soil soured by discontent and the decay of industries. France, often the pulse of Europe, first showed the symptoms of fever in the popular life. From France the contagion spread to Germany. A bloody conflict raged in the streets of Berlin for hours on March 18. Denmark's internal troubles filled Christiansfeld with billeted soldiery. In Vienna the mob sacked the palace of Prince Metternich. The kings of Saxony and Württemberg granted new and more liberal constitutions to their subjects. Bavaria had its insurrection. Mazzini and Garibaldi grasped the chance to commence their work of redeeming Italy. Lombardy was invaded.

It was in the midst of these convulsions, portending it was impossible to fortell what eventful outcome, that a general synod once more convened at Herrnhut on May 29, destined to prepare the way for the reconstruction of the constitution of the church. Bishop John G. Hermann presided. A leaning towards liberalism was apparent. On the Continent of Europe new congregations might hereafter be commenced where opportunity afforded and need arose, to be patterned moreover not after the exclusive "settlements," but after the town and country congregations. In the case of the "settlements" them-

selves the membership should not be restricted to those who resided within the locality and were subject to its civil and communal regulations, but might include persons in immediately
adjacent parts who sought fellowship. The requests of the
American congregations were practically granted, and carried
with them the pledge of a future change in the constitution of
the Unity. Provincial synods with full legislative power in
reference to purely Provincial affairs should be convened at intervals of six years in each division of the Unity—the American being regarded as two distinct Provinces in this respect.
All incumbents of Provincial offices, all pastors and brethren
in active service were to have seats and votes in these assemblies, and each congregation should enjoy lay representation.
The President of the Provincial Elders' Conference should be
ex-officio the president of the Provincial synod. The synod of the
British Province should nominate to the Unity's Elders' Conference for its approval the members of its governing board.
In America the procedure should obtain which had been mapped
out by the preparatory conference of 1847. Thus the first stage
in the development of Provincial independence was attaind. Its
influence upon the future of the Moravian Church in America
within a generation should exceed the expectations of the most
sanguine of those whose deliberations projected and whose energies secured these important concessions. The Unity's Elders' Conference was anew constituted of the same members as
previously, save that the venerable Frederick Renatus Frueauff,
eighty-five years of age, asked to be released from active service after a career of sixty-one years. Joseph Reinhold Ronner was elected to the vacancy. Not until the 6th did this important gathering bring its labors to a close.

Hardly were its members homeward bound, when the thunders of revolution again resounded. Prussia, Saxony, the
Palatinate, Baden, Denmark—all of them suffered from civil
strife. Königsfeld and Christiansfeld were both deprived of the
use of their churches, requisitioned as hospitals. But even
more important consequences were felt in the impetus given to
migration to the great western El Dorado and to Australia. In
1850 the removal of a compact body of *Diaspora* members from
Giersdorf near Herrnhut to West Salem in Illinois called forth
such sympathy that contributions were solicited to aid them
in establishing a congregation school in their new home. Nor

were the Australians forgotten. In the same year Christopher Schondorf of Gnadenfeld received a call to minister to former members and friends who had settled in South Australia, and who desired to maintain connection with the church. Arriving at Adelaide after a tedious voyage of one hundred and six days, he organized a congregation at Light's Pass, forty-five or fifty miles away, where a church was consecrated on Palm Sunday, 1854.

Characteristic of this era of the advance of political liberalism and of the formation of the Gustavus Adolphus Association, and of the foundation of the *Deutsche Zeitschrift für christliche Wissenschaft und christliches Leben*, by Neander, Nitsch and Müller, was the movement in the interest of free coöperation for the defense of the faith against the attacks of a false freedom of thought. This defensive movement found its expression in the establishment of the Church Diet (*Kirchentag*) in Wittenberg in 1848. In its annual conventions the Diet paid attention to the maintenance of an Evangelical Alliance, such as had been realized in England since 1845, and to the work of "Inner Missions." Representatives of the Unity participated in the various conventions, men like Frederick William Kölbing, Charles von Bülow, Ernest Reichel and Kleinschmidt. Moreover the purposes and characteristics of the Unity were now brought to the attention of a wide circle by the publication of a considerable historical work, Ernest William Cröger's *Geschichte der erneuerten Brüder-Kirche*, which was issued in several parts, the first being published at Gnadau in 1851. The author had been appointed historiographer in accordance with action taken by the synod of 1848. Particular interest in historical matters had then been aroused by the report of the acquirement for the Archives of Plitt's voluminous manuscript *Denkwürdigkeiten aus der alten und neuen Bruder-Geschichte*, which furnished well collated materials for a history down to 1818. And the interest had been further stimulated by the reported purchase of the large and valuable collection of "Lissa Folios." These were thirteen folio volumes of Latin and Bohemian documents, once forming a part of the old archives of the church at Lissa, collected subsequent to the destruction of the former archives in the conflagration at Leitomischl in 1546. Discovered by Frederick Emmanuel Kleinschmidt in 1836, and examined by Plitt, their value had led to their early

ERNEST WILLIAM CRÖGER.

acquirement. Cröger had indeed aimed to furnish neither a critical nor an exhaustive history of the resuscitated Unity; but he laid the church under indebtedness by his work, carried down to the centenary of the founding of Herrnhut. It ministered to edification within the pale of the Unity, afforded a ready means of acquainting others with her essential traits, and served to stimulate more critical research, besides erecting a monument to the past at a time when the transition period was about to emerge into the modern era of a more liberal constitution and ever developing activities.

Fluctuating fortunes attended the *Diaspora*, here prosperity and growth, there failure or contraction. It was judged that the time was not yet ripe to change the societies in Montmirail and Locle into fully constituted congregations. Yet Jonathan Kramer was directed to confine his services to Locle, so as to become to all intents and purposes pastor loci, with Theodore Schutz as his assistant. Elsewhere there was also an increase in the number of Brethren engaged in this phase of evangelism—in Brieg, in the Westerwald and in Poland. Livonia continued to have trying experiences. Nor did success attend the plan cherished by the Provincial synod of 1856 for a resuscitation of Herrnhaag, now vacated for more than one hundred years. Bordeaux had also to be abandoned on the death of John Louis Shiep in 1856, since the committee in charge of the Mariners' Chapel in which he had ministered procured his successor from another communion.

Several of the older men passed away just as the constitutional changes anticipated by the legislation of 1848 were beginning to be keenly agitated. In 1849 Bishop Hermann had returned to America, to succeed Bishop William Henry Van Vleck in Salem. In his place Godfrey Andrew Cunow, of the British Board, had been summoned to Herrnhut. Bishop Schneider had died on March 23, and Gregor on April 19. Frederick William Kölbing, although a much younger man, had been carried off by a stroke on May 24. Ernest Frederick Reichel and Charles Frederick Schordan were made members of the Conference. The retirement of the aged Samuel Christlieb Reichel in 1852 created another vacancy, filled by the election of Charles Frederick Kluge, administrator in North Carolina. Reichel enjoyed only a brief evening of rest. On April 2, 1853, he was called home. Born at Barby on January 30,

1774, where his father was a member of the Unity's Elders' Conference, he had served as professor in the college from 1795 to 1801, and in the seminary from 1801 to 1808, when he was appointed one of the secretaries of the Unity's Elders' Conference. In 1821 he became a member of the Board itself, two years later entering the sphere in which he should render most distinguished services—the Department of Finance. In 1848 the synod had publicly recognized that the improved financial status was due to his unwearied energy, consummate ability and painstaking fidelity, under the blessing of God. In October of the following year Joseph Reinhold Ronner resigned from the Department of Missions on account of failing health, and the venerable Bishop Curie retired from active service, to be called home on February 19, 1855. Charles William Jahn of Sarepta was chosen for the vacancy in the Department of Education and the Pastoral Office, whilst Henry Rudolph Wullschlaegel, the leader in Surinam since 1849, became a member of the Mission Board.

By this time the agitation of needful changes in the constitution of the church had been gathering headway, especially in Am.,ica.   There it had been felt for some decades that the Moravian Church could not fulfill her calling, if hampered by the remnants of the exclusive system and by an absence of home rule. These convictions had been definitely formulated in   Provincial synod held at Bethlehem from May 2 to 23, ₁855. Agreement had been reached as to various matters of fundamental importance, and a memorial had been drafted for presentation to the Unity's Elders' Conference, adducing reasons why these changes were deemed requisite, and requesting that a general synod be convened at an early day to act in the premises. Briefly the desiderata were as follows: supervision of Provincial affairs by a board, the members of which shall all be elected by the Provincial synod, and serve as its executive; power of self-organization to be granted to this board, in place of having its President selected by the Unity's Elders' Conference; accountability of this executive board to the Provincial synod, and not to the Unity's Elders' Conference for all acts that concern the Province as such; nomination of the bishops of the Province by the Province itself and not by the Unity's Elders' Conference; the appointment of the administrator in America by the Unity's Elders' Conference, and his accountability as such to this board alone, he being no longer *ex-officio* connected with the supervision of the congregations in America; and with this the implied separation of the Unity's funds and properties from Provincial funds and properties. Upon the receipt of the memorial a call was issued for a general synod in May, 1857, to be preceded by preparatory synods in each of the Provinces. Now discussions of all issues pertinent to the most fundamental principles of constitution, polity and discipline, or relating to the most divergent points and to questions only indirectly involved, followed in the *Fraternal Messenger* in England, the *Brüder-Blatt* and the *Moravian* in America—and in various pamphlets. Most noteworthy of the latter were *Die Brüder-Kirche: Was ist Wahrheit?* by "*Forscher*," which appeared anonymously in 1856, without the imprint of any publication house, and *Der Forscher beleuchtet*, by Henry Levin Reichel, issued at Löbau in the same year. "*Forscher*" was understood to be a Moravian missionary in Jamaica, whose years of faithful and efficient devotion to the cause should have been sufficient proof of his loyalty and sincerity of purpose had he chosen to come out over his own signature. He attacked especially the commonly received view of the "chief eldership" of Christ, with regard to which some since the celebration of 1841 had used language unwarranted by the position of the church as defined in her Synodal Results; the abuse of the lot; the society-theory of the Brethren's Church as contrasted with the independent churchly conception; the exclusivism of the "settlement" regulations; the alliance of secular business and spiritual life which was involved in the "Diacony system;" and he maintained that these were the causes why the Unity had fallen from her first high estate. Whilst the manner and phraseology of his presentation, unfortunately very keen and almost excessively ruthless as it still appears in certain passages, doubtless repelled the semi-conservative whom less incisively denunciatory and more calmly argumentative persuasion might have won over, and whilst the weak points in the statement of historical premises were conclusively exposed by his enlightener, the fact undoubtedly remains that "*Forscher's*" pungent pamphlet was one of the instrumentalities overruled for good, and that it did contribute to the improvement which became apparent in succeeding years. The new wine of the revived life of the Unity, revived variously in the different Provinces, could

not be kept in the old skins. These very discussions indicated
a ferment which was rending them.   Most of the results at
which "*Forscher*" aimed have been achieved during the decades
that have transpired, and the correctness of his aims has been
demonstrated, if not of his premises or of the entire process of
his argumentation.   But at the time intense feeling was
aroused.   The mere receipt of the American resolutions had
been sufficient to call forth gloomy forebodings with respect to
the future of the Moravian Church as a Unity of the Brethren.
To German minds disruption seemed not at all improbable if
the American desires were conceded.   The German preparatory synod, in session at Herrnhut from May 19 to 24, dominated by the conservative spirit, was unable to appreciate all
that was involved in the utterly divergent conditions of American religious life with its absolute freedom of operations.   The
American memorial seemed tantamount to a declaration of a
desire for the dissolution of the bonds of the Unity.   They
therefore asked the preparatory American synod in the North
to reconsider its position.   To some in America even this discussion of the American proposals by the German Provincial
synod appeared to involve a transgression of constitutional
functions.   They held that in so doing the German Province
had fallen into the error of identifying the Unity with itself, and
solemnly protested against what appeared to them equivalent
to a prejudgment of the entire case, since the German Province
at the general synod had sufficient representatives to outvote
the other two Provinces combined.   They overlooked the fact
that no preparatory synod at this juncture could do its work
without considering their memorial.   Had the strife of the pen
continued much longer, the end of the Unity might well have
followed. In the event the providence of God mercifully directed
all to the strengthening of the church's usefulness and to an enlarged apprehension of her commission.

CHAPTER XLVIII.

THE CHURCH IN BRITAIN AND IRELAND FROM 1836 TO 1857.

Soon after the synod Samuel Frederick Church died at Ock-brook, and John King Martyn was chosen a member of the Conference. In 1842, the venerable Charles Augustus Pohlman was incapacitated by a stroke whilst officiating in Bristol. Bishop John Beck Holmes, the English historian of the Moravian Church and its missions, for many years pastor of the Fulneck congregation, also died here on September 3, 1843. He was in his 76th year. His father, the captain of a Danish whaler, had been led to Christ by the missionary Beck, when a passenger on his ship en voyage for Greenland. Educated at Christiansfeld, Niesky and Barby, his activity since 1791 had found a sphere wholly in the British isles. After the death of Pohlman, Bishop Martyn became President of the Conference at Ockbrook, and as the third member Benjamin Seifferth was chosen. In autumn, 1846, however, Martyn resigned as a member of the board, owing to failing health. Seifferth now became President, and on October 26 was consecrated a bishop. The vacancy in the board was filled by the appointment of Godfrey Andrew Cunow.

For these brethren, as indeed for all those who were charged with responsibilities of office in the British isles, the closing years of the period must have been heavily burdened with anxieties. Every enterprise felt the stress of the times. On the one hand the revival of Chartism threatened unknown and vague troubles of a sort impossible to foresee. On the other hand, as far back as 1845, the poor harvests of continental Europe had their counterpart in the appearance of the potato-rot in Ireland, the disease of the chief article of Irish subsistence becoming almost universal in 1847, whilst the blight of the intervening year also led up to the intensity of general distress. At length "famine" became the dreadfully appropriate term to describe the real state of millions of human beings. One million and a quarter joined the vast tide of migration to the United States in the years just before and during and immediately after the calamity. Business failures in England demonstrated the interdependence of commercial relations in modern life.

Nevertheless there were various reachings out for a widening of influence. Wibsey (Horton) was given up in 1837, but in 1839 John Carey became pastor in Little Horton. Moravian evangelists had been known here as far back as 1742, but the present undertaking found rootage through the efforts of Joseph Hinchcliffe of Horton Hall Academy, a famous school in its day. The Bedford group also received an accession in 1839. A couple of miles northwest of Kimbolton, watered by the same brook, the purling Kym, lies the little village of Tillbrook, amid the same delightfully rural scenery. Here services were now commenced, and the pastor of Kimbolton found welcome opportunity to extend his sphere of usefulness.

Nor was the Irish work without its efforts at extension. In 1842 John Birtill purchased an unfinished mansion at Sandy Bay, and shortly after converted one of its large rooms into a place of worship. This house was but three miles from Glenavy, where Cennick had preached in September, 1750, to several thousand people. The grounds sloped down to the shores of Lough Neagh. But in 1846 Birtill was transferred to Kilkeel, and the exigencies of the day caused his former pastoral relations to be made good only by the visits of a Scripture reader. Even this substitute failed with the removal of the latter brother to Ballinderry, and ere long the property passed from the church by sale.

Meantime various efforts were made to maintain the connection of the English and Irish churches with those on the Continent, the bands of fellowship being strengthened by an official visit of Renatus Frueauff in 1837.

A Provincial conference was held at Fairfield from June 30 to July 16, 1847, Benjamin Seifferth presiding. The "Results" of 1836 were followed as the basis of business. Exception was taken to the articles on Baptism, the Lord's Supper, and Confession in the Augsburg Confession. A proposal to the forthcoming synod was adopted, abrogating assent to the Augsburg Confession on the part of the Brethren's Church, or exempting the British Province from its operation. Since 1835 there was an increase of 53 communicants, a decrease of 457 "Received Members" and a total decrease of 51. "Reception" was still to be made subject to the decision of the lot. A committee was appointed to undertake the publication of a new hymnal utilizing the work done for this purpose by James Montgomery. Peter La Trobe was commissioned to edit a cheap edition of the Tune book. A new scheme for preparing young men for the ministry was adopted, and a fund inaugurated in support of this undertaking. The Society for Propagating the Gospel in Ireland was found to be in a languid state, and efforts were to be made to revive it. For the temporal relief of the distressed congregations in Ireland £365 had been raised in the English congregations. Of this amount £150 had been expended in seed corn.

Agitation, discussion, an ever-widening desire to attain renewed vigor and usefulness—these are the chief characteristics of the British Province in the years preceding the fundamental changes in the constitution of the Unity. Opportunity for additional preparatory discussion was afforded both by the convocation of Provincial synods, in 1853 and 1856, and also by the rise of religious periodicals, the *Fraternal Messenger* and the *Moravian Magazine*. The former, a private and independent enterprise, projected and carried out by its editor, John Carey, came into existence in 1850. In its pages many a pointed inquisition was made into usages which had pursued the even tenor of their way hitherto unchallenged, warnings were uttered against actual or supposed failings of the church, bugle notes rang out clearly to challenge an advance of the cross standard, and fraternal thrusts were exchanged in numerous give-and-take debates. If something of the air of a free lance appears in his paragraphs, so abundantly militant, there is nevertheless never an absence of the deeply chivalrous consecration of a true crusader, nor can the devotion of this champion of reform to his denominational standard be ever questioned. As in the case of *Forscher*, his stoutest blows proved rather stimulative than annihilative or really detrimental. The *Moravian Magazine*, like the *Fraternal Messenger* a monthly, was published as an official organ of the church, at the instance of the synod of 1853, and had for its editors William Edwards, John England

and G. L. Herman. Its publication was suspended, however, in the following year for lack of support.

At the head of affairs, with residence at Ockbrook, were now Bishop Benjamin Seifferth, with Samuel Rudolph Reichel and Godfrey Andrew Cunow. In London, Peter La Trobe served as secretary, and William Mallalieu as agent of missions. Cunow was called to Berthelsdorf in 1849 and Bishop William Essex took his place. The death of Bishop Martyn at Bristol on August 18, this same year, only forty-five years of age, fell like a sudden blow upon the church; and this loss was followed by the death of Bishop Essex, in 1852. William Edwards, pastor of Fulneck, was given the duties hitherto discharged by the latter.

Again new beginnings were attempted. Four or five miles southeast of Glastonbury, redolent with memories of masterful Abbot Dunstan, is the little village of Baltonsborough, with about 800 inhabitants in 1852, mainly freeholders, occupying comfortable farms or neat cottages. But for years prophecy had been precious in these parts. High church preaching of morality had been succeeded by veneration of crosses and candles and vestments and altar pieces. In the midst of this spiritual dearth a Mr. Whitehead was awakened through the visits of a godly minister of a neighboring village to his mother when critically ill. Becoming acquainted with James La Trobe, the Moravian minister at Bristol, he invited him to come to Baltonsborough and preach in a neat Gothic chapel of stone, which he had recently built. Another Moravian minister, J. J. Montgomery, came hither for his health, and upon his recovery accepted the new pastorate.

In Batheaston, a suburb of Bath, on the Frome, an earnest Christian family solicited the aid of Austin Smith in endeavors to wholesomely influence this and surrounding villages. He commenced his labors on September 1, 1853. The number of stated hearers so increased that soon a room capable of accommodating upwards of three hundred persons was secured. Unfortunately this interesting undertaking did not attain permanence.

When superannuated in 1856, John Carey, on retiring to Greengates, near Apperley, Leeds, could not be contentedly inactive, but must needs inaugurate a mission.

Once more also the founding of a theological seminary was attempted in a modest way, at Bedford, in 1854, in charge of John England, who in the following year received Bennet Harvey as an assistant in the pulpit and the pastorate. Voluntary subscriptions provided largely for the support of the undertaking, but it came to an end in 1857.

As in America the preparatory synod of 1856, at Fulneck, largely voiced demands for reform, though the requests were somewhat more conservative in tenor. It was proposed that the members of the Provincial board should continue to discharge a double responsibility. The President of the Conference should be designated by the Unity's board from among those elected by Provincial synod. Thus appointed the Provincial Helpers were to be accountable to the Provincial synod for the proper management of the local concerns of the Province, and accountable to the Unity's Elders' Conference for maintaining sound doctrine, and the affairs of the Unity in general.

Synod further determined that in order to further home missions, the Province should be divided into four Districts, three in England and one in Ireland, in each of which a District conference should be statedly convened. In each of these Districts associations should be established, which should jointly form a Moravian Home Mission Society, under the direction of a committee consisting of the Provincial Helpers' Conference and one brother from each District conference, of which District conference he shall be the secretary. In addition, a general secretary, C. E. Sutcliffe, pastor of Dukinfield, and a general treasurer, Brother Phillips, the delegate of the Bristol congregation, were forthwith elected. It was suggested that each District should at the start support one home missionary.

Two deaths yet require to be chronicled. James Montgomery, the beloved hymn-writer of the Unity, died at Sheffield, April 30, 1854. Born on November 4, 1771, at Irvine, in Scotland, his father being the Moravian pastor there and later a missionary in the West Indies, he had been educated in Fulneck School. As editor of the *Sheffield Iris* twice suffering imprisonment for his devotion to liberty and personal rights, he had also deservedly earned a national reputation as a devotional poet, and more than local esteem as a philanthropist. A typical Moravian in spirit and principle, he cherished his fellowship with Fulneck, restored in matured life, and by temperance and prudence and godliness had prolonged the powers of a naturally weak constitution to more than four score years. In the same year John Willing Warren, Esq., the venerable President of the London Association in Aid of Moravian Missions ever since its organization in 1817, passed away at the advanced age of eighty-five. His successor in this office of fraternal aid was Sir Edward N. Buxton, Bart.

CHAPTER XLIX.

THE AMERICAN CONGREGATIONS, FROM 1836 TO 1857.

In both North and South the church was awakening to its responsibilities in relation to missions at home. The United Brethren's Home Missionary Society of North Carolina did not confine its operations to the districts around Mount Bethel. Its semi-annual meetings called attention to neglected neighborhoods in the immediate vicinity of Salem. Henry A. Shultz, pastor of Friedberg, was especially active in seeking out new fields, and established preaching-places at Coolspring, Goodhope and Hopewell, and as a result the New Philadelphia congregation was organized on July 6, 1846.

In the North the progress was more striking. Hope became the starting point for wider activity in Indiana, and the congregations in the Tuscarawas Valley, Ohio, extended their influence. In 1840 Herman J. Tietze, of Gnadenhütten, commenced to preach statedly at Dover, and in 1843 a separate pastoral charge was created here, in care of Lewis F. Kampmann. In 1844 Martin Hauser's zeal for a second time subordinated family comforts to the good of the church, and as the leader of another company of colonists from the southern congregations he pushed forward to the alluvial prairie between the Ohio and the Mississippi in southern Illinois, there to found New Salem—later known as West Salem. In April, 1846, Hope branched out into a filial, Enon.

Meantime significant movements were in progress in the older congregations. In 1842 the state of the financial affairs of the establishments for unmarried women and widows at Bethlehem had caused the transfer of their business management to the hands of men. During the year 1843 the proprietorship in the north had been transferred to Philip H. Goepp, the administrator. The maintenance of the old exclusive system of a typical "settlement" had been found too onerous at

Bethlehem, having frequently necessitated the purchase of property for the church to prevent its falling into the hands of others
than members. Hence the congregation council on January
11, 1844, decided on the abolition of the local exclusive arrangements; and this became the initial step which led up finally to
changes in the entire constitution of the church.

At this time also changes took place in the incumbency of the
various Provincial offices. In 1844, John Christian Jacobson,
recently principal of the school and co-pastor at Salem as well
as a member of the governing board in the South and now
about to become principal of Nazareth Hall, together with William Eberman entered the governing board in the North. The
retirement from active service of Theodore Shultz caused the
transfer of Charles F. Kluge from the principalship of Nazareth
Hall to the position of administrator at Salem and *ex-officio*
member of the Southern Conference.

At length decisive steps were initiated to effect constitutional
changes which were imperatively required. With a dispropor-
tionately small representation in the general synod American
affairs had received slight attention from this body, and in consequence its legislation embodied many regulations which were
more or less clearly inapplicable to North America. Hence
the Conferences and members of that Province did not earnestly attempt to put them into practice; nor did the Unity's
Elders' Conference require on their enforcement. Official visits
had been few of late; hence the American congregations were
impressed with the idea that they were less cared for than the
European congregations, and that it was left to themselves in
most instances to manage their own affairs, and to adopt such
regulations as the circumstances of their country together with
its prevailing modes of thought and action appeared to require.
The more the circumstances and customs of the American
Province deviated from those of the church in Europe, the more
did the internal structure of the congregations in America become different from that of the congregations in the European
part of the Brethren's Unity. Yet the existing lack of legal
autonomy prevented the American congregations from completely adapting themselves to the requirements of their surroundings and the demands of the day by a thorough change
of polity.

From May 4 to 20, 1847, twenty-six ministers and twenty lay delegates met at Bethlehem for conference, preparatory to the general synod appointed for the succeeding year. Provision was made, subject to ratification by the general synod, for the convocation of a Provincial synod at stated intervals, to which the Provincial executive, hereafter to be known as the Provincial Elders' Conference, should be more largely responsible. Two of its three members should be elected by the American Provincial synod. The administrator of the Unity's property in Pennsylvania should be *ex-officio* a member of the Provincial board, but should not be eligible to serve as its president except in case of a temporary emergency. The inconsistency which was involved in the retention of this *ex-officio* member was necessitated by the peculiar financial methods of the church, an intricate system which could not be hastily abolished.

These desires of the Northern congregations the general synod of 1848 granted. But before the northern group of churches met to take advantage of the liberty allowed, Bishop Benade resigned the presidency of the Conference and retired from active service, Goepp provisionally taking his place.

The synod of the South was convened in January, 1849. To it Bishop William H. Van Vleck presented his resignation. The southern executive was now constituted of Bishop Hermann, who resigned from the Unity's Elders' Conference, George F. Bahnson and Charles F. Kluge, the administrator.

Two important transactions now took place at Bethlehem. The first was a conference of the wardens of the "settlement" congregations with the Provincial authorities in order to consider the status of the yet remaining industries which were carried on for the benefit of the congregations as such. To these deliberations may be traced the abrogation of this system in Bethlehem in the year 1851 and at Nazareth in 1855. Lititz decided upon incorporation as a congregation in 1855. In Salem the lease system expired in 1856. The other significant movement was the formation of a "Home Missionary Society," on March 31, 1849, chiefly through the exertions of Henry A. Shultz, one of the pastors since 1847. It was to systematically prosecute the work of church extension, under the administration of eleven directors: Henry A. Shultz, President; Herman Tietze, Vice-President; Francis Wolle, Recording Secretary; Charles F. Seidel, Corresponding Secretary; John F. Rauch,

Treasurer; Jedidiah Weiss, John C. Weber, John M. Miksch, Simon Rau, Maurice Jones and Henry B. Luckenbach. Of these only three were ministers.

The Northern synod was in session from June 6 to 20, 1849. It was quick to take advantage of the opportunities for self-government and expansion now made possible. John C. Jacobson and Henry A. Shultz were elected members of the new executive board, the third member being the administrator, Philip H. Goepp. Provision was made for the readjustment of the general finances. A monthly church periodical was authorized, the *Moravian Church Miscellany*, the first number appearing in January, 1850, Henry A. Shultz being the editor. To the directors of the existing "Home Missionary Society" at Bethlehem the synod committed the general oversight of the work of extension, under the final supervision of the Provincial Elders' Conference, with the proviso that no burden should be added to the "Sustentation Diacony." The formation of auxiliary societies in the various congregations was encouraged. Several of these, however, preferred to support distinct missions for which they were to be regarded as responsible. Thus the American Moravian Church stood definitely and hopefully committed to a policy of aggressive church extension; and the long pent up energies of the people now burst forth with remarkable force.

The pioneer selected for the work was John Frederick Fett. Born in 1800 near Nuremberg of Lutheran parents, and having studied first law and then theology at Erlangen, he had been active in the *Diaspora* circles of Switzerland and South Germany. In 1848 he had been employed as a home missionary amongst the Germans of Philadelphia. To him a call was now given to undertake a tour amongst the German immigrants of the north-western territories, Milwaukee, Wisconsin, and Quincy, Illinois, being the special objective points. Correspondence had already been exchanged with Andrew M. Iverson, of Milwaukee, a native of Norway, who had learnt to know the Moravian Church through the *Diaspora* whilst a student in the mission institute at Stavanger. He was now ministering to a small congregation of Scandinavians in Milwaukee and with them sought the fellowship of the Moravian Church. Fett arrived at Milwaukee in the middle of October, 1849, and found a number of Germans formerly connected with the Moravian Church in Europe. He recommended that a home missionary be stationed in this city, to itinerate and organize preaching places amongst the surrounding settlers, and he cordially urged the ordination of Iverson and the reception of his Scandinavians into the Moravian Church. The ice prevented him from reaching Quincy by boat, as had been planned.

Next May Iverson was ordained a deacon of the church at Bethlehem. His former undertaking became fully identified with the Moravian Church. Meantime Fett's place in Philadelphia had been taken by Philip H. Gapp. Charles Pfohl, who had for some time served an extensive circuit in Hendricks County, Indiana, came into connection with the board. Henry Lauenroth was sent to the Germans of Cleveland. In June, 1850, Fett in company with Otto Tank, formerly of the Surinam mission, and a man of large ideas and liberal purposes, visited Greenbay, a town of about two thousand, with many unchurched Germans. A Moravian congregation was organized next year, and in 1852 a church built on ground presented by William B. Astor, of New York. Iverson with twenty of his Scandinavians also temporarily moved thither in August, 1850, the former mission buildings of the Protestant Episcopal Church being rented for their use by Tank. Before long Fett made the town his headquarters, to arrange for a Moravian settlement on the opposite bank of the Fox River, where Tank had purchased eight hundred acres of partly cleared land. One section of this, on the road from Fort Howard to Depere, was conveyed to the Norwegians, but later these first settlers removed to Fort Howard itself.

In January, 1851, Charles Barstow, of Staten Island, was given work in Indiana, itinerated in Hendricks, Putnam and Morgan Counties, and organized Coatesville congregation. Hauser's new settlement of West Salem in 1848 had received large additions through a colony of Germans from the vicinity of Herrnhut, and he himself extended his activity to Olney, Mount Carmel, Wanboro and Albion.

In October, 1851, John G. Kaltenbrunn, formerly of the Silesian *Diaspora*, was appointed home missionary in New York city; and next year, although not under the auspices of the board, the commencement of Moravian worship in Brooklyn was made by David Bigler, pastor in New York, and John F. Warman, an ex-missionary in Surinam.

In the early spring of 1853 Kaltenbrunn was sent to Watertown, Wis., and its vicinity. A number of his New York members, on the receipt of his favorable report determined to migrate thither, being most liberally assisted by the New York auxiliary society. Thus Ebenezer was founded, near Watertown. Kaltenbrunn's place in New York was taken by Ulrich Günther, formerly of Neudietendorf and recently a colporteur of the New York Tract Society. He soon secured an outpost at Greenville, in New Jersey.

Early in 1854, Hiram Meyers of Gnadenhütten was appointed to mission work in Iowa, where Moravia and Richland became the centers of operation. Philip H. Gapp received an assistant in Philadelphia in the person of John Praeger. They alternately visited Palmyra and Camden and Centerville, New Jersey. Reiterated calls were received from Germans in Utica, N. Y., New Haven and Bridgeport, Conn., and even from New Orleans. To Utica, in the summer of 1854 Valentine Müller was sent, formerly of Königsfeld, now of Rochester, in the employ of the Tract Society, and Leonard Rau was appointed to the New England field in 1857, after several visits had been made thither by Günther, who had meantime taken charge of a vacant German Presbyterian church in Newark in October, 1854, with the approval of the Provincial Elders' Conference, Praeger following him in New York.

In the home congregations affairs of importance were on foot. In March, 1851, the Provincial Elders' Conference became a body corporate. Henry A. Shultz resigning from its membership during this year, his place was taken by Charles F. Seidel. Beginning with January, 1854, a German monthly periodical, *Das Brüder Blatt*, was issued by Levin Theodore Reichel, pastor of Lititz.

In the South, Jacob F. Siewers labored as a missionary at Woodstock Mills in Florida among the negroes, from 1847 to 1850, being succeeded by John Adam Friebele, who prosecuted similar work in the vicinity of Salem, when the former project was given up. With the election of Charles F. Kluge as a member of the Unity's Elders' Conference, Emil A. de Schweinitz became administrator in North Carolina in April, 1853. Next year the entire Unity mourned a loss in the South. In spite of symptoms of the weakness incident to declining years Bishop Hermann had decided to pay in person a needed visit of inspection to the Cherokee Mission in Indian Territory, and left Salem by private conveyance on April 30. The fatigue of the wearisome undertaking culminated in an attack of fever on the return journey, and he died at McCullah's farm in Stone County, Missouri, on July 20. Levin Theodore Reichel was appointed his successor in the Southern board.

From May 2 to 23, 1855, a most important Provincial synod was in session at Bethlehem. Bishop Jacobson presided. A special committee was chosen to tentatively recast the constitution of the Unity so as to meet American requirements. It consisted of David Bigler, Samuel Reinke, Henry A. Shultz, Philip H. Goepp and William Eberman, ministers, and Jacob Blickensderfer, sr., and Jacob Blickensderfer, jr., delegates. Various plans, involving more or less radical changes were submitted to this committee. A memorial from the New York congregation advocated the most complete Provincial independence, and involved the adoption of diocesan episcopacy, with an upper and a lower house of synod or convention and a change of name to the "Moravian Episcopal Church in the United States of North America." But synod declined to proceed in this manner, and rested content with a maintenance of former terms. It however resolved that constitutional measures be taken for Provincial self-government and development, by vesting the supreme authority in the Provincial synod constituted of ministers and delegates and devolving executive administration upon a collegiate conference of ministers, to be known as the Provincial Elders' Conference. The first incumbents of this office, now conditionally elected, were Bishop Jacobson, President; Sylvester Wolle, Secretary, and Philip H. Goepp, Treasurer. The last named continued to serve as administrator of the Unity's property. It was understood that the independent powers of the new Conference would require the sanction of the general synod, and that the approval of the Unity's Elders' Conference must meanwhile be secured.

Furthermore provision was made for the establishment of a church publication-house and book-store in Philadelphia under the general superintendence of Francis Jordan, and for the founding of an official weekly church paper, *The Moravian*. Of this Edmund de Schweinitz, pastor of the Philadelphia church, was elected editor with power to secure associates. Later Lewis F. Kampmann and Francis F. Hagen consented to become his coadjutors, and the first issue of the new periodical appeared on January 1, 1856.

An advance in the educational work of the church was projected by the formation of a collegiate department in connection with the theological seminary. The death of Edward Rondthaler, who was at the head of this institution, had crippled its work since March. The collegiate department was placed in charge of Edward T. Kluge, with residence in the Whitefield House at Nazareth, whilst the members of the theological class temporarily removed to Philadelphia, where Edmund de Schweinitz, notwithstanding his already heavy responsibilities commenced to deliver lectures to them in August, being assisted in certain branches by George W. Perkin as special tutor.

Synod furthermore placed the administration of the home missions on a new basis. Withdrawing the control of the undertakings from the society at Bethlehem, it substituted a "Home Mission Board" representing the entire Province, and entrusted the management to it. The new board consisted of the members of the Provincial Elders' Conference together with eight others elected by the synod, not less than three of whom were required to be residents of Bethlehem. The choice of the synod fell on Charles F. Seidel, Henry A. Shultz, David Bigler and Sylvester Wolle of Bethlehem, Francis R. Holland of Sharon, Francis Wolle of Bethlehem, Abraham Clark of New York, and Frederick Wilhelm of Philadelphia. The new system did not put an end to the activity of the association at Bethlehem. It resumed its original form as a local organization, and continued its labors with unabated zeal, dividing the field with the general board. The latter took charge of the enterprises at Greenbay and Watertown, and those in Iowa, Indiana and Illinois; the former retained the missions amongst the Norwegians, and those at Worcester, Hartford and Utica. The general board, whose first President was Henry A. Shultz, superintended the work of church extension from the summer of 1855 to 1861, when a further alteration in methods of administration was adopted. Most of the auxiliary societies meanwhile gradually came to an end.

On the receipt of the memorial of the American Province with respect to amendments to the constitution the Unity's Elders' Conference granted provisional consent, and summoned a general synod to meet in the spring of 1857. Preparatory synods in the South and in the North in 1856 practically reaffirmed the position of the synod of 1855, and further developed the principles involved. In the North an "Advisory Board" was appointed to act in conjunction with the Provincial Elders' Conference in the administration of financial affairs, Matthew Krause, Jacob Rice and Francis Wolle of Bethlehem being elected.

Now sixteen centers of home missionary activity, with a number of filials, could be reported, having a membership of about 850 communicants. Associated with Greenbay, served by Fett, were Bay Settlement and New Francke. Kaltenbrunn ministered in Ebenezer, Watertown and Ixonia; and his success had induced the board to send F. J. Kilian in August, 1855, to take separate charge of Lake Mills and Germany, two of his former stations. Iverson's circuit included Ephraim, Cooperstown, Mishicott, Greenbay, Sturgeon Bay and Fish Creek. The fruits of Hauser's perseverance resulted in the organization of a home mission charge at Olney, to which Christian Bentel of New York was appointed in July, 1856. Meyers in Illinois had two additional appointments. Utica, in charge of J. J. Detterer, had attained a membership of 145 communicants. Valentine Müller in April, 1856, had been transferred to Canajoharie, under an arrangement like that of Günther in Newark, and preached also at Ilion and Mohawk. Leonard Rau was active amongst Germans of Worcester, Webster and Boston, though no congregation had been organized. From Philadelphia Gapp continued to statedly visit Palmyra and Westfield. At a number of these points churches had been built or purchased or were in the course of erection. In the Wachovia district Lewis Rights of Friedberg was privileged to see the preaching of his predecessor, Francis F. Hagen, and of himself, result in a new congregation beyond the Yadkin, Macedonia, where a church was consecrated in May, 1856.

A very significant change also took place during these years in the administration of the general finances of the church. During the summer of 1856 Philip H. Goepp resigned as administrator. The time had come to disentangle the complex system of church finance. Eugene A. Frueauff was therefore appointed administrator, and with him was associated William T.

Roepper as "responsible cashier," in order to work out the problem.

To render Provincial independence possible, and to provide for the outlays involved in the administration of the joint affairs of the congregations, for which help had hitherto been received from the funds of the Unity to the amount of about $1,500 a year, the former "settlement" congregations when winding up the affairs of their "diaconies" had made large contributions from their local resources, in recognition of the fact that a moral indebtedness rested upon them in view of the unearned increment which had accrued to them from lands purchased by them from the Unity at a fair valuation about eighty years before.   During the period of the gradual dissolution of the "Diacony system" in the years preceding 1855, the congregation at Bethlehem made over in trust to the Provincial Elders' Conference upwards of $116,000, according to an agreement in virtue of which rather more than $13,000 of this sum was applied to the discharge of the general indebtedness of the Province.   The congregation at Nazareth during these and ensuing years similarly contributed upwards of $59,000, and the congregation at Lititz relinquished all claims to the property of the church-school there, valued at $20,000.   In return it was recognized that these congregations were henceforth to be held excused from the stated annual collections in support of the joint needs of the Province which had been previously required in conformity with written agreements.   Thus came into existence what might now be appropriately named "The Sustentation Fund," since it was now for the first time actually capitalized.   Its income was to be used to make provision for those objects which had been defined by the synod of 1847 to be the purpose of the "Sustentation Diacony," including the "Diaconies of the Educational Institutions"—formerly a distinct part of Moravian economics, but recently merged into the "Sustentation Diacony" because property of the Province as such. These objects were the following:

a. To pay the salaries of such members of the Provincial Elders' Conference as hold no other office, and to discharge the unavoidable expenses of the Conferences.

b. To supply the pensions due to superannuated ministers.

c. To defray the expenses incurred by the publication of the church periodicals.

d. To aid the more destitute congregations to defray the expenses incident to the maintenance of their ministers.

e. To aid such ministers as were unable to obtain a competent support from their congregations.

f. To furnish the necessary means for the general education of the children of the ministers whose salaries were insufficient to enable them to give their children a respectable education.

g. To provide for the further education of young men engaged in a course of theological study.

Henceforth with the income of the Sustentation Fund, derived solely from the interest accruing from invested capital and from the earnings of the church schools, now that contributions from the congregations at large ceased to be expected on account of the liberality of the three, the life and development of the Province were to be very closely connected.

CHAPTER L.

Uneven pulsations mark the onrush of the incoming tide. Here it surges with a swirl and a dash; there lapping wavelets almost imperceptibly achieve and maintain their advance. Not every wave carries its front of foam as far as the preceding. Momentarily the appearance of retrogression may deceive a casual onlooker. Nevertheless all the while in the main and all along the entire line of the coast the tide is steadily adding depth to depth; where children were lately playing, the deep laden barque may now ride with even keel. Somewhat similar are the impressions received by one who observes the gradual advance of the missionary cause for any considerable period. The ultimate gains become clear, even though here and there increase has fallen below the general ratio or though retrogression has temporarily characterized specific phases of operation. The period now under review illustrates this principle. On the whole it was one of marked advance. The forty-four stations of 1836 became sixty-nine by 1857, the two hundred and eighteen missionaries became three hundred. The souls in charge increased from 51,097 to 71,347. Yet in 1840 the mission treasury was burdened with a debt of $35,000. Extraordinary exertions and the liberality of friends resulted in its removal within ten years. A mission had been attempted on a new continent, Australia, and temporarily abandoned. Some undertakings appeared to remain at a standstill; others had gone forward with a bound.

In Greenland the hopes which led to the founding of Friedrichsthal, not far from Cape Farewell, had been speedily realized through the removal thither of heathen Eskimos from the east coast. By this time comparatively few unbaptized persons could be found between Friedrichsthal and New Herrnhut, though the roving life of the Eskimos in search of a livelihood decidedly interfered with their advance in culture. For this reason since the year 1840 special attention had been directed to the founding of schools at the fishing villages. True, study had to be pursued among unfavorable circumstances, for the young men had to go fishing or seal hunting in their kayaks during the day, and could give to the instruction only the half-attention of weariness. Yet such as it was, it was appreciated, now that the New Testament was in the hands of the people. By the close of the present period rudimentary intsruction was being imparted at twenty outposts in addition to the four schools at the stations.

Ever and again the fearful drawbacks of life on the ice-mantled, fog-curtained desolation, called Greenland, inevitably reasserted themselves. Seasons of scarcity came, whose intensity was magnified by the inborn improvidence which Christian education could only slowly eradicate. Such a period of distress was the winter of 1842 to 1843 at Lichtenau, where out of five hundred adults sixty-two were carried off by an epidemic within seven weeks. The missionary in charge writes: "Owing to absolute want of hands to dig new graves, many of the corpses had to be deposited in old places of sepulture—a practice to which the baptized Greenlanders were unwilling to have recourse."

Labrador likewise had its years of leanness, the winter of 1836 to 1837 being memorable for its misery, especially at Nain, Okak and Hebron. A famine raged. Ordinary food completely failed. Tent-coverings of skin, skin-canoes, and skin-boots were masticated and swallowed to satisfy the unappeased gnawings within. Scurvy broke out. The missionaries meanwhile strained every nerve to render help, and shared their supplies with their people. When the famine was relieved, the dearth of dogs rendered impossible the remunerative pursuit of the chase in the next season. The condition of the heathen in the far north excelled in its utter distress. One savage was known to have killed his wife and children, and to have supported his own life by the horrible food thus obtained.

The new station at Hebron was completed with the dedication of its church in October, 1837. But much opposition had to be encountered from the heathen, led by an old grey haired sorcerer, Paksaut. Yet Mentzel and Barsoe and Schott labored on in hope against hope. What was their surprise, therefore, in February, 1848, to receive a visit from two men as the advance couriers of various families who desired to remove from Saeglek, the headquarters of the opposition, and settle at Hebron. By summer eighty-one of these benighted followers of the sorcerer had become inhabitants of the place, and the old sorcerer himself being drawn into the favorable environment before long expressed his deep penitence for his former satanic doings, and asked whether Jesus would hear him if he prayed. In February, 1850, the baptism of this erstwhile renowned *"angekok"* and that of his wife, after a long and thorough probation, made a deep impression as a triumph of grace.

In Labrador and the adjacent Arctic lands attempts were now made at extensions of missionary activity, though no station was actually founded. In 1847 Captain Parker, of the *Truelove*, a whaler from Hull, visited Northumberland Inlet, west of Cumberland Island. The shores of this bay and the numerous islands which studded it he found well peopled by Eskimos—at this time suffering from famine. Captain Parker at their own solicitations took an Eskimo couple to England, and there they excited much interest. The owner and the captain of the *Truelove* urged on the Moravian Church the planting of a mission on Northumberland Inlet. The negotiations resulted in an agreement, that when Captain Parker returned his Eskimos to their home together with the supplies of food furnished by British beneficence, he should touch at Greenland on the way, and take with him Samuel Kleinschmidt for the commencing of a mission. But the ice-barrier at Upernavik and the death of the Eskimo woman from consumption with the unwillingness of her husband to proceed to their former home rendered the project a failure.

During the winter of 1856 to 1857 Augustus F. Elsner of Hopedale performed a very trying sleigh journey south-west to Eskimo Bay, a settlement of the Hudson's Bay Company near the great inlet of Ivuktoke, to ascertain if some method of permanently ministering to the sparse settlements could be inaugurated. The Hudson's Bay Company was desirous of the establishment of a mission, and had extended an invitation. The adventurous party was one of five. A ten days' journey by dog-sled and snow-shoe brought them to Rigolette, the headquarters of the Company. Their report was unfavorable. In a district about one hundred and fifty miles in length only twenty-one fisher families were to be found. These with ten families of Eskimos constituted the entire population.

In June, 1857, Matthew Warmow of Lichtenfels accompanied Captain Perry in the *Lady Franklin* to Cumberland Inlet, and conversed with and preached to the people at various points, whilst he spied out the land.

Special interest attaches to the voyage of John Augustus Miertsching, for many years a missionary in Labrador, who was engaged as interpreter for the expedition fitted out in 1850 by the British Government to search for Sir John Franklin, one of the fifteen expeditions sent out by Britain and America to rescue the officers and crews of the ill-fated *Erebus* and *Terror*. On the *Investigator* Miertsching sailed from England in January, 1850, and passed the winter of 1850 to 1851 at the Princess Royal Islands, only thirty miles from Barrow Strait. A northwest passage was discovered, but could not be reached owing to a branch of the paleo-crystic ice that barred the way. As soon as possible in 1851 Captain McClure turned his ship south, and rounding Baring Island wintered next on the northern shore of Bank's Land in the "Bay of God's Mercy," musk-oxen affording food. In April, 1853, the time had been appointed for abandoning the ship, so as to reach the American continent over the ice, when three days previous to the set date the presence of the *Resolute* and the *Intrepid* became known. On May 2 the weary company were received on board the rescuing vessels. For two years their daily allowance had been two-thirds of the regulation rations. Captain Kellett of the *Resolute* showed Miertsching distinguished kindness. His services as interpreter had been invaluable, and he had contributed no little part to the efforts of the officers to systematically provide instruction and amusement as a counterpoise to the melancholy dreariness of the long Arctic nights. As a missionary exploratory tour the long voyage, ending in October, 1854, was without permanent results.

In the Danish West Indies this was a time of transition. The connection of the missions with trade for the support of the work was gradually ceasing. The creole patois step by step gave place to the English. A system of education was being inaugurated by government, with a view to prepare for the emancipation of the slaves, rendered inevitable by Britain's example. In the year 1839 Governor General Van Scholten, at the instance of the King of Denmark, paid a visit to Herrnhut, and laying before the authorities of the church his plan for the inception of elementary schools, proposed that a commencement be made on the island of St. Croix, and that the teachers be supplied by the mission, whilst the government would erect the buildings and render financial aid. It seemed a providential call. Accordingly in 1840 Bishop Breutel was dispatched to confer preliminarily with the missionaries and arrange necessary details. Eight schools were soon built, each to accommodate from one hundrd and fifty to two hundred children. With considerable ceremony the first was opened on May 18, 1841, on Great Princess Plantation, near the grave of Frederick Martin, the governor and other civil authorities lending the encouragement of their presence. Teachers were at first secured from among members of the church trained in the normal schools of the Mico Charity. In 1847 the new school system was extended to St. Thomas, having previously been inaugurated in the smaller island of St. John.

On September 18, 1847, King Christian VIII issued a decree emancipating all who should be henceforth born of slave parentage in his West Indian colonies, and providing for the cessation of all slavery at the end of twelve years. Instead of calming discontent, this proclamation rendered the negro population only the more eager to anticipate the joys of freedom, and in a quiet but determined and very thorough manner a slave insurrection was planned. Alarming reports became current on July 2, 1848, and after dark the ringing of bells and the blowing of conch shells throughout the island of St. Croix made the white population aware that something unusual was imminent. Early the next morning the plundering and rioting commenced. That same day the Governor General issued a proclamation of emancipation. This did not at once pacify the rioters—especially at the east end of the island, where a clash of arms occurred and bloodshed preceded the restoration of order. After the insurrection had been quelled, the Governor General was tried on the charge of dereliction in duty and condemned; but on an appeal to the Supreme Court of Denmark an honorable acquittal followed. Buddhoe, or "General Bourdeaux," the leader of the insurgents, was captured and exiled to Port of Spain, Trinidad, with the understanding that his life should be forfeited if he returned to the Danish islands.

Whilst the skies were reddened by the flames of burning plantations the missionaries did their utmost to restrain the rioters from violence. For weeks the attitude of the negroes remained threatening, and grave trouble was anticipated on October 1, the day set for adjusting wages. Then in particular the good offices of the Brethren proved of peculiar service. As the years passed the fruit of their efforts appeared in growing congregations requiring new and larger churches at each of the three stations prior to 1854.

In St. Thomas, Eugene Hartvig removed from Nisky to the town in 1843, to promote educational work and care for the members residing there. Thus a congregation was gradually formed, which increased in importance as the character of the island began to change after emancipation. Plantations were abandoned, but the town of St. Thomas gained from the splendid facilities offered by its magnificent harbor.

In the British islands the work of grace coincident with emancipation continued. Energetic efforts were put forth to cope with the problem of education. In 1837 Charles James La Trobe was sent out to inspect the schools at the instance of the British government, and as a result funds for the erection of the needed buildings and for the maintenance of teachers began to be gathered in England, and parliamentary grants supplemented private beneficence. In 1837 Jacob Zorn, the able superintendent of the mission, founded a normal school at Fairfield, and ten years later a similar institution was begun at Cedar Hall in Antigua for the eastern islands, in charge of Alan Hamilton. In 1854 a training institution for female teachers was likewise established at St. John's in Antigua, for female teachers, its founder being George Wall Westerby.

Jamaica presented a spectacle of rapid advance. The consecration of churches at new stations became the order of the day, Bethany (begun in 1835) being followed by Beaufort, Nazareth and New-Hope (now Salem) in 1838, Lititz in 1839, and Bethabara in 1840. It was in fact impossible to make use of all the opportunities for new work. Yet trials were not absent; the more intense the light, the deeper the shadows. In 1842 a perplexing phenomenon appeared in several parishes of the island, an outburst of one of those periodic stirrings of the deeply emotional nature of the negro peoples, that are to be observed from time to time. This was the organization of a counter-infatuation, Myalism, over against the ancient Obeahism, that dark heritage received from their African fathers. It proclaimed its purpose to be the cleansing of the world from wickedness through the possession of power to discriminate between good and evil men, and it sought the overthrow of the Obeah. The leaders of this satanic craze seemed to be veritably possessed; and for a time there appeared to be a danger of wholesale lapses into heathenism. John Henry Buchner writes: "The mark and sign of these people, who are called Myal-men, is a handkerchief tied quite fast around the waist, and another tied in a fantastical manner around the head. I have seen and spoken to several of them whom I have known before; but I should hardly have recognized them, their features being distorted, their eyes wild; in fact they had the appearance of people who are quite frantic. They are bold and daring, and there is no reasoning with them. This madness commenced on an estate where several of the late Guinea negroes were located, and now has spread over the whole parish where hundreds are now practicing this Myalism. Under these circumstances many breaches of the peace have been committed: more than one hundred cases have been tried, and the jail is filled with these people. Though they have threatened us, they have not yet come to disturb the services in our chapel; but they have molested other places of worship, and we are in constant dread of their approach. Every night the howling and singing of the votaries of Myalism reach my ear......Superstition is deeply, very deeply, rooted in a negro's mind; and it was distressing to see that so many believed in their doings as if they were from God, and that it was so difficult to persuade them that it was Satan's work......One old communicant sister, of Williamsfield, now feeble in body and mind, was persuaded by the Myal people that the shadow (soul) of her departed daughter had no rest, but was upon a cotton tree in the pasture. They directed her to procure a little coffin, covered with black merino, when upon a Saturday night they all, about twenty, went out with her to this cotton tree. A firefly upon the tree was to be the 'shadow.' After singing and dancing for some hours around the tree, they pretended to have caught the shadow, whereupon they closed the coffin and buried it.

WILLIAM MALLALIEU.

On a former occasion a white fowl had been sacrificed to the 'shadow' under the cotton tree, the tree and coffin sprinkled with its blood; and the same was that night repeated." Pitifully ludicrous though these proceedings may appear, this grotesque superstition worked much trouble, till from the very excess of its own intensity a revulsion of feeling set in, and by the close of 1844 the manifestations became infrequent. But belief in witchcraft and in the Obeah by no means died out.

The mission was greatly hampered about this time by the severe sickness of a number of useful workers, and death thinned the ranks. Seven fell from fevers or similar causes within a couple of years. A special loss was sustained when Jacob Zorn, the energetic superintendent, died in 1843. Born of missionary parents, and enthused with the true missionary spirit, wholly consecrated to his work, "a man of abundant grace and excellent gifts, humble, affectionate and discreet, yet talented, laborious and energetic," he seemed to have been stopped in mid-course, being not quite forty years of age. But to him was given the joy of seeing his labors crowned, and of perceiving the mission emerge out of many embarrassments into strength and vigor.

The official visit of Bishop Hermann and William Mallalieu in 1847 led to a reconstruction of the arrangements for the supervision of the work on the island. Conferential government was now introduced, Rudolph Wullschlaegel as superintendent having associated with him Pfeiffer, Spence, Renkewitz and Buchner. But two years later Wullschlaegel was transferred to Surinam, and Buchner took his place. In 1852 the sudden death of James Spence, a loss reminding of that of Zorn, caused the transfer of Jacob Seiler from Antigua.

In 1850 a time of severest test had to be endured. The cholera swept through the island, and death cut a broad swath. Twenty thousand persons are thought to have perished. New Fulneck and Irwin Hill suffered most, the latter losing one-fifth of its members. Here Abraham Lichtenthaler was the indefatigable missionary. Moreover, in consequence of the failure of the coffee and sugar crops ruin spread through the land. Many estates were abandoned. The laboring classes had to shift for themselves. Poverty crippled and idleness interfered with the growth of honorable qualities, the while various vices were engendered. Yet with it all the work of the

28

mission was steadily prosecuted. When the centenary was celebrated in 1854 the total membership was 12,794, as compared with 8,591 in 1836.

In Antigua also stations multiplied after emancipation; Lebanon (1837), Gracefield (1840), Five Islands (1838) and Gracebay (1848) each serving to relieve the overgrown congregation at St. John's, which at one time had a membership of upwards of seven thousand.

In the early months of 1843 repeated shocks of earthquake wrought havoc at various posts, the very heaviest being on February 8, when churches, schools, mills, sugar-works and all kinds of stone buildings were thrown down or wrecked. It was the most severe calamity that had transpired on these islands within the memory of man. In some villages scarcely a house was left standing. The south gable of Lebanon church was thrown down. Here and there the earth was full of great cracks, from which oozed a thick and slimy water, smelling strongly of sulphur. For weeks the services had to be held in the open air. On the morning of Good Friday repeated shocks drove the missionary and his people out of the church at Bethesda, St. Kitts, the building rocking like a ship. Again in August, 1848, a terrific hurricane raged on the islands of St. Kitts, St. Croix and Tobago, as well as on Antigua. St. John's, Lebanon, Gracehill and Cedar Hall were the chief sufferers. At Gracehill the loss was estimated at $6,500, at Cedar Hall from $3,500 to $4,000. The training school was completely demolished. The mission dwelling nearby resembled a dismantled hulk. Beams and furniture, clothing and books were strewn around the fields like stubble for a distance of 400 to 500 yards. During the night, whilst the lightning blazed and the thunder boomed and crashed, the howling wind had made sport with lumber and roofing, chicken-coops, grind-stones, dripstones and the like; and the fearful artillery of the elements had driven the mission family with the scholars to the cellar as a last place of refuge. All out-buildings and fences had been swept away, and the gardens were ruined.

Throughout the greater part of these years (his term of office commencing in 1844 was destined to continue till 1872) the superintendent in Antigua was the energetic and far-seeing George Wall Westerby, who was consecrated a bishop whilst on a visit to England by Bishops Seifferth and Rogers at Ockbrook on July 5, 1853. On January 3, 1856, the ordination of John Buckley as a deacon at St. John's by Bishop Westerby marked an important step in the direction of West Indian development, for with him began the line of Moravian ministers of African blood.

St. Kitts in 1845 rejoiced in the founding of a fourth station, Estridge, the Brethren Ricksecker and Klosé being specially active in this undertaking.

In Barbados, though Clifton Hill was begun in 1839, the numbers remained apparently stationary. Then in 1854 the cholera carried away one-seventh of the population. More than twelve thousand persons met with sudden death in the course of a few weeks, Sharon and Bridgetown suffering most among the mission stations. In Bridgetown for a time the burials averaged three hundred a day. Drought accompanying the pest, provisions were dear, and the misery, especially of the orphaned, was pitiful in the extreme, making incalculable demands on the good offices of the missionaries. At one time, too, riots added to the unparalleled distress.

At length the day dawned for the mission on the beautiful island of Tobago, though large numbers could not be looked for, the population being comparatively thin. And this was in spite of the frequent changes in the missionary force demanded by the treacherous climate of the beautiful island. True, Tobago escaped trials as little as other places. On September 11, 1847, Montgomery was wrecked by a hurricane, the lives of Prince and his wife, the missionaries, being spared as by a miracle. He pictures the scene of desolation thus: "When our limbs, stiff with the cold of that dreadful night, bore us tremblingly forth from the ark of refuge, what a scene met our gaze! The cocoanut trees had their graceful branches either twisted off or dangling down the trunks; those trees which are of a tougher texture showed the stumps of the branches displaying white clusters of splinters, the more brittle of them snapped short off. Spouts, rails, beams and shingles were heaped in confusion. The negro houses were a heap of ruins; the school, flat on the ground, and sliding far down the gully; the church, with the north side stove in, the roof down, and an avalanche of benches, beams, rafters, etc., protruding to a considerable distance through the rent on the north side. Our dwelling rooms were deluged—beds, books, clothes and papers

were wetted and blown together in inextricable confusion......
The crops of cane and provisions, so smiling the day before,
were all destroyed." Moriah on the other hand had been but
little injured.

In Surinam two obstacles had still to be encountered, the
first inevitable—the fever-breeding climate entailing terrible
mortality—the second about to be removed—slavery and its
attendant evils. In Paramaribo and on the plantations alike,
the sacredness of marriage among the slaves was not regarded
by their owners. Any negro husband might be sold away from
his wife and family. Again the education of the slaves was
rather dreaded than encouraged, even such rudimentary
knowledge as would serve for spelling the way through the
Bible. The number of plantations to be visited, so long as the
slaves were tied to the soil, involved most exhausting voyages
in the narrow dug-out canoes, and at best the instruction could
be imparted only at intervals. No wonder that a people barely
above the fetishism of Africa made very slow advances in Christian culture and higher life. Sometimes the secret hostility of
overseers found pretexts for hindering the visit to his plantation; it was the season of full creeks, perhaps—then the blacks
could be given no leisure, being all needed to float timber to
market, or to work the mills that crushed the canes.

Nevertheless the mission made marvellously rapid strides.
Station was added to station—Worsteling Jacobs in 1838, but
again abandoned in 1843 owing to its unsuitable situation;
Salem in the Coronie district, in 1840; Beekhuizen, near Paramaribo, in 1843; Rust-en-Werk, on the lower Comewyne, in
1844; Liliendal, on the same river, becoming an independent
station with the consecration of its church in 1848; Annaszorg,
an abandoned plantation purchased for the church as a center
of operations among the plantations on the Warappa and Mat-
appica creeks, in 1853; Catharina Sophia, on the Saramacca, in
1855; Heerendyk, the abandoned plantation Nut-en-Schadelyk,
in 1856, a relief to Charlottenburg. The congregation in Paramaribo grew remarkably—5,502 by the middle of 1856. The
total membership increased from 3,795 in 1836 to 23,316 in 1857.
All honor to the faithful workers, and to the able men in succession charged with the administration of affairs—Rudolph
Passavant, Otto Tank, Henry Rudolph Wullschlaegel and
Theopilus van Calker.

In spite of the opposition of slave owners to the education of the blacks, schools were not only commenced on a number of stations, but in 1844 Gottlieb Wünsche of Rust-en-Werk made a first attempt to train negro lads with a view to their becoming teachers of their own people; and in 1851 a normal school was successfully founded at Beekhuizen, in charge of Herman Voss, and after his early death, under Gustavus Berthold. The students were young slaves sent by planters who were favorably disposed. Beginning with the year 1856 a new sphere of usefulness was also entered upon. Government then assigned to the Moravian Church the spiritual care of the non-Catholic inmates of the hospital for lepers at Batavia on the Copename, and Theodore Dobler was assigned the duties of chaplain, with a faithful native "helper" Jacques as his assistant.

Although it had been impossible for several decades to supply the little congregation at New Bambey in the Bush country with a missionary, intercourse with Paramaribo had been maintained by the few surviving converts. Between 1830 and 1840 repeated visits were also made to them by John Henry Voigt, who found the sons of chief Arabi anxious for a renewal of fixed operations among their people. Jacobs and Rasmus Schmidt followed his example in 1838 and 1840. Thus encouraged, the remnant of the Bush negro congregation built a church and mission house—light structures with wattled walls and roofs of palm thatch. Hither Schmidt and his wife came just before the Christmas festival of 1840. The sons of Arabi, Job and John, stood by them loyally, but the determined attitude of the heathen element manifested fixed hostility. Once a heathen woman rushed on Schmidt with a drawn knife, but was fortunately disarmed in time. Fever before long did what threats and dangers could not accomplish. Schmidt died on April 12, 1845. His wife for a time maintained the post alone. Next year John Godfrey Meissner, coming out from Europe, married her, but the fatal climate claimed him as a victim in three years. Then Mads Barsoe and his wife came to the relief of the heroic woman twice a widow. But he also speedily succumbed. In the emergency another noble woman caught up the falling standard, and planted it firmly, the widow Mary Hartmann. She had come to Surinam in 1826, about twenty-nine years of age, with her husband, John Gottlieb, and with him had served in Paramaribo and at Charlottenburg till he was called to his eternal rest in 1844. In 1848 she volunteered to go alone to Berg-en-dal, on the Upper Surinam, where a small congregation had formerly been gathered, but which had diminished owing to the unavoidable removal of the missionaries. Here she had ministered, teaching the children and doing the work of a prophetess amongst the adults. Occasionally she had ventured on journeys to the Bush country, though no more proof against fevers than any other European, bodily infirmity at length becoming her cross. Nevertheless after the repeated deaths at Bambey the desolate condition of the few Christians there appealed to her, and she removed thither alone, thus cutting herself off from intercourse with her fellow countrymen. Year after year this solitary white woman lived on in the land of savage blacks, and alligators and snakes and venomous spiders and noxious vermin, breathing the heavy steaming air of the swamps. Only once and for one single day during the ensuing four years did she visit her brethren and sisters at Paramaribo, restricting her visit in this manner from the fear lest by reason of attachment to her fellow workers she might be made less willing to go back to the poor negroes of the wilderness. Testimony to the success which crowned her self-immolation is thus borne by a German commissioner sent to inquire into the condition of Surinam at this period: "Our worthy hostess was one of the rare characters of the present age. With the patience of a saint she labored in the midst of these people, imparting religious instruction, and keeping alive the spark of religious life, which so easily becomes extinct......The congregation she instructed in the church, the children she taught in her own dwelling to read and write......Bambey may well be called a Christian village in the midst of the wilderness of heathenism. The peace and quiet, which was not interrupted by any dancing and its attendant horrible yelling, together with the neat and cleanly appearance of the settlement, the inhabitants of which about one hundred in number were engaged in the manufacture of earthenware goods, cotton-weaving, and the shaping of coryars, made a pleasing impression upon us."

But on December 30, 1853, this heroine was overcome by the hardships of her situation, having been brought to Paramaribo just in time to bid her fellow missionaries farewell. Previous to this her little congregation removed from Bambey to Coffycamp, near where the Sara creek empties into the Surinam, on account of the more healthy site.

In South Africa Genadendal was prospering. Its business enterprises flourished. The cutlery had to be enlarged to meet the growing demand for its products. Smiths, carpenters, masons, wagon-makers and tanners drove a brisk trade. Distant Shiloh also advanced in externals. Fritsch and Bonatz undertook the erection of a grist-mill, the latter shaping the mill-stones with the labor of his own hands out of materials furnished by the hard sand-stone of the Klipplaat. The astonishment of the Kaffirs was boundless, when it was set in motion in 1838, the first mill in the entire region. Here a smithy was also established. Only Enon suffered a retrogression. Owing to repeated seasons of drought the Zondag ceased to flow. Irrigation became impossible. Gardens and fields ceased to be productive. The very trees, the distinguishing ornament of the place, began to perish. The necessaries of life became scanty. Water at last could be procured only by digging in the "*Zeekoegats*," the low pools in the bed of the river—"pools of the hippopotamus" as the natives called them. Remunerative labor could not be procured in the immediate vicinity, and migration to more favored spots set in. Providentially rains were sent before the station had to be abandoned; but for many years the effects of this drought continued to be felt.

Emancipation went into effect throughout this colony on December 1, 1838. It affected about 35,000 souls. Partly in anticipation of this measure, on November 1, 1838, the cornerstone of a normal school for Hottentots, a building seventy-four by twenty-three feet and two stories in height, had been laid. Next year it was opened with nine pupils, Theodore Küster having immediate charge. Before long candidates for teacherships and for the ministry were entrusted by other missionary bodies also to the care of this seminary. As in the West Indies, the church gained large accessions after emancipation. At Genadendal alone four hundred and fifty were rereceived within one year, after each case had been carefully decided on its own merits.

During the season preceding emancipation government had urged the establishment of a new station. About sixty miles west by south of Enon and north of Cape St. Franciscus a tribe of fugitive Kaffirs had taken refuge along the Zitzikamma, under the protection of the colonial government. Originally occupying land northeast of the country of the Tambookies, they had been expelled by the more warlike Fetkannas, when these in their turn had fled before the renowned Zulu chief, Chaka—hence the name Fingoos, "vagrants," given them by fellow Africans. Agreeably to the request of the civil authorities, Halter and Küster and Neuhaus in 1839 made their way to the Zitzikamma. Speedy returns justified the project. Within half a year a little village clustered around the mission, and young and old swarmed to the services from the neighboring kraals. A great awakening marked the spring of 1840. Governor Napier, who was deeply interested in the new station, selected for it the name of Clarkson, in honor of the distinguished advocate of freedom.

But now like a bolt from a clear sky, the sudden death of Bishop Hallbeck shocked the mission and its friends. He died on November 25, 1840, fifty-seven years of age. When he came to the Cape, in 1817, the mission embraced only two stations with about 1,600 souls; now seven with a native membership of nearly 4,500. "In him a powerful mind was united with an affectionate spirit; a capacity for generalization, with a readiness to enter into the smallest details; great ability in direction, with surprising facility of execution; originality of thought, with sterling sense and a decided preference for whatever was practical and useful. His plans were ordinarily marked by sound judgment, though his temper was naturally arduous and impetuous; and in the transaction of business he exhibited uncommon regularity, energy and despatch. No Hottentot or enfranchised slave found him otherwise than ready to give him counsel in temporal, as well as instruction in spiritual things. Though by no means an eloquent preacher, his discourses were Scriptural and experimental, delivered with great warmth of heart, and accompanied with the demonstration of the Spirit and of power."

Teutsch became superintendent, and Rudolph Kölbing came to take charge of the educational work. Extension was the order of the day, amongst colonists and natives. Outposts were regularly maintained—Kopjes Kasteel, Bosjesfeld and Twistwyk being served from Genadendal, Houtkloof from Elim, and Louwskloof, Goedverwacht and Wittezand from Mamre. Nor was the advance one in numbers only. Various agencies were set at work for the spiritual elevation of the people, for example, the formation of a missionary society at Genadendal in 1845.

For some time plans for a removal of the hospital for lepers from the mainland had been contemplated by government. At length in December, 1845, the transfer was effected to Robben Island, a small rocky island near the entrance of Table Bay. Joseph Lehman and his wife accompanied the seventy-two unfortunates to the new home.

Since the early thirties the movement of the Boers eastward and northward had been of significance. The exodus involved the trekkers in more or less incessant strife with the native tribes. This reacted upon the condition of the entire eastern border. Kaffir raids became frequent. Many cattle were lifted. The proportions of a state of belligerency were almost reached. At last war actually broke out—the War of the Axe, in March, 1846, so named from the fact that the immediate occasion for hostilities was the murder of a Hottentot, to whom a Kaffir thief had been manacled whilst being conveyed to Grahamstown for trial on the charge of stealing an axe. The escort was attacked en route, and the Hottentot slain. In this war the Gaikas and Tambookies played a leading part, under the generalship of Chief Sandili. With the quelling of the outbreak in 1853 British Kaffraria was created a colony. At first Shiloh was the only mission station in all Kaffraria that escaped the consequences of the strife. The hand of the Lord was wonderfully stretched over it. Thither missionaries of other societies fled. When peace was temporarily restored in 1848, the advance of the frontier to the river Kei brought it within the limits of colonial rule. But this proved no unmixed blessing; for on the founding of Whittlesea hostile traders suggested to government to order the missionaries to push on beyond the frontier and do pioneer work, that the lands which they had reclaimed might be placed at the disposal of settlers. But the authorities had a more just conception of missionary labor. Instead they encouraged the founding of Mamre on the Bicha in the vicinity of Fort Peddie; but with the renewal of hostilities this place had to be abandoned. So also Shechem, later Goshen, begun in 1850 on the Windvogelberg, not far from Shiloh, was perforce for a time deserted. At length Shiloh itself was exposed to Kaffir incendiarism. The missionaries and about seventy faithful Fingoos found refuge in Colesburg, on the Orange River. Savages applied the torch to the evidences of industry and civilization, and after the restoration of peace Shiloh and Goshen had to be completely rebuilt.

Meantime Teutsch died at Genadendal on July 16, 1852. Kölbing now became superintendent, with Frederick William Kühn as his assistant. At the synod of 1857 it could be reported that the African mission during twenty years had increased from a membership of 3,308 to one of 7,037; and that several natives, trained at Genadendal, were giving promise of distinguished usefulness, notably John Nakin, John Zwelibanzi, Nicholas Oppelt and Ezekiel Pfeiffer, the first two Kaffirs, the last two Hottentots.

CHAPTER LI.

THE THREE NEW MISSION FIELDS ENTERED BETWEEN THE YEARS
1848 AND 1857—THE MOSKITO COAST, AUSTRALIA
AND CENTRAL ASIA.

Along the Caribbean coast of Central America, from the
Wama or Sinsin Creek to Rama River, and for about forty miles
inland, lies the Moskito Reserve. From 1655 to 1850 this territory enjoyed a semi-independent status, under the protection
of Great Britain, being ruled by a so-called Indian "king." The
terms of the Clayton-Bulwer treaty in 1850, and of the treaty
of Managua in 1860, transferred the protectorate to Nicaragua,
and in 1895 all vestiges of semi-independence were swept away.

Special attention was directed to this district of Central
America about the year 1847 by an attempt of the Prussian
government to establish a colony there. But it proved difficult
to direct the tide of emigration thither owing to the reputation
of the climate. At this time Prince Schönburg-Waldenberg, a
liberal supporter of Moravian Missions, earnestly solicited the
efforts of the Moravian Church in behalf of the people of this
little known land. In response the Conference commissioned
Henry Pfeiffer and Amadeus A. Reinke, missionaries in
Jamaica, to undertake a tour of exploration. Proceeding via
Greytown, they reached Bluefields, the capital, a village with
from six to seven hundred inhabitants, on May 2, 1847. The
place itself perpetuated the cognomen of a notorious buccaneer
of the seventeenth century, one Blauveldt, and was found to be
characterized by an absence of religious observances. For the
English speaking people a catechist of the Anglican Church,
an ex-schoolmaster from Jamaica, read prayers and a sermon
on the Lord's Day. Now and then unauthorized colored persons went through a caricature of infant baptism and collected
fees from the negroes whose innate religiousness they imposed
upon.

For the Indians—Moscos, or Moskitos, Woolwas, Ramas, Sumoos and Caribs—who periodically visited Bluefields to trade in tortoise-shells and deer-skins, and pay tribute to their "king," no ray of light pierced the fog of superstition through which they groped. They were the unquestioning slaves of their "*sukias*" or medicine-men. Their religious conceptions were extremely scanty. They had a dim idea of a mighty, good and benevolent being, named "*Won Aisa*"—Our Father. But no personal relationship subsisted between him and man. It did not enter into their thoughts to honor him with any form of worship. On the other hand a great crowd of evil spirits, the "*Ulassa*," played a prominent role in their life. These spirits incessantly threaten man and bring upon him all the forms of evil and misfortune to which he is exposed. They scare off the fish which he in vain tries to catch. They cause the tree, as it is being felled, to fall so as to inflict injury. They are at fault, when the arrow or the ball happens to miss the deer caught trespassing in the corn field. They occasion sickness and death—often in league with a personal foe. Yet they were not regarded as the cause of sin, for the Indians themselves were almost unmoral, devoid of ethical judgment. But they lived in constant dread of the bad spirits, and life for them consisted largely in efforts to ward off their malevolent influence. The average man was, however, too weak for this. He required special assistance, such as could be alone rendered by the "*sukia*" or medicine man. The latter believed himself empowered to cast out Beelzebub with the aid of Beelzebub. His secret formulas and preposterous mummeries, of which his simple-minded fellow-countrymen stood in awe procured him the substantial rewards of the successful imposter. Polygamy was common, the number of a man's wives being limited only by his ability to purchase and maintain them. The great vice of the people was drunkenness, the national drink being "*machla*," an intoxicant decocted from corn. For the rest, the tropical climate induced indolence. The rudest sort of shelter beneath the magnificent shade of the forests, a bow and arrows, a dug-out canoe, an iron pot for cooking and a hammock woven from grasses or the inner bark of trees—and the Indian was content. A string of colored pearls around his neck might be the sole relief of his nakedness, even a breech-cloth being absent.

The first result of the visit was that the "king" urged the explorers to commence a mission in his territory, and offered a plot of land in Bluefields besides an island inhabited by Rama Indians. The Germans were solicitous of the establishment of stated services in their own tongue, and the British consul promised hearty coöperation.

Pfeiffer's report and his own willingness to become a pioneer led to his appointment, with Eugene Lundberg and Ernest George Kandler as his co-workers. They reached Bluefields on March 14, 1849. Most of the other Europeans, however, removed to Greytown, created a free port of entry in 1851 because of the thousands who sought the Golden Gate of California via Nicaragua.

In October, 1853, the baptism of the first convert, a negro woman, took place. Intercourse with the Indians was still limited. But as the language was mastered, visits to Indian villages, especially to Pearl Key lagoon, became fruitful. When Rudolph Wullschlaegel in June, 1855, on his way from Surinam to take his place in the Conference, rejoiced the missionaries by an unexpected visit, and consecrated their new church, the average attendance was about three hundred. The consecration was accompanied by the baptism of one of the sisters of the "king," Matilda, the first of the Indians to openly decide for Christ. Meantime reënforcements had arrived—amongst the rest Paulsen Jürgersen and wife, who proceeded to Pearl Key lagoon, and founded Magdala. As the crow flies this place was about twenty miles distant, but ten more by the waterway navigable for canoes.

In 1854 Pfeiffer retired. His successor was Gustavus Feurig, well qualified by fourteen years of experience in Jamaica. Magdala now gave large promise of results. The visits of the missionaries to Rama Key, an island fifteen miles from Bluefields, awoke a ready response among the Indians, and a church was built in 1857.

The blackfellows of Australia claimed the attention of the church in the years following the synod of 1848. Australia has been compared to "one of the atolls that lie in the tropic waters around it, being in effect a great ring of fertile soil surrounded by the barrenness of the ocean, and enclosing in its turn a desolate sea of rock and sand. In the inhospitable interior of Australia all the kindly influences of nature fail. The rain clouds shun it, or pass over it without meeting the hills that should arrest their course and pour them down in showers upon the yearning soil; rivers, wandering inland from their sources near the shore, sink into it without causing it to smile; its secrets are locked in perpetual drought, and its histories are written in the bones of men and beasts, that striving to penetrate its mysteries, only added thereto by the uncertainty of the fate that overtook them in its wilds. But along the entire coast-line, and exending inland variously for a distance of from fifty to two hundred miles, is a belt of rich land." Again between it and the sea of sand and rock that makes up the bulk of the conti- nent, is another belt of poorer soil suitable only for raising sheep, but excellent for that.

At the time of the Dutch discovery the habitable strips along the sea-coasts were occupied by the Papuans, the very lowest of savages. Such their descendants have largely remained. Divided into very small tribes, they are nomads by inherited in- stinct. A hut of branches or bark, scarcely affording shelter, is their only home, if such it may be called. For clothing at most they wear an opossum skin or a grass mat. When first discovered they had not a single cooking utensil. Without a domestic animal, and cultivating nothing, their food was the flesh of the kangaroo, opossum, wild dog, lizard, snake, rat, or loathsome reptile or grub, or even that of a fellow man. Their women were slaves and beasts of burden. Their infants were killed without compunctions, if sickly. Of religion they had very little. Their conception of God was that of a gigantic old man, lying asleep for ages with his head resting upon his arm, which is deep in the sand. One day he is expected to awake and eat up the world. Religious ceremonies were confined to circumcision and the "*corroboree.*" In connection with the former, inflicted on youths as they came to maturity, various rites were observed, like the punching of a hole through the nose for the insertion of an ornament, and the knocking out of the two front teeth with a wooden mallet. The *corroboree* was a midnight orgy, when the naked savages danced and howled till exhausted, having previously so marked their bodies with white clay, that at some distance they resembled moving skeletons. The vilest immorality accompanied these heathen rites. The dead were indeed interred with care in graves lined with bark, and kept free from weeds, whilst food, and after it had been introduced, tobacco, might be placed to supply needs in the spirit-world. In ghosts and in witchcraft they had firm faith, and in the power of the "evil eye." It was very unlucky for a man to meet his mother-in-law. To avoid the blight of her countenance, he would go far out of his way. Such were the black-fellows, when the whites arrived, and unfortunately for them the first whites with whom they came in contact were those that did them no good. In 1788, eighteen years after Captain Cook's famous explorations, the British Government began to make use of Australia as a penal colony. The convicts taught the natives the vices of civilization. Drink began to play havoc amongst them. The ex-convict who remained in the country thought no more of hunting and shooting natives than kanga-roos.

Sporadic attempts at missions amongst them had been made by various societies; but up to the middle of the nineteenth century the possibility of converting and changing the native Australians, body, soul and spirit, had not been demonstrated. Meantime they were tending to extinction in colonial Australia.

Repeated calls had come to the Moravian Church in the thirties and in the forties to have compassion on this race. In Herrnhut, Niesky and other German congregations "Australian Associations" had been formed amongst the young men, for stated prayer and systematic giving in behalf of a future mission. The synod had therefore committed the church to an attempt. Andrew Frederick Christian Täger, a member of Niesky, and Frederick William Spieseke of Gnadenberg were despatched as pioneers, and arrived at Melbourne on February 25, 1850, where a cordial welcome was accorded them by Lieutenant Governor Joseph La Trobe, a brother of the Mission Secretary in London. To his kind offices and the sympathy of Christian friends the favorable issue of negotiations for a tract of land and the first establishment of the missionaries in their new home in the "*Mallee*," or scrub, were largely owing.

Permanent operations were commenced in October, 1851, on a reserve in the Lake Boga District. The terms of the grant indeed contemplated a possibility that the course of events might render inexpedient the permanence of the missionary operations in this particular quarter. The climate proved healthy, save that Täger suffered from an affection of the eyes.

But the natives were exceedingly shy and timid, and their no-madic tendency appeared to be almost invincible.

In the year 1854 an additional missionary, Paul Hansen, ar-rived, and La Trobe, resigning office, returned to England. Now the position of the missionaries was rendered trying by the discovery of gold near Mount Alexander. The road to the dig-gings lay along the River Murray and past the station. The unbridled wickedness often attendant upon a rush to gold-dig-gings, and disputes as to the right of way through the mission-tract and the title to the mission-lands, vexed their souls. The civil authorities decided the points in dispute against the mis-sion. Täger, now in poor health, acting on his own responsi-bility as superintendent, and without consulting the authorities at home, in 1856 abandoned the field, though Spieseke pro-tested.

After a careful investigation of the whole affair the Confer-ence could not withhold censure. The promise was given, that the honor of the church should be redeemed by a new attempt as speedily as practicable.

The third new undertaking of these years had Central Asia as its objective. From almost the beginning of its missionary operations the Moravian Church under the leadership of Count Zinzendorf had directed its gaze towards the millions of Mon-golia and the Chinese Empire. Several unsuccessful efforts had been made via Russia or Persia. From the standpoint of the church the founding of Sarepta was planned as one pier of a bridge to the Orient. When the Czar Alexander I looked with favor upon the Brethren, Godfrey Schill and Christian Hübner of Sarepta in 1815 had been quick to renew efforts in behalf of the Asiatics. Two Buriats from Lake Baikal had been con-verted. The Gospels had been printed in Kalmuck Tartar by Isaac Schmidt of St. Petersburg. But in 1822 an imperial edict had peremptorily prohibited further operations.

The representations of Dr. Gützlaff, of China, when on a visit to Herrnhut in 1850, therefore received a sympathetic hearing. He wished the Moravian Church to again seek to enter the great Chinese Empire from the west, so that two streams of missionary force might meet in the heart of the land when open to Europeans.

Numerous volunteers came forward. Edward Pagell of Gnadenfrei and Augustus William Heyde of Herrnhut were selected. Calcutta was reached on November 23, 1853. Their first destination was Kotghur, where Mr. Prochnow, of the Church Missionary Society, welcomed and assisted them as laborers in a common cause. Here a considerable period was spent in linguistic study under a Tibetan lama. In April, 1855, they set out on a tour of preliminary investigation, in spite of the fact that two Roman Catholic missionaries had recently been murdered when attempting to proceed to Tibet by way of Assam. At Leh, in Ladak, they were made to feel anything but welcome. Nor did they discover a bright prospect for a mission in Chinese territory. When the frontier was crossed by passes at heights varying from 13,000 to 17,000 feet above sea level, nothing was gained. Invariably the Tibetans refused to sell provisions of any sort for man or beast; and the "*gopas*," or head men of each village, besought the Europeans to return, saying that if they did not succeed in stopping them, they themselves would have to answer to higher officials with their heads.

The next winter was therefore spent in Kotghur. Circumstances necessitated the founding of the first station amongst the Tibetan speaking Buddhists of Lahul, as near as possible to the frontier of Chinese Tibet. It was the best that could be done. Through the intervention of Major Lake of the British East India Company, in 1856 land was secured in the valley of the Bhagar, sixty miles or so from the borders, near Kyelang, and across the river from the town of Kardang, at an elevation of about 10,000 feet. Before winter the mission house was completed—a solitary outpost of Christianity amid the Western Himalayas, over against the fortress of the Dalai Lama; but again the missionaries sought the friendly hospitality of Kotghur, in order that early in 1857 they might welcome the arrival of their future leader. This was Henry Augustus Jaeschke, hitherto a professor in the college at Niesky. Appointed because of his preëminent linguistic abilities, that he might translate the Scriptures into Tibetan, he arrived at Calcutta in January, and hastened to his colleagues. With his arrival a new stage of the work of this mission began.

CHAPTER LII.

THE GENERAL SYNOD OF 1857.

The synod on whose issues so much depended convened at Herrnhut on June 8, 1857. It was constituted of sixty-one members, five of whom had been called from the mission fields at home and abroad, nine represented the American Province and twelve the British. Bishops Nitschmann presided, with Charles F. Kluge as Vice-President.

At an early stage in the proceedings a committee of twenty-one on the constitution of the church was elected, each Province being represented and selecting its own representatives. It was constituted as follows: for the German Province, Henry Levin Reichel, Gustavus Tietzen, George David Cranz, Theophilus Reichel, Ernest William Cröger, Gustavus Lilliendahl; for the British Province, William Edwards, Peter La Trobe, William Mallalieu, John England, William Okely, John Smith; for the American Province, Philip H. Goepp, Lewis F. Kampmann, Edmund A. de Schweinitz, Edward T. Senseman, Emil A. de Schweinitz and Levin T. Reichel; for the Unity's Elders' Conference, Ernest F. Reichel, Charles William Jahn and Henry Rudolf Wullschlaegel. This committee in the main followed the lead of the American proposals. As adopted, the chief features of the new constitution were the following:

As hitherto the General Synod is the highest legislative body for the entire Brethren's Unity, and in the last resort decides all questions that concern the Unity. Fullest powers inhere in this assembly, with regard alike to doctrine, ritual, polity and the administration of the missions and other joint undertakings of the three provinces. The principle of equal representation of the three Provinces in the General Synod is recognized, though the American proposal basing representation upon communicant membership is rejected. Nine elected delegates to each General Synod shall be chosen by each of the Provincial

Synods, the American church to be considered a unit in the general count, seven delegates being apportioned to the North and two to the South. By virtue of their office all the bishops of the Unity shall have seats and votes in the General Synod, and each Provincial Elders' Conference, the American church having two Conferences, shall have the right to send one representative.

To the Provincial Synods is committed full power to legislate in all purely Provincial affairs, with the proviso that any action taken by them in contravention of the transactions of the General Synod shall be invalid. The American and British Synods enjoy the right of electing their respective Provincial Elders' Conferences, responsible henceforth to the Provincial Synods for their administration of Provincial affairs. Each Provincial Synod shall further be empowered to determine the number of delegates sent by each congregation thereto, together with the mode of their election, and to regulate its own organization and methods of procedure. The Northern Synod in America also receives the right to prescribe its own method of nominating bishops. The Unity's Elders' Conference is to decide whether a Provincial Synod has transcended its powers.

The Unity's Elders' Conference, elected by the General Synod, and responsible to it, remains as hitherto the highest executive of the entire Unity. Inasmuch as a desire for Provincial independence has not as yet made itself felt on the Continent, the relationship of the Unity's Elders' Conference to the German Province is left undisturbed. The constitution of this body also remains the same, with its three departments—for financial affairs, for the oversight of the pastorates and of the educational undertakings, and for the management of the missions.

The members of the British Provincial Elders' Conference, unlike those in America, shall remain temporarily in a position of partial dependence upon the executive board of the Unity, in that their president shall be named by the latter body. In the Southern Province in America, the administrator of the Unity's property in North Carolina shall continue to be *ex-officio* a member of the Provincial executive.

With the granting of independence to the transmarine churches, there naturally was connected a financial settlement and separation. According to the arrangement which was adopted, the German Province was to become the owner of all estates to which the Unity as such now held title, including the Unity's lands in North Carolina. In compensation a fixed sum was to be paid to each of the other Provinces for the defrayal of general needs of the Province. This separation of accounts was of greater significance for the British and Wachovian Provinces than for the American Province North, whose financial independence had already commenced. Henceforth there remained as joint property of the Unity only the funds of the missions and a fund for the defrayal of the costs of general synods and of official visits undertaken by members of the Unity's Elders' Conference in Britain and America.

The newly elected Unity's Elders' Conference consisted of the following: Department of Education and the Pastoral Office, Bishop John Martin Nitschmann, Charles Frederick Schordan, Charles William Jahn, Gustavus Theodore Tietzen; Department of Finance, Bishop Christian William Matthiesen, John Ballein, Gustavus Theodore Reichel, Hermann Ludolph Mentz; Department of Missions, Ernest Frederick Reichel, Godfrey Andrew Cunow, Henry Rudolf Wullschlaegel and Levin Theodore Reichel.

Revision of the constitution did not monopolize the thought of synod. The administration of the missions during recent years received thorough scrutiny. Expressions in the Results of previous synods with reference to faith in the "chief eldership" of the Saviour were so changed as to remove due cause for objection. The lot was retained, but uniformity in the method of its use was no longer essential.

In deference to the wish of the British Province the paragraph referring to the Confession of Augsburg was omitted from the chapter on doctrine and transferred to that setting forth the relation of the German branch of the church to the Evangelical church on the Continent.

CHAPTER LIII.

THE GERMAN PROVINCE, FROM 1857 TO 1869.

The Unity's Elders' Conference organized by electing Bishop Nitschmann President and Bishop Matthiesen Vice-President. But the official circle did not long remain intact. Bishop Jahn died on January 1, 1858. In his place the pastor of Neuwied, George David Cranz, was chosen. On December 16, 1862, the venerable Bishop Nitschmann entered into rest. He was in his seventy-seventh year, and had served for almost fifty-seven years. Now Bishop Matthiesen became President, and Gustavus Tietzen Vice-President, whilst Ernest William Cröger entered the Board. On March 29, 1864, Bishop Wullschlaegel died, and on October 11 John Ballein. The vacancy in the Department of Missions was filled by the election of Augustus Clemens, superintendent of the missions in Jamaica, whilst the place of Ballein was taken by Ernest N. Hahn, warden of Neuwied. Finally Bishop Cunow, suffering in health from the fatigue of an arduous visit to the West Indies, retired in August, 1865. He died on June 24 of the following year. The superintendent of the South African missions, Frederick William Kühn, became a member of the Board.

In the "settlements" the church pursued the even tenor of its usefulness. For the German Province the synod of 1857 had involved less of immediate change than for the American and British. Nevertheless the annals were not blank. During 1858 a new congregation was organized at Goldberg, in Silesia. Gnadenberg on May 16, 1858, witnessed a counterpart of the interesting transaction at Herrnhut in 1844. Dr. Siedler having removed to Pomerania, with the consent and approval of the Royal Consistory of Posen and of the Ministry of Worship in Berlin, the highest ecclesiastical authority in Prussia, Dr. C. F. Göbel, who had been chosen his successor, was consecrated a bishop. In turn Bishop Göbel next year consecrated to the

episcopate and associated with himself Pastor Gumbrecht, of
Waschke, near Bojanowa, and thus fully secured the episcopate
to these congregations. In Poland, on October 14, 1860, the
Diaspora derived encouragement from the dedication of a new
chapel at Lodz, and on May 21, 1865, a similar dedication took
place at Zdonskawola. About this time the *Diaspora* in other
parts of the Russian Empire, and in particular in Livonia, again
occasioned gravest anxiety. Hostile Lutheran clergymen
claimed that the edict of 1834 prohibited any except ordained
ministers or candidates for the ministry from engaging in the
utterance of free speech or prayer in public assemblies for religious worship. If allowed, this interpretation would negative
the usefulness of the large body of "national helpers." The
synod of 1857 had counseled loyal obedience to the constituted
authorities, trusting that time would soften bigotry and remove
prejudice. In 1859 an unfavorable decision emanated from St.
Petersburg. Before long the General Consistory issued a mani-
festo against the formation of any *ecclesiola in ecclesia*. Inasmuch as this struck at the very existence of the *Diaspora* societies, which in Livonia now embraced a membership of from
forty to fifty thousand, the Moravian Church addressed a
memorial to the General Consistory, setting forth the unselfish
and non-proselyting character of its *Diaspora* work. In 1861
Hermann Plitt, of the seminary at Gnadenfeld, followed this up
with a polemical apologetic in defense of the Livonian work,
under the title of *"Die Brüdergemeine und die Lutherische Kirche
in Livland."* In the event the Livonian *Diaspora* continued to
prosecute its work of edification, but under very disadvan-
tageous and annoying conditions. Its superintendent was now
Christian Edward Burkhardt, who took the place of Gustavus
Müller in 1859. On the other hand in French Switzerland the
Diaspora widened its channels of usefulness, a new center being
established at Peseux, near Neuchatel, in 1859, and a third
Diaspora agent being appointed for French Switzerland in 1856.

In 1862 the German Province convened its first synod under
the conditions of the new constitution. It was in session at
Herrnhut from May 16 to July 16. Bishop Matthiesen presided. Attention was mainly directed to the inner life of the
congregations and to the needs of the *Diaspora*—especially in
Livonia. The erection of a new building for the college at
Niesky was ordered, an undertaking happily completed on Octo-

ber 17, 1865. Sanction was given to the launching of a new bi-monthly periodical, *Der Bruder Bote*, the net financial profits of which should be devoted to the *Diaspora*. Professor Plitt was appointed its editor, assisted by Joseph Reinhold Ronner, who had succeeded the venerable Christian Frederick von Schweinitz as archivist in 1859. The compilation of a history of the Unitas Fratrum previous to its overthrow in consequence of the Counter Reformation was authorized. Finally it was determined to renew activity amid the homes of the fathers in Bohemia and Moravia. This took the form of *Diaspora* labor, rather than that of actual church extension, Emanuel Kleinschmidt of Neusalz being sent this same year and a society being formed at Rosendorf. In 1865 F. D. Peter was stationed at Tschenkowitz; in 1867 William Hattwig at Rothwasser, and in the same year Andrew Köther in Prague, to be followed there two years later by Otto Bernhard.

But the peaceful activities of the church in Germany were to suffer rude interruptions. During the Schleswig-Holstein War the resources of Christiansfeld were taxed by the billeting of soldiers whose numbers sometimes exceeded one thousand, the church used as a hospital. The meetings of *Diaspora* circles in the vicinity were interrupted. Then the "Seven Weeks' War" broke out. Dreyse's needle-gun, the terribly significant efficiency of which was now to be revealed to the world, practically multiplied Prussia's battalions. Hesse-Cassel and Saxony were overrun without a battle. After a series of minor engagements the three Prussian armies converged upon Sadowa, and on July 3, 1866, the shattered Austrian army after a fearfully bloody conflict retreated in demoralization. Prussia's dominance in German affairs was assured and the foundation laid for the new empire with Austria excluded in the new unification of the Fatherland.

During this crisis several of the Moravian congregations renewed the experiences of the Napoleonic age—at least measurably—Niesky, Herrnhut and Gnadenfrei being in particular subjected to the billeting of troops, and Gnadenfrei and Gnadenberg being drawn upon for the establishment of military hospitals. Inasmuch as the railroad from Löbau to Zittau, which passes through Herrnhut, was for a time the only line open as a means of direct communication between Prussia and the seat of war, all civil traffic was suspended, and train after train, first of men to the front, then of sick and wounded on the way home, passed through by day and night. Nobly did the people rise to the opportunity to minister to suffering for humanity's sake and in the name of Christ, making no distinction between the friends and the foes of their Saxon land. Nor were the religious needs of the troops forgotten. Two thousand five hundred copies of the New Testament, besides copies of tracts and devotional works were freely given. When Herrnhut became a stated halting place for the trainloads of wounded who were being removed from the field hospital at Königinhof, an organization was effected to supply them with all manner of refreshments and to re-dress their wounds while waiting. Unstinted liberality was lavished alike upon Prussians, Saxons, Austrians and Hungarians. Moreover many men and women crossed the frontier to offer needed services as nurses upon the field and in the various temporary hospitals along the front. Abundant testimony was borne to the fact that the Prince of Peace was thus glorified amid the horrors of human strife.

From June 4 to July 21, 1868, a synod was convened preparatory to the general synod of the following year, Bishop Ernest Reichel presiding. Amongst the most important of its transactions was the recommendation that the Unity's Elders' Conference take steps to found a "mission institute," to prepare men for foreign service. When the question of the possible abandonment of the Livonian *Diaspora*, owing to the incessant hostility of the Lutheran clergy, was referred to the decision of the lot, a negative answer was received.

During the year 1868 the first weekly periodical of the German Province appeared—the *Herrnhut*, an unofficial publication. Even a cursory review of the period, however, would be incomplete without at least a passing reference to the literary labors of Hermann Plitt, President of the theological seminary at Gnadenfeld since 1853. His *Die Gemeine Gottes in ihrem Geiste und ihren Formen*, published in 1859, and his *Evangelische Glaubenslehre* in 1863—the former a presentation of the ideal spirit and calling of the Unity of the Brethren and the latter a systematic exposition of its theology—were standards for years to come.

CHAPTER LIV.

THE BRITISH PROVINCE, FROM 1857 TO 1869.

Samuel Rudolph Reichel, Treasurer of the British Provincial Board, had died at Herrnhut during the sessions of the synod of 1857. William Mallalieu, hitherto agent of missions in London, was elected to the office.

From June 29 to July 15, 1858, the Provincial synod held its sessions in Bristol, a gathering of special importance for the adjustment of affairs in Britain to the conditions created by the new constitution of the Unity. Bishop Cunow brought greetings from his colleagues and the church abroad. Baltonsborough was formally recognized as a congregation, and its pastor, John Miller, forthwith admitted to a seat and vote. Cheering news came from Ireland, where a remarkable revival of religion had characterized the past months, having had its rise in the vicinity of Gracefield. The commencement could be traced to the prayers of a few humble but earnest men. Deep concern for the essential grounds of assurance had become widespread. At times four to five thousand people had assembled for preaching and worship in the open air. Though strange excitement had been a marked feature of the awakening, the reality of the Spirit's influence was attested by the changed lives of multitudes. Samuel Connor, pastor of Gracefield, had been indefatigable in ministrations in connection with this season of grace, and he and his people had reaped marked benefit.

Having been definitely separated from the church in Germany, ministers and delegates alike recognized that a theological seminary was now absolutely essential to the Province. Therefore another attempt was ordered, the new seminary to have two departments, to train teachers for the schools and to prepare men for service in the home missions and congregations, though an absolute cessation of the sending of British ministerial candidates to Niesky and Gnadenfeld was not necessarily involved.

This new "Training Institution" should be under the immediate control of the Provincial Elders' Conference, and a committee of five was elected to coöperate with that body in conducting annual examinations, etc., viz.: William Phillips, John England, J. Slater, J. T. Purser and James La Trobe. The commodious building at Fulneck, formerly occupied by the unmarried men, was to be appropriated for this college—a measure which went into effect in October, 1860, when John England was inducted into office as its president, Henry Edwards Shawe being later appointed an additional instructor. From the separation of the financial interests of the three Provinces about $90,000 had accrued to the British Province. It appeared that the Provincial accounts were arranged under a number of distinct heads, as follows: The Ministers' Fund, for which voluntary contributions were received from time to time, was designed to supplement inadequate ministerial salaries; the Provincial Expense Account dealt with such items as the cost of official journeys and the appointment and removal of ministers; the Sustentation Fund provided pensions; the Educational Expense Account cared for the education of ministers' children, the accounts of Boarding Schools, as such, forming a distinct phase of Provincial finance. There was also a separate account for the estates of the church, at Gracehill, Gracefield, Fulneck, Fairfield, Ockbrook and Dukinfield, which were now to be all merged into one. A book account, a Superannuated Teachers' Fund, and a fund for the salaries of the Provincial Elders' Conference completed the list. The report of the Treasurer, William Mallalieu, gave great satisfaction for its clearness, and distinctly testified to the success and ability of his management and that of his predecessor, Rudolph Reichel.

Notwithstanding the fact that Bishop Edwards sought relief from the duties of a Provincial Elder, synod brought constraint upon him and paid a tribute of confidence to him and his colleagues by insisting upon a reëlection of the three.

For one congregation, whose development had been so modest and gradual as almost to escape notice, Malmesbury in Wiltshire, these were important years. In the days of Cennick, a society, affiliated with Tytherton, had worshiped here, later enjoying the ministrations of men like Münster, Cooke and Parminter. Rogers had become the first resident minister in 1768, but not until 1827 had the organization distinctly severed connection with Tytherton. Now in 1859 Malmesbury rebuilt its church, enlarging it to double the size of the old one, and in the following year opened a new Sunday-school.

On September 27, 1858, William Ignatius Okely died—one of the leaders in recent years. Born in 1804, at Mirfield, where his father was pastor, he had originally engaged in the architect's profession at Bristol, but in 1837 yielded to the constraint of an inner call, and removed to Fulneck in order to pursue a course of theological study, on the completion of which a visit in Germany enabled him to form an acquaintance with the life of the church abroad. He had been popular as a pastor in a number of congregations, and had been a British representative at the synod of 1857. The death of Bishop Rogers on July 26, 1862, seventy-six years of age, was followed by the consecration of James La Trobe at Ockbrook, on January 18, 1863, by Bishops Edwards and Seifferth.

From June 24 to July 8 of the latter year the Provincial synod was again in session, Bedford being its place of convocation, and Bishop Seifferth being again chosen President. Special attention was devoted to home missions, and Louis H. Spence was appointed Treasurer and Charles Sutcliffe Secretary of the Home Missionary Society. The enterprises to which its energies were directed, now embraced the following: Eydon, Culworth and Priors Marston, near Woodford; Risely, near Bedford; Horton and Heckmondwike, in Yorkshire; Crook, in Durham; Brockweir, affiliated with Bristol; Bakewell, on the Wye, in Derbyshire; Pendine, in South Wales; and West Pennard, near Baltonsborough. The last two owed their existence to individual self-sacrifice, rather than to associated activities. At Pendine, Charles Ellis was laboring at his own charges, and at West Pennard, Charles Cooney had started a day-school at his own risk, and had commenced to gather a congregation. Risely dated back to Cennick's day. The group in the vicinity of Woodford, like Horton and Brockweir, also belonged to the decades preceding the present. Heckmondwike a busy manufacturing town of Yorkshire, had been commenced in 1859 by members of the Mirfield congregation who resided there. Crook owed its start to William Allanson, who had removed to a neighboring farm from Baildon, and had opened his house for services conducted by J. P. Libbey. John Carey had removed hither from Greengates and had at first preached in the old Mechanics' Institute, besides statedly holding services in five neighboring villages. A permanent place of worship had been secured in May, 1860. At Bakewell, whither Brother Rose had recently gone in search of health at its springs, with restoration he had commenced to labor in a quiet way. Synod earnestly commended these undertakings. Furthermore it was resolved to establish an official monthly periodical, *The Messenger*, of which Charles Sutcliffe, of Dukinfield, was elected editor. The new Conference was constituted of Bishops Seifferth and La Trobe together with William Mallalieu.

On September 24, 1863, Peter La Trobe died suddenly of heart failure while on a visit to Berthelsdorf. For forty-two years he had been *Secretarius Unitatis Fratrum in Anglia* and Secretary of Missions in London, at first being associated with his father in the latter office. He was in his sixty-ninth year. His weighty counsels in the deliberative assemblies of the church had ever carried with them much influence, and his wide acquaintance with the missions and zeal for their furtherance had made his name a household word. William Mallalieu became *Secretarius Unitatis Fratrum in Anglia*. Thomas Leopold Badham, recently Associate Secretary of Misions, was charged with the office thus vacated, and received Henry Edwards Shawe as his assistant. The duties of *Advocatus Fratrum in Anglia*, unassigned since the death of John Frederick Foster, in April, 1858, were given to Charles Joseph La Trobe, the former Lieutenant Governor of Victoria. On November 12 of the same year Samuel Wilson died. His career had been that of an educator, having been at the head of the schools at Fulneck and Ockbrook for a long series of years. On January 27, 1867, John Carey died at Gracefield, having attained a like age, despite his indefatigable activity.

Yet with the removal of the workmen, the work went on. On October 28, 1865, the dedication of a building erected for school purposes at Westwood, Oldham, lying between Fairfield and Salem, gave notice of the intention of the Moravian Church to broaden its efforts to care for the densely packed manufacturing population of Lancashire, a notice which was followed by the consecration of a church in May, 1869. On October 13, 1867, Bishop La Trobe preached the first Moravian sermon in a house of worship at Durdham Down, recently acquired from the Wesleyans. In this suburb of Bristol persistent and effective evangelism had been in progress for quite a number of years. The neighborhood had borne a bad name when it commenced, and now the happy results were appearing.

The British synod convened a third time during the present period, in July, 1868, preparatory to the assembling of the approaching general synod. Its place of convocation was Fulneck. The experience of more than a decade confirmed the wisdom of the constitutional changes of 1857. The reëlection of the members of the Provincial Board; the appointment of Henry Edwards Shawe as Secretary of Missions, Badham, however, remaining editor of *Periodical Accounts*; an increase in the amounts to be paid as pensions to those superannuated after faithful service in the church; measures taken for the furnishing of parsonages; the appropriation of an annual sum from Provincial funds in aid of the home missions; the clothing of Provincial Elders' Conference with powers of oversight over all the church schools in the Province, with a view to promote uniformity of methods; plans for increasing the salaries of the teachers; the appointment of the new Secretary of Missions as editor of a church directory and Moravian almanac, hereafter to be issued statedly; the creating of the accountant of the Province the responsible cashier of the Provincial Elders' Conference; and the election of delegates to the coming synod were the most important transactions.

Finally several works of historical importance require notice. In 1866 Bishop Seifferth issued his "Church Constitution of the Bohemian and Moravian Brethren." This was the *Ratio Disciplinae* of Comenius reprinted in the original Latin, and also in a translation accompanied with valuable historical notes. In 1867 "Notes on the Origin and Episcopate of the Bohemian Brethren" appeared from the pen of Daniel Benham, Esq., whose diligence had already placed the church under obligation for his "The Reformation and Anti-Reformation in Bohemia," a translation of Pescheck's work, in 1846; "Memoirs of James Hutton," 1856; "School of Infancy" and "Life of Bishop Comenius," etc., 1858; and "Sketch of the Life of Jan August Miertsching," etc., 1854.

CHAPTER LV.

THE AMERICAN PROVINCE, FROM 1857 TO 1869.

Now civil war laid its burden of distress on all parts of the church. The Southern Province passed through "innumerable evils." Its resources were badly crippled. For a time all communication with the rest of the Unity was cut off. In the North, Graceham, York and Lancaster were exposed during the invasion of Pennsylvania in the summer of 1863; Minnesota learnt the terrors of Indian warfare. Everywhere distress, bereavement, heavy taxation, privation owing to the rise in the cost of necessaries of life—all the accompaniments of war—became sadly familiar. Yet patriotic loyalty and self-sacrifice ministered to a deeper sense of dependence upon God, and appreciation of the means of grace became a marked feature of the times.

In the administrative board of the church changes took place as men passed from the noon-tide to the evening of their powers. Bishops Jacobson and Peter Wolle and Philip H. Goepp remained in office until 1861, when the board was reconstituted, Bishop Jacobson still presiding, with Francis F. Hagen and Sylvester Wolle as his associates. The synod of 1867 charged with the general oversight Robert de Schweinitz, Lewis F. Kampmann and Sylvester Wolle, the first named becoming President. In the South, Bishop Bahnson, with Robert de Schweinitz and Emil A. de Schweinitz (the latter *ex-officio*) had been elected Provincial Elders in 1857. When the second of these removed to the North, in 1865, his place was taken by Lewis Rights.

Special importance attaches to the transactions of the synod at Bethlehem, convened on June 2, 1858, Bishop Jacobson presiding. A Provincial constitution was adopted in virtue of the powers granted by the general synod of the preceding year, fundamental to which were government by a Provincial Synod meeting triennially and constituted of the ministers in active service and the delegates of the congregations, and the administration of affairs in the interval by a Provincial Elders' Conference, consisting of ministers elected by and responsible to the Provincial Synod. The removal of the theological seminary from Nazareth to Bethlehem was ordered, and the commencement of a college in connection therewith planned. The resolutions of the synod of 1856 with regard to the appointment and powers of a Board of Trustees, to act in conjunction with the Provincial Elders, were rescinded. The sum of twenty thousand dollars, the greater part of the share of the Northern American Province in the division of the Unity's funds, was devoted to the endowment of the new institution. Synod also placed the administration of the home missions and the appointment of the missionaries in the hands of a "Home Mission Board," to consist of the Provincial Elders and eight other brethren elected by Synod, three of whom should be residents of Bethlehem, the said board having power to fill vacancies in its own body. By the synod of 1861, at Lititz, a further change was made in the administration of home missions. The Home Mission Board was abolished, and the management placed in the hands of the Provincial Elders as such, the various home missionary societies of the individual congregations, however, continuing their activities.

In May, 1864, the synod again met in Bethlehem. Now all ordained home missionaries were placed on an equality with other ministers in every respect. The establishment of a printing and publishing house in Bethlehem was authorized, a measure which went into effect in January, 1866. Synod elected as a "Board of Visitors," advisory to the Provincial Elders' Conference in all concerns of the college and theological seminary, Eugene A. Frueauff, Francis Jordan, George K. Reed, J. B. Tschudy, Jacob Blickensderfer, jr., C. M. S. Leslie, Augustus Wolle, William C. Reichel and Bishop Henry A. Shultz, with power to add two others to their number—in the event Edmund de Schweinitz and John C. Leibfried. It was thereby intended that some system of scholarships should be devised, and that students should also be entered as *non-gratuiti*. The founding of a church school for boys at Chaska, Minnesota, was recommended to the favorable consideration of the Provincial Elders' Conference.

Lititz was the scene of the deliberations of synod in May, 1867. At the opening Bishop Jacobson sought permission to retire from active service. He had held various appointments in the church for more than fifty years. Synod by formal vote paid a tribute to his prolonged fidelity.

Attention was drawn to the need of closer uniformity in ritual throughout the various congregations. The reintroduction of the "Brotherly Agreement" in a revised and modernized form as a bond of union between all the congregations and home missions was ordered.

Primarily the synod of 1868, at Bethlehem, in November, was to serve as preparatory to the general synod of 1869. For a second time Bishop Bigler presided. Synod instructed the delegates to ask for such a modification of the church's constitution as would empower the Northern division of the American Province to be subdivided into Districts, each having its own synod with power to legislate for the development of local interests. Sanction of an organic union with the Southern division of the Province was to be sought. In regard to purely internal affairs, synod defined the principles in acordance with which the revision of the church liturgy and hymn-book should proceed.

During all these years, in spite of all changes and notwithstanding the progress of the war and the period of inflation that followed, the home missions received energetic support.   In 1857 organization was effected in Chaska, Minnesota, with filials at Haltmyer's (later Laketown) and Rüdiger's (later Zoar).   Of this work Martin Erdmann was in charge. On November 8 in the same year a church was consecrated at Fry's Valley, Ohio, among Swiss settlers, as a filial of Gnadenhütten, of which Henry C. Bachman was pastor.   Next year a commencement was made at North Salem, Wisconsin, by Henry A. Shultz, when on an official visit. Egg Harbor, New Jersey, begun in April, 1859, was given John Christopher Israel as pastor. On July 10 Coveville (Canadensis) church was consecrated by Bishop Jacobson, as a filial of Hopedale, John Praeger being the pastor in charge. In August, Germans of New Haven and Terryville, Connecticut, having petitioned for a pastor, Christian Bentel was sent to the former city in December.   But in April he was appointed chaplain of the U. S. military hospital in New Haven, and William Henry Rice of Yale Divinity School became his successor. Providence lost Leonard Rau by dismissal in 1860, and at the end of the year the work here was given up. The German congregation in Newark in the same year fully reunited with the Presbyterian Church, and its pastor, Günther, passed with it into the service of that denomination. Over against these losses Mamre was begun in Wisconsin and Henderson was commenced as an outpost of Chaska. South Bethlehem was organized at Christmas, 1862. On December 21, 1862, a church was dedicated in Milwaukee, Wis., but in April, 1864, its pastor, William Geyer, with most of his members seceded to the Lutheran Church and the property was taken by them. Palmyra, New Jersey, obtained recognition as a home mission on January 1, 1864, and the next year witnessed an addition to its strength, through the organization of Riverside, also founded by Philip H. Gapp. In August, 1864, Watertown, Wisconsin, hitherto connected with Ebenezer, was constituted a distinct charge under Julius E. Wuensche. In January, 1866, Elizabeth, New Jersey, was organized and received Christian Neu as its pastor. On June 10 Gracehill, Iowa, was organized, Louis P. Clewell taking charge. In October the corner-stone of the church at Franklin and Thompson Streets, Philadelphia, was laid. It was to be the house of worship for the second Moravian congregation in this city, an outgrowth of the work of Herman S. Hoffman, supported by the home missionary society of the First Church, at Franklin and Wood Streets. The dedication took place on October 2, 1869. In the year 1866 Freedom, Wisconsin, was organized by George Frederick Uecke. Next year Bethany, near Winona, Minnesota, was begun by George Henry Reusswig, who also organized Oakridge, later Hebron, in 1868. In April, 1868, an English congregation was formed in South Bethlehem, distinct from the German, the former being in charge of Albert Rondthaler, the latter of Henry J. Van Vleck. In September a third enterprise was inaugurated in Philadelphia, at Harrowgate, a northern suburb, and placed in charge of John Nice. In March, 1869, a fourth was commenced in the same city, the "Bethlehem Mission," in the northeastern part of the city, David Mortimer Warner being specially active in connection with the Sunday-school which constituted the chief feature of the work. Finally on October 31, 1869, Harmony, Iowa, rejoiced in the dedication of its church.

Gradually a number of the newer enterprises received recognition from the Provincial synod as self-supporting congregations entitled to a voice and vote in synodical legislation. In 1857 West Salem, having been divided into two organizations, the German in charge of Herman Tietze and the English in charge of Martin Hauser, synod in 1858 recognized delegates from each as clothed with full powers. At the same time Ebenezer and Watertown were received into the list of regular congregations as a joint charge. Then followed Fry's Valley in 1861, Utica in 1864, and Philadelphia Second Church and Lake Mills in 1868.

Progress could also be noted in the South, although the awful experiences of the war for a time put a check to aggressive religious activity. In 1865 a mission was commenced by Isaac Prince among the freedmen at Holly Springs, Mississippi; but circumstances compelled its abandonment in the autumn of 1866. Next year the erection of the church at Kernersville marked the beginning of an era of extension in the vicinity of Salem. During the war the spacious buildings recently erected for Salem Female Academy were well filled with pupils, such confidence was placed in the church and in the Principal, Robert de Schweinitz, who was often in perplexity to make adequate provision for those committed to his charge.

In the North the educational enterprises widened out. Bethlehem in 1858 erected a fine large edifice for its parochial school in charge of Ambrose Rondthaler. Next year a seminary for boys was begun at Hope, Indiana, with John H. Kluge as teacher, which gave place to a school for girls with Eugene P. Greider as Principal—also a congregational enterprise. But in November, 1866, a school for girls was opened at Hope as an undertaking of the Northern Province, Francis R. Holland being Principal. Meantime, in November, 1864, a church school for boys had been begun at Chaska, Minnesota, in charge of Anthony Lehman and Charles B. Shultz.

For the college and seminary the period was one of changes. In 1858 it returned to Bethlehem, its home during the years 1838 to 1851. On August 30 the former Van Kirk property was dedicated to its new use, Lewis F. Kampmann being President and Lewis R. Huebener and William C. Reichel professors. Instruction was also given by Bishops Jacobson and Wolle and by Philip H. Goepp. In the summer of 1862, Professor Reichel having accepted a call to take charge of Linden Hall, William H. Bigler was appointed in his place. The invasion of Pennsylvania in 1863 caused an interruption of studies, Professors Huebener and Bigler together with a number of the students enlisting. In October, 1864, President Kampmann having been appointed to the Lititz pastorate, Professor Huebener was thereupon appointed Acting President, half a year later to be confirmed in the office. Meantime Hermann A. Brickenstein had temporarily taken the place of Resident Professor. In September, 1865, Theophilus Zorn joined the faculty, and Edmund de Schweinitz commenced to lecture on the History of the Moravian Church, Professor Brickenstein continuing to lecture on Archaeology and Introduction to the Sacred Scriptures, and Dr. A. L. Huebener giving instruction in German. In January, 1866, an additional professor was temporarily secured, Frederick Hark, who received a permanent appointment in autumn, when Professor Brickenstein and Dr. Huebener discontinued their work. In October President Huebener entered the service of the Bethlehem congregation, and Gottlieb F. Oehler took charge of the administration of the external affairs of the institution as Steward, Professor Zorn having the more immediate oversight of the students. A further change took place in July, 1867. Now Edmund de Schweinitz became President, whilst retaining his pastoral relationship to the Bethlehem congregation. Of the former members of the faculty only one remained, Professor Bigler. The vacancies were filled by the appointment of Charles B. Shultz, Edwin G. Klosé and subsequently William C. Reichel. The members of the new faculty entered upon their duties in September, taking the pledge of office required in accordance with an enactment of the recent synod.

Changes also characterized the church publications. In December, 1858, the Moravian Bookstore and Publication Concern was removed from Philadelphia to Bethlehem, and in January, 1859, Edwin T. Senseman became editor of the Moravian. In 1860 the editing of the *Brüder Blatt* passed from C. F. Seidel to Theophilus Wunderling and John C. Brickenstein; but for lack of support this periodical ceased to be issued at the end of the year 1861. In accordance with a resolution of the synod of 1864 a printing and publishing establishment was commenced at Bethlehem in January, 1866, in charge of Messrs. A. C. and

H. T. Clauder, and in April a new attempt was made to found a German church-paper, *Der Brüder Botschafter*, which at first appeared fortnightly. Soon after the synod of 1861 the founder of the *Moravian*, Edmund de Schweinitz, again became its editor. After the synod of 1864 he received an assistant editor Hermann A. Brickenstein, and Sylvester Wolle served as financial agent. In October, 1864, both the editor and the associate editor removed to Bethlehem, the former as pastor and the latter as "Secretary of Publications," with full editorial control.

Nor were the older congregations without varied experiences in connection with their activity. Lebanon's loss of its church by fire, on July 29, 1858, during the pastorate of Theophilus Wunderling, aroused deep sympathy. Lititz, under the lead of William Rauch and Francis Christ, forthwith collected the sum of $428 as its substantial token of fraternal interest, and others soon followed the good example. The new edifice was dedicated on June 5 and 6 in the following year. Similarly Ebenezer lost its parsonage by fire in December, 1857, J. G. Kaltenbrunn and his family being the sufferers. The New York congregation held its last service in its church at Houston and Mott Streets on September 3, 1865, and entered its new home at Lexington Avenue and Thirty-first Street on April 18, 1869, Amadeus A. Reinke being pastor. This church had hitherto been known as the "Church of the Mediator," and had belonged to a congregation of the Protestant Episcopal Church, from whom it was acquired by purchase. Bethlehem remodeled its old historic chapel in 1865, and modernized and renovated its large church in 1867. York dedicated a new church in October, 1868, William Henry Rice being pastor. Brooklyn entered into its new church in October, 1869, Edward Rondthaler being in charge.

Thus change followed change, and advance was achieved in the various departments of activity.

CHAPTER LVI.

THE FOREIGN MISSIONS, FROM 1857 TO 1869.

Provincial independence was coupled with the recognition of the fact that the work of evangelization amongst the heathen remains one of the strongest bonds linking each division of the Brethren's Church to the Unity as such. More complete occupation of existing fields and the extension of the entire enterprise were proclaimed to be the definite policy of the church.

In Greenland, as a consequence of the official visit paid in 1858 by Ernest Reichel mission stations were established in succeeding years at Umanak on an island up the fjord from New Herrnhut, and at Igdlorpait on an island nine miles from Lichtenau.

To supply the requisite native assistants two normal schools were commenced in 1866, at New Herrnhut by Bindschedler and at Lichtenau by Kögel and Spindler.

Labrador, like Greenland, also enjoyed official visits—that of Levin Theodore Reichel in 1861, and that of Charles Linder in 1864 and 1865 in the interests of the Society for the Furtherance of the Gospel—and had also its attempts at extension. In 1864 a spot was selected to the south of Nain—to be known as Zoar. Here Michael Ernest Beyer laid the foundation of a new mission, and hither Augustus Ferdinand Elsner and wife moved in May, 1866. It afforded special opportunity to exercise a helpful influence over European and half-caste settlers. Although previous attempts had been so fruitless, another exploratory tour was undertaken northwards. Gottlob and Daniel, two native assistants, stirred by the news of the achievements of John King in Surinam, brought the gospel to their countrymen as far as Cape Chudleigh and along the eastern shore of Ungava Bay, voyaging in a sailing vessel of their own.

They set out in July, 1867, and during the following winter returned to the missionaries to report the welcome tidings of a desire for a "teacher." Meantime Saeglek, a point north of Hebron, had been chosen as the site of a proposed mission, and a rude temporary cabin had been built. But then the Hudson's Bay Company sent an agent thither, and to avoid disputes the missionaries withdrew. Nachvak Bay, thirty miles farther to the north was next chosen; again the trading company interposed. Now Nullatatok Bay was hit upon; but circumstances compelled the postponement of active operations.

The winter of 1862 to 1863 was attended with great mortality at Hebron. One sixth of the people died. The sickness was so general that at one time frozen corpses of necessity lay unburied for a month. During the following winter influenza and erysipelas proved very fatal at Okak, Nain and Hopedale. These visitations led to the establishment of an orphanage at Okak, at Easter, 1865, in accordance with plans adopted at a general mission conference convoked some time before at Nain. Ten of the most destitute Eskimo waifs were gathered together into a home superintended by the native schoolmaster and his wife.

The West Indies had enjoyed the influence of the marked revivals of religion in America. Thoughts were consequently turned to the possibility of complete self-support on the part of the native church. Discussion of this project formed one of the main purposes of an official visit paid by Bishop Cunow and the Mission Secretary, Thomas L. Badham, during the years 1862 and 1863. But untoward externals interfered, frequent and wide-spread droughts, yellow fever, disastrous tornados and earthquakes. The civil war in America put an embargo upon many articles of commerce, whilst the stagnation of the sugar trade deprived many of their means of livelihood. Emigration, in particular to Demerara, set in—notably from Barbados. This unfavorable change is clearly disclosed in the contrast presented by extracts from two letters written from Barbados by John Henry Buchner in 1858 and 1863. When proceeding to assume the superintendence of the mission in the former year, he thus chronicles his first impressions: "On Thursday morning the steamer brought us in sight of Barbados....It delights the eye by its rich cultivation. The island is spread out like a garden, with its cane fields, its windmills, its extensive town and numerous scattered houses. When we arrived the harbor was very lively, many vessels were taking in their cargoes, and boats were passing in all directions....When we landed on the wharf, the crowd at work there, and the large number of sugar hogsheads waiting to be shipped, at once gave us the idea that we had come to a stirring and prosperous place....We passed numbers of gentlemen's houses, many of them with prettily laid out gardens, and presenting an aspect of wealth and comfort. The road was very lively. The number of carriages and vehicles of every description, as well as of pedestrians, would have reminded us of some populous district in England, had not the dark complexion of the passers-by, and the appearance of the houses, and of many natural objects convinced us that we were in the West Indies." Five years later he writes: "How many of the people of this island still live, is a mystery to us. Hundreds have no ostensible means of getting a livelihood at all. You have perhaps heard that thieves and vagabonds have been going about the country in gangs of from ten to twenty, robbing and plundering, and causing not a little alarm. Now that most of them are lodged in jail, and a proper watch is kept, all is again peaceful and quiet. Of course, all receipts are falling off, especially the school-fees and the subscriptions to the Missionary associations. But this is not what distresses us most; the church is not so well attended as formerly, and the schools are half empty. This is simply because adults and children have no clothes but rags, in which they can not show themselves. This is a state of things which is beyond our power to remedy....It is a sad, sad tale which I have to tell. The distress here is fearful; and it is not a passing depression, likely to continue but for a short time; it is a crisis which will require years to develop its results, and which will, I fear, entail severe suffering on all classes."

After having personally inspected the operations on all the various islands, Cunow and Badham convoked a general conference at St. Thomas in June, 1863. It was a gathering that marked a new epoch. The visitants embodied the results of their observations in the form of proposals to be now acted upon, and after endorsement to be laid before the Mission Board as the basis for the new methods of operation. Self-support, native agency, local management and education were the chief points involved. Conditions that varied not only as between island and island but also as between the stations in a given sub-division of the field—differences in regard to temporal prosperity, social advancement, mental culture and Christian experience—rendered very difficult the formulation of general principles universally applicable. Whilst the justice and ultimate necessity of attaining self-support were fully recognized by all, practical obstacles were often in the way, and could not be ignored. Jamaica promised to attempt it, except that the outlay for buildings and for the journeys of missionaries would still have to be met from the general mission treasury. The Danish islands together with St. Kitts and Tobago, expressed a willingness to rely upon a gradually decreasing grant for a decade, in the hope that during the interval local resources might attain a sufficient development. Antigua and Barbados, while acquiescing in the principle of self-support, and hoping later to make theory and practice equal, found present hindrances insuperable. With regard to native agency, although a commencement had been made, and although of the 687 native assistants and of the 122 school-masters many had rendered and were rendering efficient help as exhorters and evangelists, it was felt that the church must proceed with circumspection in appointing native pastors. Meantime the meetings of the "helpers" were to be developed into something resembling the sessions of congregation committees and conferences at home. The school system was to be carefully fostered, and an approach to uniformity of method attempted through the work of the four normal schools—a fourth having been commenced in 1861 at Bethabara in Jamaica for female teachers. At the same time eagerness to advance did not shut out of view a recognition of the danger of raising the standard of the mission-schools far above the real requirements of the people.

But the happy anticipations aroused by the brave plans of the general conference were rudely interrupted. In 1866 cholera and yellow fever entered St. Thomas. By January 23, 1867, 860 deaths had been recorded in the city alone. Sea captains began to avoid the port as a pest hole. Doctors and missionaries and volunteer nurses stood bravely at their posts, and the pestilence was subdued. But on October 29 a terrific hurricane passed over the Danish islands. Shingles and planks flew through the air. Then the cabins of the natives gave way. At length the very finest buildings were rent and cracked. In the town more than three hundred lives were lost. Seventy-seven vessels were wrecked. The fine new church at Nisky was in ruins, and the other houses were partly destroyed. Not a station on St. Thomas or St. John but had been seriously damaged. The fields were devastated, and the groves and woods were choked with wreckage. Then just before three o'clock on the afternoon of November 18 a terrible earthquake visited the devoted island. Shock followed shock. A huge tidal wave with an awful roar carried the sea far inland, and after dashing on shore vessels of every size and sort, receded, leaving the bottom of the sea perfectly bare and exposing sunken wrecks for about three hundred yards. Three times the terrifying experience was repeated. Royal mail steamers went down with their valuable cargoes and precious freightage of human lives. The wharves and warehouses along the shore were laid waste. Tremendous damage was done to property. Providentially the Moravian church still stood amidst hundreds of ruined houses. More damage was done to mission property elsewhere, the losses being estimated from $10,000 to $15,000. The mission school at Friedensberg, St. Croix, was turned into a hospital for the disabled seamen of the United States frigate *Monongahela*, which had been carried ashore, and left high and dry. For six weeks following shocks recurred daily with few exceptions. The sullen rumblings were an ever repeated reminder that at any moment the seismic disturbances might increase in intensity. Many people fled from the towns to the hills and open country. Not until the following February was it considered safe to renew public worship in the town of St. Thomas. That these calamities called forth the active benevolence of the membership at home goes with the saying. A large legacy received through the agency of the London Association proved a godsend in the emergency.

Meantime memorable things were transpiring in Jamaica. In August, 1858, a spirit of prayer and inquiry appeared in the normal school at Fairfield, now in charge of Sondermann and Prince, and before long spread through the congregations, until it culminated in a manifest outpouring of the Holy Spirit in 1860, especially at Carmel, Fulneck and Fairfield. Whilst strange phenomena—fits of trembling or temporary loss of speech—bore testimony to the emotional nature of the race and pointed to the close connection between the psychical and the physical, the most striking features of this experience were the deep sense of sin and utter want of comfort and peace until assurance of pardon through the grace of an atoning Saviour found entrance into hearts. Then the fruits of faith became very evident. Churches and schools were crowded, contributions became liberal, the demand for Bibles and devotional works enlarged, the sacredness of Christian marriage received wider recognition, and additions to the churches multiplied. Ere long all the mission congregations on the island shared in the happy experience. The demand for Bibles especially became so large that it could scarcely be met. The Westmoreland Bible Society alone issued about two thousand copies.

Early in the following year the work at New Hope, on account of its low and swampy site, was removed to an estate which had been purchased by Alfred B. Lind, henceforth known as Salem, where he encouraged the blacks to colonize and themselves become independent planters on a small scale. In 1865 Mizpah was also founded between Bethabara and Bethany.

Meanwhile the vacancy in the Mission Board caused by the death of Bishop Wullschlaegel in March, 1863, had deprived Jamaica of the services of Augustus Clemens. In his place Abraham Lichtenthaeler became superintendent.

On the neighboring Moskito Coast the missionaries were now slowly counteracting the nomadic tendencies of the Indians, and village-life was being successfully introduced. Hopes could be entertained that in time the scope of the work would be coextensive with the territory. At Rama and at Reitapura (Brown Bank) churches had been built, and in Bluefields the congregation was growing in numbers and in influence. Special assistance had been afforded by the gift of a small schooner, "*The Messenger of Peace*," presented by friends at Zeist in 1858.

The year 1860 was signalized by an official visit on the part of Bishop Westerby of Antigua, commissioned by the Board. At Rama Key he especially noted the decided change for the better. The people were no longer wretched savages. Now decently clad and contented and happy they were living in neat cottages, roughly built indeed, and thatched only with palm leaves and having floors of clay, but clean and divided into separate rooms that made some provision for privacy. In October of the same year the fruits of former visits up the coast appeared in the founding of Ephrata at Wounta Hallover, not far from Cape Gracias a Dios. Here Kandler was stationed. The situation required a man of courage, tact and ability. White men, mahogany-cutters from Belize, were bringing in liquors, and drunkenness and brawling were distressingly frequent. In addition to this new undertaking, on Corn Island, directly east from Magdala, Jacob Jonathan Hoch began Joppa amongst a purely negro population.

Early in this same year the political status of the coast had been readjusted. By the terms of the treaty of Managua Britain, having already in 1850 resigned all claims to ownership in the stipulations of the Clayton-Bulwer Treaty, ceded her protectorate to Nicaragua. "The local chief was induced to accept the arrangement on the condition of retaining his administrative functions and receiving a yearly subvention of $5,000 from the suzerain state for the ten years ending in 1870. But he died in 1864, and Nicaragua never recognized his successor. Nevertheless the reserve continued to be ruled by a chief elected by the natives and assisted by an administrative council which assembled at Bluefields." For the present the Indians asserted a quasi-independence under Chief George William.

Now the mission at Magdala especially prospered. Grunewald's normal school was removed thither from Bluefields. The outposts on the peninsula east of Pearl lagoon gained in every way, so that in 1864 Tasbapauni (Red Bank) could be developed into an independent station, Bethania. Here Peter Blair, a native of Jamaica, was given charge.

But this mission also had its trials. On the night of October 18, 1865, a terrible hurricane swept the coast. At Bluefields only eight houses remained, and they half-ruined. Of these eight the mission-house was one. Church, school, kitchen, teacher's residence and the boat-house were leveled. The second "Messenger of Peace"—a gift from England—lay on her beam ends, badly damaged. At Ramah only three houses remained besides the church and mission-house, and these had lost their roofs. At Magdala the home of the missionary was shattered to pieces. Bethania had been carried away by a tidal wave, and Blair had difficulty in escaping by boat. Only one solitary post showed where the station had stood. At Joppa Hoch and his family for weeks had no other shelter than the displaced roof of the church, which kept its shape when it fell from the walls. The destruction of the cocoanut palms and the devastation of the provision grounds rendered starvation a possibility. Discontinuance of the mission was under consideration. But deep sympathy was aroused in the home congregations, and liberal gifts came in. Bluefields church could be anew consecrated in July, 1867, and Ephrata in August, 1868. The development of the India rubber industry provided the people with a new source of income. A third *"Messenger of Peace"* was supplied by the young people in America, stirred by the appeals of Amandeus A. Reinke, the former pioneer. Lundberg was now superintendent.

Surinam progressed meanwhile under the wise and energetic leadership of Van Calker. New stations were commenced— Beersheba in 1858 at the edge of a savannah near La Prosperite Estate, for the Para district, and Waterloo in the Nickerie district and Clevia on the Lower Surinam near its confluence with the Comewyne, in 1859. In the Bush Country on the Upper Surinam, a spirit of inquiry was spreading, and the labors of Gottlieb, the native assistant at Gansee, and of his two coadjutors bore fruit in the application of forty of their countrymen for baptism, by August, 1861. By the providence of God a very remarkable movement was also in its incipiency.

About the end of the year 1857 a stranger made his appearance in Paramaribo, declaring that God had warned him through dreams to come hither and seek the truth. He was a heathen Bush-negro, of the Matuari tribe, John King by name. His mother had formerly lived in town, but after the death of her parents the family had removed to the Saramacca district, and had lapsed into utter heathenism. Up to manhood John King had been little better than his fellows. Like them he had been accustomed to the ancestral fetish worship of Africa, was hardened to the debauchery and immoralities and cruelties of heathenism, thought little of the frequently occurring fights with poisoned iron rings, was familiar with the *"winti"* dance and alleged witchcraft, dreaded the power of the evil eye, and trembled at the sight of an old rag fluttering in a cleft stick that had been planted as "medicine" before the door of a hut. But now he wished to follow the light that had been given to him in dreams. "In the first of these he saw a large, light and beautiful house, full of people clothed in white garments who were heard singing so delightfully, that he had never heard the like.

Then he saw a dismal building like a jail, in the courtyard of which an enormous fire was blazing. As he approached the fire the flame leaped up and touching him caused him indescriable torment. Near it he beheld vessels as large as those in the boiling house of a sugar plantation, in which he was told wicked people were tormented in burning oil. In the house itself he to his terror caught sight of the dark form of the evil spirit. A person who showed him these objects then desired him to go and tell his people what he had seen and what was the lot of the damned. With the horrible feeling that he himself belonged to this number, King followed his guide to a river, into which he sprang—and awoke. When restored to consciousness, he was almost beside himself with terror, trembled from head to foot, and was for some time unable to rise from his bed. Not until evening did he regain sufficient composure to relate his dream to those around him. What he stated filled his hearers with horror. A week later he dreamed that he was in a church at the door of which a man was standing who said, 'King, do you know what you ought to do? You must have your name set down at the church, for if you abide by what the heathen say, you will be lost for ever.'" These experiences had led him to Paramaribo as a sincere inquirer after the truth. Here he proved a man of singular capacity and endowments—sincere, energetic, desirous to learn, gifted and diligent in study and in work. On August 11, 1861, he was baptized in Paramaribo, receiving the name of John. Returning to his village of Maripastoon, on the Saramacca in the dense forests four days' journey beyond Gansee, he forthwith commenced to labor as an evangelist amongst his people, with the fervor of one possessed of the conviction of a direct call from God. The results enforced his belief. Before long his near relative, Adrai, the local chief, sought baptism and took the name of Noah. The conflict was protracted and sometimes bitter, King's life being threatened. But he destroyed the rude temples, and threw the broken idols into the river; and in October, 1865, Kalkoen, the aged supreme chief of the Matuaris, through his ministrations and those of another native evangelist, Manasseh, could be baptized by Drexler, choosing for himself the name of Joshua.

John King's career now became one of peculiar interest. Long journeys were undertaken by him in all parts of Surinam,

up sluggish and fever-breeding streams, through the dense
jungles where white men could not have lived. With an utter
abandon of fearlessness he braved the *"winti"* men, and exposed
their follies and deceptions. And though these blind leaders of
the blind, enraged at the prospect of losing their occupation,
conspired against him, he passed unscathed, their poison failing to reach him. Once indeed even he fell a victim to fever;
but the prayers of the brethren were heard for his recovery.
Related by birth to the Aukas (or Djukas) as well as to the
Matuaris, he undertook an expedition to them also, and proposed to guide the Brethren Bramberg and Lehman to their
distant villages. But before the missionaries crossed the
boundary of the colony proper, armed men presented a hostile
front, and a reluctant return was the sole resource. By this
time at Coffycamp, Gansee, Goejaba and Maripastoon, about
eight hundred Bush-negroes had been enrolled in the membership of the church.

Meantime momentous events had been transpiring. On
July 1, 1863, by royal proclamation the emancipation of the
slaves became an accomplished fact throughout Surinam.
According to the terms of the edict a ten years' apprenticeship was first provided for, the choice of masters being voluntary, and the contracts being subject to governmental supervision. Furthermore each ex-slave was required to declare himself either a Christian or a Jew in faith to be entitled to be benefits of royal favor. About two-thirds of the entire slave population had already been in connection with the Moravian Church.
Hence this wide-reaching measure specially concerned the
mission. The removal of the hindrances inherent in slavery
was a source of hearty joy to the missionaries. Yet it was
impossible that all the consequences of slavery could be at once
eradicated. The immorality and the utterly lax ethical conceptions instilled into the slave race must be a source of trouble
for a generation at least. Marriage of slaves hitherto received
no legal recognition. Even now the requirement that a civil
contract be entered into before a magistrate if a marriage were
to become valid—a regulation involving considerable expenditure of money—drove only too many of the ex-slaves into connections resembling concubinage rather than wedlock.

To counteract the heritage of the past, special attention was
now paid to the schools. Sixteen of these were being carried on

by the mission, with two thousand three hundred and thirty-eight scholars. To develop the normal school, it was transferred to the capital in 1866. In general, sudden expansion in the number of the adherents of the mission was a result of emancipation. In the city the membership had grown to more than six thousand; in the entire colony it reached a total of 24,330 by the year 1869. Discipline naturally suffered in consequence, but the missionaries kept the old standard in view.

Of the South African congregations for the greater part of the present period it could be said in apostolic language, "Then had the churches rest, and were edified; and walking in the fear of the Lord, and in the comfort of the Holy Ghost were multiplied." Yet at the beginning it seemed as though the conditions necessary to external peace would be wanting. Already in 1856 the failure of the attempt to secure the loyalty of the Kaffir chiefs by the payment of salaries in return for the surrender of certain of their rights, became evident. A would-be prophet who possessed influence with chief Sandili, aroused a wave of wild fanaticism amongst his people by pretending that if they would follow his suggestions they should secure the aid of their departed ancestors in a war of extermination against the colonists. The peculiar test to which he put their faith, was the requirement, that they should unhesitatingly slay their cattle. This act of self-sacrifice complete, he bade them await the appearance of two blood-red suns as the heaven-sent sign for the promised success and vengeance. But the omen failed to appear, though the people obeyed his injunction literally. Gaunt famine stalked through Kaffraria. Swarms of despairing beggars streamed into the colony and pitifully pleaded for food. This was the only army evolved by the delusion. In the eastern part of the country the population was reduced to almost one-third. Hundreds clamored for alms at the mission stations. Shiloh, for example, received a permanent influx of three hundred of these poor deluded refugees. The missionaries devised all manner of labor that they might not be degraded by acknowledged pauperization. Warriors distinguished for former prowess might be seen roaming through the forests for firewood; others cut pliant osiers and wove them into baskets; others shouldered pick and shovel for the unwonted labor of ditching and draining. One result of these experiences was the founding of a new station, Engotini, six miles distant on the Engoti, a tributary of the Oxkraal, begun by Henry Meyer, who had come to Africa in 1854. Under his energetic leadership rapid progress was made.

Meanwhile another extension of operations was to be noted in quite a different quarter, the Picketberg range near St. Helena Bay, eighty or ninety miles north of Cape Town. Since 1846 the little valley of Goedverwacht had enjoyed the services of a native teacher trained at Genadendal, Joshua Hardenberg. By the year 1858 the work had assumed such proportions that the establishment of a regular station seemed imperative. But the peculiar history of Goedverwacht precluded the formation of the station at the place itself. In the year 1810 a Dutch farmer, Buergers by name, had purchased nine hundred acres of fertile valley in the Picketberg, and in time rendered his estate a garden spot through the well directed labor of his Hottentot slaves. Here he lived in comfort until disturbed by rumors of impending emancipation. To keep his slaves about him in this emergency, he selected six of the most intelligent and faithful, and made an extraordinary proposal to them. If they solemnly covenanted to faithfully serve and care for him so long as he lived, he would bequeath his entire property to them. They readily agreed. He therefore drew up his last testament, bequeathing his land to the six jointly, with the proviso that it should not be sold until the death of the last of the six. Emancipation came on December 1, 1834. They remained true to their pledge. Mr. Buergers himself died in 1843, and the once despised Hottentots became the joint owners of a fine piece of property. Hither their relatives gradually removed, till there arose a village of about five hundred souls. It was in response to a request made by these people that the church sent a teacher to them in 1846. But the uncertainty of the tenure of the land, contingent as it was upon the lives of the six ex-slaves, suggested the purchase by the mission of the neighboring farm of Wittewater as the actual site of the station, Goedverwacht being served in conjunction with it.

Two deaths saddened the friends of the African mission, that of Daniel Suhl, the principal of the normal school, on April 30, 1858, and that of Charles Rudolph Kölbing, the superintendent of the mission, on December 28, 1860. Both had rendered valuable services; and the former left the school in such a condition that the enlargement of its accommodations was a necessity. Three of its graduates were now serving as assistant missionaries; fifteen were filling posts as teachers in schools of their own and sixteen in schools of sister churches. Benno Marx succeeded to the vacant office. Now special attention was paid to the operation of a printing press by the students. *De Bode*, a missionary periodical in the Dutch language, and *De Kinder Vriend*, for children, were issued at stated intervals; and a commencement was made in 1861 with the publication of parts of the Hermony of the Gospels, translated into the Kaffir tongue. Frederick William Kühn received the oversight of the mission as a whole, to be succeeded in his turn by Ferdinand Bechler in 1865, when elected a member of the Mission Board to fill the vacancy caused by the death of Bishop Cunow.

Meantime an advance was made into Kaffraria, at the request of government. John Henry Hartmann and Richard Baur advanced by ox-wagon into the Tambookie country eight or nine days from Shiloh, and found at Baziya a spot suitable for the commencement of a mission in the land of Chief Joyi, which Baur and his wife proceeded to occupy. The gradual advance into heathen Kaffraria lent special importance to a conference of missionaries engaged in the service of the eastern group of stations, held at Shiloh from February 18 to 20, 1863—a first step in the direction of separation into a distinct missionary province.

But in 1863 a sudden calamity gave a temporary check to the work in Kaffraria. Hitherto South Africa had been remarkably free from tornadoes, so far as the experience of the missionaries was concerned. Towards sunset on the evening of September 28 a cyclone struck Baziya without any warning. In a few seconds the mission-house was completely destroyed. But miraculously Baur and his family crept from the ruins unhurt, save for minor bruises. Parts of the house were found a mile away. The missionary's wagon had been broken in two and one half carried one hundred yards. Other articles were found two to three miles away. A temporary refuge was secured at the home of Mr. Gordon, the Anglican missionary at All Saints', about half a day's journey distant, until Baziya could again be made habitable.

The year 1867 finally marked an involuntary withdrawal from a sphere of activity. With the retirement of Küster and his wife from missionary service the care of the hospital for lepers

31

on Robben Island, their latest charge, at the desire of government passed from the Moravian to the Anglican Church. Thus the forty-five years' ministration to these poor sufferers in Africa came to an end. All the more opportune, therefore, was the overture received about this time from Baroness Keffenbrink-Ascheraden in respect to the founding of a similar institution at Jerusalem.

Long ago it has been said that "failures are with heroic minds stepping-stones to success." This was exemplified in connection with the mission in Australia. In May, 1858, Moravian missionaries were again at Melbourne, Spieseke, who had protested against the former retreat, being accompanied by Frederick Augustus Hagenauer. Sir Henry Barkly, the new Governor, and the Bishop of Melbourne lent their support. It was proposed by the former that the missionaries should now begin operations in the Wimmera District, a fairly watered tract and unlikely to become the scene of serious difficulties with the colonists. In accordance with this advice a site was fixed upon near Antwerp, a station belonging to a Mr. Ellerman, who gave the mission a section of his land and manifested continuous sympathy with the undertaking. The new mission received the name of Ebenezer. For a considerable time the only hopeful sign was the willingness of some of the people to give up their nomadic habits. Souls they scarcely seemed to have. If any race resembled the driest of the dry bones seen by Ezekiel, this was the one. But by and by to the amazement of their countrymen two of them, Bony and Pepper, young men, began to build something of a house in imitation of the one occupied by the missionaries. Nevertheless there did not as yet appear the faintest trace of interest in their message or of longing for salvation. For weary months it was a scattering of precious seed on bare rocks. The ingrained habit of begging, especially for tobacco, was a source of annoyance. Grossly material interests alone appealed to the blackfellows. Feuds often led to strife. Once Spieseke was in imminent danger. Spears and boomerangs were already flying. The women and children had fled or had taken to the trees. In a moment's intermission of strife he threw himself between the hostile parties, now forty or fifty paces apart. For a time it appeared as though his life would be the penalty. But calm, decided courage won the day, and peace was restored.

Suddenly in the midst of all that was unpromising, the story of Kajarnak received its counterpart. It is January 17, 1860. Hagenauer is absent, and Spieseke is showing to a group of savages pictures illustrating Scripture history. Now one is shown of a man kneeling in great distress, in a garden. An agony is on his brow. "What is that? Show me that again!" asks one of the group. "Pepper," says the missionary, "that is Jesus. He weeps; he is in great sorrow, and He weeps for thee, Pepper." It is told over and over again; and the thought of the suffering Saviour in Gethsemane awakens the long slumbering soul in the Australian savage. Hagenauer on returning recognizes that Pepper's interested question only confirms signs of an inner working of the Spirit that have already been somewhat perceptible to him. One Sunday when he is riding back from a distant appointment, one of the missionaries comes upon this same Pepper, preaching the Christ he has just found and only half knows to a company of about fifty associates. He is now given special instruction, and on August 12, 1860, is baptized, receiving the name Nathanael. On the same day the church at Ebenezer is dedicated. Gradually it became evident that the dry bones could be clothed with flesh and sinew, could receive a new heart and be filled with the inbreathing of the divine Spirit. Here progress was more rapid amongst the men than the women. Gradually the old terrible customs began to disappear, and the place commenced to assume the aspect of a neat village, good houses with nice gardens taking the place of the wretched heaps of bark-covered sticks. The "Mallee" gave place to fields. Christian family life was understood and appreciated. The school worked marvellous changes amongst the young.

Meantime the initial success encouraged friends in Melbourne, and led the Presbyterian Assembly of Australia to offer to supply the money for the establishment of another station, if the Moravian Church would furnish the men. The proposal was accepted. New recruits were sent out to the mission, and Hagenauer was appointed to explore Gippsland. On a reserve near Lake Wellington and on the banks of the Avon a new post was founded in 1863, Ramahyuk, that is in the blackfellows' tongue, "Ramah, our home." Here the first convert, James Matthews, was baptized in 1866. A vigorous school soon became characteristic of the place.

Similar success, however, was not vouchsafed to a third attempt in the wilderness eight hundred miles northwest of Ebenezer, near Cooper's Creek, whither the Brethren Walder, Meissel and Kramer were sent in 1866. Efforts put forth at Kake Kopperamanna, forty miles west of Lake Hope, had to be abandoned, owing to severe drought which scattered the blacks and compelled neighboring settlers to leave their sheep-runs. Furthermore the missionary association at Melbourne found it difficult to defray the expense of the mission. The three missionaries were therefore transferred elsewhere. Yet another point was also occupied by William Julius Kühn, namely, Yorke's Peninsula, about one hundred miles west-northwest of Adelaide; but after varying success the missionary passed into the service of another church.

Whilst Ebenezer and Ramahyuk advanced in numbers and various industries gave employment—sheep-raising at the former and the cultivation of arrowroot at the latter—it soon became evident that the church had been called to minister beside the death-bed of a race. The weaknesses inherited from generations steeped in unchecked vice had sapped the vitality of the people. Consumption and kindred diseases were almost universal. Births were few in proportion to the marriages.

When ignorance and conceit are amalgamated and fashioned into weapons of offence and defence they present an almost invincible front—invincible save by the grace of God. This the missionaries on the western Himalayas for years experienced. The opposition was one of supreme indifference and contempt. Outside of Chinese Tibet, Pagell and Heyde and Jaeschke might go where they pleased without hindrance. Buddhist monasteries might be invaded, and the folly of idolatry denounced under the shadow of prayer-mills and within the sight of shrines wreathed in incense, and yet no angry demonstrations be called forth—only dull scorn. Conviction of sin seemed impossible where the very conception of the actual nature of sin was lacking, so distorted was the mind and so benumbed the conscience of priests and people. It was often difficult even to gather an audience. If a village were entered in the course of a missionary tour, the people remained in their houses, to which the missionary had no access. If the weather permitted, the householders might be on the flat roofs. Then, the house door being fastened, the stranger must needs boldly mount up by a ladder outside. Possibly the people would meanwhile vanish. If they remained, he must be content to hear the invitation passed on to gather for the performance of the "*tadmo*," *i. e.*, juggler, merry-andrew, clown. A "holy" man will say to him: "Your religion is good perhaps; but you do not fear sin." "How so?" the surprised missionary replies. "You kill sheep." On his trying to prove that God has not forbidden this, and on his retorting that the Buddhist himself eats mutton when he can get it, the latter will say: "Yes, but I kill nothing, not even the merest insect." "But you let others do the killing for you." "That may be; but then only half the sin is mine. Besides I acknowledge and repent of my sins in the evening of each day on which I have eaten flesh."

In October, 1859, the arrival of their brides from Germany gladdens the hearts of these lonely men, and they can begin to enjoy some of the comforts of home life. Previous to this they have begun to employ a new method of making known their message. A lithographic press has been set up, and a Tibetan, Sodnom Stobkyes, who has been in their employ for some years, proves an adept at handling it. Thus Jaeschke begins to disseminate his translation of the Harmony of the Gospels. Copies can be sent into the great closed land, Chinese Tibet, by means of traders who come over the passes with their packages of salt fastened to the backs of sheep.

In 1865 Pagell and his wife establish a second station at Poo, in Kunawur, in the valley of the Sutlej, and nearer to the border which they wish to cross. Jaeschke, who will henceforth devote himself to the work of translation, is succeeded as superintendent by Theodore Rechler. But most noteworthy of all is the gleam of hope in the baptism of Sodnom Stobkyes and his son Joldan on October 11. In March of the following year their example is followed by two other men, and later by the wives of these last. Jaeschke's labor bears fruit in the publication of the gospel of St. Matthew in Tibetan by the British and Foreign Bible Society. But ill-health and the complete undermining of his wife's constitution necessitate his return to Europe in the following year. His translation of the New Testament must be completed there.

Meantime an unexpected opening offered itself. Small-pox was making fearful ravages in Chinese Thibet. Whole families had died out. In their extremity the people of Tso-Tso, one of the western provinces, sent for Pagell to stay the scourge by vaccination. Although in bed from sickness at the time the cry for help reached him, he regarded it as a providential summons, and set out over the passes scarcely free from snow. Nevertheless the officials had no intention of permitting his planting the gospel within the territory of the Dalai Lama. After he had vaccinated six hundred and thirty-nine persons, he was compelled to return. Not wholly disheartened by the inhibition of missionary labor in Tibet, Pagell persevered at Poo, and on December 15, 1868, baptized his first convert there, Baldan, now named Joseph. At Kyelang also a few others were added to the little church. Now the mission had reached the stage when indifferent tolerance passed into sharply accentuated hostility. The converts were ostracized.

CHAPTER LVII.

THE GENERAL SYNOD OF 1869.

Fifty-two representatives of the church and its missions met at Herrnhut on May 24, 1869, and organization was effected by the choice of Levin Theodore Reichel as President, with Bishop Ernest Reichel, William Mallalieu and Emil A. de Schweinitz as Vice-Presidents.

In the doctrinal position of the church only one change of significance was made, viz., it was stipulated that hereafter neither universal salvation nor the annihilation of the wicked shall be taught by any one who expects to remain in the fellowship of the Moravian Church.

In connection with the ritual, in response to petitions from America and England with reference to the mode of administering baptism, synod decided that whilst affusion or sprinkling shall continue to be the modes in use, immersion may be allowed in exceptional cases where it is a matter of conscience with the individual, provided this be not coupled with a rejection of the baptism of infants. The merits of each exceptional case are to be passed upon by the Provincial Elders' Conference having jurisdiction. Synod also gave its sanction to a usage desired by the American congregations and tentatively approved already by the Unity's Elders' Conference, viz., that candidates for ordination publicly confess their faith and pledge their fidelity to the church in answer to a series of questions addressed to them by the bishop.

The legislation with reference to church government and constitution was mainly a working out in further detail of some particulars not fully developed by the synod of 1857, or requiring readjustment, e. g., the mode of filling inter-synodical vacancies in those departments of the Unity's Elders' Conference which might be justly regarded as more narrowly constituting the governing board of the German Province. Whilst the choice was to be left with those most nearly concerned, the two other Provinces of the church should each have one vote in such an emergency, since these departments constituted a part of the board of appeal for the entire Unity. One proposed constitutional change was wholly rejected by the synod, viz., that henceforth all members of the governing boards of the Unity and of the Provinces and the superintendents of the larger mission fields should be consecrated to the episcopate, and no others, with the understanding that when they retired from active service of the church they should still be empowered to ordain but should no longer have a seat and vote *ex-officio* in general synods.

The request of the Northern synod in America for liberty to sub-divide the Province into Districts and to institute District synods, was granted, with provisos guaranteeing the rights of individual congregations and guarding against infringement of the General or the Provincial constitution. Similarly favorable action was taken in reference to the request of the Southern Provincial synod, approved already in the North, which sought to pave the way for an organic union of these two main divisions of the American Province.

In the constituency of general synods a slight change was made. With the alienation of the estates of the Unity in North Carolina by their transfer to the Southern Province, to congregations or individuals, the office of administrator ceased as a "Unity's office," and with it all reason for his presence in the general synod. The Secretary of the Missions in London, on the other hand, was added to the list of *ex-officio* members.

Obligation to have recourse to the official lot was now narrowed down to the appointment of bishops after nomination by the respective nominating bodies, and the acceptance of candidates for missionary service.

Synod definitely stated the aim of the missions amongst the heathen to be the winning of individual souls in such a manner that a self-supporting and self-dependent church might be ultimately secured. Cordial approval was given to measures taken during the past period with a view to the more systematic prosecution of the work. The first of these was the formulation of a code of regulations in 1867, designed to govern the mutual relationship of the mission board and the missionaries. The second was the introduction of cash salaries. Originally the missionaries had been merely supplied with the necessaries of life. Since 1836 circumstances had led to the gradual substitution of salaries in the West Indies. The third was the founding of an institute for the training of candidates for mission-service. On February 1, 1869, a "Mission Institute" had been opened at Niesky in Prussia by Alexander von Dewitz. It was clearly recognized that the Brethren's Houses no longer furnished either a sufficient number of men for the mission-fields or men adequately trained.

Provision was further made by synod for a uniform classification of the membership in the various mission congregations.. Detailed plans were devised for developing mission congregations in such a manner that their organization should more nearly approach that of the home churches, with church councils and the various committees or boards in vogue in the home organizations. At the request of the preparatory conference held at Shiloh, the South African work was divided into two Provinces, Shiloh, Goshen, Engotini and Baziya constituting the Eastern and the remainder of the mission stations the Western, that supervision might be facilitated, extension promoted, and the distinct problems of the two parts of the field receive the more thorough attention.

A new joint undertaking of the entire Unity was projected. Petitions had been received from England and from America of practically the same import, though there had been no preconcerted action. The one was from Bishop Seifferth, himself a descendant of members of the old Unity of the Brethren. The other had received the signature of every minister of the Moravian Church in the United States. Both memorials prayed that steps be taken to commence a work of evangelization in the twin-lands of the forefathers, Bohemia and Moravia, not on the basis of the *Diaspora*, but with a view to the reëstablishment of the Unity there as a distinct church. Synod accepted the peculiar coincidence and the fervent unity of the American ministry as tokens of a higher will. It was determined, that, while for the present good faith to sister evangelical churches required the continuance of auxiliary *Diaspora* work at Rosendorf, Tschenkowitz and Rothwasser, if openings offered elsewhere home missions like those in England and America should be undertaken in the seats of the fathers, provided permission could be secured from the Austrian government. Such enterprises were to be carried on in the name and at the cost of the entire Unity by a committee in Germany with associate members in the other Provinces, acting under the direction of the Unity's Elders' Conference. Coöperation heartily accorded, it was believed that ere long the name of the Brethren would once more become a power for good in places hallowed by the memory of ancient piety and fidelity.

Finally the Unity's Elders' Conference was reconstituted as follows: the Department of Education and of the Pastoral Office, Bishop Gustavus T. Tietzen, President, Bishop C. W. Cröger, Theophilus Reichel and William Verbeek; the Department of Finance, Gustavus Reichel, E. N. Hahn, George Frederick Martin and Henry Levin Reichel; the Department of Missions, Bishop Ernest Reichel, Levin Theodore Reichel, Augustus Clemens and Frederick William Kühn.

CHAPTER LVIII.

THE GERMAN PROVINCE, FROM 1869 TO 1879.

The German Province was granted an uneventful close to the year of the general synod, although premonitions of a coming storm were not wanting. In 1870 the tempest broke in its fury. On July 19 the formal declaration of war was delivered at the Prussian capital. Europe was speedily appalled at the rapidity with which battle followed battle, and at the awful carnage and devastation involved. Neuwied and Königsfeld dreaded a repetition of the scenes which had transpired early in the century. But after Saarbrücken had been followed by Weissenburg and Wörth and Spichern, and when the indecisive but bloody conflicts at Rezonville and Gravelotte had formed a prelude to Beaumont and Sedan, and Bazaine was content to remain in Metz, it became clear that France, not Germany, must be on the defensive. Yet the scourge of war left its marks on the victors also. There were those whose brothers or fathers or sons or husbands were carrying their lives in their hands for king and country. Neuwied, closing its schools temporarily, yielded its chief buildings, the church included, for hospital service, or for the fitting out of military establishments. The *Diaspora* in France suffered, Hillberg and Bönhof perforce leaving Bordeaux and St. Hippolyte. But Breutel at Strasburg experienced the dangers of the siege. Preliminaries of peace being signed on February 26, 1871, and the Treaty of Frankfort consummated on May 10, the union of Germany under Prussian leadership was an accomplished fact. The new status of civil affairs was followed by changes of significance for the church. Schools of every description were brought under governmental supervision. The difficulty of securing a sufficient number of thoroughly trained teachers was acutely felt. This led to the establishment of a normal school for male teachers at Niesky and of a similar institute for female teachers at Gnadau. Meanwhile a recently erected building was entered by the school for boys at Neuwied, on September 13, 1871, and in 1873 the flourishing school for boys at Lausanne in order to secure adequate accommodations effected a transfer to the castle of Prangins, near Noyon, on the west shore of Lake Geneva.

Events had also been transpiring in Switzerland, which placed the work of the Moravian Church on a new basis. There was no longer any good reason for maintaining the status of a sub-dued *Diaspora* in Canton Neuchatel. Hence, in 1873, congregations were organized at Montmirail, La Locle and Chaux-de-fonds and at Peseux, Marc Theophil Richard, Theodore Schütz and Eugene Reichel being their pastors.

In Germany itself death was busy among the leaders. Bishop Matthiesen had died on October 10, 1869, for thirty-three years a member of the governing board. Charles Frederick Schordan followed on October 31, 1870, for twenty-eight years the President of the college at Niesky, and then for nineteen years a member of the Conference. In 1874 Ernest Nathanael Hahn retired after forty years of active service, nine of them in the Conference. Augustus Clemens died on May 5, 1874, a member of the Department of Missions for ten years. On February 18, 1875, Bishop Breutel passed away, four score years of age. On February 3, 1878, Bishop Ernest William Cröger died. On May 23 Bishop Levin Theodore Reichel likewise heard the summons to come up higher. For twenty years he had been a most valuable member of the Department of Missions. America had enjoyed his services. Several times he had officially visited distant mission fields, and had also personally learnt to know the British Province and the *Diaspora* in Livonia and Esthonia. His was therefore a very thorough personal acquaintance with the work of the entire church. The most important of his recent official visits had been to the British Province in 1874, and his second visit to Labrador in 1876. The former of these was undertaken in conjunction with his colleague, Frederick William Kühn. Together they participated in the transactions of the Provincial synod held at Fairfield, from June 24 to July 8.

On May 27, 1868, a Provincial synod preparatory to the general synod of 1879 convened at Herrnhut. Henry Levin Reichel presided. A conservative tone prevailed. Two serious gaps were made in its membership before many days passed. Ernest L. Wünsche, the eloquent and influential pastor of the Berlin congregation for the past twenty-six years, had scarcely been excused from attendance by the advice of his physician, when on June 14 there came the news of his exceedingly sudden death. On the 19th of the same month Bishop Ernest Frederick Reichel, the Vice-President of the Unity's Elders' Conference, also died. He was seventy-one years of age, and had been a member of the Conference since 1850, oversight of the missions being his special sphere. Gustavus Reichel now became Vice-President. The vacancies in the Department of Missions were filled by the election of James Connor, of Ockbrook, England, and Eugene F. Reichel, of Peseux. Louis Erxleben was appointed to Berlin.

The most noteworthy of the transactions of the synod were the following: In connection with the doctrinal position of the church, the general synod was asked to refer to the Easter Morning Litany as giving in substance the faith as apprehended by the Moravian Church, and to avow acquiescence in the so-called Apostles' Creed. It was further desired to state more explicitly adherence to faith in the vicarious atonement of Christ, and to clearly confess His true divinity and true humanity. Confession of faith in the fellowship of believers in the church universal of which He is the head, and in eternal life and a blessed resurrection, should also be more definitely asserted. Synod took a position in regard to Sabbath observance in advance of continental usage. The liberal position of the Moravian Church in America respecting public vocal prayer by women in services of the church or in prayer-meetings was sharply antagonized.

Meanwhile anxieties were aroused in connection with Sarepta. Alterations in the ecclesiastical laws of Russia threatened to deprive it of its favored status. Freedom from military service was definitely abrogated, and the permanence of other privileges granted by the special concession appeared very questionable.

CHAPTER LIX.

During this decade increased liberality attests deepening appreciation of responsibility for the foreign missions, and the systematic activity of the *Juvenile Missionary Societies* established in the schools of the church trains the young to intelligently support this cause. Pensions are raised, and the movement for the equalization of ministerial salaries simplifies the problem of ministerial appointments. Union of evangelistic effort with sister churches may be observed here and there, and the visit of Messrs. Moody and Sankey with its attendant promotion of vital godliness in many parts has its significance for the Moravian Church in Great Britain and Ireland amongst the rest.

The Provincial synod assembled thrice. Fulneck welcomed the first convocation, on June 21, 1871. Bishop La Trobe presided. The following transactions may be recounted: Henceforth the general superintendence of the home missions shall be relegated to the Provincial Elders' Conference. Local committees shall assist in the management of details, and an auxiliary society is to be organized in every congregation. Heckmondwike, a filial hitherto of Mirfield, is to receive a minister of its own. Synod consents to the continuance of West Pennard, but recommends the abandonment of the field, if later developments render this step advisable. Provision is made for pensioning Irish Scripture-readers. Synod voices its deep interest in the newly commenced mission in Bohemia, and reiterates the responsibility of the Province over against the foreign missions. Bishop Seifferth and William Mallalieu on account of advancing years retire from the Conference. The new board is therefore constituted of Bishop James La Trobe, Bishop John England, and Thomas Leopold Badham; synod elects as Trustees of the Provincial Estates, William Taylor,

John William Scandrett, Robert Elliot and Herbert Edwards; as editor of the *Messenger*, Charles Sutcliffe, assisted by J. Hull, Jackson Shawe and Herbert Edwards.

Only a few weeks elapse when the entire Brethren's Unity mourns the loss of one of her most active and most widely known leaders, William Mallalieu, who died at Ockbrook on August 30, 1871. Born on November 22, 1798, at Fairfield, he commenced his service of the church in 1824, as warden of that congregation, and participated in the general synod of 1825. Ten years later he was called to London as agent of missions, and in 1847 and 1848 in conjunction with Bishop Hermann paid an official visit to the West Indies, returning by way of the United States. In 1857 his election as a member of the Provincial Elder's Conference placed in his hands the management of the Provincial finances, a task discharged with notable ability. Calm, steady, thorough and persevering in the prosecution of duties, his cheerful kindliness and large benevolence endeared him to the entire church. Repeatedly he represented his Province at general synods, and the devoted zeal of his friendly offices lightened the leave-taking of many a missionary when embarking for a distant land, or soothed the troubles of the aged or infirm or widowed or orphaned when returning. It was in keeping with his character and life, that his like-minded widow now in his memory presented the sum of $25,000 to various Provincial funds.

Besides witnessing the new advance at Heckmondwike, the year 1871 was noteworthy also for the commencement of systematic efforts to establish a home mission in the North of Ireland's busy commercial and manufacturing entrepot, Belfast. For three years the services of Scripture-readers were mainly employed, and in particular those of John James Hanna, of Kilwarlin. In December, 1874, however, William Lang was introduced as a resident home-missionary, rooms in the Abercorn Buildings, on Victoria Street, being rented. In 1877 Samuel Kershaw became his successor, and Lombard Hall was rented in 1878, to be used until 1877, when a church was erected.

In June, 1874, the synod again convened at Fairfield, owing to the desire of the Mission Board that the agency for the missions in London should be permanently undertaken by the Provincial Elders of the British Province, a change which would necessitate their removal from Ockbrook to the metropolis. Levin Theodore Reichel and Frederick William Kühn, of the Mission Board, were present to explain and urge the desirability of the change. The agency was constituted of the Provincial Elders, together with the Secretary of the missions and one other brother, at first the venerable Bishop James La Trobe. Thomas Leopold Badham was selected as the actually responsible agent, with J. F. Pemsel as the business manager in charge of affairs; and later a sub-committee of the Society for the Furtherance of the Gospel was also called in to assist. The seat of the Provincial Elders' Conference was transferred to London during the following year.

Synod ordered the removal of the college and seminary from Fulneck to Fairfield, that the students might enjoy the advantages of Owen's College (Victoria University), Manchester.

The Provincial Elders' Conference was constituted of Bishop England, Thomas Leopold Badham and William Taylor. Sutcliffe received as his assistants in charge of the church paper Jackson Shawe and John Daniel Libbey.

At the age of eighty Bishop Benjamin Seifferth entered into rest at Ockbrook, on January 31, 1876. His grandfather was Anthony Seifferth, the first Moravian minister ordained in what are now the United States of North America, and his great-grandfather was Georg Seifart, who with his wife Anna, *m. n.* Beyer, fled to Herrnhut from Zauchtenthal in Moravia. Born near Fulneck, on December 17, 1795, he had to contend with many disadvantages when young. But in men like Christian Frederick Ramftler and Charles Gotthold Reichel and Daniel Steinhauer he had found helpful friends, and by dint of perseverance had made himself acquainted with the classics and Hebrew. In 1814 he became a tutor in the prosperous academy of Joseph Hinchcliffe, first at Quarry Gap and then at Horton House. In March, 1825, his sphere of work was removed to Bristol, where he was engaged for four years as a classical and mathematical tutor. Then he accepted the directorship of a classical and academic institution on St. Michael's Hill, Bristol, a private undertaking enjoying the countenance of the church authorities. After for some time assisting Ramftler, of Bristol, in ministerial duties, in the year 1833 he agreed to undertake the temporary supply of Kingswood, though at first with hesitation and diffidence. Malmesbury became his first regular appointment after ordination in the following year. Having served in the pastorate of various congregations, he entered the Conference in 1843. For twenty-four years he was its President, and six times presided over the deliberations of Provincial synods. His consecration to the episcopate took place in 1846. One of his colleagues has paid the following tribute to his character: "He loved the Bible, he loved the classics, he loved young men, and he loved the church......Few men who have attained that honorable office have so fully come up to the inspired portrait of a bishop indeed."

In the same year another loss was widely felt, that of Jacob Amandus Eberle, pastor of Dublin, whose missionary descent had made itself perceptible in his advocacy of the mission cause, and whose methodic accuracy had been of signal value in synodical gatherings. He was in his sixty-first year.

On June 26, 1878, the synod convened at Fairfield, Bishop England presiding. By it the Irish Home Missionary Society and the Scripture Readers' Society were merged into one, under the true title of the latter organization, the Society of the Brethren's Church for Propagating the Gospel in Ireland. A revision of the hymn-book was resolved upon, and a committee appointed for the purpose—Bishop James La Trobe, James Connor, Joseph H. Willey and Bennet Harvey. "General Elders' Conferences," not for the purpose of legislation, but for mutual advice and coöperation and local supervision under the Provincial Conference, were appointed for the West of England, the Eastern counties and the North of Ireland. The benefits of this form of organization, the membership of which included practically all the ministers in active service in the District and the incumbents of such spiritual offices as "choir laborers," had already been enjoyed in Yorkshire and in Lancashire. Bishops John England and William Taylor, with William Robbins were elected Provincial Elders.

CHAPTER LX.

THE AMERICAN PROVINCE, FROM 1869 TO 1879.

In accordance with the sanction of General synod, the Provincial synod at York in the spring of 1870 sub-divided the American Province in the North into four Districts, in each of which annual conferences were to be convened, constituted of ministers and lay delegates. Legislative powers were not given to these bodies. Their function should be to promote vital religion within their district; to examine into, develop and strengthen the work of the church, collect information, hear complaints and grievances, examine into the causes thereof, endeavor to adjust and reconcile differences, examine how the enactments of synod are carried out in the district, and stimulate systematic beneficence. The congregations in the State of New York together with the congregation in Elizabeth, New Jersey, constituted the First District; those in Pennsylvania and Maryland, and the remaining congregations in New Jersey, the Second; those in Ohio, Indiana, Illinois and Michigan, the Third; those in Iowa, Wisconsin and Minnesota the Fourth. The first of these conferences took place in Brooklyn on January 25 and 26, 1871; and for several years the plan was carried out with regularity; but the financial depression of the entire country then necessitated an intermission of the conferences, especially where great distances separated the congregations and increased the cost of assembling.

Church extension meantime continued to receive paramount attention. In February, 1870, Edward J. Regennas was sent to Unionville, Huron Co., Michigan. A congregation was organized and attained successful proportions, notwithstanding severe forest fires in the autumn of 1871. Mamre, hitherto a filial of Lake Mills, in 1870 received its own pastor in the person of William Stengel. In June, 1872, the "Bethlehem Mission" in Philadelphia was founded, William H. Vogler becoming the first pastor. Coveville was separated from Hopedale, William H. Hoch taking charge. After a few years, however, this enterprise was reunited with its mother-congregation, owing to the decrease in population with the abandonment of the tanneries, the sole industry, after the clearing of the great forests of the Pocono region. The dedication of a church at Castleton Corners, on Staten Island, August 31, 1873, as a place of worship for a portion of the New Dorp congregation, practically marked a new advance, although no division of membership was made. Meanwhile in 1872 El Dorado, Wisconsin, and North English and Victor, Iowa, had been commenced. Next year Sturgeon Bay was separated from Ephraim, and received as its pastor Christian Madsen, a graduate of the mission institute at Niesky in Silesia. The steadily growing commercial importance of this thriving city, especially after the completion of the ship canal between Lake Michigan and Sturgeon Bay, rendered it one of the most important of the Scandinavian congregations. Next year Hebron, on the fertile plateaus of Winona County, Minnesota, was separated from Bethany, and placed in charge of Herman Meinert, and towards the close of the year Berea was organized. In October Joseph Mortimer Levering took charge of the new organization in Uhrichsville, Tuscarawas County, Ohio, and in the same month, Gerah, the filial of Mamre, dedicated its church. In the summer of 1875 a church was bought at Independence, Van Buren County, Iowa, and James Haman became pastor. Here as in other parts of the same state, the tendency to the consolidation of farms into large estates, with a consequent decrease of the rural population, militated against the work. More permanent, however, was the organization effected by Henry Lehman amongst German settlers at Manasseh, not far from Ephraim, Wisconsin, on October 25 of the same year.

On November 24, 1870, Bishop John Christian Jacobson died in Bethlehem. Born in 1795, at Burkal, in Denmark, he had come to America in 1816, serving first as a teacher in Nazareth Hall and then from 1824 to 1826 as a professor in the theological seminary. For eight years he had been pastor of Bethania, North Carolina, and was for ten years, 1834 to 1844, in charge of Salem Female Academy, serving also during the greater part of this period as a member of the Southern Provincial Elders' Conference. Transferred to the North, he became Principal of Nazareth Hall and a member of the Northern Conference, until his election as President of the latter body in 1849. Consecrated a bishop at Lititz in 1854, he remained President of the Conference for eighteen years, until the increasing infirmities of age compelled a retirement from active life. As one of the American delegates to the synod of 1848, he had contributed materially to the revision of the constitution of the church. Bishop Peter Wolle, who died on November 14, 1871, was born in 1792 at New Herrnhut, St. Thomas. In 1807 he became a member of the first class in the newly constituted theological seminary. His first ministerial appointment, that of assistant in Salem, was followed by service in the pastorate at Bethania, Lancaster, Philadelphia and Lititz. In Lititz he labored from 1836 to 1853, being also a member of the executive board. Here, too, he was consecrated a bishop on September 28, 1845, by Bishops Benade and Van Vleck. After an *ad interim* appointment to Canal Dover, in 1855, he was chosen a member of the Provincial Elders' Conference, and served till 1861, since which year he had been living in retirement at Bethlehem. Philip Henry Goepp, who died on Staten Island in March, 1872, was born in 1798, at Gnadenfrei. In 1852 he had been appointed a professor in the theological seminary at Gnadenfeld, and was one of the secretaries of the Unity's Elders' Conference from 1833 to 1834. His appointment as administrator in Pennsylvania brought him to America in 1834, and upon the separation of the Provinces he was elected a member of the executive board. Retiring from active life in 1861, he revisited Germany, but returned to America in 1870.

The synod which convened at Lititz in June, 1873, amended that by-law which prohibited a Provincial Elder from simultaneously holding some other ministerial appointment, and recommended that the members of the board should remove their residence from Bethlehem, if such a removal was found practicable and would result in decreasing the expenditures of the Sustentation Fund or improving its condition. This legislation led to practical results very soon. Scarcely two months had passed, when Sylvester Wolle, the Treasurer of the Conference, whose health had for several years been gradually giving way, died suddenly on August 28. He was in his fifty-eighth year, a man "full of untiring energy and zeal," "one of the most conspicuous and useful servants of the church." On November 17

Francis Raymond Holland, Principal of Hope Seminary, was elected his successor. "In order that this school might not suffer detriment, and to lessen the expenses of the Sustentation Fund, as also to test the practicability of accomplishing all that was required of an executive board having one of its members separated by a distance of nearly nine hundred miles from the other two," he continued to reside in Hope, retaining his position there, whilst his colleagues remained in Bethlehem, Robert de Schweinitz serving as President and Treasurer and Lewis F. Kampmann as Secretary. Other important changes transpired. Eugene A. Frueauff resigning the principalship of Linden Hall, was followed by Herman A. Brickenstein. In his place Jesse Blickensderfer became Secretary of Publications. On the day before Palm Sunday, 1874, Lewis R. Huebener died suddenly at Gnadenhütten. He had been a professor in the theological seminary from 1858 to 1864, and for the following two years its President. Later he had served in the pastorate at Bethlehem, Hope and Gnadenhütten. Henry J. Van Vleck was appointed his successor. Next year in July Bishop David Bigler died at Lancaster, where he had been pastor for eleven years. Born in 1806, at Hagerstown, Maryland, he had served for several years at Nazareth Hall, and then as a missionary in St. Kitts and Antigua. His pastorate in Lancaster had been preceded by similar labors in Philadelphia, New York and Bethlehem, where he had been consecrated a bishop on July 31, 1864 by Bishops Samuel Reinke, Peter Wolle and John C. Jacobson. Edmund A. Oerter succeeded him in Lancaster. Previous to this the church had lost by death, on January 21, 1875, Bishop Samuel Reinke, who had been living in retirement at Bethlehem since 1860. A companion of Bishop Peter Wolle as a member of the first class of the theological seminary, his had been long and varied pastoral service distinguished by fearless fidelity. On October 25 Martin Hauser died at Hope. To his untiring energy and zeal, Hope, Enon, West Salem and Olney owed their origin. He was now a venerable father of seventy-six years, and of late had been living in retirement.

When the Provincial synod convened at Nazareth, in May, 1876, church extension received chief attention. Synod decided to entrust this work to a "Provincial Board of Church Extension," to be constituted of four ministers and four laymen together with one Provincial Elder. To them was assigned the task of raising, prior to the next triennial synod a "Church Extension Fund" of fifty thousand dollars. The capital of this fund should ever remain intact, nor should any of the interest be used until the entire amount to be capitalized was in hand. Thereafter the interest should be loaned or donated, to assist home mission charges in the erection of churches or parsonages. The board was constituted of the following ministerial mem-- bers: Bishop Edmund de Schweinitz, Herman S. Hoffman, Edward J. Regennas and Henry Reusswig; lay members, Nath- anael S. Wolle, C. A. Zoebisch, Charles Gebhard and Joseph A. Rice; member of the Provincial Elders' Conference, Francis R. Holland. Herman S. Hoffman was elected Corresponding Secretary, and later Francis R. Holland became President, Edmund de Schweinitz and Henry Reusswig Vice-Presidents, C. A. Zoebisch Treasurer, and Joseph A. Rice Recording Secre- tary. The active canvass of the congregations was commenced by the Corresponding Secretary in September, 1876; but in June of the following year he was compelled by sickness to tem- porarily lay aside the duties of this office. The Recording Sec- retary assumed the duties of correspondence, and Edward J. Regennas continued the canvass of the congregations, visit- ing Illinois, Michigan, Wisconsin and Minnesota. By the fall of 1878 the cash assets of the fund amounted to $13,677.62.

District Boards of Church Extension were meanwhile organ- ized and although the general condition of business throughout the country was not propitious, several advances were made. An endeavor was put forth to separate Ixonia from Watertown, and Vincent Seifert was sent thither as pastor,; but in 1877 the former connection was reestablished. In October 1876 Fred- erick W. Shaw, a member of the Second Church in Philadel- phia, with the aid of a number of coadjutors from the same congregation, commenced a Sunday-school in the northern part of the city, and west of the Fourth Church. A congregation was organized on June 3, 1877, and later a church building on Germantown Avenue, above Dauphin Street was purchased. Work begun by Francis F. Hagen at Blairstown, Iowa, resulted in the formation of a congregation of which Charles L. Moench became pastor in 1878. In July, 1877, Charles Steinfort organ-- ized Osborne, Kansas. In November Henry Lehman gathered into a congregation Germans to whom he ministered at Egg

Harbor, Wisconsin, fifteen miles from Manasseh. In the same month preaching was commenced in a chapel at Giffords, on Staten Island, overlooking Great Kills. In 1878 Reusswig visited German settlers in the Red River valley in Dakota, twenty-five or thirty miles from Fargo, and the rich fertility of the wheat producing prairie suggested the name Goshen for the congregation organized in May.

Meanwhile serious trouble was arising. The summoning of the general synod for the year 1879 necessitated preparatory synods in the several Provinces. Early in 1878 the question of the time and place of convocation was discussed in *The Moravian*. The synod at Nazareth had accepted an invitation to hold its next session at Hope, and had appointed the year 1879 as the time. But since the majority of the members of the synod resided in the East, many believed that the cost of convening a synod at Hope would be materially in excess of the cost of meeting in the East. The financial condition of the Province was precarious. Owing to the panic of the early seventies, the earnings of the church schools in recent years had materially decreased, seriously affecting the general status. Every possible curtailment of expense seemed desirable. Before long it appeared that a serious difference of opinion existed between the members of the Provincial Elders' Conference in regard to their powers in relation to this subject. The two members residing in Pennsylvania held that the Provincial Elders' Conference was not merely the executive of synod, bound to carry out its resolutions in a mechanical way, but as well the directing board of the Province, qualified to initiate measures, or in an emergency to disregard formal orders of synod, with the understanding that such action on their part must be reported to the next ensuing synod for its judgment. They furthermore took the ground that the synod of Nazareth had directed that the regular triennial synod should be held at Hope; but that the Provincial Elders' Conference was competent to determine the place of convocation for this special preparatory synod. To all this their colleague took exception, and the congregation at Hope insisted upon what it believed to be its rights in the matter. Others entered into the controversy. Finally an appeal was taken to the Unity's Elders' Conference. Decision was given, that the Provincial Elders' Conference had the right to convene a preparatory synod wherever in their judgment it should be convened, but advised that the preparatory synod of 1878 be convened at Hope; and this advice was accepted, that the Province might be spared the cost of two synods in successive years. Synod, in session from October 9 to 24, with Bishop Edmund de Schweinitz as presiding officer, accepted the principle involved in the decision to the appeal, but memorialized the general synod to define more clearly and specifically the several rights, privileges, duties, powers and responsibilities of Provincial synods and Provincial Elders' Conferences, and their relations to each other and to the Unity's Elders' Conference. In respect to the constitution of the Unity's Elders' Conference, the following amendments were proposed to the general synod, with the expression of a desire that a separation be effected between the Unity's Elders' Confrence and the administrative board of the German Province: 1. That the Unity's Elders' Conference consist of seven members, to be elected by the general synod as heretofore. 2. That in future each Province be directly represented in the Unity's Elders' Conference by at least one member. 3. That when a vacancy occurs, by death or resignation of any member of the Unity's Elders' Conference, the vacancy be filled from among the ministers of that Province which has lost a representative, such Province to make nominations. 4. That in the actual election to fill a vacancy, each Province shall have an equal number of votes.

In connection with legislation of an internal character, a schedule of general collections was adopted in order to systematize benevolence and statedly meet general expenses. The Provincial Elders' Conference was reconstituted, five members being elected—Edmund de Schweinitz, Henry T. Bachman, Henry J. Van Vleck, Eugene Leibert and Herman S. Hoffman—with the understanding that not more than one of their number should receive a salary as such, and with the recommendation that two should reside west of the Alleghany mountains. The Church Extension Board was constituted of the Provincial Elders' Conference together with C. A. Zoebisch, Nathanael S. Wolle, Joseph A. Rice and Henry S. Rominger.

CHAPTER LXI.

THE FOREIGN MISSIONS, FROM 1869 TO 1879.

Significant of the place which the missions had come to assume in the life of the church were the dedication in September, 1871, of the home for missionaries on furlough at Kleinwelke, in Saxony, erected by voluntary gifts, and the presentation to the church of the "Whitefield House" at Nazareth, in Pennsylvania, designed for a similar purpose, and as the permanent residence of retired missionary couples, the gift, also in 1871, of John Jordan, jr., of Philadelphia.

Although the balance sheet presented to the synod of 1879 disclosed a deficit of $23,570, there was good reason to thank God and take courage. To thoughtful minds such a deficit emphasized the truth that the task of evangelizing the heathen world is and must remain for the Brethren's Church a work of faith, a providential provocation to renewed fidelity and yet more strenuous effort. This conviction was deepened by the action of the synod. After a searching investigation it declared that the causes of the repeated deficits in the accounts of the foreign missions "lie neither in defective administration at home nor in inconsiderate extension in the field itself. They rather lie in the considerable decrease in legacies received, and especially in the general embarrassment of business which shows itself in a decided lowering of direct contributions and in the lessening of the profits of industries carried on in various mission-provinces in behalf of the work. In addition larger demands have been made upon the mission treasury for the pensioning and educational accounts—and here the administration dare not abridge."

In Greenland it had been a very trying decade for Henry Kögel, superintendent since 1871, and for his associates. Despite the work of the two normal schools, at New Herrnhut and Lichtenau, very little advance had been achieved in the direction of self-dependence. A veritable army of misfortunes, officered by influenza and pleurisy and other diseases, had swept up and down the coast in the winters of 1871 to 1872 and of 1875 to 1876. Poor Friedrichsthal, thus far the largest and richest of the congregations, had especially suffered. Once its four hundred and sixty-nine people had been wont to bring to the Royal Trading-post one thousand three hundred barrels of seal oil in a season. After the disastrous winter of 1871 only eight seal-catchers were left, only five boats could be manned, and out of twenty-three boys in the school only three had fathers living. Of those who had died six were male "helpers" and five female "helpers," a severe loss to the mission, as it was not easy to find persons suitably qualified for the position. Missionaries and traders had to come to the relief of the widows and orphans in a most liberal manner.

By this time every station and out-station had its school. Every child connected with the mission acquired the ability to at least read, and the majority also to write and to cipher as well as to memorize Biblical history. The girls learnt sewing and the arts of feminine handiwork.

In 1871 a new and revised edition of the Greenlandic Scripture History was issued, and in 1878 a similarly improved edition of the Hymn Book. In 1873 a Catechism, in 1876 a song book for schools, with notes; and in 1877 and 1879 volumes of sermons for the use of "helpers" at the out-stations, were welcome additions to the literature of the language. Kleinschmidt also prepared a dictionary, and labored at a revised translation of the Scriptures.

In Labrador extension continued to be the goal. The attempt of Samuel Weitz at Nachvak had been frustrated by a variety of circumstances, and the house erected there had to be temporarily abandoned. But in 1871 the determined missionary with his devoted wife and Adolphus Hlavatschek—the latter to superintend the trade—were willing to go once more to the far north. They selected Nullatatok Bay, a natural, land-locked harbor, sixty miles north of Hebron, surrounded by dizzy, snow-capped crags. The waters of the bay extend inland about four miles, and the entrance is almost barred by a majestic cliff beetling up precipitously a thousand feet above the surf. A beach about five hundred yards long by three hundred wide forms the only available site for dwellings. Here, with a lake-like expanse of blue water before them, the missionary party speedily put up the little one-roomed house which was at first to serve as residence, school and church. Later the abandoned dwelling at Nachvak should be removed hither. Only two families of heathen now lived at Nullatatok. But with the founding of Ramah, as they named the new post, it was hoped that in time the nomadic savages would be induced to cluster here. In any case it was felt to be the true way to commemorate a mission jubilee, by pushing forward into the "regions beyond." On October 11, 1875, the first reward of this bold faith came in the baptism of Kangersaut (Boaz), Salome and Mary and two children.

For Theodore Bourquin, superintendent of this mission Province, the years were full of cares. His own health and that of his wife necessitated a return to Europe for a furlough in 1871. On resuming his duties he was compelled to deal with a very difficult situation. This arose from the unavoidable connection of the mission with trade. From almost the inception of the work in Labrador this had been carried on for a variety of reasons—not to make profits as a main purpose, but that the comforts and sometimes the necessaries of life might be procured by the natives without their being at the mercy of conscienceless speculators, whose transient visits moreover inevitably produced demoralizing results, and that the effort to advance the people in the scale of civilization might be facilitated by their being furnished an opportunity to dispose of the products of their industry at fair rates. Besides the maintenance of a vessel afforded the mission its only sure connection with Europe. But in the case of people with a disposition like that of the Eskimo, their two-fold relationship to the Europeans as their religious teachers and the purveyors of their external comforts, afforded occasion for misunderstandings and mistrust. In seasons of scarcity they would expect to obtain credit at the stores, and humanity compelled the granting of supplies to refuse which would mean direst want. But that obligations thus incurred must be repaid in the case of the ablebodied in seasons of plenty, was a conception not so readily apprehended or assented to by the Eskimo. The difficulties which thus arose led to a complete separation between the spiritual and the temporal administration at each settlement in the year 1866. Men were sent out from Europe or henceforth exclusively charged with a commission to act as traders, to whom no spiritual duties were assigned; and henceforth the missionaries were to have no other relationship to the people than that involved in their spiritual office. For a few years all went well. But disaffection did not wholly cease. Nor did discontent end in murmurings. On March 28, 1873, when Charles Adolphus Slotta was busy in the store at Okak, a man suddenly and without warning attacked him and threw him down. The natives who were present failed to interpose, and ran out. No serious injury was inflicted. The store was closed, and business suspended, until the culprit voluntarily withdrew from Okak and his fellow countrymen besought that it might be reopened.

Next winter there was scarcity at several places—no seals, very few foxes, few ptarmigans, little fresh meat. At Nain influenza appeared in autumn. A number of thefts occurred, attributed to the stringency of the times. William Haugk, the store-keeper shut the door, and put up the shutters, and declared that business would not be resumed till the stolen articles had been returned. This measure failed of the desired effect, but led to the holding of a mass meeting by the Eskimos on December 22. It lasted for three hours and was tumultuous in the extreme. Even the "helpers" acted with the turbulent. Happily the celebration of Christmas brought most of the lawless to their senses; many of them expressed their penitence, and the way was now open for negotiations looking toward a readjustment of affairs by Samuel Bindschedler, the superintendent of the trade and chief agent of the Society for Propagating the Gospel. Reconciliation was effected. The celebration of the Holy Communion on January 17 was characterized by deep solemnity. But alas! the feelings of the natives carried them into fanaticism and worse. Such an outburst took place a few days later as would have been thought impossible in the case of the phlegmatic Eskimos. The ringleader in what followed was the man who had been most outspoken in connection with the lawlessness of December. At an assembly held in the house of this man an actual descent of the Holy Spirit was claimed to have been experienced. "A post in the house was worshipped as the cross of Christ, and the Eskimos were fetched in from neighboring houses that they might kneel before it. The leaders then breathed upon their hands folded on their breasts, thus imparting to them the Holy Spirit. The celebration of the Lord's Supper was also travestied." Next day the missionaries had to rescue a woman from the murderous assault of her husband, who was deluded with the belief that she was possessed by a devil. It was a critical hour for the mission at Okak. But God heard his servants' prayers. The extravagances vanished as suddenly as they had appeared. Further disturbances were attempted by the ringleader in the trouble, but his former associates silenced him. A welcome calm ensued.

All these experiences rendered a visit by a number of the Mission Board desirable. Bishop Levin Theodore Reichel, in spite of his weight of years, undertook the delicate task, being especially qualified by his former visit to Labrador. His efforts during the summer of 1876 were instrumental in restoring confidence on the part of the people, whom he exhorted to sobriety in thought and act, to careful thrift and diligence. The regulations with reference to the trade were revised, with a partial return to the arrangements which obtained prior to 1866.

The visitor was gratified to observe signs of advance in civilization during the period since his former coming to Labrador. Two stations had been added. At the various missions the old sod-huts were disappearing, log houses taking their place. Neatness and order appeared within. Hunting was on the decline, but fishing was improving. Skin-canoes were being replaced by fishing-smacks. The number of dogs, the all important means of transportation in winter, had more than trebled. Family life supplanted the ancient herding of the people in the overcrowded hovels of former days. Education was making progress, and natives were able to serve as schoolmasters. All this rendered the publication of the Scriptures the more opportune. Thanks to aid given by the British and Foreign Bible Society, Erdmann's translation of the Old Testament from Joshua to the Song of Solomon had been issued in 1870 and 1871; and Bourquin's revision of the Eskimo New Testament came out in 1878. Besides a Catechism and a revised edition of the Hymn-book and a text-book for instruction in geography had been placed in the hands of the people.

Amongst the important transactions of the general synod of 1869 not the least important had been the series of resolutions to provide for the gradual emergence of the West Indian congregations from the status of missions, so that they might constitute a fourth federated province of the Brethren's Unity. Loyally the missionaries and their people accepted and responded to the demands thus made upon them by the church. Yet neither well-informed observers, nor the workers in the field itself overlooked the fact, that islands where considerable illiteracy, the superstitions of Africa, the dark practices of obeahism and poisoning and very lax conceptions of personal morality still abounded could not be spoken of in the same breath with lands where inherited tendencies of generations, that had known nothing else than the Christian standard of ethics and that had enjoyed ample facilities for enlightenment, made for at least the appearance of godliness as persistently as the West Indian environment made for the contrary. In one sense the West Indies must remain mission ground for decades, even though no longer a field for missions exclusively amongst utter pagans.

Providential circumstances interfered sorely with the solution of the financial problem of self-support, particularly in the Eastern islands. Retrogression in the general economic condition was produced by earthquakes and tornadoes—Antigua and St. Thomas, for example, experiencing a hurricane in August, 1871, which involved a loss of $10,000 to mission property, and damage to sugar estates from which it took years to recover—protracted and repeated seasons of drought that caused abandonment of estates now become unproductive, with lack of employment for very many.

Nevertheless steps were taken towards self-dependence. One important measure was the founding of a theological seminary at Fairfield, in Jamaica, in 1876. Walter L. G. Badham, at the same time Principal of the normal school, took charge. A two years' course of studies was pursued. The normal school for females at Bethabara, and its counterpart in St. John's, Antigua, continued to render valuable services. That for young men at Cedar Hall, on the other hand, was abandoned in 1871. The Mico Institution was open to members of all denominations, and its excellent equipment rendered it needless to maintain the similar school of the church.

In 1872 Abraham Lichtenthaeler retired from active service. He was succeeded as superintendent in Jamaica by Edwin E. Reinke. In the same year the venerable Bishop Westerby

GEORGE WALL WESTERBY.

closed his long period of oversight in Antigua—thirty-eight years.

The migration of West Indians to Demerara now caused an extension of the missionary activity to this South American colony. The proprietor of the extensive Bel Air estate, Mr. Quintin Hogg, well known for his philanthropy in connection with the Polytechnic Institute in London, desired the services of a Moravian missionary for his employes, and offered to provide the salaries of a missionary and of an assistant, who should serve as school-master, for five years. After visits by Henry Moore, a native minister in Barbados, in company with the superintendent of the mission on that island, James Y. Edgehill, the offer was accepted. In October, 1878, Moore, with Alexander Pilgrim as his assistant, left for Georgetown. Services were commenced early in November at Cumming's Lodge.

In addition to the direct opposition of the "*sukias*" and the difficulties inseparable from missionary effort amongst nomadic savages of the tropics, on the Moskito coast indirect hindrances were now caused by the uncertain political status of the country. Enlarging intercourse with traders, who exchanged gin and rum and brandy for the valuable india-rubber of the Indians, further ministered to the positive corruption of many.

Fevers are never wholly absent from this swampy tropical land. Hence changes in personnel were frequent, and were the more unfortunate since the idiosyncrasies of the Moskito syntax and of the Indian love of metaphors could not be acquired in a day. It was this partial lack of men which measurably accounted for the abandonment of Joppa, on Corn Island, in 1871. Its few people had gladly looked to the missionaries for medical aid, but manifested marked indifference to their message. On the more populous mainland the readiness to receive the word claimed the services of all available men. Yet Corn Island was not altogether deserted. In the same year in which Joppa was given up, a Mr. and Mrs. Hall, from Bristol, England, came to the Moskito Coast to do missionary work, and settled at Quamwatla, a small village on the shore of a little lake drained by a tributary of Prince Apolka River, and about half way between Pearl Key and Ephrata. Within less than one month Mr. Hall died. His widow first removed to Ephrata. Next year she took pity on the forsaken condition of Corn Island, and removed thither to commence a school. Here her labors were not appreciated as they deserved. Her health gave way under the strain. She was reluctantly compelled to return to England in 1875. But the memory of that lonely grave at Quamwatla led her to present the sum of $5,000 to the Mission Board for the establishment of a new station on the Moskito Coast. This gift was used for the permanent founding of Karata on the Wawa River, north of Ephrata, which Frederick Smith, a graduate of the normal school in Jamaica, had just commenced as a filial. Another out-station had also been commenced, Kukallaya, across the lagoon west of Ephrata and some distance inland, the fruit of the labor of Peter Blair, who had removed thither in 1871. Here a village of about three hundred Indians clustered along the banks of a small stream.

Experience had taught the need of a staunch little vessel for communication from station to station along this coast, but the third *"Messenger of Peace"* became unseaworthy after only five years of service. In June, 1874, moreover the little *"Meta,"* her predecessor, was driven ashore near Greytown and dashed to pieces. In response to a new appeal the keel of the *"Herald,"* a trim little schooner of forty tons, and fifty feet in length, was laid in the ship-yards at Shoreham, and in September, 1875, she cast anchor in the lagoon at Bluefields. But on the night of October 2 and 3 of the following year a mighty hurricane swept the Moskito Coast. Bluefields, Magdala, Rama and Bethany each suffered severely. During the tornado the *"Herald"* was in imminent danger. A vessel riding at anchor beside her in the harbor at Bluefields went down with several on board. She was then driven into the mangrove swamps lining the lagoon. Here she lay sheltered, and suffered no material injury. Had she not been spared to transport provisions to the stations which were now threatened with famine from the destruction of their banana groves and provision grounds and from a plague of locusts and grasshoppers that followed, the consequences of the storm might have been disastrous for the mission.

Surinam even more than the Moskito Coast experienced changes in personnel during these ten years. Theophilus van Calker had been appointed Director of the school for the sons of missionaries at Kleinwelke after the synod of 1869. His successor, Theodore Enkelmann, had scarcely become accustomed to his duties as superintendent, when he was compelled to retire owing to a painful malady, and died at Herrnhut in 1870. Herman Clemens, the next in charge, died at Salem on the Coronie in 1872. Now Eugene Langerfeld stepped into the breach. Moreover, seven other brethren and ten sisters of the missionary force died during the period, and ten brethren and sixteen sisters were compelled to retire from active service on account of age or sickness.

With it all the era was a critical one for the mission from another cause. Final and complete emancipation of the slaves went into effect on July 1, 1873, the period of apprenticeship having come to an end. Government no longer exercised control over contracts for labor. It was inevitable that the blessing of liberty would be abused in some cases, and that removals of the people hither and thither until new adjustments had been made, would sever ties that had bound many to the mission and to restraining influences as regards their morals. Immorality at times became the product of a liberty that degenerated into license. In other cases the ambitious aped after "quality," and mistook glittter for worth. The tendency which ever drives labor to the large cities in the hope of easier or more remunerative work came into full play. On many estates the planters began to feel the lack of men. This led to the importation of Chinese and of Coolies, whose heathenism exercised a depraving influence on the blacks. Efforts were forthwith set on foot to carry the war into the very camp of the new paganism; but the barrier of language could not at once be overcome. Small wonder that in the ten years the numbers of the mission fell from 24,156 to 21,636.

In the educational system of the Colony the mission began to play a more important part than ever. The normal school at Paramaribo continued to supply well qualified native teachers. Governmental examinations tended to raise the standard, and the Director himself was required to have passed a pedagogic examination in Holland. At the close of the year 1878 the scholars enrolled in the day-schools of the mission numbered 7,269. Thanks to the liberality of the missionary society in Zeist, since 1875 the scope of this branch of activity had been widened by the establishment of a primary school in the city. It soon reached an attendance of 150.

But whilst the congregation in Paramaribo and those on the estates occasioned grave solicitude during the period of transition, new life appeared in the Bush Country. On the Surinam

33

River, just north of the fifth degree of north latitude, and due east of Maripastoon, lies Berg-en-dal. This is a timber-producing estate, which the church purchased in 1870, being at a convenient distance from Gansee, Victoria and Coffycamp. At this point the river curves so as to form a kind of harbor. On the lofty bank of the stream, and approached by a flight of steps is the solidly built "great house" of the estate, seventy years old but as serviceable as if new—one story in height and fifty-five feet by twenty in dimensions. In the rear towers up the steep hill which gives the place its name. Eighty houses clustering among the mango trees along the bank constitute the village of the negroes whose thrift is instanced by the fifty or sixty boats or corials usually moored in the stream. Here in the olden "great house" the missionary Lehmann makes his home in April, 1870, with David Peter Iveraar, the son of the helper Thomas of Gansee and a graduate of the normal school, as school-master. At Gansee also a church could be opened on September 30, and before long a house was erected and provision made for a resident missionary.

In happy contrast to the perplexities of Surinam South Africa now presents in the main signs of advance both in externals and in the inner life. In general there is peace throughout the decade, and missionary labor moves on harmoniously.

In the Western Province, the division having been effected in accordance with the resolution of the synod of 1869, William Theodore Bauer succeeded Ferdinand Bechler as superintendent upon his election as a member of the Department of Missions in 1874. Special attention was paid to the efficiency of the normal school at Genadendal. Examinations by government inspectors reflected special credit upon Ballein and Zachert, the missionaries in charge. Seven of the thirty-one students whose preparation was completed during the present decade were members of the Reformed Church or of the Berlin Mission. Thus the Moravian Church was permitted to contribute to the solution of the problem of Africa's evangelization beyond the bounds of her own mission fields.

The development of the railroad system of the Colony now afforded abundant employment to the members of several congregations. But with this advantage evils were combined— the temporary removal from the wholesome influences of the religious life of the mission stations, contact with irreligious whites and temptations to fall into drinking habits, for canteens sprang up like mushrooms in the vicinity of the camps of the laborers. Yet much transpired at the mission centers themselves to warrant the hope that growth in grace was permanent and deep. Mamre, distinguished as the point of extension in the Western Province through the establishment of its filial, Johanneskerk or Pella, especially enjoyed a deepening of its religious life. At Elim an awakening amongst the school-children in 1876 gave promise of a bright future. The churches at Enon and Clarkson were enlarged in 1870 and 1871, and a new church built at Snyklip, and new schools at Mamre and Elim, without drawing upon the mission treasury.

Theodore Weitz was appointed superintendent of the newly organized "Eastern Province," with headquarters at Shiloh. Extension of labor amongst the "red" Kaffirs called forth all energy. The Kei River now formed the boundary between British and Independent Kaffraria. The natural features of the latter region were striking. "Consisting farthest from the sea of lofty plains on the slopes of the Sturm and Draken ranges, the ground is hilly and undulating nearer the coast, being intersected by the picturesque and well-wooded Amatola range and its spurs, which have been described as the home of the Kaffirs, and have always formed their chief stronghold in their wars with the Colony. The climate is healthy, and the soil in the well-watered regions wonderfully fertile. Snow at times covers the higher mountains, and appears occasionally for a very brief period in the plains. The heavy rainfalls during the winter months are often very destructive, and cause delay and peril to the traveler. The elephants, quaggas, zebras and many other kinds of antelopes, which were common here not many years since, have begun to disappear from most parts of the country before the advance of civilization." Here a still powerful people, numbering about three hundred thousand, were massed in four chief tribes. Physically resembling the Caucasian rather than the Negro or the Hottentot, with brown skin, however, and woolly hair, the Kaffir was a born warrior. His importance was reckoned by the number of his cattle and of his wives. In number the latter were limited only by his ability to purchase. His mental capacity was higher than his moral qualities. Theft and lying were not esteemed disgraceful as means to an end. Lighthearted and cheerful, sociable and hospitable, he was amiable so long as his will was not crossed; but then capable of sudden passion, he could combine ferocity and cruelty. His religion was a compound of atheism and superstition. His witch-doctors possessed even greater power than his chiefs. The *"umhlahlo,"* or smelling dance gave them good opportunity for exercising their cunning—certain mummeries by the aid of which it was pretended that they could smell out persons guilty of having inflicted sickness or misfortune on any individual through uncanny means. The most frightful tortures were meted out to the victims designated by spite or envy. Stretched out upon the ground with arms and legs extended, and hands and feet pinned to the earth by sharp stakes, ants of a peculiar kind, whose bite was very painful, were shaken all over them to torment them by creeping into eyes, nose, ears and mouth, besides stinging all over the naked body. Finally fires were kindled so as to slowly roast them to death. Amongst their religious rites, circumcision had a place, and was attended with licentious abominations. Kaffir corn, from which beer was malted, maize, melons, and tobacco were cultivated by the women. Primitive industries, like tanning, pipe-making, blacksmithing and basket-weaving and pottery, were somewhat practiced. Feudal and patriarchal features combined to characterize their mode of government. "The hereditary head of a tribe (*ukumkani*) had under him several minor chiefs (*inkosi*), whose dignity was also hereditary. The *"ukumkani"* decided questions of peace or war, and settled disputes amongst his subordinate rulers; but each of the latter had full authority over the people in his own district, subject only to the advice and control of his councillors (*ampakati*). The *"inkosi"* is appealed to for help by the poor, and as the father of his people is expected to give what is needed, a cow, or a sheep, or a *"kaross."* If it were not for the many fines imposed on transgressors, the herds and possessions of many an *"inkosi"* would rather dwindle. Generally speaking, the *"inkosi"* was endowed with sufficient business capacity to make the dignity he he held afford him a fair pecuniary return. In all judicial proceedings, which were conducted with a certain degree of dignity, the accused was considered guilty, until he had proved his innocence; if the *"inkosi"* was the accuser, he was almost sure to be condemned. Murder was punished with death, all other crimes with fines in cattle, a penalty which the Kaffir called being "eaten up." The nearest relatives of the con-demned were expected to contribute, if a man was unable to pay the full amount of the inflicted fine. From early years their laws were a matter of deep interest to the natives, which they delighted in discussing; in this occupation they often displayed a striking degree of those qualities which distinguish a lawyer."

In Independent Kaffraria there still remained a wide field for pioneer activity, and Baziya here formed a point of vantage for the future extension of the Moravian mission. When there-fore repeated requests for a missionary were presented at Shiloh from Zibi, chief of the Amahlubi, and a vassal of the great chief Ngangelizwe, it was recognized as a providential call. Hart-mann of Goshen and Richard Baur of Baziya made a tour of reconnaissance by ox-wagon in April and May, 1860. But meanwhile the settlement of various territorial disputes through the mediation of the governor of British Kaffraria had involved the removal of Zibi from the border country near Shiloh, to Nomansland, a district bounded by the Draken Mountains and the rivers Tina and Xinixa being apportioned to his Hlubis and to Lubenya's Basutos. The tour of exploration resulted in the calling of Henry Meyer of Engotini, to establish a mission in the new home of the Hlubis, with Samuel Mazwi as his assist-ant. In the early part of November the veteran, by this time an accomplished Kaffir linguist, made a lonely journey of a week through the trackless wilderness, accompanied only by two Christian Kaffirs. The chief himself was not at home; but his wife accorded a cordial welcome at Ezincuka (*i. e.* among the wolves), amid the sandstone crags of the Draken, where the primitive shelter of a cave whose front had been walled up, afforded the missionary a temporary home. Though the place was two hundred and forty miles from Engotini and seventy-five miles from the nearest white man, and four days' journey on horseback distant from the nearest point whence a letter might be despatched, he determined to bring his wife and child-ren hither. In the spring of 1870 they set out. Three weeks of exhausting travel compelled her and their four children to remain at the English mission of St. Augustine. No wagon had ever crossed the mountains. There was no path. At one impassable spot a road had to be broken with the help of Zibi's men. When Meyer reached his kraal, one of the innumerable Kaffir wars had broken out. Meyer must hasten from chief to chief to endeavor to make peace. Under the circumstances Ezincuka was untenable. But he would not retreat. Somewhat to the northwest, in a central position between five mutually hostile heathen tribes, but with the full consent of the local chief, Lehanna, who claimed jurisdiction, he drove the first stake of the new station—Emtumasi. His house was built high up amid the rocks, for safety. Then he returned for his wife. Their trip was thrillingly perilous. Hostile marauders all around, once their wagon upset. A fall of snow on the mountains drove them for shelter within a smoky Kaffir hut, without window or chimney. Sixteen days they tarried here. But it was not lost time. Some of the people were found to have formerly lived at Shiloh. The enforced halt brought them a gracious opportunity to hear God's Word daily. At last Emtumasi was reached, and the work of evangelization commenced. As many as fifty dusky warriors sought the missionary's ministrations. But scarcely were hopes awakened when muttering thunders of strife rolled around the mountains. Assegais gleamed. Zibi was on his defence. Lehanna scoured the country. Provisions were scarce. The cattle of the mission were stolen. Once during this time of terrible anxiety Meyer was compelled to be absent at Shiloh, securing provisions, and conveying word to the colonial authorities respecting the state of affairs. The wife and children are indeed "among the wolves." Swollen rivers detained the husband for weeks. Fuel failed at Emtumasi. The lonely woman and children must search for miles for brushwood and dry grass. Their candles gave out, and the evenings and nights were long. Then cruel Lehanna came and boasted of the Basuto missions which he had plundered. Two of the children were seized with typhus fever. But God was merciful. They recovered, and the husband rejoined her in her extremity. It was just in time. Presently clouds of smoke ascended from Zibi's kraal. Lehanna's threats seemed about to be verified, for Zibi's men were scattered to the crannies of the mountains. On the heights above the mission the Basuto yells rang out, and the hills echoed with the fierce beat of spears on shields. But God was merciful. For some unknown reason the foes drew off.

Then followed two years of utter solitude. The chieftain who had invited Meyer to Nomansland did not dare to show his face. But Meyer faithfully sought out the hiding places of Zibi's men, and their hearts were somewhat softened by distress. Moreover his energetic representations to the British commissioner proved a factor in hastening the restoration of peace.

Now came reward. For Zibi and his men it was good to have been afflicted. A hunger for the Word and for enlightenment arose. The assegais were gladly laid down and primers and spelling-books taken in hand. A little village sprang up beside the mission house. By August, 1873, thirteen converts met around the Lord's table, and nine candidates desired baptism. Out-stations were soon required. The cry "What must I do to be saved?" passed from kraal to kraal. On Sunday crowds came from far and near, no longer smeared with war paint, no longer in nakedness and filth, but clean and clothed.

Ludini, Zibi's uncle, was a dignified old man, somewhat laconic, but apt to speak to the point. Now he repeatedly put one question to Meyer, at each visit, "Where is my teacher?" His people also desired to learn of Christ. Their appeal could not be set aside. Building operations were therefore commenced at this new point, twenty-seven miles away; but the money at the disposal of the missionary was soon exhausted. Yet Meyer was not downcast. Gathering his Emtumasi Christians, he and they prayed for means to complete what had been begun for Ludini. The very next day a letter from America brought a sum which sufficed to complete the mission house; and so they called it *"Elokulweni"*—*i. e.*, in faith. Thither the Meyers removed, native Brethren taking care of Emtumasi and its two filials, Tinana and Mvenyane, until missionaries could come to the help of the pioneer. For he needed relief. Overwork, anxieties, exposure, and in addition to all a painful tumor in the left shoulder rendered a furlough absolutely necessary. Nevertheless he was indefatigable in pastoral visits and evangelistic labors. But at last he must bid farewell to his children in the faith. On January 6, 1876, he turned away from the Draken Mountains, and from the four mission stations planted by him in a heathen land. In London and in Holland he kindled large audiences by his enthusiasm in spite of pain. But medical experts assured him that an operation was his only hope. This was attempted in Marburg. Only beside his bed was his family circle ever fully complete on earth—a typical missionary family in this. In the wanderings of his delirium he was even yet with his Kaffirs. Their tongue had banished the speech of his boyhood. And so, in fancy still at his post, Meyer embraced his wife for the last time, and whispered the name of their youngest son and of the Saviour, and passed to reward, not quite fifty years of age.

Elukolweni and Mvenyane were in charge of Alvin Richter; at Tinana Otto Padel was stationed, whilst Emtumasi was entrusted to John Nakin, the efficient native assistant. And in the following years each steadily advanced.

Meanwhile, another "*inkosi*," Stokwe, a Tambooki living about halfway between Shiloh and Baziya, had requested that a missionary be sent to him. John Henry Hartmann, together with Paul Gwazela of Goshen were dispatched, and so in 1874 Entwanazana was founded on the Umtata River.

But now perplexities thickened. The result of many negotiations for a grant of land at Emtumasi, adjudged by the commissioners to be within the sphere of Lubenya, the Basuto chief, was a refusal on his part. Moreover his vassals persisted in regarding the work of the mission there from a tribal standpoint. For them to join a Hlubi organization would be disloyalty. Therefore a reluctant withdrawal of the missionary for a season seemed to be the only alternative. In addition rumors of a coming Kaffir war, to be of dimensions far exceeding any preceding one, filled the air. Guns and rifles with bayonets found a ready sale in frontier settlements. Soon after Christmas the Gcalekas, joined by Bowana's and Lehanna's Basutos, rose in an effort to throw off the British yoke. Stokwe joined the raiders. Nganglizwe was restless, yet loyal to those whose suzerainty he had accepted. Hence in God's providence, the entire Kaffir mission did not become involved, as had been feared. The campaign was brief. Sandili, a troubler of the peace for years, fell in a skirmish. Kreli, chief of the Gcalekas, hid in the fastnesses of the mountains. Stokwe was defeated and captured. Sir Bartle Frere, in the name of Queen Victoria, could offer amnesty to all except a few ringleaders. But Entwanazana had been looted and stood in ruins. In June, 1878, Hasting returned. His former people had been scattered, the land being taken away from Stokwe's Kaffirs. Yet seventy-eight souls could soon be reported as gathered round him.

Meantime the older congregations of the Eastern Province were beginning to assume a more distinctively Christian character. Chief hindrances remained the disorders attendant upon the war, and the abundance of canteens in the frontier districts. Nevertheless progress was observable. The beehive shaped kraals were giving place to houses after the European mode, where the decencies of life could be observed. A commencement was made at an effort to contribute to the support of the gospel. Special attention was paid to the schools. For the erection of a new church at Shiloh the people themselves contributed $2,500 in 1870 and 1871.

In Australia imposing numbers could not be expected. In all Victoria there were not more than eight hundred pure Papuans. But although the fruits of missionary labor could show an increase of only one hundred and twenty-five in 1879 as compared with sixty-eight ten years before, the improvement in quality had been remarkable. At Ramahyuk in 1872 the school earned one hundred per cent., the highest number of marks attained by any of the fourteen hundred schools under the supervision of the government inspector. Ebenezer blossomed out like an oasis, thanks to the windmill and aqueduct, constructed by Adolphus Hartmann, which had rendered irrigation possible. When the project of founding a hospital at Sale, near Ramahyuk, was agitated, the first contribution received towards the erection of the building came from the native congregation, a donation of $15. In 1876 an orphanage was begun at Ramahyuk itself, in charge of native Christians. Commissioners appointed by government in 1877 to inquire into the condition of the aborigines of the colony and to suggest the best means for furthering their interests, in spite of preëxisting prejudices against the system of reserves reported favorably, and especially gave the palm to the two stations conducted by the Moravian missionaries, as exceeding in efficiency the four under the direct management of the Board for the Protection of the Aborigines.

On the other hand, with all the expenditure of faithful labor, the Himalayan mission remained comparatively fruitless. Converts had to face the certainty of being disowned by relatives, and of losing employment, whilst local chiefs were incessant in both open and secret opposition. Great rejoicing had attended the baptism by Pagell in 1872 of a young convert, Nathanael Sodpa Gjalzan, an ex-lama from Lhassa. His linguistic attainments had been invaluable. The schools had extended their

influence, and in the spring of 1876 the baptism of the Moham-
medan teacher in the school at Kyelang had been followed by
the conversion of five of his scholars. Mission tours had been
frequent, and large numbers of copies of tracts and of parts of
the New Testament distributed. Jaschke's literary labors had
not ceased with his return home in 1868. He carried through
the press the Synoptic Gospels, the Book of Acts, the Epistle
to the Hebrews, and the Revelation, besides a translation of the
Harmony of the Gospels. Redslob, who arrived in 1872, had
completed the translation of Genesis. In hope against hope the
missionaries persevered, and laid the foundations of future
success.

Now yet another sphere of unselfish service was entered. In
1865 a benevolent German lady, Baroness von Keffenbrink-
Ascheraden, with her husband visited the Holy Land. The
misery of the lepers, crouching and begging with their hoarse
cries beside the Zion gate of Jerusalem, went to her heart. She
purchased a plot of ground outside the Joppa gate, and built a
house to serve as an asylum. A local committee of Christian
gentlemen was formed for the supervision of its affairs, with
Bishop Gobat as chairman.

But to build a house was easier than to secure men and
women willing to cope with this terrible disease at less than
arm's-length. It seemed natural to turn to the Moravian
Church, identified for forty-five years with the care of lepers
in Cape Colony. Frederick Tappe and his wife, for years previously active in Labrador, consented to undertake the work.

The asylum was dedicated in May, 1867. But deep prejudices at first thwarted its usefulness. Fanatical Moslems would
not enter the Christian dwelling. Independence and the pleas-
ures and privileges of begging were not supposed to be coun-
terbalanced by tender care, by a comfortable home, by changes
of linen and good food, conditioned by the observance of necessary rules. On the day of dedication not one solitary beneficiary was at hand. However within a year twelve patients
were sheltered, and within ten years twenty became the average
number at one time. "But now the maintenance of such an
institution, requiring about $1,500 per annum, called for the
exercise of faith in God. How was such a sum to be raised?
There was but one answer, 'Ask, and ye shall receive.' And
prayer was made and answered. It happened that while the

Baroness pondered upon this matter, a small pamphlet from the pen of Bishop James La Trobe, giving an account of the self-denying labors of our missionaries among the lepers in South Africa, fell into her hands. She at once wrote to the author, claiming his sympathy and aid for her cherished plan on behalf of the lepers in Emmanuel's land. Her touching letter, published in the *Moravian Magazine*, elicited a ready response, not only from members of the Moravian Church, but also from Chrisians of other names. And ever since that day of small things, the Lord has raised up many warm friends to this cause in England, Germany, Switzerland and in the United States. It is true there have been times when the Committee and Managers have been in sore straits, but neither compassions, nor faith, nor supply have failed. Year by year help has come seasonably and often most unexpectedly."

CHAPTER LXII.

THE GENERAL SYNOD OF 1879.

From May 26 to July 3, 1879, fifty-three representatives of the church were assembled at Herrnhut, under the presidency of Bishop Edmund de Schweinitz, with Bishops Henry Levin Reichel, William Taylor and Emil de Schweinitz as Vice-Presidents.

True to the traditional aversion of the Moravian Church in regard to the formulation of a fixed creed, synod declined to draw up any confession, but deemed it desirable to add to the statement of cardinal truths, recognized to be essential and biblical, "the doctrine of the fellowship of believers with one another in Christ Jesus, that they are all one in Him who is the Head of the body and all members one of another," and "the doctrine of the second coming of the Lord in glory, and of the resurrection of the dead, unto life or unto condemnation." Thus eight tenets were henceforth to be considered as of first consequence, though as heretofore synod refrained from defining in exact theological terminology the manner in which these tenets are to be held. In reference to these eight fundamentals it was further enacted: "The church esteems it neither necessary nor profitable to construct a creed formulated with regard to all individual points of doctrine, thus binding consciences and quenching the Spirit, nor does it consider the welfare of the church to be determined by the obligatory acceptance of such a creed on the part of its ministers, but to depend on the vivification and invigoration of the spirit of the church by the grace of the Lord. Yet just as little can the church suffer any one within its borders to teach and preach anything opposed to Holy Writ, and particularly to those statements which we, according to our understanding, consider to embody the leading doctrines of Holy Scripture. Nor can the church entrust the highly important office of preaching the Word and instructing youth in the truths of Christianity to brethren who stand in actual opposition to said statements, and least of all to such as neither can nor will take the position of conscientious believing submission to the Holy Scriptures, on which those statements rest, and as are consequently in conscious disagreement with the spirit of the church." This gave notice, that the tolerant liberality of the Moravian Church in regard to formal theology is not to be understood as equivalent to laxity.

Petitions from several congregations in Germany and the proposals of the synod of the American Province, North, brought the subject of constitutional revision into consideration. But a large number were opposed to any change. Finally it was decided that as hitherto the Unity's Elders' Conference, holding office from general synod to general synod, should consist of twelve members, assigned to three departments—those of finance, of the oversight of the pastorates and of the educational activity and that of missions. In future the eight members constituting the two former departments should be nominated by the preparatory synod of the German Province, and then formally elected by the general synod, whilst the members of the last department should be directly and immediately chosen by synod. In its entirety the Conference should administer the joint undertakings of the whole church—its missions, including that in Bohemia, and its joint finances. It should also represent the Moravian Church in negotiations with governments on the Continent of Europe, and continue to be the governing board for the German Province. In addition, however, the four members of the Department of Missions, in conjunction with one member of each of the other departments, chosen by the general synod, should constitute what was to be known as the "Department of the Unity." This body should alone be in correspondence with the British and American Provinces, and should constitute their supreme court of appeal, and an executive in so far that it should be charged with the duty of guarding against any contravention of the transactions of the general synod on the part of either Province. In purely Provincial matters, the independence of each Province was wholly unaffected by the legislation, save that synod affirmed the principle that a Provincial Elders' Conference is more than a mere executive committee of a Provincial synod, with functions limited to a perfunctory carrying out of instructions. On the contrary it has powers of initiative as an actual board of government and administration, responsible, however, for its actions to the Provincial synod. As members of the Unity's Elders' Conference the following were now elected: the Department of Missions, Eugene Reichel, James Connor, Bishop Kühn and Ferdinand Bechler; the Department of Finance, Gustavus Reichel, Ferdinand Martin, Eugene Groche, and Henry Levin Reichel; the Department of Education and of the Pastoral Office, Theophilus Reichel, Henry Müller, Theophilus van Calker and Martin Achtnich. As members of the Department of the Unity in addition to the members of the Department of Missions, the choice of synod fell upon Theophilus Reichel and Henry Levin Reichel.

One of the most important transactions of the synod was the adoption of a plan for the development of the mission in the West Indies to a status of self-dependence and self-administration. A general governing board was to be created in the West Indies, with its own President and Treasurer, to occupy temporarily a position of responsibility between the Mission Board at home and the seven general conferences of the islands. The hope was cherished that this board might assume the character of a Provincial Elders' Conference, enjoying rights and powers similar to those of the executive bodies in the British and American Provinces. For the next ten years financial aid was to be rendered according to a steadily descending scale, the starting point being $15,000, that the congregations might during their period gradually accustom themselves to the burden of self-support. The expenses of the theological seminary and of the three normal schools, repairs of buildings necessitated by earthquakes, tornadoes or other catastrophes, the costs of furloughs of missionaries and the outfit of those sent for the first time were to be considered as still devolving upon the home church, as well as the pensions of the superannuated. In carrying out the details of the plan, the Mission Board was directed to use the greatest circumspection and to deal in the fullest brotherly love, so as to guard the interests and if possible meet the wishes of those who would be most affected by the proposed change.

CHAPTER LXIII.

THE GERMAN PROVINCE, FROM 1879 TO 1889.

Although changes in the governing board followed in quick succession in the years after the creation of the Department of the Unity, official visits were frequent. Surinam received attention from Eugene Reichel and Theophilus van Calker in 1880, South Africa enjoyed the stimulus of a visit from its former superintendent, Bishop Kühn, in 1882 and 1883, Bishop Richard strengthened the bonds uniting America with the European church in 1883, Connor in the same year made a tour of the British congregations, and Bishop Romig visited the special sphere of his own life-work, the eastern islands of the West Indian mission, in 1887.

Theophilus Reichel resigned in 1881, and Marc Theophil Richard, Principal of the school at Montmirail, was elected in his place. Suddenly, on January 28 of the following year a stroke removed the aged President of the Conference, Bishop Gustavus Reichel. Bishop Henry Levin Reichel now became President, and Bishop Kühn Vice-President, Francis Krüger, warden of Herrnhut, being chosen as the new member. In September, 1884, these two officers of the Conference retiring, Bishop Müller, and Martin Achtnich replaced them. Bishop Henry Levin Reichel had now completed fifty years of service, and his declining health constrained retirement. The choice of the church now fell upon Christian Theodore Hans of St. Petersburg. Before the year was out Bishop Gustavus Theodore Tietzen died. Born in 1809, his labors had commenced in 1830, and had closed with the synod of 1879. As a professor in the college at Niesky, he had been instrumental in God's hand in connection with the revival of 1841. His counsel had been of the highest value at all of the general synods since 1848. His connection with the governing board dated from 1857. Achtnich remained a member of the Conference only two years, dying on March 15, 1886. Scarcely half a year elapsed when on November 14 the church mourned the death of a younger man, Frederick Eugene Reichel, of the Department of Missions, only fifty-five years of age. His former field had been French Switzerland, where he had met with signal success in efforts to call forth support of the missions. Of permanent value is also his *Rückblick über die Hundert und fünfzigjährige Missionsarbeit der Brüdergemeine*, published in connection with the Mission Jubilee of 1882. Conrad Beck and Arthur Guido Burkhardt stepped into the vacant places. Finally in 1887 both Hans and Kühn resigned. Theodore Bauer, Principal of the Girls' School at Kleinwelke, and Benjamin Romig, President of the Provincial Conference of the Eastern division of the West Indian Mission, became their successors.

Special attention was directed early in the decade towards the Russian Empire. During the latter part of the seventies inducements held out by government had been attracting agriculturists to the undeveloped wooded plateaus and half-drained marshlands of Volhynia. Hither by the year 1884 one hundred thousand emigrants had flocked from Poland and Bohemia, mainly people of German birth or extraction. Served by only three Lutheran pastors, their religious condition was that of extreme destitution. Many of the Polish-German emigrants to Volhynia had been connected with the *Diaspora* of the Moravian Church before they ventured into the forests. Hence they sent petitions to Herrnhut to be supplied with pastoral care. In these requests former Roman Catholics from Bohemia also joined, who had cut loose from priestly domination, and were now desirous of coming into connection with the Brethren's Church. A preliminary visit on the part of Herman Rudolph Steinberg of the Polish *Diaspora* was followed by the appointment of William Lange to Schadura, one of the German colonies eighteen German miles from Rowno. In September, 1884, he reached this village, a straggling settlement about one mile in length in the midst of dense forests of oak and birch, where wolves and other wild beasts still abounded. Here amidst extremely necessitous circumstances a numerous band of earnest people undertook to found a congregation of the Brethren's Church. Having no connection with this movement, in November of the same year, in quite a different part of the Russian Empire a similar commencement bade fair to be inaugurated. On the steppes a day's journey to the south of Sarepta a colony of Germans who had come in 1879 from Saratov, Swabians by birth, had rented an estate from the widow of a Russian general. Hungering for the Word, they sent for Bernard Fliegel of Sarepta, who visited the place to minister to them, and named the new congregation Gnadenthal with the consent of the ninety communicants. But in spite of the urgent representations of Hahn, whom the church sent to St. Petersburg, the Russian government issued its prohibition. In fact, instead of the hoped for concessions, efforts were put forth to thwart the church elsewhere. Not even was Schadura to be tolerated. But its people esteemed God's truth and liberty of conscience to be more precious than houses and fields. Under the leadership of their pastor, Lange, they once more took the wanderer's staff in hand. Two thousand five hundred acres of land were secured near Joinville, in the Province of Santa Catharina, Brazil. There Brüderthal arose in 1885 a South American counterpart of Bethel in Australia.

On June 9, 1884, the Provincial synod convened at Herrnhut. Bishop Müller presided, with Eugent Reichel and Guido Burkhardt as his assistants. Important preparations had been made for this gathering towards the close of the previous year. Special commissions had been in session at Berthelsdorf in November and December, taking counsel respecting the educational activity and the financial status of the German division of the church. These subjects now occupied the main attention of the synod. Since the late seventies, owing largely to the wide financial depression, the number of pupils at the various church schools had decreased. The school for boys at Zeist in 1881 had been changed into a day-school. Gnadenfeld girls' school was declining. The russification of the Baltic Provinces involved the school for girls at Lindheim in difficulties. Moreover the requirements of the Prussian government respecting teachers' certificates, connected with the unification of the educational system of the country, seriously affected the conditions governing the supply of teachers from the membership of the church. Amongst other measures, that there might be more uniform methods in all the church schools, the office of Inspector of schools was created with jurisdiction over all the educational undertakings of the Province. The curriculum of the college was so amended as to give it the status of a *gymnasium*.

Meanwhile the theological seminary had suffered a serious loss in the retirement of Dr. Herman Plitt from the president's chair in July, 1880, after more than thirty years' service in the institution. Preëminently the theologian of the church in this era, his intercourse with students had been an inspiration. Otto Uttendörfer became his sucessor, to be followed in the autumn of 1886 by Bernard Becker.

The resignation of Francis Müller, Director of the college, in 1885 formed a parallel to the retirement of Plitt. For thirty-four years he had been identified with its interests. Herman Theodore Bauer, hitherto Co-director, now took charge.

On January 4, 1887, Augustus von Dewitz died, in his fifty-first year. The founder of the normal school in 1872, as he had been of the mission institute in 1869, he stood at the head of both until 1879, when his energies were concentrated upon the latter only, Charles Buchner being then called to the former. Since 1883 Herman Kluge had been his chief assistant in the mission institute, and was now given the management. The death of the founder the more seriously affected it, since it interrupted the erection of its main building. In 1883 a plot of ground had been purchased, and a commodious edifice commenced, in which workshops and apparatus for manual training as well as ordinary school-rooms should find a place. The corner-stone had been laid on April 28, 1885, and the chief hall had been consecrated in June, 1886. But all this constituted only a portion of the structure as planned. In the execution of the project thus far Alexander Gruschwitz of Neusalz had laid the church under tribute by special liberality.

This same year, 1887, afforded opportunity to give proof that the old spirit of consecration survived. In the year 1880 the ownership and the full responsibility for the home for lepers near Jerusalem had been given over to the Unity's Elders' Conference. Age and the state of his health unfitted Tappe for further service in 1884. His place was taken by Francis Müller, a student of the institute at Niesky. Numbers had been increasing and the need of a better equipment was apparent. At a new site just outside the city, on the road to Bethlehem, a new and larger house was completed in 1887. Now volunteers were called for in the German Moravian Church for service in the wards and in the kitchen. Nine brave women responded. Three only were required; and Paulina Pletz, Augusta Ehrle and Magdalene Jeffe were accepted for the work.

In the closing days of May and throughout June, 1888, the synod was once more in session at Herrnhut, preparatory to the assemblage of the general synod of the ensuing year. Protracted discussions took place respecting a further revision of the constitution of the Unity's Elders' Conference. But synod contented itself with the proposal that "the German Province be allowed liberty of action in constituting the Department of Education and the Pastoral Office and the Department of Finance according to the requirement of the case" and that "General Synod devise some new mode of electing the brethren of the Department of Missions." Synod also requested that henceforth the use of the lot be not obligatory in the German Province in connection with appointments to office and in the nomination of bishops.

The decade had been prolific in additions to the literature of the church. Henry Augustus Jaeschke, who died at Herrnhut on September 24, 1883, lived to see his Tibetan Dictionary issued in an English translation. It was printed in Berlin at the expense of the East Indian Government. But the most important of his linguistic achievements was his New Testament in the Tibetan. With the exception of the Epistle to the Hebrews and the Revelation of St. John, translated by Frederick Adolphus Redslob, he himself completed the magnificent work. It formed his chief monument, coming from the press in 1884 at the cost of the British and Foreign Bible Society. Another masterly fruit of missionary labor was the Eskimo Grammar of Theodore Bourquin, issued in 1887. In the same year the official historiographer, Joseph Müller, gave to the public *Die deutschen Katechismen der Böhmischen Brüder*, in addition to sending forth from time to time reports which embodied the fruits of his researches. Ernest Arved Senft, pastor of the congregation at Peseux, laid French speaking Moravians under obligation in 1888, by his *L'Église de L'Unité des Frères (Moraves) esquisses historiques précédées d' une notice sur l'Église de l'Unité de Bohême et de Moravie et le piétisme allemand du XVIIe siècle*. And last, but of special importance for its original research and philosophic presentation of Zinzendorf and the Moravian Church of his age in its relation to the great movements of thought in the eighteenth century was Bernard Becker's *Zinzendorf im Verhältnis zu Philosophie und Kirchentum seiner Zeit*, issued at Leipsic in 1886.

CHAPTER LXIV.

THE BRITISH PROVINCE, FROM 1879 TO 1889.

For more than a quarter of a century to mention Fulneck schools called up the kindly face of their Director, Joseph Hutton Willey. Class after class of ministers' and missionaries' sons looked up to him as a second father. Under his wise administration Fulneck boys and girls made a good record in connection with the Universities' local examinations, athletics flourished, and a hearty young Christian life was nurtured. But change is inevitable everywhere. Early in 1881 he exchanged educational activity for the pastorate of Gracehill. Jackson Shawe succeeded, and signalized his entrance into office by remodeling the buildings and household appointments. About the same time the weight of years constrained Bishop John England to withdraw from the Conference, and assume the pastorate of Fairfield. Godfrey Clemens of Fulneck stepped into the vacant place, Bishop Taylor becoming President. But the constitution of the new member of the board had been already undermined by a paralytic stroke after his return from the synod of 1879. His end followed soon. His had been a career of long sustained usefulness in various pastorates and for fifteen years at Fulneck. Of German parentage, born at Mamre in Cape Colony in 1818, he had thoroughly identified himself with the British Province from the days of his first service in Fairfield as a teacher twenty years of age, and his mild, affectionate disposition, which knew how to combine firmness of principle with lovable tenderness, had endeared him to all.

Jackson Shawe received fifty of the seventy-three votes cast in the ensuing election; but never entered upon the duties of the office to which he was called by the voice of the church. During a visit to Morecambe Bay he met with a sudden death by drowning. The sorrowing congregations deferred a new election until the synod should convene. William Titterington, well prepared by a long period of service as a successful master, became Director of Fulneck school.

From June 27 to July 12, 1882, the synod was in session at Fulneck. Taylor and Robbins received as their colleague Thomas Henry Hines. Alexander Cossart Hasse was elected a bishop, and received consecration at the hands of Bishops La Trobe and Taylor. The *Messenger* was confided to Robert Elliott, with William Mallalieu as assistant editor. As a committee for the final revision of the Church Hymnal, synod appointed J. H. Willey, B. Harvey, F. Purser, J. D. Libbey, V. Drury and B. La Trobe.

On May 2, 1884, the sad news of another loss startled the congregations. Henry Edwards Shawe, the Secretary of Missions in London, whose services as editor of *Periodical Accounts* and as advocate of the missions in all parts of Britain had won him deserved prominence, died rather suddenly at Fairfield, in his fifty-second year. Never having held a pastoral position, but from the first trained for the secretaryship, and having served originally as Assistant-secretary, he had become an expert who seemed indispensable. Nevertheless providence again provided. Benjamin La Trobe, of Haverfordwest, before long proved himself true to family traditions, and worthy to carry forward the fallen standard. Next year, moreover, the former incumbent of the office, Thomas Leopold Badham, died in Dublin, aged sixty-seven. His services as a missionary in the West Indies, as Mission Secretary and as a Provincial Elder, were gratefully recalled by the church. So, too, when loss of hearing caused Bishop England to retire to Bedford in the spring of 1886, after forty-six years of service identified with the efforts of the church to better adapt itself to the requirements of the British field, it was felt that it was a veteran indeed who sought repose.

The synod of 1886, at Fulneck, although breaking the ground, by thorough discussions, for a change which was to be consummated two years later, itself scarcely did more than discharge routine business. The members of the Provincial Elders' Conference received hearty testimony of the confidence they enjoyed by obtaining a practically unanimous reëlection. Considerable time was devoted to a careful revision of the liturgical services for the new edition of the Hymnal. Arrangements were perfected whereby "associate congregations" might be recognized as enjoying the fellowship of the Brethren's Church, in virtue of agreement to certain fundamentals of doctrine and discipline, but retaining independence in matters of ritual.

On May 14, 1887, transpired the dedication of the handsome church on University Road, in Belfast, a practical evidence of church extension which ministered bright encouragement. To the energy of Samuel Kershaw, pastor since 1877, the final success of the enterprise was especially owing.

Bedford welcomed the Provincial synod in August, 1888. Its convocation was anticipated with special interest on account of lengthy discussions in the *Messenger* for some time previously with regard to the proposed creation of an "annual conference," a body of ministers and laymen, smaller in number than the constituency of the Provincial synod. But it was now feared that its duties and prerogatives might trench on those of both the Provincial Synod and of the Provincial Elders' Conference, whilst its existence would involve the creation of another piece of machinery. Instead synod therefore determined upon annual sessions of the Provincial synod, as necessitating no change in the constitution, and yet likely to reach the ends desired by those who advocated the new measure. This problem being solved, it appeared opportune to provide for the compilation of a "Church book," containing all the statutory rules and regulations of the Province, together with the necessary introductory matter of a historical and explanatory character. John Taylor of Blakewell, the successor of Charles Joseph La Trobe as *Advocatus*, was appointed the compiler, and J. D. Libbey, J. H. Edwards and Leonard Hasse were associated as a committee to revise the work in conjunction with the members of the Provincial Elders' Conference. These were now Bishop Taylor, Thomas Henry Hines and Henry Edwards Blandford, Robbins retiring from active service.

CHAPTER LXV.

THE AMERICAN PROVINCE, FROM 1879 TO 1889.

Peculiar difficulties hampered the executive board of five after the synod at Hope. The heritage of financial perplexity received from the past intimate connection of the Sustentation Fund with the life and activity of the church, intensified by the results of the financial panic of 1873, had to be taken into account at every turn. Fully aware at the outset that the funds were insufficient for the demands made upon them, the Conference attempted to lighten the burden by refraining from drawing compensation for their official labors, each member obtaining his personal support from some other source. But the burden of double duties, especially in the case of the President, Bishop Edmund de Schweinitz, charged with frequent and extensive official visits in addition to his duties as pastor of the Bethlehem congregation, was heavier than the church should have required. In November, 1880, he resigned his pastoral position, in order to devote himself wholly to the work of administration. The congregations at Bethlehem, Nazareth, Lititz and New York (English) entered into a special agreement to temporarily provide a salary, in order that the Sustentation Fund might be relieved. But the strain of the situation remained. The three schools which had formerly been a source of large revenue had not yet recovered. Hope Seminary did not pay its way, although its expenses had been reduced. A large deficiency was disclosed in the general accounts of the Province at the end of the first financial year. A still larger was the result of operations at the end of the second. Moreover the after effects of the strife which preceded the synod at Hope were felt, especially in Philadelphia. Three ministers withdrew. The disturbed state of the Second Church in Philadelphia culminated in a division, ninety-eight communicants leaving with Herman S. Hoffman to form Holy Trinity Moravian Church, at Twelfth and Oxford Streets in December, 1879. The parent congregation for a number of years maintained a difficult struggle for existence. After erecting a handsome stone church in 1880 the new congregation, under the lead of its pastor, in the autumn of 1881 transferred its fellowship to that of the Reformed Episcopal Church.

Meanwhile on May 18, 1881, the Provincial Elders' Conference convened a special synod to meet the financial emergency. Bishop Edmund de Schweinitz presided. Up to this time the income of the funded principal and the earnings of the church boarding schools and of the Publication Concern, which constituted part of the assets of the Sustentation Fund, had been employed for the general needs of the Province—the salaries of Provincial Elders under normal arrangements, the expenses involved in the appointment and transfers of ministers, the deficiencies of the periodicals, the deficiencies of the theological seminary, the current expenses of the Provincial Elders for general administration, the stipends of the superannuated, the cost of the education of ministers' children, and the salary of the Secretary of Publications. At the rate of the recent deficits it was apparent that if this system were continued without a change, the Sustentation Fund would be exhausted in fifteen years, leaving the Province without provision for the administration of its general affairs, to say nothing of the distress into which its pensioners would be brought. Moreover the church had morally no right to run through the endowment created by the liberality of the churches at Bethlehem, Nazareth and Lititz. Although legal forms had not been observed when the Fund was created, in fact and morally it was a trust fund, the integrity of which the Province was under obligation to maintain. This view of the situation was taken by the synod with practical unanimity. Radical measures were adopted to insure the payment of pensions, and at the same time to provide for the general administration of the Province. On the one hand the Sustentation Fund was temporarily relieved of all obligations save the payment of pensions. The ministers voluntarily proposed to yield the educational privileges of their children until such time as the Sustentation Fund might be in condition to resume this charge. Earnings of the schools should be applied to make good the impaired capital of the Fund. The office of Secretary of Publications was abolished, and the periodicals were to be edited gratuitously by various editorial committees. The theological seminary was severed from all connection with the Fund, the professors having signified their willingness to risk their salaries, and depend upon the liberality of the church. And finally, the most significant measure of all was the institution of what was to be known as the "Provincial Revenue." The representatives of the congregations declared their conviction that the Province was able to pay the cost of its joint expenses, and that these expenses ought to be met directly by the membership. The salary of one Provincial Elder, the office and traveling expenses of the Board, the cost of official visits, the cost of appointments and transfer of ministers should be provided for by contributions annually sent by each congregation according to ability, the dues of each congregation to be amicably determined in a joint conference of its officers and a representative of the Provincial Board. The advisory board of laymen who together with the Provincial Elders' Conference had the oversight of the Sustentation Fund should have the management and control of all the financial affairs of the Province not otherwise provided for. As members of this board synod elected Charles A. Zoebisch, Abraham S. Schropp and J. Samuel Krause; Bishop Edmund de Schweinitz, Eugene Leibert and Augustus Schultze constituting the Provincial Elders' Conference.

Much of the time of the synod was also given to the consideration of a plan of union with the Southern Province, presented by the delegates of the Southern synod, Edward Rondthaler and J. Frank Shaffner. Union had been suggested by the Southern body, and the overture was gladly welcomed by the North. In general the Southern plan was accepted, and commissioners were appointed to arrange details. Visits were made to Salem by these commissioners, and correspondence exchanged. A Southern synod subsequently passed upon the matter favorably, but with difference of opinion. A change of sentiment had become evident in the South. Ultimately the commissioners had to report to the synod at Lititz in 1884, that the project had come to nothing, though the Southern division gave assurances of its purpose to unite in the support of the theological seminary and of the periodical publications of the church.

Encouragement was derived from the report of the Conference to the synod in session at Lititz in May, 1884. The crucial
moment of the financial crisis seemed to be passed. True,
Hope Seminary had been closed in the summer of 1881. The
other schools had been able to make good impaired capital to
the amount of about four thousand dollars. A legacy of one
thousand dollars devised by George W. Dixon, of Bethlehem,
for the support of superannuated ministers, had practically
increased the Sustentation Fund by that amount. Provincial
Revenue had been a success, $8,931 having been raised in the
three years, leaving a surplus of $1,229 in the hands of the
Treasurer. However it was evident that this favorable result
had been dependent upon that fact that two members of the
Conference served gratuitously, and upon the additional uncertain feature that the number of ministerial changes of late had
been unusually small. Furthermore, notwithstanding the fact
that the editorial committees gave their services gratuitously,
the Manager of the Publication Concern, Edwin G. Klosé, who
since 1881 had combined its oversight with his professorship
in the theological seminary, reported that this establishment
was by no means as prosperous as the church had been in the
habit of supposing.

Synod reaffirmed the principle of the Provincial Revenue.
The members of the Provincial Elders' Conference and of the
advisory board were reëlected. The office of Secretary of Publications was restored, carrying with it the business management of the concern. After the synod Edwin G. Klosé consented to give his undivided attention to this responsible post,
and resigned the professorship which he had filled successfully
for eighteen years. The arrangement of editorial committees
was continued, with changes of personnel.

Meanwhile the life of the church showed various fluctuations,
here retrogression, there advance. In Iowa the tendency
towards the consolidation of the farms told unfavorably.
Moravia was sold in 1878, the enterprise coming to an end.
Next year near Florenceville, close to the Minnesota line, and
about fifty-six miles from Bethany, Henry Reusswig organized
Ramah, ministered to jointly by the pastors of Bethany, Hebron
and Northfield; but on Reusswig's appointment as traveling
missionary in 1882, and with the opening of better prospects
in western Minnesota and North Dakota, Ramah came to an

end, several of its families having removed and identified themselves with Moravian churches elsewhere. In 1878 J. J. Detterer made his home in Atlantic City, and ministered to the home mission congregation, served since 1877 from Egg Harbor; but when in 1880 its members reached the point of erecting a place of worship, they lost courage, and the undertaking came to an end. Very different features presented themselves in connection with the work in Dakota. Independent from the first, the new organizations there were characterized by stalwart self-reliance and large liberality. The Red River valley became a hopeful field. Goshen prospered, and in 1881 a second congregation was organized, consisting of former members of Minnesota and Wisconsin congregations and other settlers, living beyond Maple River. This church was named Canaan. For about a year it was served from Goshen, but in the summer of 1882 it received a pastor of its own in the person of William Strohmeier. For a number of years North Salem, Wisconsin, was a filial of Lake Mills. In 1882 William H. Romig took charge, and English services were instituted at the request of people of the vicinity. During the same year Fry's Valley was separated from Gnadenhütten, Bishop Van Vleck becoming its pastor. In December, 1883, Coopersburg was begun by Lewis P. Clewell, pastor of Emmaus, as a filial of the latter charge. But in the same year Victor, Iowa, had to be abandoned. In October a church was dedicated at Port Washington, as a result of the energetic labors of John H. Clewell, pastor of Uhrichsville, who had organized this filial the year before. And about the same time Christian Madsen, at Sturgeon Bay, gathered together the Scandinavian settlers seven or eight miles to the south, and established Shiloh. The year 1884 witnessed the erection of a chapel in West Bethlehem, as an additional place of worship for the members of the mother congregation. Castleton Corners obtained a resident pastor, Clarence E. Eberman, union with New Dorp being maintained as a collegiate church. Oakland, Missouri, begun some years before by the Southern Province, was transferred to the charge of the Northern board. On the other hand the union of Blairstown with Harmony marked a retrogression. In 1886 London, in Dane County, Wisconsin, was organized, but Olney, in Illinois, after a prolonged effort to maintain it from West Salem, was abandoned.

In the Southern Province changes had meanwhile been transpiring. Here at the outset of the period the Provincial Elders
were Bishop Emil A. de Schweinitz, Lewis Rights and Eugene
P. Greider. On November 3, 1879, after the first returned
from the synod, failure of health, manifest during its sessions,
terminated fatally. Identified with the South ever since 1849,
for many years the administrator of the Unity's estates in North
Carolina, and for the last ten years the President of the
Southern Conference, he had been indefatigable in promoting
the interests of the Province during the critical period of constitutional development and throughout the trying years of the
Civil War, and had represented it in the general synods of 1857,
1869 and 1879. Edward Rondthaler, pastor of Salem congregation, was chosen his successor, Lewis Rights becoming President. Upon Greider's retirement in 1884, Parmenio Leinbach
became the third member of the Board. Maximilian E. Gru-
nert accepting a call to Emmaus, Pennsylvania, in 1877, was
followed by Jacob Zorn as principal of Salem Female Academy.
He in his turn seven years later became Associate Principal
of Nazareth Hall, when Edward Rondthaler took charge of the
school in Salem, in addition to previous duties, with John H.
Clewell as assistant. Four years later the latter assumed full
control, entering upon a career of marked success.

The North now experienced severe losses. On October 21,
1884, Lewis F. Kampmann died at Bethlehem. First serving
in various pastorates, he had guided the affairs of the theological seminary during the important years after its removal to
Bethlehem from 1858 to 1864. Minister at Lititz for three years,
he was then elected a member of the Provincial Elders' Conference, from 1867 to 1878. For six years subsequently he had
been pastor of York, and had been living in retirement at Bethlehem for only a few months. Within a year, namely, on October 22, 1885, Bishop Henry A. Shultz followed him. Born in
Surinam, he had been educated in the schools of the church in
America, and had served in a variety of positions both South
and North from 1833 to 1871. From 1849 to 1851 a member
of the Provincial Elders' Conference, he especially enshrined
himself in the memory of his Brethren by his unflagging cham-
pionship of the new work of home missions throughout the
Northwest.

EDMUND ALEXANDER DE SCHWEINITZ.

Early in the year 1886 Eugene Leibert resigned his office as a Provincial Elder, finding the double burden too onerous and preferring to devote himself to the interests of Nazareth Hall, with which he remained identified for a quarter of a century as its honored Principal. Robert de Schweinitz was elected his successor, and again became Provincial Treasurer.

On December 18, 1887, the church was startled by the sudden death of Bishop Edmund de Schweinitz, who quietly fell asleep as he sat reading at home on the evening of the Sunday before Christmas, having presided in the afternoon at the annual lovefeast of the active workers of the Bethlehem congregation. It was a sore loss. Identified with the constitutional changes of the middle of the century, the founder of the *Moravian,* he had also been a prolific contributor to the history of the church, his *Life and Times of David Zeisberger* and his monumental *History of the Unitas Fratrum* up to the time of its resuscitation at Herrnhut—the latter published in 1885—being his chief works. Pastor of the Bethlehem congregation from 1864 to 1880, President of the college and theological seminary from 1867 to 1885, President of the Provincial Elders' Conference since 1878, and a wise counsellor of his Brethren in synods since early in the fifties, his had been a position of unique prominence. He had represented his Province at two general synods, and had been chosen President of the latter, that of 1879. Gifted with native eloquence, a profound scholar, he at the same time possessed a grasp of affairs and administrative gifts and large sympathies which impelled others to recognize him as a natural leader and to lean upon his ripe judgment. Deeply appreciating the worth of the traditions of former days, he at the same time stood for all that was progressive in the healthiest sense. Men of such preëminent qualities are given by God to any church only at rare intervals. The mourning which followed his departure was wide-spread and deep.

At the call of the church J. Mortimer Levering consented to enter the breach in the Conference, whilst retaining his position as a pastor of the Bethlehem congregation. Robert de Schweinitz combined the duties of President and Treasurer until the next convocation of the synod.

In the autumn of the year 1887 a chapel was erected at the northern outskirts of Bethlehem, on Laurel Street, as an additional place of worship for members of the widely scattered congregation. In the same year Osborne, Kansas, had been abandoned, in consequence of the removal of many of the people because of repeated failures of crops from droughts. On the other hand the church now entered into a close relationship to the interdenominational city missions in York, Pennsylvania, engaging to supply them with a minister, and an attempt was made to inaugurate a congregation in Milwaukee. Next year Reusswig's labors as a traveling missionary bore additional fruit in the consecration of a church at Hector, Renville County, Minnesota, where he had made his home since 1886, the nearest railroad station to Elim, and served in conjunction with it. In the spring of 1888 a congregation was organized in Easton, Pennsylvania, under promising auspices. Finally the application of Scandinavians at Centralia and Grand Rapids, Wisconsin, being looked into by Jacob Hoyler, Christian Madsen accepted a call thither.

When therefore the synod assembled at Bethlehem on September 19, 1888, the outlook was hopeful. Bishop Amadeus A. Reinke was chosen President. Provincial Revenue was found to have stood the test of time, and could be regarded a permanent arrangement. The schools were on the whole recovering from the effects of the financial depression, Jesse Blickensderfer of Bethlehem reporting a decided gain in the number of scholars, and Linden Hall rejoicing in the erection of its chaste memorial chapel, dedicated in February, 1885. This was the gift of George W. Dixon of Bethlehem in memory of his daughter Mary, a former pupil. Synod endeavored to provide for Provincial development, changing the District conferences into District synods, as had been originally contemplated. The expenses of all synods in the Northern Province were henceforth to be met by annual per capita assessment of the membership, that the weaker Districts might be helped by the stronger. Further it was determined that a new theological seminary should be erected, and a building committee was created with full power to act in the premises. This committee consisted of Amadeus A. Reinke, Henry T. Bachman and Jesse Blickensderfer, the members of the new Provincial Elders' Conference, together with Augustus A. Schultze, the President of the seminary, J. Taylor Hamilton, the Resident Professor, and Joseph A. Rice, Joseph H. Traeger and Ashton C. Borhek.

CHAPTER LXVI.

THE FOREIGN MISSIONS, FROM 1879 TO 1889.

A net gain of thirteen stations and of eleven thousand and thirty-one adherents and of sixteen missionaries as compared with the figures at the beginning of the decade, gave proof that divine favor rested upon the work. This very extension, however, carrying as it did with it an increasing outlay not only for current expenses but also for the training and outfit of missionaries, for the education of missionaries' children and for pensions, as well as for the erection and care of additional buildings, and complicating the work of administration, involved an ever increasing strain upon resources. Seven of the ten years showed deficits in the annual accounts, ranging from $6,866 to $16,951. Nevertheless by the blessing of God the liberality of members and friends made it possible for the general synod of 1889 prior to the close of its sessions to rejoice at the announcement that the last deficit had been made good.

Greenland saw a slight increase in the number of members, although only the most southern station, Friedrichsthal, any longer came into contact with actual heathen, and these for the most part visitors from the east coast. In the year 1881 Jacob Brodbeck undertook a tour of exploration thither in the company of heathen Eskimos who were returning home, but met with no other persons whatsoever. In 1883 Nordenskjöld, the Swedish explorer, contemplating an expedition to the same region, requested the aid of Brodbeck as interpreter. The wish was granted, in the hope that missionary work might be done. The expedition reached the 66th degree of northern latitude. Having spent the winter in Europe, Brodbeck set sail from Copenhagen in the barque *Albaon*, March 30. On April 1 the ship was running under close-reefed sails. A storm had been raging since the previous day. About ten o'clock, the night being very dark, breakers were suddenly seen right ahead. In a moment there was a fearful crash. The vessel had struck on a reef near the Shetland Islands. Only the mate, two seamen and one passenger managed to crawl out onto the rocks, to which they clung till morning, when they were rescued by a boat from the shore. Of the others, including Brodbeck, nothing was ever seen.

With this exception, the life of the mission in Greenland moved on in an uneventful manner, but the gradual impoverishment of the people scattered along the west coast became more and more painfully evident. The prospect of ultimate self-support on the part of this mission field was becoming more and more problematic. The normal school at New Herrnhut was closed in 1884; and whilst that at Lichtenau was theoretically retained, during several years its usefulness was practically suspended for lack of adequate forces.

Labrador, at the end of the decade showed a slight decrease in the number of Eskimos, but an increase in the number of white settlers, attached to the church, a total of 1,283 in all. The trade carried on in connection with the defrayal of the costs of the mission still occasioned no little perplexity. Conducted by the Society for the Furtherance of the Gospel, its agents since 1876 were regarded as in the service of the Mission Board, although not charged with spiritual duties. At their head stood a warden. Trouble again arose in connection with the debts of the natives and assumed such a character that the society commissioned Benjamin La Trobe to visit Labrador as its representative. Zoar had been the chief center of dissatisfaction. Ever since 1882 the unpaid indebtedness of the Eskimos of this station had been steadily increasing, in spite of considerable advances from the "poor fund," until the twenty-six men who were heads of families there owed in all about $2,715. From its founding in 1865 this place had earned a reputation as a poor point for fishery, etc. And the character of its people left a good deal to be desired in regard to amenability to regulations. During the autumn of 1887 their industry was attended with complete failure. Much distress arose. Instead of humbling themselves under the afflictive providence, certain of the people planned to plunder the store. The trader was however warned in time, and sent for Bourquin, the superintendent of the mission, who came from Nain to allay the dissatisfaction. His earnest representations for a time appeared to have quieted the restless spirits. But later a man shot twice into the store where the Rinderknecht and Lundberg were busied, because they had refused his unjustifiable demands. After a thorough examination into the whole affair, La Trobe with the missionaries decided upon the abandonment of the store at Zoar. This carried with it the probable withdrawal of the missionaries. The decision had a wholesome effect at the other stations.

In yet another respect the Society for the Furtherance of the Gospel was occasioned perplexity during the decade. The *Cordelia*, an auxiliary supply ship used in the trade between Labrador and London, was run down by a steamer in the Thames in 1881. All hands were saved, but the cargo perished, a considerable loss to the treasury of the society.

The Indian missions in North America had passed through severe trials. During the Civil War lawless bands ranged through the Cherokee country. On September 2, 1862, Ward, a native missionary, was shot by Indians as an alleged southern sympathizer. New Springplace founded in the early forties was pillaged. Gilbert Bishop, the missionary in charge, after suffering arbitrary arrest by a subordinate Northern officer, made his way with his family to Pennsylvania. Canaan, the first station to be established, in 1841, after the removal from Georgia, was destroyed. In both places the converts were scattered. Yet in 1866 Edwin J. Mack had returned from Salem and reoccupied New Springplace. Later a church was built at Talequah, the capital of the "nation."

In 1837 two-thirds of the people of New Fairfield had removed with their missionary, Jesse Vogler, to the west of the Mississippi, ultimately settling near Fort Leavenworth, in Kansas, where New Westfield was founded on a reserve of twenty-four thousand acres, a mission doomed almost from the outset by the tide of white migration westwards. Meanwhile the remnant at New Fairfield pursued the uneventful tenor of their life. After a period marked by prevailing indifference, the heart of Adolphus Hartmann—missionary here since his transfer from Australia in 1870—was gladdened in 1887 by an awakening whereby sixty persons were brought to Christ or renewed in an earnest desire for a consecrated life. At New Westfield, Kansas, the church was twice burnt by incendiaries (November 15, 1880, and January 1, 1886)—presumably by bad whites or half-

35

breeds. The greater attractions of the government industrial school at Lawrence having induced the people to send their children thither, the day-school at New Westfield was closed in December, 1884. Retrogression in this period also marked the work amongst the Cherokees. The church at Talequah, for lack of attendance was sold to the Presbyterians in 1880. The consequent removal of one missionary for a time placed the entire field in charge of Theodore M. Rights, having care of Springplace and Woodmount and preaching occasionally in Talequah. But in 1884 Benjamin Lineback was called as a co-worker, and two years later a church was consecrated at Woodmount, the Cherokees themselves contributing $575 towards this purpose. Meanwhile attempts were made to open out-stations; but the membership remained small—less than two hundred in all.

On the other hand with the approval of the Mission Board· in 1884 the American Province, under the leadership of the Northern Provincial Elders' Conference and the Society for Propagating the Gospel at Bethlehem, energetically undertook new labors in behalf of the aborigines of the American continent. In 1885 a mission was permanently established in western Alaska.

For the Moskito territory God had special blessings in reserve. The first traces of the awakening manifested themselves in May, 1881, at Magdala. Soon the awakening became general, and spread to Bluefields, Bethany, Ephrata, Karata and Kukallaya. All the neighboring villages felt the effects. Though in addition to the proofs of a genuine work of the Spirit of God fanatical excesses also appeared, caricatures wrought by the enemy, the entire revival approved itself a work of God and did not burn out hastily. Indians, Negroes, Creoles and Spaniards felt the mighty movement of the Spirit in their hearts. Men wrestled with God under a crushing sense of sin for days, it might be, and then light dawned upon their darkness. Sins were confessed openly. Restitutions were made. In November, 1882, a conspiracy against the government in Bluefields came to naught because of the religious movement. More than a dozen "*sukias*," the forefront of the opposition, surrendered to the truth. Liberal offerings were made by some who had formerly strenuously resisted even the entrance of light. "At the reopening of the chapel at Magdala,

January 19, 1883, an aged Indian, named Fox, rose and said: 'Brethren, I can not make long speeches, but I will say this: make ten collections for the chapel, and I will give something each time.' All the brandy and rum shops in the village were closed, with one exception. The people went to the chapel instead of to the public house. At Quamwatla two hundred Indians returned to the village, which they had left eight years before owing to superstitious dread of poison supposed to be buried there. They rebuilt their huts and awaited the arrival of a missionary. As in apostolic times, the Lord added to the church daily such as should be saved. The chapel at Karata, built seven years before with considerable misgivings, was filled with an auditory of two hundred persons. Sixty-six Indians were baptized there on November 16, 1881; the next day eighteen couples received the blessing of the church upon their union." Several hundred heathen asked for instruction and applied for baptism. Before the end of the year 1887 nine hundred and sixty-one adults were baptized. During the decade the adherents of the mission increased in number from 1,030 to 3,294. Three out-stations were added. Indians across the border of Nicaragua also desired instruction; but the government of the republic interposed a prohibition, on the ground that the Roman Catholic was the only church recognized by their constitution. Yet in 1888 the regulations were in so far relaxed as to permit visits on the part of Augustus Erdmann and Frederick Smith, and negotiations were begun for the placing of a "helper" at Sandy Bay in Nicaragua. One result of the revival was the erection of chapels in a number of villages not regularly occupied, and in many cases without assistance from the treasury of the missions.

Whilst the course of the mission as such throughout these years afforded special satisfaction, the political situation became grave. So long as the little strip of undeveloped coast remained wilderness there was little inducement for any power to place a new interpretation on the terms of the Treaty of Managua, according to which it enjoyed independent government whilst recognizing the suzerainty of Nicaragua. But after the establishment of trade in tropical fruits and the exportation of mahogany and other valuable timber as a consequence of the civilizing effects of missionary labor, and with the influx of traders and gold-seekers and adventurers from many lands, the situation changed. During the early summer of 1879 Chief Henry Clarence was poisoned, and died suddenly. Great excitement ensued. The absorption of the coast by Nicaragua appeared likely to follow. But the election of a new chief was effected, Albert Hendy by name, a convert of the mission. Yet ominous signs reappeared from time to time, and his sudden death at Magdala, on November 8, 1888, once more threw affairs into confusion, and threatened both the independence of the territory and the free prosecution of missionary activity. But once more fears were dispelled by the election of Jonathan Charles Frederick, a nephew of the late chief, in March, 1889, and the quiet and orderly conduct of affairs was maintained.

By the year 1884 the *Herald* began to succumb to the influences of tropical seas that shorten the life of all kinds of craft. Liberal contributions again came in. A serviceable schooner, the *Adele*, built for use along this coast, was therefore bought, and renamed the *Meta*, in 1888. But of yet greater importance to the mission as an auxiliary to the faithful efforts of the Brethren, and rendered especially desirable since the revival, was the completion of the translation of the New Testament into the Moskito Indian tongue by William Siebörger, who brought his manuscript to Europe in 1888, to be printed at the expense of the Herrnhut Bible Society.

In November, 1879, an important conference of ministers and delegates was convened at Nisky, St. Thomas, in order to take the steps necessary to carry out the legislation of the general synod, which should prepare the way for Provincial autonomy. The resolutions of the synod and the proposals of the Mission Board were discussed with frank thoroughness, and various conclusions reached from the standpoint of the mission itself. The first of these, which sought a division of the work into two Provinces, met with the approval of the Mission Board. It was recognized that Jamaica presented features different from those prevailing in the eastern islands, and that the distance of this western sphere of operations from the Lesser Antilles would involve large outlays, if the West Indian mission were hereafter maintained as one organic whole. Moreover in Jamaica such a degree of organization had already been developed, that few changes were necessary to adapt the situation to the desires of the general synod. Supervision was already exercised by an executive conference under the direction of the

Department of Missions. Here, therefore, the five members of this executive were retained in office—Edwin E. Reinke, President; George Henry Hanna, Treasurer; John Paul Pulkrabek, Secretary; Peter Larsen, and Alfred Lind—until 1884, when a new executive of three was chosen, after the analogy of the order of affairs introduced in the Eastern islands—George Henry Hanna, President; Alfred Lind, Treasurer, and Callender Smyth, Secretary. General mission conferences were appointed in both missionary provinces for every five years, when a new election of the executive should take place. Provision was made for the convening of this assembly in the Eastern Province in such a manner that each island should be adequately represented. Here the executive was constituted of Benjamin Romig, President; Samuel Warner, Treasurer, and John Lewis Hasting, Secretary—reëlected in 1884. In every case the election, whether proceeding from the general conference, or as in the Eastern islands in 1884 by the vote of all the ordained missionaries, was subject to the approval and confirmation of the Mission Board. Upon the removal of Benjamin Romig to Berthelsdorf in 1887, Theodore Niebert was chosen his successor as President of the Eastern executive, and when Hasting retired from active service on account of ill health in 1887, Frederick Clemens became Secretary. A further change was necessitated in the following year, when both the Treasurer and the Secretary returned home owing to illness. Samuel L. Thaeler undertook the duties of the former, whilst those of the latter fell to Henry Weiss.

Unfortunately for both divisions with the increase in the production of European beet-sugar, the cane industry, West India's chief source of wealth, steadily declined. Employment became uncertain, and wages constantly fell. Under the circumstances the steady decrease in the appropriation from the mission treasury in aid of the West Indian work caused hardship, and the achievement of self-support within the decade was found an impossibility, notwithstanding the loyal efforts of missionaries and people.

An indispensable condition of self-support was the development of a native ministry. The death of Badham in 1879 had resulted in the temporary closing of the theological seminary in Jamaica. The task of establishing a like institution at Nisky in St. Thomas was now assigned to Augustus Romig. But an affection of the throat compelled him to relinquish the task after a few months in 1886, and Edward Foster was called from England as his successor. Later the Western Province renewed an attempt to prepare candidates for the ministry in connection with the normal school at Fairfield, but in 1888 this was once more abandoned owing to untoward circumstances.

Progress in numbers characterized the work in both portions of the field throughout the decade, Jamaica making a gain of more than fifteen hundred, and the Eastern islands of more than two thousand five hundred.

Of special importance for the future of the mission in Jamaica was the recognition of the church as a body corporate in 1884, title to the mission property in the island being vested in the Provincial Conference of the island together with the President of the British Provincial Elders' Conference and the Mission Secretary in London.

In the Eastern islands a noteworthy event was the erection of a memorial church in the city of St. Thomas, to commemorate the one hundred and fiftieth anniversary of Moravian missions, large gifts being received for this purpose from all parts of the Brethren's Unity. The foundation of a massive stone structure was laid on August 21, 1882, and the dedication took place on May 16, 1884. The queen of Denmark on this occasion took opportunity to convey her warm appreciation of the beneficent results of the missionary labors of the Brethren.

As in Jamaica, steps were also taken in the Eastern islands to secure the title to mission property; but here the varied condition of things on the different islands and the fact that different governments had to be dealt with protracted the negotiations.

In the early part of the year 1879 Mr. Quintin Hogg, the patron of the mision in Demerara, paid a visit to his estates in that colony. Now he asked that Alexander Pilgrim might be sent to the Reliance plantation near the Essequibo. This took place in April. A further extension followed in 1882. In the village of Beterverwachting there lived a number of members of the Congregational church, who had separated from their parent organization in 1863, and since then had been served by their own deacons. Once a month an ordained minister had administered the sacraments. But in the course of years he had accepted a call elsewhere. Now fifty-seven of these people asked to be received into the Brethren's Church and regarded as constituting a filial of Graham's Hall. The request was granted. By the end of the year 1888 there were one hundred and twenty communicants here alone, whilst the membership at Graham's Hall had grown to four hundred and forty-five, of whom two hundred and twenty-one were communicants. Reliance on the other hand failed of success, chiefly through the opposition of a high church clergyman, and was therefore abandoned. Moreover at the end of the year 1884 the patron of the mission gave notice that the decline of the sugar industry rendered it impossible for him to as largely sustain the work in Demerara as heretofore.

Meantime in the Surinam mission numbers grew very rapidly. At the end of the year 1888, 26,106 adherents could be reported, an increase of more than 5,000 when compared with the total ten years before. The growth was not an even one. On the plantations, especially those near the capital, a decline followed the abandonment of sugar production, and the consequent removal of the people to town. Along the Coronie and Nickerie, where the negroes cultivated their own land, an increase was perceptible, for instance at Salem and Waterloo. In Paramaribo itself, the seven thousand three hundred in church connection had become thirteen thousand. Distinct organizations had been budded off, Rust en Vrede in 1882 and Wanika in 1886. These with Combé and the old church grew rapidly, the central organization leading with a total membership of 8,280.

This rapid growth in numbers in the city proved no unmixed blessing. Slavery's heritage of evil in connection with sexual morality, and the practical difficulties placed in the way of poor persons by the cost attendant upon the recognition of marriages by the civil authorities, rendered necessary numerous exclusions from church membership. At the same time arrangements that sufficed for the administration of discipline whilst the congregation remained small, were now inadequate. To add to the difficulties a prominent missionary in August, 1879, became conscientiously insubordinate, carried away by peculiar views concerning church discipline, holding that exclusion must be determined by the congregation and not by the missionaries. He refused to yield either to the Provincial authorities or to the Unity's Elders' Conference. An official visit on the part of Eugene Reichel and Theophilus van Calker

in 1880 resulted in his dismissal and the remodeling of the
arrangements for the cure and care of souls.   For a time
trouble still made itself felt beneath the surface.   But gradually
a better state of things arose.   The erring missionary made
acknowledgment, and besought reinstatement.   After a time
he was given the means of earning a livelihood in connection
with secular employment carried on for the benefit of the mission.   The erection of the Rust en Vrede church afforded
opportunity for the employment of energies, and caused a beam
of light to radiate the darkened sky.   But new difficulties arose
in connection with problems of church discipline.   John Haller,
the missionary now charged with the general oversight in this
connection, like his predecessor but from a different standpoint
in his turn failed to act in agreement with his colleagues in
Paramaribo, and with the Mission Board, being inclined to
compromise that tended to laxity, from his appreciation of the
perplexity in which the colored people were placed by the cost-
liness of civil regulations regarding marriage.   For a brief
period discipline was at a low ebb.   The controversy in time
so preyed upon Haller's health, that in 1885 a furlough became
necessary.   He was not destined to return to Surinam.   In
December, 1886, he died, at the age of forty-five, a brother of
rare personal gifts, but of a temperament which unfitted him
for collegiate labors.   Now the "native helpers" themselves
commenced a movement for the attainment of a higher
standard of discipline, and in 1893 the colonial government
altered the laws which had impeded true marriage on the part
of the negroes.

An increase in numbers also characterized the work in South
Africa, more particularly that among the Kaffirs.   In the Western Province the drift of population to the capital took thither
many young people from the mission stations.   During the
visit of Bishop Kühn in 1882 and 1883, the advisability of gathering these scattered children of the mission into a congregation in Cape Town was discussed.   On his return the Mission
Board entered into the project, and Philip Emil Hickel was
called.   He met with hearty sympathy from Christian friends,
and the consecration of a church and school on Moravian Hill
took place in 1886 and 1887.

In November, 1887, it became possible to take a step in advance in connection with the normal school at Genadendal, the

formation of a class of theological students, definitely destined for the ministry. Prior to this the first ordinations of native brethren had already transpired, Bishop Kühn having received John Nakin, Charles Jonas and John Zwelibanzi into the ranks of the ministry on January 7, January 28 and February 11, 1883, at Shiloh, at Enon and at Clarkson. Throughout the congregations also the desirability of attaining self-support was beginning to manifest itself more plainly in the steady increase in contributions, alike for meeting the stated expenses and for defraying the cost of repairs to churches and schools, and this in spite of the gradual impoverishment of the Colony. The decline in colonial prosperity meanwhile had its embarrassing effect upon the various enterprises prosecuted for the benefit of the mission; nor did the desired success attend the effort to introduce new industries, silk-culture, the growth of arrowroot, the production of castor oil, etc. With it all the future of one congregation was temporarily placed in jeopardy by the death of aged Christina Lewis of Goedverwacht, the last of the slaves of Mr. Buergers, in December, 1888. It could scarcely be foreseen that the thirteen persons whom the government determined as his heirs, should reject the tempting offers of neighboring planters, desirous of purchasing their valuable patrimony, and in a spirit of splendid self-sacrifice should offer it to the church at a nominal figure, and then individually make liberal contributions towards the erection of a permanent house of worship.

The Kaffir mission, embracing the three older posts in the Colony proper, Shiloh, Goshen and Engotini, together with the two widely separated groups in Tembuland and East Griqualand (Nomansland) experienced fluctuations, expansion prevailing on the whole. In consequence of the war with insurgent Basutos and Tambookies, in 1880 and 1881, Entwanazana had to be abandoned and was looted and burnt. Baziya and Tabase experienced similar misfortunes in 1880, but were reoccupied and rebuilt. On the other hand Bethesda and Ezincuka in 1883 and 1887 advanced to the status of fully equipped stations, and Mnari or Nxotschane and Magadla in Hlubiland became out-stations.

In both divisions of the South African field difficulties arose in relation to the title to the stations and mission property, complicated especially in Shiloh and Goshen by restiveness of a

minority of members under certain municipal regulations—
difficulties shared at the same time and in a similar manner by
the Anglican and Wesleyan missions. Negotiations were set
on foot, with a view to secure a permanent decision from the
colonial parliament. A tendency decidedly favorable to the
desires of the mission became apparent in this high court during the summer of 1888, but the proceedings protracted themselves beyond all expectation. Meanwhile it was the more
desirable that a decision on all points at issue should be
obtained, since the opportunities for evangelization were widening. Amongst the Hlubi and Tembu Kaffirs alone it was estimated that about eight thousand heathen were yet to be found.

In hope against hope the West Himalayan mission continued
to be prosecuted, the scanty results that came to the surface
exercising no deterrent effect upon the fidelity of missionary
zeal, as little as did the lamented death of Pagell and of his wife
in 1883. Here the most notable occurrence was the founding
of a station in Leh, the capital of Ladak, and the most important town in Western Tibet. This transpired in December, 1886,
thanks to the friendly influence which the British commissioner,
Mr. Elias, brought to bear in seconding the efforts of Heyde
to obtain concessions from the Maharajah of Cashmere. Success had been conditioned on the sending of a medical missionary to take charge of the polyclinic and hospital of the city.
For this purpose Charles R. Marx had taken a degree in medicine at Edinburgh, and now came with his wife as the coadjutors of Brother and Sister Redslob, transferred to Leh. The
dedication of a place of worship transpired on September 2,
1888.

Jaeschke, whose broken constitution had compelled a return
to Europe in 1868, lived long enough to see the publication of
his invaluable Tibetan-English dictionary; but his death in 1883
anticipated the completion of his translation of the New Testament. Redslob with the aid of the converted lama Nathanael
supplied the missing books. In 1884 the entire New Testament
in Tibetan was printed in Berlin at the cost of the British and
Foreign Bible Society. The first copies reached Leh in 1885.
Redslob next undertook the translation of the Old Testament;
and Genesis, in addition to the translations of a treatise on the
Catechism and other works by Heyde, could speedily be sent
forth from the lithographic press at Kyelang.

In Australia, the slow but steady decrease in the native population pointed to the inevitable certainty of the extinction of the Papuans in the southern colonies. All the greater interest therefore attached to the tribes of wild aborigines believed to exist in the northern portions of Queensland. Three or four beckonings of circumstance indicated a call to commence missionary operations there. But as often as an opening commanded attention, other circumstances interfered, even after an important tour which Hagenauer made in 1885, when he met with the representatives of eighteen tribes near Cookberg and the Bloomfield River. Nevertheless the Mission Board and the United Synod of the Presbyterian Churches in Australia kept steadily in view the importance of evangelizing these poor savages and the Kanaka laborers on the sugar plantations, whenever a favorable oportunity should offer.

CHAPTER LXVII.

THE FOUNDING OF THE MISSION IN ALASKA.

Discovered by Vitus Bering in 1742, and a Russian dependency for more than a century, the vast territory of Alaska was purchased from Russia in 1867 by the United States for $7,200,-000. The climate of the southern part is comparatively mild, and very humid, owing to the warm Kuro-Siwo, or Japanese current, of the Pacific. The northern portion experiences the terrible cold of protracted arctic winters. Its people, estimated at about 35,000 prior to the discovery of gold on the Yukon, have been classed as Americans, Russians, Haidas, Thlingits, Aleuts, Innuits or Eskimos, and Athapascan Indians. Eight distinct languages and several dialects are spoken. As a rule the natives are strongly built, and inured to hardship. The men have slight beards or none at all, and frequently trim closely the scattering hairs on their chins or pluck them out. An Asiatic cast of features predominates. The Eskimos are distinguished from the Eskimos of Greenland and Labrador, by being taller and more robust. All the various races of Alaska are characterized by a rather massive head, straight and coarse dark brown or black hair, dark eyes, high cheek-bones and a nut-brown or yellow complexion.

The natives of southeastern Alaska, taught by contact with civilization, have frame or log houses, wholly above the ground, with sleeping apartments partitioned off from the main or living-room, where the central fire-place is built; and many of the Thlingits use a modern cooking-stove. On the other hand, the Eskimos, being largely nomads, in summer occupy tents constructed of the best material that is at hand, skins or cotton canvas. In making a winter house, a cellar from twenty to twenty-five feet square is dug, from three to five feet deep. At the corners and along the sides of the excavation are set posts. On the outside of these poles pieces of drift-wood are laid one upon another to the top. Other timbers are placed across the top, forming the roof or ceiling. Against the outside, and upon the roof, dirt and sod are piled, until the whole has the appearance of a mound. A narrow platform extends along one side or several sides of the room, upon which are stowed the belongings of the family and bedding of furs. This platform is also the sleeping place. Large shallow dishes of earthenware, bone or stone, filled with seal oil and with wicks of moss, are the combined stove and lamp of the family. Sometimes these lamps are of huge dimensions, two to four feet in length and eight to ten inches in width, with thirty or forty wicks. In one corner of the hut frames are suspended in which snow or ice may be placed, which thawing and trickling into a tub below shall furnish the water supply of the family. At one side of some rooms, and in the floor near the center in others, there is a small opening. This is the doorway and opens into a hall twelve to fifteen feet long and very narrow and low, leading to a well or shaft. This shaft is six or seven feet deep and leads up a rude ladder to the open air. Within, the combined smell of reeking oil-lamps, rancid blubber and the effluvia of human beings and dogs, becomes malodorous in the extreme. When on hunting or traveling expeditions, temporary snow huts are built, peaked, or in the shape of an inverted bowl.

All villages of any consequence have their public hall, resembling the private dwellings, only much larger. Some of these are sixty feet square, twenty feet high and contain three tiers or platforms. These buildings are known as the *kashima* or *kashka*. Here the public festivals are held and dances take place. They are also the common workshops in which the men make their snowshoes, dog-sleds, spears and other implements.

Fishlines and nets and bird-snares are constructed of sinews and raw hide. Arrows, spears, nets, traps and harpoons with floats made of whole seal-skins inflated, are used in hunting, though guns are being introduced by the traders. For transportation on land the people have snowshoes and dog-teams and sleds, and on the water the kayak or *bidarka* and umiak or *bidarra*. With a frame-work of drift-wood, these canoes are made of skins; the kayak being a long, narrow, light, graceful craft, from sixteen to eighteen feet long, tapering at either end, with one, two, or three holes for the paddlers. The umiak is the family-boat, and may be from twenty-four to forty feet long, with a carrying capacity for fifteen persons and twenty tons of freight.

The food supply of the arctic Alaskans consists of the white whale, the walrus, seal, deer, squirrels, hares, beavers, land otters, etc., and of many varieties of birds, especially geese and ducks and gulls. Fish also form a large portion of the diet, raw, frozen, broiled or dried. Berries are used either in a fresh state or are mixed with whale or seal oil, or with fat chopped fine and beaten into a paste—"native ice cream." Love of strong drink, in spite of all law to the contrary, is a special curse.

Ignorant and savage, and with a religion built out of belief in ghosts and evil spirits, the Eskimos are superstitious to an extreme, and ascribe everything they do not understand to occult influences, thus falling ready victims to the chicanery of shrewd men who choose to drive the profitable trade of "*shamans*" or witch-doctors. Believers also in the transmigration of souls, they fancy that spirits enter even into rocks and winds and tides and animals, and that their favor or malevolence determines the business of the community as successful or unsuccessful. They also suppose that these conditions may be changed by sorcery. By suitable incantations, nonsensical mummeries and ventriloquism, the *shaman* can control the winds and tides, and can reward friends and punish enemies. Marriage is entered upon with no special ceremony. If the parties are young people, the affair is largely arranged by the parents. Perhaps the young husband joins his wife's family, and is expected to hunt and fish for them. If he refuses to give his father-in-law the furs he takes, he is driven out of the house, and some one else more active or more obedient is installed as the husband of the girl. Sometimes a woman has ten or twelve husbands before she settles down. In this condition of things it is not at all strange that the women become indifferent and often false to their husbands, and that childhood is a pitiful stage of experience. Love has little to do with family-life, and husbands and wives may be exchanged by mutual agreement. Polygamy also prevails to a limited extent. There are various festivals which involve heathen rites—a whale dance, seal, walrus and reindeer dances, etc. There are festivals for the spirits of wives, of dead friends, of *bidarkas*, etc.

Inhuman cruelty is sometimes practiced towards the sick.

The prevailing diseases are scrofula, diphtheria, catarrhal disorders, pneumonia, ulcerations and consumption; and the death rate is large. A superstitious fear exists with reference to a death in a house, so that when the sick are thought to be nearing their end they are carried out and placed in an out-house. If they do not die as soon as was expected, they are killed, usually by the *shaman*.

The dead are wrapped in skins and drawn on a sled to the rear of the village, where they are placed on scaffolds, out of the reach of animals, or upon the ground and covered over with drift-wood, or, as among some of the tribes, are left upon the ground to be soon torn in pieces and devoured by the dogs of the village.

The commencement of a Moravian mission in Alaska was quite unforeseen by the members of that church until soon before its inception; and the call came from an unexpected quarter.

At the annual meeting of the "Society for Propagating the Gospel Among the Heathen," held on August 23, 1883, at Bethlehem, its President, Bishop Edmund de Schweinitz, communicated a letter from the Rev. Sheldon Jackson, D.D., of New York, then Secretary of the Board of Missions of the Presbyterian Church, and since 1885 "United States General Agent of Education in Alaska," in which he urged the establishment by the Moravian Church of a mission in Alaska among the Indians and Eskimos. Instrumental himself in founding the Presbyterian mission at Sitka a few years before, Dr. Jackson considered the Moravian Church to be especially fitted for this much-needed work, in view of the long experience of Moravian missionaries in evangelizing tribes of degraded savages; and stated that he had unsuccessfully applied to other denominations on behalf of these neglected heathen. The society having favorably entertained his appeal, with the sanction of the Department of Missions, Adolphus Hartmann, missionary among the Indians in Canada, and William H. Weinland, a member of the graduating class of the theological seminary at Bethlehem, were appointed to undertake a tour of exploration.

Steaming out of San Francisco on May 3, 1884, in the U. S. Revenue Cutter *Corwin*, they reached Unalaska on May 16, and thence proceeded in the *Dora*, of the Alaska Commercial Company, across Bering Sea to the mouth of the Nushagak.

Here was a Greek church whose priest claimed the district of the Nushagak and Togiak Rivers as his parish. Passing on to the Kuskokwim, they traveled up this river beyond Kolmakovsky in two large *bidarkas*. Their interpreter was Mr. Lind, an agent of the Alaska Commercial Company. The natives they found approachable. The land seemed to be prevailingly flat, sandy soil on either side of the river, covered with *tundra,* though wooded mountains appeared in the distance. Retracing their way overland with the frequent use of *bidarkas* to Nushagak, the return voyage to San Francisco was made without special event; and on September 25 they reached Bethlehem in safety, recommending that a mission station be founded on the Kuskokwim, near the native village of Mumtrekhlagamiut, about eighty miles from the mouth of the river.

The spring of 1885 sees a company of missionary pioneers in San Francisco, *en route* for Bethel, as this projected station is to be named. They are William H. Weinland and John Henry Kilbuck, a lineal descendant of Gelelemend, a Christian king of the Delawares in the last century, recent graduates of the theological seminary, with their wives, and Hans Torgersen, a practical carpenter, who as a lay-missionary will assist in establishing the mission. He has left his wife at New Fairfield, where he has hitherto been engaged. They charter a schooner, the *Lizzie Merrill,* to convey themselves and their building material and supplies to the mouth of the Kuskokwim, taking with them a small sail-boat, the *Bethel Star,* with which to navigate that river. Weighing anchor on May 18, they arrive at the Kuskokwim on June 19. Before ever their goods are all at the site of the mission, Torgersen on August 10 is drowned in the river. The situation is most serious. Two young men, utterly inexperienced in house-building, with their brides of a few months, face to face with an arctic winter, and not having a roof over their heads; Kilbuck, moreover, suffering from an affection of the eyes that at times almost blinded him; the material which they have brought for the construction of a house so wet from the frequent rains that they doubt whether they can use it; and, to crown all, both of them able to communicate with the natives only by "sign language," except for the aid of Mr. Lind. Less brave souls might have searched for some possible means of a retreat. Not so, these missionary couples. They dry their lumber as best they can in the *kashima* which Lind kindly places at their disposal. They erect their dwelling according to the best of their ability; and it is taken possession of by them on October 10. They write concerning this time of test, "You see that we can say, 'The Lord is our Helper.'"

The winter, which soon set in, was unusually severe. On December 29, the thermometer reached 50 6-10 degrees below zero. In October neighboring lakes were like rock in the grasp of the cold; and it was the end of May before the river was clear of ice.

In the summer of 1886 a second station was founded, in order to insure communications, and named Carmel, on the Nushagak River, near Fort Alexander, by Frank Wolff, who resigned his pastorate at Greenbay, Wisconsin, to volunteer. Returning the same year, next spring he proceeded thither with his wife and two children and Mary Huber of Lititz.

In the same year, the summer of 1887, Weinland and his family were compelled to return, owing to severe sickness—a retreat which preserved them for a successful career of pioneer mission-work in Southern California; but it was too late to send reënforcements to Bethel.

A weary, weary time was the early part of the winter of 1887 to 1888 at the lonely outpost of civilization and Christianity on the Kuskokwim. Work enough there was to do. At times troops of natives covered with boils, the heritage of a period of semi-starvation, clamor for salves and medicines; the school must be taught, its seventeen children clothed and fed—often washed, or even disinfected, when first received; there is a log-house to be built with native help; there are heavy parental anxieties about little Katie, the missionaries' child, and sometimes the utter cruelty of the unfeeling heathen is such that it would depress any except the stoutest-hearted.

But dawn is at hand. It is the Passion Week, 1888. Daily services, such as are customary throughout the Moravian world, have been commenced on Palm Sunday. Twice, or even thrice a day, there have been natives who are willing to listen for an hour and a half to two hours at a time, to what of the language the missionary can command. It is Good Friday. He is explaining that the blood shed by Jesus Christ on the cross was for the taking away of all sin, when some of the older men exclaim, "*Kou-já-nah!* (Thanks) We, too, desire to have our badness taken away by that blood." It is Easter Sunday,

36

at day-break, and forty people have gathered about *the grave of Torgersen*. They sing, in the native language, three hymns of the Resurrection. It seems the message, that "He died for our sins and rose again for our justification," is balm for the wounds of the hearts of Eskimos, as well as of the Caucasians who have sent the messenger, and of the Indian messenger who brings them the glad tidings. They leave the grave, having sung "Praise God from whom all blessings flow."

A number of natives soon apply for membership in the church—some have already months ago hinted at such a desire, before they realized the full significance of this step. A period of instruction and probation follows, and on September 10, 1888, eight are gathered in as the first fruits of the mission amongst the Eskimos in Alaska.

On May 12, 1888, Ernest Weber, of Gracehill, Iowa, who had volunteered and had been ordained for service in Alaska, left San Francisco, and arrived at his destination on June 16. He is soon quite at home in his work, his arrival making it possible to hasten the erection of the log-house planned for a school and chapel.

At the beginning of December he takes Kilbuck's place as teacher in the school, for the latter on the third of the month starts off with a dog-team for a five weeks' visit to Carmel, where he would confer with the missionaries about their work. But though man may propose, it is God who disposes. The difficulties of travel and the heavy rains so prolong the journey thither that Christmas has passed before he reaches the other mission-station. Then terrible storms and intensest cold delay the return. *Seventy-three* days elapse before he reappears at home, like one risen from the dead, "his hair and beard long and his face all covered with black spots where it had been frozen." The thermometer during this period had registered 59° below zero. It had been a miracle that he got through with his life. "No wood but green willow brush to burn, and very little food to be gotten for his teams of fifteen dogs." Meantime his wife, worn out with overwork at home, had been seized with serious illness, and was confined for several weeks to her bed. Yet grace sustained her, so that she could write: "Never before did I feel the nearness and dearness of my Saviour so thoroughly."

This visit to Carmel made it possible to send tidings home in February instead of mid-summer, by the kind offices of Lord Lonsdale, who was about to close an adventurous tour in the arctic regions. Already the conviction had become fixed, that additional help should be sent to both stations, and a call had gone forth for volunteers. Now, it appeared as though the brave woman who had so long toiled to the utmost of her strength without female help at Bethel might be compelled to return home, for a time at least. The news sent a thrill through the Moravian Church in America. Fully nineteen volunteers came forward for service in Alaska. Two were selected. John Herman Schœchert, of Watertown, Wisconsin, who was subsequently ordained, was appointed to go to Carmel; and Carrie Detterer, of Riverside, New Jersey, a daughter of a former pastor of the Moravian congregation there, was chosen for Bethel. In addition, the wife of Bishop Henry T. Bachman, one of the Provincial Elders of the American Moravian Church, North, offered to go to Bethel for one year, with her youngest son, in order to give Mrs. Kilbuck the rest she so much needed.

Accordingly this new company of missionaries sailed from San Francisco on May 15, 1889, separating at Unalaska, to arrive safely at their respective destinations about a week apart in June. At Bethel health had been restored to Mrs. Kilbuck, so that her absence from her post was not required. About twenty children were attending the school. The little congregation numbered twenty-two, not counting the missionaries. At Carmel the absence of the Greek priest, who had left for San Francisco, rendered labor more agreeable. During the summer the ministrations of Wolff to the men of the canneries seemed to be not wholly resultless. Louis Günther, a German sailor, had confessed his faith and joined the church. Two of the girls of the school were, moreover, candidates for membership in the church. Here the number of scholars in October, 1889, was thirty-one.

In this year a *"Brief Grammar and Vocabulary of the Eskimo Language of North-Western Alaska"* was prepared and published by Augustus Schultze, D.D., President of the Moravian College and Theological Seminary, as a help to future missionaries. A new and greatly enlarged edition came out in 1894.

CHAPTER LXVIII.

A BRIEF SURVEY OF THE CLOSING YEARS OF THE NINETEENTH
CENTURY.

Vigorous maintenance of active interest in the prosecution of
the missions among the heathen, as manifested in the volunteering of men and women already in the active service of the home
churches, in the hearty approval of the inception of new spheres
of activity and in the zealous coöperation for the removal of
financial burdens resting on the work—this appears a marked
trait of the life of all portions of the Unity during the decade
now in review.   The British and American divisions in particular feel and heartily respond to the world-wide movement for
the culture of the religious life of the young through the agency
of the Society of Christian Endeavor and kindred organizations.
All the Provinces are affected by the drift of population to the
cities, involving the removal thither of those in search of a livelihood or a career, in many instances tending to deplete the
centers of Moravian operation, and rendering the maintenance
of the old institutions identified with the inner life of the congregations on the continent of Europe a matter of increasing
difficulty.

For the German Province the decade proved critical in
various ways.   It became evident that the old financial arrangements involved in the *Diacony* system must give place to a somewhat less centralized and less closely interconnected method.
In place of the general federation of the congregations and
choirs, a measure of local independence and local responsibility
must be devised without destroying a general community of
interests.   In a modified form it was for German Moravianism
the counterpart of the problem which had confronted American
Moravianism in a far less intricate fashion in the fifties of the
century now closing.   The solution was hastened by the experience of heavy losses in the business establishment maintained

by the church in St. Petersburg, which necessitated its being closed in 1890. Therewith the very influential *Diaspora* activity in the Russian capital came to an end in the following year. Affairs were next complicated by troubles in Sarepta. In contravention of the privileges accorded by the imperial ukase which was the charta of this congregation's foundation, on July 30, 1891, a Russian official appeared before the church council and demanded the cessation of the civil regulations inseparably connecting the religious and the communal life of the village, and declared the warden deposed. The demands involved the diversion of church property to the commune and the interference of the people of the commune in the administration of the affairs of the Moravian congregation. Accusation of malfeasance in office was brought against the warden because of his acting in accordance with congregation rules and administering affairs in the interests of the Moravian Church and not in the interests of the commune. Government required the identification of the commune with the congregation and the recognition of every member of the commune as *ipso facto* a member of the Moravian congregation. Church discipline was thus made impossible. Unfortunately personal interests led a portion of the membership of the congregation to acquiesce in the demands. Nothing was left, but that the Unity's Elders' Conference must recall the pastor and his assistant together with the warden and on March 20, 1892, communicate to the people of the place the decision that Sarepta could no longer be recognized as a congregation of the Brethren's Unity.

Other shrinkages of the period were the union of Goldberg with Gnadenberg and the abrogation of a separate establishment in Norden, in 1891 and 1898. On the other hand in 1892 Breslau received recognition as a congregation and in 1893 Rixdorf was separated from Berlin, and given an independent organization.

In view of the Russian experiences it was inevitable that the chief attention of the Provincial synod, in session in Herrnhut from June 13 to July 2, 1892, and in adjourned session from September 25 to October 30, 1893, Bishop Richard and William Schultze respectively presiding, should devote its attention to a complete revision of the Provincial constitution, a rearrangement of the administration of the affairs of the congregations and a reconstruction of the entire financial system and busi-

ness methods of the Province and of its congregations. In the
interval between the two sessions of the synod, and on the basis
of resolutions preliminarily adopted, a special committee of nine
in conjunction with the governing board of the Province
worked out the details of the proposed reconstruction, which
was referred to the synod in its adjourned convocation and duly
considered, amended and approved. Practical unanimity prevailed. Neuwied and Zeist, however, in the application of the
principles arrived at, dissented in respect to certain details connected with the declaration that all business undertakings carried on for the church should henceforth become the property
of the Province as a whole. Special exceptions were made in
reference to these two congregations. Further consequences
of the principles now agreed upon were worked out by the Provincial synod which met on May 27, 1894, and remained in session almost five weeks. Now at length the new Church Book
(*Kirchenordnung*) with practical unanimity was finally constituted the law of the Province. According to its terms, the
administration of Provincial affairs should henceforth reside in a
board known as *Die Deutsche Unitäts-Direktion*, divided into two
departments: one having charge of all spiritual and educational
affairs, consisting of five brethren, and one of three, having
charge of all financial and secular matters. Each department
should be measurably independent of the othe ·, but should submit its decisions and transactions to the other for review, and in
certain cases the two should act together, constituting one board
over against the state and in all legal transactions. In the constitution of the synod provision was made for a larger proportion of laymen. Official members should be: the members of
the Directing Board, two representatives of the Department of
Missions of the Unity's Elders' Conference; the Bishops residing in Germany (until the next general synod); the Director of
the theological seminary. Elected members should be: three
Brethren engaged in the service of the *Diaspora*, called by the
Directing Board; twelve representatives of the clergy; representatives of the congregations, grouped together into seventeen
groups, but sending representatives in proportion to their membership—one from those with 500 members or less, two from
those with more than 500 but less than 1000, and three from
those having 1,000 or more members. In place of the two
boards hitherto existing in each congregation, there was to be

one board, the Elders' Council, which was entrusted with the administration of all matters, spiritual and temporal, connected with the congregation. This Council was to consist of the pastor and co-pastor and the chaplain of the unmarried men, and of from three to eleven members elected by the congregation and holding office for six years, the terms being so arranged that half the number were to be elected every three years. A separation having been effected between the property of the Province and that of the congregations, the following arrangements were effected for the payment of current expenses: The Province as such should pay the costs of administration and the salaries of all who receive appointment from the Directing Board, including pensions; the expenses of the educational establishments, in so far as the income of each is insufficient; certain costs of the *Diaspora* work; contributions to the Unity as a whole and certain special expenses. Each congregation should meet the needs of its local requirements, save in reference to the salaries of pastors.

Time was needed in order to carry into effect these far-reaching changes. William L. Kölbing was commissioned to visit the separate congregations, and rearrange the business affairs, attending to all legal requirements. Accordingly the first election of Elders' Councils in the several congregations took place in September, 1895. Meanwhile the Saxon Government recognized the Brethren's Church as a body corporate, under the title of *"Die evangelische Brüder Unität in Deutschland,"* and gave legal status to the two Saxon congregations. Similarly by an edict on June 2, 1894, the Mission Board had received corporate rights under the title of *"Die Missions-anstalt der Evangelischen Brüder Unität."*

The year 1897 was again memorable for the convocation of the synod, from September 23 to October 30. Apart from its serving to prepare for the general synod of 1899, its chief business was an inquiry into the work of the theological seminary at Gnadenfeld, of which Paul Kölbing was President. For a number of years earnest apprehensions had been felt in various circles, on account of the influence which was believed to be exerted in the seminary by the Ritschlian type of theology, prevalent amongst many of the scholars of Germany. These apprehensions had been shared by friends of the church in the *Diaspora* and by supporters of its missions. Amongst the members of the synod itself, when it convened, various views prevailed. Whilst some could declare their unreserved confidence in the seminary and its professors, others felt that the critical tendency could not be conscientiously tolerated, if it actually characterized the teaching. It appeared that synod had before it the alternative, either to disband the seminary, or to continue it with changes in its staff and an essential modification of its present methods. At the same time it was admitted that the abrogation of the institution would be attended with the most serious consequences for the German Province, whilst on the other hand a complete change in the personnel of the instructors was impracticable. In every respect the situation was anxious. But once more in the history of the Unity the power of prayer was manifested. The Lord granted a peaceful solution. The synod did not degenerate into an arena, nor did its members divide into two irreconcilably hostile parties. On the contrary in brotherly openness the issues were thoroughly debated. In brotherly fashion searching inquiries were made and met, so that many of the apprehensions respecting the position of the Gnadenfeld professors disappeared, and it was possible to declare that confidence in them was restored. It became more and more evident that the solution of the situation was to be found in anew emphasizing the Christo-centric position of the theology of the Brethren's Unity. All true theology must be unquestionably and definitely founded on the doctrine of the atonement. This must be made the test by which to try the theology characteristic of Gnadenfeld. After the President of the seminary had made a complete statement in the name of and in conjunction with his colleagues in reference to this test, by a vote of forty-three to four synod expressed its conviction, that although the prevalent theologico-scientific methods of the age affected the mode of presentation, nevertheless the theology of Gnadenfeld came within the limits of that which the Brethren's Church can tolerate, being in harmony with its teaching concerning the way of salvation, and that the seminary may continue as at present organized.

Many changes had characterized the administrative Board of the Province during the past years. As now constituted it consisted of the following: Theodore Bauer, William Jacky, Paul Dober, Bishop Conrad Beck and Paul Reichel, members of the Department of Education and the Pastoral Office, and

Max Bertram, Otto Uttendörfer and Daniel Schärf, members of the Department of Finance, with William L. Kölbing as a supernumerary member for the effecting of legal arrangements not yet complete. Theodore Bauer became President of the Unity's Elders' Conference, and Otto Uttendörfer Vice-President. But next year failing health compelled the resignation of the former, whereupon Bishop Jahn received a seat in the Board and Uttendörfer became President of the Unity's Elders' Conference, with Paul Reichel as Vice-President. Amongst the changes of the past, throughout the Unity special mourning had been called forth by the deaths of Bishop Richard on January 31, 1894, of William Schultze on January 4, 1895, and of Bernard Becker on December 15, 1894. The two former had been members of the Board, and had previously rendered valuable services in connection with the educational undertakings of the church, Richard especially in Switzerland, and Schultze in adapting the schools to meet the requirements of inspection by the state. The official visit of Bishop Richard in the eighties had peculiarly endeared him to the American congregations. Dr. Becker, as President of the theological seminary, in whose management he had been succeeded some time before his death by Paul Kölbing, had added a most valuable contribution to the historical literature of the Unity and through his lectures in Pastoral Theology had placed a high ideal before the younger ministers of the German Province. Similarly Herrnhut congregation in particular mourned over the deaths of Bishop Hermann Jahn and of Theodore Bauer in the spring of 1899. The former, dying on June 14, for many years prior to his election as a member of the Directing Board had served Herrnhut as its pastor, and was borne to his last resting place amid the sorrow of many. The latter had previously resigned office on account of increasing physical sufferings, but remained in Herrnhut, where he had also sustained the relation of co-pastor prior to taking charge of the school for the children of missionaries at Kleinwelke and his subsequent service in the Board. He died on May 26. The vacancy was filled by the election of Herman Bauer, for many years President of the college at Niesky. In like manner the services of the venerable Bishop Henry Müller, who retired from active engagements in 1896, and of Guido Burkhardt, who resigned from the Mission Board in 1894, were held in grateful remembrance. The latter became editor of the new *Mitteilungen aus der Brüdergemeine*.

Meantime the work of evangelization in Bohemia and Moravia, the undertaking of the entire church, was beginning to attain significant proportions. Promptly upon the adjournment of the synod of 1869, which had directed its inception, steps were taken to carry the resolve into effect. But until 1880 innumerable difficulties stood in the way. It was one thing to be filled with a high purpose, and quite another thing to carry out that purpose. According to Austrian law Moravians were creedless separatists, entitled to no legal consideration. Therefore services conducted by Moravian ministers might be attended only by persons who could show that they had been individually invited by card, as to a social gathering. Prosecutions on the ground of attempts to make proselytes were also inevitable. The imposition of fines and the being annoyed with all manner of vexations were things to be expected as a matter of course. But in spite of all this, the resolutions of 1869 were to be carried out, providence permitting.

On October 16, 1870, the congregation of Pottenstein was organized, in the Richenau district so thoroughly occupied by the Brethren in former days. In May and October, 1871, congregations were founded at Dauba and at Rothwasser. In August the prayer-hall at Pottenstein had been dedicated.

Now trouble burst like a thunderstorm. The judge of the circuit in which Pottenstein is situated issued an order peremptorily prohibiting Moravian services. But at the other center, which was in another jurisdiction, for a time no notice seemed to be taken of the enterprise. However, before Theobald Wunderling, the chairman of the committee charged with the oversight of the mission, arrived at the place when on his way to install Eugene Schmidt in October, the judge of the district forbade the services, and further threatened Schmidt with banishment if he attempted to baptize. He applied to the provincial government at Prague, and was informed that religious services would be within the law, if held in private houses and if restricted to guests who had received an invitation individually and by name. Divine worship in the morning of that installation Sunday was rudely interrupted by the entrance of police, one of whom was armed with a bayonet. In spite of this, the services proceeded, and the Holy Communion was celebrated in the afternoon. Scarcely had the visitors from Germany left, when the officers arrived with an order for their arrest and conveyance to the frontier.

In December, 1874, the dedication of a new building for the orphanage at Rothwasser, the old one having been destroyed by fire, made public proclamation of the determination to labor on in spite of obstacles, trusting that the God of the fathers would overrule affairs and so change the hearts of authorities, that liberty of operations might at length be secured. But during this period it did not come, notwithstanding that no lawful means were omitted for the obtaining of the desired change. However, preparations were made in these days of frequent discouragement, that the prophecy of the Zerotins might be fulfilled, and the gravestone at Brandeis truly set forth the future, that "out of the ashes of the forefathers there should grow a blossom and out of their deeds ripe fruit."

At length on March 30, 1880, the energetic and persistent representations of the leaders of the work were crowned with reward, in the issuing of an imperial edict which accorded recognition to the Brethren's Church and its directing board, though the resultant negotiations were protracted until 1883. Meantime Pottenstein received as filials, in addition to Rothwasser, Tschenkowitz, Wildenschwert, Landskron, Reichenau and Prague. A significant step in advance was the ordination on July 5, 1885, by Bishop Henry Levin Reichel, at Pottenstein, of Joseph Mikulastik, the first native Bohemian to receive ordination in Bohemia at the hands of a bishop of the Brethren's Church for more than two centuries. Other ordinations followed. In 1889 an important change was made, the transfer of Eugene Schmidt to Dauba, and the appointment to Pottenstein of Theophilus Reichel, hitherto chaplain of the unmarried men at Herrnhut. In 1890 the endeavor was put forth to specially develop the work at Prague, by the stationing of a local pastor, Wenceslaus Betka. Next year Moravia was entered, a congregation being organized on June 17, 1891, at Herzogwald, near Hof, of which Francis Spiegler became the pastor. Dauba meanwhile blossomed out into filial organizations at Grottau, Gablonz-Reichenberg, Jungbunzlau, Turnau, Hühnerwasser, Bodenbach-Dux, Leitmeritz-Lobositz (Michsen). Yet the numbers at each place did not proclaim that the day of small things was past, and for the most part the membership was drawn from the humble in the land. Nor did the cunning and craft of priestly opposition cease to render the efforts of faithful ministers laborious in the extreme. Friendly relations were on the other hand maintained with the ministers of other evangelical bodies and with the "Old Catholics," and the sympathy of people of culture no less than the ever accelerating momentum of the national movement to be "free from Rome" gave reason to hope that in time brighter days must dawn.

In the British Province the policy of convening annual synods was inaugurated at Ockbrook in August, 1890. This involved the annual election of the Provincial Elders' Conference, but not necessarily a change in the personnel of the board. In point of fact the first change took place in 1894, when J. Herbert Edwards was chosen to fill the vacancy caused by the retirement of Hines—and at that by an intersynodal election. In 1896 Bishop Taylor's declination of a reëlection after a service of twenty-two years as a Provincial Elder and of upwards of forty-seven years in the active ministry was followed by the election of John M. Wilson. Finally after the death of Bishop Blandford in May, 1899, Robert Elliott entered the Board.

By the Ockbrook synod the *Messenger* was changed from a monthly to a fortnightly periodical and its form enlarged, Robert Hutton becoming editor, to be succeeded in 1894 by J. M. Wilson, with Henry England as his associate, and after two years England becoming editor-in-chief, with Samuel King as assistant, to be followed in two years by Harold Mumford as editor, whilst in 1899 Wilson once more assumed the chief responsibility, King meanwhile retaining his position.

For the extension of the church at home this synod was also of significance. Kershaw's faithful and successful labor in Belfast had demonstrated the possibility of growth in that busy center of industry, whither members of the Irish congregations were removing. Now it was determined to commence a second enterprise, University Road being given a companion in Shankhill Road, at first in charge of Edwin Zippel. Later the second congregation established its church home in Perth Street. Nor was this the only move for the extension of home missions during the period. In 1893 the old Methodist chapel at Crediton was leased by William Gribble, who labored in the interests of the Brethren's Church. In the same year the rapid growth of a suburb of the ancient city of Bedford, known as Queen's Park, through the removal thither of the works of one of the great railways, led to the purchase of land, and on February 2, 1896, a congregation was organized. It was served as a filial of the church in St. Peter's parish. The similar growth of the town of Swindon through its importance as a railway center caused the renting of its Good Templars' hall for services in 1897, the first celebration of the Lord's Supper taking place on September 27, Arthur Ward of Malmesbury being especially diligent in furthering the new undertaking, until in the summer of 1899 it received its own pastor, W. H. Mellowes, and steps were taken towards the purchase of a church formerly occupied by a Presbyterian congregation. In 1898 at Abbey Hey, a suburb of Manchester, about one mile from Fairfield, a site for a church was purchased, and in the following year a temporary structure of iron erected. Thus in various directions progress characterized the work. Moreover through the generosity of Mr. Morton of London, the liberal benefactor of Moravian Missions, a new sphere of usefulness was opened in the British Province. Desirous of supplying religious opportunities to the people of neglected country districts, the while all proselytism should be absent, he offered first of all in 1895 to furnish the salaries of five rural missionaries. These were soon forthcoming, and commenced to labor in the districts about Wickwar, near Bristol, and around Kimbolton, Tytherton, Woodford and Campden, in the north of Gloucestershire. In imitation of the *Diaspora* on the continent, the purpose was to promote true godliness and evangelical faith, without organizing congregations, or urging a separation from previous religious affiliations. By January, 1897, thanks to the generosity of the same benefactor, eleven missionaries were thus employed, and by the end of the period the number rose to twenty, though the death of Mr. Morton rendered a reduction in these forces inevitable.

By the synod of 1890 a change was inaugurated in connection with the college and theological seminary, the junior students being assigned quarters in the former boys' school in Fairfield, whilst the seniors should attend Edinburgh or some other university. Meantime the juniors should continue to enjoy the advantages offered by Owen's College. But the synod of the following year, at Leominster, found the experiment unsatisfactory, and resolved upon the reconstruction of the institution, by providing for a resumption of theological lectures. In November Joseph Waugh was appointed President. In 1895 an exchange was effected between Waugh and Leonard Hasse, pastor of the congregation in London.

Ever active in the support of the missions of the church, the British congregations and their friends were aroused to new interest by the volunteering of James Ward, pastor of Ballinderry, and his wife to become the pioneers of a new undertaking about to be inaugurated amongst the blackfellows of North Queensland. Together with Nicholas Hey they set out in 1891, and Ward's early death with the faithful continuance of his brave wife at her post served as an additional incentive to fidelity at home. The death of James Connor, at Berthelsdorf, January 13, 1896, deprived the Province of the valued services of Benjamin La Trobe, Secretary for the missions in London, and editor of *Periodical Accounts*, being chosen to fill the vacancy thus created. His successor was Charles J. Klesel, hitherto missionary in the West Indies, and pastor of Devenport.

Other deaths of men in the active ministry or in retirement after long years of service deeply moved the Province, notably those of Bishop Alexander Hasse in 1894, Bishop John England and Thomas Hines in 1895, Frederick La Trobe and Maurice O'Connor in 1896, Bishop James La Trobe—a venerable patriarch of ninety-four—in 1897, and Bishop Blandford and Edward Shawe in 1899, the last receiving his summons with startling suddenness whilst on his wedding tour. So, too, the retirement of Joseph H. Willey in 1899, and his death in the following spring, removed one who for long years had been intimately identified with the life of the church in Britain.

Special importance attaches to the synod of Wellhouse in 1898, preparatory to the general synod of the following year. In 1892 the Church Book of the British Province, collated by John Taylor, *Advocatus Fratrum in Anglia*, had been issued as the authoritative code of the Brethren's Church in this Province. Its preparation, adoption and publication had directed special attention to the study of the constitution of the Unity, and discussion had been quickened by a pamphlet issued by Bishop Buchner, of the Department of Missions. Furthermore the synod of 1897 had appointed a committee to prepare proposals for submission to the present convocation with reference to proposed constitutional changes. The report of this committee, of which Edward Shawe was spokesman, embodied the following seven main suggestions:

"1. That the management of the Missions in all their branches, inclusive of the Home for Lepers at Jerusalem, be entrusted to a Board, constitutionally independent of the German Provincial Elders' Conference.

"2. That this Board be called 'The Mission Board,' and consist of five members, elected by the General Synod, three of them being respectively regarded as representative of the German, British and American Provinces, and the other two being, if possible, missionaries.

"3. That the Unity's Elders' Conference be discontinued.

"4. That the Department of the Unity be discontinued.

"5. That the four Provincial Elders' Conferences shall form the supreme board of appeal from any Province, each Provincial Elders' Conference to give one vote, except it be a case when appeal is made against one of the Provincial Elders' Conferences, in which case that particular Provincial Elders' Conference shall have no vote.

"6. That the Bohemian work be administered by the German Province, with the assurance of the financial assistance of the other Provinces as heretofore.

"7. That the several Provincial Elders' Conferences be requested to act as Advisory Boards to the Mission Board, as and when requested by that Board."

In the main the suggestions of the committee were adopted as proposals of the British Synod.

Mention should yet be made of the publication in 1895 of "*A Short History of the Moravian Church*" by J. E. Hutton, M.A. (Vict.), a popular account of the Unity from its inception in 1457, presented in a very readable style. Its appearance was welcomed on both sides of the Atlantic, as meeting a felt want.

Meanwhile the American division of the church, like its sister Provinces, strove to fulfill its calling. In the North the home missions gradually advanced, one after another being admitted into the class of recognized congregations, and new enterprises were commenced. In the South the era was one of remarkable progress, the occupation of neglected rural districts in the vicinity of Salem being a marked feature of the decade, the year 1892 moreover being noteworthy for the addition of more than 500 communicants to the membership of the Province. In the

North, Spring Grove, Missouri, was organized in 1890; and Mount Carmel, in Kansas, though failing of permanence, constituted for a time a promising mission amongst Scandinavian settlers, and secured a church building in 1891, whilst in the former year Fort Howard received Aschwaubenon as a filial. In 1891 the two congregations in North Dakota each branched out, Bethel and Casselton being founded, and in the same year Maple Grove in Ohio was organized as a filial of Uhrichsville, whilst in Bethesda, Minnesota, a prayer-hall was consecrated in the parsonage, this congregation receiving its own pastor in the following year. Furthermore in 1892 Riverside was separated from Palmyra, and became a separate pastoral charge. In 1894 Berea was separated from Bethany. In 1895 William H. Vogler undertook the organization of a congregation in Indianapolis, and West Rudolf was formed as a filial of Centralia. In 1897 a second congregation, Scandinavian, the other being German, was formed in Centralia, and each obtained its own pastor and acquired its own house of worship by 1899. Further in 1897 Sister Bay was founded as a filial of Ephraim, Wisconsin.

But an advance of peculiar interest was the new work undertaken in connection with emigration into the Canadian territory of Alberta. In the Russian province of Volhynia families had long been settled, whose acquaintance with the Moravian Church dated from the activity of the *Diaspora* amongst the Germans of Poland soon after the Napoleonic wars. In 1884 two congregations had been formally organized amongst these people, one at Kremenka, the other at Schadura. Owing to the intrigues of the state clergy government had adopted measures so repressive, that the former organization had been dissolved very shortly, and the members of the other had migrated to Brazil. Meantime whilst the attempted russification of these Germans, who had entered Russia in reliance upon promises of religious liberty, was being actively prosecuted, the thoughts of many had turned to the western continent. The Canadian government held out inducements to intending emigrants, and offered on very favorable terms abundant lands well adapted for producing cereals. When in 1894 word reached the persecuted Germans of Volhynia, that land, well-wooded and fertile, and endowed with mineral riches, was available in the territory of Alberta, a number of families forthwith disposed of their properties and set out. On their arrival in Canada, they put themselves in correspondence with the Provincial Elders' Conference at Bethlehem, constituted of Edward T. Kluge, Edmund A. Oerter and Morris W. Leibert, elected at the Provincial synod of 1893, the successors of Henry T. Bachman, Augustus Schultze and Jesse Blickensderfer. Land was acquired about eighteen miles from Fort Saskatchewan, and forty acres secured for uses of the church, whilst a congregation was organized on May 6, 1895, the name Brüderheim being selected. Then on the 27th of the following month, under yet more favorable circumstances, organization was effected five miles from Edmonton, the name Brüderfeld being chosen. Here eighty acres were deeded to the church. Then in November and December Morris W. Leibert, by commission of the Conference and the Board of Church Extension, paid a visit of inspection, ministering encouragement to those who had ventured so much for the faith's sake. He reported most favorably in regard to both their spirit of devotion and the material prospects of the land. The Province responded to the appeal for special aid. Help also came from Europe, for general sympathy was aroused. In the summer of 1896 Clement Hoyler, pastor at Elizabeth, New Jersey, and William N. Schwarze, a recent graduate of the seminary, were appointed to the new field. A third congregation, Heimthal, was formed on July 26, 1896, soon after Hoyler's arrival. Churches were dedicated at the two older congregations in May and June of 1897, and by the autumn of 1899 each had its parsonage and resident minister, whilst outposts were established at Spring Creek and Limestone Lake. At the latter Norwegian was the language in use, whilst English was spoken at the former. Moreover in 1897 the arrival of Godfrey Henkelmann from Russia, a school-master and a devoted member of the church, who was licensed to preach, furnished welcome aid.

Meantime, under the leadership of two of its business men, Joseph A. Rice and Joseph H. Traeger, the building committee appointed at the instance of the synod of 1888, had been diligently canvassing the congregations, the President, Dr. A. Schultze, and the Resident Professor visiting most of the churches in the North and Joseph A. Rice the South. Everywhere the response was generous, and the congregation at Bethlehem donated a very eligible site. On September 27, 1892,

37

Comenius Hall, named in memory of the great Moravian bishop and educator, could be dedicated free of debt. It had commodious appointments for fifty students. Next year, thanks to the lavish liberality of Ashton and Louisa Borhek, the members of their family coöperating with special gifts of memorial windows, a beautiful chapel was likewise consecrated, in memory of their daughter, Helen Stadiger. In order to increase the usefulness and efficiency of the institution thus provided with an adequate equipment, and in order to keep it prominently before the church, the synod of 1893 relieved the Provincial Elders' Conference of the *ex-officio* trusteeship, and substituted a specially elected body of thirteen, the majority of whom were lay-men, provision being made furthermore for the representation of every District of the Province in the new board. Similar boards of trustees were also created for the several schools of the church, and a larger number of business men added to the Advisory Finance Board. But the complete severance of the Provincial administration from the educational institutions did not meet with permanent approval, the synod of 1898, at Lititz, appointing the Provincial Elders, viz., Bishop E. A. Oerter (President), Paul de Schweinitz (Treasurer and Secretary), and J. Taylor Hamilton, and the President of the college and seminary trustees *ex-officio*, and giving the former an advisory voice in the affairs of the boarding schools. Another important measure of the synod of 1898 was the separation of these schools from the Sustentation Fund, that henceforth the financial standing of the Province as such should be no longer bound up with the prosperity of these undertakings or the reverse.

In its character as a preparatory synod, this convocation approached the constitutional problems from a standpoint differing from that of the British synod. It asked for the creation of a central executive for the entire Unity, to which the several Provincial Elders' Conferences should be in certain respects subordinated, as are the governments of the several States of the American Union to the national government. At the same time this central executive, constituted of representatives of the various Provinces of the church, should be charged with the administration of the missions.

Meanwhile in the South, Centerville had been organized in 1887, Calvary chapel was built in Winston in the latter part of

1889; Fulp and Wachovia Arbor were founded in 1893; the organization of Christ Church in Salem, Mayodan, Mizpah, Bluff, Pleasant Fork, Enterprise and Moravia followed in 1896; Advent in 1897, and Willow Hill and Union Cross in 1898. In the autumn of 1892 a remarkable awakening marked the life of the Girls' School at Salem, now numbering more than 300 scholars, about three-fourths of the boarders making confession of faith in Christ. In this year the death of Parmenio Leinbach caused a vacancy in the Provincial Board, and Bishop Edward Rondthaler and Dr. N. S. Siewers received as their new colleague James E. Hall of Friedberg, and thus the Board remained until ill health compelled Siewers to decline a reëlection in the autumn of 1899, when John W. Fries took his place.

Meanwhile, especially in the North, death had deprived the church of the services of a number of ministers of prominence. The necrology of the period embraced the following amongst other names well known throughout the American Moravian Church—in 1889, Bishop Amadeus A. Reinke; 1890, Jacob Hoyler and Henry Reusswig; 1891, C. L. Rights; 1892, R. P. Leinbach; 1893, F. W. Detterer, J. J. Detterer and Francis Wolle; 1894, Francis R. Holland and Edwin G. Klosé; 1895, J. G. Kaltenbrunn; 1896, Bishop Henry T. Bachman; 1897, C. C. Lanius—a roll of honor, men closely identified with the advance of the church during the past quarter of a century.

With the constant extension of operations Moravian Missions during the closing years of the century became more than ever a work of faith. To the previously existing fields four were added in 1890—Trinidad, California, North Queensland and Nyasaland, and in 1896 Urambo in Unyamwesi, in German East Africa.

The first practically constituted an extension of the West Indian work, a considerable nucleus of members being to hand, emigrants from less fortunate centers of industry in British or Danish islands. Commenced by way of experiment at St. Madeleine, in 1892 a church was dedicated on August 2 in the capital, Port of Spain, Marc Richard being in charge. Later, out-stations were established at Chaguanas and Manantao. In a few years nearly five hundred members were enrolled, and the enterprise could be regarded as an important strategic point for labor in behalf of the eighty thousand Coolies of the island.

In California the destitute condition of the "Mission Indians," former proteges of the Roman Catholics, but forsaken for nearly sixty years, since the secularization of the church by Mexico, had appealed to the Women's National Indian Association. In turn these ladies had applied to the Moravian Church, and William Weinland had been sent on his recovery from the effects of the Alaskan climate. Potrero, "The Ramona Mission," was speedily founded near Banning, and in 1896 Martinez in the desert was occupied by David Woosley.

The call to Queensland came from the Federal Assembly of the Presbyterian Church of Australia, the veteran Hagenauer having made a tour of exploration. The Presbyterians offered to bear the cost, if the Moravians would furnish the missionaries for the cannibal blackfellows. James Ward and his devoted wife volunteered to leave their comfortable parsonage at Ballinderry, and Nicholas Hey accompanied them. They selected Mapoon, near Cullen Point, within the north-western corner of Cape York Peninsula, as the scene of operations, and soon gained the confidence of the dangerous savages, through their influence moreover securing kind treatment for a shipwrecked crew in place of barbarity. Ward's early death from fever, January 3, 1895, was a severe blow. But his brave wife and her sister, with her brother-in-law, Hey, maintained their post, and next year were rewarded with the baptism of the first converts. In 1897 Edwin Brown commenced the establishment of a second station, at Weipa, somewhat farther south.

The Nyasa Mission originated in the receipt of a large and quite unexpected legacy from a gentleman of Breslau, John Daniel Crakau, who died in 1887, combined with an appeal from the well-known Alexander Mackay of Uganda conjointly with Bishop Parker of Equatorial Africa, in 1888. Other missionary leaders, like Dr. Warneck, urgently seconded this call. The directors of the East Africa Colonial Company in Berlin assured Bishop Buchner of their readiness to coöperate in ways within their power. Accordingly in the spring of 1890 Theodore Meyer, Theophil Richard, George Martin and John Häfner set out for the country to the north of Lake Nyasa, *via* the Suez Canal, Zanzibar and the Shire River. Martin's grave paved the way for the advance, at Kararamuka, and all suffered from fever. But Rungwe was founded among the Konde people in August. Other coadjutors came out. Fever proved fatal to three of these. But Rutenganio and Ipiana were founded in 1894 and Utengule, among the Safuas and Sangos, in 1895.

This commencement of operations north of Nyasa led the London Missionary Society in 1896 to ask the Moravian Board to take over the unsuccessful mission at Urambo, in Unyamwesi, lying in the heart of the German colony. After considerable hesitation and a period of delay the Board became convinced of the Lord's leading, and accepted the additional responsibility, Edmund Dahl and Conrad Meyer being sent from the Mission Institute, and Rudolph Stern being transferred from Surinam to serve as superintendent. In the Nyasa district baptisms began to reward effort in February, 1897, notwithstanding the barriers of an exceeding difficult speech. Thus the Moravian Church practically assumed responsibility for the evangelization of the vast region constituting the western half of German East Africa.

Small wonder that the men in charge of mission-administration were often driven to their knees. As elected by the synod 1889 the Department of Missions was constituted of James Connor, Guido Burkhardt, Benjamin Romig and Charles Buchner. In 1894 Burkhardt resigned owing to considerations of health, and Connor was called home in 1896. Their places were taken by Otto Padel, superintendent in South Africa, East, and Benjamin La Trobe, Secretary of the missions in London.

Small wonder, too, that with the steady advance in the old fields, the cost of the world-wide work frequently exceeded the income of the mission treasury. During the decade the annual cost of the work increased by $92,640. Deficiencies of specially large amounts were those of the years 1894, 1896 and 1897, viz., $26,390, $25,334 and $62,068. Yet by the providence of God each was in its turn made good, the last just before the convening of the general synod. That of 1896 was wiped out by a single stroke of the pen on the part of a generous friend of the church, John Thomas Morton, of London, who had already on more than one occasion lent liberal aid. At his death, in September, 1897, he constituted Moravian Missions the beneficiary of a large part of his residuary estate under certain conditions. His trustees were directed to pay over the money, estimated at several hundred thousand dollars, during a period of ten years, *and the sums so received were to be used solely in behalf of out-posts which should be thereby developed into fully equipped stations. The money should not be employed to relieve existing missions.*

In connection with the administration of the missions an important step was taken in 1894, when on June 2 by a decree of the Saxon government the rights of a corporation were extended to the board, under the title of *"Missions-anstalt der evangelischen Brüder-Unität."*

Varied features characterized the special fields of operation. As for *Greenland*, a sufferer in more than ordinary degree through shipwrecks, four vessels carrying supplies being lost in 1895, 1896 and 1897, it became more and more evident that with all the faithful endeavors of the missionaries self-support could not be achieved. Meanwhile work among actual heathen was no longer being carried on, the people having been Christianized Under all these circumstances plain intimations had been received of the desire of the Danish government and church that a transfer of the Moravian stations to the latter should be effected.

In *Labrador* Albert Martin had been superintendent since the return of Bourquin to Germany in 1889. It had been a decade distinguished by severe epidemics, and the total number of Eskimos in care of the mission had decreased, whilst the number of white settlers connected with the church had so increased as to counterbalance this loss. The abandonment of Zoar, whence many natives had removed after the closing of the store in 1889, was determined by the mission conference in 1893. Ramah, on the other hand, was rebuilt, and during the years 1896 and 1897 Makkovik was founded to the south of Hopedale, Herman Jannasch dedicating its church on Christmas Day of the latter year. And preparations were made to establish a station at Rigolette yet farther to the south.

In *Alaska* the membership expanded from 84 to 987 by the end of the year 1899. Ugavigamiut was founded eighty miles up the Kuskokwim from Bethel; Bethel numbered six out-stations, Ugavigamiut two, and Carmel three. More than twenty native helpers rendered efficient assistance. But sad experiences caused sorrow throughout the church. To the dismissal of three missionaries was added the loss by drowning of Ernest Weber and his wife and child in Kuskokwim Bay on one of the last days in June, 1898, when returning from furlough, their small steamer foundering with all on board. Upon Herman

Romig, medical missionary at Bethel, devolved the burden of leadership on the Kuskokwim, a burden rendered the heavier by the failure of the vessel with supplies to make a landing in the summer of 1899.

In 1896 the Mission Board transferred to the Home Mission Board of the American Province, North, the care of the work amongst the *Cherokees* in Indian Territory, long languishing. As a consequence of national legislation, which cut down the mission farms upon whose produce the missionaries had been largely dependent, to the paltry size of four acres in each case, this branch of activity came to an end in the spring of 1899. Meanwhile the new work in *California* compensated in some measure for this loss.

In the *West Indies* the constant movement of the population, intensified by the stagnation of the sugar industry, together with the impoverishment of the masses had rendered the effort to attain self-support impossible, though loyal effort had been strenuously put forth and heavy sacrifices made. In 1897 the superintendents of the eastern islands met in conference, and after thorough discussion agreed to a general reduction in the salaries of missionaries, already none too high. However, numbers indicated a slight advance—of one station and three out-stations in the Eastern Province, and of six stations or out-stations and four preaching-places in Jamaica, whilst the membership in each Province was marked by a net gain of rather more than one thousand in ten years. Trinidad was a new and hopeful field, rapidly developing under Marc Richard. Since 1897 Edwin C. Greider had been President of the Eastern and Frank P. Wilde of the Western board.

For the *Moskito Mission* the year 1894 was critical in the extreme. Then the nominal suzerainty of Nicaragua developed into complete ownership, the Reserve being wholly incorporated into the Republic. Business being unsettled, and various regulations altered, the expense of maintaining the undertakings of the church was heavily increased. Yet with all the anxiety, and in spite of many changes in personnel occasioned by the climate, there was a steady advance, the number of stations and outposts being increased by five, and the membership by nearly two thousand. Here after many years of faithful labor, Augustus Martin resigned his office of superintendent, to be followed by Augustus Erdmann, who was called higher within a year. In turn William Siebörger, whose translation of the Gospels and Acts was published by the Herrnhut Bible Society in 1890, assumed the reins.

Demerara suffered a heavy loss in the death of the founder of the work at Graham's Hall, Henry Moore, in November, 1896. John Dingwall, teacher in the high-school at Bluefields, became his successor. The abandonment of the Bel Air estates, owing to the fact that the maintenance of the dikes more than absorbed the profits from the sugar, led to a removal from Graham's Hall to Cumming's Lodge prior to the death of Moore. A new beginning was also made in Georgetown, and an attempt was made to evangelize Coolies and Chinese who were pressing into the colony. As in the case of the West Indian field, the fluctuation of the people, and especially the removal of many to gold diggings along the Demerara River militated against large increase in numbers.

Surinam, where Frederick Stähelin succeeded Jonathan Kersten as superintendent in 1894, continued to be characterized by growth, a net gain of more than three thousand, and of five stations in ten years. Specially significant was the spread of the work amongst the Bush Negroes of the interior, though the self-sacrifice of Kersten at Albina demonstrated once more the impossibility of a white man's permanently enduring the climate. In 1891 the appointment of the first Chinese "helper," Lazarus Fu Ahing, gave promise of happy labor amongst the immigrant Asiatic heathen, and yet higher hopes were raised by the fidelity of another Coolie convert and evangelist, Abraham Lincoln by name. A further development of usefulness was the appointing of a missionary and two deaconesses, in 1897, to minister to the Protestants among the inmates of the leper hospital at Groot Chatillon.

South Africa, West, where the founding of Etembeni and Elinde, near Enon, reminded that the day for labor amongst pagans was not over, though for the most part the work had to be restricted to the "settlements," rejoiced in a gain of rather more than one thousand members in ten years, the total rising from 7871 to 9181. Moreover the steady advance towards self-support and self-discipline was most gratifying. The increasing tendency of the young people to seek employment in the towns occasioned a repetition in Port Elizabeth of the procedure attended with such good results in Cape Town, and the ministrations first of a native brother and then of Rudolph Schmitt prepared for the establishment of a congregation in this busy port. William Bauer dying in August, 1892, Paul Hennig had been charged with the leadership in the Province.

Similarly in the *Eastern Province*, where Ernest van Calker had succeeded Otto Padel, there was marked growth, peace had blessed the land and missionary labor could be uninterruptedly pursued. As a result of the visit of Bishop Buchner in 1892-1893, Tabase, Elokolweni and Mvenyane were raised to the rank of stations, and a number of out-stations were commenced. The membership rose from 3671 to 5314. Thanks to the liberality of Mr. Morton in 1896 a training school for native teachers and ministers was founded at Mvenyane.

The *Himalayan* field, distinguished for many years for almost fruitless toil, and during this decade characterized by severe sickness and death amongst the staff of missionaries, limited towards the west by agreements with other societies and to the east by the impenetrable boundaries of Tibet proper, gave out a gleam of hope, Poo especially showing signs of life. The native evangelists Paulu and Ga Puntzog, boldly itinerated amongst their countrymen. New outposts were established at Chot and Gui, near Kyelang, and at Scheh, near Leh.

At the close of the year 1899 the statistics of the missions were as follows:

Income from Home Sources,	$142,533.62
" " Foreign "	128,100.00
Total Cost,	416,007.50
Ordained Missionaries,	166
Physicians (already included),	(2)
Lay Missionaries (unordained),	23
Married Women,	180
Unmarried Women,	21
Total Missionaries,	390
Ordained Natives,	18
Other Native Helpers—Men,	1089
" " " Women,	756
Total Native Workers,	1863
Principal Stations,	146
Sub-Stations,	68
Organized Churches,	214
Communicants,	34,054
Sabbath-schools,	126
Membership of Sabbath-schools,	18,091
Total Contributions of Native Members,	$129,100
Total Membership,	96,380

CHAPTER LXIX.

THE FOUNDING OF THE MISSION IN GERMAN EAST AFRICA.

About mid-way in the route of the Cape to Cairo railway, the great trans-continental line of Africa, lies the sphere of influence assigned to Germany by the Conference of the Powers in Berlin in 1885. Victoria Nyanza and snowy Kilimanjaro form its northern boundary marks. The Indian Ocean washes its eastern shore. Lakes Nyasa and Tanganyika fix its limits to south and west.

With good reason Caucasians have been wont to shudder at the thought of tropical Africa. Its sluggish waterways and tangled jungles symbolize death. "There the voyager drives his paddle through a waste of fetid mire, where mangroves spread their dingy leaves to hide foul depths of putrefaction among their rotting roots. Sour odors of decay mingle with the sickly sweetness of blossoms in the hot fever-laden mist, that shrouds the rankness of vegetation on either bank except at noon." Such a characterization suits the flat lowlands of equatorial Africa near the sea. But the East Africa of Moravian missionaries is happier land, though even here the white man must run the gauntlet of fever, before reaching the healthier highlands.

Directly north of Lake Nyasa, and to east and west of its northern end, rise mighty peaks joined by glorious ranges of hills. Six to seven thousand feet are often reached. Rungwe towers up nearly ten thousand feet above the sea. Here on one of the foot hills is a point occupied by white men early in the nineties. Amid a clearing on this mountain, about four thousand feet up, houses of brick with shady verandahs and thatched roofs form their homes. Rungwe rears its mighty head three miles to the northeast. Its precipitous sides are mostly naked rock. Yet soft grass clothes the ledges, and on the shoulders of the passes and in the ravines a luxuriant forest growth abounds. About the station the fertile soil has accorded a propitious welcome to fruit trees and garden plants. Many springs gush from the slopes, and a clear stream dashes down a stony ravine. The air is pure, and the climate healthy though hot. To south and southeast and west and north the charms of Kondeland lie spread to view, the east shut in by the great wall of the Livingstone Range, twelve thousand feet high and more. Elsewhere the lofty fertile plateau, broken by peaks and cut by gorges, presents glimpses of villages of round, conical roofed huts, peeping out from among glossy dark green banana groves or well tilled fields of maize or mighty forests of mag-- nificent *Muave* trees, the lindens of Kondeland. Gigantic tree ferns curtain the steeps, down which mountain torrents roar. In the long grass of the lowlands buffaloes and wild swine and panthers and hyenas are hiding. Twenty-five miles away shim- mers the clear blue of the great lake.

Here dwells a veritable tangle of tribes. They all belong to the superior Bantu stock; but the internecine wars of centu- ries and the raids of Arab slavers have driven to these highlands a variety of peoples, distinguished by differences of speech and tribal peculiarities. An inability to organize, reciprocal strife of village with village; unconditional subjection to their petty chiefs, and the insidious corruptions of Arab slavers, who intro- duce weapons, powder and brandy, the while they foment mutual strife, explain in large measure the failure of the men of equatorial Africa to work out a worthy destiny.

The people themselves present traits of superiority, as com- pared with other Africans. Physically and intellectually the Bantus are a fine stock, manly and erect in form and gait. Their women, if clad in civilized dress, would many of them claim a certain type of beauty. All esteem cleanliness. Their houses, circular and palm-thatched, are kept tidy and their vil- lages neat. For savages they are comparatively good-natured, and peace loving. On the whole they enjoy contentment and happiness. Brave in war, their fortune is deserved.

Yet after all credit has been given, they remain pagan sav- ages. Mistrust, innate beggary, greed, and unblushing theft, and amazing conceit and self-righteousness meet in them. Litigation and strife over ownership of cattle constantly dis- turb family peace. Theirs is a curious idea of justice. A favorite method of deciding the merits of a suit is by the ordeal of drinking *Muafi*. *Muafi*, a juice pressed from the leaves and tender twigs of a certain tree, is a strong poison. But it may be so diluted as to become only an emetic. When resort is had to this ordeal the sorcerer prepares the drink in two cups—and here is his opportunity for fraud, and thereby for increasing his influence. The two litigants drink in the presence of the villagers. He who is first compelled to vomit is the man who has justice on his side. His opponent must pay him a fine of so and so many cattle.

The position of woman may be higher among the Konde people than among many Africans. But here, too, polygamy is limited only by a man's ability to buy and keep wives. An ox or two is the price. An old man with adult children will buy as a new wife a young girl of ten, who is not to leave her parents' house until grown up. Yet the transfer of cattle is made. When the maiden becomes conscious of her charms, she prefers some stalwart young warrior and elopes with him. The aggrieved bridegroom that was to be seeks to recover his cattle. The father protests he could not hinder the flight, and the cattle are his. So a feud arises between the venerable bridegroom and his younger father-in-law and the family of his successful rival. As among all savages, moreover, toil belongs to women. They till the fields of maize, and gather bananas, whilst lordly man enjoys the chase, or glories in battle, or lolls at his ease with his pipe.

Mighty influence is possessed by the medicine-men, for firm belief in witchcraft prevails, and with it cruel penalties are imposed on those thought to be convicted of injuring others through its means.

These people have some conception of God, a conception elevated above that of fetish worship. Yet dark ignorance and confused contradictions inhere in their religious sense and usages. That there must be a divine creator, they appreciate. But his very dignity renders him unseen, inapproachable, and carries with it the impossibility of a revelation. They name him "*Mbamba*," the Good, or "*Kiara*," the Heaven. He is absolute goodness, but absolutely removed from men. They neither worship him nor offer sacrifices. Yet in special exigencies the village chief may guide his people into the depth of the forest, where echoes of nature's sounds are divine voices. Under the chief's lead they dance there, and call on "*Mbamba*." Then they place the leaves of a certain tree in their mouths, chew them lightly, and take a sip of beer. Now the beer is blown out through the leaves as a fine spray. This is their only form of devotion. The ceremony concludes with feasting and diligent drinking of beer. They suppose that the unseen god dwells in the forest depths, and is pleased to be honored thus.

In 1891 four young missionaries of the Moravian Church came to these people of the Konde highlands. About the same time the Berlin Missionary Society began operations to the east. Isolated in the almost trackless wilderness, the Moravians commenced to build about forty miles from the nearest outpost of the German government, with great mountains intervening. An utterly unknown language had to be learnt. Their base of supplies, at Quilinave on the coast, was several hundred miles and several weeks' journey distant. Dreadful fevers were inevitable. George Martin died before the first house was built. Other missionaries died within a few years. Though not hostile, the people were wholly indifferent, feeling no need of a Saviour because without a true sense of sin. Ingratitude on the part of slaves who were nursed out of sickness after being rescued from the Arabs by German soldiers, had to be endured.

At Utengule, a station begun some twenty miles to the northwest, Chief Merere forbade his people to attend the services, and for a time they refused to sell provisions. Merere had sold land for a mission with the purpose of gaining the white men as valuable allies in war. He had been driven from his old home by the fierce Wahehes, and plotted revenge. When the favorable time came he sent for missionary Theophil Richard. The interview took place in an open court before his fortress, where Merere lay in the sun haughtily lolling on an ox-hide. Instead of consenting to join the raid, Richard warned him against robbery and murder. But he spoke only of victory and revenge. "Victory?" asked Richard, "how do you know you will conquer? You may be defeated and fall in the fight. In that case, are you ready to go before the presence of God, whose will you have not done?" The war commenced. A pitched battle was followed by a hasty flight back to Utengule. And now the position of Richard became critical indeed. Merere might vent his wrath on him who had been a prophet of evil. The pursuing conquerers might identify the missionary with their foes. But God held his hand over him, and kept him safe from both, though the breach between Merere and the mission now became fixed. Merere ordered Richard to leave. But he refused to go. Thereafter even in Utengule the gospel began to conquer.

At Rungwe peculiar interest attended the first baptism. The missionary Traugott Bachman was to leave Rungwe for Ipiana, a station recently established on the north-west shore of Lake Nyasa. On February 7, 1897, he preached his farewell sermon on the parable of the tares among the wheat. When he had closed, all unexpectedly a woman who had been under instruction, Fiabarema by name, arose. She stepped up to the pulpit and said: "I have risen to say that I belong to God. I wish to follow Jesus and to belong to Him alone. By the power of God I must shun sin. God is my father." A death-like stillness prevailed in the church as the missionary replied, "God has heard what you have said, Fiabarema! Do this, and God will take you as His child." Then followed the closing prayer, as usual. The people said, "The woman is drunk." But her confession of faith had made a deep impression. That evening she was baptized in the church, hastily decorated with flowers, and took the name *Numuagire*, that is, "I have found him— Jesus."

After less than nine years the status of the work was as follows: four stations were manned in the Nyasa country, Rungwe, Ipiana, Rutengania and Utengule, and foundations were being laid at Mbozi (Nika). About them was a population of from forty-five to fifty thousand souls according to the missionaries' estimate, or of from seventy to eighty thousand according to the reckoning of government officials. Nineteen missionaries were engaged. More than one hundred converts formed the membership of the Christian church in their care. Theodore Meyer from the first has been superintendent of the undertaking in the Nyasa region, and Theophil Richard manager of its external interests.

In consequence of the founding of this mission, the church in 1896 took over from the London Missionary Society the Urambo mission some three hundred miles to the north, near where the Gombe River makes its way towards the northern end of Lake Tanganyika. Thus, by agreement with other missionary organizations on the continent and in Britain, the Moravian Church assumed responsibility for the evangelization of the western half of German East Africa.

Moreover the men and women who went thither in response to the call were characterized by a spirit worthy of the best missionary traditions of the church. When prior to the synod of 1899 the great deficit rested like a load upon the undertakings of the Unity and retrenchment appeared inevitable, they met in conference to discuss their relation to this deficit. They realized that East Africa had entailed heavy outlays since 1891. They knew also that it had involved for themselves much that men reckon as sacrifice. Near them were the graves of companions and co-workers. But they wrote home to the Board: "Brethren, if retrenchment is unavoidable, we beg you not to recall us. Rather than abandon the work God has given us, we will relinquish claim to your support, and will do our work wholly at our own cost." Resolves like this are a wholesome demonstration, that the instinct of Christianity remains essentially what it was in the apostolic age. Happy is the church privileged from time to time to receive and loyally respond to such stimulus from its standard bearers in the field. Made universal, and everywhere yielded to, this spirit would enable "the hosts of God to fill the whole world with a knowledge of Christ in this generation."

CHAPTER LXX.

For the last time in the century the general synod convened at Herrnhut on May 16, 1899. Fifty-four voting members represented the several Provinces and mission-fields, and were assisted in their deliberations by nine advisory members. Special provision had been made that the interests of the missions should receive full attention. In addition to the exhaustive report of the Mission Board, their affairs were presented by the superintendents summoned from Labrador, Jamaica, Antigua, Surinam, Cape Colony and Kaffraria. Moreover for the first time men of the African race participated, as advisory members, in the transactions of a general synod—John Dingwall, of Demerara, Oliver Haynes, of Antigua, and James Carnegie, of Jamaica.

Organization was effected by the election of Morris W. Leibert, of Bethlehem, Pennsylvania, as President, and Otto Uttendörfer and Robert Elliott as Vice-Presidents.

The divergent action of the several preparatory synods in the different Provinces had made it evident that a recasting of the constitution of the church was inevitable, and that it would be attended with difficulties. After much earnest discussion in the open assembly and in committee, harmony was at length attained.

As adopted, section 1 of the constitution enumerated the divisions of the Brethren's Unity in triple classification: *A*. the self-supporting and independent divisions, four—the Brethren's Unity in Germany, the British Province, the American Province, North, and the American Province, South; *B*. the fifteen Mission Fields, and *C*. the Evangelical Brethren's Church in Austria. Section 2 provided that no individual shall be recognized as a member of the Brethren's Church unless he is a member of some congregation in one particular part of the church.

Sections 3 and 4 set forth the fact that the general synod is the supreme legislative body for the whole Brethren's Church, constituted of representatives who, whilst considering the welfare of their own Provinces and whilst in general being guided by the directions of the bodies that elected them, are nevertheless to be primarily solicitous for the good of the whole church. Section 5 treated of the functions and powers of the general synod, practically the same as hitherto; but general synod henceforth relegates to the various Provincial synods the right to elect the bishops of the church in the self-dependent Provinces, whilst it reserves to itself the power of electing bishops for the work of missions amongst the heathen. Sections 6 and 7 set forth the constituency of the general synod in the future. Voting members are the following:

A. Ex-officio: The members of the Mission Board, two members of the governing board of the German Province, one member of the governing boards of each of the other self-supporting divisions of the church. One member of each of the administrative boards in the West Indies. Two bishops from each of the home Provinces, elected by their Provincial synods, and finally the Mission Secretary in London. *B. Elected Members*: Nine delegates from each of the three divisions of the church, the two Provinces in America being regarded in this respect as one—seven from the Northern and two from the Southern Province; one delegate from each mission-field entitled to such representation (the West Indian Provinces at the present stage in their development), one delegate of the Brethren's Church in Austria. *C.* Not more than five missionaries, called by the Mission Board. Section 7 enumerated the advisory members of general synod. Then followed a number of details of minor significance.

With section 15 the most fundamental constitutional change was reached, rendering the Moravian Church a federation hereafter rather than an organic unit. The Unity's Elders' Conference gives place to a coördination of the four several Provincial Boards with the Mission Board, to be known as the "Directing Board of the Unity." In accordance with the decrees of the Saxon government in 1844 and 1895, it has its seat at Berthelsdorf. The President of the Board is authorized to sign legal documents in its name. He is to be elected by the general synod from the membership of the Mission Board.

38

The President of the Mission Board, however, is not eligible for this office. The rights, functions and duties of this board are essentially those of the former Unity's Elders' Conference, in so far as they can be assigned to a board constituted of distinct corporations at such a distance from each other. The Mission Board is empowered to refer to this Board of the Unity questions of principle and problems of weighty importance that go beyond the sphere of mere administration, such as the entrance upon new mission-fields or the transfer or abandonment of old fields. Should the Mission Board feel the necessity of it, a decisive vote may be demanded, but in other instances a mere expression of opinion. In this way it was hoped that the Mission Board might learn the will of the membership at large. This general board will also decide in the last result with reference to the Evangelical Church of the Brethren in Austria and the Leper Hospital. The resolutions and the results of the various Provincial Synods shall be communicated to the various corporations constituting the Unity's Board; so also must resolutions of Provincial Boards which touch matters of principle set forth in the Results of General Synod, or which may perhaps be held to clash with these Results.

During the next decennial period the Directing Board of the Unity shall hold meetings in person two or three times. For this purpose each corporation shall be represented by one delegate, with the exception of the Mission Board, which shall send two delegates. The six shall meet at a place selected by the Unity's Board, having each previously received instructions from the Board he represents. The entire scope of the work of the Unity's Board is within the purview of the delegates so assembled. At all other times the current business of the board will lie primarily in the hands of an executive committee of three, consisting of the two members who are at the same time members of the Mission Board and one member of the Provincial Board of the German Province. As a rule each of the three chief nationalities (German, English and American) shall have its representative in this executive committee. When any subject must be decided upon by vote, each of the Provincial Boards and the Mission Board shall have one vote, five in all, the American church here counting as two Provinces.

With section 19 of the constitution the Mission Board came into consideration, the responsible board of administration for the entire work of evangelization amongst the heathen. Berthelsdorf remains its seat. Being elected by general synod, of its five members three must be representatives of the German, British and American Provinces respectively. When it shall become necessary to fill a vacancy during an inter-synodal period, if the vacancy affects the representation of any of the home Provinces, the Province in question shall first nominate its representative, and in the case of the other members the remaining members of the Mission Board shall suggest the names of not less than three Brethren from whom a selection shall be made. The formal election itself in either case takes place through coöptation on the part of the Directing Board of the Unity. Whilst the duties and prerogatives of the Mission Board remain the same as hitherto, provision was made in the new constitution whereby they are authorized to come to an understanding with the board of each Conference in regard to the manner in which their mutual relationship to the missions, *i. e.*, in reference to calls, education of candidates, furloughs, pensions, education of children, etc., shall be adjusted.

One of the most important transactions of the synod was the resolution to transfer the mission in Greenland to the Danish Lutheran Church. The Mission Board had previously prepared a mass of information very compactly packed into twenty-eight printed pages. The proposal was not new. Ten years previously the general synod contemplated the possibility of the step. One of the most significant facts was that with one possible exception the missionaries now laboring in Greenland did not oppose the measure, but rather welcomed it. In its favor were the following considerations: First, Moravian work as a *mission* is accomplished in Greenland. There are no actual heathen, in the full sense of the word, to be found in Greenland, at least on the west coast, which is alone really habitable. For the few East Greenlanders Denmark has appointed a minister, Pastor Ryttel. The Eskimos are descendants of Christians for several generations. The ultimate aim of a mission is the upbuilding of a fully organized and self-dependent national church. This will be an impossible achievement amongst the proteges of the Moravian Church, the circumstances and conditions of their winning a livelihood rendering intellectual labor, needful for the training of native pastors, out of the question.

The State Church, on the other hand, which has the care of 8,000 to 10,000 Greenlanders, many of whom are halfbreeds and more vigorous and intelligent than the full-blooded Eskimos, is ready and willing to assume charge of the 1,700 souls at the Moravian stations. By the transfer a native Greenland church can be established. Further, whilst Denmark recognizes with gratitude the work done by Moravians, she believes that they are now standing in her way. The honorable thing for the successors of those who went out *primarily as assistants* of Hans Egede, is to withdraw, now that the time is ripe for Hans Egede's successors to take charge of the entire field, and now that they are able and willing so to do. In this manner an example of Christian comity will be set, and the Protestant world assured that Christian comity is more than a mere theory. Furthermore, the Danish Church is in a good condition to care for these people. A better state of spiritual life characterizes the Danish Church now than in many periods of the past. There is an abundance of candidates for service in Greenland. These candidates learn the language in a special seminary at home, where they study it for two years prior to their appointment. When appointed, the married men engage to serve at least nine years in Greenland, the unmarried at least six. Some remain for life. In Greenland they are assisted by native catechists, many of them half-breeds, who are trained for the work and who are able to visit the scattered population with ease, being expert with the kayak, a canoe few Europeans ever learn to manage. Finally the withdrawal is likely to redound to the temporal benefit of the people; for the conditions of life seem to render it necessary, and the Danish government requires, that they be removed from their present limited environment and scattered from the mission stations. Such a scattering will be of double advantage from a physical and temporal standpoint. On the one hand it will render more easy the sucessful catch of fish and furs, on which they depend for a livelihood. On the other hand they may then be more free to marry with Greenlanders of the Danish Church. It is evident that the present narrow village life, with its isolated conditions, villages being quite cut off from each other, promotes a degree of intermarriage that is to some extent a cause of numerical decrease. It is due to them to remove every crippling influence upon their race as such. In addition to these considerations, it was reported that the Bishop of Zealand, who is at the same time Bishop of Greenland, and the Danish minister of Public Worship had given assurances that they will conscientiously do their duty by former members of the Moravian missions when the transfer shall have been effected.

An attempt was made to solve the West Indian problem by granting to these Provinces practical independence with certain restrictions. A fixed annual grant, normally of $3,500, shall be allowed to each Province for ten years, and certain specific donations were voted. The cost of maintaining one theological seminary on the islands, under the jurisdiction of the Mission Board, shall be a charge of the general mission treasury. Mission Board will continue to bear the expenses, as hitherto, for foreign brethren now in service, i. e., pension, etc. For foreign missionaries appointed after December, 1899, Mission Board will undertake half of the expenses connected with outfit, pension, education of children, etc.; the other half must be borne by the Province.

In connection with the mission in Surinam, synod resolved upon a separation between the management of the business interests in Paramaribo and the administration of the mission itself. The former shall be placed in charge of an experinced business man.

The investments, business methods and accounts of the Mission Board, with the complete coöperation of its members, were subjected to a thorough and searching examination by the Finance Committee of synod. This committee, and in particular John W. Fries, of the American Province, South, and William Mallalieu, of the British Province, bore unequivocal and reassuring testimony to the prudent management of the mission administration. The deficits in recent years were attributed to the wide extension of the work and not to bureaucratic errors. The investments of the various funds were found to have been effected with sound conservatism. At the same time an advisory committee was created, to share with Mission Board the burden of responsibility in future, and the publication of a budget at the commencement of each year was required.

The negotiations of Mission Board with the heirs of Mr. Morton and with the trustees of his estate in relation to his munificent legacy, were reviewed. Besides paying a tribute of gratitude to his memory, synod expressed its approval of the decisions arrived at as a result of these negotiations, viz.:

1. That the payments from the Morton Bequest shall not be used for the entrance upon new mission fields, but only for the extension and the completion of existing fields.

2. That the Mission Board shall give the first consideration to those Mission Districts in which extension and completion are indispensable, and in which such an extension would have taken place even had the Morton Bequest not come to us.

3. That the decision, i. e., suggestion to the trustees, in which mission fields the money shall be employed, and in what ways it shall be expended in detail, shall lie in the hands of the Mission Board alone, and not in those of the local authorities of the Mission Provinces.

4. That besides the single payments for the founding of a station, and for the outfit and journeys of the additional workers, and besides the current annual salary of the missionary and the native teacher no other figures from the Bequest shall appear in the usual annual statement of the Mission Board. The payments for pension and education, which do not belong to the account for the current year, shall be entered to the respective funds (Pension Fund, Education Fund, Native Pension Funds), but in such a way that they stand as a separate item until the residuary estate is exhausted. Nor shall the interest on these sums appear in the current statement as long as the installments of the Bequest continue to be paid, but shall be added to the respective capitals. This will eventually constitute a reserve capital, whose interest shall not be drawn upon until the support of the newly founded stations falls entirely on the General Mission Fund.

5. That on every mission field which receives a gift from the Morton Bequest, there shall be laid the duty, as far as possible, to gather a Reserve Fund for the station so founded, by collections and contributions which shall similarly be capitalized, and neither capital nor interest shall be drawn upon until the cessation of the payments from the Morton Legacy.

The members of the Mission Board were reëlected and received as their additional colleague John Bau, Principal of the school for the daughters of missionaries at Kleinwelke. Bishop Buchner became President and Bishop Romig Vice-President of the Board.

The mission in Bohemia and Moravia was a subject of very solicitous consideration. Here the final decision in matters of administration was placed in the hands of the Directing Board of the Unity. In the actual management of this work the Directing Board is to be assisted by the Bohemian-Moravian Committee, consisting of two sections, namely, the executive section and the circle of non-resident members. *A.* The executive section is to be constituted of eight persons: three members of the Directing Board of the Unity, residing in Berthelsdorf, one of whom must be a member of the Mission Board; three brethren living in Herrnhut or its vicinity, and two of the pastors of congregations in Austria recognized by the government. *B.* The circle of non-resident members shall be composed of a number of brethren in each Province of the Unity. These are to be appointed by the governing board of each Province in accordance with its own needs. Provincial Elders' Conference in each case also appoints the chairman of its branch of the committee, who conducts the correspondence with the executive session.

As a rule conferences of all the brethren who are in the service of the Bohemian-Moravian Mission shall take place twice a year. The congregation-councils of the recognized congregations and of each filial having a membership of more than one hundred souls shall each be represented in these conferences by one member, who shall be chosen to serve for three years. This conference is given a measure of autonomy, and within the limits of the annual budget determined by the executive section of the Bohemian-Moravian Committee shall also control the expenditure of money donated for the work.

The executive section of the Bohemian-Moravian Committee was constituted of Paul Reichel, Otto Padel, Herman Schneider, Theodore Bechler, A. Christoph, Eugene Schmidt and Theophilus Reichel.

The election of the executive committee of the Directing Board of the Unity resulted as follows: President, Bishop Benjamin Romig; Vice-Presidents, W. Jacky, Benjamin La Trobe. Finally the executive committee for the Leper Hospital at Jerusalem was constituted of William Kölbing, Benjamin La Trobe and Paul Dober, Kölbing being selected as the chairman, primarily charged with the conduct of the business interests and correspondence of the Committee.

A Committee of nine representatives of the various Provinces had been appointed to consider all proposals bearing on points of doctrine or discipline. As a result of its deliberations, the following resolutions were adopted with unanimity:

Synod again declares its adherence to the fundamental doctrines of our Church, as given in the second chapter of the General Synodal Results of 1889. Synod holds that all that is essential is expressed there, and that nothing therein should be changed either by additions or by omission. At the same time Synod declares, that it accepts *all* Holy Scripture, Old and New Testament, which is the source of these doctrines, as the Word of God, given by God as the rule of our faith and life, and that we are determined to adhere thereto with all earnestness and faithfulness.

In view of the fears entertained by some, lest there be divergence from the truth as received and taught in our Church hitherto, Synod urges the Provincial Boards in the appointment of Ministers and teachers to be the more faithful and conscientious in carrying out the regulations of the General Synodal Results, Chapter II, Section 11, paragraphs 2, 3 and 4, so as effectually to meet the danger of error.

Synod earnestly and affectionately urges the members of our Church in all provinces to examine themselves as in the Lord's sight, whether they are firmly grounded in living faith in the Divine truth of the Gospel and in the fundamental doctrines of our Church, and thus whether they are true disciples of the Lord and true and living members of our Brethren's Church. Further Synod affectionately and earnestly admonishes all who serve in the Word in the Home Churches and the Mission Fields to pray anew for the power and anointing of the Holy Spirit, that their preaching may both awaken and edify when they publicly set forth the Gospel in accordance with the convictions of our Church as described in the General Synodal Results, and when they apply the same to individual souls for admonition and comfort. Thus we may confidently expect fresh outpourings of Divine grace and true conversions in our congregations.

As to the request of the Synod of the Northern American Province, to the effect that the staff of every educational establishment in the Unity shall be called upon publicly to declare their adherence to the fundamental doctrines of the Brethren's Church, Synod declares such profession of faith to be the concern of the individual provinces. At the same time all intrusted with the management of our schools and especially of our theological colleges are admonished and requested conscientiously to do all in their power to bring up our young people in the spirit, the doctrines and the princ.ples of our Church.

Adjournment was reached in the afternoon of June 30. In the evening the consecration of Reinhold Becker, Paul Dober and Arved Senft, recently elected bishops, took place at the hands of Bishops Beck, Müller and Rondthaler.

Again, in the providence of God, disruption of the Brethren's Unity, which at one time appeared not impossible, had been averted and a readjustment effected, that further usefulness in promoting His kingdom might be assured. To Him be glory ever!

The united membership of the four Provinces of the Moravian Church, according to the latest published statistics, those of January 1, 1899, was 35,385; the Bohemian Mission numbered 597; in Australia and in Russia there were 283 members; 53 missionaries were engaged in the work of the *Diaspora* in various European lands; 390 missionaries were laboring in the foreign field—a total of 36,705 belonging to the Home Provinces. In the congregations gathered from among the heathen a membership of 96,380 was reported. The *Diaspora* societies included about 70,000. Hence the total number of those in fellowship with the Moravian Church was about 203,000.

APPENDIX A.

THE BISHOPS OF THE RESUSCITATED MORAVIAN CHURCH.

TOTAL NO. FROM 1467.	NO. FROM 1735.	NAME.	WHERE AND WHEN CONSECRATED.	BY WHOM CONSECRATED.	PROVINCE.	YEAR OF DEATH.
63	1	David Nitschmann,	Berlin, March 13, 1735,	Jablonski (Sitkovius),	Missionary,	1772.
64	2	Nicolas Louis Count Zinzendorf,	Berlin, May 20, 1738,	Jablonski, Nitschmann (Sitkovius),	Missionary, Silesian,	1760. 1747.
65	3	Godfrey Polycarp Müller,	Marienborn, July 9, 1740,	Nitschmann and Zinzendorf,	German and American,	1772.
66	4	John Nitschmann, Sr.,	Herrnhaag, July 22, 1741,	Zinzendorf and P. Müller,	German,	1777.
67	5	Frederick de Watteville,	Gnadeck (Silesia), Aug. 25, 1743,	Zinzendorf and P. Müller,	German,	1748.
68	6	Martin Dober,	Herrnhaag, June 15, 1744,	Zinzendorf and P. Müller,		
69	7	Augustus Gottlieb Spangenberg,	Marienborn, July 26, 1745,	Zinzendorf, David Nitschmann, Sr., P. Müller, John Nitschmann,	American and German,	1792.
70	8	David Nitschmann, the Syndic,	Zeist, Jan. 14, 1746,	Zinzendorf and Watteville,	German,	1779.
71	9	Frederick Wenceslaus Neisser,	Zeist, Jan. 14, 1746,	Zinzendorf and Watteville,	German,	1777.
72	10	Christian Frederick Steinhofer,	Zeist, Jan. 14, 1746,	Zinzendorf and Watteville,	German,	1761.
73	11	John Frederick Cammerhof,	London, Sept. 25, 1746,	Zinzendorf, M. Dober and Steinhofer,	American,	1751.
74	12	John de Watteville,	Herrnhaag, June 4, 1747,	Zinzendorf, D. and J. Nitschmann,	German,	1788.
75	13	Leonhard Dober,	Herrnhaag, June 4, 1747,	Zinzendorf, D. and J. Nitschmann,	German,	1766.
76	14	Albert Anthony Vierorth,	Herrnhaag, June 4, 1747,	Zinzendorf, M. Dober and Steinhofer,	German,	1761.
77	15	Frederick Martin,	Herrnhaag, Jan'y 10, 1748,	Zinzendorf, J. Watteville,	Danish West Indies,	1750.
78	16	Peter Böhler,	Herrnhaag, Jan'y 10, 1748,	Zinzendorf, J. Watteville, J. Nitschmann,	American,	1774.
79	17	George Waiblinger,	Herrnhut, Dec. 6, 1750,	Watteville and L. Dober,	Silesian,	1775.
80	18	Matthew Hehl,	London, Sept. 24, 1751,	Watteville, Spangenberg and Böhler,	American,	1787.

TOTAL NO. FROM 1467.	NO. FROM 1735.	NAME.	WHERE AND WHEN CONSECRATED.	BY WHOM CONSECRATED.	PROVINCE.	YEAR OF DEATH.
81	19	John Gambold,	London, Nov. 14, 1754,	Watteville, L. Dober,	British,	1771.
82	20	Andrew Grasmann,	Herrnhut, July 5, 1756,	Watteville, L. Dober, J. Nitschmann,		
83	21	John Nitschmann, Jr.,	Herrnhut, May 12, 1758,	Zinzendorf, Watteville, L. Dober, J. Nitschmann,	German,	1783.
84	22	Nathanael Seidel,	Herrnhut, May 12, 1758,	Zinzendorf, Watteville, L. Dober,	German,	1783.
85	23	Martin Mack,	Bethlehem, Pa., Oct. 18, 1770,	Nitschmann, Hehl and Seidel,	American,	1782.
86	24	Michael Graff,	Bethlehem, Pa., June 6, 1773,	Hehl and Seidel,	Danish West Indies,	1784.
87	25	John Frederick Reichel,	Barby, Oct. 8, 1775,	Spangenberg, Watteville, Grasmann,	American, South,	1782.
88	26	Paul Eugene Layritz,	Barby, Oct. 8, 1775,	Spangenberg, Watteville, Grasmann,	German,	1809.
89	27	Philip Henry Molther,	Barby, Oct. 8, 1775,	Spangenberg, Watteville, Grasmann,	German,	1788.
90	28	Henry von Bruiningk,	Herrnhut, Oct. 2, 1782,	Watteville, Spangenberg, J. F. Reichel, P. E. Layritz,	British,	1780.
91	29	Gotlieb Clemens,	Herrnhut, Oct. 2, 1782,	Watteville, Spangenberg, J. F. Reichel, P. E. Layritz,	German,	1785.
92	30	Jeremiah Risler,	Herrnhut, Oct. 2, 1782,	Watteville, Spangenberg, J. F. Reichel, P. E. Layritz,	German,	1788.
93	31	George Traneker,	Zeist, Aug. 14, 1783,	Watteville, et. al.,	German,	1811.
94	32	John Ettwein,	Bethlehem, Pa., June 25, 1784,	Watteville and Hehl,	British,	1802.
95	33	Gustavus Schaukirch,	Bethlehem, Pa., June 25, 1785,	Watteville and Ettwein,	American,	1805.
96	34	Richard George Müller,	Herrnhut, Jan'y 11, 1786,	Spangenberg and Layritz,	West Indies,	1799.
97	35	Christian Gregor,	Herrnhut, Aug. 25, 1789,	Spangenberg, Reichel, Risler,	German,	1801.
98	36	Samuel Liebisch,	Herrnhut, Aug. 25, 1789,	Spangenberg, Reichel, Risler,	German,	1809.
99	37	Christopher Duvernoy,	Herrnhut, Aug. 25, 1789,	Spangenberg, Reichel, Risler,	German,	1808.
100	38	Christian David Rothe,	Herrnhut, Aug. 25, 1789,	Spangenberg, Reichel, Risler,	German,	1802.
101	39	John Andrew Hübner,	Bethlehem, April 11, 1790,	John Ettwein,	American, South,	1809.
102	40	John Daniel Köhler,	Lititz, May 9, 1790,	Ettwein and Hübner,	British,	1805.
103	41	Thomas Moore,	Herrnhut, Aug. 26, 1801,	Reichel, Liebisch, Duvernoy,	German,	1823.
104	42	Christian Solomon Dober,	Herrnhut, Aug. 26, 1801,	Reichel, Liebisch, Duvernoy,		1827.

TOTAL NO. FROM 1467.	NO. FROM 1735.	NAME.	WHERE AND WHEN CONSECRATED.	BY WHOM CONSECRATED.	PROVINCE.	YEAR OF DEATH.
105	43	Samuel Traugott Benade,	Fulneck, Eng., Nov. 13, 1801,	Traneker and Moore,	British,	1830.
106	44	Charles Gotthold Reichel,	Bethlehem, Dec. 6, 1801,	Ettwein,	American,	1825.
107	45	George Henry Loskiel,	Herrnhut, March 14, 1802,	J. F. Reichel, Liebisch, Hübner,	American,	1814.
108	46	John Gottfried Cunow,	Herrnhut, Dec. 26, 1808,	J. F. Reichel, Liebisch, Hübner,	German,	1824.
109	47	Herman Richter,	Herrnhut, Dec. 26, 1808,	J. F. Reichel, Liebisch, Hübner,	German,	1821.
110	48	John Herbst,	Lititz, May 12, 1811,	Loskiel and Gotthold Reichel,	American, South,	1812.
111	49	Lawrence Wilhadus Fabricius,	Herrnhut, Aug. 24, 1814,	C. Dober, J. Cunow, H. Richter,	German,	1825.
112	50	Christian Gottlieb Hüffel,	Herrnhut, Aug. 24, 1814,	C. Dober, J. Cunow, H. Richter,	American,	1842.
113	51	Charles Augustus Baumeister,	Herrnhut, Aug. 24, 1814,	C. Dober, J. Cunow, H. Richter,	German,	1818.
114	52	John Baptist von Albertini,	Herrnhut, Aug. 24, 1814,	C. Dober, J. Cunow, H. Richter,	German,	1831.
115	53	Jacob Van Vleck,	Bethlehem, May 7, 1815,	Gotthold Reichel,	American, South,	1831.
116	54	Gottlob Martin Schneider,	Herrnhut, Sept. 2, 1818,	Moore, Cunow, Richter,	German,	1849.
117	55	Frederick William Foster,	Herrnhut, Sept. 2, 1818,	Moore, Cunow, Richter,	British,	1832.
118	56	Benjamin Reichel,	Herrnhut, Sept. 27, 1818,	Fabricius, Moore, G. Reichel,	German,	1835.
119	57	Andrew Benade,	Lititz, Sept. 15, 1822,	Hüffel, Van Vleck,	American,	1859.
120	58	John Wied,	Herrnhut, Aug. 18, 1825,	Baumeister, Schneider, Foster,	German,	1837.
121	59	Lewis Fabricius,	Herrnhut, Aug. 18, 1825,	Baumeister, Schneider, Foster,	German,	1838.
122	60	Peter F. Curie,	Herrnhut, Aug. 18, 1825,	Baumeister, Schneider, Foster,	German,	1855.
123	61	John Holmes,	Herrnhut, Aug. 18, 1825,	Baumeister, Schneider, Foster,	British,	1843.
124	62	John Daniel Anders,	Herrnhut, Sept. 26, 1827,	Albertini, Wied, Curie,	American,	1847.
125	63	Frederick Louis Kölbing,	Herrnhut, March 13, 1835,	Hüffel, Curie, Wied,	German,	1840.
126	64	John Christian Bechler,	Lititz, May 17, 1835,	Anders, Benade,	American,	1857.
127	65	Charles Aug. Pohlmann,	Herrnhut, Sept. 5, 1836,	Curie, Wied, Anders,	British,	1842.
128	66	Hans Peter Hallbeck,	Herrnhut, Sept. 5, 1836,	Curie, Wied, Anders,	South Africa,	1840.
129	67	Jacob Levin Reichel,	Herrnhut, Sept. 5, 1836,	Curie, Wied, Anders,	German,	1853.
130	68	Daniel Frederick Gambs,	Herrnhut, Sept. 5, 1836,	Curie, Wied, Anders,	German,	1854.
131	69	William Henry Van Vleck,	Bethlehem, Nov. 20, 1836,	Benade, (Anders),	American, South,	1853.
132	70	John King Martyn,	Ockbrook, Dec. 23, 1836,	Pohlman and Hallbeck,	British,	1849.
133	71	John Ellis,	Fulneck, Dec. 29, 1836,	Holmes and Hallbeck,	West Indies,	1855.
134	72	John Martin Nitschmann,	Herrnhut, Sept. 17, 1843,	Curie, Wied, Anders,	German,	1862.
135	73	Christian Conrad Ultsch,	Herrnhut, Sept. 17, 1843,	Curie, Wied, Anders,	German,	1862.
136	74	John Stengörd,	Herrnhut, Sept. 17, 1843,	Curie, Wied, Anders,	German,	1848.

TOTAL NO. FROM 1467.	NO. FROM 1735.	NAME.	WHERE AND WHEN CONSECRATED.	BY WHOM CONSECRATED.	PROVINCE.	YEAR OF DEATH.
137	75	William Wisdom Essex,	Ockbrook, March 30, 1844,	Martyn, (Curie),	British,	1852.
138	76	Peter Wolle,	Lititz, Sept. 28, 1845,	Benade, Van Vleck,	American,	1871.
139	77	John Gottlieb Hermann,	Herrnhut, Sept. 27, 1846,	Curie, L. Reichel, Nitschmann,	German and American,	1855.
140	78	Benjamin Seifferth,	Ockbrook, Oct. 26, 1846,	Martyn, Hermann,	British,	1876.
141	79	Christian William Matthiesen,	Herrnhut, Sept. 5, 1848,	Curie, L. Reichel, Van Vleck,	German,	1869.
142	80	Francis Joachim Nielsen,	Herrnhut, Sept. 5, 1852,	Nitschmann, Reichel, Matthiesen,	German,	1867.
143	81	John Rogers,	Ochbrook, Sept. 19, 1852,	Seifferth, Ellis,	British,	1862.
144	82	John Christian Breutel,	Herrnhut, June 26, 1853,	Matthiesen, Curie, Bechler,	German,	1875.
145	83	Henry Theodore Dober,	Herrnhut, June 26, 1853,	Matthiesen, Curie, Bechler,	German,	1867.
146	84	George Wall Westerby,	Fulneck, July 5, 1853,	Seifferth, Rogers,	British West Indies,	1886.
147	85	John Christian Jacobson,	Lititz, Sept. 20, 1854,	Peter Wolle, (Benade),	American,	1870.
148	86	Godfrey Andrew Cunow,	Herrnhut, Aug. 30, 1857,	Nitschmann, Matthiesen, Nielsen,	German,	1866.
149	87	William Edwards,	Herrnhut, Aug. 30, 1857,	Nitschmann, Matthiesen, Nielsen,	British,	1879.
150	88	Charles William Jahn,	Herrnhut, Aug. 30, 1857,	Nitschmann, Matthiesen, Nielsen,	German,	1858.
151	89	Henry Rudolph Wullschlaegel,	Herrnhut, Aug. 30, 1857,	Nitschmann, Matthiesen, Nielsen,	German,	1864.
152	90	Samuel Reinke,	Lititz, Oct. 3, 1858,	Wolle, Jacobson,	American,	1875.
153	91	George Frederick Bahnson,	Bethlehem, May 13, 1860,	Wolle, Jacobson,	American, South,	1869.
154	92	Ernest F. Reichel,	Herrnhut, July 13, 1862,	Matthiesen, Cunow, Dober,	German,	1878.
155	93	Ernest William Cröger,	Niesky, Aug. 31, 1862,	Nitschmann, Matthiesen, Cunow,	German,	1878.
156	94	James La Trobe,	Ockbrook, July 18, 1863,	Edwards, Seifferth,	British,	1897.
157	95	David Bigler,	Bethlehem, July 31, 1864,	Reinke, Wolle, Jacobson,	American,	1875.
158	96	Henry A. Schultz,	Bethlehem, July 31, 1864,	Reinke, Wolle, Jacobson,	American,	1885.
159	97	Gustavus T. Tietzen,	Herrnhut, April 22, 1866,	Matthiesen, E. F. Reichel, Cröger,	German,	1882.
160	98	Levin Theodore Reichel,	Herrnhut, July 7, 1869,	E. Reichel, La Trobe, Bahnson,	German,	1878.
161	99	Augustus Clemens,	Herrnhut, July 7, 1869,	E. Reichel, La Trobe, Bahnson,	German,	1874.

TOTAL NO. FROM 1467.	NO. FROM 1735.	NAME.	WHERE AND WHEN CONSECRATED.	BY WHOM CONSECRATED.	PROVINCE.	YEAR OF DEATH.
162	100	Gustavus B. Müller,	Herrnhut, July 7, 1869,	E. Reichel, La Trobe, Bahnson,	German,	1898.
163	101	John England,	Herrnhut, July 7, 1869,	E. Reichel, La Trobe, Bahnson,	British,	1895.
164	102	Edmund A. de Schweinitz,	Bethlehem, Aug. 28, 1870,	Bigler, Wolle, Jacobson, Reinke, Shultz,	American,	1887.
165	103	Amadeus Abraham Reinke,	Bethlehem, Aug. 28, 1870,	Bigler, Wolle, Jacobson, Reinke, Shultz,	American,	1889.
166	104	Emil Adolphus de Schweinitz,	Salem, N. C., Oct. 11, 1874,	Shultz, Bigler, G. F. Tietzen,	American, South,	1879.
167	105	John Frederick William Kühn,	Herrnhut, July 7, 1878,	G. B. Müller, G. F. Tietzen,	German,	1890.
168	106	William Taylor,	Fairfield, July 10, 1878,	La Trobe, England, Edwards,	British.	
169	107	Henry Levin Reichel.	Herrnhut, June 29, 1879,	Tietzen, England, Edmund de Schweinitz,	German.	
170	108	Henry Müller,	Herrnhut, June 29, 1879,	Tietzen, England, Edmund de Schweinitz,	German.	
171	109	Theobald Wunderling,	Herrnhut, June 29, 1879,	Tietzen, England, Edmund de Schweinitz,	German,	1893.
172	110	Henry J. Van Vleck,	Bethlehem, Sept. 18, 1881,	Shultz, Reinke, E. deSchweinitz,	German, American.	
173	111	Alexander C. Hasse,	Fulneck, July 5, 1883,	La Trobe, Taylor,	British,	1895.
174	112	Mark Theophilus Richard,	Herrnhut, June 25, 1888,	Henry Müller, Henry Levin Reichel, Theobald Wunderling,	German,	1894.
175	113	Conrad Beck,	Herrnhut, June 25, 1888,	Henry Müller, Henry Levin Reichel, Theobald Wunderling,	German.	
176	114	Louis H. Erxleben,	Herrnhut, June 25, 1888,	Henry Müller, Henry Levin Reichel, Theobald Wunderling,	German.	1894.
177	115	Herman F. Jahn,	Herrnhut, June 25, 1888,	Henry Muller, Henry Levin Reichel, Theobald Wunderling,	German,	1899.
178	116	Clement L. Reinke,	Bethlehem, Sept. 30, 1888,	A. Reinke, H. J. Van Vleck,	American.	
179	117	Henry T. Bachman,	Bethlehem, Sept. 30, 1888,	A. Reinke, H. J. Van Vleck,	American.	1896.
180	118	Joseph Mortimer Levering,	Bethlehem, Sept. 30, 1888,	A. Reinke, H. J. Van Vleck,	American.	
181	119	George Henry Hanna,	Bristol, Eng., Aug. 21, 1889,	La Trobe, Taylor,	West Indian, Western.	
182	120	Benjamin Romig,	Herrnhut, Aug. 3, 1890,	Miller, Richard, Beck,	Missionary.	
183	121	Charles Edward Sutcliffe,	Ockbrook, Aug. 7, 1890,	La Trobe, Taylor, Hasse,	British.	
184	122	Edward Rondthaler,	Salem, N. C., April 12, 1891,	Levering, Van Vleck, Bachman,	American, South,	

TOTAL NO. FROM 1467.	NO. FROM 1735.	NAME.	WHERE AND WHEN CONSECRATED.	BY WHOM CONSECRATED.	PROVINCE.	YEAR OF DEATH.
185	123	Henry Weiss,	Gracehill, Antigua, May 28, 1891,	Romig,	West Indian, Eastern,	1895.
186	124	Charles Buchner,	Herrnhut, Aug. 21, 1892,	Müller, Romig, Beck,	Missionary.	
187	125	Henry Edwards Blandford,	Baildon, Aug. 8, 1894,	Taylor, Sutcliffe,	British,	1899.
188	126	Frederick Ellis,	Baildon, Aug. 8, 1894,	Sutcliffe, Taylor,	British.	
189	127	Herman Otto Padel,	Herrnhut, Sept. 28, 1896,	Müller, Romig, Buchner,	Missionary.	
190	128	Edmund A. Oerter,	Lititz, Pa., Sept. 18, 1898,	Rondthaler, Levering, Reinke,	American.	
191	129	Charles L. Moench,	Lititz, Pa., Sept. 18, 1898,	Rondthaler, Levering, Reinke,	American.	
192	130	Reinhold Becker,	Herrnhut, June 30, 1899,	Beck, Müller, Rondthaler,	German.	
193	131	Paul Dober,	Herrnhut, June 30, 1899,	Beck, Müller, Rondthaler,	German.	
194	132	Arved Senft,	Herrnhut, June 30, 1899,	Beck, Müller, Rondthaler,	German.	
195	133	Frederick Stähelin,	Herrnhut, Oct. 22, 1899,	Buchner, Romig, Padel,	Surinam.	
196	134	Paul Hennig,	Herrnhut, Oct. 22, 1899,	Buchner, Romig, Padel,	South Africa, West.	
197	135	Ernest van Calker,	Herrnhut, Oct. 22, 1899,	Buchner, Romig, Padel,	South Africa, East.	
198	136	Albert Martin,	Herrnhut, Oct. 22, 1899,	Buchner, Romig, Padel,	Labrador.	
199	137	Edwin Carpenter Greider,	Nazareth, Pa., June 27, 1900.	Moench, Levering, Oerter,	West Indies, Eastern.	
200	138	J. Herbert Edwards,	London, Oct. 16, 1900.	Sutcliffe, Ellis,	British.	

APPENDIX B.

THE DOCTRINAL POSITION OF THE MORAVIAN CHURCH.

Placing life before the merely intellectual apprehension of and assent to any fixedly formulated creed (see pages 18, 23, 57, etc., of the *Results of the General Synod of 1899*), the Moravian Church seeks to exemplify a living church of Jesus Christ, constituted of regenerated men and women, while it offers a common meeting point for Christians who apprehend dogmas variously. Personal faith in the crucified Saviour constitutes the chief foundation for the fellowship thus established.

"We aim at the *comprehension*, in a higher *living unity*, of the diversity of doctrinal views, in so far as this diversity turns on the interpretation of Scripture, and arises from the different modes in which the same scriptural truth is apprehended by different minds. This aim, however, we do not seek to attain by simply shutting out differences of opinion, or by leaving them unnoticed. On the contrary, we desire that such differences should find expression and be recognized as legitimate. Nor again, would we establish unity by allowing all possible opinions to subsist, and letting love bear the sway over their heads. We seek rather a *positive* and *living unity*. This we find in the *faith in the crucified Christ, in whom, as in the Son of God, we have reconciliation to God—that is, the forgiveness of our sins.* (Rom. v, 10; Eph. i, 7.) This faith, and the *personal living fellowship with the Saviour* which goes with it, we place, with all emphasis, in the very center of the Christian life; indeed, we give these so high a place that for us everything else, *in comparison therewith*, is relegated to a relatively subordinate place."—*Results of the General Synod of 1899, p. 23.*

"The chief thing, then, for us all as members of this Brethren's Unity is, and remains, to strive to be *One*, and to become more and more *One* in all that is *essential*, so that we may have *a sure ground for our state of grace*, and may become true members of the *One* body whose Head Christ is."—*Results of the General Synod of 1899, p. 24.*

At the same time the doctrinal position of the Moravian Church is not constituted of colorless negations. Statements affirmed by its synods and the language of its authorized catechisms and liturgies, especially of its Easter Morning Litany, and the doctrinal contents of the hymns embodied in the hymnals published by authorization of synods, present a clear and readily apprehended position in reference to the cardinal truths of salvation. Whilst carefully guarding the right of private judgment the Moravian Church jealously provides against the dissemination of error and unfaith in its pulpits and schools.

The inspired word of revelation, found in the Old and New Testaments, constitutes the sole norm of faith. Nothing is posited as to the mode of inspiration, for this pertains to the mysteries which it has not pleased God to reveal.

"The Holy Scriptures of the Old and New Testaments are, and shall remain, the only rule of our faith and practice. We venerate them as God's Word, which He spake to mankind of old time in the prophets, and at last in His Son and by His apostles, to instruct us unto salvation through faith in Christ Jesus. We are convinced that all truths that declare the will of God for our salvation are fully contained therein."

"We continue strictly to hold to what has ever been the principle among the Brethren, that it is not our business to determine what Holy Scripture has left undetermined, or to contend about mysteries impenetrable to our human reason."—*Results of the General Synod of 1899, p. 26.*

An explicitly and outspokenly trinitarian position is taken, especially in the Litany for Easter Sunday (pages 10 to 15 of the Hymnal of the Moravian Church in America). The entire structure of this Litany is based on the doctrine of the Holy Trinity. Here, however, is one of those mysteries of the faith which the church does not undertake to define in human phraseology, whilst firmly holding that Holy Scripture reveals God as triune, Father, Son and Holy Ghost. However, the Easter Morning Litany reads, "I believe in the Holy Ghost, who proceedeth from the Father, and whom our Lord Jesus Christ sent, after he went away, that he should abide with us for ever." The Catechism of the American Province, North, in connection with the doctrine of the Trinity, cites the "Apostles' Creed." In the Catechism the attributes of the Godhead are classified as "eternal, omnipresent, omniscient, almighty, all-wise; God is holy, true and righteous; God is love."

The fall of Adam is affirmed and the consequent inheritance of sin and death by the whole human race; but all dogmatizing in respect to infralapsarianism or supralapsarianism, imputation and the like, carefully avoided. "Total depravity" is

39

taught, but discussions of a theoretical character concerning "original sin" are shunned.

"The doctrine of the Total Depravity of human nature, that, since the fall, there is no health in man, and that he has no strength to save himself. (John iii, 6; Rom. iii, 23; vii, 18; i, 18–32; iii, 9-18; Eph. ii, 8–13.)" — *Results of the General Synod of 1899, p. 27.*

"What do we mean when we say that human nature is sinful? We mean that there is in it a natural tendency to sin, a love of evil, an indisposition to that which is good, and a predominance of evil passions over better convictions."—*Catechism, question 32.*

Sin is shown to be essentially alienation from God, as well as the concrete act of disobedience, and its awful consequences are set forth in terms that admit of no uncertain meaning.

"What is sin, therefore, in its very essence, or true nature? Sin, in its true nature or essence, is a falling away, or an estrangement from God, and is therefore in itself hateful and evil, as darkness is darkness."

"What is the punishment of sin called? The punishment of sin is called death."

"What is meant in Scripture by the word death? By the word death is meant, not only that the body dies and is exposed to external sufferings, but especially the misery of the souls of the wicked in this world and in the world to come. Temporal or natural death denotes the external consequences of sin, as shown in this world, as pain, suffering, dishonor and natural death (or the death of the body). Eternal death denotes the consequences of sin in the life to come, everlasting condemnation."—*Catechism, questions 33, 34, 35.*

But Moravian teaching rejoices especially in bearing clear testimony to the love of God, manifested in redemption through Jesus Christ, the incarnate Son of God, the Redeemer, and is wholly evangelical in holding up His vicarious atonement as the sole objective means of salvation. Yet it insists on the acceptance of no forensic theory of redemption, nor as such on assent to any other merely scholastic presentation of the method and manner of justification. It magnifies the merits of His entire perfect life on earth, whilst it emphasizes the truth that by His sufferings and death He purchased redemption, becoming the propitiation for our sins.

"The doctrine of the Love of God the Father, who 'has chosen us in Christ before the foundation of the world,' and 'so loved the world that He gave His only-begotten Son, that whosoever believeth in Him should not perish, but have everlasting life.' (John iii, 16; Eph. i, 3, 4; 1 John iv, 9; Eph. ii, 4.)

"The doctrine of the real Godhead and the real Humanity of Jesus Christ—that the only-begotten Son of God, by whom all things in heaven and earth were created, forsook the glory which He had with the Father before the world was, and took upon Him our flesh and blood, that He might be made like unto His brethren in all things, yet without sin. (John i, 1–3; John i, 14; John xvii, 5; 1 John v, 20; Cor. i, 17–19; Phil. ii, 6, 7; Heb, ii, 14, 17; iv, 15.)

"The doctrine of our Reconciliation unto God, and our Justification before Him through the sacrifice of Jesus Christ—that Christ 'was delivered for our offences, and was raised again for our justification,' and that by faith in Him alone we obtain through His blood forgiveness of sin, peace with God, and freedom from the bondage of sin. (Rom. iii, 24, 25; v, 1; 1 Cor. i, 30; Heb. ii, 17; ix, 12; 1 Pet. i, 18, 19; 1 John i, 9; 2 Cor. v, 18, 19.)"—*Results of General Synod of 1899, pp. 27, 28.*

" They (Moravians) believe that, in His great mercy, God from all eternity formed a plan for the salvation of man, because He 'will have all men to be saved;' that Jesus Christ, the Son of God, who by the overshadowing of the Holy Ghost was born of the Virgin Mary, and Who therefore was true God true man in one person, came into the world to accomplish this salvation; and that He, by His holy life, sufferings and death on the cross redeemed us from the power of sin and Satan, and enabled us to become children of God and heirs of heaven.

"They believe that Christ rose from the dead, ascended into heaven and is seated at the right hand of God; but that He is, at the same time, invisibly with us always, and through the Holy Ghost rules His spiritual kingdom, the Church, as the absolute sovereign and king of His people."—*What do Moravians believe? Tract, by A. Schultze, D.D.*

Justification by faith alone, and the necessity of regeneration, the work of the Holy Spirit in the human heart are posited not as tenets of scientific theology but as facts of personal experience.

" The doctrine of the Holy Ghost and the operations of His grace, that without Him we are unable to know the truth; that it is He who leads us to Christ by working in us the knowledge of sin and faith in Jesus, and who 'beareth witness with our spirit that we are children of God.' (John xvi, 8-11; John xvi. 13, 14; 1 Cor. xii, 3; Rom. viii, 16.)"

" Living heart-faith is necessary, for one becomes a true Christian only through faith; but it is also necessary that the soul be brought to a deep and thorough conviction of its sin and misery, of its worthiness of damnation, and of its need of redemption. For the more earnest is the longing for peace the more confidently, on the evidence of God's faithful word, can the redemption wrought out by Christ be laid hold of by faith."

" *Through faith* the sinner receives from God, through grace, the *forgiveness of his sins, purification in the sight of God, and peace with God;*

and he receives the power (the right) to become *a child of God.* (Luke vii, 48-50; Rom. v, 1; John i, 12.)"

" As to the manner in which God, in His merciful compassion, effects this great change in the human heart, both Holy Writ and the experience of believers show that there is a great diversity in God's ways of leading souls to their eternal salvation. Some, like Paul, are able to give the hour of the decisive turning in their inner life, when, called and awakened by the voice of God, they found justification and peace in believing. With others, again the experience of their awakening and pardon cannot be defined as belonging to any one particular moment."—*Results of the General Synod of 1899, pp. 28 and 29.*

The Moravian Church does not teach perfectionism, but it rejoices in the reality of sanctifying grace. It holds that to those who have received the forgiveness of sins and a conviction of their sonship with God, is given divine power for the resistance of evil and the overcoming of sin. It is their duty and privilege to follow after holiness, and to prove their faith by works of love, the while they reach towards the goal in imitation of their perfect example, Christ Jesus.

"The doctrine of Good Works as the fruit of the Spirit, inasmuch as faith manifests itself as a living and active principle by a willing obedience to the commandments of God, prompted by love and gratitude to Him who died for us. (John xiv, 15; Rom. vi, 11-14; 1 Cor. vi, 20; Gal. v, 6; Gal. v, 22–24; 1 John v, 3-5; Eph. ii, 8-10; James ii, 17.)"—*Results of the General Synod of 1899, p. 28.*

"The same grace which effects in the soul the knowledge of sin, and justifies the sinner before God and makes him a child of God, works in him further also true *sanctification.* This sanctification, however, consists not merely in the laying aside of certain sinful habits and vices, but far more in the renewal of the inmost mind, and the decision of the whole heart and will to be the Lord's. We love Him who first loved us, with the whole heart, the whole soul, and the whole mind, and we give proof of our love by doing the will of God with the whole heart, and obeying his commandments."

" The concurrent *mark of all true children of God* is this, that they have received *the Spirit of Christ.* (Rom. viii, 9.) It is this spirit of Christ who first certifies them by his witness that they have the forgiveness of sins, that they are children of God and heirs of eternal life. *He* works in them, instead of the spirit of a slave and of fear of the wrath of God, the spirit of sonship in which they cry, 'Abba, Father!' He impels them to follow after that sanctification, without which no man shall see the Lord. He sheds abroad in their hearts the love of God, by which they receive power no longer to let sin reign in their mortal body that they should obey it in its lusts. He reproves them, makes them sorry with a godly sorrow for the sin that is still present with them, and at the same time produces in them heartfelt confidence in their Lord, so that they ever and again confess their sins to Him who is faithful and just to forgive them their sins, and to cleanse them from all their unrighteousness. In view of the *goal* of sanctification in Christ the child of grace in deep humility, and also with holy and earnest decision, confesses with Paul, 'not that I have already obtained, or am already made perfect; but I press on, if so be that I may apprehend that for which I was apprehended by Christ Jesus.' (Phil. iii, 12.)

"But all the power thus to press forward towards the goal is given us by the gracious operation of the Holy Ghost, if we do not cease to look in faith unto Jesus, the Author and Perfector of our faith—that is, do not cease to look in faith at the whole merit of His life, sufferings, death and resurrection —and if we abide in that constant confidential intercourse with Him which a pardoned sinner has with his Saviour. That intercourse is none other than the abiding of the branch in the vine, of which Christ says: 'As the branch cannot bear fruit of itself, except it abide in the vine ; so neither can ye, except ye abide in me ; for, apart from me, ye can do nothing.' (John xv, 4, 5.)

" Thus the new life of the regenerate child of God is safely carried forwards towards its maturity, according to the measure of the stature of Christ, toward its glorification in the image of Christ and its perfection in eternity." —*Results of General . ynod of 1899, pp. 30, 31.*

Stress is laid upon the need of employing prayer and other private and public means of grace, for the culture of spiritual life. The Moravian conception of the church avoids narrow denominationalism on the one hand and a perverted ecclesiasticism on the other hand. Community with Christ is held to be of more importance than details of ritual, and polity, though all things should be done decently and in order, when worship is rendered in spirit and in truth. Whilst a complete liturgical ritual is enjoyed, including forms for use on the Lord's Day, and for the administration of the sacraments and the celebration of various rites, like confirmation, marriage and burial, and whilst the Christian Year is observed, free prayer is allowed, and ministers are not restricted in their choice of themes for the pulpit to the lessons assigned in conformity with the church seasons. The three orders of the ministry are perpetuated, but with no hierarchical conception of the functions of the episcopate. The congregations themselves, through their elders particpate in the administration of discipline. Fellowship with believers of every name is encouraged, and members of evangelical churches are received at their desire into communicant membership by certificate.

" What is our part and duty in the work of sanctification? We should watch over ourselves, and maintain our communion with God our Saviour by means of prayer."

" What do the Holy Scriptures teach us with regard to prayer? It is our privilege and our duty to bring all our feelings, wishes and desires in prayer before God, in all places and at all times."—*Catechism, questions 113, 114.*

" What was founded through the preaching of the Apostles? Through the preaching of the Apostles the first Christian congregation was founded, and this was the beginning of the Christian Church, which has since been spread over the whole world."

" Where is the true Church of Christ to be found? To the true Church of Jesus Christ belong all those who have been saved by faith in Him, and who, from love to Him, keep His commandments. But this true Church of Christ is not to be found anywhere on earth in a pure and unmixed state.

[The *visible* Church comprehends all those who have outwardly accepted the Gospel of Christ. These are called *Christians.* (Acts xi, 26.) The *true* or *invisible* Church is contained in the visible one, and is also called the *holy catholic* (universal) Church. Nominal Christians and real Christians.]"

" What has Christ instituted for the establishment and the spread of His Church on earth? Christ instituted the sacred ministry for the purpose of maintaining the knowledge of the Gospel, and spreading the same, by means of living witnesses."—*Catechism, questions 55, 56, 58.*

" The Christian Church has not considered it sufficient to dwell upon our Lord's redeeming work in general only on Sundays, but has also recommended the commemoration of the essential parts of that redemption by special festivals. From these has arisen the *course of festive seasons,* which embrace in historical sequence the whole counsel of God for the salvation of the human race, and occupy the first half of our Church year."—*Results of General Synod of 1899, p. 41.*

" Regulations belonging to our ritual and liturgy must never be allowed to become a dead letter, or to degenerate into dry, cold form. It is rather a principle of our Church to be highly esteemed, that we have and maintain liberty to introduce changes and improvements in our ritual as circumstances may require.

" Every minister presiding at a service must be at liberty in unessential points of ritual to act as the spirit moves him."—*Results of the General Synod of 1899, p. 38.*

" The ministry in the Protestant Church of the Brethren, by means of which it can enjoy an independent an undisputed activity in the kingdom of God in the same manner as every other organized Church, rests on the consecration of Bishops, Presbyters, and Deacons."

" The diaconate is the first degree of orders in the Church. It entitles to the exercise of the ministry of the Word and of the sacraments. After the example of the Apostolic Church, this consecration be also imparted to those brethren to whom the control of the temporal affairs of the Church is committed."

" The degree of presbyter is primarily to be conferred upon such deacons as are appointed to the ministry of the Word, and to the charge of a congregation in one of the three Provinces of the Unity, or are entrusted with the direction of any particular branch of Church work."

"The office of a bishop imparts in and by itself no manner of claim to the control of the whole Church, or of any part of it ; the administration of particular dioceses does therefore not belong to the bishops. A bishop, like every other minister of the Unity, must receive a special commission from the Synod, or from the Directing Board of a Province, for every office which he may have to fill.

"A bishop alone is authorized to perform ordinations to the various grades of the Ministry of the Church."—*Results of the General Synod of 1899, pp. 87, 88, 89, 90.*

From the first the Moravian Church has refused to formulate definitions in connection with the sacraments, holding that these are eminently to be classed among the "mysteries" of revelation, and observing with regret how these very means of grace, intended by the Lord Jesus Christ to promote union among His followers, have become causes of contention and division when men have attempted to bind the conscience concerning them. This, however, the Moravian Church does affirm : that "baptism is a sacred rite, by which under the emblem of water, we receive a pledge of the forgiveness of sin and admission into the covenant of God, through the blood of Christ; and that children also may be baptized as a sign and pledge to them of the promise of Christ that their's is the kingdom of heaven; furthermore that in the Lord's Supper the believer receives a divine seal of the covenant which was ratified by the blood of Christ, and that he is thereby drawn into the most intimate communion with Jesus Christ."

" What are Sacraments ? Sacraments are sacred rites, which Jesus Christ has ordained in His Church, in order to communicate and to confirm to us the gifts and promises of the Gospel."

"How many Sacraments has the Christian Church ? The Christian Church has two Sacraments : Holy Baptism, and the Lord's Supper or the Holy Communion."

¶ ¡" What is Baptism ? Baptism, as an external rite, is a sign of dedication to God, and of reception into the Christian Church."

¡²" What is the higher and spiritual signification of Baptism ? The external emblem signifies a dying of the old man, and at the same time an admission into the covenant with God."

" What do we, therefore, receive by Baptism ? By Baptism we receive, under the condition of faith, the promise of the grace of God in Christ Jesus for the forgiveness of sins, and at the same time the communication of the Holy Spirit for sanctification."

" What, then, is the Lord's Supper ? It is a sacrament instituted by Jesus Christ in memory of His death."

" What is it besides ? It is also a COMMUNION, or COVENANT-RITE, and as such a Divine seal of the Testament (or covenant) which was ratified by the blood of Christ for our salvation and reconciliation with God. ' Take, eat : this is My body. This is My blood of the New Testament, which is shed for many for the remission of sins.' Matt. xxvi, 26, 28. The Holy Communion is, therefore, a mysterious enjoyment of the body and blood of Christ ; that is, *when the Lord's Supper is enjoyed according to the mind of Jesus Christ*, the partaking of the bread and wine is connected with the enjoyment of the body and blood of Jesus, in a manner incomprehensible to us, and therefore inexpressible."

" The fourfold fruit of the Communion, therefore, is : 1. The assurance of the forgiveness of sins ; 2. The strengthening of faith ; 3. The increase of mutual love ; 4. The confirmation of the hope of eternal life, and of a glorious resurrection."

" What is requisite in order that we may really become partakers of all these blessings? We can become partakers of the fruits and promises of the Lord's Supper only by approaching the table of the Lord in a worthy manner."

" What is necessary if we would approach the Lord's table in a worthy manner ? Serious preparation and self-examination are requisite to a worthy participation in the Lord's Supper."—*Catechism, questions 60–65, 70, 71, 75–77.*

Questions of eschatology have not been entered upon by Moravian synods, for the purpose of defining dogma. Here as in connection with predestination and the sacraments, it is preferred that individual members grow in knowledge by personal search of the Scriptures and by personally seeking to apprehend so much as they can of the mysteries of revelation. Premillenarians and postmillenarians may both be found in the membership of the church. However, the Moravian Church plainly teaches a conscious existence of every individual soul after death, and affirms the resurrection of the body. It confesses faith in the visible return of the Lord Jesus Christ in power and great glory, in order to judge the living and the dead and establish his kingdom of glory, and that those who are His will enjoy the consummation of perfect life for ever, but those whom he condemns will suffer eternal punishment.

" I have a desire to depart, and to be with Christ, which is far better ; I shall never taste death ; yea, I shall attain unto the resurrection of the dead ; for the body which I shall put off, this grain of corruptability, shall put on incorruption ; my flesh shall rest in hope.

"And the God of peace, that brought again from the dead our Lord Jesus, that great Shepherd of the sheep, through the blood of the everlasting covenant, shall also quicken these our mortal bodies, if so be that the Spirit of God hath dwelt in them.

" The Lord will descend from heaven with a shout, with the voice of the archangel, and with the trump of God, to judge both the quick and the dead.

" This is my Lord, who redeemed me, a lost and undone human creature, purchased and gained me from sin, from death, and from the power of the devil ;

" Not with gold or silver, but with His holy precious blood, and with His innocent suffering and dying ;

" To the end that I should be His own, and in His kingdom live under Him and serve him, in eternal righteousness, innocence, and happiness ;

Even as he, being risen from the dead, liveth and reigneth, world without end."—*Easter Morning Litany.*

" When will the work of grace be completed ? At the glorious coming of our Lord Jesus Christ."

" When will He come ? The day and the hour no man knows, for He will come unexpectedly."

" What will then take place ? Then all the dead will be raised up by Jesus Christ ; but the dead in Christ (believers) will rise first."

" What will happen to those believers who are still alive at the coming of Christ ? Those believers who are still alive at the coming of Christ will be changed ; and their bodies will be made like unto the glorified body of Jesus Christ, in the same manner as the risen bodies of the saints."

" What will take place after the general resurrection ? After the *general* resurrection of the dead, the FINAL JUDGMENT will take place."

" Who will be the Judge ? Jesus Christ, the Judge of the quick and the dead, will recompense to every man according to his works."

" What will be the condition of man after death ? After the resurrection and final judgment, man will partake either of everlasting happiness or of everlasting misery."

"Who will be partakers of everlasting life ? The righteous, that is, all who have believed in Jesus Christ, will attain to everlasting happiness, being released from sin, from death and from all pain, admitted to the most intimate communion with God and Jesus Christ, and made partakers of His glory."

" What will become of the wicked ? The wicked, that is, all who hold the truth in unrighteousness, and are not obedient to the Gospel, shall go into everlasting punishment, and shall be separated from God and all the saints."

" What will then happen to the universe ? The whole visible creation (heaven and earth) will then undergo an entire change. This is called THE END OF THE WORLD !

"And I saw a new heaven and a new earth ; for the first heaven and the first earth were passed away." (Rev. 21 : 1.) "We, according to his promise, look for new heavens and a new earth wherein dwelleth righteousness." (2 Peter 3: 13.)—*Catechism, questions 123–130.*

INDEX.

The references are to page numbers.

Abbey Hey, 557.
Aberford, 134.
Abini, 273.
Abraham, the Mohican, 262.
Abraham of New Fairfield, 365.
Abraham, negro of St. Thomas, 53.
Abyssinia, 178, 179.
Achtnich, Martin, 510, 511.
Acolytes, 338.
Act of N. Y. Assembly against the Moravians, 135, 142, 143.
Adams, Samuel, 252.
Administrators of the Unity's Estates in America, 241, 291, 357, 361, 389, 400, 404, 524.
Adrai (Noah), 461.
Advent, 563.
"Advisory Board," The, 407, 521.
Advocatus Fratrum in Anglia, 286, 380, 444, 518.
Africa (see Cape Colony, Egypt, Guinea Coast).
Africa, East Equatorial, 570–575.
Africo, 64, 276.
Agricola, 206.
Alaska, 530, 540–547, 566.
Albany, 142.
Alberta Territory, 560–561.
Albertini, John Baptist, 341, 343–347, 357.
Albion, Ill., 403.
Albina, 568.
Alexander I of Russia, 311, 382, 432.
Algeria, 65, 95.
Allanson, William, 443.
Allen, William, 82.
Allegheny River, The, 244.
Allemaengel, 140.
Almond, Thomas, 288.
Alphen, Van, 62.
Altona, 285.
America (see Pennsylvania and North Carolina).
American congregations in 1790, The, 257 note.
Amsterdam, 62, 63, 94, 95, 97, 113, 114, 122, 149, 284, 285.
Amsterdam, Classis of, 151.
Amtrup, Niels, 303, 339, 344.

Anders, John Daniel, 357, 359, 360, 380, 381.
Anderson, 200.
Andrew, negro of St. Thomas, 56.
Anna, negress of St. Thomas, 53.
Annaszorg, 420.
Antes, Henry, 104, 106, 145, 170, 176.
Antes, John, 179.
Anthony, the Mohican, 244.
Anthony, the negro, 50, 51.
Antigua, 184, 269, 329, 331, 373, 415, 418, 494.
Anton, Paul, 3, 4, 18, 20, 32, 171.
Aporo, 332.
Arabi, 273, 421.
Arawacks, The, 185-188.
Arbalik, 61.
Archangel, 65.
Archives, The Unity's, 96, 207, 305, 340, 380.
Argyle, Lord, 136, 215.
Arkansas Territory, 362, 364.
Arran, 288.
Artrea, 166.
Arva, 288.
Aschwaubenon, 560.
Ashton, 165.
"Associate congregations," 518.
Associated Brethren of Schippack, The, 104.
Astor, Wm. B., 403.
Astrakhan, 210-212, 230.
Atlantic City, 523.
Aufseher Collegium, The, 144, 218.
Augsburg, Confession of, 72, 113, 124, 196, 198, 436.
August Thirteenth, 1727, 38.
Augustus, The Strong, 23.
Augustus, Indian, 365.
Aukas, The (Djukas), 462, 568.
Aulibissi Creek, The, 331.
Australia, 387, 388.
Australia, Missions in, 429-432, 466-468, 505, 539, 564.
Australia, Presbyterian Assembly of, 467, 539.
" Australian Associations," 431.
Awakening amongst the Children,The, 40.
Ayr, 215, 249.

40

ERRATA.

Circumstantial narration of events and transactions in the closing years of the nineteenth century has not been regarded as within the scope of the present work. Yet for the sake of completeness, it may be added that the general synod was in session at Herrnhut from May 27 to July 1, 1889. Bishop William Taylor was elected President with Bishops Henry Müller and J. M. Levering as Vice-Presidents. The main attention of this synod was given to administrative details in relation to the joint undertakings of the Brethren's Unity. The use of the lot as a part of the required methods of church activity and life, was abrogated. As reconstituted by synod the Unity's Elders' Conference consisted of the administrative board of the German province, together with James Connor, Benjamin Romig, Guido Burkhardt and Charles Buchner, the members of the Department of Missions.

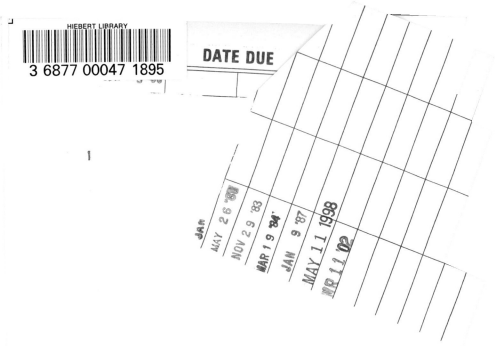

DATE DUE